SEX AND GENDER

Using both scientific and feminist approaches in its analysis, *Sex and Gender: A Biopsychological Approach* provides a current and comprehensive understanding of its titular topics, making it an invaluable textbook for instructors and students.

Sex and gender can only be properly understood when examined in the contexts of biological, psychological, and social processes and the interactions between those processes. The structure of this book facilitates this necessary exhaustive discussion:

- First section: a biological analysis that discusses evolutionary, cellular, and genetic processes, and their effects on physical and behavioral development
- Second section: a psychological and sociological analysis that discusses stereotypes, sexism, and theories of gender
- Final section: a discussion of the current global challenges surrounding sex and gender, such as discrimination and religious and social oppression of various groups
- Across chapters: bonus features that can be used as discussion topics, student essay topics, or special topics for instructors to expand the text's discussion into the classroom

The text's unique focus on biological, psychological, and social processes – as separate entities and interacting processes – makes *Sex and Gender* crucial for a comprehensive and advanced understanding of the subject. This is an essential resource for instructors who want to bring a thorough and complex analysis of sex and gender studies to their classrooms.

Heidi R. Riggio is Professor of Psychology at Cal State LA. She has been teaching in Southern California since 1996. She is a social psychologist with published research on sibling relationships, parental marital conflict and divorce, relationship attitudes and their strength, sexual health, religiosity and cognitive biases, and political attitudes.

SEX AND GENDER

A Biopsychological Approach

Heidi R. Riggio

First published 2021
by Routledge
52 Vanderbilt Avenue, New York, NY 10017

and by Routledge
2 Park Square, Milton Park, Abingdon, Oxon, OX14 4RN

Routledge is an imprint of the Taylor & Francis Group, an informa business

© 2021 Taylor & Francis

The right of Heidi R. Riggio to be identified as author of this work has been asserted by her in accordance with sections 77 and 78 of the Copyright, Designs and Patents Act 1988.

All rights reserved. No part of this book may be reprinted or reproduced or utilized in any form or by any electronic, mechanical, or other means, now known or hereafter invented, including photocopying and recording, or in any information storage or retrieval system, without permission in writing from the publishers.

Trademark notice: Product or corporate names may be trademarks or registered trademarks, and are used only for identification and explanation without intent to infringe.

Library of Congress Cataloging-in-Publication Data
A catalog record for this title has been requested

ISBN: 978-0-367-47978-7 (hbk)
ISBN: 978-0-367-47979-4 (pbk)
ISBN: 978-1-003-04187-0 (ebk)

Typeset in Interstate Light
by Newgen Publishing UK

Visit the eResources: www.routledge.com/9780367479794

To my students, past, present, and future
To my daughter, Clara

CONTENTS

Preface		ix
Acknowledgements		xi
1	Human Evolution	1
2	The Cellular Basis of Life	21
3	Genetics	39
4	Human Sexual Reproduction	59
5	Gender Stereotypes	82
6	Theories of Gender	112
7	Global, Historical Sexism	154
8	Human Sexuality	198
9	Personality, Emotions, and Health	251
10	Intimacy and Interpersonal Relationships	297
11	Aggression	344
12	Occupational Roles and Power	389
13	Current Issues and Social Problems	424
Index		459

PREFACE

When I first started teaching at Cal State LA (I won't reveal how long ago that was), I was asked to teach a course called Sex & Gender. This course was unique for me, for a few reasons. First, the course was an upper-division general education course, with students required to complete three courses outside their major. Cal State LA's upper-division general education was at that time coordinated around so-called "themes," with this course included in Theme C, "Sex in the Diversity of Human Experience." So while the course served as an upper-division elective in Psychology for Psychology students, it was also open to all majors, with students from many different majors taking the course. Second, the course was cross-listed with Biology, with the course occasionally being taught by Biology faculty. As such, it had substantial biology content, which had apparently been standardized across instructors because the course was a general education course (with specific required student learning outcomes). Third, the course was also unique to me because I had never taught such a course; my teaching up to that point had centered around Critical Thinking, Social Psychology, Statistics, Introduction to Psychology, and various Management/Organizational Psychology courses. I did not consider myself an expert in biological psychology. When I was asked to teach Sex & Gender, I was initially hesitant for all of the reasons just listed. I preferred Psychology students and teaching within the major, which felt somehow safer. Although I had very much enjoyed Biology courses as an undergraduate student, I did not consider myself an expert in human biology. And, preparing a new course? Who needs that extra work?

At the same time, I felt challenged. The only person in the Department who had taught the course previously was retiring; my Department needed me! I could expand my teaching experience, expand my own knowledge, show my Department what I was made of, and learn some new stuff. I was also a social psychologist and feminist who was fascinated with and passionate about issues associated with sexual health and the social-psychological construction of gender. I was further challenged when I accepted the course and the chair of the Biology Department emailed, inquiring as to my abilities to properly teach the course. As a junior faculty member, I was challenged again to prove myself, by my senior colleagues.

Teaching the course for the first time was challenging, to say the least. Two books for the course were required; a slim volume on human reproductive biology, and a larger, more expansive textbook focusing on gender from a psychological perspective. The first half of the course focused entirely on biology, starting with evolution and genetics, up to human reproduction and pregnancy. I learned right along with the students that first term, and I've been learning more and more ever since in an attempt to become as expert as possible on the first half of this course. The second half of the course was much less but still challenging, as I expanded my knowledge of human sexuality, sexual health and rights, gender differences in behavior, and historical and modern inequalities around the world. As I continued to teach the course over time, it became a favorite course to teach. However, over time, I and the students became increasingly frustrated over the necessity of two texts, and I decided one comprehensive textbook would be a useful tool in teaching and learning about sex and gender.

I approached writing this book with a fascination for understanding human evolution and behavior, and a passion for the importance of gender equality, gender freedom, and sexual health and happiness. I hope you enjoy reading this book as much as I enjoyed writing it.

Heidi R. Riggio
Department of Psychology
California State University, Los Angeles
Los Angeles, CA 90032 USA
December 12, 2019

ACKNOWLEDGEMENTS

I would like to thank my colleagues and friends within Psychology for their superlative support, kindness, and encouragement over the years. I would like to thank my wonderful students for their continuing hard work and sharing their talents with me. I would like to thank my daughter, Clara, for her support and encouragement in everything, including writing every word of this book. Thank you to my nephew Sam and my niece Sadie for giving me more good reasons for everything I do. Special thanks to my friend Dr. Brigitte Matthies for her constant presence as a friend who understands me; and Dr. Brian Johnson for his helping me understand myself. Lots of love and gratitude, I am truly blessed by the people in my life.

1 Human Evolution

The Beginnings of Life on Earth	4
Evolution: Basic Principles, Supporting Evidence	5
Evolution of Human: Hominids and Early *Homo* Species	8
Modern Human Variation	15
The Evolution Controversy	16

INEQUALITIES AND INJUSTICES

Intimate Partner Violence in the Cave?

Human beings have a violent history. Homicide is a leading cause of premature death among young adults in the United States (Centers for Disease Control & Prevention, 2010), and war after war have been fought across time. People fight over territory, possessions, and people, and violence occurs between people who are in the same family, people we are supposed to love. Even in the modern, civilized world, with laws prohibiting violence and law enforcement and courts punishing violence, violence is a major social issue around the world. If modern humans are so violent, what were ancient humans like? Human skeletal remains from fossil remains of campsites and group living areas provide data on the violent behavior of ancient people. An anthropologist who examined research on antemortem (before death) and perimortem (at death) skeletal injuries among ancient human remains, Phillip L. Walker (2001), asserts that the human species has always been quite violent, especially men. Throughout the history of Homo Sapiens, cannibalism was a regular and widespread practice, and there is plentiful evidence of mass killings and individual homicides/assaults across the globe. With humans having a tendency toward aggression and interpersonal violence, how would this come into play in intimate relationships among ancient peoples? The average man is much bigger and stronger than the average woman; this fact alone allows men to control women with violence. In the cave, with no formal laws and fewer sophisticated ideas on the importance of equality between the sexes, it is clear that cave men used physical force to control their cave women. Anthropological research must continue to gather evidence of physical violence used against women as a means of controlling the other half of the human race, beginning in the cave.

LEARN MORE

Early Hominid and *Homo* Groups

This entire book isn't long enough to describe every group representing human evolution over time. There are many other early hominid and early *Homo* groups that you might be interested in reading about. Here is a list for you to check out, groups we missed in our chapter:

Orrorin tugenensis
Ardipithecus ramidus
Australopithecus anamensis
Kenyanthropus platyops
Australopithecus garhi
Australopithecus sediba
Australopithecus aethiopicus
Australopithecus robustus
Australopithecus boisei
Homo georgicus
Homo ergaster
Homo sapiens idaltu

CRITICAL THINKING

Top Ten Myths about Evolution

Top 10 Myths about Evolution **(Skeptics Society, 2010)**
www.skeptic.com/downloads/top-10-evolution-myths.pdf

1.   If Humans Came from Apes, Why Aren't Apes Evolving into Humans?

Human beings and apes evolved from a common ancestor about six to seven million years ago. Apes are our cousins; we did not evolve from them.

2.   There Are Too Many Gaps in the Fossil Record for Evolution to Be True

There are of course gaps in the fossil record; fossils have only been systematically collected for about 200 years. In addition, accurately describing fossil finds takes time. Many intermediate fossils exist, including interesting creatures like the *Tiktaalik*, intermediate between fish and amphibians. Multiple intermediate forms in the evolution of humans have also been found. As more discoveries are made, the progression of evolution becomes clearer.

3.   If Evolution Happened Gradually over Millions of Years, Why Doesn't the Fossil Record Show Gradual Change?

Most successful species live for relatively long periods of time. The history of life shows long periods of stability with little change, with speciational change happening rather rapidly. The **equilibrium** of life is thus **punctuated** by bursts of change.

4. *No One Has Ever Seen Evolution Happen*

This is first an appeal to ignorance, a poor argument tactic. Secondly, if there are no witnesses to an event, that doesn't mean people cannot figure out what happened. For example, accident reconstruction specialists determine what happened in traffic accidents based on evidence at the scene. Crime scene specialists and law enforcement experts recreate crimes, including sequences of events, causes of injuries, even the mindset of perpetrators. Understanding something from evidence left behind is reasonable and logical; eyewitnesses are not necessary (and sometimes not all that accurate; Loftus & Palmer, 1996). Finally, independent observations and evidence from every branch of science support that evolution is a fact. Strong, consistent, and continuing convergence of evidence strongly supports that evolution is indeed the process by which life evolved on our planet.

5. *Science Claims That Evolution Happens by Random Chance*

This argument is completely false. Natural selection is not random at all; rather, survival is determined by individual qualities that enhance ability to survive and reproduce in a particular environment. There is nothing random about that.

6. *Only an Intelligent Designer Could Have Made Something as Complex as an Eye (or Whatever)*

Eyes are actually not well put together. They are in fact upside down and backwards. Among human beings, about 75% require some vision correction (Vision Council of America, 2017). The structure and function of eyes across species is very well understood from an evolutionary perspective, with initial primitive light-sensing cells the precursors to similarly-structured eyes across many different species.

7. *Evolution Is Only a Theory*

This is also a poor argument tactic called a **straw person**, where a solid argument is changed into something easily knocked down ("only" a theory). A **theory** is an explanation; good theories explain most or all of the known evidence, provide testable hypotheses, are guided by natural law, and are falsifiable. Evolution is supported by abundant, converging evidence, and guides new predictions. It is a superior theory, the singular theory that unites all of science.

8. *Evidence for Human Evolution Has Turned out to Be Fake, Fraudulent, or Fanciful*

Some "evidence" produced by scientists has indeed turned out to be fake. *Piltdown Man*, offered by Charles Dawson and Arthur Smith Woodward in England, is an example of a fake. Honest scientists also make mistakes in research, like the case of *Nebraska Man*. But fakes do not define all of science, and mistakes usually turn out to be useful in the progression of science. Science as a method is designed intentionally to stop fakes and frauds and to minimize mistakes. Scientific evidence is subject to peer-review and the greatest scrutiny. Mistakes often lead to new directions and discoveries, and a few fakes do not undermine the totality of evidence supporting evolution. To claim that one part or one piece invalidates an entire body of evidence is a poor argument tactic called the **part-whole fallacy**.

9. *The Second Law of Thermodynamics Proves That Evolution Is Impossible*

This physical law applies to closed, isolated systems. The Earth is an **open system**, with constant energy provided by the sun. The Second Law of Thermodynamics does not apply to life existing and evolving on Earth, nor to many other processes on Earth.

10. *Evolution Can't Account for Morality*

Morality is observed across the animal kingdom. We see love, attachment bonds, relationships, and altruism happening among animals. For example, mothers across species care for their children, show obvious affection toward them, help them in time of need, and show great distress when they are missing or injured. **Pair bonding** of mates across a lifetime is also common. As social species, **primates**, including humans, show great respect for social processes such as **reciprocity**, cooperation, and sharing with others. Evidence of caretaking and kinship bonds is abundant in the fossil record of hominid groups. **Morality** enhances ability of a species to survive because it enhances group bonds, which aids individual survival and reproduction. Evolution can and does account for moral behavior in humans and other animals.

The Beginnings of Life on Earth

The story of the origins of life on our planet is obviously very complicated, and there is much that scientists still do not know about the origins of life. The universe is said to be over 13 billion years old (Planck Collaboration, 2015), while the Earth is said to be about 4.5 billion years old (Braterman, 2013). Evidence of early microbial life is found in rocks about 3.5 billion years old in Western Australia (Noffke, Christian, Wacey, & Hazen, 2013). Microfossils about 4 billion years old have also been found in Canada. Early bacteria are found in rocks in Greenland, about 3.7 billion years old (Nutman, Mojzsis, & Friend, 1997). Evidence of the most likely beginning of organic life on the planet comes from a series of experiments conducted by Sutherland (Powner, Gerland, & Sutherland, 2009). The young Earth was covered in oceans, with many different forms of energy present, including sunlight, lightning, volcanoes, deep-sea vents, and meteorites from space. In addition to water, oxygen, hydrogen, nitrogen, sulphur, phosphorus, and carbon were all present, the basic elements of life. Sutherland and colleagues actually created **ribonucleic acid (RNA)**, which is essential for protein production in living cells, in their laboratory. The earliest life was likely prokaryotic bacterial cells (cells without nuclei), such as the ones found in ancient fossils. Once life existed on Earth, it would not be stopped, and over billions of years, very slowly, everything alive that has ever existed on the planet and that exists today evolved from these earlier simpler forms. As every branch of science continues to test the predictions of evolutionary theory, including modernly, the evidence supporting evolution continues to mount. Today, the theory of evolution is largely regarded as factual. A theory is an explanation of a particular phenomenon that provides a testable hypothesis. The explanation of life provided by the theory of evolution has been supported by numerous observations since its inception over 150 years ago.

Evolution: Basic Principles, Supporting Evidence

Charles Darwin is the English naturalist who first published on **evolutionary theory** in his famous book, *On the Origin of Species* (Darwin, 1859). Darwin had traveled on his ship, *The Beagle*, observing various life forms in different types of ecosystems and environments all over the world. Based on his observations, Darwin concluded that life forms evolved slowly over time to survive in changing environments. For example, in the Galapagos Islands (an island group about 600 miles off the west coast of South America) he observed various types of finches, all of which belonged to the same species. The finches all originally flew from the mainland to the Islands. On some of the islands the birds ate nuts and seeds and lived on the ground. On other islands the finches ate fruit and lived in trees. On other islands the finches ate insects. Depending on their main diet, the finches possessed different features, particularly different shaped beaks, with some beaks better for cracking open seeds and other beaks adapted for drinking nectar from flowers. All the same species, yet different features had evolved over time, depending on the environment and food supply on each particular island. Darwin concluded that life forms changed slowly over time depending on the dynamic, changing environment in which each creature lived (see Figure 1.1).

Darwin asserted two main premises underlying the process of **evolution**. First is the idea of **common ancestry**, that all life on the planet evolved over time from earlier simpler forms. In this way, all life on the planet is based on the same essential amino acids, the building blocks of protein; and **adenosine triphosphate**, or ATP, a small molecule (a nucleotide) that supports energy transfer and metabolism at the cellular level. All eukaryotic cells (cells with a nucleus), that compose the bodies of nearly 99.9% of the world's organisms, function in a similar fashion

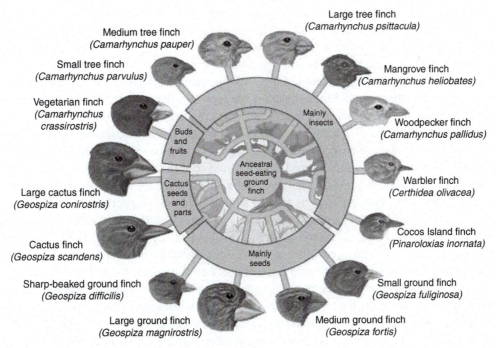

Figure 1.1 Adaptive radiation in Galapagos finches
Source: © 2005 Encyclopedia Britannica, Inc.

as well. These molecular, chemical, and cellular similarities would not exist if all of life was not interrelated, if all of life did not come from the same early simple life forms. The fact that this biochemistry and cellular function is identical across all life forms is very strong evidence of common ancestry.

A second main premise underlying the process of evolution is that of natural selection, the process by which the natural environment "selects" some species members for survival and reproduction because they possess qualities that are particularly well-suited for that environment. There are four basic elements of the process of natural selection. First is the central idea of variation, the fact that individual organisms within each species vary widely in their individual characteristics. For example, the Galapagos finches: within one species many varieties of bird features existed, including very different shapes of beak. Human beings modernly vary widely in their features, including height, eye color, skin color, hair type, body type, diseases, and many other genetic qualities. All species vary widely in their traits and qualities. If all members of a species were alike, one disease or illness could wipe out the entire species at once. To enhance survival, to support unstoppable life, species vary widely across many different characteristics.

A second essential element of natural selection is the struggle for existence. It's not easy being a zebra, or a fox, or a salmon, or an eagle. The world is dangerous, full of predators and hazards, and staying alive is not easy. Human beings, although we have altered our world so much for safety and to preserve life, face literally lethal dangers on a daily basis. It is not easy to survive. Who among a species is most likely to survive? This is the third element of natural selection, survival of the fittest. Among any species, there will be individual members who will possess characteristics that are especially well-suited to survival in a particular environment. A finch with a long pointy beak is better able to survive on an island where flowers provide a main source of food, nectar. A finch of the same species with a short beak may not survive very long on that particular island. Over time, as the fittest live longer and have more offspring, their adaptive characteristics become more numerous within the species. This is the fourth essential element of natural selection, adaptation. An adaptation is any characteristic that enhances the ability of a species to survive in a particular environment. As the characteristic enhances survival, it also enhances ability to reproduce, resulting in more species members having adaptive qualities, and those species members without those qualities not surviving, not reproducing. As such, nature "selects" for survival those individual species members that possess particularly adaptive characteristics. Over millions of years, within a changing planet, ecosystem, and immediate environment, the result is many changes in life forms, eventual divergence of species, and a planet covered in different creatures that are adapted for survival in their environment (see Figure 1.1).

As indicated earlier, there is an abundance of evidence supporting the common ancestry of life on Earth. First, biogeography, as studied by Darwin himself, supports common ancestry. Biogeography is the study of plant and animal life as it varies in different environments all over the world. Dolphins, sharks, squid, and other marine life obviously possess characteristics that enable them to survive in the ocean. No one would argue that a dolphin could survive in a desert or a forest. Creatures all over the world possess qualities that enable them to survive in their particular environment; if the environment changes dramatically and suddenly, the species will be wiped out. Darwin made the particular observation of the Patagonian hare, a rodent living in the grasslands of South America (which had no rabbits during Darwin's time). The hare is quite similar in many features to rabbits in England, except it is much bigger and is a completely different species. Darwin concluded that these completely distinct species, living thousands of miles apart, have similar features because both the hare and the English rabbit live in similar grassland environments.

Fossil evidence also supports common ancestry and evolution of life on our planet. A **fossil** is any remains of past life: bones, shells, pottery, tools, footprints, etc. Scientists date fossils based on various chemical tests and where they are found in the geologic column. Many extinct species and intermediate forms are present in the fossil record. The ancient horse is different from the modern horse and fossil evidence (dated to a theory-predicted date within the geologic column) clearly shows this. Earlier, more primitive versions of many species are present in the fossil record. Evidence of human evolution is also present in the fossil record, including clear changes in physical characteristics over time.

Anatomical evidence also supports common ancestry. Many body structures and processes are similar across species; the structures are **homologous**. A widely used example is the forelimb of vertebrate species, which has the same number of bones arranged in highly similar manner across species (i.e., a bat wing is like a dolphin fin is like a bird wing is like a horse's front leg is like the human arm; see Figure 1.2). Fetal development in mammals also follows a similar progression and morphology across species, as does sexual reproduction across even more species. There is no particular reason for this similarity; the similarity itself does not enhance survival of species. Rather, the similarity exists because all of these creatures are descended from the same earlier, simpler forms. These early structures were modified by natural selection over long periods of time into their current forms across many species. Animals of all kinds are anatomically and biologically similar because we are all interrelated.

Finally, modern biochemical evidence, unavailable to Darwin in his scholarly work, also supports common descent. **DNA** (**deoxyribonucleic acid**) exists in every cell of all living things and composes the genetic code. Genes determine the production of proteins at the cellular level, which in turn determines how different creatures look and function (we will talk much more

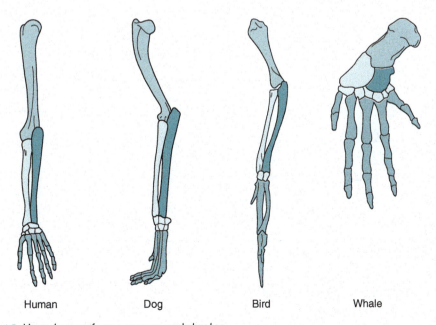

Human   Dog   Bird   Whale

Figure 1.2 Homologous forms among vertebrates

about cells and genes in the next chapters). It is clear from research in genetics that all creatures have very similar genetic codes, with closely related species being more similar genetically than species less closely related. For example, human beings share about 50% of the same genes with bananas, but nearly 99% of the same genes with chimpanzees. In fact, genetically humans and chimpanzees are nearly identical, except chimps have 48 chromosomes (24 pairs), while humans have 46 chromosomes (with 23 pairs). The major difference is that human beings have one chromosome 2, which appears to be a fused version of two separate chromosomes possessed by chimps, generally called 2A and 2B (Yunis & Prakash, 1982).

Major genetic differences between humans and chimps relate to body hair, skeletal structure, and structure of the larynx and mouth (structures relating to speech). This genetic similarity is actually unnecessary for life to occur. Life on Earth would be supportable with other genetic codes. The genetic similarity of all life on Earth is very strong evidence of our common ancestry.

Evolution of Human: Hominids and Early *Homo* Species

A common misperception is that human beings evolved directly from apes (see "Critical Thinking"). Human beings are closely related to apes, with both having evolved along separate lines from a common ancestor who existed about 7 million years ago. Apes (including chimpanzees, gorillas, orangutans) and humans, along with monkeys (including marmosets and baboons) and prosimians (lemurs, tarsiers), are all considered primates (see Figure 1.3). Primates are related to the first mammals to enter trees, with eventual divergence of larger classes, orders, and families of

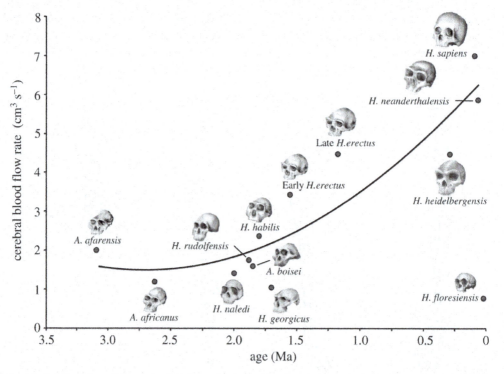

Figure 1.3 A timeline of human evolution
Source: Royal Society Publishing

creatures. Humans are most closely related to chimpanzees and bonobos, a bit less to gorillas, a bit less to orangutans, and even less to monkeys.

Primates have several characteristics that make them unique in relation to other mammals, qualities that are particularly adaptive for living in trees. Ancient ancestors of humans originally lived in trees and we still see qualities well-suited for that in modern humans. First, part of the greater reliance on vision of primates relates to the importance of depth perception. Primates perceive depth better than other creatures because their eyes face forward on a flatter face, with a shorter snout (due to a decreased reliance on smell over time). Depth is important for judging distances, including from tree limb to tree limb and from tree to the ground. Second, primates have mobile limbs and grasping hands, important for moving about, swinging, climbing, and gripping tree limbs. Our hands are very sensitive and powerful, with shorter claws better and sensitive fingertips highly adaptive for gripping and climbing. Primates also have large complex brains, larger than most other mammals. Such brains are important for living in groups, for communication, for movement and balance, and for processing spatial information retrieved from larger vision areas. A hallmark of human evolution is a trend toward a larger and larger brain, especially growth in the frontal lobe areas of the brain, which are important for planning, learning, consciousness and identity, and empathy. Finally, primates have a reduced reproductive rate relative to other mammals, having usually only one baby at a time. Having a baby is difficult, but if you're living in a tree, it can be more difficult and one needs to be able to carry a baby all the time. Having multiple babies while living in a tree is dangerous and makes one (and babies) vulnerable to falls, predators, and other mishaps. Having fewer offspring at a time is essential for successful life in the trees.

Along the path of human evolution, various hominid (meaning "man-like") species have been discovered in the fossil record (see Figures 1.3 and 1.4). The most obvious changes that occur over long periods of human evolution involve brain size (and thus skull size and shape), changes in brain structures (growth in some structures but not in others, as evidenced by changes in skull shape), changes in body hair (because the human cooling system relies on perspiration much more so than other animals), and changes in the facial structures (including the teeth as our diets became more varied and we began cooking food). All of these changes are actually the result of the most important change affecting how we evolved: the trend toward and eventual reliance on bipedalism, walking upright on two feet.

Dramatic climatic changes in Africa during early human evolution would have resulted in many fewer trees, with forests becoming grasslands over time. This change in the environment requires more time on the ground, looking for food and traveling from tree to tree. As our early ancestors spent more time on two feet, there were many advantages to be had: two free hands (no longer used for movement), being able to view an entire surrounding landscape, and a fast efficient gait and eventual run. As we began running, not just in sprints but over long distances, a sophisticated and unique cooling system developed, involving less body hair allowing cooling of more of the body with watery sweat from eccrine sweat glands (versus panting and oily apocrine sweat glands among other mammals). The nose is also large and longer on a flatter face, better for our cooling system. Freedom of the hands allows carrying and use of tools to a better degree, resulting in brain growth over time as intelligence and planning become more important for survival. Planning also involves the frontal lobe areas of the brain, structures rather unique to human beings. As we evolved we communicated better, also linked with brain growth over time, especially in language areas of the brain. Communication evolved with changes in mouth

10   Human Evolution

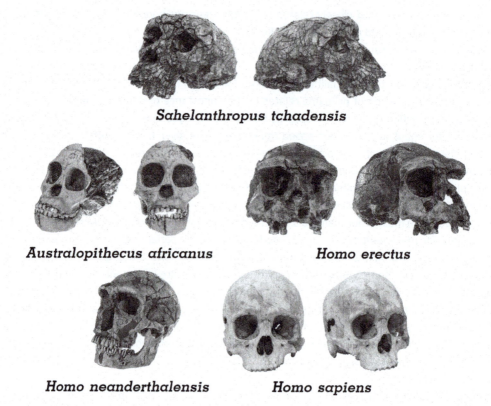

Figure 1.4 Evolution of human: skulls
Source: 123RF

structure and tongue size, strength, and flexibility. Bipedalism is the main force behind all of these gradual, cumulative changes.

Hominids and Early Homo Species

Many different species are represented along the timeline of human evolution; it is not possible to describe them all in one chapter, so we will discuss a few major players. The oldest known hominid species documented, which is believed to be a species variation close to the common ancestor of humans and other primates, is called **Sahelenthropus Tchadensis**, who was found in Chad in central Africa in 2002 (see Figure 1.4). Sahelenthropus Tchadensis dates to between 6 and 7 million years ago (MYA), so she is thought to have existed close to the time of the divergence between creatures that eventually became chimpanzees and those that eventually became human. She had a very small brain (about 350cc), and still lived in the trees. It is not yet known to what degree she was bipedal.

Two important hominid groups that existed are called Australopithecines, or "southern apes." The first and oldest is called **Australopithecus Afarensis**, whose skeletal remains upon discovery (in Ethiopia, 1974) were named "Lucy" by paleontologist Donald Johansen. Afarensis is dated to about 3.2 to 3.5 MYA, and is thought to have spent more and more time on the ground, due to declining numbers of trees, but still largely lived in trees, in groups. Afarensis was small, under

4 feet tall and only weighing about 70-80 pounds. She had a small brain (about 400cc), but her skeletal structure indicates she was indeed bipedal. Additional evidence of bipedalism is found in footprints found in a lava bed dated to around the same time as Afarensis, about 3.8 MYA, with footprints from three individuals walking on two feet, side by side.

Afarensis is the ancestor of later Australopithecine groups, including **Australopithecus Africanus.** Africanus is about the same size as Lucy, but more recent in our history, dated to around 2.8 to 2.5 MYA. Africanus also lived in groups, but spent more time on the ground than Afarensis. About the same size, the brain is slightly bigger, between 440 and 500cc. The first discovery of Africanus was in a place called Taung in South Africa, in 1924 by Professor Raymond Dart, who found a small child's skull. For these reasons, Africanus is sometimes called "Taung Child." Africanus used rudimentary tools, such as using unfashioned rocks to break open animal bones to retrieve the rich, nutritious marrow inside. The Taung Child is thought to have been killed at about age 3 years by an eagle, because of the talon markings found inside the eye sockets (see Figure 1.5).

Although many early hominid groups, and other primates today, use rudimentary tools in obtaining food (e.g., chimpanzees use sticks to get bugs out of their nests), a most important leap in human evolution took place when we got smart enough to actually make tools (i.e., change a rock or a stick into something else that is useful). The first example of tool making in human evolution is the creation of the hand axe, or working on, shaping, and sharpening a rock so that it is more effective as a tool. The first groups identified with the genus **Homo** have three main

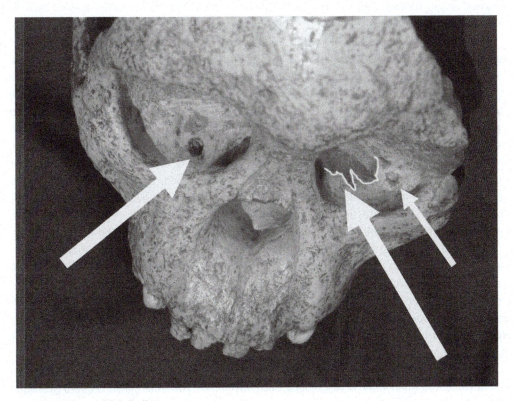

Figure 1.5 Taung child skull
Source: Wiki

12 *Human Evolution*

features: 1) brain size is larger than 600cc; 2) jaw and teeth are similar to modern human teeth; and 3) tool making is evident.

Many different *Homo* groups existed simultaneously at different times over the millions of years of human evolution. Modern humans are not descended from all of them; many of them died out, became extinct, and their lines went no further. Homo groups are characterized by living in large groups, fending off many predators, sometimes changing immediate environments to find additional food sources. Early Homo groups generally showed very broad subsistence patterns. Definitely omnivorous, they would eat pretty much anything, including meat, plants, eggs, insects, fruit, honey, and roots. These broad subsistence patterns are definitely adaptive across environments, especially in instances of drought. Living in groups is also adaptive, as it maximizes safety against predators, effective hunting, and likelihood of finding a willing mate. Group living also allows caretaking of the sick, elderly, and children.

The hand axe is the hallmark of **Homo Habilus**, literally the "Handy Man." The first discovery of Habilus was by the famous married team Louis and Mary Leakey, in the 1960s in Kenya. Habilus shows the increases in brain growth characteristic of human evolution, with a much larger brain than Australopithecines (up to about 775cc). Standing between 4 and 5 feet tall, Habilus likely weighed about 80 pounds. The shape of Homo Habilus' skull suggests larger speech areas in the brain, with language communication increasing along with brain size and creation of tools. Homo Habilus remains have been found along with remains of very large campsites, suggesting Habilus lived in large groups where communication would be essential for effective functioning of the group. Evidence also indicates that Habilus was likely not an active hunter, but that meat was obtained largely through scavenging. The broad subsistence patterns of Habilus allowed them to survive without hunting.

One of the most successful Homo groups to ever exist, existing far longer than modern humans, is **Homo Erectus** ("upright man"), fossils of which have been found all over Africa, Asia, and Europe, dating to about 2 MYA to 300,000 years ago (see Figure 1.6). The first discovery of Erectus was called *Java Man*, as he was discovered on the island of Java, by Eugene DuBois in 1891. The brain size of Erectus is much bigger than that of Habilus, nearly 1000cc, with a rounder, flatter forehead, and a much more human-like face and appearance. Body hair is also much less than in previous species, with more eccrine sweat glands and a longer nose for cooling, and Erectus is more like modern humans in terms of height (5-6 feet tall, with males taller than females), and in terms of communication, which is increased. The whites of the eyes have become more and more visible among Homo groups, because the eyes are so important for accuracy of emotional expression and communication. Homo Erectus was clearly a hunter, using more sophisticated compound tools including spears and knives, and hunting in large groups. Homo Erectus is thought to have been the first species to have captured fire, a major achievement that changed the lives of early groups, allowing cooking, warmth, a source of light in the night (and a reason to stay up late and tell stories). Highly successful, Homo Erectus migrated from Africa to Europe and to Asia. Various groups are descended just from Homo Erectus, including **Homo Heidelbergensis** and **Homo Neanderthalensis**. Heidelbergensis is an early form of us, **Homo Sapiens** ("Thinking Man"); Neanderthalensis is a close cousin, but not a direct ancestor of modern humans.

Fossil finds in Europe and Africa are evidence of Heidelbergensis, so named because he was first documented when found in Heidelberg, Germany in 1907. Heidelbergensis is dated to around 700,000 to 200,000 years ago. Scholars assert that the skulls of this group are rather an intermediate form of Erectus and Sapiens, less primitive than Erectus with an increasingly rounded

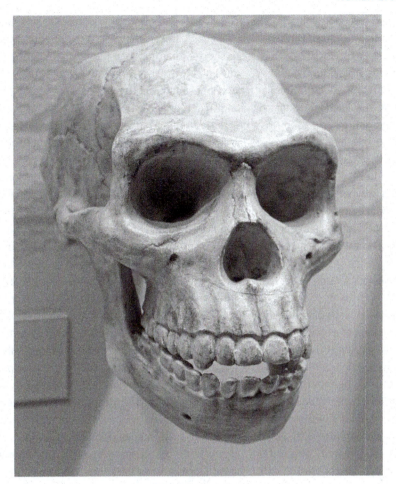

Figure 1.6 Reconstruction of a *Homo Erectus* skull
Source: Wiki

and large forehead. This frontal lobe development would support planning, creativity, and communication, superior compared to other animals. Communication is particularly advanced compared to other earlier Homo groups. The teeth also show support for an intermediate form (see "Critical Thinking"), a form in between Erectus and Sapiens, which would not only support greater oral communication but also continuously growing variety in diet, especially with availability of fire and cooking. Heidelbergensis were nomadic, traveling long distances depending on season and herds of large animals they followed, including woolly mammoths. Although many groups did migrate to Europe, some stayed in Africa. Scholars today argue that Heidelbergensis evolved into two separate but related groups, Homo Neanderthalensis in Europe, and Homo Sapiens in Africa, with the two regions undergoing very different climatic changes (Ice Age in Europe, drought in Africa).

Perhaps the most fascinating group of early Homo are Neanderthals, so called because they were found in the Neander Valley in Germany, in 1856 (although they were first found in Belgium in 1829). Despite common ideas, Homo Sapiens is not directly descended from Neanderthal Man; they are a distinct species (Hublin, 2009). Neanderthal evolved from Homo Heidelbergensis in

14   *Human Evolution*

Europe around 400,000 years ago, and survived, co-existing with Homo Sapiens, until around 30,000 years ago (Pinhasi, Higham, Golovanova, & Doronichev, 2011). The Neanderthals looked like the typical image of the cave person; shorter than modern humans (5.5 feet on average), but rather large (180 pounds) and very muscular, with shorter limbs. Neanderthals had a large head and brain (1450cc) but a smaller frontal lobe compared to humans. Archaeological evidence indicates that they lived in groups, including structures built for homes. They most certainly created tools and hunted and used fire. They buried their dead with gifts and artifacts, suggesting complex social relationships and close family bonds. Like other groups of human ancestors, like other animals on Earth, Neanderthals loved each other.

Science did not realize that Neanderthal Man was not a direct ancestor of human beings until the 1990s, when with modern technology geneticists discovered that Neanderthal genes were not in fact human. While Neanderthals and humans are 99.8% genetically similar, some genes are turned on in Neanderthals but not in humans, and vice versa, mainly genes affecting brain function and the shape and length of arms, hands, and legs (Gokhman et al., 2014). Additional genetics research indicates that among modern human beings alive today, about 9% possess genes shared with Neanderthals, with about 1–4% of genes being shared. Clearly, Neanderthal and Homo Sapiens were interbreeding and producing offspring. Interestingly, humans and Neanderthal do not share mitochondrial DNA, DNA that is present within the mitochondria (engines) of every human body cell that is inherited always from one's mother. Because of this, scholars suggest that matings between female humans and male Neanderthals produced viable offspring, while matings between female Neanderthals and male humans apparently did not. Humans with Neanderthal genes are exclusively non-African, of European or Asian descent; the ancient humans in Africa did not interbreed with Neanderthals because there were no Neanderthal neighbors in Africa.

In close competition with Neanderthals for most fascinating early humans are **Homo Floresiensis**, nicknamed "The Hobbit," who was first discovered in 2003; and **Homo Sapiens Denisovans**, first discovered in 2010. Homo Floresiensis existed at the same time as Homo Sapiens and Neanderthalensis, about 200,000 to 50,000 years ago, but only on the small island of Flores in Indonesia. Apparently this group had become isolated on the island, and over time had evolved into a unique species. Speciation often involves this kind of geographic isolation, with traits adaptive to the specific environment becoming more frequent in successive generations, eventually resulting in a new species. Living on this tiny island resulted in tiny people, only about 3 feet, 6 inches tall, about 65 pounds, with a small brain (450cc), large teeth, and large feet. They created tools, hunted live prey, and used fire.

Homo Sapiens Denisovans, a subspecies of human, also existed at the same time as Homo Sapiens and Neanderthalensis, but their fossil remains have only yet been found in the Denisova caves in Siberia. Scholars argue that their origins are the same as Neanderthals, and that they also interbred with ancestors of modern humans. Like all advanced Homo groups, the Denisovans lived in groups and used tools. People alive today who are of Melanesian or Aboriginal Australian descent possess some Denisovan genes (about 3 to 5%) (Gibbons, 2011).

With all of these cousins and ancestors and subspecies, all of them now extinct, where in the world did we come from? There is ample evidence indicating support for the Out-of-Africa hypothesis, the idea that modern human beings, Homo Sapiens (sometimes called **Homo Sapiens Sapiens**), evolved as a separate species within Africa around 150,000 to 200,000 years ago, and then migrated all over to populate the planet, beginning around 80,000 years ago. Groups of Homo Heidelbergensis that stayed in Africa are currently thought to be our most direct ancestor. Homo Sapiens has long arms and legs, and a large brain (1360cc), with a particularly large frontal lobe for thinking, planning, experiencing consciousness, and forming identity and empathy. The skull is unique; it is called "high-vaulted" (Puiu, 2020), with a nearly vertical and wide forehead. It is relatively thin compared to earlier hominid skulls. Brow ridges are very small compared to prior species, as are teeth and jaws, so modern humans have less of the caveman look. Although height and weight clearly vary depending on genes, living conditions, childhood well-being, food supplies and so on, among North Americans today, the average man is 5 feet, 9 inches tall, weighing 172 pounds, while the average woman is 5 feet, 4 inches tall, weighing 137 pounds. Men are about 15-20% larger than women and much stronger, on average. Men possess 50-80% greater upper body strength and 30-60% greater lower body strength than women (Lassek & Gaulin, 2009). I mention these size and strength differences now because they are important and meaningful for understanding nearly everything else in this book. As we move forward, ask yourself this question every time you hear about some way in which men and women are different: how do size and strength differences come into play here? This is certainly not the only question you should ask, but it is an important one.

Modern Human Variation

Every human being alive today is a member of the same species, Homo Sapiens Sapiens. And yet, human beings are clearly very different in many ways. Like other species, we see great variability among humans in physical height and body build, facial features, hair color and texture, skin color, and in behavioral traits, including personality, intelligence, and mental health. Think of all the breeds of dog you know. Giants like Great Danes, and tiny dogs like Chihuahuas. There is fur of all kinds, all colors and textures, and different personalities across different breeds. All dogs alive today are one species, *Canis lupus familiaris*, but there are clearly genetic variations among them.

For humans, one variation that has consumed the psychology of people over human history is that of skin color. This is a natural variation determined by genes, with differences in **melanin** production responsible for skin color differences. Variations in melanin are important for survival in a very basic way, because environments around the globe vary significantly in terms of sun exposure and correspondingly ambient temperature. In Africa, the sun is hot and intense; it is visible most of the day, so people are exposed to it all day long. This is true for practically the whole year, across seasons. In such an environment, darker skin is much more adaptive; it is less likely to burn and less likely to produce cancer, with melanin protecting the body from damaging ultraviolet light (Brenner & Hearing, 2008). Sunlight to some degree is essential for human life, however; the body produces Vitamin D from absorption of sunlight through the skin. While people in Africa are exposed to lots of sunlight, in more northern areas of the planet, including Europe, especially Scandinavia, sunlight is rather scarce, and when the sun is out it is not intense. For this reason, lighter skin is more adaptive in these types of environments, because it absorbs more of the relatively scarce sunlight than darker skin. Over many years, variations in hominid skin color arose because different groups were living in different environments.

Another variation that is obvious across people involves differences in body size and shape, really for the purposes of thermal regulation of the body. There are two rules to describe variations in body shape and body size, called **Allen's Rule** and **Bergmann's Rule**. Allen's Rule (Allen, 1877) asserts that in warm-blooded animals, species will vary in the shape of ears and appendages depending on the climate of their environment. In colder, northern environments, limbs, digits, and ears will be rounder and more compact, to conserve body heat, whereas in warmer climates, they will be longer, to allow greater surface-to-air ratio and greater cooling of the body through the skin. Bergmann's Rule (Bergmann, 1847) is similar but applies to body size, with humans being generally larger overall in colder climates, smaller and leaner overall in warmer climates, with larger, more compact bodies having lower surface-to-air ratios, again so that body heat is preserved.

Human beings vary in many other respects, because variation within species is so important for survival. Modern variations that are said to be recent evolutionary changes include lactose tolerance and eye color. Among nearly all mammals, the capacity to digest lactose, a sugar found in milk, turns off when offspring are no longer in infancy, because the animals are no longer dependent on mother for food (Swallow, 2003). Human beings are believed to be the only mammal with the ability to digest lactose after early childhood. **Lactose persistence** is genetic; it varies widely, with very high proportions of people descended from Northern and Western Europe being able to digest lactose well, and lower proportions among people in Asia and much of Africa (Bersaglieri et al., 2004; Gerbault et al., 2011). The gene for lactose tolerance is recently evolved, estimated to have occurred first around 10,000 years ago (Bersaglieri et al., 2004), coincidentally around the time when people started keeping animals for food. Another recent genetic change, caused by a genetic mutation in one single person, led to blue eyes, and is thought to have occurred between 6,000 and 10,000 years ago (Eiberg et al., 2008). That person is the relative of every blue-eyed person who has ever lived and who will ever live on Earth.

The Evolution Controversy

Evolution is supported by evidence from every branch of science; from geology, archaeology, and paleontology, to biogeography, biology, microbiology, physiology, zoology, and psychology. Evolution as the process behind all of the life on Earth is supported by 97% of the world's scientists (Pew Research Center, 2009). So why then is there still controversy surrounding this explanation (see "Critical Thinking")? Only 33% of Americans accept evolution as a completely natural process responsible for biological diversity on Earth (Pew Research Center, 2015). Why?

The following is from a sticker placed into all science textbooks by the Alabama Department of Education in 1995 (Dawkins, 1997):

• *This textbook discusses evolution, a controversial theory some scientists present as a scientific explanation for the origin of living things, such as plants, animals and humans. No one was present when life first appeared on earth, therefore, any statement about life's origins should be considered as theory, not fact.*

Please note the appeal to ignorance used in this official government statement (see "Critical Thinking"). Indeed, the current Vice President of the United States, Mike Pence, referred to evolution as "just a theory" in a speech to Congress in 2002, at the same time asserting that **creationism** should be taught in every high school biology course. The United States Department of Education Secretary Betsy DeVos is in favor of teaching "intelligent design" (another term for creationism) in public schools (Waldman, 2017). Let's be clear on this issue: there is no evidence supporting creationism. First, the Biblical account, taken literally, that the Earth and life on it were created in six days, is not naturally possible. Second, even if the Biblical account is not taken literally and days are interpreted in millions or billions of years, the account is not true and does not explain the existing evidence. There is no systematic, scientific evidence supporting any creator of the universe or the Earth. Human beings did not arise from dust and bones. We know that human beings and all of life on Earth evolved over time based on the abundant and clear evidence from every branch of science supporting that fact. To deny the observed evidence, to deny our senses in pursuit of a false idea, is unreasonable and not at all adaptive.

In addition to being false, teaching creationism is harmful, because it encourages ignorance of evidence, and modernly, a mistrust and dismissal of science (Pew Research Center, 2015). Conservative and religious thinking are also linked with negative attitudes toward higher education (Brown, 2018). In 1984, the U.S. Committee on Science and Creationism concluded that teaching creation science is anathema to the need for a *"scientifically literate citizenry"* and a large pool of technically and scientifically qualified workers. Science is a method for discerning truth about the natural world. It uses empirical, systematic observation, precise measurements and analyses, and peer review. The fruits of science are all around us and benefit humankind greatly on a daily basis. Yes, sometimes people misuse science; they fake the evidence somehow (see "Critical Thinking"). But science is not the culprit here, the person using the science is. Science as a method for discovering truth is superior because it works. As a student in this kind of course, you are here to study what science says about women and men on our planet today, how they are similar and how they are different, and why that variation exists.

Chapter Summary

Abundant evidence indicates that life on our planet evolved over billions of years from earlier, simpler forms. Common descent from earlier forms is supported by biogeography, anatomical evidence, the fossil record, and genetic evidence. Natural selection is the process by which life evolved, with individual organisms possessing characteristics enhancing survival better able to reproduce and pass along such adaptive qualities. Human beings began to evolve about 7 million years ago, when there was a lineage split between apes and humans. Human beings evolved from Australopithecine creatures who were very ape-like and lived in trees, across various groups of early "man-like" creatures in the same genus called *Homo*. Bipedalism was particularly important in our evolution, enabling the use of hands which then accelerated brain growth, which accelerated development of planning, intelligence, and language. Various species co-existed with early Homo Sapiens, including different (and now extinct) species, Homo Floresiensis and Homo Neanderthalensis. Modern variations in our species include skin color, body shape, eye color, and lactose persistence. Although controversial mainly because it conflicts with religious accounts of life on our planet, evolution is the best explanation for the origins of life on our planet because it is supported by abundant evidence from nearly every branch of science.

Thoughtful Questions

- Explain how a decrease in the number of trees in Africa millions of years ago affected human evolution.
- Describe the physical qualities shared by primates that are adaptations for living in trees.
- Imagine a distant planet, very far from Earth, that is populated by two groups, the Biggies and the Littles. The Biggies are taller and much stronger than the Littles. They

18 *Human Evolution*

are similar in intelligence. Describe how society might be structured on this planet. Who's in charge?

- How might sex differences in physical size and strength affect daily tasks and responsibilities of individuals in early *Homo* groups?
- Imagine that women and men were on average the same size, with on average the same physical strength. How do you think the world would be different?
- Describe three early hominid groups.
- How do the examples of human evolution presented here show intermediate forms?
- Why have blue eyes spread so rapidly across the human population, having only occurred as a genetic mutation about 6,000 to 10,000 years ago?
- Explain how lactose persistence is adaptive using evolutionary theory.

Glossary

Adaptation: any characteristic that enhances the ability of a species to survive in a particular environment. A basic dimension of natural selection.

Adenosine triphosphate (ATP): a small molecule (a nucleotide) that supports energy transfer and metabolism at the cellular level. A biochemical necessary for life that is present in all living things.

Allen's Rule: warm-blooded species will vary in the shape of ears and appendages depending on the climate of their environment (rounder, more compact in colder climates; longer and leaner in warmer climates).

Bergmann's Rule: warm-blooded species will be larger overall in colder climates, smaller overall in warmer climates, with larger, more compact bodies having lower surface-to-air ratios, so that body heat is preserved.

Biogeography: the study of plant and animal life as it varies in different environments all over the world.

Common descent: a central premise of evolutionary theory, that all life on the planet evolved over time from earlier simpler forms.

Creationism: the religious idea that a deity created the universe, the Earth, and all life on Earth through magical processes.

Deoxyribonucleic acid (DNA): a protein structure that exists in every cell of all living things and composes the genetic code. DNA composes genes, which are present on chromosomes in the nuclei of cells.

Evolution: the process by which all life forms came to be on our planet, evolving from earlier, simpler forms through the process of **natural selection**.

Evolutionary theory: the scientific explanation that life on our planet evolved over millions and millions of years from earlier, simpler forms. Evolutionary theory is supported by evidence in every branch of science and is accepted as fact by the vast majority of scientists.

Fossil: any remains of past life (bones, teeth, shells, tools, footprints, etc.).

Homo: in Latin, "man"; the genus of human beings (Homo Sapiens) and many other now extinct groups. Three criteria for the genus are a large brain, small teeth and jaws, and tool making.

Human Evolution   19

Homologous forms: many body structures and processes are similar across species; the forms are the same. Homologous forms are evidence of common descent.

Lactose persistence: a genetic trait involving ability to digest lactose (milk sugar) with ease.

Melanin: a protein substance that produces pigment in the body, particularly skin color.

Morality: ideas about right and wrong. Moral behavior involves doing the right thing for the greatest well-being of all, even with self-sacrifice.

Mutations: random changes in genetic material that lead to variations in phenotype (see Chapter 3).

Natural selection: the process by which the natural environment "selects" some species members for survival and reproduction because they possess qualities that are particularly well-suited for that environment.

Open system: a system where energy is expended and acquired from the environment. Earth is an open system, with constant energy provided by the sun.

Out-of-Africa hypothesis: the idea that Homo Sapiens evolved only in Africa, then migrated to populate the Earth.

Pair bonding: development of a strong emotional bond between sexual mates. Occurs across species, including primates.

Part-whole fallacy: the poor argument tactic that if one part or one piece of a group or body is fake or bad, then the whole group or body is fake or bad.

Primates: various mammalian species characterized by qualities evolved for living in trees. Includes the great apes (humans, gorillas, chimpanzees, orangutans), monkeys, tarsiers, lemurs, and many other species.

Punctuated equilibrium: evolution of species involves long periods of stability followed by sudden periods of rapid change, usually caused by sudden changes in the living environment or mutations.

Reciprocity: the norm of giving and receiving. Receiving from others typically entails giving back to them in some form at some time.

Ribonucleic acid (RNA): a nucleic acid that is essential for protein production at the cellular level; RNA carries genetic instructions provided by DNA in the cell nucleus.

Straw person: a poor argument tactic whereby a solid argument is labeled as something easily knocked down (like a straw person) or easily dismissed ("only" a theory).

Struggle for existence: the fact that life is difficult; existence is a struggle for all species on the planet and always has been. A basic dimension of natural selection.

Survival of the fittest: the fact that those species members who possess the most adaptive characteristics for living in a particular environment will survive and reproduce in that environment. Those members who do not possess adaptive qualities will not survive, and thus will not reproduce or will reproduce less. A basic dimension of natural selection.

Theory: an explanation. Good theories explain most or all of the known evidence, provide testable hypotheses, are guided by natural law, and are falsifiable.

Variation: all species show variability in physical and behavioral traits and abilities. Variation within species is essential for species survival. A basic dimension of natural selection.

References

Ade, P. A. R., Aghanim, N., Ahmed, Z., Aikin, R. W., & Partridge, B. (2015). Joint analysis of BICEP2/Keck array and Planck data. *Physical Review Letters, 114*(10), 1-17. doi:0031-9007=15=114(10)=101301(17).

Allen, J. A. (1877). The influence of physical conditions in the genesis of species. *Radical Review, 1,* 108-140.

Bergmann, C. (1847). Über die Verhältnisse der Wärmeökonomie der Thiere zu ihrer Grösse. *Göttinger Studien 1:*595-708.

Bersaglieri, T., Sabeti, P. C., Patterson, N., Vanderploeg, T., Schaffner, S. F., Drake, J. A., Rhodes, M., Reich, D. E., & Hirschhorn, J. N. (2004). Genetic signatures of strong recent positive selection at the lactase gene. *American Journal of Human Genetics, 74*(6), 1111-1120. doi:10.1086/421051.

Braterman, P. S. (2013). How science figured out the age of Earth. *Scientific American, 20,* 4-12.

Brenner, M. & Hearing, V. J. (2008). The protective role of melanin against UV damage in human skin. *Photochemistry Photobiology, 84*(3), 539-549. doi:10.1111/j.1751-1097.2007.00226.x.

Brown, A. (2018). Most Americans say higher ed is heading in wrong direction, but partisans disagree on why. Pew Research Center. www.pewresearch.org/fact-tank/2018/07/26/most-americans-say-higher-ed-is-heading-in-wrong-direction-but-partisans-disagree-on-why/.

Darwin, C. R. (1859). *On the origin of species by means of natural selection, or the preservation of favoured races in the struggle for life.* London: John Murray.

Dawkins, R. (1997). The "Alabama insert": A study in ignorance and dishonesty. *Journal of the Alabama Academy of Science, 68*(1), 1-19.

Eiberg, H., Troelsen, J., Nielsen, M., Mikkelsen, A., Mengel-From, J., Kjaer, K. W., & Hansen, L. (2008). Blue eye color in humans may be caused by a perfectly associated founder mutation in a regulatory element located within the HERC2 gene inhibiting OCA2 expression. *Human Genetics, 123*(2), 177-187. doi:10.1007/s00439-007-0460-x.

Gerbault, P., Liebert, A., Itan, Y., Powell, A., Currat, M., Burger, J., Swallow, D. M., & Thomas, M. G. (2011). Evolution of lactase persistence: An example of human niche construction. *Philosophical Transactions of the Royal Society, 366*(1566), 863-877. doi:10.1098/rstb.2010.0268.

Gibbons, D. W., Wilson, J. D., & Green, R. E. (2011). Using conservation science to solve conservation problems. *Journal of Applied Ecology, 48*(3), 505-508. doi:10.1111/j.1365-2664.2011.01997.x.

Gokhman, D., Lavi, E., Prüfer, K., Fraga, M. F., Riancho, J. A., Kelso, J., Pääbo, S., Meshorer, E., & Carmel, L. (2014). Reconstructing the DNA methylation maps of the Neandertal and the Denisovan. *Science, 344,* 523-527.

Lassek, W. D. & Gaulin, S. J. C. (2009). Costs and benefits of fat-free muscle mass in men: Relationship to mating success, dietary requirements, and native immunity. *Evolution and Human Behavior, 30,* 322-328. doi:10.1016/j.evolhumbehav.2009.04.002.

Loftus, E. F. & Palmer J. C. (1996). Eyewitness testimony. In Banyard, P., & Grayson, A. (Eds.), *Introducing psychological research* (pp. 305-309). London: Palgrave.

Mojzsis, S. J., Arrhenius, G., McKeegan, K. D., Harrison, T. M., Nutman, A. P., & Friend, C. R. (1996). Evidence for life on Earth before 3,800 million years ago. *Nature, 384*(6604), 55-59. doi:10.1038/384055a0.

Noffke, N., Christian, D., Wacey, D., & Hazen, R. M. (2013). Microbially induced sedimentary structures recording an ancient ecosystem in the ca. 3.48 billion-year-old dresser formation, Pilbara, Western Australia. *Astrobiology, 13*(12), 1103-1124. doi:10.1089/ast.2013.1030.

Pew Research Center (2009). Global attitudes & trends. July 23. www.pewresearch.org/global/2009/07/23/lessons-from-the-2009-global-attitudes-survey-transcript/.

Pew Research Center (2015). Strong role of religion in views about evolution and perceptions of scientific consensus. October 22. www.pewresearch.org/science/2015/10/22/strong-role-of-religion-in-views-about-evolution-and-perceptions-of-scientific-consensus/.

Puiu, T. (2020). The timeline of human evolution. ZME Science. February 13. www.zmescience.com/science/timeline-human-evolutio-423/.

Powner, M. W., Gerland, B., & Sutherland, J. D. (2009). Synthesis of activated pyrimidine ribonucleotides in prebiotically plausible conditions. *Nature, 459,* 239-242. doi:10.1038/nature08013.

Skeptics Society (2010). Top 10 myths about evolution. www.skeptic.com/downloads/top-10-evolution-myths.

Swallow, D. M. (2003). Genetics of lactase persistence and lactose intolerance. *Annual Review of Genetics, 37,* 197-219. doi:10.1146/annurev.genet.37.110801.143820.

Waldman, S. A. & Terzic, A. (2017). Clinical pharmacology and therapeutics: Past, present, and future. *Precision Medicine, 101*(3), 300-303. doi:10.1002/cpt.592.

Walker, P. L. (2001). A bioarcheological perspective on the history of violence. *Annual Review of Archeology, 30,* 573-576. doi:0084-6570/01/1021-0573$14.00.

Yunis, J. J. & Prakash, O. (1982). The origin of man: A chromosomal pictorial legacy. *Science, 215*(4539), 1525-1530. doi:10.1126/science.7063861.

2 The Cellular Basis of Life

The Human Body: Cells and Their Basic Structure and Function	23
Organelles, Chromosomes, Genes, DNA	23
Mitosis and Meiosis	25
Meiosis and Variability	27
Autosomes and Sex Chromosomes	29
Problems in Meiosis	29

INEQUALITIES AND INJUSTICES

Baby Boys Are More Valuable?

Historically and across cultures, it is quite common to find that sons are considered more valuable than daughters (Bandyopadhyay & Singh, 2003). The Bible says a woman is doubly unclean after giving birth to a daughter compared to a son (Leviticus 12:2, 12:5), suggesting lower value of female children. An obvious preference for sons rather than daughters has persisted across centuries and into the modern era in China, India, and Korea (Gupta et al., 2003), Pakistan (Saeed, 2015), and Vietnam and Taiwan (Jha et al., 2006). Most scholars assert that sons are preferred because of their economic benefits to families. In agrarian and nomadic cultures, the greater physical strength of sons is potentially more useful in daily labor requiring physical strength (e.g., hunting, digging, carrying, lifting). In the modern world, men still earn more money on average than women (United States Bureau of Labor Statistics, 2017; World Economic Forum, 2016), with sons clearly able to then give more back to their parents in old age, when assistance is more likely to be required. India and China in particular favor sons, including by high rates of selective abortion of female fetuses (Chen, Li, & Meng, 2012; Ganatra, Hirve, Walawalker, Garda, & Rao, 2000; Jha et al., 2011). Brides in India also bring a high dowry, so daughters are expensive at marriage (Rahman & Rao, 2004), and if they are divorced or abandoned by their husbands, they are a shame to the family. Brides in situations of conflict over dowries are increasingly victims of physical abuse, suicide, and homicide in India (Natarajan, 1995; Rastogi & Therly, 2006).

In modern times, physical strength is less important for daily survival and occupational success, yet old traditions favoring boys over girls persist. This chapter highlights the cellular underpinnings of biological sex, natural, rather simple, common, predictable cellular processes that have very meaningful implications for survival and success.

LEARN MORE

Different Kinds of Human Body Cells

Not being an anatomy book, there are so many parts of the human body and different kinds of cells that we can't discuss. But there is a lot of information available on different kinds of cells, what they do, which kinds divide and replicate and which kinds don't, and how long they actually live. For example, nerve cells do not reproduce; this is why spinal cord and brain injuries are so devastating, because they are usually irreversible and the body cannot heal them. Blood cells also do not reproduce; blood cells are produced by bone marrow in the body when new cells are needed. Find out more about different kinds of cells at http://sciencenetlinks.com/student-teacher-sheets/cells-your-body/.

CRITICAL THINKING

Genes and Aggression?

Genes are the recipe for each of us as individual human beings. They determine physical body structures and even behavioral qualities, including personality traits, tendency toward alcoholism (Heath & Martin, 1994) and mental illness (Hennah, Thomson, Peltonen, & Porteous, 2006), and even aggressive behavior (Blonigen et al., 2003; Tellegen et al., 1988). What are some potential bases for these links? There is no denying the importance of society and important social institutions (family, community, school, religion) in affecting a person's behavior; someone who receives love, affection, and plenty of resources (good education, health care, healthy food, etc.) will develop as a healthy person and will be less likely to be aggressive or criminal. However, genes are linked with criminal behavior (Bohman, Cloninger, Sigvardsson, & von Knorring, 1982), including violent criminal behavior (Tiihonen et al., 2015). Jacob's Syndrome (when a person has XYY sex chromosomes) at one point was thought to be linked to aggressive, criminal behavior by men, as if the "extra maleness" provided by a second Y chromosome contributes to masculine, aggressive behavior (Jacobs et al., 1965). This claim has largely been refuted (Beckwith, 2002), but evidence remains of the link between genes and criminality. How do you think this happens, genes translating into criminal or aggressive behavior? Think of some potential *mechanisms* by which genes may determine behavioral qualities.

BONUS BOX

Moms Give More (Genetically) Than Dads

Each of us commonly knows that we inherit certain qualities from our moms, and other qualities from our dads. Within eggs and sperm, 23 chromosomes exist; when they combine, they create us, with 46 chromosomes, 23 from mom, and 23 from dad. The common understanding of genetics is that we get "half from mom, half from dad." But what most people don't know is that DNA doesn't only exist within a cell nucleus; DNA also exists inside mitochondria, the tiny organelles inside our cells that are vital for energy conversion. The DNA inside mitochondria (called mitochondrial DNA) contains the same recipe that every single body cell follows for taking nutrients entering the cell and converting them to energy to be used by the cell. We only inherit this DNA from our mothers. Why, you might ask? Because sperm contain no organelles; they only contain 23 chromosomes ready to unite with the egg's 23. The egg, however, is rich in nutrients and ready for fertilization, having been nurtured by the ovaries in preparation for reproduction. The egg contains nutrients and all the organelles our cells need, including mitochondria. These mitochondria are reproduced billions of times, beginning with fertilization and ending with each person's death. So thank you moms everywhere, for providing us with this important structure and the instructions needed to survive and grow every day!

The Human Body: Cells and Their Basic Structure and Function

The human body is composed of over 37 trillion cells, all of which are alive and contributing something to our bodies. Some cells die and replace themselves; other cells die and are not replaced. New cells are created when children grow and when wounds heal. Different cells have different and various functions. Muscle cells enable movement; brain cells enable thoughts, consciousness, feelings, and commands to other cells. Blood cells carry oxygen and nutrients to the other cells in our bodies. Every cell has a particular and specific function, which is usually carried out based on the production of proteins at the cellular level. Cells produce proteins that sustain life. Proteins communicate to other cells and allow the body to function (muscles to move, nutrients to be absorbed, hair to grow, hormones to be released). The same is true of the body cells of other species, which have similar structure and function, evidence of our common ancestry.

Organelles, Chromosomes, Genes, DNA

All living cells have a similar structure (there are some differences that are beyond the scope of this book). Cells in the human body and nearly every other organism on Earth (except bacteria) are eukaryotic cells, cells with a nucleus (see Figure 2.1). Cells are bound by a cellular membrane that is permeable; substances are able to enter and exit the cell. Inside the cell are many different little organs, or organelles. The command center of the cell, which tells the cell what proteins to produce and therefore how to function, is the nucleus. The nucleus is bound by its own membrane called the nuclear envelope. Within the nucleus are chromosomes, long thin protein structures that contain genes. Most of the time, except when the cell is dividing, chromosomes exist in the nucleus in an indistinct form called chromatin.

24 Cellular Basis of Life

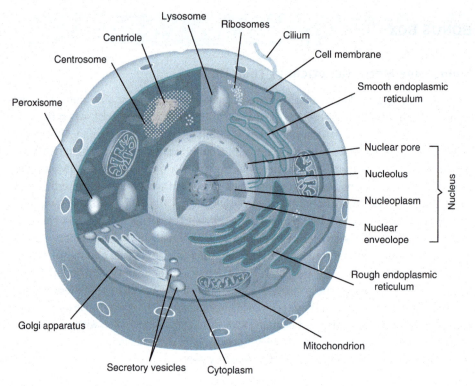

Figure 2.1 A eukaryotic cell
Source: Shutterstock

Genes are inherited from our parents (and in turn from all of our other ancestors as well) and determine the cellular organization and operation of our bodies. Because the cellular organization and operation of our bodies is determined by genes, genes determine many physical and behavioral traits. For example, blue eyes are produced by cellular production of proteins that is determined by genes. Brown eyes are determined by different proteins at the cellular level, also specified by genes. Genes specify the sequence of amino acids to be used in protein production within each cell. Genes in a sense contain the recipe or instructions for cellular function. Genes are composed of long strands of **deoxyribonucleic acid (DNA)**. DNA is a basic nucleotide chain that is essential to life on our planet, composed of amino acids, sugars, and phosphates.

Although all of our genes (46 chromosomes' worth, 23 **homologous** pairs, about 20,000 individual genes arrayed across those 46 chromosomes) are present inside every nucleus inside every one of our body cells, each cell is obviously not operated by all of our genes. Some genes are turned on within individual cells; those genes tell that cell how to function. Different genes are active in brain cells than are active in muscle cells than are active in skin cells. Cell differentiation is thus, of course, determined by genes; working as a whole, our genes determine how we look, grow, develop, age, what diseases we might develop, whether we are susceptible to mental illness, even our personality traits, and many other qualities and body functions. This is why we might resemble a parent or other relative, because we possess the same genes they do for those qualities. We will talk much more about genes and inheritance in our next chapter (Chapter 3, Genetics).

Cellular Basis of Life 25

Other organelles inside each body cell are also important for sustaining life; they are best understood in terms of their role in protein production. The genes in the nucleus specify the production of proteins in each particular cell. Inside the nucleus, the DNA instructions create molecules called **RNA (ribonucleic acid)**. These RNA molecules literally read the recipe inside the nucleus for the proteins produced by that particular cell. These RNA molecules (often called *messenger RNA*) then leave the nucleus and enter the cell to begin protein production. The RNA takes the instructions first to a structure called the **endoplasmic reticulum**, or **ER**. This is where protein production begins. The beginning protein then leaves the ER packaged in what's called a **vesicle**, which then travels through the **cytoplasm** (fluid inside each cell that contains the organelles) to another organelle called a **Golgi apparatus**. The Golgi apparatus continues processing and modifying the protein, which is released in a vesicle back into the cytoplasm. The protein then either leaves the cell for some body function or stays in the cell for its own functioning. Other organelles include the **mitochondria**, the energy factories inside each cell. The mitochondria take in nutrients and convert them into energy for the cell to use. Also inside the mitochondria are essential genes (inherited only from one's mother, more in Chapter 3) that control energy conversion. Other organelles, called **centrioles**, are important for creating a **spindle apparatus** that helps the cell to divide when cells reproduce.

Mitosis and Meiosis

The human life cycle is characterized by two main processes, growth and reproduction. Growth of course begins in utero and continues throughout the lifespan, although much of it is accomplished in early childhood and adolescence. Certain features continue to grow as we get older; in a cruel twist of fate, it is noses, ears, and feet that continue to grow! All growth, including repair of torn skin, broken bones, and other injuries, is accomplished through the cellular process of **mitosis**, a cell replication and division process that produces two identical body cells, with each having the same number and type of organelles, and a nucleus that contains all 46 chromosomes within. Mitosis occurs when children grow, when a cut heals itself, when body cells need to be replaced because they die. Understanding mitosis is important because it is a process that is essential for human development.

Mitosis is a rather straightforward process. Most of the time, cells are engaged in their typical function: producing body chemicals, transmitting information, producing movement. But within the **cell life cycle**, at some point mitosis will occur, again, whenever new cells are needed. Before mitosis begins, in preparation for it, the cell duplicates all of its organelles, so each has an exact copy. The chromosomes also duplicate themselves, with each chromosome bound to its duplicate by a **centromere**. A chromosome that has replicated itself is now composed of two copies called **sister chromatids**. The cell also synthesizes proteins that are important for cell division.

Mitosis itself occurs in several stages. First, in **prophase**, the nuclear envelope becomes fragments and the sister chromatids become visible, scattered throughout the cytoplasm. The centrioles begin to form the **spindle apparatus**, a network of fibers that will help the cell to divide by both pulling chromosomes to each side and pushing the cell apart. During **metaphase**, the chromosomes align down the center of the cell, with each centriole moving to each side, to the poles of the cell. **Anaphase** is when the cell begins to divide; the spindle pulls each sister chromatid (representing each single chromosome) to one side. During **telophase**, the chromosomes arrive at the poles, 46 at each (called the **diploid** number of chromosomes, or **2n**). The spindle apparatus disappears, and new nuclei form around each set of 46 chromosomes. The last stage

26 Cellular Basis of Life

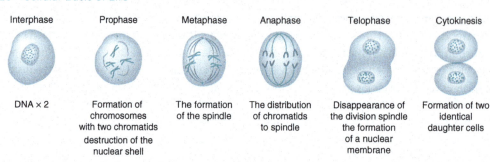

Figure 2.2 Mitosis
Source: Viktoriya Kabanova/Alamy Stock Vector

is **cytokinesis**, the division of the cytoplasm and organelles. The cell membrane forms a **cleavage furrow** in the middle of the cell to separate the two new cells. At the end of mitosis, there are two identical cells, each having formed from one original parent cell. This is how cell replication occurs, and it occurs millions of times in a lifetime, whenever new cells are needed (see "Learn More") (see Figure 2.2).

Meiosis is a very similar but altogether different process that is mainly concerned with what might happen during adulthood, reproduction. Your entire life, your body has been preparing itself to reproduce, to produce offspring. The follicles of eggs within each girl and woman begin forming in utero, when she is in the uterus of her mother. Viable sperm are produced at the very beginnings of puberty in boys. **Meiosis** is a type of cell division that is called reduction division; it does not involve production of identical cells with 46 chromosomes each, but rather begins with a 2n parent cell and results in four daughter cells with the **haploid** number of chromosomes, 23 (aka **1n** or just **n**). Human chromosomes are organized into 23 **homologous** pairs, with the paired chromosomes similar in length, number of genes, and gene location, but they are not identical to each other. One is inherited from each parent. Meiosis essentially separates the 23 pairs, so that one pair member ends up in each daughter cell. The daughter cells are not genetically identical; each is unique. Meiosis only occurs in the production of **gametes**, sex cells that combine to produce offspring in sexual reproduction. Gametes are produced within the **gonads**, ovaries in women and testes (aka testicles) in men. Gametes are commonly called eggs and sperm. Because each sperm and each egg contain only 23 chromosomes, their combination results in a cell that contains 46 chromosomes, 23 inherited from the egg (one's mother) and 23 inherited from the sperm (one's father). So that each parent is equally represented in the offspring, each gamete contains exactly half of the species' genetic code (although see Bonus Box!).

The cell division in meiosis occurs in the same manner as in mitosis, with some exceptions. Because meiosis begins with one parent cell and results in four, very different and not genetically identical daughter cells, meiosis requires two cellular divisions, formally called **Meiosis I** and **Meiosis II** (see Figure 2.3). As in the beginning of mitosis, in Meiosis I the organelles of the parent cell (which is 2n) duplicate themselves, including each of the 46 chromosomes. Each chromosome has duplicated itself, so now each of the 23 homologous pairs is composed of a pair of sister chromatids, bound together at the centromere. At the beginning of Meiosis I, the homologous pair members line up next to each other, forming what is called a **tetrad** (meaning four, with each pair member now duplicated).

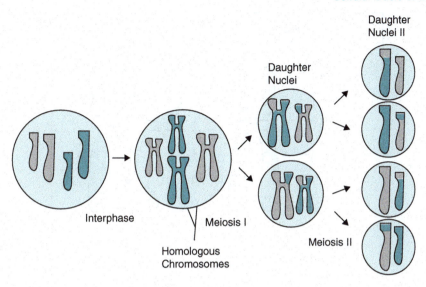

Figure 2.3 Meiosis

The alignment of the homologous pair members is called **synapsis**, and it occurs from a process that scientists still do not completely understand. During synapsis, the nonsister chromatids touch each other and seem to embrace; during this process of **crossing over**, the chromatids exchange genetic information (see Figure 2.4). For example, pair 1 has two members, A and B. A and B duplicate themselves before synapsis, so there are now two identical copies of each (e.g., A1 and A2, both of which are exact copies). When crossing over occurs, the A copies exchange genetic information with the B copies (so A1 exchanges with B1 and B2, A2 with both B1 and B2 as well perhaps). In this way, entirely new chromosomes are formed, chromosomes that now contain genes from both parents together (A1 and A2 are now no longer identical). In other words, a grandchild may inherit a chromosome made up of genes inherited from both his maternal grandmother and grandfather; or a chromosome containing genes from both his paternal grandmother and grandfather. This unique chromosome has never ever existed before, combining the genetic information of two people. Crossing over doesn't always happen, but it happens a lot.

After crossing over occurs, the still doubled homologous pair members are separated from each other, with 23 still doubled (but no longer exact duplicates) chromosomes pulled to each pole of the dividing cell. Meiosis I results in two daughter cells, each containing one member of each of the 46 homologous pairs, with each member still doubled. The daughter cells are not genetically identical; each only has one pair member (that is now likely different from crossing over), and there is no determination of which pair member ends up in each daughter cell. In Meiosis II, both of the new daughter cells divide, with one sister chromatid from each doubled chromosome going into each resulting cell. This second division results in four genetically unique daughter cells (eggs or sperm), ready to combine with the other gamete to create a totally genetically unique human being.

Meiosis and Variability

Why does meiosis occur in this way, ensuring that the resulting gametes are all genetically different from each other? Meiosis is nature's way of making sure there is great genetic variability within each species. **Variability** refers to the fact that there is great variety in the characteristics

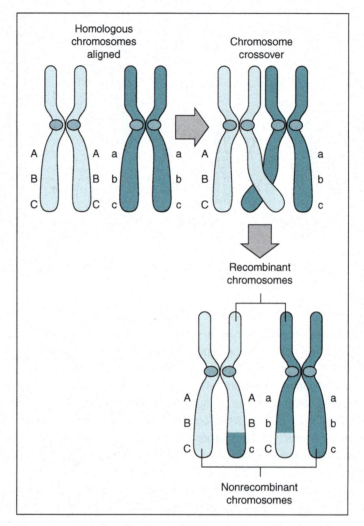

Figure 2.4 Crossing over of chromatids during meiosis

of any species; variations in size, shape, color, texture, and many other qualities. Remember, if every member of a species was genetically identical, one virus could kill the entire species very quickly. Variability means that some members may be susceptible to the virus, while some are not; that some have a good immune system to fight it, while others may not. Meiosis in people is one reason behind our great genetic variability.

There are three ways that each new individual, each human baby born, is assured a different combination of genes than either parent has. First, crossing over recombines genes on sister chromatids during Meiosis I, resulting in new combinations of genes, from genetically unrelated people (e.g., maternal grandmother and grandfather), that may have literally never existed before. Second, also during Meiosis I, there is no determination of which pair member from the 23 pairs ends up in which daughter cell. Imagine that for each chromosome pair, you have member A and B, across all 23 pairs, so there is A1 and B1, A2 and B2, and so on, all the way to the last pair, A23 and B23. Any of the pair members can be combined with any combination of all the other pair members. In other words, there is no systematic way that the As and the Bs separate during Meiosis I. One daughter cell could have mostly As and some Bs; mostly Bs and some As; about half As and Bs; or nearly all As (or Bs) and only a few Bs (or As). The number of possible combinations is enormous. Finally, with sexual reproduction, the genes of genetically unrelated individuals are combined, resulting in a unique combination of 46 chromosomes, one pair member inherited from each parent. All three of these processes result in human beings who are genetically unique, who have a specific combination of particular genes that is by itself statistically very unlikely (but did happen to result in one unique person). Meiosis is so powerful in creating diversity within species, it is almost magical (I said almost!).

In human beings, gamete production through meiosis is called **spermatogenesis** in men and **oogenesis** in women. **Spermatogenesis** is the production of sperm in the testes; it always results in four sperm, each of which has the haploid (n) number of chromosomes, 23, one from each homologous pair. **Oogenesis** is a bit different. Meiosis I results in one oocyte with 23 chromosomes (n) and organelles that is ready to be fertilized. The other daughter cell becomes what is called a **polar body**, which contains genetic material but no organelles. Meiosis II is not complete in oogenesis until actual fertilization occurs; eggs that are not fertilized have not completed the process of meiosis.

Autosomes and Sex Chromosomes

Of the 23 pairs of homologous chromosomes that human beings possess, 22 of those pairs contain genes that determine various physical characteristics of the body as well as behavioral and health qualities. Those chromosomes are called **autosomes**. The last pair of chromosomes is called the **sex chromosomes** because they determine all of the qualities that are related to biological sex (female, male, intersex, or some combination) (they actually determine lots of other non-sex-related qualities as well which we will discuss in Chapter 3). While there are multiple influences on the development of a fetus into a female, male, or intersex baby, the type of chromosomes in this pair of sex chromosomes determines biological sex and related functions for the most part.

The sex chromosomes can be X or Y. Every person, whatever the sex, possesses an X; a zygote (a fertilized egg) must have at least one X chromosome to survive (indicating how important this X is to life). That leaves the other spot in the pair open to another X (XX) or a Y (XY). Usually, XX in the sex chromosomes results in a female baby, XY results in a boy baby. In gamete production, every egg produced in oogenesis contains an X (because women are XX). In spermatogenesis, half of the sperm cells will contain an X, the other two will contain a Y. Upon fertilization, the sex chromosome carried within the sperm determines the sex of the fetus. Other outcomes, besides XX and XY, are possible as a result of anomalies in gamete formation.

Problems in Meiosis

Sometimes meiosis does not proceed as it usually does, resulting in four genetically unique daughter cells, each with 23 chromosomes (one member of each pair). Problems in meiosis can occur during Meiosis I or during Meiosis II, a problem called **nondisjunction** (failure of chromosomes to separate). When nondisjunction occurs in Meiosis I, the homologous pair members fail to separate, so that both (in the form of sister chromatids) end up in one daughter cell. When Meiosis II occurs in that daughter cell which has both pair members (still in the form of sister chromatids), the two daughter cells that result have two copies of the same chromosome. With fertilization, another copy of that homologue is added; the result is what is called a **trisomy**, or three copies of homologous chromosomes instead of two. The resulting zygote has 47 rather than 46 chromosomes (see Figure 2.5).

When nondisjunction occurs in Meiosis II, the sister chromatids fail to separate. This results in two daughter cells, one which has two copies of the same chromosome, and one which is missing a chromosome from that pair. So you have two gametes, one with 24 chromosomes, and one with only 22. If fertilization occurs here, the resulting zygote will have 45 or 47 chromosomes, not 46. When a person only has one member of a chromosome pair, they have what is called a **monosomy**. With the autosomes, a trisomy or monosomy may result in the zygote not surviving, or a fatal problem later in fetal development. But there are some children who are born with an autosomal monosomy or trisomy who survive.

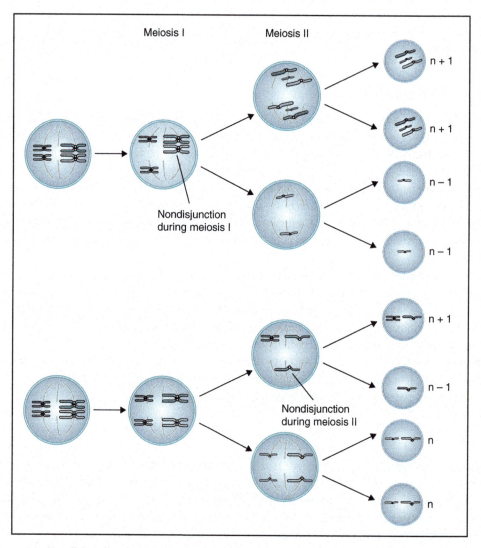

Figure 2.5 Nondisjunction in Meiosis I and Meiosis II

Cellular Basis of Life 31

Cri du Chat Syndrome is a condition where a child is born with only one member of chromosome pair 5, or is missing some genetic material from pair 5. These children have a misshapen larynx, which is responsible for the name of the syndrome ("Cat's Cry" in French), as they have a cat-like voice or cry. They are born with low birth weight and weak muscle tone. They have small heads with misshapen eyes and ears; widely spaced eyes; their face is sometimes said to be like a "moon face." Sadly they are also likely to have severe cognitive disabilities. Cri du Chat is rare and occurs in about 1 in 50,000 births. If these children live past age 1 year, they have a normal life expectancy (National Human Genome Research Institute, 2017) (see Figure 2.6).

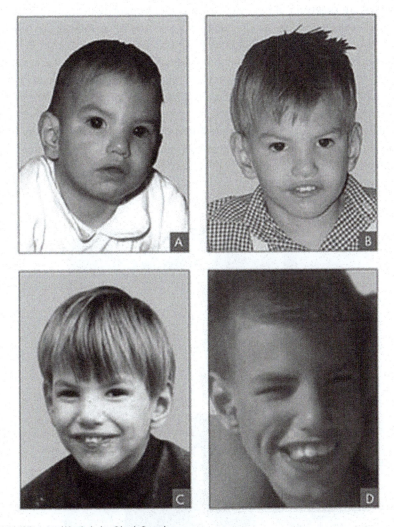

Figure 2.6 Children with Cri du Chat Syndrome
Source: Paola Cerruti Mainardi. Cri du Chat syndrome. Orphanet Journal of Rare Diseases. 1, 33. 2006 (www.ojrd.com/content/1/1/33).

Down Syndrome is much more common and well known, occurring in about 1 in 700 births. The likelihood of Down Syndrome increases with age of the mother, suggesting that nondisjunction in gamete formation is linked with age. Down Syndrome involves a trisomy of chromosome pair 21, such that the person has three rather than two copies of chromosome 21. There are physical features of Down Syndrome, including short stature, a round head, a rather large tongue that is fissured down the middle, larger gaps between the toes, stubby fingers, and what is called a folded eyelid. Unfortunately heart and respiratory problems are also common, as are hearing and thyroid problems. Cognitive disabilities, from mild to severe, are also apparent. The average lifespan of people with Down Syndrome has increased dramatically from age 25 years in 1983 to age 60 to 70 years today (Global Down Syndrome Foundation, 2018). This increase is largely thought to have resulted from an increase in the quality of care of individuals with Down Syndrome. Instead of institutionalization, more common before the modern era, people with Down Syndrome are receiving better medical care, more opportunities to live as independent adults, and more respect and love as individuals. My amazing niece Sadie Grace has Down's, and we couldn't love her any more than we do (see Figure 2.7, she's so cute!).

With the sex chromosomes, nondisjunction issues also result in particular syndromes, all of which generally involve the sex characteristics and reproductive organs. The idea that biological sex involves only two categories (i.e., that sex is *binary*) is incorrect. There are many chromosomal combinations that can result in various sex characteristics, both so-called "female" and "male" characteristics, as well as **intersex** conditions that are a combination of female and male or ambiguous (more in Chapter 3). As we will see also in later chapters, multiple forces operate in affecting both biological sex and gender identity (Bussey, 2011).

Figure 2.7 The author's niece, Sadie Grace, who has Down Syndrome
Source: Author

Sex chromosome monosomy results in XO, called **Turner Syndrome** (remember that a YO, or just a Y without an X, cannot survive). Turner Syndrome individuals generally appear female. They are short in stature with a broad chest, sometimes with what is called "neck webbing". They often have vision and hearing problems; they are susceptible to having hypothyroidism, heart disease, and diabetes. There can be some cognitive deficits, although they are generally mild. These girls often have underdeveloped reproductive organs, including uterus and ovaries, and as such they do not go through puberty and they do not menstruate. In this way they are infertile and cannot have children. Turner Syndrome occurs in about 1 in 2,000 to 1 in 5,000 female births (Sybert, McCauley, & McCauley, 2004).

Another condition is called **Klinefelter Syndrome** and results from sex chromosome trisomy, specifically XXY. Anytime a Y chromosome is present, male characteristics will develop (more in Chapter 4), so people with this syndrome are generally considered male with male features. Their internal and external sex organs are immature, with underdeveloped testes (called **hypogonadism**) and prostate glands. Because the testes are responsible for the production of **testosterone**, testosterone is below normal. These individuals are infertile, they do not produce viable sperm, or their fertility is lower than normal. They show little facial and body hair and they may show some breast development. They tend to have long limbs, large hands and feet. They tend to be taller than most people, and are often quiet, shy, and unassuming. There may be some learning difficulties as well, although they are generally intellectually normal. Klinefelter Syndrome occurs in 1 in 500 to 1 in 1,000 male births (National Institutes of Health, 2013).

Another trisomy of the sex chromosomes is XXX, called **Poly-X**. A greater number than three sex chromosomes is possible; Poly-X girls and women may have four or five X chromosomes. These individuals are always female internally and externally; they are generally fertile but may have underdeveloped **secondary sex characteristics** (e.g., breasts, body hair). Interestingly, they tend to be tall and thin, evidence of the importance of the X chromosome for inheritance of height. A trisomy X condition generally involves normal cognitive development and abilities; however, more than three X chromosomes generally involves cognitive impairment, including at a severe level. This condition is also linked with older maternal age. It occurs in about 1 in 1,000 female births (Otter, Schrander-Stumpel, & Curfs, 2010).

Yet another trisomy of sex chromosomes is called **Jacob's Syndrome**, which involves an XYY trisomy. These individuals have internal and external male sex organs, and they generally have normal testosterone. They tend to have normal fertility. They do tend to be tall (evidence of the importance of Y and male characteristics in physical growth), but may have hypotonia (poor muscle tone). Some learning and speech difficulties are associated with Jacob's Syndrome, including emotional and behavioral issues and attention problems. Babies who are XYY may show developmental delays, including in movement and motor skills. Jacob's occurs in about 1 in 1,000 male births (Gravholt, 2013). Early research suggested a link between Jacob's Syndrome and aggressive, criminal behavior (Jacobs et al., 1965), but this has largely been refuted (Beckwith, 2002) (see "Critical Thinking").

Chapter Summary

The basic unit of life is the cell, which contains the necessary instructions and equipment to produce proteins and sustain life. The basic human cell contains a nucleus (which contains chromosomes) and various other organelles used in protein production. Chromosomes contain genes

34 *Cellular Basis of Life*

which are composed of DNA; DNA provides the instructions for protein production for each particular cell. RNA carries the instructions from the nucleus into the cytoplasm of the cell, which contains organelles. Mitochondria are particularly important for energy conversion within the cell, while endoplasmic reticulum and Golgi apparatus are used in protein production. Cell division occurs every time new cells are needed. Mitosis is cell replication; it results in one cell dividing into two genetically identical daughter cells. Mitosis occurs during growth and cellular repair, including when injuries heal. Meiosis occurs only for gamete production, the production of sex cells (eggs in women, oogenesis; sperm in men, spermatogenesis). Meiosis involves two separate cell divisions, resulting in four daughter cells that are haploid and not genetically identical. Homologous chromosome pairs exchange genetic information in synapsis during Meiosis I. Problems in meiosis can occur, including nondisjunction in Meiosis I (failure of homologous pairs to separate) and Meiosis II (failure of sister chromatids to separate). Nondisjunction results in gametes with one extra and one missing chromosome. Various nondisjunction syndromes occur, including Down, Jacob's, Klinefelter, and Turner.

Thoughtful Questions

- Explain the basic process of protein production at the cellular level, including organelles involved and how it occurs.
- How do genes determine structure, appearance, and function of the body?
- Explain the differences between mitosis and meiosis.
- Explain how variability within species is ensured by gamete formation.
- Explain monosomy and trisomy conditions, including examples of each.
- How is it that mothers actually contribute greater genetic material to offspring than fathers do?
- How are the processes of spermatogenesis and oogenesis similar? How are they different?
- Can one determine whether nondisjunction occurs during Meiosis I or Meiosis II in development of a monosomy or trisomy? How so?
- Explain crossing over, including when it occurs and its outcomes.
- Explain how the lifespan of people with Down Syndrome changed dramatically from the 1980s to today.
- Zygotes with YO sex chromosomes (only a Y, with no X) cannot survive. What does this tell us about the function of (the genes contained on) the X chromosome?

Glossary

Anaphase: the cell division stage where sister chromatids (duplicated chromosomes) separate from each other.

Autosomes: chromosomes containing genes that affect body structure and functions; all 22 pairs of human chromosomes besides the sex chromosomes.

Cell life cycle: interphase (during which organelles and DNA are duplicated) and cellular division (mitosis).

Cellular membrane: the permeable membrane that surrounds eukaryotic cells. Nutrients may enter the cell and proteins and waste may exit the cell.

Cellular Basis of Life 35

Centromere: a small structure that holds sister chromatids (duplicated chromosomes) together until they divide.

Chromatin: the indistinct state of chromosomes within the nucleus, when the cell is not preparing to divide.

Chromosomes: long thin protein structures that contain genes; located within cell nuclei. Humans have 46 chromosomes, 23 homologous pairs; one pair member is inherited from mother, the other pair member is inherited from father.

Cleavage furrow: the furrow or groove that develops and grows within a dividing cell in mitosis; it tightens and eventually splits the cellular membrane in two, resulting in two daughter cells.

Cri du Chat Syndrome: a genetic condition resulting from nondisjunction, where a person is born with only one member of chromosome pair 5, or is missing some genetic material from pair 5.

Crossing over: an exchange of genetic information between homologous chromosome pair members during synapsis in Meiosis I.

Cytokinesis: division of the cytoplasm and organelles in mitosis.

Cytoplasm: fluid within cells that surrounds the nucleus and contains the organelles.

Deoxyribonucleic acid (DNA): a basic nucleotide chain that is essential to life on our planet, composed of amino acids, sugars, and phosphates.

Diploid: the full complement of chromosomes, 46, or 2n (with n = number of pairs, 23 in humans).

Down Syndrome: a genetic condition resulting from nondisjunction, where a person is born with three copies of chromosome 21, also called trisomy 21.

Endoplasmic reticulum (ER): a cell organelle that is responsible for protein production; messenger RNA brings the instructions for protein production first to the ER.

Eukaryotic cells: cells with a nucleus; human cells are eukaryotic cells. Bacteria are examples of **prokaryotic** cells (cells without a nucleus).

Gametes: sex cells (eggs and sperm) that combine to produce offspring in sexual reproduction. Gametes have the **haploid** number of chromosomes (23).

Genes: the units of inheritance. Genes are composed of DNA, which provides instructions for protein production within each cell of the body. We inherit 23 chromosomes containing genes from our mother, and 23 chromosomes containing genes from our father. Human beings have about 20,000 genes.

Golgi apparatus: a cell organelle that participates in protein production; modifies proteins and packages them into a vesicle.

Gonads: the main sex organs, ovaries in women, testes in men. Gametes (eggs and sperm, respectively) are produced in the gonads, which also release hormones.

Haploid: the half number of chromosomes; when a cell contains only one pair member of each of the pairs of chromosomes (n). In humans, n = 23. **Gametes** are the only human cells that are haploid.

Homologous: chromosomes exist in pairs, with the paired chromosomes similar in length, number of genes, and gene location. Pair members are not identical to each other; within each person, one pair member of all 23 pairs is inherited from mother, the other pair member of all 23 pairs is inherited from father.

Hypogonadism: underdevelopment of the gonads, resulting in lower fertility, infertility, or hormone deficiencies.

36   *Cellular Basis of Life*

Intersex: various conditions where an infant shows neither clearly female nor clearly male sex characteristics at birth. Commonly, genitals are ambiguous or external genitalia do not match internal reproductive organs.

Jacob's Syndrome: a sex chromosome trisomy (XYY), resulting in a person with normal sex characteristics who may have some learning disabilities or motor impairment.

Klinefelter Syndrome: a sex chromosome trisomy (XXY), resulting in a male person with immature sex characteristics.

Meiosis: *reduction division*; in gamete production, begins with a 2n parent cell and results in four daughter cells with the haploid (n) number of chromosomes. Meiosis occurs in two stages, Meiosis I and Meiosis II.

Meiosis I: the first meiotic division, where homologous chromosome pairs align (**synapsis**), share genetic information (**crossing over**), and then separate, with one pair member going to each of two resulting daughter cells.

Meiosis II: the second meiotic division, where sister chromatids separate. Each of the two daughter cells resulting from Meiosis I divides, resulting in four daughter cells.

Metaphase: the cell division stage where chromosomes align along the equator of the cell; the centrioles move to the poles of the cell.

Mitochondrial DNA: DNA inside mitochondria that contains the recipe for taking nutrients entering the cell and converting them to energy to be used by the cell. Inherited only from mothers, never from fathers.

Mitosis: cell replication that leads to growth and healing. Cells produced through mitosis are genetically identical.

Monosomy: a genetic condition where a person is missing a chromosome (i.e., of a particular chromosome pair, they only have one chromosome instead of two).

Nondisjunction: a problem in meiosis when homologous pair members fail to separate (**Meiosis I**), or when sister chromatids fail to separate (**Meiosis II**). Results in gametes that have an extra chromosome and a missing chromosome.

Nuclear envelope: the membrane surrounding a cell nucleus; it fragments to release chromosomes in mitosis and meiosis.

Nucleus: the command center of human cells; contains human chromosomes and produces ribosome subunits of RNA.

Oogenesis: the formation of mature eggs in the ovaries. The result of Meiosis I is an oocyte that is ready to be fertilized and a polar body (or two). Meiosis II is not complete unless fertilization occurs.

Organelles: tiny organs inside human cells (e.g., mitochondria, Golgi apparatus).

Polar body: an outcome of oogenesis, contains chromosomes but no organelles.

Poly-X Syndrome: a genetic disorder involving a trisomy with an extra X sex chromosome (XXX). Poly-X may also involve other genotypes (XXXX, XXXXX). Symptoms include tallness, thinness, cognitive deficits.

Prokaryotic cells: cells without a nucleus (e.g., bacteria).

Prophase: the first stage in cell division, when the nuclear envelope fragments, organelles are already copied, and the chromosomes appear in the cytoplasm as sister chromatids.

Ribonucleic acid (RNA): produced inside cell nuclei, RNA reads the instructions provided by the **DNA** in genes. Messenger RNA then takes the recipe for protein production outside the nucleus to other organelles in the cell.

Cellular Basis of Life 37

Sex chromosomes: one pair of chromosomes that determine biological sex. XX generally results in a female person; XY generally results in a male person. Other outcomes are possible, including **trisomy** (XXX, XXY, XYY) and **monosomy** (XO).

Sister chromatids: duplicated chromosomes. Chromosomes copy themselves in preparation for cell division.

Spermatogenesis: the process of sperm production in the testes; meiosis normally results in four genetically unique sperm.

Spindle apparatus: the structure that develops from the centrioles, long fibers that pull chromosomes apart and push the cell apart in cell division.

Synapsis: the alignment of homologous chromosomes during Meiosis I; crossing over occurs during synapsis.

Telophase: the cell division stage where chromosomes arrive at the dividing cell's poles, new nuclei for daughter cells begin to form, and the spindle apparatus disappears.

Testosterone: a male sex hormone that affects sexual development, sexual behavior, and aggression.

Tetrad: the alignment of chromosome pairs when they are in the form of sister chromatids (forming a set of four chromosomes).

Trisomy: a condition where a person has an extra (or third) chromosome. Down Syndrome results from trisomy 21 (three copies of chromosome 21 instead of the normal two).

Turner Syndrome: a genetic disorder involving a monosomy of the sex chromosomes (XO). Characteristics include hypogonadism, immature secondary sex characteristics, infertility, neck webbing, some cognitive deficits.

Variability: the fact that there is great variety in the characteristics of any species; variations in size, shape, color, texture, and many other qualities.

References

Bandyopadhyay, S. N. & Singh, A. (2003). History of son preference and sex selection in India and in the west. *Bulletin of the Indian Institute of History of Medicine, 33*(2), 149-167.

Blonigen, D. M., Hicks, B. M., Krueger, R. F., Patrick, C. J., & Iacono, W. G. (2005). Psychopathic personality traits: Heritability and genetic overlap with internalizing and externalizing psychopathology. *Psychological Medicine, 35*(5), 637-648. doi:10.1017/S0033291704004180.

Buddelmeijer, N. & Beckwith, J. (2002). Assembly of cell division proteins at the E. coli cell center. *Current Opinion in Microbiology, 5*(6), 553-557. doi:10.1016/s1369-5274(02)00374-0.

Bussey, K. (2011). Gender identity development. In S. J. Schwartz, Luyckx, K., & Vignoles, V. L. (Eds.) *Handbook of identity theory and research* (603-628). New York: Springer. doi:10.1007/978-1-4419-7988-9_25.

Cloninger, C. R., Sigvardsson, S., Bohman, M., & von Knorring, A. L. (1982). Predisposition to petty criminality in Swedish adoptees: Cross-fostering analysis of gene-environment interaction. *Archives of General Psychiatry, 39*(11), 1242-1247. doi:10.1001/archpsyc.1982.04290110010002.

Ganatra, B. R., Hirve, S. S., Walawalker, S., Garda, L., & Rao, V. N. (2000, February). Induced abortion in a rural community in western Maharashtra: Prevalence and patterns. Paper presented at the Workshop on Reproductive Health in India: New Evidence and Issues, Pune, India.

Global Down Syndrome Foundation (2018). FAQ and facts about Down Syndrome. www.globaldownsyndrome. org/about-down-syndrome/facts-about-down-syndrome/.

Groth, K. A., Skakkebaek, A., Hast, C., Gravholt, C. H., & Bojesen, A. (2013). Clinical review: Klinefelter syndrome - a clinical update. *The Journal of Clinical Endocrinology and Metabolism, 98*(1), 20-30. doi:10.1210/jc.2012-2382.

Gupta, S. S., Ton, V. K., Beaudry, V., Rulli, S., Cunningham, K., & Rao, R. (2003). Antifungal activity of amiodarone is mediated by disruption of calcium homeostasis. *Journal of Biological Chemistry, 278*(31), 28831-28839.

Heath, A. C., Cloninger, C. R., & Martin, N. G. (1994). Testing a model for the genetic structure of personality: A comparison of the personality systems of Cloninger and Eysenck. *Journal of Personality and Social Psychology, 66*(4), 762-775. doi:10.1037//0022-3514.66.4.762.

Hennah, W., Thomson, P., Peltonen, L., & Porteous, D. (2006). Genes and schizophrenia; beyond schizophrenia: The role of D1SC1 in major mental illness. *Schizophrenia Bulletin, 32*(3), 409-416.

Holy Bible, New International Version. (2011). Leviticus 12:2-5.

Jacobs, P. A., Brunton, M., Melville, M., Brittain, R. P., & McClement, W. F. (1965). Aggressive behaviour, mental sub-normality and the *XYY* male. *Nature, 208,* 1351.

Jha, P., Chaloupka, F. K., Corrao, M., & Jacob, B. (2006). Reducing the burden of smoking world-wide: Effectiveness of interventions and their coverage. *Drug and Alcohol Review, 25*(6), 597-609. doi:10.1080/09595230600944511.

Jha, P., Kesler, M., Kumar, R., Ram, F., Ram, U., Aleksandrowicz, L. ... Banthia, J. K. (2011). Trends in selective abortions of girls in India: Analysis of nationally representative birth histories from 1990 to 2005 and census data from 1991 to 2011. *The Lancet, 377,* 1921-1928. doi:10.1016/S0140-6736(11)60649-1.

Natarajan, M. (1995). Victimization of women: A theoretical perspective on dowry deaths in India. *Feminist Psychological Perspectives, 3*(4), 297-308.

National Human Genome Research Institute (2017). About Cri du Chat Syndrome. www.genome.gov/Genetic-Disorders/Cri-du-Chat.

National Institutes of Health (2013). Klinefelter syndrome. *Genetics Home Reference.* http://ghr.nlm.nih.gov/condition/klinefelter-syndrome.

Otter, M., Schrander-Stumpel, C. T., & Curfs, L. M. (2010). Triple X syndrome: a review of the literature. *European Journal of Human Genetics, 18*(3), 265-271. doi:10.1038/ejhg.2009.109.

Rahman, L. & Rao, V. (2004). The determinants of gender equity in India: Examining Dyson and Moore's thesis with new data. *Population and Development Review, 30*(2), 239-268. doi:10.1111/padr.2004.30.

Rastogi, M. & Therly, P. (2006). Dowry and its link to violence against women in India. *Trauma, Violence, and Abuse, 7*(1), 66-77.

Saeed, A., Belghitar, Y., & Clark, E. (2015). Political connections and leverage: Firm-level evidence from Pakistan. *Managerial and Decisions Economics, 36*(6), 364-383. doi:10.1002/mde.2674.

Tellegen, A., Lykken, D. T., Bouchard Jr., T. J., & Wilcox, K. (1988). Personality similarity in twins reared apart and together. *Journal of Personality and Social Psychology, 54*(6), 1031-1039. doi:10.1037/0022-3514.54.6.1031.

Tiihonen, J., Rautianen, M. R., Ollila, H. M., Repo-Tiihonen, E., Virkkunen, M., Palotie, A., ... & Paunio, T. (2015). Genetic background of extreme violent behavior. *Molecular Psychiatry, 20*(6), 786-792.

United States Bureau of Labor Statistics (2017). Women's median earnings 82 percent of men's in 2016. The Economics Daily, March 8. www.bls.gov/opub/ted/2017/womens-median-earnings-82-percent-of-mens-in-2016.htm.

World Economic Forum (2016). The simple reason for the gender pay gap: work done by women is still valued less. April 12. www.weforum.org/agenda/2016/04/the-simple-reason-for-the-gender-pay-gap-work-done-by-women-is-still-valued-less/.

3 Genetics

Chromosomes, Genes, Alleles: Basic Definitions   43
One-Trait Crosses   44
Simple and Polygenic Inheritance   46
Sex-Linked Traits   46
Sex-Linked Genetic Disorders   47
Autosomal Genetic Disorders   48
    Autosomal Dominant Disorders   49
    Autosomal Recessive Disorders   50
Epigenetics   52

CRITICAL THINKING

Do Genes Determine Social Power?

It is an American cultural value to work hard, do your best, and strive for individual achievement. The American ideal is a person who is motivated to succeed and who works effortfully to make successes happen. Our culture is called **individualistic**; individual goals are elevated above group goals, and individual achievement is emphasized (Hofstede, 2001). Social psychologists have found that Americans have a greater tendency than people from other cultures to make **dispositional attributions**, that is, explanations of cause that emphasize the actions of individual people, rather than situational or societal factors (Krull et al., 1999). In explaining poverty, many Americans focus on individual actions; e.g., "Poor people are lazy, they just don't work hard enough." United States Senator Jason Chaffitz (R-Utah, retired) is rather famous for asserting that people who can't afford health care should just not buy an iPhone (http://fortune.com/2017/03/07/gop-health-care-plan-chaffetz-iphone/), an explanation that focuses on individual choices and actions. Other Americans, and people from other cultures as well (Masuda, Gonzalez, Kwan, & Nisbett, 2008), pay greater attention to situational factors in explaining poverty, including being born poor, lack of opportunity, oppression, racial and gender discrimination, U.S. corporate culture, and so on. Senator Bernie Sanders (I-Vermont) is well-known for emphasizing situational factors in explaining poverty, including record-breaking income and wage disparities between U.S. corporate CEOs and workers in their companies, tax breaks for the wealthiest

Americans, and systematic, historical discrimination against African Americans, immigrant Americans, and women. Another example of attributions and explanations involves the fact that the United States has never had a female President. Is that because women have lacked opportunities for formal education, for political experience, for attaining power? Is it because the world sees women fundamentally differently, as if a woman could not handle the job of most powerful person in the world? Or is it because women haven't worked hard enough, because they don't have the capabilities necessary to do the job?

The reading in Chapter 2 and this chapter focuses on genes, including their influence on the development of biological sex and skin color. Do these genetic variations, sex and skin color, relate to social power in society? Do they relate to poverty? Do these qualities affect how people are treated, evaluated, valued in society? How is it individualistic to evaluate a person based on nearly immutable, ascribed characteristics? These are some questions that require lots of critical thinking, including an examination of inner beliefs and values. Thinking about such issues can be challenging, even mentally uncomfortable or unpleasant; this alone is reason enough to take on these thinking activities, to challenge oneself to think in a more complex, educated, expansive, and courageous way. Changing one's mind in response to evidence and careful critical examination is an admirable act; thoughtful educated people do this routinely.

INEQUALITIES AND INJUSTICES

The Curious Case of Rosalind Franklin

One of the most important discoveries of the 20th century was the discovery of DNA by James Watson, Francis Crick, and Maurice Wilkins (for which they received the Nobel Prize in 1962). The discovery may not have belonged solely to these male scientists, however. Rosalind Franklin, a scientist who worked with x-ray diffraction in the 1950s at King's College in London, had apparently been the first person known to have produced an image of a DNA molecule, showing its double-helix structure (see Figure 3.1). Maurice Wilkins worked in the same laboratory with Rosalind Franklin and, some assert, shared the image with Watson and Crick without Franklin's permission. Rosalind Franklin received and still receives no formal credit of any kind for the discovery of the properties of the DNA molecule. A play written by Anna Ziegler, called *Photograph 51* (the infamous double-helix image), dramatizes the competition and complex relationships that can sometimes surround important scientific discoveries, and depicts the plight of women within male-dominated professions, both historically and modernly. Read more in a blog by *Scientific American* (Lloyd, 2010; https://blogs.scientificamerican.com/observations/rosalind-franklin-and-dna-how-wronged-was-she/).

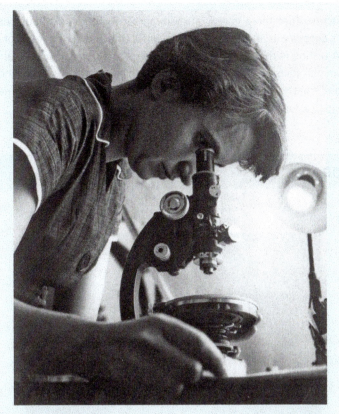

Figure 3.1 Rosalind Franklin
Source: Alamy

BONUS BOX

The Human Genome Project

https://www.genome.gov/10001772/all-about-the-human-genome-project-hgp/

The Human Genome Project (HGP) was an international project with which the United States National Institutes of Health collaborated through the National Human Genome Research Institute. The goal of the project, one of the most important scientific projects of the 20th century by far, was to completely map the genetic code of the human species (all approximately 20,000 genes on all 46 chromosomes). All of a species' genes comprise its so-called genome. The entire human genome was mapped by 2003. The HGP has provided detailed information about the organization and function of the human genome, including which genes are involved in disease, mental illness, cognitive abilities, and physical features. The importance of the findings of the HGP cannot be overestimated. The HGP serves as a catalyst for research and for development of medical technologies and treatments; and it gives us a much greater understanding of who we are as human beings, based on this recipe provided in our cells. Also thanks to the HGP, DNA technology has progressed rapidly, so much so that there is now a retail market for obtaining your genetic profile, including one's ancestry (makes a great holiday gift!). One interesting result of easy, affordable, fast DNA testing is that questions of paternity are no longer so relevant for human society. How might such questions affect relationships between women and men? How does questionable paternity relate to poverty and single parenthood for women and men?

LEARN MORE

Imprinting

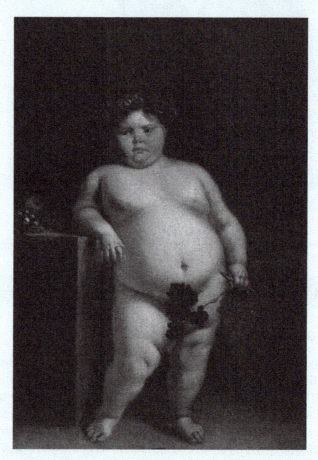

Figure 3.2 A portrait of a child with Prader-Willi Syndrome (Juan Carreno de Miranda, 1614-1685)
Source: Wiki

Geneticists are discovering more and more about DNA and the genetic codes for all life on Earth every single day. One important recent discovery concerns **imprinting**, which occurs when only the allele of a gene pair inherited from one parent is expressed; the allele inherited from the other parent is silenced, or imprinted. In this way, only one allele in the gene pair, or only the alleles on one chromosome, affect the phenotype (appearance) of the individual. When a disordered chromosome (involving missing or deleted genes) is inherited from one parent, and the corresponding chromosome from the other parent is silenced, various disorders may result. Two disorders occur as a result of a gene deletion or inactivation on chromosome 15, with imprinting of the corresponding genes on the other member of chromosome pair 15. Prader-Willi Syndrome is the outcome when the mother's genes on 15 are imprinted (silenced) and the father's are deleted/inactivated. Physical features include excessive weight gain, small stature, small feet and hands. Hypogonadism (underdevelopment of the gonads) may occur, with delayed puberty and underdeveloped sex characteristics. There are cognitive problems, including speech delays and learning disabilities, as well as sleep difficulties (see Figure 3.2). Angleman Syndrome involves the opposite pattern of gene imprinting and deletion (father's genes silenced, mother's deleted). Physical effects include particular facial features, including a wide mouth with a larger tongue, and hypopigmented skin and eyes. There are profound developmental delays, severe language impairment, and movement and balance problems. These children show a characteristically happy disposition, leading this syndrome to be previously called "Happy Puppet" Syndrome (Angleman, 1965). Both of these syndromes are rather rare (1 in 10,000-15,000/20,000 births). Yet another imprinting disorder is Beckwith-Wiedemann Syndrome (1/13,000 births), which involves imprinting and problems with genes on chromosome 11 (Viljoen & Ramesar, 1992). These children are born with large birth weight and length, have low blood sugar (hypoglycemia) at birth, have abdominal wall defects, and macroglossia (a large tongue). They show characteristic creases in their ears, called "pits." They may also have musculoskeletal abnormalities and hearing loss. There are few cognitive deficits, with intelligence generally considered normal. Sadly, they have a predisposition to developing cancer (Henry et al., 1991).

You can learn more about Prader-Willi, Angleman, and Beckwith-Wiedemann Syndromes, and imprinting of genes, by checking out a great research article by Jill Adams (2008) (at www.nature.com/scitable/topicpage/imprinting-and-genetic-disease-angelman-prader-willi-923).

Chromosomes, Genes, Alleles: Basic Definitions

Before we begin any meaningful discussion of genetics and inheritance, an introduction to basic definitions comes first. We have already defined some of these terms in Chapter 2; here, we will use slightly different definitions, to fit in the context of this chapter. Chromosomes are organized protein structures that contain genes; they are located within the nucleus of every cell. Human beings have 23 pairs of chromosomes, 23 inherited from their mother, 23 inherited from their father. The pairs of chromosomes are called homologous because they are similar in length, number of genes they carry, and gene location on the chromosome.

A gene is a locus (or region) of DNA on a chromosome that encodes a cell function or protein product. Genes are the molecular units of heredity; they contain recipes for protein production within certain kinds of cells, proteins that affect human growth, appearance, functions of the body, and daily physiology. Because chromosomes occur in pairs, genes occur in pairs as well. An allele is an alternative form of a gene having the same position (locus) on a pair of chromosomes.

Because we inherit one chromosome in each pair from each parent, we inherit different alleles of the same gene from each of our parents. Sometimes alleles are what is called **dominant**; the existence of one allele always leads to the expression of trait, regardless of the other allele. In other words, possessing that allele affects a person's **phenotype**, or the physical expression of a trait. Sometimes alleles are **recessive**; multiple copies of the allele must be present for the trait to be expressed, for the phenotype to be affected. The particular combination of alleles one actually possesses is called a **genotype**; the phenotype is how the genotype is physically expressed, either in appearance, in body function, in physiology, or in behavior. If a person possesses one of each type of allele (one dominant and one recessive), the person is said to be **heterozygous** for the trait, and the dominant trait will be expressed. If a person possesses two alleles of the same type (dominant or recessive), they are **homozygous**, and the corresponding trait will be expressed in the phenotype.

Twenty-two pairs of human chromosomes are called **autosomes**, which are chromosomes containing genetic information for formation, structure, function, appearance, and behavior of the person. The last pair of chromosomes are the **sex chromosomes** (called **allosomes**), distinct from the autosomes in important and interesting ways. First, the sex chromosomes (especially the Y chromosome) determine biological sex; the autosomes do not. Second, the sex chromosomes are not necessarily homologous. Female humans (and other species) possess two X chromosomes as their sex chromosomes, which are clearly homologous, like any autosomal chromosome pair. Male humans possess XY as their sex chromosomes; this pair is not homologous, because the Y chromosome does not contain similar genes at the same location as the X. The X chromosome contains about 1,100 genes; the Y chromosome only contains about 200 genes, and of those the most important are those that determine maleness, genes referred to as the **sex-determining region of Y**, or **SRY**. The X and Y chromosomes are homologous for some genes; these genes are called "**pseudoautosomal**" (Ross & Capel, 2005, p. 325), and do engage in crossing over during meiosis (see Chapter 2). However, there are many genes that are X-only, for which men are called **hemizygotic**, because they have only half the normal genetic material. Third, the sex chromosomes determine multiple human characteristics, particularly the X chromosome, that are not specifically related to biological sex, including tendency toward cancer (Ross & Capel, 2005) and intelligence (Skuse, 2005; Zhao, Kong, & Qu, 2014). Fourth, with a female offspring's cells, one X is inactivated early in fetal development; this inactivation is replicated millions of times in somatic cells thereafter. As such, women are also hemizygotic for certain qualities, with only one X (either the one from mother, or the one from father) operating in nearly all of their body cells (Ross & Capel, 2005). Interestingly, an X chromosome alone (without any homologue, X or Y) will result in a person who is more likely female, a person with Turner Syndrome (XO; see Chapter 2). A Y chromosome alone, without an accompanying X, will result in failure, the zygote will not form properly and pregnancy will not occur or will end in spontaneous abortion (U.S. National Library of Medicine, 2017).

One-Trait Crosses

The operation of dominant and recessive alleles is easily illustrated by using what is called a **one-trait cross**, or a **Punnet Square**. Some human traits are rather simple in their inheritance; only one pair of genes determines the phenotype. If one of those genes is dominant, it will appear in the phenotype. If both of those genes are recessive, that quality will appear in the phenotype. Human earlobes for example, are either attached or unattached (see Figure 3.3). The allele for unattached earlobes is dominant; if a person possesses just one dominant allele, their earlobes

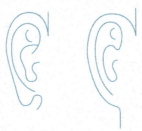

Figure 3.3 Unattached and attached earlobes

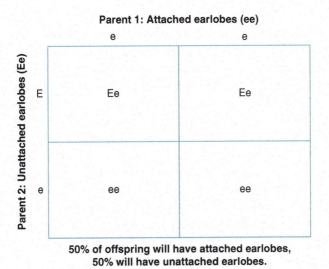

Figure 3.4 Outcomes of heterozygous and homozygous recessive crossing

will be unattached. The allele for attached earlobes is recessive; one must possess both recessive alleles (be homozygous) for earlobes to be attached. The different possible combinations are easily displayed in a one-trait cross (see Figure 3.4). Other human qualities determined by only two alleles include freckles (present or not), finger length (short or long), and hair line (widow's peak or not). Having a widow's peak, shorter fingers, and freckles are all dominant traits; only one allele must be inherited from either parent for the trait to be expressed. Not having a widow's peak, longer fingers, and not having freckles are all in fact recessive traits.

Table 3.1 shows different genotypic outcomes and their probabilities for a simple trait determined only by two alleles. Whenever either parent is homozygous dominant for a trait, that trait will dominate the phenotype, regardless of the other parent's genotype. There is 100% likelihood of the dominant phenotype, and 0% likelihood of the recessive phenotype. It's when parents are heterozygous that outcomes become interesting. Two heterozygous parents have 75% of the offspring showing the dominant phenotype, and only 25% of the offspring showing the recessive phenotype. A 50-50 outcome is only possible when one parent is heterozygous and the other is homozygous recessive. A certainty of having the recessive trait show in offspring is only possible with two parents both with the homozygous recessive genotype. Usually, it's pretty clear when a person is homozygous recessive for a trait. It's never clear from the phenotype if a person is homozygous dominant or heterozygous; so if you desperately want your child to have attached earlobes but your potential mate has unattached lobes, a DNA test might be in order!

46 *Genetics*

Table 3.1 Likelihood of various phenotypic outcomes for a simple (two-allele) trait

Genotype of parents	Chance of dominant phenotype	Chance of recessive phenotype
EE x EE	100%	0%
EE x Ee	100%	0%
EE x ee	100%	0%
Ee x Ee	75%	25%
Ee x ee	50%	50%
ee x ee	0%	100%

Simple and Polygenic Inheritance

Unlike earlobes and whether they are attached or not, most human qualities are determined by multiple genes. Simple inheritance is when one pair of genes pretty much determines an entire phenotype; whether a person has attached or unattached earlobes, or shorter or longer fingers. Polygenic inheritance is more complicated and characterizes inheritance of most human qualities; polygenic inheritance is when two or more pairs of alleles influence expression of a trait. Skin color is a good example, being determined by multiple pairs of genes. Skin color is also an example of codominance, where multiple dominant alleles are equally expressed in the appearance of a trait. Researchers assert that skin color is determined by numerous genes; with all of these genes combined in the phenotype, all dominant alleles, which contain a recipe for greater amounts of melanin (coloring) in the skin, are expressed. As such, as a person possesses a greater number of dominant alleles, their skin will be darker; as a person possesses fewer dominant alleles, their skin contains less melanin and appears lighter. Another more complicated gene pattern is called incomplete dominance, where dominant and recessive alleles are equally expressed in a phenotype. Curliness of hair is an incompletely dominant trait, where one allele for curly hair matched with a second allele for straight hair will result in wavy hair for offspring. Another example of incomplete dominance is sickle-cell anemia, a genetic disorder whereby blood cells are abnormally shaped, like sickles, and so carry less oxygen to the body. Individuals with the homozygous recessive genotype for sickle-cell suffer from the disease, including poor circulation, anemia (lack of hemoglobin), poor resistance to infection, and possibly internal bleeding and strokes. Incomplete dominance is apparent for individuals who are heterozygous for sickle-cell, having one allele for normally shaped blood cells and one allele for sickle-shaped blood cells. Heterozygotes have what is called sickle-cell trait, where blood cells become sickle-shaped, but only under certain circumstances (e.g., at high altitudes). This pattern of incomplete dominance is actually quite adaptive, because the blood cells also become sickle-shaped when under attack by malaria, which cannot survive in the abnormal blood cells. As such, in regions where malaria is prevalent and quite deadly, including in Africa, sickle-cell trait may actually help a person to survive. As such, alleles for sickle-cell continue to be passed on to offspring as individuals are more likely to survive and reproduce in a particular environment when they possess a heterozygous genotype. Because a heterozygous genotype is an adaptation in Africa, the carrier rate in Africa is higher (25%; Akinyanju, 1989) than in other areas of the world (e.g., an 8% carrier rate in the United States) (Centers for Disease Control and Prevention, 2016).

Sex-Linked Traits

Because they are determined by the sex chromosomes, some traits are called sex-linked. Very simply, the formation of the genitals, internal reproductive organs, the production of gametes, and development of secondary sex characteristics (e.g., body hair, changes in musculature and body shape, voice changes at puberty) are sex-linked. However, other qualities that are unrelated to biological sex or reproduction are also sex-linked. One sex-linked quality is **color blindness**, which involves compromises in normal color vision such that a person has difficulty seeing some colors (e.g., red-green, blue-yellow). This quality is sex-linked because the alleles for normal color vision (and abnormal color vision) are carried on the X chromosome. Thankfully, the allele for normal color vision is dominant; as such, women who are heterozygous for color vision will have normal vision but will be a carrier of the color blindness allele. Unfortunately for boys and men, who possess only one X chromosome, if that X carries the recessive allele for color blindness, because they have only one allele and no corresponding second allele, they will be color blind. Boys and men will only have normal color vision if they inherit the allele for normal color vision from their mother. Because of this lack of a corresponding color vision allele on the Y chromosome, boys and men are much more likely to have color blindness than women are (8% of Caucasian men versus 0.5% of Caucasian women). When a color blind woman has offspring with a color blind man, there is a 100% probability that any and all offspring will also be color blind.

Other traits are called **sex-influenced**, because expression of the phenotype is affected by the presence of hormones. Baldness is an example of a sex-influenced trait. Men only need one allele for baldness to have some form of pattern baldness, which is hastened by testosterone. Women must be homozygous to show baldness (Küster & Happle, 1984). Sex-influenced traits are numerous; one reason is that hormones are so important for function and morphology of the body, and for sleep, homeostasis, mood, sexuality, and reproduction.

Sex-Linked Genetic Disorders

Several genetic disorders involve recessive alleles carried on the X chromosome; because of their lack of a second X chromosome with alleles that dominate the phenotype, such disorders are more common in male offspring. **Muscular dystrophy** (MD) is an X-linked disorder (Bulfield, Siller, Wight, & Moore, 1984); it is very rare among female offspring, but sadly much more common for male births (1 in 7,000–8,000; Centers for Disease Control and Prevention, 2009). MD is a degenerative muscle disease, whereby the muscle cells lack a protein called dystrophin, which releases calcium from cells. As calcium builds up in the cells, the cells produce an enzyme that destroys muscle fibers (Hoffman, Brown, & Kunkel, 1987), leading to physical disabilities (see Figure 3.5).

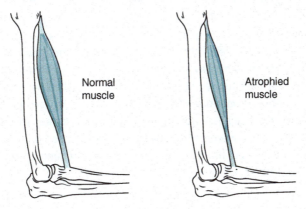

Figure 3.5 Muscular Dystrophy leads to muscle atrophy

48 *Genetics*

The survival rate for people with MD to young adulthood is only about 60% (Centers for Disease Control and Prevention, 2009).

Hemophilia, a blood disorder whereby a person lacks clotting factors in the blood, is also X-linked, and is thus much more common in male offspring than in females (National Heart, Lung, & Blood Institute, 2013). With hemophilia, the blood does not clot, so any injury can in fact be very dangerous, especially injuries to internal organs, major blood vessels, and the brain. Exsanguination is quite possible for hemophiliacs, as are strokes (NHLBI, 2013). Modernly there are medicines used to help with blood clotting; death from hemophilia was much higher before the advent of such drugs (Soucie et al., 2000), including early in childhood (Agaliotis, Zaiden, & Ozturk, 2009). Hemophilia was called the "Royal Disease," mainly because it ran in the family of Queen Victoria, who is believed to have passed the disorder onto several of her offspring, eventually including members of royal families in Germany, Russia, and Spain (Rogaev, Grigorenko, Faskhutdinova, Kittler, & Moliaka, 2009).

Because we inherit all of our mitochondria in every one of our billions of somatic cells from our mothers only (see Chapter 2), any problems our mom has with her mitochondria will be passed on to us. Remember that mitochondria are organelles within each somatic cell responsible for converting nutrients and oxygen into energy. As such, any problems with energy conversion that affect the body may result from problems in the mitochondria or genes contained inside the mitochondria. Mutations in mitochondrial DNA affect muscles and nerves, because they are particularly sensitive to problems with energy supply and conversion in the cells (Wallace, 1989). One such problem is optic neuropathy, which is an inherited disease that leads to degeneration of the optic nerve, eventually resulting in partial or complete blindness. Because this disease comes from the mitochondria, if a mother has optic neuropathy of this genetic sort, then all of her offspring will as well (Wallace et al., 1988).

Autosomal Genetic Disorders

So far we have discussed several genetic disorders that are sex-linked because they occur on the X chromosome and affect female and male offspring differently. Many other genetic disorders occur because of mutations on an autosomal chromosome. A mutation is a permanent change in DNA that is replicated in all of the body cells and the gametes; the person's DNA is different from what normally occurs in most other people (U.S. National Library of Medicine, 2017). Mutations can be very small, involving alterations in one small part of DNA, or large, involving large spans of a chromosome. Different types of mutations include deletion (D) of an entire gene, point mutations (an insertion or deletion entirely inside one gene) (P), chromosomal abnormalities (part of or a whole chromosome is extra, missing, or both) (C), and trinucleotide repeat disorders (where a gene is larger than normal). If the person survives the mutation, the mutation will be expressed in the phenotype in some way and perhaps passed on to offspring. Sometimes mutations are beneficial or not harmful; recall our discussion of lactose persistence and blue eyes from Chapter 1. If a mutation is adaptive (it enhances ability to survive and reproduce within a particular environment), it will be passed on to offspring and will spread throughout the species. Many mutations are harmful, however, and because they are passed on to offspring, they continue to occur in the general population. See Table 3.2 for a list of genetic disorders, their type of mutation, and the chromosomal location.

Table 3.2 Autosomal genetic disorders: mutation type and location

Disorder	Mutation	Chromosome
Cri du Chat Syndrome	D	5
Down Syndrome	C	21
Jacob's Syndrome	C	Y
Klinefelter's Syndrome	C	X
Poly-X Syndrome	C	X
Turner's Syndrome	C	X
Color blindness	P	X
Hemophilia	P	X
Muscular dystrophy	D	X
Neurofibromatosis	?	17/22
Huntington's Disease	P	4
Marfan Syndrome	P	15
Achondroplasia	P	4
Cystic fibrosis	P	7
Phenylketonuria	P	12
Tay-Sachs Disease	P	15
Albinism	P	11, 15 (9, 5)
Sickle-cell disease	P	11

Autosomal Dominant Disorders

Like for other genetic traits, alleles for autosomal genetic disorders can be dominant or recessive. If a disorder is dominant, only one allele is necessary for the disorder to show in the phenotype, and there is a 50% likelihood of passing the disorder onto offspring. One very common genetic disorder is neurofibromatosis (1 case per 3,000 people; Norden, Reardon, & Wen, 2010), which involves a problem in the production of a protein that blocks cell growth (neurofibromin), with parts of the body growing uncontrollably, including on the skin and the fibrous covering of nerves (see Figure 3.6). In severe cases, a person with neurofibromatosis may have blindness and deafness (because of tumors in the ears and eyes), severe learning disabilities, and skeletal deformities. Neurofibromatosis is highly variable in its expression; very mild cases may appear as birthmarks or what are called café au lait spots (Carey, Laub, & Hall, 1979; Korf & Rubenstein, 2005; Riccardi, 1981). Because many cases are mild, a person may be a carrier of the gene and not realize it until the disease affects offspring.

Huntington's Disease (about 5-10 cases per 100,000 people) is an autosomal dominant neurological disorder that involves production of an abnormally shaped protein called huntingtin; the protein builds up and forms large clumps inside nerve cells, including brain cells. This leads to progressive degeneration of brain cells, resulting in seizures, loss of muscular control, and severe effects on the brain including dementia. Sadly, Huntington's Disease may not be apparent without a genetic test until adulthood, so that the disease can be unknowingly passed on to offspring. There is no effective treatment for the disease, and once onset occurs, life expectancy is about 10-15 years (Dayalu & Albin, 2015; National Institute of Neurological Disorders and Stroke, 2016; Walker, 2007).

Marfan Syndrome (about 1 in 3,000 to 10,000 births; Keane & Pyeritz, 2008) is an autosomal dominant genetic disorder involving production of a protein called fibrillin, which is critical

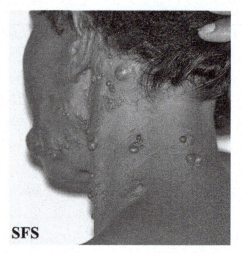

Figure 3.6 A person with Neurofibromatosis
Source: Wiki

to development and maintenance of elastic fibers throughout the body, including in the heart, lungs, spinal cord, ligaments, and eyes, all of which are negatively affected by the mutation. People with Marfan Syndrome are commonly very tall, with very long limbs, hands, and fingers (see Figure 3.7). The most serious complications involve cardiopulmonary complications, which can be fatal. Like neurofibromatosis, Marfan Syndrome is quite variable in its expression, and with proper medical care, life expectancy is normal (NHLBI, 2010).

Another autosomal dominant disorder is **achondroplasia dwarfism** (about 1 in 25,000 births), which may be inherited from a parent or may occur as a sporadic mutation. The mutation affects bone growth and cartilage formation, resulting in short stature and shortened bones. Average height with dwarfism is between 4 feet and 4 feet, 5 inches (Wynn, King, Gambello, Waller, & Hecht, 2007). The famous actor Billy Barty (1924-2000) had achondroplasia dwarfism (he appeared in the 1988 Ron Howard film *Willow* as the village sorcerer, and many other top films in his career; see Figure 3.8). Fetuses that inherit two genes for dwarfism die in utero or do not live past infancy. The sporadic mutation involved in dwarfism is associated with advanced paternal age (Orioli, Castilla, Scarano, & Mastroiacovo, 1995).

Autosomal Recessive Disorders

Autosomal recessive genetic disorders require multiple alleles for the disorder to show itself in the phenotype. As such, two affected individuals (homozygous recessive) would definitely pass disorders on to offspring, while two carriers of the recessive allele (heterozygotes) would have a 1 in 4 chance of having offspring with the disorder. One lethal autosomal recessive disorder is **cystic fibrosis (CF)**, which is the most common lethal genetic disorder in the United States (about 1 in 25 European Americans is a carrier of the recessive allele, while 1 in 2,500 newborns has the disorder). The disorder is least common among people of Asian and African descent (Massie & Delatycki, 2013; O'Sullivan & Freedman, 2009). The disordered genes affect the ability of water to penetrate cells in the bronchial tubes, resulting in abnormally thick mucus in the lungs which causes breathing problems and chronic respiratory infections. The pancreas,

Genetics 51

Figure 3.7 A person with Marfan Syndrome
Source: Mike Ehrmann/Getty Images

kidneys, intestines, and liver can also be affected (Hodson, Geddes, & Bush, 2012). There is no cure for cystic fibrosis; however, because of advancements in medical treatments, the survival rate for CF has increased to about 37 years old for women and about 40 years old for men (MacKenzie et al., 2014).

Another lethal recessive disorder is **Tay-Sachs Disease**, with involves mutation of genes for production of an enzyme called *Hex A*, which is needed to store fat in cells, including the important fatty sheaths covering the body's nerve cells. Without needed levels of Hex A, there is progressive neurological deterioration in the brain and spinal cord, resulting in blindness, severe cognitive deficits, and paralysis. Death usually results by age 3 or 4 years. The disease is most common among individuals of Ashkenazi Jewish, French Canadian, and Louisiana Cajun descent (1 in 27 is a carrier), with 1 in 250 people a carrier of the disordered gene in the general population (National Institutes of Health, 2012; National Tay Sachs & Allied Diseases Association, 2016).

Another autosomal recessive disorder is **phenylketonuria (PKU)** (1 in 10,000 to 15,000 newborns), a disorder involving a lack of an enzyme for metabolism of phenylalanine, an amino acid found in proteins and other foods. Without this enzyme, phenylalanine builds up in the body, which becomes toxic. Serious cognitive deficiencies, seizures, and behavioral problems may

Figure 3.8 The famous actor Billy Barty had Achondroplasia
Source: Everett Collection Inc/Alamy Stock Photo

result. If PKU affected the infant prior to birth, the baby may be born with low birth weight, microcephaly (a small head), and heart problems (National Institutes of Health, 2017).

A final autosomal recessive disorder we will discuss is **albinism** (1 in 5,000 among African people, 1 in 20,000 in the U.S.; Greaves, 2014), which involves malfunction of melanin-producing genes because of a mutation (see Figure 3.9). The mutation affects the operation of multiple other genes, a phenomenon called **epistasis**. Like most disorders affecting the skin, there is wide variability in phenotypic expression of albinism, ranging from mild to a complete lack of melanin. Typically individuals with albinism lack pigment in the skin, eyes, and hair. The disorder may also affect eyesight because of effects on the optic nerve and the retina. Because the skin lacks protection from the sun, skin cancers and burns are more likely (King & Summers, 1988).

Epigenetics

The influence of genes on human characteristics, traits, and even abilities and behaviors is undeniable, thanks to modern research in genetics. But does the environment affect our genes? Until recently, it was thought that only harmful effects of the environment, like exposure to radiation, could affect genes through mutation. However, recent research indicates multiple epigenetic effects on our genes. An **epigenetic** effect occurs when an environmental experience, disease, or increasing age determines which genes are active within an individual. Research indicates environmental stressors experienced prenatally or early after birth can affect whether a person develops certain disorders and diseases, including heart disease, obesity, and even serious mental illnesses like schizophrenia (Painter, Roseboom, & Bleker, 2005; van Os & Selten, 1998).

Figure 3.9 Mr. Salif Keita, a man with Albinism
Source: Kpa/Zuma/Shutterstock

Apparently, stressful environments can also affect which genes are active within particular gametes as they are being formed (Messerschmidt, Knowles, & Solter, 2014). A person's lifestyle, including use of and exposure to toxins (alcohol, drugs, smoking, occupational and environmental toxins), may affect epigenetics, such that different genes are turned on or off in response to lifestyle. Such changes may then be reproduced in gametes, resulting in transgenerational epigenetic inheritance (Nelson & Nadeau, 2010; Skinner, Manikkam, & Guerrero-Bosagna, 2010). "Good genes" may serve as a foundation of good health and longevity; however, whether good genes stay good can be a question of lifestyle and environmental stressors more than we ever thought before.

Chapter Summary

Human beings have 46 chromosomes organized into 23 pairs, with one of each pair inherited from mothers, and the other pair member inherited from fathers. Chromosomes contain genes, with different versions of the same gene called alleles. Some alleles are dominant (they will always be expressed in the phenotype, even with only one allele present), while others are recessive (two alleles, one inherited from each parent, are required for the phenotype to be expressed). Which alleles a person possesses is called their genotype; how the gene is expressed in the person's appearance or behavior is called the phenotype. Simple inheritance involves only two alleles; such traits as finger length and hair line are determined through simple inheritance. Many traits however involve polygenic inheritance, or more than one pair of alleles. Some traits are sex-linked because genes for those traits are carried on the X or the Y chromosome (the sex chromosomes). Sex-linked traits include color blindness and disorders like muscular dystrophy (MD) and hemophilia, all of which are affected by genes on the X chromosome. Because boys and men only possess one X chromosome, if the disordered allele is present they will show the disorder and the disorder will be more common in male births. Other genetic disorders are carried on the autosomes (chromosomes not involved in sex determination) and can be dominant or recessive. Autosomal dominant disorders included Marfan Syndrome, Neurofibromatosis, and Huntington's Disease. Autosomal recessive disorders include cystic fibrosis (CF), Tay Sachs Disease, and albinism. Modern research indicates that epigenetic effects (effects of the environment on which genes are active or inactive within an individual) can be linked with prenatal environmental trauma and lifestyle.

Thoughtful Questions

- Explain imprinting and epigenetic effects.
- Explain the likelihood of simple allelic traits for offspring of parents who are heterozygous for those traits.
- What are the outcomes for the daughters and sons of a color blind father and a mother who is a carrier of color blindness?
- Explain the difference between dominant and recessive disorders.
- Why does Huntington's Disease continue to affect individuals around the world?
- Explain the different kinds of mutations described in the chapter.
- Explain the difference between sex-linked and sex-influenced traits.

Glossary

Achondroplasia dwarfism: an autosomal dominant genetic disorder (and sporadic mutation) that involves abnormal cartilage formation and bone growth, resulting in stature that is between 4 and 4 feet, 5 inches on average.

Albinism: an autosomal recessive disorder that involves malfunction of melanin-producing genes, resulting in skin, eyes, and hair with less or no pigment. Vision problems and skin cancers are common.

Allele: an alternative form of a gene having the same position (locus) on a pair of chromosomes.

Allosomes: the sex chromosomes (XX female, XY male).

Angleman Syndrome: a genetic disorder where the father's genes on chromosome 15 are imprinted and the mother's are deleted/inactivated. Characterized by a wide mouth, large tongue, hypopigmented skin and eyes, profound developmental delays, severe language impairment, and movement and balance problems.

Autosomal dominant disorders: a disorder is dominant when only one allele is necessary for the disorder to show in the phenotype, and there is a 50% likelihood of passing the disorder onto offspring.

Autosomal recessive disorders: multiple alleles for the disorder are required for it to show itself in the phenotype.

Beckwith-Wiedemann Syndrome: a genetic disorder which involves imprinting and problems with genes on chromosome 11. Characterized by large birth weight and length, neonatal low blood sugar, abdominal wall defects, macroglossia, ear pits, musculoskeletal abnormalities, and hearing loss.

Chromosome: an organized protein structure that contain genes.

Chromosomal abnormality: a mutation involving part of or a whole chromosome extra, missing, or both.

Codominance: when multiple dominant alleles are equally expressed in the appearance of a trait. An example of codominance is skin color.

Color blindness: a sex-linked trait, with normal color vision the dominant allele, and color blindness (difficulties in seeing certain colors, including red-green and blue-yellow color blindness) the recessive allele. Because the gene for color vision is carried on the X only (and not on the Y chromosome), it is a sex-linked trait, such that males only require one recessive allele to show color blindness.

Cystic fibrosis: an autosomal recessive disorder that involves inability of water to penetrate cells in the lungs, bronchia, and digestive organs, resulting in abnormally thick mucus and chronic respiratory infections and digestive problems.

Deletion: a mutation involving deletion of a gene or genes.

Dispositional attributions: explanations of cause that emphasize the actions of individual people rather than situational or societal factors.

Dominant: an allele that will always be expressed in a phenotype; only one dominant allele will lead to expression of the trait.

Epigenetic effect: an effect that occurs when an environmental experience, disease, or increasing age determines which genes are active within an individual.

Epistasis: when one gene affects the operation of other genes.

Gene: a locus (or region) of DNA on a chromosome that encodes a cell function or protein product; the molecular units of heredity.

Genotype: the particular alleles of genes that a person possesses (e.g., one dominant, one recessive, or Ee).

Hemizygotic: having only half genetic material for a trait (e.g., men are hemizygotic for X-only traits).

Hemophilia: a genetic blood disorder involving a lack of clotting factor; hemophilia is sex-linked, with genes for normal or abnormal blood clotting carried on the X chromosome.

Heterozygous: having a genotype made up of one dominant and one recessive allele.

Homologous: chromosomes that are not identical but that are similar in length, number of genes they carry, and gene location on the chromosome; chromosomes in each pair are homologous.

Homozygous: having a genotype made up of two dominant or two recessive alleles.

Huntingtin: an abnormal protein produced in people with Huntington's disease; the protein is the wrong shape and forms large clumps inside nerve cells, including brain cells.

Huntington's disease: an autosomal dominant neurological disorder that involves production of an abnormally shaped protein called **huntingtin**; the protein builds up and forms large clumps inside nerve cells, including brain cells, leading to progressive degeneration of the brain.

Imprinting: when a gene allele inherited from one parent is silenced, such that it does not operate and does not affect the phenotype.

Incomplete dominance: where dominant and recessive alleles are equally expressed in a phenotype. Curliness of hair is an incompletely dominant trait.

Individualistic: a cultural dimension, whereby within a culture individual goals are elevated above group goals and individual achievement is emphasized. The United States is highly individualistic.

Marfan Syndrome: an autosomal dominant disorder that involves problems in production of elastic fibers, affecting growth, the heart, lungs, spinal cord, and eyes. Affected individuals are often very tall with long limbs and fingers.

56   *Genetics*

Mitochondria: organelles within cells that convert nutrients to energy that the cell needs to function.

Muscular dystrophy: an X-linked degenerative muscle disease; the person lacks a protein needed to release calcium from muscle cells (dystrophin).

Mutation: a permanent change in DNA that is replicated in all of the body cells and the gametes.

Neurofibromatosis: an autosomal dominant genetic disorder that involves a problem in the production of a protein that blocks cell growth (neurofibromin), with parts of the body growing uncontrollably, including fibrous covering of nerves.

Optic neuropathy: an inherited disease that leads to degeneration of the optic nerve; it is inherited through a mutation in mitochondrial DNA.

Phenotype: the physical expression of a trait (e.g., long fingers or blue eyes); the genotype determines the phenotype.

Phenylketonuria (PKU): an autosomal recessive genetic disorder, whereby a person lacks an enzyme for metabolism of phenylalanine, an amino acid present in many foods. Without diet regulation beginning in infancy, results in severe cognitive deficits.

Point mutation: a mutation involving any insertion or deletion entirely inside one gene.

Polygenic inheritance: when a trait is determined by more than one pair of genes (alleles).

Prader-Willi Syndrome: a genetic disorder where the mother's genes on chromosome 15 are imprinted and the father's are deleted/inactivated. Characterized by excessive weight gain, small stature, small feet and hands, hypogonadism, and cognitive problems.

Pseudoautosomal: genes for which the X and Y chromosomes are homologous (they mimic autosomes in this way). These genes engage in crossing over during meiosis.

Punnet Square: a simple illustration of a one-trait cross, where two pairs of alleles combine one allele per pair to produce a trait outcome for offspring.

Recessive: an allele that will only be expressed in a phenotype when two of the same alleles are present; two recessive alleles are necessary for expression of the trait.

Sex-determining region of Y (SRY): one gene on the Y chromosome that is responsible for the production of testis-determining factor, a protein substance that triggers development of the testes in a developing fetus. Without this one gene (or with its mutation or malfunction), the fetus will develop into a female.

Sex-linked traits: traits for which genes are carried on the sex chromosomes (X or Y).

Sex-influenced traits: traits for which gene expression is influenced by hormones. For example, baldness is more likely to be expressed in men because the expression of baldness is influenced by the presence of testosterone, which men have more of than women.

Sickle-cell anemia: a genetic disorder whereby blood cells are abnormally shaped, like sickles, and so carry less oxygen to the body; symptoms include poor circulation, anemia, poor resistance to infection, and internal bleeding.

Simple inheritance: when one pair of genes determines a phenotype.

Tay-Sachs Disease: an autosomal recessive disorder involving the body's failure to produce *Hex A*, an enzyme necessary to store fat in cells, including nerve cells, resulting in progressive neurological deterioration and death in young childhood.

Trinucleotide repeat disorders: a mutation involving a gene that is extended in length.

References

Adams, J. (2008). Imprinting and genetic disease: Angelman, Prader-Willi and Beckwith-Weidemann syndromes. *Nature Education, 1*(1), 129.

Agaliotis, D. P., Zaiden, R. A., & Ozturk, S. (2009). Hemophilia overview. eMedicine from webMD. Updated: November 24, 2009. http://emedicine.medscape.com/article/210104-overview.

Akinyanju, O. O. (1989). A profile of sickle cell disease in Nigeria. *Annals of the New York Academy of Sciences, 565*, 126-136.

Angelman, H. (1965). "Puppet" children: A report of three cases. *Developmental Medicine and Child Neurology, 7*, 681-688.

Bulfield, G., Siller, W. G., Wight, P. A., & Moore, K. J. (1984). X chromosome-linked muscular dystrophy (mdx) in the mouse. *Proceedings of the National Academy of Sciences of the United States of America, 81*(4), 1189-1192.

Carey, J. C., Laub, J. M., & Hall, B. D. (1979). Penetrance and variability in neurofibromatosis: A genetic study of 60 families. *Birth Defects, 15*(5B), 271-281.

Centers for Disease Control and Prevention (2009). Prevalence of Duchenne/Becker muscular dystrophy among males aged 5-24 years - four states, 2007. *Morbidity and Mortality Weekly Report, 58*(40), 1119-1122.

Centers for Disease Control and Prevention (2016). Sickle Cell Disease, www.cdc.gov/ncbddd/sicklecell/data.html.

Dayalu, P., & Albin, R. L. (2015). Huntington disease: pathogenesis and treatment. *Neurologic Clinics, 33*(1), 101-14. doi:10.1016/j.ncl.2014.09.003.

Franklin, R. (2015). All about the Human Genome Project (HGP). National Human Genome Research Institute, National Institutes of Health, www.genome.gov/10001772/all-about-the--human-genome-project-hgp/.

Greaves, M. (2014). Was skin cancer a selective force for black pigmentation in early hominin evolution? *Proceedings of the Royal Society B: Biological Sciences, 281*(1781), 20132955. doi:10.1098/rspb.2013.2955.

Henry, I., Bonaiti-Pellié, C., Chehensse, V., Beldjord, C., Schwartz, C., Utermann, G., & Junien, C. (1991). Uniparental paternal disomy in a genetic cancer-predisposing syndrome. *Nature, 351*, 665-667. doi:10.1038/351665a0.

Hodson, M., Geddes, D., & Bush, A. (2012). *Cystic fibrosis* (3rd ed.). London: Hodder Arnold.

Hoffman, E. P., Brown, R. H. Jr., & Kunkel L. M. (1987). Dystrophin: The protein product of the Duchenne muscular dystrophy locus. *Cell, 51*(6), 919-928.

Hofstede, G. (2001). *Culture's consequences: Comparing values, behaviors, institutions, and organizations across nations*. Thousand Oaks, CA: Sage.

Keane, M. G., & Pyeritz, R. E. (2008). Medical management of Marfan syndrome. *Circulation, 117*(21): 2802-2813. doi:10.1161/CIRCULATIONAHA.107.693523.

King, R. A., & Summers, C. G. (1988). Albinism. *Dermatologic Clinics, 6*(2), 217-228.

Korf, B. R., & Rubenstein, A. E. (2005). *Neurofibromatosis: A handbook for patients, families, and healthcare professionals*. Stuttgart: Thieme.

Krull, D. S., Loy, M. H.-M., Lin, J., Wang, C.-F., Chen, S., & Zhao, X. (1999). The fundamental fundamental attribution error: Correspondence bias in individualist and collectivist cultures. *Personality and Social Psychology Bulletin, 25*(10), 1208-1219.

Küster, W., & Happle, R. (1984). The inheritance of common baldness: Two B or not two B? *Journal of the American Academy of Dermatology, 11*(5, Pt. 1), 921-926.

Lloyd, R. (2010). Rosalind Franklin and DNA: How wronged was she? *Scientific American*, November 3, https://blogs.scientificamerican.com/observations/rosalind-franklin-and-dna-how-wronged-was-she/.

MacKenzie, T., Gifford, A. H., Sabadosa, K. A., Quinton, H. B., Knapp, E. A., Goss, C. H., & Marshall, B. C. (2014). Longevity of patients with cystic fibrosis in 2000 to 2010 and beyond: Survival analysis of the Cystic Fibrosis Foundation Patient Registry. *Annals of Internal Medicine, 161*(4), 233-241. doi:10.7326/m13-0636.

Massie, J., & Delatycki, M. B. (2013). Cystic fibrosis carrier screening. *Paediatric Respiratory Reviews, 14*(4), 270-275.

Masuda, T., Gonzalez, R., Kwan, L., & Nisbett, R. E. (2008). Culture and aesthetic preference: Comparing the attention to context of East Asians and Americans. *Personality and Social Psychology Bulletin, 34*(9), 1260-1275.

Messerschmidt, D. M., Knowles, B. B., & Solter D. (2014). DNA methylation dynamics during epigenetic reprogramming in the germline and preimplantation embryos. *Genes & Development, 28*, 812-828. doi:10.1101/gad.234294.113.

National Heart, Lung, & Blood Institute (2010). What is Marfan Syndrome? www.nhlbi.nih.gov/health/health-topics/topics/mar#.

National Heart, Lung, & Blood Institute (2013). What are the signs and symptoms of hemophilia? July 13. www.nhlbi.nih.gov/. Retrieved September 8, 2016.

National Institute of Neurological Disorders and Stroke (2016). Huntington's Disease information page. www.ninds.nih.gov. Retrieved July 19, 2016.

National Institutes of Health (2012). Tay-Sachs Disease. Genetics Home Reference. https://ghr.nlm.nih.gov/condition/tay-sachs-disease.

National Institutes of Health (2017). Phenylketonuria. Genetics Home Reference. https://ghr.nlm.nih.gov/condition/phenylketonuria.

National Tay Sachs and Allied Diseases Association (2016). Phenylketonuria. Genetics Home Reference. www.ntsad.org/index.php/tay-sachs.

Nelson, V. R., & Nadeau J. H. (2010). Transgenerational genetic effects. *Epigenomics, 2*(6), 797-806.

Norden, A. D., Reardon, D. A., & Wen, P. Y. (2010). *Primary central nervous system tumors: Pathogenesis and therapy.* New York: Springer Science + Business Media.

Orioli, I. M., Castilla, E. E., Scarano, G., & Mastroiacovo, P. (1995). Effect of paternal age in achondroplasia, thanatophoric dysplasia, and osteogenesis imperfecta. *American Journal of Medical Genetics, 59*(2), 209-217.

O'Sullivan, B. P. & Freedman, S. D. (2009). Cystic fibrosis. *Lancet, 373*(9678): 1891-1904. doi:10.1016/s0140-6736(09)60327-5.

Painter, R. C., Roseboom, T. J., & Bleker, O. P. (2005). Prenatal exposure to the Dutch famine and disease in later life: an overview. *Reproductive Toxicology, 20*, 345-352.

Riccardi, V. M. (1981). Von Recklinghausen neurofibromatosis. *New England Journal of Medicine, 305*, 1617-1627. doi:10.1056/NEJM198112313052704.

Rogaev, E. I., Grigorenko, A. P., Faskhutdinova, G., Kittler, E. L. W., & Moliaka, Y. K. (2009). Genotype analysis identifies the cause of the "Royal Disease". *Science*, 326(5954), 817. doi:10.1126/science.1180660.

Ross, M., Darren, V., Grafham, A. J., Coffey, S., Scherer, K., McLay, D., & Muzny, M. (2005). The DNA sequence of the human X chromosome. *Nature, 434*(7031), 325-337. doi:10.1038/nature03440.

Skinner, M. K., Manikkam, M., & Guerrero-Bosagna, C. (2010). Epigenetic transgenerational actions of environmental factors in disease etiology. *Trends in Endocrinology and Metabolism, 21*(4), 214-222.

Skuse, D. H. (2005). X-linked genes and mental functioning. *Human Molecular Genetics, 14*(Suppl 1), R27-R32. doi:10.1093/hmg/ddi112.

Soucie, J. M., Nuss, R., Evatt, B., Abdelhak, A., Cowan, L., Hill, H., Kolakoski, M., Wilber, N., & Hemophilia Surveillance System Project Investigators (2000). Mortality among males with hemophilia: Relations with source of medical care. *Blood, 96*, 437-442.

U.S. National Library of Medicine (2017). What is a gene mutation and how do mutations occur? Genetics Home Reference. https://ghr.nlm.nih.gov/primer/mutationsanddisorders/genemutation.

van Os, J., & Selten, J. P. (1988). Prenatal exposure to maternal stress and subsequent schizophrenia. The May 1940 invasion of The Netherlands. *British Journal of Psychiatry, 172*, 324-326.

Viljoen, D., & Ramesar, R. (1992). Evidence for paternal imprinting in familial Beckwith-Wiedemann syndrome. *Journal of Medical Genetics, 29*, 221-225.

Walker, F. O. (2007). Huntington's disease. *Lancet, 369*(9557), 218-228. doi:10.1016/S0140-6736(07)60111-1.

Wallace, D. C. (1989). Mitochondrial DNA mutations and neuromuscular disease. *Science, 5*, 9-13.

Wallace, D. C., Singh, G., Lott, M. T, Hodge, J. A., Schurr, T. G., Lezza, A. M. S., Elsas, L. J. II, & Nikoskelainen, E. K. (1988). Mitochondrial DNA mutation associated with Leber's hereditary optic neuropathy. *Science, 242*(4884), 1427.

Wynn, J., King, T. M., Gambello, M. J., Waller, D. K., & Hecht, J. T. (2007). Mortality in achondroplasia study: A 42-year follow-up. *American Journal of Medical Genetics A, 143*(21), 2502-2511. doi:10.1002/ajmg.a.31919.

Zhao, M., Kong, L., & Qu, H. (2014). A systems biology approach to identify intelligence quotient score-related genomic regions, and pathways relevant to potential therapeutic treatments. *Scientific Reports, 4*. doi:10.1038/srep04176.

4 Human Sexual Reproduction

Sex Differentiation in Utero: Body and Mind	63
Genes and Biological Sex	64
Gonads and Hormones	65
Hormones and Fetal Brain Development: Sex and Identity	66
Genetic and Hormonal Disorders Affecting Sex and Gender	67
Congenital Adrenal Hyperplasia (CAH)	68
Androgen Insensitivity Syndrome (AIS)	68
Puberty: Developing Body and Sexuality	69
Female and Male Reproductive Systems	69
Fertilization, Pregnancy, and Childbirth	71
Prenatal Health: Nutrition and Teratogens	73

INEQUALITIES AND INJUSTICES

Women's Reproductive Health and Health Care

There is a principle of capability (Nussbaum, 1999) called bodily integrity, which refers to the right of individuals to not have their physical body violated, and emphasizes the importance of personal autonomy and self-determination of every person over their own physical body (Miller, 2007). Violating the bodily integrity of other people is commonly considered unethical, unfairly intrusive, and likely to be criminal (e.g., assaulting a person) (Alldridge & Brants, 2001). Based on this principle, people have a right to decide what to do with their own bodies, and other people should not be allowed to choose what happens to other people's bodies. In this way, a person cannot be forced to give blood, to have a surgery they don't want, to not have a surgery they do want and need. For decades, especially in the United States, people have been attempting to control what women are allowed to do with their own bodies, including whether they should be able to prevent pregnancy and whether they should be able to choose to abort a pregnancy that is not wanted or that is harmful to the mother (which essentially all pregnancies are; World Health Organization, 2010). Some Americans assert that because they have a belief that life is "sacred" (a religious belief), women should not be allowed access to safe, medical, legal abortion. The same people also tend to believe that women should not be able to prevent pregnancy, that if they have sex, they should face the possibility of pregnancy and having a child. In direct contrast to these beliefs, the United States' Constitution very clearly states that each American has a right to freedom of religion (the First Amendment), including freedom from any religion and from having any religions imposed on oneself. Imposing beliefs that life is "sacred" and that life "begins" at conception are religious impositions; they are against the law and a violation of every American's civil right to not be forced to follow edicts of religion. In addition, making birth control and abortion illegal is an assault on women's bodily integrity, forcing them to have pregnancies they do not want and not allowing them the right of bodily autonomy. Just as a man has a right to not have his genitals surgically altered or to have an appendectomy when he needs one (or to not have an appendectomy if he doesn't want one), women have a right to control their own bodies. There is no evidence linking the experience of safe, legal abortions to poor outcomes for women (Rocca et al., 2015). In fact, quite the opposite, with research indicating that women who have abortions report positive emotions about it (Kero, Högberg, & Lalos, 2004). Safe, legal abortion saves women's lives (World Health Organization, 2010) and allows women to control their own destinies.

CRITICAL THINKING

Infant Gender "Assignment"

As you may discover within the chapter, sometimes babies are born with genitals that look different from what parents and doctors expect. Sometimes the genitals are not clearly female and not clearly male, but a mix of each. This is called **intersex**; the genitals are ambiguous or not distinctly one sex or the other. This condition occurs in about 2% of live births (Blackless et al., 2000). Traditionally, when babies were born intersex, a "corrective" surgery was used to assign a gender to the child, usually early in infancy (only about 0.1% to 0.2% of births; Blackless et al., 2000). Unfortunately, many problems may arise with this type of surgery, resulting in genitals that are not normal in appearance or configuration, loss of sexual sensation, or other permanent injuries to the genitals (Köhler et al., 2012).

Research indicates that some girls with **Congenital Adrenal Hyperplasia (CAH)**, who are often born with ambiguous genitals, have surgeries in infancy that are not entirely successful in differentiating genitals to be more female. As girls and women, they report having feelings of shame and discomfort regarding their genitals, which results in their lack of interest in or avoidance of sexual activity (Creighton, 2004; Minto, Liao, Woodhouse, Ransley, & Creighton, 2003). Other individuals, male and female, who were assigned a gender through surgery in infancy develop the opposite gender in childhood, because parents and doctors apparently made the wrong choice. Those individuals then have to deal with growing up with surgically altered genitals that do not match their identity (Greenfield, 2014). One famous case involved "botched" circumcision of a boy infant that resulted in his penis being destroyed. The boy, eventually known as David Reimer, was "reassigned" surgically to be a girl in infancy and was raised as a girl. In early childhood, however, the

Human Sexual Reproduction   61

child knew he was male, and transitioned to live as a male finally when he was 15 years old. Tragically, David suffered from serious depression throughout adulthood and eventually committed suicide at age 38 years old (Associated Press, 2004).

There are clearly serious ethical issues here. How fair is it to alter someone's body, including their genitals, when they are a powerless, helpless, voiceless infant? When they cannot give any kind of consent, let alone informed consent where they know all the possible consequences and side effects of such surgery? Is it ethical for parents and doctors to decide a baby's sex, before that baby ever has a chance to understand their own body and their own identity? An ability to distinguish between female and male categories, including the category to which one belongs, occurs very early in life, around age 2 to 3 years (Money & Ehrhardt, 1972). How ethical is it to assign a gender and treat a child as that gender, even if they may develop a rudimentary sense of their own gender before they can speak (Leinbach & Fagot, 1993; Walker-Andrews, Bahrick, Raglioni, & Diaz, 1991)? These ethical concerns extend also to the practice of circumcision, removal of the foreskin of the penis soon after birth, a worldwide and historical practice affecting millions of boys and men (World Health Organization, 2007). How is surgically altering a baby's genitals for gender assignment more or less unethical or invasive than circumcision? Is circumcision medically necessary? What are the benefits and drawbacks of circumcision of infant boys? These are questions for everyone to think critically about!

BONUS BOX

Reversible Inhibition of Sperm Under Guidance (RISUG)

Although we will talk more about various contraceptive devices in Chapter 8 (Sexuality), one revolutionary but not yet widely used method of contraception will be discussed here as a bonus. This method is called RISUG, which stands for reversible inhibition of sperm under guidance. RISUG is a 100% effective, long-lasting, inexpensive method of contraception. Here's how it works (see Figure 4.1): a polymer gel is injected into the vas deferens, the male internal ducts that carry sperm from the testes to the penis for ejaculation. This gel is the reverse ionization of seminal fluid (semen), so that when the semen comes through the tubes for ejaculation, the sperm in the fluid are shredded into bits! All of them are killed! As such, ejaculation, orgasm, and sexual performance are not at all affected, nor are hormone levels, but there are no viable sperm. The gel apparently lasts for several years, can be easily reversed with injections of baking soda and water, and is cheaper than the syringe used to inject it. There are apparently also very few side effects as well, except some pain and swelling at the injection sites (Jha, Jha, Gupta, & Guha, 2010). Why is it not widely used, this cheap, safe, effective, easy birth control method? It is a rather recent development, and testing of it in India was slowed because of a lack of volunteers (come on fellas, it's just an injection!) (Jyoti, 2011). RISUG is being developed by a non-profit organization called the Parsemus Foundation under the product name of Vasalgel. Animal trials are currently in progress in the United States, but apparently no human testing has occurred in the U.S. as

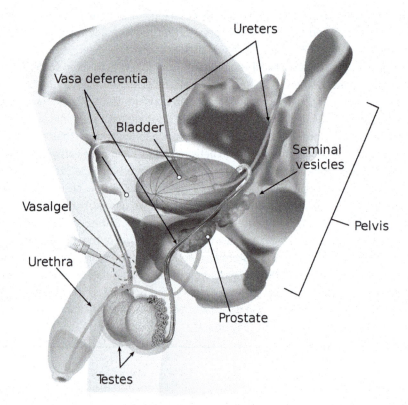

Figure 4.1 RISUG (reversible inhibition of sperm under guidance), currently marketed as Vasalgel
Source: Wiki

of yet (www.parsemusfoundation.org/vasalgel-faqs/). Maybe some conscientious, brave male students reading this book might consider signing up for clinical trials, to hasten the approval of RISUG in the United States. When compared to the many other types of contraceptives that are widely used, which are more expensive, invasive, and may involve alteration of hormones with accompanying negative side effects, an effective, affordable, safe contraceptive alternative is definitely needed.

LEARN MORE

So Many Hormones!

Living creatures on Earth are swimming in hormones, chemicals produced by various body structures that travel through the bloodstream to affect the operation of other body structures. Hormones can affect current functioning (including emotions), but they generally

Human Sexual Reproduction   63

Table 4.1 Glands of the body, hormones, and effects

Gland/organ	Hormones secreted	Target tissues	Effects
Adrenal glands	adrenaline, cortisol	many	fight/flight, anti-stress
Hypothalamus	gonadotropin-releasing	pituitary gland	sexuality
Ovaries	estrogens, progesterone	brain, uterus	sexuality, reproduction, body fat, mood
Pancreas	insulin, glucagon	liver	metabolism
Pineal gland	melatonin	many	sleep
Pituitary gland	luteinizing, follicle stimulating	many (gonads)	sexuality, oxytocin, growth hormone
Testes	testosterone	many	sexuality, reproduction, male characteristics
Thyroid	thyroxine	liver	metabolism

work over time to affect different body processes, including sexuality and reproduction, growth, and metabolism. For example, the adrenal glands on top of the kidneys secrete hormones like adrenaline, that rush through the bloodstream to act on the brain and body, producing a particular and immediate reaction (fight or flight behaviors). However, properly functioning adrenal glands and normal hormone levels are critical for long-term health outcomes as well. I can't cover everything about hormones and their importance in this book, but I can tell you about some hormones that humans produce and what they do.

There are several organs in the body that produce hormones: the **gonads** (ovaries, testes), the brain (the pituitary gland, the pineal gland), the adrenal glands, the pancreas, and the thyroid. These structures are also listed in Table 4.1.

Learn more about hormones from the U.S. National Library of Medicine (www.ncbi.nlm. nih.gov/pubmedhealth/PMHT0022075/).

Sex Differentiation in Utero: Body and Mind

There are multiple determinants of human biological sex, beginning with genes and continuing over the lifespan as we continue to grow and change in predictable ways. Many people are born with physical features (genitals, internal reproductive organs) that have been labeled all over the world as "male." Many other people are born with physical features that have been labeled as "female." Still other people are born **intersexual**, with less distinct biological sex. Sometimes genotype is male, but the person is born with female physical features (or the genotype is female and the features are male). Sometimes a person is born with indistinct genitals or organs (or both), or genitals that seem to not match the internal organs. When the sex organs (especially the **gonads**) are not completely developed, their typical functions are also affected, including production of hormones (called **hypogonadism**) that are related to other biological sex qualities, physical features as well as behaviors. Some people are also born with an identity (a **gender**) that may not match their physical features, because of pre- and postnatal hormonal influences on brain development. An important distinction exists between **biological sex** (a person's structural, biological sex as indicated by genotype, genitals, and internal reproductive organs) and **gender** (cultural ideas about what is feminine and what is masculine). **Biological sex** is about physical

64   Human Sexual Reproduction

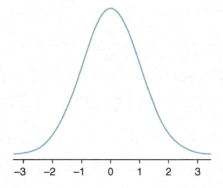

Figure 4.2 The normal distribution

characteristics that are determined by genotype and in utero processes; gender is about beliefs about femininity and masculinity and one's identification as one, the other, both, or neither.

Variability in terms of human qualities refers to the individual differences we see in different qualities, for example physical height. Some people are very short, while some are very tall, but these people are not typical. Most people have a physical height somewhere in the middle (the average for women around the world is 5 feet, 2 inches; the average for men around the world is 5 feet, 6 inches; human height ranges on average between 5 and 6.5 feet; Baten & Blum, 2012). Physical height is normally distributed within the population (see Figure 4.2). The normal distribution is a bell-shaped symmetrical curve representing variable traits across large numbers of people. Many other human qualities are also normally distributed, with the greatest number of people being moderate on a quality or dimension, and fewer and fewer people showing extremely low or extremely high scores or values. Scientists are fascinated with variability; some scholars may devote entire careers to understanding the variability of people along a single trait or quality. Like other human qualities, biological sex is variable in both genotype and phenotype. Sex is not a simple binary; complicated sets of features that result from complicated biological and physiological processes are rarely so simple. Gender is even more complicated and more variable, because it is so strongly influenced by biological processes (one's biological sex as well as hormonal and brain functions) and by environmental forces (socialization processes, cultural ideals and traditions, social institutions, and so on). An understanding of this fundamental variability of sex and gender is essential for understanding gender differences in behavior (sexuality, relationships, communication, aggression, and so on).

Genes and Biological Sex

As we discussed in Chapter 3 (Genetics), the pair of sex chromosomes in a person's genotype (in addition to the other 22 pairs of autosomes) are an important cause of biological sex. Typically, girls and women have two X chromosomes (XX), while boys and men have one X chromosome and one Y chromosome (XY). The X chromosomes contain around 1,100 genes each, while the Y chromosome contains only around 200 genes. The most important area of the Y chromosome for determining maleness is one gene called SRY (sex-determining region of Y) (Ross & Capel, 2005). This SRY gene triggers the release of hormones which then triggers a sequence of events that lead a fetus to develop into a male baby. The SRY gene operates through epistasis;

its presence and activation affects activation of other genes, also involved in determining maleness. If the SRY gene is lacking, because there is no Y chromosome or because that part of the Y chromosome is missing or not functioning properly, the fetus will by default develop into a female (Ohno, 1978).

Gonads and Hormones

Up to around week 8, all normal fetuses are the same in terms of sex. First, they all have similar parts between their legs. They have a urogenital groove, a shallow opening surrounded by labioscrotal swelling. They have a small glans organ called a genital tubercle. Second, their internal undeveloped sex organs, within the abdomen, are identical. All of them have two sets of ductwork, one set is called the Wolffian ducts, and the other set is called the Müllerian ducts. They also all possess a pair of indistinct undeveloped gonads. Around week 8, the process of sex differentiation begins. If the SRY gene is present in the genes within all the body cells, it will become activated, and will trigger the release of a hormone called testis determining factor (TDF; also called H-Y antigen) (Ohno, 1978). This hormone triggers the indistinct gonadal structures to develop into testes, the main male reproductive organ. The testes then begin to release other hormones, namely testosterone and a protein called Müllerian inhibiting substance (MIS), both of which trigger the Müllerian ducts to deteriorate and the Wolffian ducts to develop into the internal male reproductive organs. Externally, the genital tubercle will develop over the course of fetal development into a penis; the labioscrotal swelling becomes the scrotum. In the absence of SRY, the fetus develops into a female, the indistinct gonadal structures develop normally into ovaries, the Müllerian ducts flourish and grow into the internal reproductive organs (uterus, uterine tubes), the Wolffian ducts degenerate and disappear. The ovaries begin to secrete hormones prenatally (estrogens), affecting fetal development and causing the external organs to develop into a clitoris (from the genital tubercle), labia, and vagina (from the labioscrotal swelling and the urogenital groove) (Wilson, George, & Griffin, 1981). Other parts of the urogenital groove develop into the urethra in both female and male fetuses (Callahan, 2009; Holland & Smith, 2000). Testosterone continues to be present in elevated levels throughout gestation for male fetuses compared to female fetuses, affecting other developing organs, including the brain (Warne, Faiman, Reyes, & Winter, 1977).

Multiple different problems may occur during this process, many of which we will discuss in the next section on genetic disorders and sex differentiation. Sometimes the genitals are not clearly female or male; they may be indistinct, more like one than the other, or appear to be both. These individuals are generally described as intersex. Sometimes internal organs are underdeveloped or not matched with external genitalia. One issue is failure of the Müllerian ducts to degenerate within an XY fetus. Although other sexual development occurs, including the gonadal structures becoming testes and the external genitalia becoming male, the Müllerian ducts develop into a uterus and uterine tubes (although perhaps not completely). This situation is called persistent Müllerian duct syndrome (U.S. National Library of Medicine, 2017). Typically, problems result with the testes descending (which normally occurs around 6 months of age), or the person may suffer hernias. When surgery is performed to correct these problems, the uterus and uterine tubes are discovered. If this condition is not treated, undescended testes may degenerate or cancer can develop. Infertility may also result from this condition (Rey, 2005).

Hormones and Fetal Brain Development: Sex and Identity

Maternal and fetal hormones are clearly important for fetal brain development. Maternal hypothyroidism (low thyroid functioning) can disrupt fetal brain development, resulting in cognitive problems including learning disabilities (de Escobar, Obregón, & del Rey, 2004). Other prenatal and neonatal hormone influences are said to link with later sex-typed behavior in childhood and even sexual orientation in adulthood, particularly exposure to the gonadal hormones (testosterone and estrogens) (Hines, 2011). Gonadal steroids affect brain development in utero mainly by affecting the organization of the brain, with relatively enduring effects (Phoenix, Goy, Gerall, & Young, 1959). These persistent effects of hormones on the brain are thought to occur because they affect several aspects of neural development, including neurochemical specification and neuroanatomical connectivity (McCarthy, De Vries, & Forger, 2009). It is extremely difficult to study hormonal influences on prenatal development, because it is unethical to study such influences experimentally (e.g., by exposing some fetuses to excessive hormones and others not) and because links in humans are by necessity correlational (i.e., hormones and other behaviors co-occur, but are not necessarily causally related). But many studies of animals and abnormal conditions in humans have been conducted to try to understand how prenatal influences are linked with **gender behaviors** (behaviors that are sex-typed within a given culture), **gender identity** (an individual's identification as female, male, both, or neither), and **sexual orientation** (patterns of sexual attraction to people of different sexes in adulthood).

The **hypothalamus** is a brain structure in the mid-brain (beneath the thalamus, so "under thalamus"). Activity of the hypothalamus is linked with drives and needs, including thirst, hunger, sexuality, sleep, and **homeostasis** (temperature, metabolism). The hypothalamus is part of the limbic system because it is important in the experience of pleasure and emotions. The hypothalamus, the **pituitary gland** (a pea-sized gland protruding from the hypothalamus), and the **gonads** (ovaries, testes) work together on a daily basis, to affect reproduction, growth, and development. Although the brain and the gonads are not located near each other in the body, the structures are intertwined in their functions and processes across the lifespan. In utero, hormones, along with genes, act on developing fetal brain cells, affecting brain structure, which some argue has substantial influence on gender behavior in childhood and adulthood (Garcia-Falgueras & Swaab, 2010). Early research on rats indicated that exposure to greater than normal hormones prenatally can affect later sexual behavior in rats. Rats exposed prenatally to excessive androgens expressed male sexual behavior in adulthood, whether they were female or male rats. In the absence of androgens, female and male rats express female-typed sexual behavior in adulthood (Ehrhardt & Money, 1971). During human fetal development, the presence of testosterone is said to directly affect developing nerve cells, steering brain development in the "male direction." When testosterone is absent in utero, the brain is said to develop in the "female direction" (Garcia-Falgueras & Swaab, 2010, p. 22). Scholars argue that because gonadal, genital, and brain development occur at different stages, with the brain developing in the latter half of pregnancy, changing or different levels of hormones at those different times may result in biological sex organs that do not match with brain development. As such, a person may be born biologically male but, because of hormone changes, develop a brain that has more female and fewer male characteristics (Swaab & Garcia-Falgueras, 2009).

Researchers assert that an interaction between sex hormones and the developing brain determines gender identity and sexual orientation (Zhou, Hofman, Gooren, & Swaab, 1997). Researchers have linked differences in several brain structures to sexual orientation, two in particular being the **sexually dimorphic nucleus** (**SDN**) and the **suprachiasmatic nucleus** (**SCN**). Both of these brain structures are said to be maximally affected in development between age 2 and 4 years old, with much of sex differentiation in these structures occurring after birth. However, researchers argue that this sexual differentiation of the brain in early childhood is based on processes already programmed into the brain during mid-pregnancy and at birth (Swaab, Chung, Kruijver, Hofman, & Ishunina, 2001). The **SDN** is a cluster of cells within the hypothalamus, with heterosexual men in young adulthood having an SDN that is about twice as big as that of heterosexual young women. The **SCN** is a small structure within the hypothalamus that is linked with **circadian rhythms** (the body's daily "clock" which regulates needs for sleep, food, and other physiological processes), but is also linked to sexuality, with the SCN of homosexual men found to be twice as large as that of heterosexual men (Swaab, Gooren, & Hofman, 1995). Other areas of the hypothalamus (involving the **hypothalamic uncinate nucleus**) have also been found to differ in size by sex, with male-to-female transsexuals having a size more similar to that of females than males (Garcia-Falgueras & Swaab, 2008). These size differences are also linked to differences in circulating hormone levels in adulthood (Garcia-Falgueras & Swaab, 2008; Swaab et al., 2002). Swaab and his colleagues strongly assert that differences in genes, brain structures, and hormones, occurring largely during fetal development, are predictive of sexual orientation and gender identity in adulthood (Garcia-Falgueras & Swaab, 2010; Swaab et al., 2002). The prenatal influence of hormones and links with later gender behavior are also supported by outcomes associated with some genetic disorders.

Genetic and Hormonal Disorders Affecting Sex and Gender

Several genetic disorders involve the sex chromosomes. We have already discussed **Turner Syndrome** (Chapter 2), where a person is missing a sex chromosome and born with only one X (XO) (Sybert, McCauley, & McCauley, 2004). We have also already discussed **Klinefelter Syndrome** (genotype XXY), **Poly-X females** (XXX or more; Gravholt, 2013), and **Jacob's Syndrome** (XYY; Jacobs et al., 1965). All of these can involve hypogonadism (lower than normal functioning of the gonads, particularly in terms of hormone production); as such, because normal hormone production is affected by having underdeveloped gonads, many other developmental processes and sexuality qualities are affected. The syndromes are associated with distinct physical features (including immature secondary sex characteristics), and lower than normal fertility or infertility. Other features include greater physical height (Klinefelter and Poly-X females) and cognitive delays or disabilities (all of the above syndromes). Sexual orientation among Klinefelter men appears to be majority heterosexual (Liester, 1989), as does that among women with Turner Syndrome (Ehrhardt, Greenberg, & Money, 1970). There is little to no evidence indicating that sexual orientation is related to sex chromosome genotype. There is, however, growing evidence that hormones affect early brain development, which then links with gender behavior and sexual orientation later in life (Garcia-Falgueras & Swaab, 2010; Hines, 2011).

Other genetic abnormalities occur that affect biological sex and sex-linked behaviors, because they are linked to the production of hormones that affect early development in a relatively permanent way and because they affect sexual behavior in a regular physiological process in adulthood (Phoenix et al., 1959). Sometimes XY individuals are born appearing female, because the Y they possess is missing the SRY gene or it is mutated. This is called **Swyer Syndrome** (about 1 in 30,000 births). The external genitalia appear as typically female, but the gonads are underdeveloped. Because of the hypogonadism, the gonads do not produce normal amounts of

68 *Human Sexual Reproduction*

estrogens, which can affect secondary sex characteristic development and fertility, as well as gender-typed and sexual behaviors (Arver et al., 1996; Hines, 2011; Michala, Goswami, Creighton, & Conway, 2008).

Another genetic abnormality is called de la Chapelle Syndrome (about 1 in 20,000 births), and it involves individuals who are XX genotype but are born appearing male. In this syndrome, the SRY gene has somehow become attached to one of the X chromosomes, a problem thought to occur with crossing over in meiosis. Because the SRY gene is present, sex differentiation with male features occurred when the SRY stimulated gonadal development of testes (de la Chapelle, 1972). These individuals also have hypogonadism and will have effects related to insufficient sex hormones unless they are medically treated. Even with medical treatment to maintain hormone levels, these individuals are typically infertile (they do not produce viable sperm because testes are underdeveloped). Swyer Syndrome may also be medically treated with hormones taken over long periods of time to maintain hormone levels.

Congenital Adrenal Hyperplasia (CAH)

Another genetic disorder affecting sex differentiation in utero and sexual development over the lifespan is Congenital Adrenal Hyperplasia (CAH), a disorder that involves excessive production of androgens in the adrenal glands. The recessive genetic disorder occurs in about 1 in 10,000 to 1 in 20,000 births (U.S. National Library of Medicine, 2017). When a boy is born with CAH, there are usually no problems with sex differentiation in utero, given that androgens are present but elevated. While excess androgens can cause what is called *precocious* sexual development (pubertal changes at earlier than normal ages) in boys, they can be managed with medications over the lifespan. For girls born with CAH, changes are more dramatic. First, the genitals at birth may be somewhat ambiguous or even more male, while the internal organs are likely to be underdeveloped. Puberty may be absent, delayed, or precocious, they are likely to be infertile because they do not ovulate, and they may have excessive facial hair. They may not develop female secondary sex characteristics normally. Interestingly, many CAH girls are described as "tomboys" in childhood and prefer male-typed play activities (active, rough-and-tumble play involving toy guns and vehicles) instead of female-typed play (quieter play involving dolls and domestic objects) (Hines & Kaufman, 1994; Pasterski et al., 2005). A growing number of studies indicate that in adulthood, CAH women are significantly more likely to report homosexual or bisexual orientation compared to women who do not have CAH (Dittmann, Kappes, & Kappes, 1992; Meyer-Bahlburg, Dolezal, Baker, & New, 2008; Zucker et al., 1996).

Androgen Insensitivity Syndrome (AIS)

Androgen Insensitivity Syndrome (AIS) occurs in about 1 in 20,000 births, and involves a genetic mutation whereby the body's cells are insensitive to the influence of androgens (Grumbach, Hughes, & Conte, 2003). As such, XY individuals in utero will develop infantile testes which release androgens, but the body's cells do not respond. Because the body is not affected by androgens, it develops female qualities, with female external genitalia and underdeveloped internal structures. Being born appearing female, these XY babies are often raised as girls and commonly identify as girls. No one may realize the child is XY until puberty, when menstruation does not occur. While hormone replacement therapy can help with those XY AIS individuals who identify as male, research indicates that many XY girls continue to identify as female in adulthood

Human Sexual Reproduction 69

and are attracted to male romantic partners (Hines, Ahmed, & Hughes, 2003; Money, Schwartz, & Lewis, 1984). AIS is not a serious problem for individuals with an XX genotype, because they are female and androgens are less important for development.

Puberty: Developing Body and Sexuality

Sex differentiation does not end when a child is born. **Puberty** is the period of development later in childhood where secondary sex characteristics develop because of an increase in hormone release in the body. Usually occurring between ages 10 and 14 years for girls and between ages 12 and 16 years for boys (Kail & Cavanaugh, 2010), puberty begins with signals from the pituitary gland to the gonads to release more sex hormones (estrogen and testosterone). These hormones then cycle through the body affecting growth and development. **Menstruation** begins for girls, whereby the lining of the uterus (the **endometrium**) produces a nutrient-rich environment in preparation for implantation of a fertilized egg and pregnancy. When pregnancy does not occur, the rich environment of the uterine lining is shed and discharged from the body through the vagina. Girls also develop breasts and body hair (pubic hair and in the underarms), the hips may widen, and fat deposits on the body may change. For boys, puberty begins the process of **spermatogenesis**, the production of viable sperm. Boys may experience so-called "wet dreams" (**nocturnal emissions**), where orgasm and ejaculation occur during sleep. The first ejaculation ever for a boy may not occur until puberty. The surge in testosterone that comes with puberty increases skeletal and muscular growth (with boys growing quickly taller), growth of body hair, and deepening of the voice. Girls and boys are likely to experience **acne** (clogging of the facial and body pores, resulting in irritation and redness) and moodiness (because of the influence of hormones on mood and emotion). Both girls and boys are also likely to experience increases in sexual feelings and desires, and **masturbation** (**self-pleasuring**), the stimulation of one's own genitals to orgasm, may begin or increase during puberty. Young people are also likely to begin stimulating other people's genitals at this time, as well as other parts of the body, as sexual feelings increase and sexual exploration with others begins. While a greater discussion of sexuality will occur in Chapter 8, it is important to note here that during puberty, bodies are developing to successfully reproduce, a biological, physiological process that has great importance for personal and social processes and outcomes.

Female and Male Reproductive Systems

Before discussing pregnancy, let's remind ourselves of the important parts of the female and male human reproductive systems, which will help us better understand the process of human reproduction altogether. Typical genital structures for girls and women include the **vulva**, which is composed of several features, including the outer **labia** (lips), the inner **labia**, the **urethra** (a small opening from which urine leaves the body), the **clitoris** (the organ of sexual excitement and orgasm), and the vaginal opening. The **vagina** is the birth canal, the opening for the shedding of menstrual blood, and receives the penis during sexual intercourse. Internal structures for girls and women include the **ovaries** (the gonads), the primary sexual organ, which produce hormones and hold egg follicles. Once a month, one of the ovaries will release a mature egg (resulting from **oogenesis**) that is ready to be fertilized; this is **ovulation**. The average baby girl is born with about 1 to 2 million **oocytes**, or egg follicles, of which only about 400,000 are left at puberty (Krogh, 2010). The mature egg is released by the ovary into the body cavity, where the **fimbriae** at the end of the

uterine or Fallopian tube captures it; the egg then travels down the length of the uterine tube toward the **uterus** (which prepares itself each month for pregnancy and houses the developing fetus when pregnancy does occur). The lining of the uterus is the **endometrium**. At the bottom of the uterus is the opening to the vagina called the **cervix** (the bottom part of the uterus that projects into the very back of the vagina) (see Figure 4.3a). It is the uterine tubes that are severed during a **tubal ligation**, so that mature eggs cannot travel along the tubes and cannot be fertilized.

Typical external genital structures for boys and men include the **penis** (the organ for sexual excitement and ejaculation, which enters the vagina during sexual reproduction) and the **scrotum** (the sac which houses the **testicles** or **testes**) (see Figure 4.3b). The **testes** are the

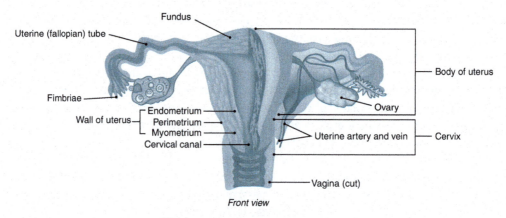

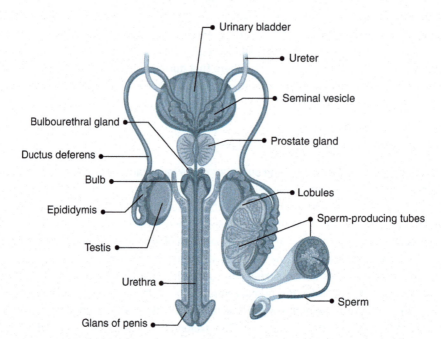

Figures 4.3a and 4.3b
Source: PATTARAWIT CHOMPIPAT/Alamy Stock Vector

Human Sexual Reproduction 71

primary reproductive organ for men, producing hormones across the lifespan and responsible for the production of sperm. Inside the body, the tubes that carry mature sperm to other organs for seminal fluid are the **vas deferens**. It is the vas deferens that are cut during a **vasectomy**, a rather simple surgical procedure that essentially serves to prevent viable sperm from entering semen. The **epididymides** are tubes on top of each teste which connect to the vas deferens. The **seminal vesicles** are glands under the bladder behind the prostate that contribute fluid and nutrients to semen, including fluids called prostaglandins that cause uterine contractions (which draw sperm up toward the uterine tubes). The **bulbourethral glands** (also called **Cowper's glands**) are behind the root of the penis and add mucosal fluid to semen, including an initial bit of mucosal fluid before intercourse for lubricant. The **prostate gland** (under the bladder, behind the root of the penis) also contributes to seminal fluid, including prostatic fluid, which enhances motility (movement and speed) of sperm. The **urethra** carries urine outside the body through the penis, and seminal fluid (semen) outside the body through the penis during **ejaculation**.

Fertilization, Pregnancy, and Childbirth

Although there are clearly variations in fertility throughout the human population, the typical adult human body is working toward reproduction most of the time, male and female. The typical man's body manufactures millions of **spermatids** (immature sperm cells) each day; sperm are stored in the testes for two to three months to mature. A woman's **fertile (follicular) phase** begins after the end of menstruation, when the lining of the uterus again begins to prepare itself for a fertilized egg. **Ovulation** (release of a mature egg by one of the ovaries) occurs about two weeks after the end of the last menstrual period. Although for much of the month the cervix is tightly closed, about three to five days prior to ovulation the cervix is more open and is covered with a thick mucosal fluid. The fluid actually works to bring any semen up toward the openings of the uterine tubes to facilitate **fertilization** (a mature sperm enters and is absorbed into a mature egg, resulting in a **zygote**). When ejaculation occurs, anywhere from 40 million to over one billion mature sperm are present in the semen that is released (about one teaspoon of fluid). Talk about overkill! Those sperm are then in a race to reach the uterine tubes, within which a mature egg may sit, waiting to be fertilized. If an egg is not fertilized within about 12 to 24 hours, it will die. Sperm can travel for over two days to reach the uterine tubes (although some are much faster and can reach an egg within an hour); sperm live around 48 to 72 hours once ejaculation occurs. If the implantation of a fertilized egg does not occur, the lining of the uterus will again be shed and released from the body as menstrual flow, about 25 to 28 days after the beginning of the last menstrual period.

If fertilization does occur, the zygote exists and immediately begins to grow through mitosis. Within around eight or nine days, the zygote has become a **blastocyst**, which burrows itself into the rich protective and nutritious lining of the uterus. If all has gone normally and the woman's body is producing hormones to protect the pregnancy and prevent the immune system from attacking the microscopic invader, within two weeks the endometrium will begin forming the **placenta** (responsible for sharing blood and nutrients between the woman and fetus through the umbilical cord); and part of the placenta and the **amniotic sac** (the membrane which holds the developing fetus within **amniotic fluid** that the fetus drinks and breathes) form from the blastocyst itself. By four weeks the blastocyst is now called an **embryo** and is about as big as a poppy seed. By ten weeks the embryo has become a **fetus** and internal organs are forming. There is a heartbeat and the fetus has limbs and eyes (which are fused closed). The second trimester begins around 14 weeks and lasts until about 27 weeks of pregnancy. The fetus' body is essentially organized and it moves about and grows during this middle period. Hearing develops so the fetus is stimulated by outside noises; the eyes open and close; the fetus will suck on its fingers during this time. The fetus sleeps and wakes at regular intervals, and weighs over one pound at the end of the second trimester. The third trimester is all about growth and brain development; the greatest period of brain development occurs here in the last trimester. The lungs are also developing in this trimester in preparation for living outside of the amniotic fluid. The fetus is considered full-term, ready to be born, at 39 to 40 weeks. The average full-term baby weighs about 7 to 7.5 pounds and is around 20 inches long. Premature births often involve many complications for the baby, especially if they occur before 34 weeks or so. Many "preemie" complications occur because of low birth weight and problems with lung development.

Childbirth can be a harrowing, very painful and life-changing experience for any woman. Labor can last for hours, usually from about 12 to 19 hours, but sometimes more than 24 hours, during which the cervix is shortening and opening for the baby to exit the uterus. Labor involves painful contractions of the uterus which are felt in the abdomen, pelvis, and back. Contractions last about 30 seconds and are several minutes apart, occurring more closely together as the cervix shortens and widens. During a vaginal delivery, which can take an additional one to two hours after labor, the woman pushes with uterine contractions to expel the baby out of the vaginal canal. This can be very difficult, dangerous, and painful, particularly because of the typical size of a human infant's head and the width of the infant's shoulders. The last stage of childbirth is delivery of the placenta (Kitzinger, 2003). While most births are in fact vaginal, around 15-20% of births worldwide occur via Cesarean section (an incision in the lower abdomen to remove the baby; Molina et al., 2015).

Pregnancy is actually very dangerous for women; a woman's life is most at risk when she is pregnant. Complications from childbirth and pregnancy are among the leading causes of death for women, especially within countries that are still developing, where high-quality health care is not available (World Health Organization, 2010). Having multiple pregnancies, an outcome that is obviously much more likely when contraception is not accessible and affordable, magnifies health risks of pregnancy and childbirth for women. Pregnancy and childbirth complications are *the* leading cause of death among women aged 15 to 19 years old in developing countries (Mayor, 2004). According to the World Health Organization (2010), there are four major causes of death for pregnant women: bleeding after childbirth, infections, hypertensive disorders (high blood pressure), and unsafe abortion (usually because abortion is illegal in that country or region). Each year around the world about 500,000 women die from pregnancy or childbirth, 7 million women develop serious long-term health problems from pregnancy or childbirth, and about 50 million women experience negative health outcomes after childbirth (World Health Organization, 2008). Conditions during pregnancy that can endanger women's lives include infections, high blood pressure (risking heart attack and stroke), anemia, gestational diabetes, hyperemesis (uncontrolled vomiting), and others. Depression and other psychological difficulties can occur during pregnancy and after childbirth, in which case it is sometimes called "post-partum depression" (Chabrol et al., 2002). Pregnant women are also particularly vulnerable to injuries. Unfortunately, some research indicates that women who are pregnant are particularly susceptible to intimate partner violence, and are more likely to be abused by a male partner compared overall to women who are not pregnant (Coid, 2000; Department of Health, 2005) (see Chapter 11). Women have made huge sacrifices, including their own lives, in carrying and giving birth to every single

Human Sexual Reproduction   73

member of the human race. Let's appreciate women and the enormous gift they have given to every person who has ever lived. Now go hug your mom!

Prenatal Health: Nutrition and Teratogens

Nutrition is extremely important during pregnancy, for the health of the woman and the additional demands being placed on her body, and the health of the developing fetus. Pregnant women should of course do their best to eat healthy, fresh foods, especially plenty of fruits and vegetables. Pregnant women need to drink lots of water and get plenty of rest. Vitamins for pregnant women often include folic acid (a form of Vitamin B-9), which is important to prevent defects of the **neural tube** (the embryonic structure that becomes the brain and spinal cord) in the fetus (Czeizel & Dudas, 1992). Calcium is important for pregnant women to help with bone growth of the fetus (Villar & Belizan, 1986), and iron is important to prevent maternal anemia (Beaufrère et al., 1995). Pregnant women should get plenty of sleep and rest throughout the day to prevent fatigue. Emotional support is extremely important for pregnant women also, not just for emotional health but also to prevent maternal stress.

Stress during pregnancy can lead to multiple complications for women and fetuses. Research indicates that stress reactions can influence thyroid functioning, which can have very deleterious effects on a developing fetus, including damage to cognitive development (King & Laplante, 2005; Schneider, Roughton, Koehler, & Lubach, 1999). One study found that exposure to stress in the second trimester of pregnancy increases the likelihood that the child will develop schizophrenia in young adulthood (Van Os & Selton, 1998). Very recent research suggests that the microbial environment of the vagina can be altered by stress, which can then be passed on to babies during childbirth, affecting the microbial environment of the newborn's stomach, its immune system and metabolism, and eventually, neurological development of the child (Jašarević, Howerton, Howard, & Bale, 2015). Unhealthy or disabled children become unhealthy and disabled adults who require greater financial and social resources, and who are less likely to make multiple positive contributions to society than healthy, normally functioning adults. Maternal stress is best reduced, and fetal health maximized, by ensuring that pregnant women have sufficient social, emotional, and financial support. If the pregnancy is accidental or unwanted, this support is likely to be reduced and mothers are likely to be more stressed. Women's and infants' health is maximized when pregnancies are planned for and wanted. Affordable, accessible reproductive health care for all women, including options for contraception and abortion, is a public good that benefits all of society.

Teratogens are toxins in the environment that can affect fetal development. If something is dangerous or poisonous in some way to people who are not pregnant, it is definitely dangerous to a pregnant woman and her fetus. Poisons, lead, carcinogens, pollutants, all are to be avoided. Potentially especially harmful to a developing fetus are teratogens that are ingested or inhaled by the mother, because these substances may enter the bloodstream of the fetus. Smoking cigarettes is dangerous for everyone, but particularly for pregnant women. Infants born of smoking mothers are more likely to be born prematurely and with low birth weight, risk factors for many infant health problems, including long-term problems (Hack, Klein, & Taylor, 1995). Smoking is linked with birth defects like cleft lip and cleft palate, and is also linked with problems with the placenta during pregnancy and infant death (Centers for Disease Control and Prevention, 2017).

Alcohol is also a known teratogen for pregnant women and may result in a complex syndrome of outcomes called **Fetal Alcohol Syndrome (FAS)** (with milder forms referred to as *Partial*

Fetal Alcohol Effect or *alcohol-related neurodevelopmental disorder, ARND*). Symptoms of Fetal Alcohol Syndrome include physical abnormalities (facial features, small head, short height); hearing and vision problems; and cognitive problems (including low intelligence, poor motor skills and coordination) (Chudley et al., 2005). As they get older, FAS kids sometimes have behavior problems, including aggression and low self-control, resulting in school and legal problems, participating in risky behaviors, and substance abuse (Coriale et al., 2013). Other drugs are also harmful to fetal development, including prescription medications (Sachdeva, Patel, & Patel, 2009). An obstetrician must always be informed of all drugs a woman is prescribed or is taking while pregnant. Along with nutritious, healthy foods, vitamins, sleep, regular exercise, and a low-stress environment, a teratogen-free pregnancy will promote health for both mother and baby.

Chapter Summary

Sex is not a simple binary; complicated sets of features that result from complicated biological and physiological processes are rarely so simple. Numerous factors affect sex differentiation in utero, including genes (XX or XY, or another combination) and hormones (androgens and estrogens). Sex differentiation begins around the eighth week of pregnancy, with all embryos up to that point possessing indeterminate genitals and indistinct internal organs. At week 8, if the SRY gene is present, it will trigger the gonads to become testes, which will then produce and secrete hormones, which cause male internal structures and genitals to develop. If the SRY gene is not present at week 8, the fetus will develop female characteristics. Various anomalies may occur that affect sex differentiation, including genetic (de la Chapelle Syndrome, Swyer Syndrome) and hormonal disorders (CAH, AIS). Hormones in utero also affect sex differentiation by affecting brain development, with a growing body of research indicating that prenatal hormonal influences in the second half of pregnancy are linked with gender identity in childhood and adulthood and adult sexual orientation. Puberty involves major body changes including development of secondary sex characteristics and growing sexual feelings. Fertilization is a complicated process that may result in pregnancy, a life-threatening 40-week experience for women. Many factors influence fetal development, including mother's nutrition and teratogens.

Thoughtful Questions

- Consider human reproduction and dangers to women and fetuses throughout pregnancy. How does high-quality maternity health care, or a lack thereof, affect society? Should everyone have to pay for maternity care? Why or why not?
- Explain how hormones may influence the developing fetal brain. How are these influences linked with feelings of identity later in childhood and adulthood?
- How might hormones influence the gender identity of a person with Swyer Syndrome? With de la Chapelle syndrome? With Androgen Insensitivity Syndrome? With Congenital Adrenal Hyperplasia?
- Why do you think women may be more vulnerable to intimate partner violence (IPV) during pregnancy? What factors may affect severity of injuries from IPV during pregnancy?
- Consider and explain how bodily integrity is linked with civil rights for women and for men.

Human Sexual Reproduction   75

- Consider your opinion on abortion. Do you think your opinion should affect women's bodily autonomy? Why or why not?
- Explain the physical processes involved in sex differentiation in utero.

Glossary

Abortion: various medical procedures used to terminate a pregnancy.

Acne: clogging of the facial and body pores with oil and dirt, resulting in irritation and redness. Oil changes in the skin occur during puberty, commonly resulting in acne for girls and boys.

Amniotic fluid: watery fluid in the amniotic sac which a developing fetus will breathe and drink.

Amniotic sac: formed from the outer layer of the blastocyst, the membranes that hold the developing fetus during pregnancy.

Androgen Insensitivity Syndrome (AIS): a genetic disorder whereby the body's cells are insensitive to androgens (male hormones); for XY individuals, this means that although the gonads are male and produce androgens, the body is insensitive to them, and so the external genitals appear female.

Androgens: male hormones linked with growth, development, sexuality, and behavior.

Biological sex: a person's structural, biological sex as indicated by genotype, genitals, and internal reproductive organs; determined largely by genes and in utero processes.

Bodily integrity: the right of individuals to not have their physical body violated, and the importance of personal autonomy and self-determination of every person over their own physical body.

Bulbourethral glands (also called **Cowper's glands**): glands behind the root of the penis that add mucosal fluid to semen, including an initial bit of mucosal fluid before intercourse for lubricant.

Cervix: the bottom part of the uterus that projects into the vagina.

Circumcision: removal of the foreskin of the penis, usually done in infancy.

Congenital Adrenal Hyperplasia (CAH): a genetic disorder whereby the adrenal glands produce excessive androgens. For XY individuals, precocious puberty may occur, but CAH can be controlled with medication. For XX individuals, the genitals may be ambiguous at birth and the internal organs are underdeveloped. Male characteristics may develop, including during puberty.

de la Chapelle Syndrome: a genetic disorder where the genotype is XX but the SRY gene has become attached to one of the X chromosomes. Because the SRY gene is present, sex differentiation with male features occurs, but hypogonadism affects sexual development.

Embryo: the developing human during weeks 4 to 10 of pregnancy.

Endometrium: the lining of the uterus. The endometrium becomes thick with an outer coating in preparation for a fertilized egg; this lining is shed during menstruation. An essential part of reproduction that forms part of the **placenta** in pregnancy.

Epididymides: part of the male reproductive system, a network of tubes on top of each teste which connect to the vas deferens.

Estrogens: female hormones linked with growth, development, sexuality, and behavior.

Fertilization: a mature sperm enters and combines genetic material with a mature egg, resulting in a zygote.

76 *Human Sexual Reproduction*

Fetal Alcohol Syndrome (FAS): a syndrome of characteristics of babies born of women abusing alcohol during pregnancy, including distinctive facial features, small head, small stature, vision and hearing problems, cognitive problems (including low intelligence), and behavioral problems.

Fimbriae: finger-like structures at the end of the uterine or Fallopian tubes which capture eggs that are released, sweeping them into the uterine tube.

Gender: cultural ideas about what is feminine and what is masculine; strongly influenced by in utero biological processes as well as socialization processes (gender norms provided by culture and social institutions).

Gender behaviors: behaviors that are sex-typed within a given culture.

Gender identity: an individual's identification as female, male, both, or neither.

Genital tubercle: in the early embryo, the indistinct genitalia that become the clitoris in a female fetus and the penis in a male fetus.

Gonads: the primary sex organs, ovaries in women and testes in men. The gonads produce hormones, which have major effects on brain development in utero and childhood and sexual development and behavior starting in puberty.

Homeostasis: controlled by the hypothalamus, the maintaining of body temperature, metabolism, and other physiological processes at a relatively constant level.

Hormones: chemicals produced by the body that enter the bloodstream and cause reactions in other structures. Hormones are linked with growth, development, sexuality, and emotions.

Hypogonadism: under-functioning of the gonads, sometimes caused by underdevelopment in utero linked with genetic disorders. The gonads do not produce sufficient hormones, affecting brain and sexual development and behavior.

Hypothalamic uncinate nucleus: a brain structure that differs in size by gender identity.

Hypothalamus: a structure in the middle of the brain beneath the thalamus that is responsible for regulating needs (including hunger, thirst, sex, sleep) and homeostasis; also a pleasure center that is linked with emotions.

Intersex: a person who is born with indistinct biological sex. Possibilities include ambiguous genitalia, genotype not matching phenotype, female genitalia with male internal structures and vice versa.

Jacob's Syndrome: a sex chromosome trisomy (XYY), resulting in a person with normal sex characteristics who may have some learning disabilities or motor impairment.

Klinefelter Syndrome: a sex chromosome trisomy (XXY), resulting in a male person with immature sex characteristics.

Labioscrotal swelling: indistinct genitals of the human embryo before week 8; for XY, develops into the scrotum; for XX, develops into the labia.

Masturbation (self-pleasuring): stimulating one's own genitals, usually to orgasm.

Menstruation: the shedding of the thick coating lining the uterus in preparation for pregnancy; menstruation occurs each month if a fertilized egg is not implanted.

Müllerian ducts: internal ductwork of the embryo that becomes internal organs of the female reproductive system (uterine tubes, uterus) when the SRY gene is absent.

Müllerian inhibiting substance (MIS): a hormone produced by the embryonic testes that triggers degeneration of the Müllerian ducts.

Neural tube: the embryonic structure that becomes the brain and spinal cord.

Nocturnal emissions: "wet dreams," or ejaculation that occurs during sleep for boys in puberty.

Oocytes: immature egg follicles contained in the ovaries.

Human Sexual Reproduction 77

Ovaries: part of the female reproductive system, the primary sexual organ which produces hormones and holds egg follicles.

Ovulation: once a month, one of a girl's or woman's ovaries releases a mature egg that is ready to be fertilized.

Penis: part of male external genitalia, the organ for sexual excitement and ejaculation, which enters the vagina during sexual reproduction.

Persistent Müllerian duct syndrome: when the Müllerian ducts fail to degenerate early in fetal development and an XY person is born with a uterus and uterine tubes, as well as male reproductive organs and male external genitalia.

Pituitary gland: a pea-sized gland protruding from the hypothalamus that secretes hormones affecting blood pressure, sexuality, metabolism, growth, and reproduction.

Placenta: the organ formed from the **endometrium** and the outer layer of the blastocyst; responsible for sharing blood and nutrients between the woman and fetus through the umbilical cord during pregnancy.

Poly-X Syndrome: a genetic disorder involving a trisomy with an extra X sex chromosome (XXX). Poly-X may also involve other genotypes (XXXX, XXXXX). Symptoms include tallness, thinness, cognitive deficits.

Prostate gland: part of the male reproductive system, a large gland under the bladder, behind the root of the penis, that contributes to seminal fluid, including prostatic fluid, which enhances motility (movement and speed) of sperm.

Puberty: the period of development later in childhood (beginning age 10–12 years) when menstruation (in girls) and sperm production (in boys) occur; secondary sex characteristics develop because of an increase in hormone release in the body; the body is preparing itself for sexual reproduction.

RISUG (reversible inhibition of sperm under guidance): a contraceptive method involving injection of a polymer gel into the vas deferens, which reverses the ionization of sperm and shreds them when ejaculation occurs. Effective, safe, cheap, reversible; currently being researched in the U.S. as Vasalgel.

Scrotum: part of male external genitalia, the sac which houses the **testicles** or **testes.**

Seminal vesicles: part of the male reproductive system, glands under the bladder behind the prostate that contribute fluid and nutrients to semen.

Sex differentiation: the process whereby an embryo develops female or male genitalia and internal reproductive organs.

Sexually dimorphic nucleus (SDN): an area of the hypothalamus that is twice as large in adult men as in adult women.

Spermatids: immature sperm cells.

Spermatogenesis: the production of viable sperm in the testes; begins at puberty.

SRY (sex-determining region of Y): the gene responsible for maleness; SRY triggers undifferentiated embryonic gonads to become testes, which then release testosterone and trigger development of the genitals and internal reproductive organs into male organs.

Suprachiasmatic nucleus (SCN): an area of the hypothalamus that is twice as large in adult homosexual men as in adult heterosexual men.

Swyer Syndrome: a genetic disorder where the genotype is XY but the SRY gene is missing or mutated. The external genitalia appear as typically female, but the gonads are underdeveloped which affects later sexual development during puberty and adulthood.

Teratogens: toxins in the environment that can affect fetal development.

Testes: the primary reproductive organ for men (the gonads), producing hormones across the lifespan and responsible for the production of sperm.

Testis determining factor (TDF; also called *H-Y antigen*): a hormone that triggers the indistinct gonadal structures of an embryo to develop into **testes**; triggered by the SRY gene.

Testosterone: a male hormone that triggers male fetal development, development of male secondary sex characteristics in puberty, production of sperm, and sexual behavior; also linked with aggressive behavior.

Tubal ligation: when the uterine tubes are severed so that mature eggs cannot travel along the tubes and cannot be fertilized.

Turner Syndrome: a genetic disorder involving a monosomy of the sex chromosomes (XO). Characteristics include hypogonadism, immature secondary sex characteristics, infertility, neck webbing, some cognitive deficits.

Urethra: in the male reproductive system, carries urine outside the body through the penis, and seminal fluid (semen) outside the body through the penis during ejaculation. In the female reproductive system, the small opening in the vulva from which urine is released.

Urogenital groove: part of the embryonic undifferentiated genitalia; with XX, becomes the urethra, bladder, vagina; with XY, becomes the urethra, bladder, and other membranes.

Uterine (Fallopian) tubes: part of the female reproductive system, the internal tubes through which mature eggs travel toward the uterus.

Uterus: part of the female reproductive system, the uterus prepares itself each month for pregnancy and houses the developing fetus when pregnancy does occur.

Vagina: part of the female external genitalia, it is the birth canal, the opening for the shedding of menstrual blood, and receives the penis during sexual intercourse.

Vas deferens: part of the male reproductive system, the tubes that carry mature sperm from the testes to other organs for the addition of seminal fluid.

Vasectomy: a simple surgical procedure involving cutting of the vas deferens, which serves to prevent viable sperm from entering semen.

Vulva: the female external genitalia, composed of several features including the outer **labia** (lips), the inner **labia**, the **urethra** (a small opening from which urine leaves the body), the **clitoris** (the organ of sexual excitement and orgasm), and the vaginal opening.

Wolffian ducts: the internal ductwork of the embryo which becomes the internal tubing of the male reproductive system if the SRY gene is present.

Zygote: a combination of one mature sperm and one mature egg; in humans, begins as one cell with 46 chromosomes in its nucleus, 23 from the egg and 23 from the sperm, with organelles provided by the egg.

References

Alldridge, P. & Brants, C. H. (Eds.) (2001). *Personal autonomy, the private sphere and criminal law*. Oxford: Hart Publishing.

Arver, S., Dobs, A. S.. Meikle, A. W., Allen, R. P., Sanders, S. W. & Mazer, N. A. (1996). Improvement of sexual function in testosterone deficient men treated for 1 year with a permeation enhanced testosterone transdermal system. *The Journal of Urology, 155*(5), 1604-1608.

Associated Press (2004). David Reimer, 38, subject of the John/Joan case. *The New York Times*, May 12, 2004. Retrieved May 19, 2015.

Baten, J. & Blum, M. (2012). Growing tall but unequal: New findings and new background evidence on anthropometric welfare in 156 countries, 1810-1989. *Economic History of Developing Regions, 27*(Suppl 1), S66-S85. doi:10.1080/20780389.2012.657489.

Beaufrère, B., Bresson, J. L., Briend, A., Farriaux, J. P., Ghisolfi, J., Navarro, J., Rey, J., Ricour, C., Rieu, D., & Vidailhet, M. (1995). Iron and pregnancy. *Archives de Pediatrie: Organe Officiel de la Société Française de Pediatrie 2*(12), 1209-1218.

Blackless, M., Charuvastra, A., Derryck, A., Fausto-Sterling, A., Lauzanne, K., & Lee, E. (2000). How sexually dimorphic are we? *The American Journal of Human Biology, 12*(2), 151-166.

Callahan, G. N. (2009). *Between XX and XY: Intersexuality and the myth of two sexes.* Chicago: Chicago Review Press.

Centers for Disease Control and Prevention (2017). *Tobacco use and pregnancy: How does smoking during pregnancy harm my health and my baby?* www.cdc.gov/reproductivehealth/maternalinfanthealth/tobaccousepregnancy/index.htm.

Chabrol, H., Teissedre, F., Saint-Jean, M., Teisseyre, N., Sistac, C., Michaud, C., & Roge, B. (2002). Detection, prevention and treatment of postpartum depression: A controlled study of 859 patients. *L'Encéphale, 28*(1), 65-70.

Chudley, A. E., Conry, J., Cook, J. L., Loock, C., Rosales, T., & LeBlanc, N. (2005). Fetal alcohol spectrum disorder: Canadian guidelines for diagnosis. *CMAJ, 172*(5), S1-S21. doi:10.1503/cmaj.1040302.

Coid, J. (2000). *Domestic violence. A health response: Working in a wider partnership.* London: Department of Health.

Coriale, G., Fiorentino, D., Di Lauro, F., Marchitelli, R., Scalese, B., Fiore, M., Maviglia, M., & Ceccanti, M. (2013). Fetal Alcohol Spectrum Disorder (FASD): Neurobehavioral profile, indications for diagnosis and treatment. *Rivista di psichiatria, 48*(5), 359-369. doi:10.1708/1356.15062.

Creighton, S. M. (2004). Long-term surgical outcome of feminization surgery: The London experience. *BJU International, 93*, 44-46.

Czeizel, A. E., & Dudas, I. (1992). Prevention of the first occurrence of neural tube defects by periconceptional vitamin supplementation. *New England Journal of Medicine, 327*, 1832-1835.

de Escobar, G. M., Obregón, M. J., & del Rey, F. E. (2004). Maternal thyroid hormones early in pregnancy and fetal brain development. *Best Practice & Research: Clinical Endocrinology & Metabolism, 18*(2), 225-248.

de la Chapelle, A. (1972). Analytic review: Nature and origin of males with XX sex chromosomes. *American Journal of Human Genetics, 24*(1), 71-105.

Department of Health (2005). Interventions to reduce violence and promote the physical and psychosocial well-being of women who experience partner violence: A systematic review of controlled evaluations. London: Department of Health.

Dittmann, R. W., Kappes, M. E., & Kappes, M. H. (1992). Sexual behavior in adolescent and adult females with congenital adrenal hyperplasia. *Psychoneuroendocrinology, 17*, 153-170.

Ehrhardt, A. A., Greenberg, N., & Money, J. (1970). Female gender identity and absence of fetal gonadal hormones: Turner's syndrome. *Johns Hopkins Medical Journal, 126*(5), 237-248.

Garcia-Falgueras, A., & Swaab, D. F. (2008). A sex difference in the hypothalamic uncinate nucleus: Relationship to gender identity. *Brain: A Journal of Neurology, 131*(12), 3132-3146.

Garcia-Falgueras, A., & Swaab, D. F. (2010). Sexual hormones and the brain: An essential alliance for sexual identity and sexual orientation. *Endocrine Development, 17*, 22-35. doi:10.1159/000262525.

Gravholt, C. H. (2013). Sex chromosome abnormalities. In Pyeritz, R. E., Rimoin, D. L., & Korf, B. R. (Eds.), *Emery and Rimoin's principles and practice of medical genetics* (6th ed.). San Diego: Elsevier Academic Press, 1180-1211.

Greenfield, C. (2014). Should we 'fix' intersex children? Standard medical practice is often to operate to "normalize" genitals, but some families are fighting back. *The Atlantic*, July 8.

Grumbach, M. M., Hughes, I. A., & Conte, F. A. (2003). Disorders of sex differentiation. In Larsen, P. R., Kronenberg, H. M., Melmed, S., & Polonsky, K. S. (Eds.), *Williams textbook of endocrinology*. Philadelphia: Saunders, pp. 842-1002.

Hack, M., Klein, N. K., & Taylor, H. G. (1995). Long-term developmental outcomes of low birth weight infants. *Future Child, 5*(1), 176-196.

Hines, M., & Kaufman, F. R. (1994). Androgen and the development of human sex-typical behavior: Rough-and-tumble play and sex of preferred playmates in children with congenital adrenal hyperplasia (CAH). *Child Development, 65*, 1042-1053.

Hines, M., Ahmed, S. F., & Hughes, I. (2003). Psychological outcomes and gender-related development in complete androgen insensitivity syndrome. *Archives of Sexual Behavior, 32*, 93-101.

Hines, M. (2011). Prenatal endocrine influences on sexual orientation and on sexually differentiated childhood behavior. *Frontiers in Neuroendocrinology, 32*(2), 170-182. doi:10.1016/j.yfrne.2011.02.006.

Holland, A. J., & Smith, G. H. (2000). Effect of the depth and width of the urethral plate on tubularized incised plate urethroplasty. *The Journal of Urology, 164*(2), 489-491. doi:10.1016/S0022-5347(05)67408-3.

Jacobs, P. A., Brunton, M., Melville, M. M., Brittain, R. P., & McClemont, W. F. (1965). Aggressive behavior, mental sub-normality and the XYY male. *Nature, 208*(5017), 1351-1352. doi:10.1038/2081351a0.

Jašarević, E., Howerton, C. L., Howard, C. D., & Bale, T. L. (2015). Alterations in the vaginal microbiome by maternal stress are associated with metabolic reprogramming of the offspring gut and brain. *Endocrinology, 156*(9), 3265-3276. doi.org/10.1210/en.2015-1177.

Jha, P. K., Jha, R., Gupta, B. L., & Guha, S. K. (2010). Effect of γ-dose rate and total dose interrelation on the polymeric hydrogel: A novel injectable male contraceptive. *Radiation Physics and Chemistry, 79*(5), 663-671.

Jyoti, A. (2011). Poor response from male volunteers hits RISUG clinical trial. *The Pioneer.* New Delhi.

Kail, R. V., & Cavanaugh J. C. (2010). *Human development: A lifespan view* (5th ed.). Belmont, CA: Cengage Learning.

Kero, A., Högberg, U., & Lalos, A. (2004). Well-being and mental growth - long-term effects of legal abortion. *Social Science and Medicine, 58*(12), 2559-2569. https://doi.org/10.1016/j.socscimed.2003.09.004.

King, S., & Laplante, D. P. (2005). The effects of prenatal maternal stress on children's cognitive development: Project Ice Storm. *Stress, 8*(1), 35-45.

Kitzinger, S. (2003). *The complete book of pregnancy and childbirth* (revised). New York: Knopf.

Köhler, B., Kleinemeier, E., Lux, A., Hiort, O., Grüters, A., Thyen, U., & DSD Network Working Group (2012). Satisfaction with genital surgery and sexual life of adults with XY disorders of sex development: Results from the German clinical evaluation study. *Journal of Clinical Endocrinology & Metabolism, 97*(2), 577-588, doi.org/10.1210/jc.2011-1441.

Krogh, D. (2010). *Biology: A guide to the natural world.* San Francisco, CA: Benjamin-Cummings Publishing Company.

Leinbach, M. D., & Fagot, B. I. (1993). Categorical habituation to male and female faces: Gender schematic processing in infancy. *Infant Behavior & Development, 16*(3), 317-332.

Liester, M. B. (1989). Psychiatric aspects of Klinefelter's Syndrome. *Journal of the Multihandicapped Person, 2*(3), 241-250.

Mayor, S. (2004). Pregnancy and childbirth are leading causes of death in teenage girls in developing countries. *British Medical Journal, 328*(7449), 1152. doi:10.1136/bmj.328.7449.1152-a.

McCarthy, M. M., De Vries, G. J., & Forger, N. G. (2009). Sexual differentiation of the brain: mode, mechanisms, and meaning. In Pfaff, D. W., Arnold, A. P., Etgen, A. M., Fahrbach, S. E., & Rubin, R. T. (Eds.), *Hormones, brain and behavior.* San Diego: Academic Press, 1707-1744.

Meyer-Bahlburg, H. F. L., Dolezal, C., Baker, S. W., & New, M. I. (2008). Sexual orientation in women with classical or non-classical congenital adrenal hyperplasia as a function of degree of prenatal androgen excess. *Archives of Sexual Behavior, 37,* 85-99.

Michala, L., Goswami, D., Creighton, S. M., & Conway, G. S. (2008). Swyer syndrome: presentation and outcomes. *British Journal of Obstetrics & Gynaecology, 115*(6), 737-741. doi:10.1111/j.1471-0528.2008.01703.x.

Miller, R. A. (2007). *The limits of bodily integrity: Abortion, adultery, and rape legislation in comparative perspective.* Aldershot, UK: Ashgate.

Minto, C. L., Liao, L.-M., Woodhouse, C. R. J., Ransley, P. G., & Creighton, S. M. (2003). The effect of clitoral surgery on sexual outcome in individuals who have intersex conditions with ambiguous genitalia: A cross-sectional study. *The Lancet, 361.*

Money, J. & Ehrhardt, A. A. (1971). Fetal hormones and the brain: Effect on sexual dimorphism of behavior—A review. *Archives of Sexual Behavior, 1*(3), 241-262.

Money, J. & Ehrhardt, A. A. (1972). *Man and woman, boy and girl: Differentiation and dimorphism of gender identity from conception to maturity.* Oxford: Johns Hopkins University Press.

Money, J., Schwartz, M., & Lewis, V. (1984). Adult erotosexual status and fetal hormonal masculinization and demasculinization: 46 XX congenital virilizing adrenal hyperplasia and 46 XY androgen-insensitivity syndrome compared. *Psychoneuroendocrinology, 9,* 405-414.

Nussbaum, M. C. (1999). *Sex and social justice.* Oxford: Oxford University Press, 41-42.

Ohno, S. (1978). The role of H-Y antigen in primary sex determination. *Journal of the American Medical Association, 239*(3), 217-220.

Pasterski, V. L., Geffner, M. E., Brain, C., Hindmarsh, P., Brook, C., & Hines, M. (2005). Prenatal hormones and postnatal socialization by parents as determinants of male-typical toy play in girls with congenital adrenal hyperplasia. *Child Development, 76,* 264-278.

Phoenix, C. H., Goy, R. W., Gerall, A. A., & Young, W. C. (1959). Organizing action of prenatally administered testosterone propionate on the tissues mediating mating behavior in the female guinea pig. *Endocrinology, 65,* 163-196.

Rey, R. (2005). Anti-Müllerian hormone in disorders of sex determination and differentiation. *Arquivos Brasileiros de Endocrinologia & Metabologia, 49*(1), 26-36.

Rocca, C. H., Kimport, K., Roberts, S. C.M., Gould, H., Neuhaus, J., & Foster, D. G. (2015). Decision rightness and emotional responses to abortion in the United States: A longitudinal study. *PLoS ONE 10*(7): e0128832. doi. org/10.1371/journal.pone.0128832.

Ross, A. J., & Capel, B. (2005). Signaling at the crossroads of gonad development. *Trends in Endocrinology and Metabolism, 16*(1), 19-25. https://doi.org/10.1016/j.tem.2004.11.004.

Sachdeva, P., Patel, B. G., & Patel, B. K. (2009). Drug use in pregnancy; a point to ponder! *Indian Journal of Pharmaceutical Sciences, 71*(1): 1-7. doi:10.4103/0250-474X.51941.

Schneider, M. L., Roughton, E. C., Koehler, A. J., & Lubach, G. R. (1999). Growth and development following prenatal stress exposure in primates: An examination of ontogenetic vulnerability. *Child Development, 70*, 263-274.

Swaab, D. F. & Garcia-Falgueras, A. (2009). Sexual differentiation of the human brain in relation to gender identity and sexual orientation. *Functional Neurology, 24*(1), 17-28.

Swaab, D. F., Chung, W. C.J., Kruijver, F. P.M., Hofman, M. A., & Ishunina, T. A. (2001). Structural and functional sex differences in the human hypothalamus. *Hormones and Behavior, 40*(2), 93-98.

Swaab, D. F., Chung, W. C., Kruijver, F. P., Hofman, M. A., & Ishunina, T. A. (2002). Sexual differentiation of the human hypothalamus. *Advances in Experimental Medicine and Biology, 511*, 75-105.

Swaab, D. F., Gooren, L. J.G., & Hofman, M. A. (1995). Brain research, gender and sexual orientation. *Journal of Homosexuality, 28*(3-4), 283-301. doi:org/10.1300/J082v28n03_07.

Sybert, V. P., & McCauley, E. (2004). Turner's syndrome. *New England Journal of Medicine, 351*(12), 1227-1238. doi:10.1056/NEJMra030360.

US Library of Medicine (2017). Persistent Mullerian Duct Syndrome. Genetics Home Reference. https://ghr. nlm.nih.gov/condition/persistent-mullerian-duct-syndrome#sourcesforpage.

U.S. National Library of Medicine (2017). Congenital adrenal hyperplasia. Medline Plus. https://medlineplus. gov/ency/article/000411.htm.

Van Os, J., & Selton, J. (1998). Prenatal exposure to maternal stress and subsequent schizophrenia. *British Journal of Psychiatry, 172*, 324-326.

Villar, J., & Belizan, J. M. (1986). Calcium during pregnancy. *Clinical Nutrition, 5*, 55-62.

Walker-Andrews, A. S., Bahrick, L. E., Raglioni, S. S., & Diaz, I. (1991). Infants' bimodal perception of gender. *Ecological Psychology, 3*(2), 55-75.

Warne, G. L., Faiman, C., Reyes, F. I., & Winter, J. S. D. (1977). Studies on human sexual development. V Concentrations of testosterone, 17-hydroxyprogesterone and progesterone in human amniotic fluid throughout gestation. *Journal of Clinical Endocrinology and Metabolism, 44*, 934-938.

Wilson, J. D., George, F. W., & Griffin, J. E. (1981). The hormonal control of sexual development. *Science, 211*, 1278-1284.

World Health Organization (2007). Male circumcision: Global trends and determinants of prevalence, safety and acceptability.

World Health Organization (2008). *Education material for teachers of midwifery: Midwifery education modules* (2nd ed.). Geneva.

World Health Organization (2010). Maternal deaths worldwide drop by third. Geneva/New York, Report, 15 September.

Zhou, J.-N., Hofman, M. A., Gooren, L. J.G., & Swaab, D. F. (1997). A sex difference in the human brain and its relation to transsexuality. *International Journal of Transgenderism, 1*(1).

Zucker, K. J., Bradley, S. J., Oliver, G., Blake, J., Fleming, S., & Hood, J. (1996). Psychosexual development of women with congenital adrenal hyperplasia. *Hormones and Behavior, 30*, 300-318.

5 Gender Stereotypes

Sex versus Gender	87
The Human Information-Processor: Schematic versus Controlled	87
Expressivity and Communality, Agency and Instrumentality	95
Gender Stereotypes Are Prescriptive and Proscriptive	97
Sources of Gender Stereotypes: Biology, Social Roles, and Cultural Institutions	99
Purposes of Gender Stereotypes: Division of Labor and Social Dominance	102

INEQUALITIES AND INJUSTICES

That *Feisty* Guy? Words That Are Only Used for Women

The following list of words appeared in an online article in the *Telegraph* (a newspaper in the United Kingdom) as words that are reserved for descriptions of women (Sanghani, 2017). What do you think? Consider each word, and whether you've heard it in descriptions of women, and in descriptions of men. How might you use each to describe a woman, or a man?

P.S., I admit it, I added one word (strident), having been called that a time or two. I also took out two words that were quite British as I thought they weren't highly recognizable.

Airhead, noun
Slang for stupid, not smart.
Abrasive, noun
Harsh, annoying, irritating in manner.
Bitch, noun, or *Bitchy*, adjective
A mean woman who criticizes others and complains; being like a bitch.
Bombshell, adjective
A sex pot, a "brick house," you get the idea. Bombshell implies her sexuality is dangerous.
Bossy, adjective
Women who assert their will, who tell people what to do (maybe because they're the boss?). But see Table 5.1 Pancultural Adjective Checklist.
Breathless, adjective

Gender Stereotypes 83

That sexy flustered look, like you're almost going to faint.

Bridezilla, noun

What about the husband who beats his wife the first time on the day after the wedding?

Bubbly, adjective

Lively, excitable, gregarious, like a glass of champagne.

Curvy, adjective

Real men have curves? Hmmm.

Ditsy, adjective

Silly, airheaded, dimwitted.

Emotional, adjective

Aka fragile, weepy, clingy, needy.

Feisty, adjective

Lively, not easily tamed or subdued, like a wild pony. Troublemaking.

Frigid, adjective

Sexually frozen, like trying to make out with a popsicle.

Frumpy, adjective

A combination of dumpy and frazzled? Maybe dumpy and frigid?

High-maintenance, adjective

Needs a lot of attention and gifts.

Hormonal, adjective

Everyone has hormones and hormones affect physical, physiological, and emotional processes.

Hysterical, adjective

Meaning neurotic, extremely emotional and irrational. Based on the Latin word for "uterus."

Illogical, adjective; and *Irrational*, adjective

Gaslighting involves calling women illogical or irrational when they express concern about something.

Pushy, adjective

Like bossy, abrasive. Asserting your will because you can.

Sassy, adjective

A spitfire, spark plug (see feisty). A cute little word for a little girl, not a woman.

Shrill, adjective

A woman speaking loudly in an octave that is higher than the average man's. Only bossy and abrasive women are shrill.

Strident, adjective

Loud, harsh, insistent. See shrill, abrasive.

Voluptuous, adjective

Nothing wrong there.

Working mom/mother/mum, noun

Working dad? No qualifier needed, apparently.

Adapted from Radhika Sanghani (2017). Feisty, frigid and frumpy: 25 words we only use to describe women. *The Telegraph*, March 17. www.telegraph.co.uk/women/life/ambitious-frigid-and-frumpy-25-words-we-only-use-to-describe-wom/.

CRITICAL THINKING

What's So Bad about Atheists?

Stereotypes are schemas we have for broad social categories of people, including ideas about their typical qualities, traits, and attributes. Most people have stereotypes for people of different religions: what Christians are like, what Buddhists are like, what Muslims are like, and so on. People also apparently have stereotypes for atheists, people who don't believe in any gods. The content of those stereotypes is apparently provided mainly by, you guessed it, religion. Christians believe they are more moral than atheists (Simpson & Rios, 2016). Most people report perceiving theists (believers in a god or gods) to be trustworthy and moral (Hall, Cohen, Meyer, Varley, & Brewer, 2015). Theists are viewed as more likely to be helpful, kind, reliable, and responsible than atheists (Saroglou, 2002), even by people who are not themselves religious (Galen, Williams, & Ver Wey, 2014). Atheists are perceived to be not trustworthy and very immoral, seriously lacking in inhibitions, willing to engage in almost any perverse, evil behavior (Gervais, 2014). Religious people are apparently motivated to follow social norms of good behavior to avoid punishment from a god (Norenzayan et al., 2014); because of that motivation, they are perceived by others to be more prosocial (caring of others) in their behavior (Tan & Vogel, 2008).

Religion is clearly tied to ideas about morality, yet research indicates that people who are not religious are just as likely to engage in moral and immoral acts as people who are religious (Hofmann, Wisneski, Brandt, & Skitka, 2014). There is no systematic research linking atheists to any kind of seriously immoral behavior, yet it is so condemned by society that atheists are afraid to "come out" as atheist (Brewster, 2013). So what gives? How are religious people more moral than atheists if they're engaging in the same frequency of moral and immoral acts? What do you think about atheists? Do you think that religion is required for morality? Research evidence indicates that the development of the prefrontal cortex of the human brain is important to judgments of morality, feelings of empathy for others, and acting prosocially (Forbes & Grafman, 2010; Masten, Morelli, & Eisenberger, 2011; Seitz, Nickel, & Azari, 2006). Is this biological process affected by religion? Is belonging to a group enough to somehow increase moral behavior? Do religious people merit moral authority over people who don't share the same mystical beliefs? I'm most interested in if you have a stereotype of atheists, what it contains, and if you've ever actually met an atheist? Actual direct experience is helpful in forming accurate stereotypes; information provided by others and social institutions might not be reflective of actual experience and may have other purposes (read more about legitimizing myths below).

BONUS BOX

Confirmation Bias or Belief Bias?

Confirmation bias is a pervasive human bias for information that confirms what we already believe. A bias is a preference; people prefer information that confirms an assertion. Correspondingly, people tend not to notice or to ignore information that disconfirms an assertion. A classic study by Smedslund (1963) involved trained nurses, who were asked to examine 100 patient cases and determine if a certain physical symptom was an indicator of the presence of a particular disease. The nurses were provided with 100 cards indicating two pieces of information: whether or not the patient had the symptom, and whether or not the patient had been diagnosed with the disease. The proportion of cards of each category are below:

Is having the symptom evidence of the disease?

	Disease Present	No Disease	
Symptom Present	37/100	33/100	70/100
No Symptom	17/100	13/100	30/100
	54/100	46/100	

What do you think? Do you think that if a patient has a certain symptom, they can be diagnosed with having the disease? Decide your answer before reading further.

If your answer was "yes," like the nurses, then you are the victim of confirmation bias. In deciding if there was a symptom-disease relationship, which a majority of the nurses in the Smedslund study did, they paid attention only to the information in the chart above that confirmed there was a symptom-disease relationship: the disease and symptom present, 37 of 100 cases; and the disease and symptom absent, 13 of 100 cases. But that's only half the evidence. The other 50% of the cases provided information disconfirming the symptom-disease relationship (disease without the symptom, symptom without the disease). Don't feel too bad if you showed confirmation bias, it's common, that's the point! People show a particularly strong preference for information that confirms their strongly held beliefs. This kind of bias, called belief bias, goes beyond a preference for confirmatory information. This kind of bias is motivated and leads individuals to actively ignore information that disconfirms their beliefs. They will screen it out, avoid it, or dismiss it with false claims of falsity ("Fake news!") without producing any evidence to support their argument. This is not just a failing or weakness or flaw in the human information-processing system; this is intentional ignorance, intentionally ignoring information because it doesn't fit with one's strongly held beliefs. This kind of thinking is dangerous and harmful to everyone.

For example, although the vast majority of the world's scientists agree about the reality of global climate change and how human activity contributes to it (NASA, 2018), many people (mostly not scientists) actually think that climate change is not happening. They dismiss climate change even though climate change is negatively affecting them and their families and friends and futures as well, in spite of that danger. Why? Religion plays a role in acceptance of climate change research and feeling concern about nature and the environment. Research shows that conservative Christians have a lower concern about climate change and the global environment because they trust their god, not science, and they believe in the Biblical assertion of man's dominion over the Earth (Genesis 1:26) (Guth, Green, Kellstedt, & Smidt, 1995; Hand & van Liere, 1984; Morrison, Duncan, & Parton, 2015). Research indicates that scientists are actually viewed as lacking real emotions and as rather immoral, valuing knowledge instead of morality (Rutjens & Heine, 2016), which likely helps to legitimize dismissal of scientific findings. Unfortunately, when that type of thinking is allowed to affect laws and regulations that affect millions of people, including people who do not share the same strongly held beliefs, everyone loses. Dear student, as an educated person, it is your duty to actively process important (i.e., about our planet) information in terms of its evidentiary bases, with the most solid reliable evidence yielded by the scientific method. This is a science book intended for science courses; the careful, systematic, intentionally objective, peer-reviewed information provided by science will be considered the most valuable in making any determinations or conclusions. I hope you will adopt the same standard.

LEARN MORE

Distracted Anything Is Hazardous to Your Health

People all over the world today are engaged in constant contact with each other and the internet. Everyone has a smartphone or handheld device through which they access work materials, entertainment, and communication with people in the next room or on another continent. People are constantly on their phones, when they're eating, when they're in class, when they're in bed, when they're watching television, sitting next to people they love, we are just always on the phone (which is rarely actually used as a telephone anymore). How this constant stimulation, communication, and online lifestyle will affect people in the long run is still a pertinent question with not enough answers. But how does it affect us in the short term, on a daily basis? The National Highway Traffic Safety Administration (www.nhtsa.gov/risky-driving/distracted-driving) reports that in any typical day in the U.S. nearly half a million people drive while distracted by using their cell phones or handheld devices (see Figure 5.1). The results are deadly, with 3,450 people killed in the United States in 2016 from distracted driving (someone driving while texting or otherwise distracted in the car), with texting being the most dangerous distraction; 391,000 people were injured in 2015 in the U.S. in car accidents involving distracted drivers. Human consciousness is called **working memory** or **short-term memory**, and it is seriously limited. We can only pay attention to five to nine separate pieces of information at one time with full attention. It is physically impossible for anyone to effectively operate a car (a piece of machinery capable of killing people) while intentionally focused on a text message or an email or a Facebook post. Please don't kill yourself or someone else over a text. Don't be distracted when you drive!

Figure 5.1 Don't text and drive, even on a quiet country road!
Source: Stevanovicigor/iStock Photo

Sex versus Gender

The title of this book is *Sex and Gender*, and as such, we continually examine biological sex and ideas of gender in multiple chapters. **Sex** refers to biological sex; one's sexual **genotype** (genetic profile) and to some degree, one's sexual **phenotype** (the appearance of a trait) in terms of genitalia, gonads, other internal sex organs, and secondary sex characteristics (e.g., body hair, breasts) (see Chapter 3). **Gender** refers to the social construction of what it means to be female, male, or another gender; ideas about **femininity** and **masculinity** that are developed within a particular culture, including traditions, **roles**, and expectations of behavior for women and girls, men and boys. Gender also encompasses **gender identity**, one's identification as female, male, both, or neither. Sex is more easily explained, as it is dependent on gamete formation, sexual reproduction, and sex differentiation processes in utero (see Chapters 2, 3, 4). Gender is clearly a more complex, nuanced topic, involving individual psychological development of identity, socialization and enforcement of gender through culture and social institutions, and **social cognition**, using information we possess about gender to process information about people (and ourselves) on a daily basis. In this, our first chapter that addresses the psychology of gender, we focus on social cognitive processes related to gender, including the function and content of **gender stereotypes**. The learning of gender, development of gender identity, and gendered behaviors are more appropriately and thoroughly discussed in later chapters.

The Human Information-Processor: Schematic versus Controlled

Human cognition is amazing. The accomplishments of humankind, in terms of art, literature, scientific discoveries and creations, are essentially unfathomable. The human mind, existing in the wonder of nature, is responsible for all of it. **Cognition** refers to processes of human thought, including perceiving, thinking, reasoning, remembering, and awareness. Cognitive psychology

88 *Gender Stereotypes*

is the subdiscipline of psychology that is focused broadly on understanding human thought. Current psychological approaches to understanding human thought often take an **information-processing** approach (with computers as a model), while recognizing the strengths and limitations of human thought. The human information-processing system is capable of theoretically limitless storage. The capacity of human **long-term memory** is massive and allows the storage of mass amounts of information in a relatively permanent manner. Yes, forgetting occurs all the time, but usually because of a lack of proper memory storage to begin with (Simons & Levin, 1998) or problems in locating information that is stored in memory (Brown, 1991).

So storage of information is not really a problem. Weaknesses in the human information-processing system occur more often at the level of **short-term memory**, or **consciousness**, which is only capable of processing a few separate pieces of information at one time, for a few seconds at a time (Conway et al., 2005). We are easily overwhelmed by too much information and must focus our attention on information to truly process it and to be able to remember it later. Multi-tasking is cognitively difficult and can actually be dangerous (texting while driving, for example; you think you can do it, but you can't; see "Learn More"). Attention is limited; we "pay" attention because it requires energy to fully engage it. With the constant sensations and changes happening around us in any given situation, with our limited conscious workspace and attention, how is it that any of us survive each day, let alone make discoveries and creations that change the world?

Several models within social and cognitive psychology describe the human information-processor as a **motivated tactician** (Fiske & Taylor, 1991; Operario & Fiske, 1999). Human beings choose what information they pay a lot of attention to and what they spend a lot of cognitive energy on each day. We have a variety of tactics (strategies, tools) for use in our cognitive toolbox. We can choose to engage in careful, deliberate, thorough processing of information, a cognitive process called **elaboration** (Petty, Cacioppo, Strathman, & Priester, 2005). Elaboration is highly controlled; it is engaged with conscious effort (it is effortful). Elaboration often involves thinking about new information by relating it to older information stored in memory, thinking about information in depth in terms of how it is similar to and different from what we already know. Because it is effortful, we only use it when we are **motivated** to do so, because the information is important, self-relevant, or otherwise meaningful. When you are studying for this course, for example, if you are truly motivated to understand the material, you will engage all of the effortful cognitive skills you have to process, understand, and remember the information you are reading right now. As physical creatures with organic bodies, however, our energy to process is not limitless. Even if we are motivated to process information carefully and thoroughly, we must be **able** to expend effort (we must be rested, well fed, not sick) and conscious attention (we must not be distracted by talking a ringing phone, the lawn mower running outside). The motivated tactician needs to actually be motivated to process, must possess the right tools to process (reasonable, rational processing; previous information needed to process), and must be physically and situationally able to process the information before effortful, controlled processing can be engaged.

So what happens when we don't have the ability (energy, etc.) or motivation to process information? What do we do then? Well, we can shut down and ignore the information to the best of our ability. Or we can process it rather quickly, with very little effort or even any conscious awareness, in terms of **knowledge** we already possess (knowledge is information that has been processed). The human cognitive system is full of knowledge that is stored not in a chaotic, haphazard way, but in terms of interconnected categories, sets of ideas that are linked through **associative networks**. Because information is stored by association, we are able to locate information in memory much more quickly than if it was stored haphazardly. For example, all of the knowledge you possess about colors is interconnected; different colors are connected to each other (when you think of red you instantly think of other colors as well) and we group objects together by color (making it easy to think of things that are red). Knowledge is stored in mental knowledge structures called schemas. This is our first exposure to this idea, but it is certainly not the last. Schemas are repeatedly accessed patterns of thought about some stimulus that are built up from experience and that are used to guide the processing of new information. They are mental knowledge structures that contain everything we know about a particular topic or subject. You have schemas for fruit, for animals, for countries, for people you know, for movie stars, for yourself (self-schemas that comprise the self-concept), and for broad social categories of people. Evolved for functionality and efficiency, namely processing lots of information very quickly but not very thoroughly, our processing system is the hardware, and data storage and organization are part of that. Socialization provides the content of schemas (the software), knowledge we use to process information that comes next.

Different kinds of schemas have been identified. Traits are actually schemas; they are words that describe how people are different, qualities and attributes we have knowledge of from interaction with other people. For example, the trait of friendliness; we know what behaviors and attitudes friendliness involves (kind, open, accepting, helpful), and we have examples of people attached to that trait schema. Other kinds of schemas include scripts (schemas for actions and events associated with particular social setttings) and roles (rules for the parts people play in different settings). Prototypes are exemplars, another kind of schema; representations of a particular type of person (e.g., the housewife/mother, the religious leader, the college professor) (see Figure 5.2). We also have schemas for individual people, including ourselves. Schemas we possess for broad social categories of people are called stereotypes. Stereotypes contain the traits, qualities, and attributes we associate with people within particular social groups, like ethnic and racial groups, religious groups, and age groups. Stereotypes are widely shared within a society, meaning most people will report having similar ideas about what particular groups of people are like, even if they don't necessarily believe in the accuracy of stereotype content (Clark & Kashima, 2007). Gender stereotypes contain ideas we have about the typical qualities, traits, and attributes of women and men, girls and boys. Everyone possesses stereotypes, because that's how the human information-processor works. The existence of stereotypes is not the problem. It is the content of stereotypes and use of negative stereotypes to discriminate against people that are the problems.

So with potentially limitless storage, but little capacity for current online processing of information, how do human beings function? Because we have so much information stored, we are able to use it rapidly and rather effortlessly to process most mundane information most of the time. For example, I take a train every day to my campus. Before I started the position, knowing I would be taking the train, I sought out information on schedules, purchasing tickets, obtaining a monthly pass, stops from my town to campus, and so on. I even found out ahead of time that only the first three cars open up at the campus station; if you're in the last two cars toward the back of the train, the doors don't open and you'll miss your stop! All of this important information guided me on my first trips on the train. After 13 years, I barely think about it anymore and my mind is free to focus on more important, current information that needs my attention. The same process is true for our processing of almost everything; we don't need to reinvent the wheel every day when we wake up. We use stored information to navigate easily through the world and pay attention to tasks that actually require it (and that we are motivated to focus on). Complex tasks (driving to work, taking the train) are accomplished effortlessly and automatically, with

Figure 5.2 The fictional all-American idealized housewife/mother type
Source: Pictorial Press Ltd/Alamy Stock Photo

our minds focused elsewhere (why you sometimes miss your exit or even your stop on the train). Each day, we process much information automatically, with little conscious awareness and little effort. We can do that because of our efficient information-processing system that allows for fast, consciousless, automatic **schematic** processing.

Schematic processing is highly adaptive for several reasons. First, it frees up our cognitive energy and consciousness to focus on more important tasks. I don't have to think about driving to the grocery store, instead I can make a mental list of what I need to buy. Instead of thinking about washing your hair and your body in the shower, you engage in these activities effortlessly so your mind can rehearse important facts about sex and gender for your upcoming exam. Second, schemas allow us to make quick social judgments in situations where we have little information. I've never been to the airport in Poland, but when I travel there in the future, I have a good idea of what to expect, having been in numerous airports all over the world. Similarly, when meeting a new group of students at the beginning of the semester, I pretty much know what to expect, generally speaking, having worked with many different groups of students. I don't have to get to know each student on the first day to have some understanding of their needs, goals, purposes in taking the course. Third, schemas are usually based on probabilities, not on irrational ideas. That is, schemas, including stereotypes, do contain factual information, information that is accurate.

That doesn't mean that all people can be accurately described in terms of stereotypes or that all stereotype content (e.g., women are stupid) is accurate. What it does mean is that stereotypes, like other schemas, are based on direct experience and evidence, not just **socialization** or messages we receive from culture and social institutions. For example, would it be inaccurate for me to assume that your grandmother or grandfather is retired? Maybe hard-of-hearing? Wears glasses, bald and wrinkly? These are qualities that are indeed common among older people and so my schema is based on likelihoods. Your grandmother could have a full head of gorgeous red hair, in which case my assumption would be wrong. But an individual's stereotype content is not necessarily negative, misinformed, or inaccurate.

Schemas are retrieved for use in processing social information in several ways. Sometimes we use schemas because they are cued or activated by the situation. At the dentist's office, you act like you do at the dentist's office. Sometimes a person serves as a cue. A person wearing workout clothes might lead to retrieval of our athletic or physically fit person schema. Sometimes our own recent experiences cause us to retrieve and use particular schemas. When you're leaving campus, you might be more likely to perceive any young adult as a college student. Your current emotions can also affect which schemas you use to process people. If you've been recently angered or exposed to angry stimuli (angry words, someone yelling), you might be harsher in your interpretations of others' behaviors. One classic study exposed research **participants** to words, but very briefly, flashed so quickly on a computer screen that participants had no conscious recollection of actually seeing the words (flashed for 100 milliseconds). Some participants were exposed to words that were hostile (e.g., punch, stab, hate are hostile words); other participants were exposed to neutral words (e.g., long, always, between). Participants then completed an "unrelated" task involving reading a paragraph about a target person named Donald and evaluating Donald in terms of his traits. Participants exposed to hostile words were harsher in their impressions and judgments of Donald (Bargh & Pietromonaco, 1982). Other studies support the influence of recent experience (which may **prime** particular schemas for use) and current mood on impressions we form of other people (Zupan, Hammen, & Jaenicke, 1987).

Schema accessibility refers to the ease and frequency with which individuals use particular schemas. Schemas that are highly accessible are easily brought to mind and frequently used to process social information. They are easily retrieved, with little conscious effort, and people use them in processing information about others and in interacting socially. Sometimes schemas are highly accessible to people because they are habitually and chronically used; they are ways of viewing the world that the person has developed over time that they now use all the time, automatically, without awareness, to process the world. These are called **personal constructs** (Kelly, 1955); they are traits, types, or stereotypes that an individual characteristically uses most often in understanding and evaluating other people. People who rely more on socialized, negative racial and gender stereotypes are faster at categorizing target people into racial and gender categories (Zarate & Smith, 1990). Research indicates that people who report greater racial **prejudice** (negative feelings toward members of particular racial groups) are faster at identifying and categorizing stereotypical traits associated with racial groups (McConnell & Leibold, 2001). People are more likely to be **schematic** for traits that they see as important within themselves and others. These traits will then be used to understand other people. For example, race is extremely important to **white supremacists** (they think being white is supreme); race is a chronically accessible personal construct for white supremacists, who evaluate every person primarily based on their skin color and other visible features. People for whom gender is an important concept that they use in evaluating themselves and others are called **gender schematic.**

Figures 5.3a and 5.3b The Ku Klux Klan and modern White supremacists
Source: Universal History Archive/Getty Images

Overreliance on schematic processing has many shortcomings. Processing everything quickly is not necessarily a good goal to have, especially if you are really trying to learn new information, form new cognitive schemas, or change existing schemas (a cognitive process called **accommodation**). If you are trying to learn about sex and gender, so you can be an expert on the topic and talk about it with authority, that requires a lot of effort and attention. Skimming a paragraph three times while watching television and checking out Facebook does not work. Accommodation is difficult cognitive work; it requires energy and the experience of troubling emotions in realizing one has been wrong or incorrect or ill-informed. Human beings have a strong tendency to seek out information that confirms what they already believe and ignore information that disconfirms what they believe (**confirmation bias**; see Bonus Box). We have a preference for behavior that confirms what we already think we know. People are motivated toward confirmation because it feels good; it confirms we are correct in our understanding of the world and that everything is fine (Heider & Benesh-Weiner, 1988). To achieve a state of cognitive balance where we have confidence in our knowledge and belief systems, people are more likely to rely on their schemas and existing knowledge and less likely to actively engage in changing their cognitions.

For example, hiring interviews are the most widely used method of screening new employees used around the world (Judge, Cable, & Higgins, 2000). Unfortunately, they are often highly ineffective, most commonly because they are biased (Bargh, Chen, & Burrows, 1996). Upon meeting someone for the first time, many social categories can be activated. Does it affect what you think about a person immediately if they are female? If they are male? If they are darker skinned or lighter skinned? If they have a hearing aid or a back brace or glasses? If they are very short or very tall? If they have wrinkles and gray hair? If they have an accent? Physical features we associate with particular groups are included in stereotypes (Eagly, Ashmore, Makhijani, & Longo, 1991) and thus serve to activate (prime) stereotypes we have about broad social categories of people (Moskowitz, Stone, & Childs, 2012). Once a stereotype is activated into consciousness, it will be used to process information about people and may cause our evaluations to be biased toward confirming the stereotype (Bargh et al., 1996; Fiske & Taylor, 1991). As such, if a hiring manager thinks women are not very smart, he will find information to confirm that by processing everything female job applicants do in a negative manner that confirms his belief. Similarly, a racist who thinks that darker skinned people are criminals will automatically rely on that stereotype and use it to process information about darker skinned people, including in everyday decisions that affect the outcomes of those people. In the long term and on a wide scale, negative stereotypes are used by the powerful as **legitimizing myths**, false beliefs that justify discrimination against and oppression of less powerful groups (Pratto & Walker, 2004). If most people in a society share the same negative stereotypes over long periods of time, because of the messages of religion, the government, and media, systemic marginalization and oppression of such stereotyped groups will result.

There are various ways in which confirmation biases can affect our social perception of people and the structure of our schemas. First, they affect how we interpret ambiguous information. In a classic study, participants watched a film clip of a little girl being interviewed and answering questions in an academic setting. The setting was either rather posh and expensive looking, or appeared impoverished and run-down. Participants were then asked to judge the girl's academic abilities based on her responses to the questions. Although the girl's responses remained the same regardless of the setting, participants who viewed her performance in the wealthier setting judged her academic abilities as very good, while those who viewed her performance in the poorer setting judged her academic abilities as poor (Darley & Gross, 1983). Rather than changing the schema, participants "changed" the information (the girl's performance) so that it fit better with the schema that was activated by the setting. This process is called **assimilation**; information is assimilated into the schema and thus changed, leaving the schema intact. This process requires much less cognitive effort than accommodation. Importantly, assimilation can require no conscious effort and no conscious awareness at all, with biases toward social groups **implicit** in our thinking. **Implicit bias** is racial, gender, sexuality, or religious bias that is so deeply ingrained through socialization that it has become automatic, without conscious control (Amodio & Mendoza, 2010; Sabin, Riskind, & Nosek, 2015). People automatically interpret social information as fitting with their social biases against particular groups or individuals.

Second, when people are presented with strong disconfirming information, they are likely to **discount** it rather than changing their schema. One method of discounting (explaining away) disconfirming information is to restructure the schema to include subtypes. **Subtypes** are seen as different from the overall stereotype category, but are seen as odd and infrequent. Rather than change the whole stereotype, the person creates a small "fenced off" area of the stereotype for odd cases that don't fit in. So, for example, the strong female Chief Executive Officer who is assertive and interpersonally powerful is put into her own subtype. She is not integrated into the entire "woman" schema because that would lead to cognitive pressures to change the whole schema (Crano & Chen, 1998). The schema is defended through creation of the subtype. Another way people discount disconfirming information is by creating **attributions**, or explanations for how something happened, explanations about the causes of a particular event or outcome (Morris & Larrick, 1995). So what are the causes of the female CEO's success? If a high-achieving woman doesn't fit the schema of women as interdependent, caring for others, self-sacrificing, and incapable of men's work, one might be motivated to explain her success as being caused by her wealthy father or her relationships with powerful men or some other cause than her high-level skills and abilities. As such, her success does not violate the rigidly traditional stereotype, and the schema remains intact.

Processing social information quickly in terms of rigid, biased, or automatic stereotypes is also ineffective and is reflective of low **social interest**, a lack of engaging positively and productively with other people, which is associated with maladjustment (Crandall, 1980, 1984). People who chronically process social information in terms of racial and gender stereotypes that contain negative content provided through socialization (from parents, media, religion, government, etc.) are **racist** and **sexist**. They think in terms of simplistic categories that are rigidly defined (e.g., they're all the same, they are all this way), with no change allowed in stereotype content. They impose their rigid categories on nearly every person they interact with (racial and gender stereotypes are chronically accessible) and intentionally ignore information that challenges their strongly held beliefs about people (**belief bias**; see Bonus Box). It is very difficult if not impossible to change the minds of those who are so completely convinced of the rightness of their beliefs. In fact, attempting to change their beliefs may make their beliefs even more strongly held (Byrne & Hart, 2016; Rhine & Severance, 1970).

Some people are motivated to not be prejudiced, to not use stereotypes in processing information about individuals and groups. Those people are called accepting, **humanistic**, **liberal**. How do we as individuals prevent negative stereotypes from affecting our own evaluations of and interactions with people that we encounter every day? Consciously and effortfully processing information about every single person we meet each day is not cognitively or physically possible. But we can try to exert conscious control over the content of our stereotypes and become more aware of our reliance on them in processing social information. This is exceedingly difficult, however, with automatic processes being very powerful and insidious in affecting our thoughts, feelings, and behaviors (Bargh, 1999). First, challenge negative content that might be included in your stereotypes by examining actual evidence. For example, years and years of research on gender differences in cognitive abilities indicate that there are no differences in intelligence between women and men (Halpern & LaMay, 2000). So ideas about women as not being as smart as men are just plain wrong, they are false and inaccurate. Altering one's stereotypes in response to disconfirming information, **accommodation**, requires cognitive effort and is not usually accomplished quickly (Hewstone & Hamberger, 2000; Johnston, 1996; Piaget, 1970). In addition, consciously recognizing one's use of stereotypes and feeling negatively about that use (**compunction**) can also lead to a reduction in reliance on negative stereotypes (Devine, Monteith, Zuwerink, & Elliot, 1991).

Expressivity and Communality, Agency and Instrumentality

So now that you know what stereotypes are, what they are for, and how automatically and frequently we use them, let's discuss gender stereotypes specifically. Williams and Best (1994) asked children and adults in 30 countries questions about what they think women are like, and what they think men are like, in a program of research spanning 15 years. In one aspect of the research, they gave university students from all over the world a set of 300 adjectives and asked them to indicate whether the word was used equally to describe each gender, or if it was used most frequently in describing one gender. From the responses they selected the words that were most reliably associated with each gender within each country, and they found a high degree of agreement across the 30 countries on which words those were. Those words comprise the **Pancultural Adjective Checklist** (see Table 5.1). Research indicates that although there are some cultural variations, gender stereotypes, ideas we have about the traits, qualities, and abilities of women and men, are quite similar all over the world, and reflect overall dimensions of **femininity** (soft, caring, gentle, kind, emotional) and **masculinity** (hard, strong, tough, unemotional, independent) (Wood & Eagly, 2010).

Femininity and masculinity as broad categories of traits essentially represent gender stereotypes. Those traits differ along a few dimensions. First, femininity around the world involves the broad personality dimension of **emotionality**. **Emotionality** includes emotional behaviors and emotional expressiveness, so women are seen as highly emotional and expressing of that emotion. They are perceived as loving, kind, anxious, fearful, submissive, emotional. Qualities attributed to women also include the dimension of **communality**, which involves qualities such as caring for others, behaving communally. Women are seen as caretakers for everyone, even when they are not directly engaged in motherhood. So women are perceived as caring, understanding, nurturing, and self-sacrificing, putting their needs after the people for whom they are caring (Abele, 2003; Costa, Terracciano, & McCrae 2001; Löckenhoff et al., 2014). Research indicates that people react negatively to women who are perceived as harsh, aggressive, loud, not nurturing (Fiske, Cuddy, & Glick, 2007; Fordham, 1993); and to women who succeed in typically masculine tasks (Heilman, Wallen, Fuchs, & Tamkins, 2004). Common words for women who do not behave communally, but independently and with assertion, include "shrill," "pushy," and "bitch" (see "Inequalities and Injustices"). Women engaged in caretaking are idealized as the **housewife/mother**, the loving, reliable grandmother (Gaunt, 2013).

Ideas about masculinity around the world are centered on the dimensions of **agency** (activity, strength, power, competence) and **instrumentality** (effective action, getting things done) (Abele,

96 *Gender Stereotypes*

Table 5.1 The 100 items of the Pancultural Adjective Checklist

Male-Associated		Female-Associated	
Active	Loud	Affected	Modest
Adventurous	Obnoxious	Affectionate	Nervous
Aggressive	Opinionated	Appreciative	Patient
Arrogant	Opportunistic	Cautious	Pleasant
Autocratic	Pleasure-seeking	Changeable	Prudish
Bossy	Precise	Charming	Self-pitying
Capable	Progressive	Complaining	Sensitive
Conceited	Rational	Confused	Sexy
Confident	Realistic	Curious	Shy
Courageous	Reckless	Dependent	Softhearted
Cruel	Resourceful	Dreamy	Sophisticated
Cynical	Rigid	Emotional	Submissive
Determined	Robust	Excitable	Suggestible
Disorderly	Serious	Fault-finding	Superstitious
Enterprising	Sharp-witted	Fearful	Talkative
Greedy	Show-off	Fickle	Timid
Hardheaded	Steady	Foolish	Touchy
Humorous	Stern	Forgiving	Unambitious
Indifferent	Stingy	Frivolous	Understanding
Individualistic	Stolid	Fussy	Unintelligent
Initiative	Tough	Gentle	Unstable
Interests wide	Unfriendly	Imaginative	Warm
Inventive	Unscrupulous	Kind	Weak
Lazy	Witty	Mild	Worrying

Source: Best, D.L., & Williams, J.E. (1994). Masculinity/femininity in the self and ideal self descriptions of university students in fourteen countries. In A. Bouvy, F.J.R. van de Vijver, P. Boski, & P.G. Schmitz (Eds.), *Journeys into cross-cultural psychology* (pp. 297–306). Lisse, Netherlands: Swets & Zeitlinger.

2003; Costa et al., 2001; Glick et al., 2004; Löckenhoff et al., 2014). Men are described as leaders, workers, fighters, decision-makers, people who are assertive, aggressive, dominant, brave, and determined. Masculinity involves an unflinching pursuit of one's goals, bystanders and collateral damage be damned. Men are unfriendly and unscrupulous; they can be dangerous and so approach at your own peril.

Children all over the world by age 5 years old show excellent knowledge of gender stereotypes, with increasingly stereotypical, traditional beliefs about women and men developing within most children across childhood into adulthood. Children across cultures identified female characters in stories as emotional, weak, and soft-hearted; male characters are aggressive, strong, and cruel (Williams & Best, 1994). Women all over the world describe themselves using similar adjectives reflecting femininity, and men all over the world describe themselves using the same masculine trait terms. Reflections on the **ideal self** (the self one desires to be, one's better self) indicate that masculinity is highly valued by both women and men, and women describe their ideal self as more masculine (Best & Williams, 1994). There are some cultural variations in gender stereotypes depending on the cultural dimension of **individualism-collectivism** (whether a culture values individual or communal goals more highly; Triandis, 1989), with dominant cultural values viewed as more masculine, and thus preferred, within each type of culture (Cuddy et al., 2015). Researchers have also identified specific gender subtypes (various prototypes of women and

Gender Stereotypes 97

Figure 5.4 The sexy woman type
Source: Johnny Greig/iStock Photo

men). Female subtypes include the **housewife/mother**, the sexy woman, the athletic woman, and the **career woman**; male subtypes include the blue-collar man, the businessman, the athletic man, and the macho man (Coats & Smith, 1999; Deaux et al., 1985; Eckes, 1994) (see Figures 5.4 and 5.5). In most studies, the housewife/mother is evaluated most positively, as especially warm but not necessarily competent (Fiske, Cuddy, Glick, & Xu, 2002). The career woman is seen as competent but not very likable (Rudman & Fairchild, 2004) (see Chapter 12).

Gender Stereotypes Are Prescriptive and Proscriptive

More so than racial or ethnic stereotypes, or stereotypes for various religious or age groups, gender stereotypes are highly **prescriptive** and **proscriptive** (Delacollette, Dumont, Sarlet, & Dardenne, 2013; Prentice & Carranza, 2002). That is, they describe the ways women and men "should be," not just how women and men "are." Stereotypes are **prescriptive** when they prescribe a certain way of being as a better or preferred way. So to say women should be gentle is a prescription. Gender stereotypes contain **proscriptions**, or prohibitions or punishments for being a certain way. Some prescriptions and proscriptions are described as **intensified**; it is very important for women and men to be (or not be) these qualities. Other prescriptions and proscriptions are described as **relaxed**; it is more okay for a woman or man to violate these prescriptions (valuable, but not necessary) and proscriptions (not desirable, but not a huge problem) (Prentice & Carranza, 2002; see Table 5.2). For example, it is very proscribed for women to be highly sexual. Promiscuous women are condemned by every world religion and words for the highly sexual woman are uniformly negative (I'm sure you can think of them, but also see Chapter 7). Wanton sexuality is highly proscribed for women, not really proscribed for men. Highly sexual men are

Figure 5.5 The Macho Man, pro-wrestler Randy Savage (11/15/1952–5/20/2011)
Source: B Bennett/Getty Images

Table 5.2 Relaxed and intensified prescriptions and proscriptions for women and men.

Intensified Prescriptions		*Intensified Proscriptions*	
For Women	*For Men*	*For Women*	*For Men*
Warm and kind	Good business sense	Rebellious	Emotional
Loves kids	Athletic	Stubborn	Approval-seeking
Loyal	Leadership ability	Controlling	Impressionable
Sensitive	Self-reliant	Cynical	Yielding
Friendly	Dependable	Promiscuous	Superstitious
Clean	Ambitious	Arrogant	Childlike
Attentive to appearance	High self-esteem		

Relaxed Prescriptions		*Relaxed Proscriptions*	
For Women	*For Men*	*For Women*	*For Men*
Intelligent	Happy	Yielding	Rebellious
Mature	Friendly	Emotional	Solemn
Common sense	Clean	Impressionable	Controlling
Sense of humor	Warm and kind	Childlike	Stubborn
Concern for future	Enthusiastic	Shy	Promiscuous
Principled	Optimistic	Naïve	Self-righteous
		Superstitious	Jealous

Source: Prentice, D. A., & Carranza, E. E. (2002). What women and men should be, shouldn't be, are allowed to be, and don't have to be: The contents of prescriptive gender stereotypes. *Psychology of Women Quarterly, 26*, 269-281.

seen as normal, healthy, as regular men (Hust, Brown, & L'Engle, 2008), with women serving as objects for men's healthy sexual desire (Fredrickson & Roberts, 1997; Ward, 2003).

There is a strong dichotomy in stereotypes of women between two extremes: the pure, angelic mother versus the devilish, evil, feminist loose woman (insert derogatory word for sexually active woman here). The dichotomy is part of the legitimization of women's oppression; if women can only be good by being one way (strongly prescribed by dominant religious ideology within a culture; Connell, 1987; Conrad, 2006), any variation from those requirements is dangerous and subjects women to social ridicule and rejection (with gender a **stigma**; Schur, 1984). "Good" women as defined by the Abrahamic religions (Christianity, Islam, Judaism) are obedient and submissive to men (Colossians 3:18; Ephesians 5:22-24; Qu'ran 4:34, 33:33, 33:59); they are virginal at marriage (or else; Deuteronomy 22:13-21; Hebrews 13:4; Qu'ran 56:36) and devoted to their roles in the family (Genesis 3:16; Titus 2:5; Qu'ran 33:33). Women outside of this role are loudly condemned by religion (Proverbs 5-7, 11:22; Psalms 140:2; Qu'ran 66:5); they are called whore and witch (Exodus 22:18; Jeremiah 3:1; Revelations 17:1-18). These messages, claimed to be provided by an almighty all-powerful supernatural being, obviously affect not just what everyone within a culture thinks about women, but women's self-concepts as they exist within cultures that endorse these ideas (Gupta, Szymanski, & Leong, 2011; van Es, 2016). We will discuss religion as a source of socialization of gender ideology throughout this book.

Sources of Gender Stereotypes: Biology, Social Roles, and Cultural Institutions

Although we more thoroughly address explanations for gender differences in Chapter 6 (Theories of Gender), the sources of and processes of learning about gender stereotypes must be noted here. Biological processes related to sex inform ideas about gender. **Social role theory** (Eagly, 1987; Eagly & Wood, 1999) asserts very clearly that the content of gender stereotypes largely stems from the social groups to which people belong, and the social roles associated with that group. The primary source of social roles for women and men is biologically assigned roles in reproduction and physical differences between women and men, which informed social roles in hunter-gatherer societies and still inform social roles in the modern world. Social role theory is biosocial because it emphasizes the interplay between human biology and the living environment in affecting ideas we have about ourselves, and about women and men in general. Because men are much stronger on average than women, men have been assigned to labor that requires more strength, including hunting, fighting, lifting and carrying, building (Sell, Hone, & Pound, 2012). Women can certainly engage in these tasks successfully, but the average man is more effective in these roles than the average woman because of large strength and speed differences. Because men more typically occupy these social roles, men as a group are seen as possessing the qualities of these roles (strong, agentic, dominant qualities) and individual men adopt qualities of the role (Eagly & Wood, 1999).

A major biological characteristic defining femaleness is the ability to carry and give birth to children and to feed children. These are roles that only women occupy, those of pregnancy, childbirth, and breastfeeding. According to social role theory, because women are much more typically in the role of parent and caretaker, ideas about women and femininity involve conceptions of kindness, nurturance, tenderness, and communal behaviors that care for other people. In addition to informing stereotypes about women, these disproportionate reproductive responsibilities

100 *Gender Stereotypes*

Figures 5.6a and 5.6b Stereotypical and traditional female and male roles
Source: Pixdeluxe/iStock Photo and Morsa Images

interfere with women's abilities to engage in other productive work, reinforcing the traditional **division of labor** between women (family responsibilities) and men (earning income) (Wood & Eagly, 2002).

Another approach to understanding gender stereotypes is also based on biological qualities, the structure of various aspects of the human face. Friedman and Zebrowitz (1992) suggest that women are expected to be childlike (i.e., gentle, timid, submissive, sweet) more so than men because women have faces that are more like those of children. This approach emphasizes "babyfacedness" as affecting how women are perceived and then treated by others. Because women's faces are more like those of babies and children (small chin, large eyes, full lips, long eyelashes, small nose) than are men's faces (strong jaw, hairy, rough, large nose), women are seen as a group to be childlike, weaker than men. Unfortunately for women, another aspect of being childlike is being not as smart or as knowledgeable as the "grown-ups." Treating women like children is called infantilizing, and it involves diminishing women's experience, knowledge, and opinions relative to those of men. Treating women like children can also involve a technique known as gaslighting, which involves manipulating people psychologically so that they begin to question their own knowledge or their own right mind. Men have a tendency to over-explain issues to women, including women's issues back to women, a behavior known as mansplaining. Treating women like children who need to be protected by someone is a component of benevolent sexism, sexism involving paternalistic protection of women as fragile, delicate (Glick & Fiske, 1996; see Chapter 7).

Social cognition theorists assert that people have evolved the ability to automatically and instantly process information about a target person's warmth (approachability, safety, kindness, positivity) and competence (strength, ability, agency). Upon first encountering any person, especially a stranger, our mind instantly examines the person's physical being (their gender, race, age, height, visage, etc.) and forms an instant impression about whether the person is warm (essentially safe), and whether they are powerful (competent). This happens within seconds of meeting a person. These initial impressions function to inform the person of how to engage the target, either by approaching them (if they are safe or have the ability to provide good things) or avoiding them (if they are not safe, incompetent for one's purposes, or have the ability to hurt or punish). In this way, scholars assert, people make essential distinctions between people based on liking (they are warm and trustworthy) and respect (they are efficient, competent) (Fiske et al., 2007). Because physical size is linked with instant impressions of high power and competence, men on average will be instantly perceived as more competent than smaller others, namely women, making respect for men an essentially automatic judgment (Riggio & Riggio, 2012). In other words, men are ascribed respect by virtue of being men, while women have to earn respect through repeated demonstrations of competence (Glick et al., 2004).

Once social roles are constructed for women and men, those roles are promulgated, disseminated, and reinforced by cultural and social institutions, from the moment we are born, even before, as parents develop expectations about their girl or boy child, their dispositions, likes and dislikes, as they shape the living environment for the child (Pomerleau, Bolduc, Malcuit, & Cossette, 1990). As children grow and learn within any particular culture, they are socialized; they learn the norms, rules, traditions, and beliefs of the culture through multiple avenues, including religion, the media (television, print, social media, music), and government. Multiple psychological theories explain how socialization occurs, particularly social learning or social cognitive theory, which emphasizes children learning through observation and imitation of important others, especially parents (Bandura, 1997, 2001). Various behaviors are rewarded, other behaviors are punished, leading the child to adopt behaviors encouraged by the culture for their gender (Bwewusa, 2008; Klinger, Hamilton, & Cantrell, 2001). We will discuss theories of gender in greater depth in Chapter 6, and socialization of gender ideology and gendered behavior in later chapters.

Purposes of Gender Stereotypes: Division of Labor and Social Dominance

The informing and reinforcement of social roles and gender stereotypes by social institutions occurs for many reasons. First, division of labor increases efficiency within any means of production. It is inefficient to have duplication of functions and division of labor increases individual expertise as they practice the same behaviors repeatedly (Romer, 1990). As such, the division of labor between women and men does in fact increase efficiency, especially in primitive societies such as agrarian or hunter-gatherer groups (Marlowe, 2007). In the modern world, however, with increases in technology and educational opportunities, confining women to parenting and domestic roles is not efficient; it retards social and economic development, and is inhumane and unjust. So why do gender stereotypes persist? Another reason is that gender stereotypes are **internalized** and incorporated into **self-concept**; it is very difficult to change ideas one has about oneself, even if those ideas are negative (that's why therapy can take years and years). Self-concept change is difficult to accomplish (Swann, 1997). In this way, gender stereotypes are played out every day in individual identities and well-learned gendered cognitions and behaviors, reinforcing their utility and existence (West & Zimmerman, 1987).

A primary explanation, from a **feminist** perspective, for why people continue to view themselves and each other in terms of gender stereotypes is particularly relevant to women, who are more strongly negatively stereotyped than men, specifically in terms of competence, intelligence, and capabilities. I and others assert that gender stereotypes are used as **legitimizing myths**, false beliefs about a group that justify their continued oppression. Please note the presence in the Pancultural Adjective Checklist of words like "unintelligent," "confused," and "foolish" to describe women, conditions that clearly preclude such a person from any important or difficult task or role. There are no gender differences in general intelligence (Halpern & LaMay, 2000), and this is not a secret anymore. Yet people continue to ignore evidence and characterize women as less capable so that they are systematically excluded from opportunities for greater social power. This exclusion is intentional; women are excluded from increasing power in society because promoting women's equality would threaten **hegemonic patriarchy**, prescribed hierarchy with men at the top, the current social system characterizing the world today. Women are not equal to men in terms of financial, political, and social power in any country in the modern world, a global inequality that was even worse in the past (Iversen, 2017).

As described by **social dominance theory** (Pratto & Walker, 2004), groups and individuals who enjoy a disproportionate (i.e., unfair) share of society's resources (money, power) will work very hard to maintain that power. One way to maintain it is to continue to oppress those who have less power and fewer resources, through socialization of legitimizing myths which justify systematic oppression. For example, many people in relatively powerful positions, from wealthier groups, believe that poor people are lazy and that is why they are poor. Not because they were born poor, or because it is virtually impossible in a capitalistic society to drag oneself out of poverty, but because they are lazy, good-for-nothing, and as such deserve their poverty. This is the **Protestant work ethic** or **achievement ideology** that is particularly strong in the United States (Barnes, 2002; Furnham, 1982), the belief that hard work leads to success. Unfortunately, many people also believe that the reverse is true, that success means one worked hard (an **illicit conversion**, a reasoning error). People who endorse the work ethic have more negative attitudes toward disadvantaged groups (i.e., the poor, racial minorities, women) and are less likely to endorse social programs designed to help the poor (Barnes, 2002; Rosenthal, Levy, & Moyer,

2011). Similarly, women and men who are higher in power and in social dominance orientation (a preference for inequality between groups) are likely to endorse negative gender stereotypes about women (e.g., sexism doesn't really exist anymore, women are just low-achieving, a form of modern sexism) (Radke, Hornsey, Sibley, & Barlow, 2017). Global, historical sexism continues today because it benefits the powerful, a disproportionate number of whom are white, Western, Christian men (Bump, 2015; Iversen, 2017). We will address sexism in Chapter 7, and social dominance as a primary reason for the existence of gender ideology throughout this book.

Chapter Summary

Human beings think very efficiently. With theoretically limitless long-term memory, but limited online processing capacity, we tend to process lots of information efficiently but not very thoroughly. To engage in thorough, effortful, careful processing of information, we must be both motivated and able to engage that processing. If we are not motivated or not able, we generally process information schematically, that is, in terms of stored knowledge structures (schemas) that are easily brought into consciousness and that guide the processing of new information. Processing information schematically is highly efficient, which is why our cognitive system evolved the way it did. However, overreliance on schematic process leads to a short-circuiting of the social interaction process and can lead to use of negative stereotypes in processing information about people and treating them unfairly. Over long periods of time, negative stereotypes are used throughout a culture to legitimize oppression of subordinate groups. Gender stereotypes all over the world depict women as communal and emotional; men are viewed in terms of qualities associated with agency and instrumentality. Ideas about what women and men are like stem from the social roles which they typically occupy, largely roles linked to physical, biological differences between women and men, including differences in strength and differential roles involved in reproduction. In addition to becoming internalized into individual self-concepts, gender stereotypes are promulgated and reinforced by culture and social institutions (media, religion, parents, government), largely in the service of maintaining hegemonic patriarchy, as described by social dominance theory.

Thoughtful Questions

- Explain confirmation and belief bias. How do such biases relate to gender stereotypes?
- Explain the current view of the human information-processor.
- What are the benefits of schematic processing? What are the drawbacks?
- Is it possible to control automatic use of stereotypes? How?
- Explain schemas as highly accessible personal constructs. How do such personal constructs relate to sexism and racism?
- Explain gender stereotypes and their content.
- Explain how the content of gender stereotypes is derived from social roles.
- Explain internalization of gender stereotypes.
- Explain how evolved fight-or-flight responses affect perceptions of women and men.
- Explain social dominance theory, including the use of legitimizing myths and social dominance orientation.
- Explain the Protestant work ethic and how it is linked to attitudes toward social programs.

Glossary

Ability: in this context, the ability to process information effortfully. Requires sufficient energy and wellness and lack of distraction.

Accommodation: changing a schema in response to new information.

Agency: a quality involving activity, strength, power, competence; a primary dimension of ideas about masculinity.

Assimilation: changing information to fit with an existing schema; perceiving information as being more similar to a schema than it actually is.

Associative networks: the way knowledge is stored in the human mind, a vast network of interrelated concepts. Associative network storage allows nearly instant retrieval of information from long-term memory.

Atheists: people who don't believe in any gods.

Attributions: explanations for how something happened, about the causes of a particular event or outcome. Attributions can be used to **discount** information that is inconsistent with existing schemas.

Babyfacedness: the fact that women's faces are more like the faces of babies and children than men's faces. Because of babyfacedness, women are more likely to be perceived as childlike (low in competence) compared to men.

Belief bias: a strong preference for information that confirms one's strongly held beliefs.

Benevolent sexism: sexism involving warmth, trust, and desire for intimacy, along with paternalistic ideas that subordinate women.

Career woman: a subtype (**prototype**) of women included in stereotypes. The career woman is usually viewed as competent but not very likable.

Cognition: processes of human thought, including perceiving, thinking, reasoning, remembering, and awareness.

Communality: emotions and behaviors motivated toward caring for the well-being of others; a primary dimension of ideas about femininity.

Competence: instant impressions about strength, ability, agency. Affect approach–avoid responses.

Confirmation bias: a pervasive human preference for information that confirms what we already believe. People prefer information that confirms an assertion.

Discounting: a cognitive strategy to explain away disconfirming information that can't be ignored, keeping the existing schema intact and unchanged.

Discrimination: any attitude, act, or institutional structure that subordinates a person because of their group membership. For example, sexism involves treating people differently because of their gender.

Division of labor: assigning different tasks, duties, and responsibilities to women and men, traditionally family responsibilities to women and earning income to men.

Elaboration: effortful processing of information; processing new information by relating it to existing knowledge.

Emotionality: emotional behaviors and emotional expressiveness; a primary dimension of ideas about femininity.

Empathy: the ability to feel what other people are feeling; feelings of compassion for those who are suffering.

Femininity: the content of stereotypes of women; women are viewed as soft, caring, gentle, kind, emotional.

Gender Stereotypes 105

Feminist: a person who promotes and strives for equality between women and men. Feminist approaches emphasize global historical patriarchy in the oppression of women.

Functional: traits that exist because they are adaptive and enhance ability to survive and reproduce.

Gaslighting: manipulating people psychologically so that they begin to question their own knowledge or their own right mind.

Gender: the social construction of what it means to be female, male, or another gender; ideas about femininity and masculinity that are developed within a particular culture, including traditions, roles, and expectations of behavior for women and girls, men and boys.

Gender identity: one's identification as female, male, both, or neither.

Gender schematic: when a person habitually uses gender stereotypes to process information about the self and other people.

Gender stereotypes: schemas we have about women and men, including ideas about their typical qualities, traits, and attributes, which comprise ideas of femininity and masculinity within a culture.

Genotype: one's genetic profile for a particular quality. For example, the genotype for femaleness is XX.

Hegemonic: a dominant or ruling social system.

Hegemonic patriarchy: a social system that promotes and justifies men's control and dominance of the majority of a society's financial, social, and political power.

Housewife/mother: a prototype of women as loving, nurturing, caretaking; highly valued all over the world. The housewife/mother is viewed as warm (loving) but not high in competence.

Humanist: a person with a genuine, positive interest in the well-being of individual persons and humankind.

Illicit conversion: a reasoning error where the reverse of an "if, then" statement is assumed to be true. This is an error because it is unknown under what other conditions the "then" event may occur.

Implicit bias: racial or gender or sexuality bias that is so deeply ingrained through socialization that it has become automatic, without conscious control.

Infantilizing: diminishing women's experience, knowledge, and opinions by referring to them as childlike.

Information-processing: an approach to human cognition that uses computers as a model.

Instrumentality: a quality involving effective action, getting things done; a primary dimension of ideas about masculinity.

Intensified: commands about what women and men should and should not be like that are very strong.

Internalized: incorporating stereotypes into individual self-concept during socialization.

Knowledge: information that has been cognitively processed.

Legitimizing myths: false beliefs that justify the oppression of less powerful groups.

Liberal: a person who is open-minded, tolerant of differences.

Liking: a feeling that a person is warm and trustworthy.

Long-term memory: the human memory system for storage of large amounts of information in a relatively permanent manner.

Mansplaining: when men over-explain issues to women, including women's issues back to women.

Masculinity: the content of stereotypes of men; men are viewed as hard, strong, tough, unemotional, independent.

Modern sexism (aka neosexism): beliefs that women have already achieved equality, and that women who say otherwise are whining or trying to gain unfair advantage.

Moral authority: having some kind of special knowledge or possession of morality; serving as a guide to others on what morality and proper moral conduct are. A person or organization with moral authority is presumed to know better than most people about what comprises moral behavior.

Motivated tactician: a modern model of the human information-processor, who processes depending on motivation and ability and has a variety of cognitive strategies at their disposal.

Motivation: in this context, the will or personal need to process information thoroughly.

Participant: a person who is observed in scientific research.

Personal construct: a chronically accessible schema; a schema a person uses repeatedly and habitually in understanding other people and social information.

Phenotype: the physical appearance of a trait.

Prejudice: negative feelings toward people who belong to certain social groups.

Prescriptions: commands to be a certain way; ideas about what women and men should be like.

Prime: to activate a schema with a cue.

Proscriptions: commands to not be a certain way; ideas about what women and men should not be like.

Prosocial behavior: behavior designed to help other people.

Protestant work ethic (achievement ideology): the belief that hard work leads to success.

Prototypes: exemplars; representations of a particular type of person.

Racist: a person who treats people differently because of their apparent race or ethnicity.

Relaxed: commands about what women and men should and should not be like that are not very strong.

Respect: a feeling that a person is efficient and competent.

Roles: rules for the parts people play in different settings.

Schema accessibility: the ease and frequency with which individuals use particular schemas.

Schemas: repeatedly accessed patterns of thought about some stimulus that are built up from experience and that are used to guide the processing of new information. Mental knowledge structures that contain everything we know about a particular topic or subject.

Schematic: processing information in terms of pre-existing categories (schemas).

Scripts: schemas for actions and events associated with particular social settings.

Self-concept: the sum total of an individual's feelings and ideas about the self.

Self-schemas: schemas about the self that comprise the self-concept.

Sex: biological sex; one's sexual genotype (genetic profile) and phenotype (the physical appearance of a trait).

Sexist: a person who treats people differently because of their apparent gender.

Short-term memory: working memory, consciousness. The human memory system that holds limited amounts of information in consciousness for relatively brief periods of time.

Social dominance orientation (SDO): individual preference for inequality between groups. People high in SDO prefer inequality and believe that some groups are inferior to others.

Social dominance theory: an explanation for inequality between social groups that emphasizes that the powerful will maintain disproportionate power and resources by legitimizing oppression of subordinate groups.

Gender Stereotypes   107

Social interest: the desire to relate positively and productively with other people.

Social learning/social cognitive theory: an explanation of socialization which emphasizes children learning through observation and imitation of important others, especially parents.

Social role theory: an explanation for gender stereotypes that asserts that the content of gender stereotypes largely stems from the social groups to which people belong.

Socialization: learning through living in a particular culture; learning from messages about reality provided by culture and social institutions (parents, religion, media).

Stereotypes: schemas we have for broad social categories of people, including ideas about their typical qualities, traits, and attributes.

Stigma: any identifiable condition that subjects a person to social ridicule.

Subtyping: creation of a small subgroup, a "fenced off" area of the schema for odd cases that don't fit in. A method of discounting.

Theists: people who believe in one or more gods.

Traits: a type of schema containing personality qualities, words that describe how people are different.

Warmth: instant impressions about approachability, safety, kindness, positivity. Affect approach-avoid responses.

White supremacist: a racist who thinks that white people are genetically superior and that white people should oppress all other groups and rule the world.

References

Abele, A. E. (2003). The dynamics of masculine-agentic and feminine-communal traits: Findings from a pro-spective study. *Journal of Personality and Social Psychology, 85,* 768-776.

Amodio, D. M., & Mendoza, S. A. (2010). Implicit intergroup bias: Cognitive, affective, and motivational underpinnings. In Gawronski, B. & Payne, B. K. (Eds.), *Handbook of implicit social cognition: Measurement, theory, and applications* (pp. 353-374). New York: Guilford Press.

Bandura A. (1997). *Social learning theory.* New York: Prentice-Hall.

Bandura, A. (2001). Social cognitive theory: An agentic perspective. *Annual Review of Psychology, 52,* 1-26.

Bargh, J. A., & Pietromonaco, P. (1982). Automatic information processing and social perception: The influ-ence of trait information presented outside of conscious awareness on impression formation. *Journal of Personality and Social Psychology, 43*(3), 437-449.

Bargh, J. A., Chen, M., & Burrows, L. (1996). Automaticity of social behavior: Direct effects of trait construct and stereotype activation on action. *Journal of Personality and Social Psychology, 71*(2), 230-244.

Bargh, J. A. (1999). The cognitive monster: The case against the controllability of automatic stereo-type effects. In Chaiken, S. & Trope, Y. (Eds.), *Dual-process theories in social psychology* (pp. 361-382). New York: Guilford.

Barnes, S. L. (2002). Achievement or ascription ideology? An analysis of attitudes about future success for residents in poor urban neighborhoods. *Sociological Focus, 35*(2), 207-225.

Best, D. L. & Williams, J. E. (1994). Masculinity/femininity in the self and ideal self descriptions of university students in fourteen countries. In Bouvy, A.-M., van de Vijver, F. J. R., Boski, P., & Schmitz, P. G. (Eds.), *Journeys into cross-cultural psychology.* Lisse, Netherlands: Swets & Zeitlinger, pp. 297-306.

Brewster, M. E. (2013). Atheism, gender, and sexuality. In Bullivant, S. & Ruse, M. (Eds.), *The Oxford handbook of atheism.* New York: Oxford University Press.

Brown, A. S. (1991). A review of the tip-of-the-tongue experience. *Psychological Bulletin, 109*(2), 204-223.

Bump, P. (2015). The new Congress is 80 percent white, 80 percent male and 92 percent Christian. *Washington Post,* January 5. www.washingtonpost.com/news/the-fix/wp/2015/01/05/the-new-congress-is-80-percent-white-80-percent-male-and-92-percent-christian/?utm_term=.18d4eef1377e.

Bwewusa, W. (2008). The representation of gender in media: Role of media in reinforcing gender stereotypes. *EPU Research Papers, 5*(8), 1-20.

Byrne, S. & Hart, P. S. (2016). The boomerang effect: A synthesis of findings and a preliminary theoreti-cal framework. *Annals of the International Communication Association,* 3-37. https://doi.org/10.1080/23808985.2009.11679083.

Clark, A. E., & Kashima, Y. (2007). Stereotypes help people connect with others in the community: A situated functional analysis of the stereotype consistency bias in communication. *Journal of Personality and Social Psychology, 93*(6), 1028-1039. https://doi.org/10.1037/0022-3514.93.6.1028.

Coats, S., & Smith, E. R. (1999). Perceptions of gender subtypes: Sensitivity to recent exemplar activation and in-group/out-group differences. *Personality and Social Psychology Bulletin, 25*(4), 516-526. https://doi.org/10.1177/0146167299025004009.

Connell, R. W. (1987). *Gender and power.* Stanford, CA: Stanford University Press.

Conrad, B. K. (2006). Neo-institutionalism, social movements, and the cultural reproduction of a mentalité: Promise keepers reconstruct the Madonna/Whore Complex. *The Sociological Quarterly, 47*(2), 305-331. doi:10.1111/j.1533-8525.2006.00047.x.

Conway, A. R. A., Kane, M. J., Bunting, M. F., Hambrick, D. Z., Wilhelm, O., & Engle, R. W. (2005). Working memory span tasks: A methodological review and user's guide. *Psychonomic Bulletin & Review, 12*(5), 769-786.

Costa Jr., P. T., Terracciano, A., & McCrae, R. R. (2001). Gender differences in personality traits across cultures: Robust and surprising findings. *Journal of Personality and Social Psychology, 81*(2), 322-331.

Crandall, J. E. (1980). Adler's concept of social interest: Theory, measurement, and implications for adjustment. *Journal of Personality and Social Psychology, 39*(3), 481-495. http://dx.doi.org/10.1037/0022-3514.39.3.481.

Crandall, J. E. (1984). Social interest as a moderator of life stress. *Journal of Personality and Social Psychology, 47*(1), 164-174. http://dx.doi.org/10.1037/0022-3514.47.1.164.

Crano, W. D. & Chen, X. (1998). The leniency contract and persistence of majority and minority influence. *Journal of Personality and Social Psychology, 74*(6), 1437-1450.

Cuddy, A. J. C., Wolf, E. B., Glick, P., Crotty, S., Chong, J., & Norton, M. I. (2015). Men as cultural ideals: Cultural values moderate gender stereotype content. *Journal of Personality and Social Psychology, 109*(4), 622-635.

Darley, J. M., & Gross, P. H. (1983). A hypothesis-confirming bias in labeling effects. *Journal of Personality and Social Psychology, 44*(1), 20-33.

Deaux, K., Winton, W., Crowley, M., & Lewis, L. L. (1985). Level of categorization and content of gender stereotypes. *Social Cognition, 3*(2), 145-167. https://doi.org/10.1521/soco.1985.3.2.145.

Delacollette, N., Dumont, M., Sarlet, M., & Dardenne, B. (2013). Benevolent sexism, men's advantages and the prescription of warmth to women. *Sex Roles, 68*(5-6), 296-310. https://doi.org/10.1007/s11199-012-0232-5.

Devine, P. G., Monteith, M. J., Zuwerink, J. R., & Elliot, A. J. (1991). Prejudice with and without compunction. *Journal of Personality and Social Psychology, 60*(6), 817-830.

Eagly, A. H. (1987). *Sex differences in social behavior: A social role interpretation.* Hillsdale, NJ: Erlbaum.

Eagly, A. H., & Wood, W. (1999). The origins of sex differences in human behavior: Evolved dispositions versus social roles. *American Psychologist, 54*, 408-423.

Eagly, A. H., Ashmore, R. D., Makhijani, M. G., & Longo, L. C. (1991). What is beautiful is good, but...: A meta-analytic review of research on the physical attractiveness stereotype. *Psychological Bulletin, 110*(1), 109-128.

Eckes, T. (1994). Explorations in gender cognition: Content and structure of female and male subtypes. *Social Cognition, 12*(1), 37-60. https://doi.org/10.1521/soco.1994.12.1.37.

Fiske, S. T., & Taylor, S. E. (1991). *Social cognition* (2nd ed.). New York: McGraw-Hill.

Fiske, S. T., Cuddy, A. J., Glick, P., & Xu, J. (2002). A model of (often mixed) stereotype content: Competence and warmth respectively follow from perceived status and competition. *Journal of Personality and Social Psychology, 82*(6), 878-902. doi:10.1037//0022-3514.82.6.878.

Fiske, S. T., Cuddy, A. J. C., & Glick, P. (2007). Universal dimensions of social cognition: Warmth and competence. *Trends in Cognitive Sciences, 11*(2), 77-83. https://doi.org/10.1016/j.tics.2006.11.005.

Forbes, C. E., & Grafman, J. (2010). The role of the human prefrontal cortex in social cognition and moral judgment. *Annual Review of Neuroscience, 33*, 299-324. https://doi.org/10.1146/annurev-neuro-060909-153230.

Fordham, S. (1993). "Those Loud Black Girls": (Black) women, silence, and gender "passing" in the academy. *Anthropology and Education Quarterly, 24*(1), 3-32. https://doi.org/10.1525/aeq.1993.24.1.05x1736t.

Fredrickson, B. L., & Roberts, T.-A. (1997). Objectification theory: Toward understanding women's lived experiences and mental health risks. *Psychology of Women Quarterly, 21*, 173-206.

Friedman, H., & Zebrowitz, L. A. (1992). The contribution of typical sex differences in facial maturity to sex role stereotypes. *Personality and Social Psychology Bulletin, 18*(4), 430-438. https://doi.org/10.1177/0146167292184006.

Furnham, A. (1982). The Protestant work ethic and attitudes toward unemployment. *Journal of Occupational Psychology, 55*, 277-285.

Galen, L. W., Williams, T. J., & Ver Wey, A. L. (2014). Personality ratings are influenced by religious stereotype and ingroup bias. *International Journal for the Psychology of Religion, 24*(4), 282-297.

Gaunt, R. (2013). Ambivalent sexism and the attribution of emotions to men and women. *Revue Internationale de Psychologie Sociale, 26*(2), 29–54.

Gervais, W. M. (2014). Everything is permitted? People intuitively judge immorality as representative of atheists. *PLoS ONE, 9*, e92302. http://dx.doi.org/10.1371/journal.pone.0092302.

Glick, P., & Fiske, S. T. (1996). The ambivalent sexism inventory: Differentiating hostile and benevolent sexism. *Journal of Personality and Social Psychology, 70*, 491–512. doi:10.1037/0022-3514. 70.3.491.

Glick, P., Lameiras, M., Fiske, S. T., Eckes, T., Masser, B., Volpato, C., Manganelli, A. M., Pek, J. C. X., Huang, L.-I., Sakallı-Uğurlu, N., Castro, Y. R., D'Avila Pereira, M. L., Willemsen, T. M., Brunner, A., Six-Materna, I., & Wells, R. (2004). Bad but bold: Ambivalent attitudes toward men predict gender inequality in 16 nations. *Journal of Personality and Social Psychology, 86*(5), 713–728. https://doi.org/10.1037/0022-3514.86.5.713.

Gupta, A., Szymanski, D. M., & Leong, F. T. L. (2011). The 'model minority myth': Internalized racialism of positive stereotypes as correlates of psychological distress, and attitudes toward help-seeking. *Asian American Journal of Psychology, 2*(2), 101–114.

Guth, J. L., Green, J. C., Kellstedt, L. A., & Smidt, C. E. (1995). Faith and the environment: Religious beliefs and attitudes on environmental policy. *American Journal of Political Science 39*, 364–382.

Hall, D. L., Cohen, A. B., Meyer, K. K., Varley, A. H., & Brewer, G. A. (2015). Costly signaling increases trust, even across religious affiliations. *Psychological Science, 26*, 1368–1376. http://dx.doi.org/10.1177/0956797615576473.

Halpern, D. F. & LaMay, M. L. (2000). The smarter sex: A critical review of sex differences in intelligence. *Educational Psychology Review, 12*(2), 229–246.

Hand, C. M., & van Liere, K. D. (1984). Religion, mastery-over-nature, and environmental concern. *Social Forces, 63*, 555–570.

Heider, F., & Benesh-Weiner, M. (Eds.) (1988). *The notebooks, vol. 4: Balance theory.* Weinheim: Psychologie Verlags Union.

Heilman, M. E., Wallen, A. S., Fuchs, D., & Tamkins, M. M. (2004). *Penalties for success: Reactions to women who succeed at male gender-typed tasks. Journal of Applied Psychology, 89*(3), 416–427.

Hewstone, M., & and Hamberger, J. (2000). Perceived variability and stereotype change. *Journal of Experimental Social Psychology, 36*(2), 103–124. https://doi.org/10.1006/jesp.1999.1398.

Hofmann, W., Wisneski, D. C., Brandt, M. J., & Skitka, L. J. (2014). Morality in everyday life. *Science, 345*(6202), 1340–1343. doi:10.1126/science.1251560.

Hust, S. J. T., Brown, J. D., & L'Engle, K. L. (2008). Boys will be boys and girls better be prepared: An analysis of the rare sexual health messages in young adolescents' media. *Mass Communication and Society 11*(1), 3–23. https://doi.org/10.1080/15205430701668139.

Iversen, K. (2017). 7 charts that show gender inequality around the world. World Economic Forum. www.weforum.org/agenda/2017/08/charts-gender-inequality-women-deliver.

Johnston, L. (1996). Resisting change: Information-seeking and stereotype change. *European Journal of Social Psychology, 26*(5), 799–825. https://doi.org/10.1002/(SICI)1099-0992(199609)26:5<799: AID-EJSP796>3.0.CO;2-O.

Judge, T. A., Cable, D. M., Higgins, C. A. (2000). The employment interview: A review of recent research and recommendations for future research. *Human Resource Management Review, 10*(4), 383–406. https://doi.org/10.1016/S1053-4822(00)00033-4.

Kelly, G. A. (1955). *The psychology of personal constructs. Volume 1: A theory of personality.* New York: W.W. Norton.

Klinger, L. J., Hamilton, J. A., & Cantrell, P. J. (2001). Children's perceptions of aggressive and gender-specific content in toy commercials. *Social Behavior and Personality, 29*, 11–20.

Löckenhoff, C. E., Chan, W., & McCrae R. R. (and 40+ others) (2014). Gender stereotypes of personality: Universal and accurate? *Journal of Cross-Cultural Psychology 45*(5), 675–694. doi:10.1177/0022022113520075.

Marlowe, F. W. (2007). The human sexual division of foraging labor. *Cross-Cultural Research, 41*(2), 170–195. https://doi.org/10.1177/1069397106297529.

Masten, C. L., Morelli, S. A., & Eisenberger, N. I. (2011). An fMRI investigation of empathy for 'social pain' and subsequent prosocial behavior. *NeuroImage 55*(1), 381–388. https://doi.org/10.1016/j.neuroimage. 2010.11.060.

McConnell, A. R., & Leibold, J. M. (2001). Relations among the Implicit Association Test, discriminatory behavior, and explicit measures of racial attitudes. *Journal of Experimental Social Psychology 37*, 435–442. doi:10.1006/jesp.2000.1470.

Morris, M. W., & Larrick, R. P. (1995). When one cause casts doubt on another: A normative analysis of discounting in causal attribution. *Psychological Review, 102*(2), 331–355.

Morrison, M., Duncan, R., & Parton, K. (2015). Religion does matter for climate change attitudes and behavior. *PLoS ONE, 10*(8): e0134868. https://doi.org/10.1371/journal.pone.0134868.

Moskowitz, G. B., Stone, J., & Childs, A. (2012). Implicit stereotyping and medical decisions: Unconscious stereotype activation in practitioners' thoughts about African Americans. *American Journal of Public Health, 102*(5), 996-1001.

NASA (2018). Scientific consensus: Earth's climate is warming. *Global climate change: Vital signs of the planet.* https://climate.nasa.gov/scientific-consensus/.

Norenzayan, A., Shariff, A. F., Gervais, W. M., Willard, A. K., McNamara, R. A., Slingerland, E., & Henrich, J. (2014). The cultural evolution of prosocial religions. *Behavioral and Brain Sciences, 39*, 1-86.

Operario, D., & Fiske, S. T. (1999). Social cognition permeates social psychology: Motivated mental processes guide the study of human social behavior. *Asian Journal of Social Psychology, 2*(1), 63-78.

Petty, R. E., Cacioppo, J. T., Strathman, A. J., & Priester, J. R. (2005). To think or not to think: Exploring two routes to persuasion. In Brock, T. C. and Green, M. C. (Eds.), *Persuasion: Psychological insights and perspectives.* Thousand Oaks, CA: Sage, pp. 81-116.

Piaget, J. (1970). Piaget's theory. In Mussen, P. H. (Ed.), *Carmichael's manual of child psychology 1* (3rd ed.). New York: Wiley.

Pomerleau, A., Bolduc, D., Malcuit, G., & Cossette, L. (1990). Pink or blue: Environmental gender stereotypes in the first two years of life. *Sex Roles, 22*(5-6), 359-367. https://doi.org/10.1007/BF0028833.

Pratto, F., & Walker, A. (2004). The bases of gendered power. In Eagly, A. H., Beall, A. E., & Sternberg, R. J. (Eds.), *The psychology of gender.* New York: Guilford Press, pp. 242-268.

Prentice, D. A., & Carranza, E. E. (2002). What women and men should be, shouldn't be, are allowed to be, and don't have to be: The contents of prescriptive gender stereotypes. *Psychology of Women Quarterly, 26*, 269-281. doi:10.1111/ 1471-6402.t01-1-00066.

Radke, H. R.M., Hornsey, M. J., Sibley, C. G., & Barlow, F. K. (2017). Negotiating the hierarchy: Social dominance orientation among women is associated with the endorsement of benevolent sexism. *Australian Journal of Psychology*, August 7.

Rhine, R. J., & Severance, L. J. (1970). Ego-involvement, discrepancy, source credibility, and attitude change. *Journal of Personality and Social Psychology, 16*(2), 175-190.

Riggio, R. E., & Riggio, H. R. (2012). Face and body in motion: Nonverbal communication. In Cash, T. F. (Ed.), *Encyclopedia of body image and human appearance*, vol. 1 (pp. 425-430). San Diego: Elsevier Academic Press.

Romer, P. (1990). Endogenous technological change. *Journal of Political Economy. 98*, S71-S102.

Rosenthal, L., Levy, S. R., & Moyer, A. (2011). Protestant work ethic's relation to intergroup and policy attitudes: A meta-analytic review. *European Journal of Social Psychology, 41*(7), 874-885.

Rudman, L. A., & Fairchild, K. (2004). Reactions to counterstereotypic behavior: The role of backlash in cultural stereotype maintenance. *Journal of Personality and Social Psychology, 87*(2), 157-176. https://doi.org/10.1037/0022-3514.87.2.157.

Rutjens, B. T., & Heine, S. J. (2016). The immoral landscape? Scientists are associated with violations of morality. *PLoS ONE, 11*(4), April 5.

Sabin, J. A., Riskind, R. G., & Nosek, B. A. (2015). Health care providers' implicit and explicit attitudes toward lesbian women and gay men. *American Journal of Public Health, 105*(9), 1831-1841. doi:10.2105/ AJPH.2015.302631.

Sanghani, R. (2017). Feisty, frigid and frumpy: 25 words we only use to describe women. *The Telegraph*, March 17. www.telegraph.co.uk/women/life/ambitious-frigid-and-frumpy-25-words-we-only-use-to-describe-wom/.

Saroglou, V. (2002). Religion and the five factors of personality: A meta-analytic review. *Personality and Individual Differences, 32*, 15-25. doi:10.1016/S0191-8869(00)00233-6.

Schur, E. M. (1984). *Labeling women deviant: Gender, stigma, and social control.* Philadelphia: Temple University Press.

Seitz, R. J., Nickel, J., & Azari, N. P. (2006). Functional modularity of the medial prefrontal cortex: Involvement in human empathy. *Neuropsychology, 20*(6), 743-751.

Sell, A., Hone, L. S. E., & Pound, N. (2012). The importance of physical strength to human males. *Human Nature, 23*, 30-44. doi 10.1007/s12110-012-9131-2.

Simons, D. J., & Levin, D. T. (1998). Failure to detect changes to people during a real-world interaction. *Psychonomic Bulletin & Review, 5*(4), 644-649.

Simpson, A., & Rios, K. (2016). How do U.S. Christians and atheists stereotype one another's moral values? *International Journal for the Psychology of Religion, 26*(4), 320-336.

Smedslund, J. (1963). The concept of correlation in adults. *Scandinavian Journal of Psychology, 4*, 165-173.

Swann, W. B., Jr. (1997). The trouble with change: Self-verification and allegiance to the self. *Psychological Science, 8*(3), 177-180. doi.org/10.1111/j.1467-9280.1997.tb00407.x.

Tan, J. H. W., & Vogel, C. (2008). Religion and trust: An experimental study. *Journal of Economic Psychology, 29*, 832-848. http://dx.doi.org/ 10.1016/j.joep.2008.03.002.

van Es, Margaretha (2016). *Stereotypes and self-representations of women with a Muslim background: The stigma of being oppressed*. Basingstoke: Palgrave Macmillan.

Ward, L. M. (2003). Understanding the role of entertainment media in the sexual socialization of American youth: A review of empirical research. *Developmental Review, 23*, 347-388.

West, C., & Zimmerman, D. H. (1987). Doing gender. *Gender & Society, 1*(2), 125-151. https://doi.org/10.1177/0891243287001002002.

Wood, W., & Eagly, A. H. (2002). A cross-cultural analysis of the behavior of women and men: Implications for the origins of sex differences. *Psychological Bulletin, 128*, 699-727.

Wood, W., & Eagly, A. H. (2010). Gender. In Fiske, S. T., Gilbert, D. T., & Lindzey, G. (Eds.), *The handbook of social psychology* (5th ed., pp. 629-667). New York: Wiley.

Zarate, M. A., & Smith, E. R. (1990). Person categorization and stereotyping. *Social Cognition: 8*(2), 161-185. https://doi.org/10.1521/soco.1990.8.2.161.

Zupan, B. A., Hammen, C., & Jaenicke, C. (1987). The effects of current mood and prior depressive history on self-schematic processing in children. *Journal of Experimental Child Psychology, 43*(1), 149-158.

6 Theories of Gender

Theories of Gender	120
Biological Explanations	124
Social Learning/Social Cognitive Theory	125
Cognitive Development Theory	127
Gender Schema Theory	128
Social Role Theory	129
Parental Investment	131
Social Dominance Theory	134
Feminist Approaches	139
Gender Role Strain and Precarious Manhood	140

CRITICAL THINKING

Gender Dysphoria

A very small percentage of people around the world identify with a gender that they are not assigned at birth (e.g., a child identified as a boy by his parents at birth develops a gender identity of a girl). A person who identifies with a gender they are not assigned at birth is called transgender (see Figure 6.1). A person experiences gender dysphoria when they suffer significant emotional distress because their assigned sex does not match their gender identity (American Psychiatric Association, 2013). Only around 1% of the human population identifies with a gender they are not assigned at birth, and an even smaller percentage of people suffer gender dysphoria. But they suffer greatly. Gender dysphoria among children and adolescents is associated with social isolation, harassment by peers at school, anxiety, depression, and loneliness (Clark et al., 2014; Davidson, 2012). Unfortunately, because of lack of awareness and resources for these young people, they are also more likely to experience foster care, residential treatment programs, and the juvenile justice system compared to other kids (Ansara & Hegarty, 2012). Adults with gender dysphoria suffer from anxiety, depression, and are more likely to suffer other psychological disorders as well (Davidson, 2012). Very sadly, suicide and suicide attempts are quite common among transgender individuals (Grant et al., 2011).

Theories of Gender 113

Figure 6.1 Caitlyn Jenner, a transgender woman
Source: ITV/Shutterstock

The American Psychiatric Association originally identified a condition termed *gender identity disorder*, which they changed to gender dysphoria in the fifth edition of the *Diagnostic and Statistical Manual of Mental Disorders* (*DSM-5*; APA, 2013) based on professional recommendations from treatment providers and scholars (Fraser, Karasic, Meyer, & Wylie, 2010). The terminology was changed because it was recognized that calling gender identity conflict a "disorder" was pathologizing and stigmatizing for transgender individuals and because it reinforced a hegemonic binary model of gender (Bryant, 2007; Newman, 2002). As you recall from Chapter 4, there are multiple genetic conditions that can result in intersex conditions, including ambiguous genitalia or internal organs that do not match genitals. In addition, much research indicates that prenatal exposure to hormones affects brain development and gender identity, after the genitals are already formed (Garcia-Falgueras & Swaab, 2010; Swaab & Garcia-Falgueras, 2009). As such, individuals may be born with a brain that forms a gender identity that does not necessarily match their genitals or internal reproductive organs.

Transgender individuals face tremendous prejudice and discrimination in our world (Rodriguez, Agardh, & Asamoah, 2017), and there is a current social outcry condemning the existence of transgenderism, arguing that there are "only two genders," and that those genders are based on having a penis or a vagina (Rutledge, 2017). We already know this is false, and very simplistic, based on numerous conditions resulting in indistinct or mixed genitalia, atypical hormone conditions, or other outcomes that do not represent a gender binary. Part of this current and hostile climate stems from controversies surrounding use of public restrooms, with conservatives arguing that transgender women (men who are becoming or have become women) are dangerous for girls and women in public restrooms (Dastagir, 2016; Mathers, 2017). Transgenderism is not linked with violence at all, except that transgender individuals are likely to be physically attacked themselves, especially by heterosexual men (DiFulvio, 2015; Hutton, 2016; Peitzmeier et al., 2015). In fact, the greatest

Theories of Gender

perpetrators of sexual assaults against girls and women all over the world are heterosexual men who identify as such (Sedgwick, 2006). Some might argue that a public restroom is safer than a church given the epidemic of sexual abuse from clergy (Park, 2017).

Gender is not a simple construct; it is extremely complex and involves interactions of mind and body, hormones and physiology, social constructions of gender, sexuality, and cultural ideologies. The binary view of gender is simplistic and ill-informed; it is not accurate. Transgender people have always existed, including across history and cultures. They have not always been stigmatized; an example is the case of the two-spirit person in North American indigenous culture, a person said to possess male and female spirits simultaneously who represented a third identified gender (Pruden & Edmo, 2016). Intolerance of differences in people is immature, unsophisticated, and unfair. People all over the world show **individual differences**, variations in traits, qualities, and attributes throughout the human species. Feeling hostility toward someone because they are different is **xenophobic** and just plain wrong. Fair-minded, compassionate, knowledgeable people are tolerant of everything but intolerance (Popper, 1945). A greater understanding of gender identity and social constructions of gender includes recognition of gender complexity and individual differences in human biological and psychological qualities.

INEQUALITIES AND INJUSTICES

You Throw Like a Girl!

Athough the sexes are much more similar than they are different (Hyde, 2005), psychologists and other scientists have examined differences in many qualities, traits, and abilities based on sex. A search on PsychInfo (the main database in Psychology) for articles, books, and chapters with "sex differences" or "gender differences" in the title yields 16,440 results (as of January 8, 2018; American Psychological Association, www.apa.org/pubs/databases/psycinfo/). Sex differences in a quality are sometimes expressed statistically in terms of an **effect size**, a statistical indicator of the strength of the relationship between two variables. Larger effect sizes indicate greater sex differences; small effect sizes indicate a small average difference between women and men or boys and girls. One common indicator of effect size is called Cohen's d, which is a statistic that indicates the average difference between groups in terms of standard deviation units. A d of 1 indicates one standard deviation difference on average between the two groups. A d value close to zero (0) indicates no real difference between groups. Cohen (1988) provides guidelines for interpreting d, with values around .20 indicating a small average difference between groups; values around .50 indicating a moderate average difference; and values around .80 indicating a large average difference (positive values indicate men are higher; negative values indicate women are higher, a convention when sex differences are examined). A review by Janet Shibley Hyde (2005) provides many effect sizes reflecting overall sex differences on many qualities yielded from multiple **meta-analyses** (studies examining the statistical results of many other studies to obtain an overall indicator of an effect). For example, women and girls show superior verbal abilities (e.g., reading comprehension) compared to men and boys, but the effect is quite small at -.09. Similarly, boys and men show superior spatial skills compared to girls and women, but the effect is also small at .20 (Hedges & Nowell, 1995). Differences in personality have been documented, with women higher in traits like gregariousness (d = -.07), and men higher in traits like assertiveness (d = .51). These personality differences are generally small to moderate (Feingold, 1994; see Chapter 9).

The largest effect sizes are found in sex differences in physical strength. The d value for throwing distance difference between women and men is 1.98, an absolutely huge difference, larger than any difference in any psychological variables. For throwing velocity, d is 2.18 (Thomas & French, 1985). This huge difference in physical strength has had and still has enormous consequences for women (see Figure 6.2). Statistically, this large difference means that approximately 98% of men are stronger than the average woman, and that if a man and woman are randomly chosen, there is a 92% chance that the man will be physically stronger than the woman (go to https://rpsychologist.com/d3/cohend/ to calculate overlap between distributions of different scores). Being the much smaller half of the human race makes one extremely vulnerable to physical oppression by larger others. Do the larger others always use physical force to get their way? No, not always. Do they use it at all? Of course they do. Men have used and continue to use physical force to get their way, to coerce weaker and smaller women to comply. This physical oppression may not be as typical or obvious as it once was, before the codification of norms against interpersonal violence. But let's not forget that laws all over the world still exist that permit husbands to beat their wives (Alfred, 2014). The physical oppression of women in our world today is evident in intimate partner violence (IPV) and murder and rape statistics, with perpetrators overwhelmingly male and victims overwhelmingly female, especially in less developed countries (Bassuck, Dawson, & Huntington, 2006; World Health Organization, 2012, 2017; see Chapter 11). Yes, women can be abusive, including toward men. But men are more likely to use their superior strength against women, and when they do, they do more damage than women, who are typically smaller and physically much weaker.

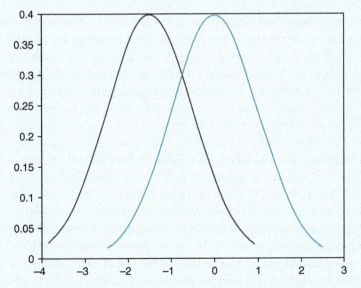

Figure 6.2 A two standard deviation difference between groups (Cohen's d = 2.00) representing overall differences in physical strength between women and men

On top of the physical oppression of women, the statement "You throw like a girl!" is an insult. Describing a male person as in any way feminine can be incredibly insulting and stressful to boys and men, including American men (O'Neil, Helm, Gable, David, & Wrightsman, 1986; Kierski & Blazina, 2009; Vandello, Bosson, & Cohen, 2008). The *Oxford English Dictionary*, in 2018, offers one definition of the word "female" as *"befitting or characteristic of a woman (as perceived as inferior to a man); weak, petty; inferior (now rare). Of a man or boy: possessing womanly qualities; effeminate."* The *Macmillan Dictionary* provides a list of "insulting words for a man" in its thesaurus (www.macmillandictionary.com/us/thesaurus-category/american/insulting-words-for-a-man), including "pansy" (*"a man who is weak or easily afraid"*), "pussy" (*"an insulting word for a man who is not strong, brave, or determined,"* clearly common slang in reference to female genitals), and "sissy" (*"an insulting word for a boy or a man who does things that girls or women usually do"*). Saying a man or boy is like a woman or girl is insulting because of the cultural imperative for men to be strong, powerful, aggressive, brave (Bergling, 2001; Gilmore, 1990). So women are not only actually physically weaker than men as a group (not a strong position to start in); that inborn comparative physical weakness is derogated, derided, and shamed, a psychological oppression that is grossly unfair. Women comprise one-half of the human race; they have an equal stake in the survival of us and our planet. It is far past time for each individual person to consider women as human beings equal to men.

BONUS BOX

Changing Roles in the Family

Traditional roles for wives and husbands, mothers and fathers, even sisters and brothers, are pretty clearly laid out in classic television situation comedies like *Leave it to Beaver*, *I Love Lucy*, *The Brady Bunch*, and *Happy Days* (Coats & Smith, 1999) (see Figures 6.3 and 6.4). Women work in the home to support the comfort and well-being of the family, while men work outside the home and earn resources to support the comfort and well-being of the family. Research supports that when people think about the typical woman, although an increasing number of people think of the career woman (a woman in professional dress in a professional setting), their first idea is typically that of the *housewife/mother*, a nice woman in a traditional role who takes care of others in the family by cooking and cleaning. The typical man is a man in a business suit and/or in a professional setting, a role that is not tied to the family or work in the home (Vonk & Ashmore, 2003). Despite the relative automaticity of such **prototypes** (representations of a typical group member) (Greenwald & Banaji, 1995), these types actually do not represent the most frequently occurring type of wife or husband, mother or father. Fifty-seven percent of all American women work outside the home, earning an income; around 70 percent of American men work outside the home. Seventy percent of American women with minor children work outside the home, while about 93% percent of fathers work outside the home. Among women with

Figure 6.3 The stereotypical housewife/mother (please note how slender and attractive she is)
Source: H. Armstrong Roberts/ClassicStock/Getty Images

children under the age of 3 years, about 61% percent of them work outside the home (United States Department of Labor, 2014). The majority of college graduates are now women (United States Department of Labor, 2017). How is it, then, that the traditional prototype still prevails when people think about the word "woman"? Why do most people think of June Cleaver or Betty Crocker as the "typical" woman instead of a woman in a business suit or in a professional setting? Among men, research indicates that fathers are becoming more involved in the daily work of raising children (Pew Research Center, 2013). There are greater numbers of men who stay home and care for the home and children, not working outside the home, today than in the past (Pew Research Center, 2014). Although women still complete the majority of household tasks, even though they are also likely to be employed outside the home, men are engaging in more housework today than in the past (Pew Research Center, 2013). How is it, then, that for men, home and family roles have little do with ideas about "typicality"? **Schemas** (knowledge structures,

Figure 6.4 June Cleaver, mother on the popular series Leave it to Beaver, played by Barbara Billingsley
Source: Everett Collection Inc/Alamy Stock Photo

stereotypes) we have about gender are difficult to change when they are embedded in cultures and permeate socialization processes from birth. Because they are so strongly socialized, ideas about gender are **implicit**; they occur automatically with little effort and conscious awareness (Greenwald & Banaji, 1995). Becoming consciously aware of biased and negative stereotypes and their automaticity is one first step in combatting their use, both individually and in wider social contexts.

Families are changing in many ways. There are greater numbers of same-sex marriages and families (Gates, 2015). Many families are blended families, including stepparents and step- and half-siblings, and a growing number of couples don't marry but have children and live as families (Pew Research Center, 2015). So-called "nontraditional" family structures are changing the way people think about families, slowly but surely. Partners and parents in modern families, and artistic and cultural depictions of them (*Modern Family*), are representing new family roles that will eventually permeate our culture and our ideas, perhaps changing our ideas of the "traditional" mother, father, and family.

LEARN MORE

Psychoanalytic Theories of Gender

Sigmund Freud (1856-1939) (see Figure 6.5) is the originator of psychoanalytic approaches to understanding human personality, including gender identity. While these approaches are perhaps more central to a book on personality psychology, Freud's ideas about gender are important because they are so well-known and have been influential for other approaches in understanding ideas about gender and gender identity (Person & Ovesey, 1983). Freud emphasized the importance of early childhood experiences and relationships with parents in impacting personality development. He asserted that ideas about gender and the self as being a particular gender arise during early childhood, between the ages of 3 and 6 years old, during what he called the phallic stage (*phallic* refers to phallos, the Greek word for penis). During this stage, the child is developing ideas about love, jealousy, and sexuality, chiefly based on observation and relations with parents. An understanding of their own genitals is also developing here and impacts gender identity. According to Freud, boys during this period have an experience called the *Oedipus Complex*, whereby they fall in love with their mother (as in the Greek tragedy *Oedipus Rex*). In feeling so much love

Figure 6.5 Sigmund Freud
Source: Science History Images/Alamy Stock Photo

for mother, boys develop intense jealousy of her relationship with father, and experience feelings of anger and hatred toward father. Boys project their own hatred onto their father and become fearful that their father will discover the jealousy and cut off their penis (*castration anxiety*). Because these feelings are so intrapsychically intense and frightening for the child, the ego in response uses a defense mechanism of *reaction formation*, whereby they form an identification with the father and idealize him as a man. As such, boys who successfully resolve the *Oedipus Complex* identify with their father and form a male gender identity. Successful resolution also involves the development of actual contempt or fear of women because of the overwhelming fears associated with mother. The **Superego**, the structure of the mind responsible for morality and feelings of conscience, is said to emerge from the conflict.

Girls have an altogether different experience according to Freud. Girls experience something called the *Electra Complex*, which begins with an originally intense bond with mother, until the child recognizes that she is missing a penis, which the daughter fears has been cut off. Her *penis envy* leads to feelings of inferiority relative to boys and men. To replace the missing penis, the girl develops a desire for a child and father becomes the romantic love target, with corresponding jealousy of father's relationship with mother. In a successful resolution of this conflict, the girl recognizes that mother will not be usurped, and she re-identifies with mother and establishes a female gender identity. Becoming attractive to men as love objects to obtain children becomes an important part of feminine gender identity, and girls and women will also have a contempt for and jealousy of other women in competition for men, according to Freud. The Superego also emerges as for boys, but it is weaker, which is the reason for the compromised morality and weak ego strength of women in adulthood (Freud, 1925/1974).

Freud's approach has multiple weaknesses that are rather obvious. First and foremost, the theory is **sexist**; it assumes inferiority of women relative to men. The world is certainly sexist and always has been, but in the Victorian era (1837 to 1901) when Freud was around, the Western world was even more sexist and very sexually repressed. The cultural norms during Freud's theorizing were obviously sexist and, as such, scholarly works during that time are also sexist. Additionally, the approach offers pretty complicated explanations, with processes largely occurring inside the mind (thus not observable) and perhaps somewhat unconsciously (with Freud very strongly emphasizing the unconscious mind throughout his theory). So these processes may in fact be ultimately unmeasurable as well as not subject to direct observation, making this approach decidedly unscientific (Popper, 1963). Freud's theorizing was also based on his own clinical work with clients, data that were not shared publicly (an important feature of science). Freud's approach is extremely influential throughout psychology, and it is interesting in its historic relevance, and thus important for students of gender to understand.

Theories of Gender

A **theory** is an explanation. In science, a theory is an overarching explanation of a particular phenomenon that is subject to empirical testing. A theory explains a particular process, event, or behavior in such a way that features of the explanation can be observed or tested. For example, arguably the greatest theory in all of science is the theory of evolution, which explains the origins of life on our planet as changes in life forms over long periods of time based on changes in survival needs in changing environments. If evolution is a good explanation, or an accurate explanation, one should be able to test its premises, including the essential assertion of changes in life forms. Are there changes in life forms that can be observed? Of course! If we reflect back on Chapter1, we see multiple hominid forms in the fossil record of human evolution, with changes over time moving toward walking upright and a larger brain, both of which served to enhance ability of hominid species to survive over time. Scientific theories are testable; their assertions are subject to observation, to empirical testing, by anyone. Sometimes people argue against theories by arguing that they are somehow hypothetical or amorphous, only a supposition of how things might work. So the word "theory" to some people means that it is an idea that is not substantiated or supported by fact. Quite to the contrary, scientific theories are subject to rigorous testing, and those that are not supported by empirical observations, by evidence, do not last very long as explanations. Unsupported theories are jettisoned from science; theories that are supported by evidence are retained and continuously explored as possible explanations for phenomena. No theory has been more strongly tested and examined than the theory of evolution, and it has stood the test of time.

Theories have key purposes. First, as theories describe a particular process or event, they make predictions about that particular process or event. Theories make predictions about the phenomena of interest, including predictions about future and unobserved events. For example, if evolution is true, we would expect to see species evolving continuously over time depending on changes in the environment. If this process is absent, evolution is refuted. If this process is indeed observed, repeatedly, including in as yet unknown species, evolution is supported (between 15,000 and 18,000 new species are discovered on Earth each year; Nosowitz, 2015). Second, theories organize known findings; they serve as an organizing explanation for the known research evidence. Powerful theories explain processes across a variety of contexts and explain a lot of evidence. And third, theories serve as a guide for researchers. A scholar interested in a particular topic examines prominent theories within the discipline about that topic and decides which theory they will test, which explanation they will use to guide their observations.

There are several features of "good" theories that bear outlining. First, because they make predictions, good theories are **comprehensive**; they explain most or all of the available empirical evidence. Not all studies will support a theory and, in fact, some research findings may contradict a theory. But good theories are supported by the overall body of evidence concerning a particular phenomenon. The theory of evolution serves as an explanation of the fossil record of hominids and every other species for which fossils have been found. The theory of evolution also explains evidence from research examining the geologic column, the distribution of plants and animals all over the planet, research in microbiology and genetics, and much more. It is a very comprehensive theory. Second, and also because good theories make predictions, they have **heuristic value** in that they serve as a guide to researchers.

Third, good theories are highly **testable**; they provide many testable **hypotheses**, or statements concerning the supposed relationship between things or events called **variables**. The assertions and concepts of the theory must be subject to empirical observation by anyone. For example, I once went to a psychic (just for kicks). The psychic made multiple predictions about events that were going to happen in the future, involving personal outcomes. She very strongly asserted that only she was able to make these predictions; no one else was able to access the information she received in a magical way. The psychic's assertions are not testable; there is no way to observe the magical process that provides her with information about the future. It happens in a magical way that only she can perceive. Scientific theories provide testable, observable assertions and predictions. If something is not subject to careful, structured observation, by anyone, it is essentially a magical or **pseudoscientific** process. Testable theories are **falsifiable**; one can set up a situation where some aspect of the theory can be shown to be false. If a statement cannot be falsified, it is a pseudoscientific concept. One can assert that a psychic's methods are false, but because the phenomena are not observable, they are not truly falsifiable. Because they cannot be falsified, they cannot be proven either.

Fourth, good theories are **parsimonious**; that is, they provide straightforward, rather simple explanations, with a minimum number of **assumptions** (a notion that is taken for granted or assumed to be true though not observed). Complicated explanations are not necessarily better explanations. For example, both Freudian (psychoanalytic) and social learning theories provide explanations for development of **gender identity**, individual identification as a female, male, or other gender. According to psychoanalytic theory, young boys come to identify as male through the experience of the *Oedipus Complex*, whereby boys fall in love with their mother and want to murder their father out of jealousy, but instead through defense mechanisms identify with their father as a representation of maleness (Freud, 1925/1974) (see "Learn More"). Social learning theory argues that boys form gender identity through observation and **modeling** (imitation) of the same-sex parent and other male role models (Bandura, 1986). Which explanation is simpler? Which explanation is more observable or testable? Arguably, the social learning explanation is more straightforward and more easily observed, with key concepts (observation, modeling) rather clearly defined and not difficult to see or measure. The psychoanalytic prediction is not straightforward and involves key concepts that are deeply psychological and not easily measured or observed. Good theories provide clear definitions of key concepts and simple explanations.

Finally, good theories integrate findings from multiple domains. Evolutionary theory is the preeminent example of this. There is no substantive body of evidence from any science that contradicts or refutes evolution as the explanation for the diversity of life on our planet. Evolutionary theory explains research findings from every branch of science, including Earth sciences, biological sciences, and social sciences. **Evolutionary psychology** is the branch of psychology that examines how animal and human behaviors are adaptive for survival. For our purposes here, how is individual human development of **gender identity** (personal experience of the self as female, male, or other) linked with survival of the species over time? How is group development of ideas about **gender** (the social construction of what it means to be female, male, or other) adaptive across environments and over long periods of time? How do **gender roles** (roles that a society deems appropriate for each gender) affect group survival? Answers are provided by evolutionary explanations of human behavior.

Theories of gender may involve explanations of individual development of gender identity, social and cultural development of gender ideology, and how those two processes interact with each other. A mature individual sense of self as female or male (or other) would necessarily involve learning of sociocultural ideas about femininity and masculinity, about women and men, including norms for behavior and gender roles, with **gender-congruent** behavior tending to be rewarded by others and favored by norms. Although ideas about gender roles are always changing, and in more modern times are more liberal for women in general, **gender-incongruent**

Theories of Gender   123

behavior is still punished and condemned in many cultures, experiences that are clearly mean-ingful for ideas and feelings about the self. In this way, questions about gender identity and the sociocultural construction of gender are necessarily intertwined. This is perhaps why there are multiple theories describing one or the other or both; how gender identity is formed, how social constructions of gender arise, or how social constructions of gender influence gender identity content and formation.

Evolutionary psychology provides one perspective, emphasizing how individual gender iden-tity and ideas and norms about gender enhance ability of humans to survive and reproduce. Many other explanations are offered, with different theories providing insight into and explana-tion of how gender identity and sociocultural ideas about gender develop and how they influence individual and group behavior. Why are there so many explanations, with not one single theory necessarily standing out as the best and most comprehensive? As with most human behaviors, the development and experience of gender identity is complex; it is linked with genetic pro-cesses, physiological and hormonal processes, in utero events, socialization, family experiences in early childhood, exposure to various media, experiences with developing sexuality, and so on. It influences individual self-concept, self-esteem, feelings of belonging and well-being, lifestyle, relationships, career pursuits, and many other important psychological and social outcomes. How about ideas that societies and cultures develop to explain what it means to be female, or what it means to be male? Gender as a social construction, as an ideology involving traditions, expectations, and norms for behavior, is extremely complex in trying to observe, understand, and explain. Because of the complexity involved in human behavior, sometimes there are vari-ous complementary and competing explanations for particular phenomena. As such, there are various theoretical approaches one can use in attempting to explain individual and social con-structions of gender. This chapter will present prominent, important, and "good" theories of gender.

Another uniqueness of theories of gender bears asserting up front, and that is the fact of inherent sexism in explanations of gender. The earliest explanations of gender from Greek philos-ophers (Plato, 428–348 BCE; Aristotle, 384–322 BCE) and physicians (Hippocrates, 460–370 BCE; Galen, 129–210) focused on women as incomplete or inferior or underdeveloped men. Men are seen as fully developed, life-giving forces of nature, while women are seen as dependent, inferior, with undeveloped genitals and weaker morality and intellect (King, 1993; Laqueur, 1990; Smith, 1983). Such negative descriptions and emphasis on female inferiority are not just inaccurate, biased, disrespectful and insulting to women; such explanations, relied upon by formal social structures including education, medicine, science, and government, have negatively impacted personal and social outcomes for women for centuries (see Chapter 7). If Plato asserts that women are inferior, even like children, there is justification for their oppression, including excluding them from edu-cation and professions, even from civic engagement. If subsequent scientific explanations rely on such ideas, their usefulness as a guide for researchers is compromised, because hypotheses are biased toward confirmation of female inferiority and male superiority. If all of society asserts female inferiority, from parents to religion to teachers to laws to science, women's ideas and feelings about themselves are influenced, beginning in infancy for every girl who has ever lived. Ideas so deeply embedded throughout a culture become automatic, implicit; they are used by most people in a rather unthinking, effortless manner, with women automatically viewed as infe-rior compared to men (Greenwald & Banaji, 1995). Such ideas influence behaviors toward women, sometimes resulting in discrimination (Fiske & Taylor, 1991). So thanks a lot, Plato!

Biological Explanations

There is a clear distinction between sex and gender, presented throughout this book. As a reminder, **sex** refers to biological sex; one's sexual **genotype** (genetic profile) and **phenotype** (the appearance of a trait) (see Chapter 3). The phenotype of sex includes gonads, genitalia, other internal sex organs, and secondary sex characteristics (e.g., body hair, breasts). **Gender** refers to the social construction of what it means to be female, male, or another gender; ideas about femininity and masculinity that are developed within a particular culture, including traditions and norms of behavior for women and girls, men and boys. Some explanations of gender focus on sex and other biological processes in determining gendered behavior and roles. Some of these are rather strictly biological; they focus nearly completely on biological processes in determining gender identity, with little concern for socialization processes. Others are more strictly social; they consider socialization and learning processes, with little regard for biological processes. Still other approaches are called **biosocial**; they consider the interaction of biological and social forces in determining gender identity and social constructions of gender. Let's look at more strictly biological approaches first.

As we read about in Chapter 4 on human sex differentiation, the process of biological sex begins in utero, with various hormonal processes triggered by the presence of the Y chromosome which determines maleness. Once gonads are formed, hormones differ between the sexes, with testes producing androgens, especially testosterone, and the ovaries producing estrogens. Other hormones are produced in the brain by the hypothalamus and released by the pituitary gland (Chiras, 2012). They can also vary by sex because their production and effect depend on the presence of the sex hormones (Goldstein, Meston, Davis, & Traish, 2005). Hormonal differences between the sexes are present at birth and continue throughout the lifespan. Hormones influence body formation and daily physiology; they affect growth, moods, sexual behavior, and social behavior. By adulthood, the XX genotype results in a person who appears female, having female genitalia, internal organs, and secondary sex characteristics (breasts, wider hips, greater adipose tissue). The XY genotype results in a person who appears male, with male genitals and internal organs, little breast tissue, greater musculature, taller physical height, greater body hair, and greater physical strength.

Recall from Chapter 4 our discussions about research indicating that gender identity is largely determined by in utero brain processes that are affected by exposure to hormones prenatally. Fetal brain development is affected by hormones, affecting brain structures, largely structures that interact with the gonads across the lifespan. Some researchers argue that these brain structures affect gendered behavior in childhood and adulthood. When **testosterone** is present during fetal development, brain development is steered toward the "male direction." When testosterone is absent in utero, the brain develops "in the female direction" (Garcia-Falgueras & Swaab, 2010, p. 22). These in utero influences on the brain are also argued to affect sexual orientation (Zhou, Hofman, Gooren, & Swaab, 1997). These explanations of gender identity and sexual orientation are nearly purely biological, asserting that fetal brain development is the determining factor of both (Swaab et al., 2001). Other researchers also argue for the importance of fetal and baseline hormones in determining gender identity and sexual orientation, including those examining Congenital Adrenal Hyperplasia (CAH) in girls and women and its behavioral correlates (Dittmann et al., 1992; Meyer-Bahlburg et al., 2008; Zucker et al., 1996).

For psychologists, hormones are importantly linked specifically with sex differences in relationship and aggressive behaviors. In terms of forming close relationships with others, women produce greater amounts of an estrogen called oxytocin, a hormone that is present during child-birth and promotes mother-infant bonding (Yang, Wang, Han, & Wang, 2013). Oxytocin is also produced in response to daily social interactions; people who engage in cooperative social inter-action with others produce this relaxing, feel-good hormone (Spengler et al., 2017). Oxytocin is said to underlie feelings of trust and love (Bernaerts et al., 2017; Zak, Kurzban, & Matzner, 2005). Women and men produce oxytocin at orgasm (Meston & Frohlich, 2000), which promotes pair bonding (Meyer, 2007) and may also promote relationship fidelity (Scheele et al., 2012). Women produce more oxytocin than men on a regular basis because its production is influenced by the presence of estrogens (Carter, 2006). As such, women should be higher in feelings of closeness, trust, and intimacy with others than are men, with oxytocin both motivating closeness and rein-forcing it. Indeed, much research in social psychology indicates that women tend to report more intimate feelings and behaviors in both romantic and same-sex friendship interactions (Burda, Vaux, & Schill, 1984; Caldwell & Peplau, 1982; Cozby, 1973; Drescher & Schultheiss, 2016; Wada, 2000). While society certainly reinforces the notion that women should be loving, kind, caring for others, and engaged in more communal and caretaking behaviors than men, naturally-occurring hormones are also involved in being motivated toward close, supporting, loving interactions and relationships (see Chapter 9). As women and men behave naturally, societal ideas about women and men are affected.

Aggression is another broad category of social behavior that is influenced by hormones, par-ticularly **testosterone** (Book, Starzyk, & Quinsey, 2001). Testosterone differs by sex; men produce much more testosterone on a daily basis, through the testes (Southren et al., 1967; Torjesen & Sandnes, 2004). Women also produce testosterone in the ovaries. Boys are higher in testos-terone than girls, including at birth (Tomlinson, Macintyre, Dorrian, Ahmed, & Wallace, 2004). Testosterone is linked with aggressive behavior in humans and animals. People and animals injected with testosterone are more aggressive in laboratory settings (Sandnabba, Lagerspetz, & Jensen, 1994; Terburg, Aarts, & van Honk, 2012). Men with higher baseline levels of testosterone are more aggressive than men with lower baseline levels of testosterone (Archer, 2006). Higher levels of prenatal testosterone are linked with more aggressive behavior later in childhood for boys (Liu, Portnoy, & Raine, 2012). While there are clearly many factors involved in aggressive behavior, including direct provocation (Bettencourt & Miller, 1996), emotional arousal (Knight, Guthrie, Page, & Fabes, 2002), and aggressive learning experiences (Bandura, 1979), testosterone as a male hormone is linked with greater aggression and even criminality (Dabbs, Carr, Frady, & Riad, 1995). Norms for men's dominance, power, bravery, and yes, aggression, continue to char-acterize ideas about masculinity and men all over the world (Steinberg & Diekman, 2016), in part because of boys and men engaging in complex behaviors that involve autonomic physiological processes. We discuss aggression in depth in Chapter 11 of this book (also see "Inequalities and Injustices").

Social Learning/Social Cognitive Theory

Multiple theories of gender identity and gender as a social construction focus on socialization and learning processes. A primary approach to understanding gender identity (and individual and social psychology in general) is Bandura's approach first called **social learning theory** (Bandura, 1977), then termed **social cognitive theory** (Bandura, 1986). According to the theories, children learn much about the world, including ideas about femininity and masculinity, through observa-tion of people who are important to them (especially parents, but other **role models** as well).

126 *Theories of Gender*

Children observe important people behaving and imitate those behaviors, especially behaviors that they see rewarded by others. Through **modeling** (imitating or reproducing behavior that is observed), and through trial-and-error testing of different behaviors, children eventually learn and adopt behaviors that society rewards and deems appropriate, including gendered behavior. Same-sex parental models are particularly influential for children learning about gender and gender roles. As children become aware of gender rather early in life (generally by age 3 years; Thompson, 1975), at young ages they are more likely to imitate same-sex than other-sex models (Bussey & Bandura, 1984), and they show a preference for same-sex peers (Powlishta, Serbin, & Moller, 1993). Exposure to explicit messages about gender (e.g., "boys are tough and girls are sweet") and implicit messages about girls and boys (e.g., surrounding girls with pink and flowers, boys with blue and cars), women and men (e.g., the prevalence of women in some professions, men in others), also affects children's learning of gender roles and stereotypes (Bigler & Liben, 2006). Learning about gender roles continues into adulthood as adults strive to achieve a coherent, socially competent sense of self (Bandura, 2001; Bussey & Bandura, 1999).

There is abundant evidence that children are reinforced by parents and others for **gender-congruent behavior** (behavior deemed acceptable by a particular culture for one's identified gender) and punished or not rewarded for **gender-incongruent behavior** (behavior of the opposite sex deemed not acceptable by a particular culture). Children are treated according to their gender, beginning at birth (Laflamme, Pomerleau, & Malcuit, 2002); their rooms are decorated and furnished based on gender stereotypes (Pomerleau, Bolduc, Malcuit, & Cossette, 1990). Infant girls are talked to more by mothers than infant boys (Clearfield & Nelson, 2006), and fathers engage in more physical play behaviors with boys than with girls, beginning around age 7–8 months (MacDonald & Parke, 1986; Power & Parke, 1983). Caldera, Huston, and O'Brien (1989) observed that parents acted most excited when playing with their infants with gender-congruent toys than with neutral or incongruent toys. Both mothers and fathers were also more engaged in play with their infants with gender-congruent toys. Parents are more likely to choose gender-congruent than incongruent toys for toddlers (Idle, Wood, & Desmarais, 1993). Parents are more likely to read to girls (Baker & Milligan, 2016) and engage in relationship play (e.g., with dolls) with girls (Caldera & Sciaraffa, 1998) and to engage in rough-and-tumble play with boys (Jacklin, DiPietro, & Maccoby, 1984). Boys are discouraged from crying and emotional behaviors by parents, while girls' emotionality and expression are encouraged (Bronstein, 2006). Gender-congruent toys are very heavily marketed to children (Fine & Rush, 2018), and television shows and films geared to children show children in highly stereotypical roles (Hust & Brown, 2008). Society rewards girls for being girls and boys for being boys, and that fact is quite evident early in life. Boys (Lauer, Ilksoy, & Lourenco, 2018) and men (Gal & Wilkie, 2010) show particular preferences for gender-congruent behaviors.

As individuals mature, the learning experiences that occur over time become a fundamental part of how they process information about the world, including about themselves. As **self-concept** (one's ideas and knowledge about the self, including gender identity; Hoffman, Hattie, & Borders, 2005; Larson, 2012) develops in childhood, it is used as a guide to individual behavior on a daily basis, and becomes more complex and sophisticated as a person grows and socialization and experiences continue. Individuals then come to rely on internal (**intrinsic**) rewards, or good feelings about the self in response to behavior that fits with one's self-concept, including gendered behavior (Bussey & Bandura, 1999). In support of the importance of modeling by parents for learning and gender identity, children's gender role attitudes are influenced by parents' gendered behaviors, even more than by parents' explicit gender ideology (Halpern & Perry-Jenkins,

2016). Children who grow up with traditional gender roles are more likely to follow and endorse those roles in adulthood. Children exposed to nontraditional gender roles and behaviors are likely to be less traditional themselves in their behavior as adults (Riggio & Desrochers, 2006; Serbin, Powlishta, & Gulko, 1993).

Children also learn about relationship dynamics and conflict resolution in observing their parents interact with each other. Children who grow up in homes characterized by high levels of family conflict are likely to repeat those patterns in their own relationships in adulthood (Feerick & Haugaard, 1999; Heise & Garcia, 2002; Johnson, 2003). It is true that there is an intergenerational transmission of divorce, where offspring of divorced parents are more likely to experience their own marital dissolution (Kunz, 2000). Does that intergenerational transmission of divorce occur because young people learn loose relationship commitment norms, rules that ending relationships, including marriages, is acceptable; or because young people with divorced parents likely observed higher than average levels of conflict between parents? Research suggests that learning about conflict and its resolution from parents is more likely to be a determinant of offspring marital dynamics and quality (Amato, 1996). Research also indicates that one of the most important determinants in the perpetration of intimate partner violence is observations of parents using violence against each other (World Health Organization, 2012; see Chapter 11).

Cognitive Development Theory

There are several cognitive theories of gender identity that are similar to social cognitive theory in their focus on children's development of cognitive conceptualizations of gender that they use to process information about the self and others and to fit in to the social world. Classic cognitive development approaches assert that while children may recognize gender categories from their experiences, including that most of the world is divided into female and male, they do not understand their own gender and its stability over time until they are cognitively capable of that, usually around age 4 years and later (up to age 7 years or so) (Kohlberg & Ullian, 1974; Slaby & Frey, 1975). Around age 5 years, children are said to develop **gender constancy**, the awareness that a person's gender remains unchanged regardless of behaviors or circumstances. So while a 3-year-old girl may think she "becomes" a boy when wearing "boys'" clothing, older children have self-concepts that are based on psychological rather than physical and behavioral qualities (Harter, 1983). Older children recognize that they are a girl or a boy and that they always will be (Karniol, 2009; although see "Critical Thinking").

Once children develop gender constancy and identify as female or male (or another gender identity), they use that category to process information about the self, others, and social situations and experiences (Martin, Ruble, & Szkrybalo, 2002). Because children tend to value their own gender identity and gender group (Powlishta, 1990; Zucker, Wilson-Smith, Kurita, & Stern, 1995), they are motivated to understand and comply with gender norms, recognizing their importance as a social distinction. Children actively try to understand more about gender roles, norms, and stereotypes. Like everyone else, they are motivated to seek out information that confirms what they already believe about gender, so they seek out behaviors and activities that are consistent with their gender. Such consistency is rewarding to children (Kohlberg, 1966). Younger children (5-7 years) tend to be more rigid in their gender categories; they are reinforced by experiences and observations of gender-congruent behavior and are likely to prefer behavior that is unambiguous with regard to gender roles (Lauer, Ilksoy, & Lourenco, 2018). Older children become more flexible and recognize that gender categories are rather permeable, although

128   *Theories of Gender*

they have more knowledge of gender stereotypes and gender roles than younger children. Girls are more flexible in their stereotyping than boys (Dinella, Claps, & Lewandowski, 2017; Katz & Boswell, 1986).

Empirical evidence indicates that children's behavior is strongly guided by gender, beginning in infancy, based on modern research that examines infant gaze as an expression of motivation or interest. Infants can apparently distinguish between men and women at an early age. Infants aged 6 months and older can discriminate female from male voices (Miller, 1983), and by 9 months infants can distinguish between female and male faces (Leinbach & Fagot, 1993). Infants will gaze longer at images of toys that "fit" their gender (e.g., dolls for girls, trucks for boys) (Campbell, Shirley, Heywood, & Crook, 2000; Lauer, Udelson, Jeon, & Lourenco, 2015). Before gender constancy is established, preschool children prefer gender-congruent toys (Todd et al., 2017) and activities (Golombok et al., 2008). Lauer and colleagues (2017) found that preference for gender-congruent toys in infancy (as indicated by gaze) is predictive of toy preference at age 4 years. Children's play preferences in preschool are also predictive of gender identity later in adolescence (Golombok, Rust, Zervoulis, Golding, & Hines, 2012), with preschoolers preferring typically feminine play activities likely to identify as female as a teenager, and preschoolers preferring masculine-typed play identifying as male.

Gender Schema Theory

Gender schema theory is similar to social cognitive theory and cognitive development theory, in that it emphasizes the importance of learning gender and development of **schemas. Schemas** are mental knowledge structures that represent what we know about particular concepts. We have schemas representing ideas about women and femininity, men and masculinity, including a **self-schema** (a mental knowledge structure comprising all one's knowledge and beliefs about the self; also known as **self-concept**), which includes gender identity. It is considered more of a cognitive theory in that it focuses on how cognitive structures are formed and then used to guide social information processing. Gender schema formation begins early in life, in infancy, as we have seen in studies showing infant ability to distinguish between genders (Leinbach & Fagot, 1993) and infant gaze preference for gender-congruent toys (Campbell et al., 2000; Lauer et al., 2015). We have also discussed how parents begin to socialize children as their assigned gender at birth, modifying their behaviors and environments to emphasize the child's gender (Clearfield & Nelson, 2006; Pomerleau et al., 1990). Parents emphasize gender-congruent toys and play activities (Caldera, Huston, and O'Brien, 1989; Idle, Wood, & Desmarais, 1993), which inform gender stereotypes, roles, and norms for children (Bem, 1984; Martin & Halverson, 1981). Parents who are highly traditional in their gender roles are likely to encourage children's development of traditional gender ideology (Kane, 2009; Riggio & Desrochers, 2006). As children grow, they are exposed to even more influence and socialization sources, including education and mass media (Katz & Boswell, 1986; Singer, 2001). This exposure obviously informs schema formation.

Accessibility of schemas is an important concept in all schema theories. **Accessibility** refers to the ease with which a category schema is brought to mind; how long it takes for a schema to be activated and retrieved for processing current information. Some schemas are highly developed and highly accessible; they are easily brought to mind and often used to process social information, sometimes implicitly, without cognitive effort or awareness. Chronically accessible schemas are habitual; they are **personal constructs** (Kelly, 2003) that are used normally and frequently when processing information about the self, others, and social experiences. For example, a person who is very health-conscious is always thinking about and processing information in terms of health and how it fits with their lifestyle. A person who is a racist habitually and rather automatically uses racial categories to evaluate people; people are judged almost immediately based on apparent race and the content of the racist's schema (usually highly negative) (Chin, 2010; Taylor & Falcone, 1982). When gender categories are important and chronically used to process self and other information, the person is said to be gender schematic; they actively seek out and use information concerning gender to process information, using gender schemas to interpret and evaluate social information. Schematicity can be measured in terms of how much individuals see feminine or masculine traits as characteristic of them and important to them; extreme scores are associated with gender schematicity (Markus, 1977).

Research indicates that some people are indeed gender schematic; they habitually use gender schemas (stereotypes, roles, etc.) to process information. For example, boys tend to rely more on gender stereotypes than girls in play activities (Eisenberg, Murray, & Hite, 1982), friendships (Zucker et al., 1995), toy preference (Turner, Gervai, & Hinde, 1993), and choice of gender role (Edelbrook & Sugawara, 1978), suggesting greater schematicity. Gender schematicity in girls and boys is associated with gender-congruent toy preference (Carter & Levy, 1988). Gender schematic adults tend to see themselves as highly representative of their gender and they tend to be rather traditional in their gender stereotypes and roles (Bem & Lenney, 1976). Other people are relatively gender aschematic; that is, they do not pay much attention to gender and do not rely heavily on gender stereotypes and roles to understand other people. These people are likely to be more androgynous (showing a mixture of typically feminine and masculine traits) in their own behavior (Schmitt & Millard, 1988).

It is important to point out the difference between cognitive development theory and gender schema theory. Cognitive development theory is more concerned about how gender identity develops and how that is reflected in children's thoughts, feelings, and behaviors. Gender schema theory is more concerned with how gender schemas are used in processing social information, including one's own gender identity. Schema theories explain that schematic processing is associated with automaticity, low effort. Schemas are easy to use and help process information very quickly, even instantly, according to a stereotype. An example is meeting a woman and instantly processing her in terms of gender stereotypes rather than other individuating information (e.g., she is Latina-American, she is a doctor, she is older; Signorella, Bigler, & Liben, 1993). As you recall from Chapter 5, people use schemas when they are not motivated or able to process information carefully and thoroughly (Petty, Cacioppo, Strathman, & Priester, 2005). Thus we are more likely to process quickly and schematically when we are not interested or have no stake in a person or issue (e.g., they are a stranger) or when we are tired or fatigued or cognitively engaged with another task. Importantly, schematic processing is highly adaptive; it allows us to engage in multiple tasks at once and to consciously decide which social information we will pay attention to. In this way, gender schema theory can be viewed as more explicitly evolutionary in its emphasis on functionality of human information-processing than other theories.

Social Role Theory

Strictly biological models, while useful as theories in providing testable hypotheses and guiding researchers' explorations, do not provide a whole picture of gender identity or gender as a social construction. Models that focus exclusively on socialization and learning processes are comprehensive and useful to researchers, but may not fully consider biological factors. A very important explanation offered by scholars Alice Eagly and Wendy Wood (Eagly, 1987; Eagly & Wood, 1999; Wood & Eagly, 2002) focuses on how social constructions of gender and individual social behaviors are influenced by features of biological sex that relate to the division of labor. This biosocial model is called **social role theory**, and its fundamental assertion is that the content of social constructions of gender (including stereotypes about women as communal and men as agentic) stems largely from the social roles that women and men typically occupy. Because gender roles were strongly in the past and are still today influenced by biological differences between women and men (in terms of size, strength, and reproductive roles), this model is highly biosocial. Men are about 15-20% larger than women and much stronger, on average. Men possess 50-70% greater upper body strength and 30-50% greater lower body strength on average than women. Because of these strength differences, over the centuries men have been assigned to labor that requires more strength, including hunting, fighting, lifting and carrying, building. Women can certainly engage in these tasks successfully and many women have done so and still do; but the average man is more effective in these roles than the average woman because of large strength and speed differences. Because men more typically occupy these social roles, men as a group are seen as possessing the qualities of these roles (strong, agentic, dominant qualities) and individual men adopt qualities of the role (Eagly & Wood, 1999).

A major biological characteristic defining femaleness is the ability to carry and give birth to children and to feed children. These are roles that only women occupy, those of pregnancy, childbirth, and breastfeeding. How does this affect society's view of women? First, pregnancy is a vulnerable state; a woman's life is definitely more in danger from a variety of conditions while she is pregnant than when she is not (Chabrol et al., 2002; World Health Organization, 2008). Childbirth and post-partum complications are also deadly for women (World Health Organization, 2010). So women are very physically vulnerable during pregnancy, which affects their ability to engage in various roles. In the cave, it would be much more likely that a woman would stay near the campsite and care for the sick, elderly, injured, and children while pregnant than travel long distances on a hunt or to fell trees. Second, women, being able to produce the perfect food for their infants, are obviously going to be the parents who tend to dominate the role of infant caretaking, much more so than men, especially during pre-modern times when substitutes for breast milk were not available. According to social role theory, because women are much more typically in the role of parent and caretaker, ideas about femininity involve conceptions of kindness, nurturance, tenderness, and communal behaviors that care for other people. In addition to informing stereotypes about women, these disproportionate reproductive responsibilities interfere with women's abilities to engage in other productive work (Wood & Eagly, 2002).

People do not follow roles robotically; there is a dynamic interplay between gender identity, social constructions of gender, and gender roles in which individuals are engaged. Because men are typically in positions of power and status and women are not, men come to act in more powerful, status-oriented ways while women come to act in less powerful, subservient ways (Lips, 1991). Because men's social roles and activities are associated with power and dominance, men over time have dominated social, political, and financial power, across cultures, with women having much less power and fewer resources (Hughes & Hughes, 2001; Lerner, 1986; Pew Research Center, 2017; World Economic Forum, 2017). Further, when cultures provide women with little control over their own bodies in terms of contraception (Hock, 2007; Soller, 2014) and sexual consent (Sanday, 1981), women have significantly less opportunity to engage in learning and training activities, formal education, and paid employment. Such inequalities further cement power differences and a hierarchical social structure favoring men and oppressing women (Pratto & Walker, 2004).

Physical differences between men and women obviously exist. But what if they didn't? What if men and women were equally sized, with no physical strength, height, or speed differences between the two sexes? Ask yourself if there was a foreign planet, deep in outer space, with two groups, the Biggies and the Littles, who would be in charge? The groups are identical except the Biggies are bigger, stronger, and faster than the Littles. No intellectual or cognitive or emotional or personality differences at all, just that the Biggies are bigger. Who is in charge on that planet? Which group has more social, political, financial power? The physical size and strength differences between women and men, coupled with the disproportionate vulnerability and physical responsibility of human reproduction, have left women at a distinct disadvantage over all of human history. Men have more power just by virtue of greater strength; they have seized the vast majority of power across history because they can. Women as individuals and as a group can be physically compelled, forced to comply, much more easily than men. The idea that men have not taken advantage of their greater physical strength to compel women is naïve and not true. Imagine those two groups on another planet were not different in size, they were not Biggies and Littles but Oranges and Greens, exactly the same size and strength on average. Now who is in charge? The answer becomes much less obvious.

Parental Investment

Another biosocial model is more explicitly evolutionary in nature and posits that women's and men's reproductive roles and differences in **parental investment** (the degree of physical and temporal investment required by each of the sexes in producing an offspring; Trivers, 1972) are primary determinants of gender roles and behaviors and, as such, ideas about gender (Buss, 1995). According to these evolutionary approaches, women and men have evolved different strategies for mating and reproduction, with an innate drive to reproduce. Men can theoretically produce new children every day; all they need are fertile partners. Ejaculating is fun and easy for men and they have no further physical or biological responsibilities associated with reproduction. Because mating and reproduction are so easy for men, they develop so-called *short-term mating strategies*, whereby they seek to mate with as many fertile women as possible and devote little time and investment to offspring. Because men are always seeking sexual partners, they have evolved competitive and aggressive tendencies as they compete with other men for women. Theoretically, men are also sexually aggressive toward women, seeking to mate with as many women as possible. Genghis Khan (1162–1227) is said to have produced up to two thousand children, and not only with wives, because he had many concubines and because he was a rapist (Zerjal, Xue, & Bertorelle, 2003). Descendants of Genghis Khan today are estimated at approximately 16 million. Interestingly, when National Geographic reported the results of the Zerjal et al. 2003 study on Genghis Khan, including that he raped women in conquered lands and took the most beautiful women as sex slaves, that he was a violent rapist and predator, they titled him "a prolific lover" (National Geographic News, 2003). National Geographic, rape is not love.

Women, on the other hand, invest a great deal in each and every offspring that is produced. Producing a mature egg takes time, conception is not guaranteed, and pregnancy is nine months of physical consequences for women and their health. In addition, women cannot produce new children every day; in fact, women have a limited fertility span of time (compared to men) and even if they worked hard at it, there is a reasonable upper limit to the number of children one woman can have in her lifetime (the greatest number of births to one woman is recorded as 69 from 27 pregnancies, with 16 sets of twins, 7 sets of triplets, 4 sets of quadruplets; Guinness World Records, 2018). Because of the limits on their reproductive abilities, each offspring is precious, and women therefore devote much time and resources to each individual offspring in an attempt to ensure their survival into adulthood. Because of their much greater investment as a parent, women have evolved *long-term mating strategies* and are much more selective of their mates, seeking out partners with enough resources and inclination to support their offspring in the long term. Because of evolutionary pressures to produce viable offspring, women have evolved nurturing and attachment behaviors so their children's survival is maximized. Because they are more sexually selective, women desire fewer sexual partners. As such, they have evolved to be lower in aggression, because they do not typically have to compete for sexual access (Buss & Schmitt, 1993).

There are differences in mating and sexual behaviors between women and men that correspond to such explanations. Men around the world show greater valuing of physical attractiveness in selecting sexual partners than women do, reflective of a focus on health and fertility when choosing mates. Men show a strong preference for younger female partners. Women all over the world place greater emphasis on a partner's earning capacity than men do and prefer mates who are older than them (Eagly & Wood, 1999). Men are much more approving of casual sex than women are and men tend to have more sex partners over their lifetimes than women do (Oliver & Hyde, 2000). Men also think about sex more than women do, thinking about sex nearly 34 times every day, compared to 19 times per day on average for women (Fisher, Moore, & Pittenger, 2012). Men are clearly much more sexually aggressive than women, being perpetrators of reported rapes nearly 99% of the time (United States Department of Justice, 1997). Men are also more likely to respond with jealousy to sexual infidelity by partners, which evolutionary theorists argue is because of **paternity uncertainty**, uncertainty about the paternity of children, especially when women have multiple sex partners (Mathes, 2005). Women on the other hand respond more strongly with jealousy when men are emotionally unfaithful, when they establish an emotional connection with another woman. It is the emotional bond with another that threatens women most because her partner may no longer be available to support her and her offspring in the long term. These sex differences in jealousy have been found using self-report (Buunk, Angleitner, Alois, & Buss, 1996) and physiological measures (Pietrzak, Laird, Stevens, & Thompson, 2002). They have been documented around the world, including the U.S. and countries in Europe (Buunk et al., 1996) and Asia (Buss et al., 1999; Geary, Rumsey, Bow-Thomas, & Hoard, 1995).

Sex differences in reproductive roles and parental investment interact with society and culture, a biosocial process. The cross-cultural study by Eagly and Wood (1999) found that in traditional, less egalitarian cultures, where men have greater power over women and women's activities and opportunities are more limited by men, mating strategies of women and men are the most different. In more egalitarian countries, where women have greater access to education, paid employment, and social power (including freedom of choice), they are less likely to choose a partner based on his ability to provide resources and more likely to value qualities like personality and physical attractiveness. Thus, when power differences between women and men are smaller, women show even greater selectivity in choosing a mate and do not rely on earning capacity as a primary determinant. For men, sexual jealousy is correlated with wanting to have children, with men who desire children reporting greater sexual jealousy. Antipathy toward adopted and stepchildren (offspring not genetically linked to oneself) is also positively correlated with self-reports of sexual jealousy (Mathes, 2005).

Let's also consider today's world and the desire for offspring. The average number of kids Americans want is 2.5 (Carroll, 2007). Men around the world desire a slightly higher number of children than women (United States Agency for International Development, 2010). In countries where sex outside of marriage (**fornication** in legal terms) is not punishable by law (it is still illegal in seven U.S. states; Los Angeles Times, 2001; Sweeny, 2014), most people use contraception, because they do not want to have children every time they have sex. This is true especially among women, with 99% of women using contraception at some point (Centers for Disease Control and Prevention, 2010). If the biological imperative, reproducing viable offspring, was a pure force affecting human behavior, everyone would desire and attempt to produce as many offspring as possible. At certain times in history, having a greater number of children was highly desirable, because children served as helpers and essentially laborers for adults. In some environments, those characterizing agrarian, agricultural societies, families have more children. In more traditional or developing societies, women have less reproductive control, less control over their own bodies (see Figures 6.6 and 6.7). Contraception is likely to be limited or unavailable, abortion is likely to be completely banned, and there are likely to be few prohibitions against marital rape. Marital rape is still not a crime in a majority of countries (127 of 195). In wealthier, more technologically advanced societies, women have greater access to contraception, including abortion, and marital rape is considered a crime (although not in all 50 U.S. states until 1993). In such modern cultures, where women have more freedom to choose life roles, women have fewer or, increasingly, no children because they are engaged in other professional, artistic, scientific activities. Women are more equal to men in many indicators of status in countries where contraception is available and accessible (Nargund, 2009; U.N. Women, 2011).

Figure 6.6 A woman and her children in a developing country
Source: Leonid Plotkin/Alamy Stock Photo

134 Theories of Gender

Figure 6.7 The Duggar family of the hit reality show *19 Kids and Counting*
Source: Wiki

The dynamic interplay between biological and social forces in affecting behavior is also observed in other animals. **Ethologists** (scholars who observe animal behavior over time, usually in natural settings) are increasingly verifying social learning processes occurring within various species, particularly other primates. For example, skills learned in obtaining food are quickly learned by other primates through observation and imitation, and are eventually passed on to successive generations. A learned skill is apparently genetic to an observer who is not familiar with the history of a particular species (Fausto-Sterling, 1992). Differences in so-called "instinctive" behaviors (e.g., courtship behaviors) have also been observed in different groups of the same species. For example, one community of chimpanzees observed by primatologist Jane Goodall and colleagues exhibited nearly 40 behaviors involved in grooming, courtship, and tool use that were not common to other communities of chimpanzees living nearby (Whiten et al., 1999). Once again, animal behaviors that appear instinctive or innate may be learned and specific to the one particular animal group that is observed. Only long-term observations of such behaviors may reveal their social bases and the biosocial nature of interpersonal behavior.

Social Dominance Theory

Other approaches to understanding gender focus explicitly on social structures in affecting gender identity and broader sociocultural ideas about gender. An extremely influential theory examining hierarchies in society is **social dominance theory** (Pratto, 1996; Pratto & Walker, 2004). Social dominance theory asserts that within any hierarchical society, individuals at the top of the hierarchy enjoy a disproportionate share of society's benefits and resources (e.g., money, education, political power), while those at the bottom of the hierarchy suffer a disproportionate share of society's shortcomings and liabilities (e.g., poverty, low-quality education, few opportunities, lack of social and political power). People at the top have greater access to resources and to prominent, powerful social and political positions. They have greater power than those lower in the hierarchy to influence cultural ideas about gender (Pratto & Walker, 2004). People at the top of the hierarchy are generally enjoying their greater proportion of political, economic, and social power; they are loath to give it up, and so engage in hierarchy-enhancing behaviors, behaviors that help to maintain and support the hierarchy itself and their position at the top. People at the bottom of the hierarchy are clearly not happy; they are being unfairly deprived of society's resources by the people at the top. They are in fact oppressed. These people engage in hierarchy-attenuating behaviors, behaviors that strike against the hierarchy by promoting equality and social change. One hierarchy-enhancing behavior is the creation of legitimizing myths, false ideas about the people at the bottom that justify their oppression. The people at the top use such ideas about the people at the bottom to control and oppress them and thus enjoy a disproportionate share of society's power and resources.

There has never been a truly gender-equal society on the planet; a hierarchy based on sex has existed in nearly every known culture, where men are at the top and have greater access to power and resources (Rosaldo, 1974). These rather automatic differences in power between the sexes in more primitive societies are based very simply on biological differences in physical strength, size, and speed. Today, men have greater social status and power in virtually every society in the world (United Nations Development Programme, 2013). In the United States and other Western cultures, there are clear hierarchies based on social class, race and ethnicity, religion, and sex, with white European-American Christian men, especially those of the middle to upper classes, still in charge of pretty much everything (see Figures 6.8a, 6.8b and 6.8c). Eastern cultures are also characterized by patriarchies, hierarchical systems based on sex, with men maintaining the majority of social, economic, and political power in the society.

What are the legitimizing myths that justify the oppression of other groups by white Christian men? There are clearly legitimizing myths based on race, with stereotypes of people of color more negative in content than those of white, European-American people. For example, white young men's stereotypes of African Americans in the 1930s included the traits *lazy*, *ignorant*, and *happy-go-lucky* (Katz & Braly, 1933). These ideas are false; they are imposed on African Americans by European Americans and justify oppression and control of black people (Sidanius, Levin, & Pratto, 1996). Religions other than Christianity? Some Christians say that those religions are false, that those believers are following a false religion. The Bible says that people who "serve other gods" are without God (2 John 9), that they are deceivers and antichrists (2 John 7), that they should be killed (Deuteronomy 13:6–10). And women? Recall from Chapter 5 the traits that are commonly attributed to women from all over the world based on the Pancultural Adjective Checklist (Best & Williams, 2001; Williams & Best, 1990). More negative traits are attributed to women than to men, including traits like "foolish," "unintelligent," "weak," "confused." These words, common features of stereotypes of women all over the world, describe a child; someone who is illogical, silly, not mature or competent or smart. Such people must be controlled! My goodness, how can they even be allowed to drive a car or leave the house? Based on these stereotypes, it sounds like grown women might need an escort to help them survive on a daily basis. Such ideas clearly allow men to dismiss women's work, achievements, talents, strengths, ideas, and emotions, and men (along with their greater physical strength) have been using such gender stereotypes to oppress women since the dawn of time (or at least since Plato). Thanks again, Plato!

An important part of social dominance theory is an individual difference, a trait-like variable called social dominance orientation (SDO), which refers to one's preference for inequality in society. People high in SDO think that groups rightly exist in a hierarchy because some groups are better than others. They believe superior groups should possess most of the power and resources society has to offer, while inferior groups should stay at the bottom of the hierarchy

136 Theories of Gender

Figures 6.8a, 6.8b, and 6.8c Some of the richest people in the world: Jeff Bezos, Bill Gates, Mark Zuckerberg
Source: Andrew Harrer/Bloomberg via Getty Images; Nicolas Liponne/NurPhoto via Getty Images; FLDphotos/iStock Photo

Table 6.1 Items from a measure of social dominance orientation (SDO)

1. Some groups of people are simply inferior to other groups.
2. In getting what you want, it is sometimes necessary to use force against other groups.
3. It's OK if some groups have more of a chance in life than others.
4. To get ahead in life, it is sometimes necessary to step on other groups.
5. If certain groups stayed in their place, we would have fewer problems.
6. It's probably a good thing that certain groups are at the top and other groups are at the bottom.
7. Inferior groups should stay in their place.
8. Sometimes other groups must be kept in their place.
9. It would be good if groups could be equal.
10. Group equality should be our ideal.
11. All groups should be given an equal chance in life.
12. We should do what we can to equalize conditions for different groups.
13. Increased social equality is beneficial to society.
14. We would have fewer problems if we treated people more equally.
15. We should strive to make incomes as equal as possible.
16. No group should dominate in society.

Respondents indicate degree of agreement with each item, with 1 = *strongly disagree*, 7 = *strongly agree*. Items 9 through 16 are reverse-scored (i.e., strong agreement indicates low SDO). Higher scores indicate greater SDO.

Source: Pratto, F., Sidanius, J., Stallworth, L.M., & Malle, B.F. (1994). Social dominance orientation: A personality variable predicting social and political attitudes. *Journal of Personality and Social Psychology, 67*, 741-763.

with few resources and little power (see Table 6.1). The people at the top of the hierarchy are commonly high in SDO. Men are higher in SDO than women; European Americans are higher in SDO than African Americans and Latino/a Americans; and heterosexuals are higher in SDO than LGBTQ individuals (Pratto, 1996).

When people are not at the top of the hierarchy (especially in terms of wealth), but still high in SDO, they are likely to also be high in **authoritarianism** (Choma & Hanoch, 2017; Osborne, Milojev, & Sibley, 2017), a trait-like quality involving blind obedience to traditional authorities, strong respect for tradition and status, rigid conservatism, convergent (low-effort, categorical) thinking, and use of negative stereotypes about outgroups who are hated and feared (Duckitt & Bizumic, 2013). Authoritarians tend to be racist (Radkiewicz, 2016) and sexist (Christopher & Wojda, 2008). People at the bottom of the hierarchy who are not authoritarian tend to be low in SDO; they prefer equality between groups and see all groups as equally important in society. A good measure of SDO is provided by Pratto and colleagues (1994) (see Table 6.1). Unfortunately, SDO can actually increase in people who are initially low in SDO, if they become part of a high-status group (Morrison, Fast, & Ybarra, 2009). So people who originally fight the hierarchy, once they get power and resources, become more status-oriented and supportive of the hierarchy. The point is to get to the top and use that power to smash the hierarchy and create real social change, because inequality is bad for individuals and for society as a whole (Rodriguez-Bailon et al., 2017).

While stereotypes as legitimizing myths and physical strength are certainly useful in maintaining patriarchy, men and women engage in gender roles that reinforce status and power differences between men and women. Men have greater access to powerful positions in society, as evidenced by political power all over the world today (see Figure 6.9). Women are clearly underrepresented in positions of political power all over the world, including in the United

Figure 6.9 White men running the United States
Source: Drew Angerer/POOL/Getty Image

States, with only 21 current female U.S. Senators, only four U.S. Supreme Court Justices who have been female (three currently), and not one single female President of the United States. Time Magazine (2011) offered their "Complete List of Top Female Leaders Around the World" (http://content.time.com/time/specials/packages/completelist/0,29569,2005455,00.html); the list has 13 names. There are 195 countries in the world today, and women are leading only 13 (6.7%). Among management positions in the U.S., women are a slight majority compared to men (at 51.5%), but they comprise only 27% of Chief Executive Officers and 30% of General Operations Managers. Women are the majority in management positions that are about helping people, including human resources, fundraising, and education. Women hold the majority (65%) of jobs in community and social services, including social work and counseling. They occupy 73% of positions in education. Men hold the majority of jobs as lawyers (64%) and judges (66%) (United States Department of Labor, 2017). As of this writing, there are 32 female CEOs in Fortune 500 companies in the U.S. That's about 6-7%. These proportions reflect a division by sex; men's positions are about action, assertion, decision-making, power; women's positions are about helping others. Women also engage in more parenting (Albritton, Angley, Grandelski, Hansen, & Kershaw, 2014; Ishii-Kuntz & Coltrane, 1992) and housework than men (Lachance-Grzela & Bouchard, 2010), including when both partners work full-time (Cinamon & Rich, 2002). In spite of historical oppression, women in the United States are increasingly seeking positions of power (see Figure 6.10).

Do women lack powerful occupations and political power because of lack of ability? Are women lacking in the professions and politically because they can't do it, because they're not capable, they don't work hard enough? Such legitimizing myths are just that, myths. There are

Figure 6.10 Female members of the U.S. House of Representatives
Source: Cheriss May/NurPhoto via Getty Images

very few and rather small differences between men and women in terms of cognitive abilities (Hyde, 2005; see "Injustices and Inequalities") or academic effort or motivation (in fact girls and women are often higher in motivation; Bugler, McGeown, & St. Clair-Thompson, 2015; D'Lima, Winsler, & Kitsantas, 2014; Yeung, Craven, & Kaur, 2012). So for work that does not require physical strength or speed, women are equally as capable as men given similar training and education. It is true that men and women can prefer different activities and may have different goals for their careers (Kirkcaldy & Cooper, 1992). But role preference is clearly not the only explanation, especially given the prevalence and amount of power differences characterizing human societies and codified prohibitions against women's participation in politics and education that have always existed and that still exist in some cultures (Brand, 1998; Goldin, 1994; McCammon, Campbell, Granberg, & Mowery, 2001). It is social structures and cultural institutions that promote such gendered division of labor, with women expected to be loving, kind, and communal in their behaviors and roles and men expected to be strong and powerful in their behaviors and roles. Men have greater access to positions of power and the resources, influence, and opportunity they afford (Pratto & Walker, 2004).

Feminist Approaches

A **feminist** is a person who desires and strives for equality between women and men in social, financial, and political power. Feminist approaches to gender have focused primarily on gender identity development, including the difficulties associated with developing female and male identity. An early approach is psychoanalytic and strongly influenced by Freud, the work of Karen Horney (1885–1952). Horney (1939) asserted that both girls and boys have difficulties in developing gender identity, but not because of penis envy or the Oedipus Complex. She argued that girls might have some difficulty with gender identity because mothers are typically dominated by fathers, which girls initially resent. Eventually, girls develop an identity that they are inferior to boys and men and that their primary appeal is in relation to them, including sexually. Girls learn to focus on physical appearance and exist in relation to men (fathers, husbands, sons) all their lives. Because parents devalue and sexualize girls, they become dependent on others and anxious about their identity and abilities. Boys have difficulty with gender identity because they are reproductively inferior to women and are jealous of women's abilities to produce and feed children with their bodies.

A second feminist psychoanalytic approach was developed by Dorothy Dinnerstein (1976), and emphasizes the dominance of mothers in the infant experience. Infants are typically most strongly attached to their mothers (Klaus, 1978), and being totally helpless and dependent, the infant is overwhelmed by the power of the mother. The bond is so powerful that children come to fear female power and become alienated from it; they flee from it in developing identity. Eventually girls and boys find it easier to recognize male power, and girls always feel inadequate relative to mother's formidable power, while boys become men who fear dependency on women. These children become adults who reinforce and support male domination. A similar theory is the **gynocentric** approach of sociologist Nancy Chodorow, who asserts that mothers indeed overwhelm children with their power, mainly because society is lopsided in parenting roles, with mothers pushed into taking on the majority of parenting responsibilities (Chodorow, 1978). This domination by mother results in problems for gender identity development, including for girls who become dissatisfied with relationships with men because they cannot compare to their relationship with mother. Girls also feel devalued in their identity because society devalues women. Boys are particularly likely to experience gender identity difficulties, because in their bond with mother, they share her identity and develop a sense of femaleness; the inability to completely separate from mother interferes with and undermines a sense of maleness (Chodorow, 1989). Because fathers have little involvement with parenting, boys also lack clear ideas about masculinity. Eventually, boys reject the power of mother and masculinity becomes over-valued and women are viewed as inadequate.

Gender Role Strain and Precarious Manhood

As we discuss in "Learn More," psychoanalytic approaches are particularly difficult to examine empirically, mainly because of constructs that are difficult to directly observe or measure. However, these psychoanalytic feminist approaches paved the way for examinations of difficulties men may experience in following traditional gender roles. **Gender role strain** is an approach offered by Pleck (1981, 1995), which emphasizes that individuals can have difficulty conforming to gender roles because society's expectations are contradictory and inconsistent. Pleck argued that men are particularly likely to experience gender role strain, as they are expected to be both aggressive and dominant and sensitive as husbands and fathers. When men behave sensitively, they are often derided and shamed, which threatens masculinity. A related and modern construct is that of **precarious manhood**, the assertion that modern masculinity is fragile and easily threatened (Vandello & Bosson, 2013), especially among men who have had difficulty achieving a masculine gender identity. Across cultures, manhood is seen as more of an accomplishment, something boys earn through initiation, direct instruction, and effort. Boys and men must prove their masculinity through actions and public demonstrations. In contrast, womanhood

Theories of Gender 141

is seen as developing naturally, without effort, specifically with sexual maturity and ability to produce children (Gilmore, 1990). Women are women quite easily, just by existing, while men have to earn masculinity (Vandello, Bosson, Cohen, Burnaford, & Weaver, 2008). Because of this, along with excessive demands for men's tough, strong, dominant behaviors from society (Addis, Mansfield, & Syzdek, 2010; Ducat, 2004), masculinity is precarious. When gender status is challenged or threatened, especially when women outperform them, men experience anxiety and feel compelled to prove their masculinity through demonstrated action, which includes maladaptive and risky behaviors, including aggression (Bosson, Vandello, Burnaford, Weaver, & Wasti, 2009). Masculine gender role stress is linked with increased perpetration of intimate partner violence (Jakupcak, Lisak, & Roemer, 2002). Not all men have fragile or precarious manhood; boys and men obviously can and do develop positive gender identity that is linked with positive social behaviors (Kiselica & Englar-Carlson, 2010; Levant, 1992; O'Neil, 2008). But these feminist theories point out the devaluing of women and the inequality between the sexes in cultures all over the world, inequalities resulting in women's oppression, victimization, and mistreatment. Understanding how cultural ideology about female inferiority and male superiority interacts with male gender identity, interpersonal behavior, and physical dominance over women around the world is critical for establishing true equality between women and men.

Chapter Summary

Theories of gender may address individual gender identity development, adoption of gender roles, and development of social and cultural ideology about gender. Good theories are comprehensive, testable, and falsifiable, integrate findings from multiple domains, and serve as a guide to researchers. Biological explanations focus on genetic and physiological processes in development of gender identity, and links between hormones and gendered behaviors, including nurturance and aggression. Social learning and social cognitive approaches emphasize the learning of gender roles and identity through observation and modeling of others' behaviors, especially important models of feminine and masculine behavior like parents. Cognitive development theories focus on gender identity as a developmental milestone and achievement of gender constancy, the recognition that one's gender is stable and immutable. Gender schema theory emphasizes development of mental knowledge structures (schemas) representing gender categories and roles and the use of those structures in processing social information. Social role theory is a biosocial approach that links differences in reproductive roles and other physical differences between women and men to societal division of labor. Because women and men typically occupy certain roles, they come to be seen as possessing the characteristics necessary for role accomplishment, even when they do not occupy those specific roles. Parental investment is an evolutionary approach that predicts gender differences in aggressive and sexual behavior based on sex differences in reproduction and differential investment in each individual offspring. Social dominance theory asserts that societies exist in hierarchies, with people at the top of the hierarchy enjoying a disproportionate share of societal resources and benefits, while people at the bottom suffer a disproportionate share of societal shortcomings and liabilities. Finally, feminist approaches are psychoanalytic and focus on how mothers and their powerful presence in infancy affect gender identity development of girls and boys. Sometimes, men may experience gender role strain because of inconsistent and contradictory demands placed on men. Precarious manhood occurs when masculine identity is fragile and easily threatened, resulting in men's compensatory demonstrations of masculine-typed behavior, including aggression.

Thoughtful Questions

- Explain the current prejudice against transgender individuals, including in terms of public restrooms.
- Explain the difference between gender dysphoria and gender identity disorder.
- Explain the roles of physical strength differences, gender stereotypes, and gender roles in patriarchy.
- Compare and contrast psychoanalytic and social cognitive theories of gender identity development.
- Compare and contrast cognitive development theory and gender schema theory.
- Explain how biological differences between the sexes affect the division of labor and social constructions of gender.
- Why do you think some low-status people are motivated toward a hierarchical structure? Even though they are at the bottom of the hierarchy, why do they support a hierarchical structure?
- How does gender role strain differentially affect women and men?
- Describe precarious manhood and why it is linked with aggressive behavior.

Glossary

Accessibility: the ease with which a category schema is brought to mind; how long it takes for a schema to be activated and retrieved for processing current information.

Assumption: a notion that is taken for granted or assumed to be true though it is not observed.

Authoritarianism: a trait-like quality involving blind obedience to traditional authorities, strong respect for tradition and status, rigid conservatism, convergent (low-effort categorical) thinking, and use of negative stereotypes of outgroups who are hated and feared. Stems from punitive domineering childrearing practices.

Biosocial: theories that consider the interaction of biological and social forces in determining gender identity and social constructions of gender.

Comprehensive: a feature of a good theory; a theory is comprehensive when it explains most or all of the available empirical evidence.

Discrimination: treating a person differently than others because of their group membership. Sexism is discrimination based on sex.

Effect size: a statistical indicator of the strength of the relationship between two variables.

Ethologists: scholars who observe animal behavior over time, usually in natural settings.

Evolutionary psychology: the branch of psychology that examines how animal and human behaviors are adaptive for survival.

Falsifiable: one can set up a situation where some aspect of a theory can be shown to be false.

Feminist: a person who desires and strives for equality between women and men in social, financial, and political power.

Fornication: the legal term for premarital sex or sex outside of marriage when it is deemed against the law.

Gender: the social construction of what it means to be female, male, or other genders; ideas about femininity and masculinity that are created within a particular culture, including traditions and norms for behavior.

Gender-congruent behavior: behavior deemed acceptable by a particular culture for one's identified gender. In contrast to gender-incongruent behavior, behavior of the opposite sex that is not acceptable for one's gender.

Gender constancy: the awareness that a person's gender remains unchanged regardless of behaviors or circumstances.

Gender dysphoria: A psychological condition where a person experiences significant emotional distress because their assigned sex does not match their gender identity.

Gender identity: individual identification as a female, male, or other gender; an idea about the self as female, male, or other gender.

Gender role strain: individuals can have difficulty conforming to gender roles because society's expectations are contradictory and inconsistent.

Gender roles: roles that a society deems appropriate (and correspondingly inappropriate) for women and men, girls and boys.

Gender schema theory: emphasizes the importance of learning about gender and development of schemas representing ideas about women and femininity, men and masculinity, in developing gender identity.

Gender schematic: when gender schemas are highly accessible and frequently used by a person, they actively seek out and use information concerning gender to process information, using gender schemas habitually to interpret and evaluate social information.

Genotype: the particular combination of genes one possesses for a trait.

Gynocentric: an approach that centers on women's roles and behaviors in influencing society or individuals, especially children in terms of gender identity development. Contrasts with the phallocentric (male-centered) approach of Freud.

Heuristic value: a *heuristic* is a tool or guide to a problem. Good theories have heuristic value because they serve as a guide to researchers; they provide testable hypotheses which guide researchers' observations.

Hierarchy-attenuating behaviors: behaviors that strike against the hierarchy by promoting equality and social change.

Hierarchy-enhancing behaviors: behaviors that help to maintain and support the hierarchy itself and the position of the people at the top.

Hypotheses: statements concerning the supposed relationship between things or events called variables provided by theories. Hypotheses must be *testable*.

Implicit: schemas, attitudes, or other knowledge structures that are highly accessible to consciousness and used rather automatically (effortlessly, without thought) to process current social information. Implicit attitudes are highly socialized, accepted beliefs; they are automatically activated frequently and easily in social information processing.

Intrinsic: an internal, intangible reward, often a good feeling about the self in response to behavior that fits with one's self-concept.

Legitimizing myths: false ideas about women created by society that justify their oppression by men. Men use these false ideas about gender to oppress women and enjoy a disproportionate share of society's power and resources.

Meta-analyses: a study examining the statistical results of many other studies to obtain an overall indicator of an effect.

Modeling: in social learning theory, observing and reproducing behavior of another person, facilitating learning.

Oxytocin: a hormone (an estrogen) that is present at childbirth and promotes mother-infant bonding; also released at orgasm for women and men and in close intimate interactions with others.

Parental investment: the degree of physical and temporal investment required by each of the sexes in producing an offspring.

Parsimonious: a straightforward, rather simple explanation, with a minimum number of **assumptions** (notions that are taken for granted or assumed to be true though not observed).

Paternity uncertainty: uncertainty about the paternity of children, especially when women have multiple sex partners.

Patriarchy: a hierarchical social structure based on sex, with men maintaining the majority of social, economic, and political power in the society.

Personal constructs: schemas that are used normally and frequently when processing information about the self, others, and social experiences.

Personality psychology: the subdiscipline of the science of psychology that examines characteristic ways of thinking, feeling, and behaving.

Phallic stage: the psychic period between the ages of 3 and 6 years when children develop gender identity, according to Freud. *Phallic* refers to penis, the physical focus of psychic energy during this period. Girls also focus on the penis because of *penis envy*.

Phenotype: the physical appearance of a trait as determined by the genotype and environmental effects.

Precarious manhood: the assertion that modern masculinity is fragile and easily threatened, resulting in anxiety and maladaptive behaviors on the part of men.

Prototype: a mental representation, usually including an image, of a typical group member. While *stereotypes* describe characteristics of large social groups, prototypes describe exemplars within particular groups (e.g., used car salesman, housewife/mother, career woman).

Pseudoscientific: a doctrine, practice, or theory that is without scientific foundation because it is untestable and not falsifiable; an assertion based on magical, supernatural processes.

Psychoanalytic theory: an intrapsychic approach from Sigmund Freud that emphasizes young children's feelings of sexuality and jealousy toward their parents in the development of gender identity.

Role model: a person a child observes and imitates; someone whose behavior is modeled by another person. A central component of social learning theory.

Schemas: repeatedly accessed patterns of thought about some stimulus, that are built up from experience, and that guide the processing of new information.

Self-concept: a mental knowledge structure (a **self-schema**) representing the totality of one's ideas and knowledge about the self. Includes gender identity.

Sex: biological sex; one's sexual **genotype** (genetic profile) and **phenotype** (the appearance of a trait). The phenotype of sex includes gonads, genitalia, other internal sex organs, and secondary sex characteristics (e.g., body hair, breasts).

Sexism: discrimination (being treated differently than others) based on sex.

Sexist: holding negative attitudes toward women based on a belief in their inferiority relative to men; treating women differently because of those attitudes.

Social cognitive theory (earlier social learning theory): the theoretical approach that emphasizes children's learning of gender norms and identity through observation of others' behaviors.

Social dominance orientation (SDO): one's preference for inequality in society. People high in SDO think that groups rightly exist in a hierarchy because some groups are better than others. They believe superior groups should possess most of the power and resources society has to offer, while inferior groups should stay at the bottom of the hierarchy with few resources and little power.

Social dominance theory: a theory of the social construction of gender that asserts that the powerful and dominant in society (men) create *legitimizing myths*, false ideas about women that justify their oppression by men. Men use ideas about gender to oppress women and thus enjoy a disproportionate share of society's power and resources.

Social role theory: a biosocial approach that asserts that the content of social constructions of gender (including stereotypes about women as communal and men as agentic) stems largely from the social roles that women and men typically occupy.

Superego: according to Freud, the structure of the mind responsible for morality and feelings of conscience.

Testable: the assertions and concepts of the theory are subject to empirical observation by anyone.

Testosterone: a male hormone (an androgen) that is linked with sexual development and behavior, energy, and aggression.

Theory: an overarching explanation of a particular phenomenon that is subject to empirical testing.

Transgender: a person who identifies with a gender they are not assigned at birth.

Variable: in research, any measurable characteristic that can take on more than one value.

References

Addis, M. E., Mansfield, A. K., & Syzdek, M. R. (2010). Is "masculinity" a problem? Framing the effects of gendered social learning in men. *Psychology of Men & Masculinity*, *11*, 77-90. doi:10.1037/a0018602.

Albritton, T., Angley, M., Grandelski, V., Hansen, N., & Kershaw, T. (2014). Looking for solutions: Gender differences in relationship and parenting challenges among low-income, young parents. *Family Process*, *53*(4), 686-701.

Alfred, C. (2014). These 20 countries have no law against domestic violence. *Huffington Post*, March 10. www.huffingtonpost.com/2014/03/08/countries-no-domestic-violence-law_n_4918784.html.

Amato, P. R. (1996). Explaining the intergenerational transmission of divorce. *Journal of Marriage and the Family*, *58*(3), 628-640.

American Psychiatric Association (2013). *Diagnostic and statistical manual of mental disorders* (5th ed.). Arlington, VA: American Psychiatric Publishing.

Ansara, Y. G., & Hegarty, P. (2012). Cisgenderism in psychology: Pathologising and misgendering children from 1999 to 2008. *Psychology and Sexuality*, *3*(2), 137-160. doi:10.1080/19419899.2011.576696.

Archer, J. (2006). Testosterone and human aggression: An evaluation of the challenge hypothesis. *Neuroscience and Biobehavioral Reviews*, *30*(3), 319-345. doi:10.1016/j.neubiorev.2004.12.007.

Baker, M., & Milligan, K. (2016). Boy-girl differences in parental time investments: Evidence from three countries. *Journal of Human Capital*, *10*(4), 399-441.

Bandura, A. (1979). The social learning perspective: Mechanisms of aggression. In Toch, H. (Ed.), *Psychology of crime and criminal justice*. Prospect Heights, IL: Waveland, pp. 198-236.

Bandura, A. (1986). *Social foundations of thought and action: A social cognitive theory*. Englewood Cliffs, NJ: Prentice-Hall, Inc.

Bandura A. (1997). *Social learning theory*. New York: Prentice-Hall.

Bandura, A. (2001). Social cognitive theory: An agentic perspective. *Annual Review of Psychology*, *52*, 1-26.

Bassuck, E., Dawson, R., & Huntington, N. (2006). Intimate partner violence in extremely poor women: Longitudinal patterns and risk markers. *Journal of Family Violence*, *21*, 387-399.

Bem, S. L. (1984). Androgyny and gender schema theory: A conceptual and empirical investigation. *Nebraska Symposium on Motivation*, *32*, 179-226.

Bem, S. L., & Lenney, E. (1976). Sex typing and the avoidance of cross-sex behavior. *Journal of Personality & Social Psychology, 33*, 48-54.

Bergling, T (2001). *Sissyphobia: Gay men and effeminate behavior*. New York: Harrington Park.

Bernaerts, S., Prinsen, J., Berra, E., Bosmans, G., Steyaert, J., & Alaerts, K. (2017). Long-term oxytocin administration enhances the experience of attachment. *Psychoneuroendocrinology, 78*, 1-9.

Best, D. L., & Williams, J. E. (2001). Gender and culture. In Matsumoto, D. (Ed.), *The handbook of culture and psychology*. New York: Oxford University Press, pp. 195-219.

Bettencourt, B. A., & Miller, N. (1996). Gender differences in aggression as a function of provocation: A meta-analysis. *Psychological Bulletin, 119*(3), 422-447.

Bigler, R. S., & Liben, L. S. (2006). A developmental intergroup theory of social stereotypes and prejudice. *Advances in Child Development and Behavior, 34*, 39-89.

Book, A. S., Starzyk, K. B., & Quinsey, V. L. (2001). The relationship between testosterone and aggression: A meta-analysis. *Aggression and Violent Behavior, 6*(6), 579-599.

Bosson, J. K., Vandello, J. A., Burnaford, R. M., Weaver, J. R., & Wasti, S. A. (2009). Precarious manhood and displays of physical aggression. *Personality and Social Psychology Bulletin, 35*(5), 623-634.

Brand, L. A. (1998). *Women, the state, and political liberalization: Middle Eastern and North African experiences*. New York: Columbia University Press.

Bronstein, P. (2006). The family environment: Where gender role socialization begins. In Worell, J., & Goodheart, C. D. (Eds.), *Handbook of girls' and women's psychological health: Gender and well-being across the lifespan*. New York: Oxford University Press, pp. 262-271.

Bryant, K. E. (2007). *The politics of pathology and the making of gender identity disorder*. Ann Arbor, MI: ProQuest Dissertations & Theses.

Bugler, M., McGeown, S. P., & St Clair-Thompson, H. (2015). Gender differences in adolescents' academic motivation and classroom behaviour. *Educational Psychology, 35*(5), 541-556.

Burda. P. C, Jr., Vaux, A., & Schill, T. (1984). Social support resources: Variation across sex and sex-role. *Personality and Social Psychology Bulletin, 10*, 119-126.

Buss, D. (1995). Psychological sex differences: Origins through sexual selection. *American Psychologist, 50*(3), 164-168.

Buss, D. M., & Schmitt, D. P. (1993). Sexual strategies theory: An evolutionary perspective on human mating. *Psychological Review, 100*, 204-232.

Buss, D. M., Shackelford, T. K., Kirkpatrick, L. A., Choe, J. C., Lim, H. K., Hasegawa, M., …, Bennett, K. (1999). Jealousy and the nature of beliefs about infidelity: Tests of competing hypotheses about sex differences in the United States, Korea, and Japan. *Personal Relationships, 6*(1), 125-150.

Bussey, K., & Bandura, A. (1999). Social cognitive theory of gender development and differentiation. *Psychological Review, 106*(4), 676-713.

Buunk, B. P., Angleitner, A., Oubaid, V., & Buss, D. M. (1996). Sex differences in jealousy in evolutionary and cultural perspective: Tests from the Netherlands, Germany, and the United States. *Psychological Science, 7*(6), 359-363.

Caldera, Y. M., Huston, A. C., & O'Brien, M. (1989). Social interactions and play patterns of parents and toddlers with feminine, masculine, and neutral toys. *Child Development, 60*(1), 70-76.

Caldera, Y. M., & Sciaraffa, M. A. (1998). Parent-toddler play with feminine toys: Are all dolls the same? *Sex Roles, 39*(9-10), 657-668.

Caldwell, M. A., & Peplau, L. A. (1982). Sex differences in same-sex friendship. *Sex Roles, 8*, 721-732.

Campbell, A., Shirley, L., Heywood, C., & Crook, C. (2000). Infants' visual preference for sex-congruent babies, children, toys and activities: A longitudinal study. *British Journal of Developmental Psychology, 18*(4), 479-498. https://doi.org/10.1348/026151000165814.

Carroll, J. (2007). Americans: 2.5 children is "ideal" family size. Gallup News, June 26. http://news.gallup.com/poll/27973/americans-25-children-ideal-family-size.aspx.

Carter, C. S. (2006). Sex differences in oxytocin and vasopressin: Implications for autism spectrum disorders? *Behavioural Brain Research, 176*(1), 170-186. doi:10.1016/j.bbr.2006.08.025.

Carter, D. B., & Levy, G. D. (1988). Cognitive aspects of early sex-role development: The influence of gender schemas on preschoolers' memories and preferences for sex-typed toys and activities. *Child Development, 59*(3), 782-792.

Centers for Disease Control and Prevention (2010). Use of contraception in the United States: 1982-2008 data from The National Survey of Family Growth (United States Department of Health and Human Services). DHHS Publication No. (PHS) 2010-1981.

Chabrol, H., Teissedre, F., Saint-Jean, M., Teisseyre, N., Sistac, C., Michaud, C., & Roge, B. (2002). Detection, prevention and treatment of postpartum depression: A controlled study of 859 patients. *L'Encéphale, 28*(1), 65-70.

Chin, J. L. (Ed.) (2010). *The psychology of prejudice and discrimination. A revised and condensed edition*. Westport, CT: Praeger.

Chiras, D. D. (2012). *Human biology* (7th ed.). Sudbury, MA: Jones & Bartlett Learning.

Chodorow, N. (1978). Mothering, object-relations, and the female oedipal configuration. *Feminist Studies, 4*(1), 137-158.

Chodorow, N. J. (1989). *Feminism and psychoanalytic theory.* New Haven, CT: Yale University Press.

Choma, B. L., & Hanoch, Y. (2017). Cognitive ability and authoritarianism: Understanding support for Trump and Clinton. *Personality and Individual Differences, 106,* 287-291.

Christopher, A. N., & Wojda, M. R. (2008). Social dominance orientation, right-wing authoritarianism, sexism, and prejudice toward women in the workforce. *Psychology of Women Quarterly, 32*(1), 65-73.

Cinamon, R. G., & Rich, Y. (2002). Gender differences in the importance of work and family roles: Implications for work-family conflict. *Sex Roles, 47*(11-12), 531-541.

Clark, T. C., Lucassen, M. F. G., Bullen, P., Denny, S. J., Fleming, T. M., Robinson, E. M., & Rossen, F. V. (2014). The health and well-being of transgender high school students: Results from the New Zealand Adolescent Health Survey (Youth'12). *Journal of Adolescent Health, 55*(1), 93-99. doi:10.1016/j.jadohealth. 2013.11.008.

Clearfield, M. W., & Nelson, N. M. (2006). Sex differences in mothers' speech and play behavior with 6-, 9-, and 14-month-old infants. *Sex Roles, 54*: 127-137. https://doi.org/10.1007/s11199-005-8874-1.

Coats, S., & Smith, E. R. (1999). Perceptions of gender subtypes: Sensitivity to recent exemplar activation and in-group/out-group differences. *Personality and Social Psychology Bulletin, 25*(4), 516-526. https://doi.org/10.1177/0146167299025004009.

Cohen, J. (1988). *Statistical power analysis for the behavioral sciences* (2nd ed.). Hillsdale, NJ: Erlbaum.

Cozby, P. (1973). Self-disclosure: A literature review. *Psychological Bulletin, 70,* 73-91.

D'Lima, G. M., Winsler, A., & Kitsantas, A. (2014). Ethnic and gender differences in first-year college students' goal orientation, self-efficacy, and extrinsic and intrinsic motivation. *The Journal of Educational Research, 107*(5), 341-356.

Dabbs, J. M. Jr., Carr, T. S., Frady, R. L., & Riad, J. K. (1995). Testosterone, crime, and misbehavior among 692 male prison inmates. *Personality and Individual Differences, 18*(5), 627-633. https://doi.org/10.1016/0191-8869(94)00177-T.

Dastagir, A. E. (2016). The imaginary predator in America's transgender bathroom war, *USA Today.* www.usa-today.com/story/news/nation/2016/04/28/transgender-bathroom-bills-discrimination/32594395/.

Davidson, M. R. (2012). *A nurse's guide to women's mental health.* New York: Springer.

DiFulvio, G. T. (2015). Experiencing violence and enacting resilience: The case story of a transgender youth. *Violence Against Women, 21*(11), 1385-1405.

Dinella, L. M., Claps, J. M., & Lewandowski, G. W. Jr. (2017). Princesses, princes, and superheroes: Children's gender cognitions and fictional characters. *The Journal of Genetic Psychology: Research and Theory on Human Development, 178*(5), 262-280.

Dinnerstein, D. (1976). *The mermaid and the minotaur: Sexual arrangements and human malaise.* New York: Harper & Row.

Dittmann, R. W., Kappes, M. E., & Kappes, M. H. (1992). Sexual behavior in adolescent and adult females with congenital adrenal hyperplasia. *Psychoneuroendocrinology, 17,* 153-170.

Drescher, A., & Schultheiss, O. C. (2016). Meta-analytic evidence for higher implicit affiliation and intimacy motivation scores in women, compared to men. *Journal of Research in Personality, 64,* 1-10.

Ducat, S. J. (2004). *The wimp factor: Gender gaps, holy wars, and the politics of anxious masculinity.* Boston: Beacon Press.

Duckitt, J., & Bizumic, B. (2013). Multidimensionality of right-wing authoritarian attitudes: Authoritarianism-conservatism-traditionalism. *Political Psychology, 34*(6), 841-862.

Eagly, A. H. (1987). *Sex differences in social behavior: A social role interpretation.* Hillsdale, NJ: Erlbaum.

Eagly, A. H., & Wood, W. (1999). The origins of sex differences in human behavior: Evolved dispositions versus social roles. *American Psychologist, 54,* 408-423.

Edelbrook, C., & Sugawara, A. I. (1978). Acquisition of sex-typed preferences in preschool-aged children. *Developmental Psychology, 14,* 614-623.

Eisenberg, N. H., Murray, E., & Hite, T. (1982). Children's reasoning regarding sex-typed toy choices. *Child Development, 53,* 81-86.

Fausto-Sterling, A. (1992). *Myths of gender* (rev. ed.). New York: Basic Books.

Feerick, M. M., & Haugaard, J. J. (1999). Long-term effects of witnessing marital violence for women: The contribution of childhood physical and sexual abuse. *Journal of Family Violence, 14,* 377-398.

Feingold, A. (1994). Gender differences in personality: A meta-analysis. *Psychological Bulletin, 116,* 429-456.

Fine, C., & Rush, E. (2018). 'Why does all the girls have to buy pink stuff?' The ethics and science of the gendered toy marketing debate. *Journal of Business Ethics, 149,* 769-784. https://doi.org/10.1007/s10551-016-3080-3.

148 *Theories of Gender*

Fisher, T. D., Moore, Z. T., & Pittenger, M.-J. (2012). Sex on the brain? An examination of frequency of sexual cognitions as a function of gender, erotophilia, and social desirability. *Journal of Sex Research, 49*(1), 69-77.

Fiske, S. T., & Taylor, S. E. (1991). *Social cognition* (2nd ed.). New York: McGraw-Hill.

Fraser, L., Karasic, D., Meyer, W., & Wylie, K. (2010). Recommendations for revision of the DSM diagnosis of gender identity disorder in adults. *International Journal of Transgenderism, 12*(2), 80-85.

Freud, S. (1925/1974). Some psychical consequences of the anatomical distinction between the sexes. In Strachey, J. (Ed. and Trans.), *The standard edition of the complete psychological works of Sigmund Freud* (Vol. 19, pp. 241-260). London: Hogarth Press and the Institute of Psychoanalysis.

Gal, D., & Wilkie, J. (2010). Real men don't eat quiche: Regulation of gender-expressive choices by men. *Social Psychological and Personality Science, 1*(4), 291-301.

Garcia-Falgueras, A., & Swaab D. F. (2010). Sexual hormones and the brain: An essential alliance for sexual identity and sexual orientation. *Endocrine Development, 17*, 22-35. doi:10.1159/000262525.

Gates, G. J. (2015). Marriage and family: LGBT individuals and same-sex couples. *Future of Children, 25*(2), 67-87.

Geary, D. C., Rumsey, M., Bow-Thomas, C. C., & Hoard, M. K. (1995). Sexual jealousy as a facilitative trait: Evidence from the pattern of sex differences in adults from China to the United States. *Ethology and Sociobiology, 16*, 355-383.

Gilmore, D. D. (1990). *Manhood in the making.* New Haven, CT: Yale University Press.

Goldin, C. (1994). *Understanding the gender gap: An economic history of American women.* New York: Oxford University Press.

Goldstein, I., Meston, C. M., Davis, S., & Traish, A. (2005). *Women's sexual function and dysfunction: Study, diagnosis and treatment.* New York: CRC Press.

Golombok, S., Rust, J., Zervoulis, K., Croudace, T., Golding, J., & Hines, M. (2008). Developmental trajectories of sex-typed behavior in boys and girls: A longitudinal general population study of children aged 2.5-8 years. *Child Development, 79*, 1583-1593. http://dx.doi.org/10.1111/j .1467-8624.2008.01207.x.

Golombok, S., Rust, J., Zervoulis, K., Golding, J., & Hines, M. (2012). Continuity in sex-typed behavior from preschool to adolescence: A longitudinal population study of boys and girls aged 3-13 years. *Archives of Sexual Behavior, 41*, 591-597.

Grant, J. M., Mottet, L., Tanis, J., Harrison, J., Herman, J., & Keisling, M. (2011). *Injustice at every turn: A report of the National Transgender Discrimination Survey.* Washington: National Center for Transgender Equality and National Gay and Lesbian Task Force.

Greenwald, A. G., & Banaji, M. R. (1995). Implicit social cognition: Attitudes, self-esteem, and stereotypes. *Psychological Review, 102*, 4-27. http://dx.doi.org/10.1037/0033-295X.102.1.4

Guinness World Records (2018). Most prolific mother ever. |www.guinnessworldrecords.com/world-records/most-prolific-mother-ever.

Halpern, H. P., & Perry-Jenkins, M. (2016). Parents' gender ideology and gendered behavior as predictors of children's gender-role attitudes: A longitudinal exploration. *Sex Roles, 74*(11-12), 527-542.

Harter, S. (1983). Developmental perspectives on the self-system. In M. Hetherington (Vol. Ed.) & P. H. Mussen (Series Ed.), *Handbook of child psychology: Vol. 4. Socialization, personality, and social development* (pp. 275-386). New York: Wiley.

Hedges, L. V., & Nowell, A. (1995). Sex differences in mental test scores, variability, and numbers of high-scoring individuals. *Science, 269*, 41-45.

Heise, L., & Garcia Moreno, C. (2002). Violence by intimate partners. In Krug, E. G., et al. (Eds.), *World report on violence and health.* Geneva: World Health Organization, pp. 87- 121.

Hock, H. (2007). The pill and the college attainment of American women and men. Working Paper. Florida State University. Cited in Sonfield, A., et al. (2013). *The social and economic benefits of women's ability to determine whether and when to have children.* New York: Guttmacher Institute.

Hoffman, R. M., Hattie, J. A., & Borders, L. D. (2005). Personal definitions of masculinity and femininity as an aspect of gender self-concept. *The Journal of Humanistic Counseling, Education and Development, 44*(1), 66-83. doi:10.1002/j.2164-490X.2005.tb00057.x.

Horney, K. (1939). *The neurotic personality of our time.* New York: Norton.

Hughes, S. S., & Hughes, B. (2001). Women in ancient civilizations. In Adas, M. (Ed.), *Agricultural and pastoral societies in ancient and classical history.* Philadelphia: Temple University Press, pp. 118-119.

Hust, S. J. T., & Brown, J. D. (2008). Gender, media use, and effects. In Calvert, S. L., & Wilson, B. J. (Eds.), *The handbook of children, media, and development.* Malden: Blackwell Publishing, pp. 98-120.

Hutton, A. (2016). Sexual violence against transgender college students. In Paludi, M. A. (Ed.), *Campus action against sexual assault: Needs, policies, procedures, and training programs*. Santa Barbara, CA: Praeger/ABC-CLIO, pp. 140-144.

Hyde, J. S. (2005). The gender similarities hypothesis. *American Psychologist, 60*, 581-592.

Hyde, J. S., & Oliver, M. B. (2000). Gender differences in sexuality: Results from meta-analysis. In Travis, C. B., & White, J. W. (Eds.), *Psychology of women, vol. 4, Sexuality, society, and feminism*. Washington, DC: American Psychological Association, pp. 57-77.

Idle, T., Wood, E., & Desmarais, S. (1993). Gender role socialization in toy play situations: Mothers and fathers with their sons and daughters. *Gender Roles, 28*, 679-691.

Ishii-Kuntz, M., & and Coltrane, S. (1992). Predicting the sharing of household labor: Are parenting and housework distinct? *Sociological Perspectives, 35*(4), 629-647.

Jacklin, C. N., DiPietro, J. A., & Maccoby, E. E. (1984). Sex-typing behavior and sex-typing pressure in child/parent interaction. *Archives of Sexual Behavior, 13*(5), 413-425.

Jakupcak, M., Lisak, D., & Roemer, L. (2002). The role of masculine ideology and masculine gender role stress in men's perpetration of relationship violence. *Psychology of Men & Masculinity, 3*, 97-106. doi:10.1037/1524-9220.3.2.97.

Johnson, J. G. (2003). Intergenerational transmission of partner violence: A 20-year prospective study. *Journal of Consulting and Clinical Psychology, 71*, 741-753.

Kane, E. W. (2009). Policing gender boundaries: Parental monitoring of preschool children's gender nonconformity. In Nelson, M. K., & Garey, A. I. (Eds.), *Who's watching? Daily practices of surveillance among contemporary families*. Nashville: Vanderbilt University Press, pp. 239-259.

Karniol, R. (2009). Israeli kindergarten children's gender constancy for others' counter-stereotypic toy play and appearance: The role of sibling gender and relative age. *Infant and Child Development, 18*(1), 73-94.

Katz, D., & Braly, K. (1933). Racial stereotypes of one hundred college students. *The Journal of Abnormal and Social Psychology, 28*(3), 280-290. https://doi.org/10.1037/h0074049.

Katz, P. A., & Boswell, S. (1986). Flexibility and traditionality in children's gender roles. *Genetic, Social, and General Psychology Monographs, 112*(1), 103-147.

Kelly, G. A. (2003). A brief introduction to personal construct theory. In Fransella, F. (Ed.), *International handbook of personal construct psychology*. Chichester, UK: John Wiley, pp. 3-20.

Kierski, W., & Blazina, C. (2009). The male fear of the feminine and its effects on counseling and psychotherapy. *Journal of Men's Studies, 17*, 155-172. doi:10.3149/jms.1702.155.

King, H. (1993). Once upon a text: Hysteria from Hippocrates. In Gilman, S., King, H., Porter, R., Rousseau, G.S., Showalter, E. (Eds.), *Hysteria beyond Freud*. Berkeley: University of California Press, pp. 3-90.

Kirkcaldy, B., & Cooper, Cary L. (1992). Work attitudes and leisure preferences: Sex differences. *Personality and Individual Differences, 13*(3), 329-334.

Kiselica, M. S., & Englar-Carlson, M. (2010). Identifying, affirming, and building upon male strengths: The positive psychology/positive masculinity model of psychotherapy with boys and men. *Psychotherapy Theory, Research, Practice, Training, 47*, 276-287. doi:10.1037/a0021159.

Knight, G. P., Guthrie, I. K., Page, M. C., & Fabes, R. A. (2002). Emotional arousal and gender differences in aggression: A meta-analysis. *Aggressive Behavior, 28*(5), 366-393.

Kohlberg, L. A. (1966). A cognitive-developmental analysis of children's sex-role concepts and attitudes In Maccoby, E. E. (Ed.), *The development of sex differences* (pp. 82-172). Stanford, CA: Stanford University Press.

Kohlberg, L., & Ullian, D. Z. (1974). Stages in the development of psychosexual concepts and attitudes. In Friedman, R. C., Richart, R. M., Vande Wiele, R. L., & Stern, L. O. (Eds.), *Sex differences in behavior*. Oxford: John Wiley & Sons.

Kunz, J. (2000). The intergenerational transmission of divorce: A nine generation study. *Journal of Divorce & Remarriage, 34*(1-2), 169-175.

Lachance-Grzela, M., & Bouchard, G. (2010). Why do women do the lion's share of housework? A decade of research, *Sex Roles, 63*(11-12), 767-780.

Laflamme, D., Pomerleau, A., & Malcuit, G. A. (2002). Comparison of fathers' and mothers' involvement in childcare and stimulation behaviors during free-play with their infants at 9 and 15 months. *Sex Roles, 47*, 507-518. https://doi.org/10.1023/A:1022069720776.

Laqueur, T. (1990). *Making sex: Body and gender from the Greeks to Freud*. Cambridge, MA: Harvard University Press.

Larson, P. C. (2012). Sexual identity and self-concept. *Journal of Homosexuality, 7*(1), 15. doi:10.1300/J082v07n01_03.

Lauer, J. E., Ilksoy, S. D., & Lourenco, S. F. (2018). Developmental stability in gender-typed preferences between infancy and preschool age. *Developmental Psychology*, 54(4), 613-620. https://doi.org/10.1037/dev0000468.

Lauer, J. E., Udelson, H. B., Jeon, S. O., & Lourenco, S. F. (2015). An early sex difference in the relation between mental rotation and object preference. *Frontiers in Psychology*, 6, 1-8.

Leinbach, M. D., & Fagot, B. I. (1993). Categorical habituation to male and female faces: Gender schematic processing in infancy. *Infant Behavior & Development*, 16(3), 317-332.

Lerner, G. (1986). *The creation of patriarchy. Women and history*. Oxford: Oxford University Press.

Levant, R. F. (1992). Toward the reconstruction of masculinity. *Journal of Family Psychology*, 5, 379-402. doi:10.1037/0893-3200.5.3-4.379.

Lips, H. M. (1991). *Women, men, and power*. Mountain View, CA: Mayfield Publishing Co.

Liu, J., Portnoy, J., & Raine, A. (2012). Association between a marker for prenatal testosterone exposure and externalizing behavior problems in children. *Development and Psychopathology*, 24(3), 771-782. doi:10.1017/S0954579412000363.

Los Angeles Times (2001). 7 states still classify cohabitation as illegal - Laws: Couples living together outside marriage can be cited for "lewd, lascivious" conduct and rejected for certain jobs, by Robin Fields, August 20. http://articles.latimes.com/2001/aug/20/news/mn-36308.

MacDonald, K., & Parke, R. D. (1986). Parent-child physical play: The effects of sex and age of children and parents. *Sex Roles*, 15, 367-378.

Markus, H. (1977). Self-schemata and processing information about the self. *Journal of Personality and Social Psychology*, 35(2), 63-78.

Martin, C. L., & Halverson, C. F. (1981). A schematic processing model of sex typing and stereotyping in children. *Child Development*, 52(4), 1119-1134.

Martin, C. L., Ruble, D., & Szkrybalo, J. (2002). Cognitive theories of early gender development. *Psychological Bulletin*, 128(6), 903-933.

Mathers, L. A. B. (2017). Bathrooms, boundaries, and emotional burdens: Cisgendering interactions through the interpretation of transgender experience. *Symbolic Interaction*, April 3.

Mathes, E. W. (2005). Men's desire for children carrying their genes and sexual jealousy: A test of paternity uncertainty as an explanation of male sexual jealousy. *Psychological Reports*, 96(3), 791-798.

McCammon, H. J., Campbell, K. E., Granberg, E. M., & Mowery, C. (2001). How movements win: Gendered opportunity structures and U.S. women's suffrage movements, 1866 to 1919. *American Sociological Review*, 66(1), 49-70.

Meston, C. M., & Frohlich, P. F. (2000). The neurobiology of sexual function. *Archives of General Psychiatry*, 57(11), 1012-1030.

Meyer, D. (2007). Selective serotonin reuptake inhibitors and their effects on relationship satisfaction. *The Family Journal*, 15(4), 392-397.

Meyer-Bahlburg, H. F. L., Dolezal, C., Baker, S. W., & New, M. I. (2008). Sexual orientation in women with classical or non-classical congenital adrenal hyperplasia as a function of degree of prenatal androgen excess. *Archives of Sexual Behavior*, 37, 85-99.

Miller, C. L. (1983). Developmental changes in male/female voice classification by infants. *Infant Behavior and Development*, 6(2-3), 313-330.

Nargund, G. (2009). Declining birth rate in developed countries: A radical policy re-think is required. *Facts, Views and Vision in ObGyn*, 1(3), 191-193.

National Geographic News (2003). Genghis Khan a prolific lover, DNA data implies. Hillary Mayell, February 14. https://news.nationalgeographic.com/news/2003/02/0214_030214_genghis.html.

Newman, L. (2002). Sex, gender and culture: Issues in the definition, assessment and treatment of gender identity disorder. *Clinical Child Psychology and Psychiatry*, 7(3), 352-359. doi:10.1177/1359104502007003004.

Nosowitz, D. (2015). Why thousands of new animal species are still discovered each year. *Atlas Obscura*, June 1. www.atlasobscura.com/articles/new-animal-species. Retrieved January 5, 2018.

O'Neil, J. M. (2008). Summarizing 25 years of research on men's gender role conflict using the Gender Role Conflict Scale: New research paradigms and clinical implications. *The Counseling Psychologist*, 36(3), 358-445.

O'Neil, J. M., Helm, B., Gable, R., David, L., & Wrightsman, L. (1986). Gender Role Conflict Scale (GRCS): College men's fears of femininity. *Sex Roles*, 14, 335-350.

Osborne, D., Milojev, P., & Sibley, C. G. (2017). Authoritarianism and national identity: Examining the longitudinal effects of SDO and RWA on nationalism and patriotism. *Personality and Social Psychology Bulletin*, 43(8), 1086-1099.

Park, M. (2017). Timeline: A look at the Catholic Church's sex abuse scandals. CNN. www.cnn.com/2017/06/29/world/timeline-catholic-church-sexual-abuse-scandals/index.html.

Peitzmeier, S. M., Yasin, F., Stephenson, R., Wirtz, A. L., Delegchoimbol, A., Dorjgotov, M., & Baral, S. (2015). Sexual violence against men who have sex with men and transgender women in Mongolia: A mixed-methods study of scope and consequences. *PLoS ONE, 10*(10).

Person, E. S., & Ovesey, L. (1983). Psychoanalytic theories of gender identity. *Journal of the American Academy of Psychoanalysis and Dynamic Psychiatry, 11*(2), 203-226.

Petty, R. E., Cacioppo, J. T., Strathman, A. J., & Priester, J. R. (2005). To think or not to think: Exploring two routes to persuasion. In Brock, T. C., & Green, M. C. (Eds.), *Persuasion: Psychological insights and perspectives* (2nd ed.). Thousand Oaks, CA: Sage, pp. 81-116.

Pew Research Center (2013). Modern parenthood, social & demographic trends. March 4. www.pewsocial-trends.org/2013/03/14/modern-parenthood-roles-of-moms-and-dads-converge-as-they-balance-work-and-family/. Retrieved January 4, 2018.

Pew Research Center (2014). Growing number of dads home with the kids: Statistics on stay-at-home dads. National At-Home Dad Network. *Social & Demographic Trends*, June 5. www.pewsocialtrends.org/2014/06/05/growing-number-of-dads-home-with-the-kids/. Retrieved May 16, 2016.

Pew Research Center (2015). The American family today. *Social & Demographic Trends*, December 17. www.pewsocialtrends.org/2015/12/17/1-the-american-family-today/. Retrieved January 4, 2018.

Pew Research Center (2017). Number of women leaders around the world has grown, but they're still a small group, by Abigail Geiger and Lauren Kent, March 8. www.pewresearch.org/fact-tank/2017/03/08/women-leaders-around-the-world/. Retrieved January 8, 2018.

Pietrzak, R. H., Laird, J. D., & Stevens, D. A. (2002). Sex differences in human jealousy: A coordinated study of forced-choice, continuous rating-scale, and physiological responses on the same subjects. *Evolution and Human Behavior, 23*(2), 83-94.

Pleck, J. H. (1981). *The myth of masculinity*. Cambridge, MA: MIT Press.

Pleck, J. H. (1995). The gender role strain paradigm: An update. In Levant, R. F., & Pollack, W. S. (Eds.), *A new psychology of men*. New York: Basic Books, pp. 11-32.

Pomerleau, A., Bolduc, D., Malcuit, G., & Cossette, L. (1990). Pink or blue: Environmental gender stereotypes in the first two years of life. *Sex Roles, 22*(5-6), 359-367. https://doi.org/10.1007/BF0028833.

Popper, K. (1945). *The open society and its enemies, vol.1, The spell of Plato* (London: Routledge).

Popper, K. (1963). *Conjectures and refutations: The growth of scientific knowledge.* London: Routledge and Kegan Paul, pp. 33-39.

Power, T. G., & Parke, R. D. (1983). Patterns of mother and father play with their 8-month-old infant: A multiple analyses approach. *Infant Behavior and Development, 6*, 453-459.

Powlishta, K. K. (1990). Salience of group membership: The case of gender. *Dissertation Abstracts International, 50*(12-B, Pt. 1), 5903.

Powlishta, K. K., Serbin, L. A., & Moller, L. C. (1993). The stability of individual differences in gender typing: Implications for understanding gender segregation. *Sex Roles, 29*, 723-737. https://doi.org/10.1007/BF00289214.

Pratto, F. (1996). Sexual politics: The gender gap in the bedroom, the cupboard, and the cabinet. In Buss, D. M., & Malamuth, N. M. (Eds.), *Sex, power, and conflict: Evolutionary and feminist perspectives* (pp. 179-230). New York: Oxford University Press.

Pratto, F., & Walker, A. (2004). The bases of gendered power. In Eagly, A. H., Beall, A. E., & Sternberg, R. J. (Eds.), *The psychology of gender*. New York: Guilford Press, pp. 242-268.

Pruden, H., & Edmo, S. (2016). Two-spirit people: Sex, gender and sexuality in historic and contemporary Native America. National Congress of American Indians Policy Research Center.

Radkiewicz, P. (2016). Does authoritarianism imply ethnocentric national attitudes: A revised look at the "authoritarian triad" and right-wing ideology. *European Journal of Social Psychology, 46*(2), 224-236.

Riggio, H. R., & Desrochers, S. J. (2006). Maternal employment: Relations with young adults' work and family expectations and self-efficacy. *American Behavioral Scientist, 49*(10), 1328-1353.

Rodriguez, A., Agardh, A., & Asamoah, B. O. (2017). Self-reported discrimination in health-care settings based on recognizability as transgender: A cross-sectional study among transgender US citizens. *Archives of Sexual Behavior, 47*(4), 973-985.

Rodriguez-Bailon, R., Bratanova, B., Willis, G. B., Lopez-Rodriguez, L., Sturrock, A., & Loughnan, S. (2017). Social class and ideologies of inequality: How they uphold unequal societies. *Journal of Social Issues, 73*(1), 99-116.

Rosaldo, M. (1974). Theoretical overview. In Rosaldo, M. Z., & Lamphere, L. (Eds.), *Woman, culture, and society* (pp. 17-43). Stanford, CA: Stanford University Press.

Rutledge, D. (2017). I'm sorry, but there will never be more than 2 genders. www.theodysseyonline.com/there-are-only-two-genders. Retrieved June 6, 2017.

152 *Theories of Gender*

Sanday, P. (1981). The socio-cultural context of rape: A cross-cultural study. *Journal of Social Issues, 37*, 5-27.

Sandnabba, N. K., Lagerspetz K. M., & Jensen E. (1994). Effects of testosterone exposure and fighting experience on the aggressive behavior of female and male mice selectively bred for intermale aggression. *Hormones and Behavior, 28*(3), 219-231.

Scheele, D., Striepens, N., Güntürkün, O., Deutschländer, S., Maier, W., Kendrick, K. M., & Hurlemann, R. (2012). Oxytocin modulates social distance between males and females. *The Journal of Neuroscience, 32*(46), 16074-16079.

Schmitt, B. H., & Millard, R. T. (1988). Construct validity of the Bem Sex Role Inventory (BSRI): Does the BSRI distinguish between gender-schematic and gender-aschematic individuals? *Sex Roles, 19*(9-10), 581-588.

Sedgwick, J. L. (2006). Criminal victimization in the United States, 2005 statistical tables: National Crime Victimization Survey. Washington, DC, U.S. Department of Justice, Bureau of Justice Statistics, NCJ 215244.

Serbin, L. A., Powlishta, K. K., & Gulko, J. (1993). The development of sex typing in middle childhood. *Monographs of the Society for Research in Child Development, 58*(2)[232], v-74.

Sidanius, J., Levin, S., & Pratto, F. (1996). Consensual social dominance orientation and its correlates within the hierarchical structure of American society. *International Journal of Intercultural Relations, 20*(3-4), 385-408.

Signorella, M. L., Bigler, R. S., & Liben, L. S. (1993). Developmental differences in children's gender schemata about others: A metaanalytic review. *Developmental Review, 13*, 147-183.

Singer, D. G., & Singer, J. L. (Eds.) (2001). *Handbook of children and the media*. Thousand Oaks, CA: Sage.

Slaby, R. G., & Frey, K. S. (1975). Development of gender constancy and selective attention to same-sex models. *Child Development, 46*(4), 849-856.

Smith, N. D. (1983). Plato and Aristotle on the nature of women. *Journal of the History of Philosophy, 21*(4), 467-478. doi:10.1353/hph.1983.0090.

Soller, K. (2014). The birth control pill advanced women's economic freedom. *Bloomberg Businessweek*, December 4.www.businessweek.com/articles/2014-12-04/birth-control-pill-advanced-womens-economic-freedom.

Southren, A. L, Gordon, G. G, Tochimoto, S., Pinzon, G., Lane, D. R., & Stypulkowski, W. (1967). Mean plasma concentration, metabolic clearance and basal plasma production rates of testosterone in normal young men and women using a constant infusion procedure: Effect of time of day and plasma concentration on the metabolic clearance rate of testosterone. *The Journal of Clinical Endocrinology and Metabolism, 27*(5), 686-694. doi:10.1210/jcem-27-5-686.

Spengler, F. B., Scheele, D., Marsh, N., Kofferath, C., Flach, A., Schwarz, S., Stoffel-Wagner, B., Maier, W., & Hurlemann, R. (2017). Oxytocin facilitates reciprocity in social communication. *Social Cognitive and Affective Neuroscience, 12*(8), 1325-1333.

Steinberg, M., & Diekman, A. B. (2016). The double-edged sword of stereotypes of men. In Wong, Y. J., & Wester, S. R. (Eds.), *APA handbook of men and masculinities*. Washington, DC: American Psychological Association, pp. 433-456.

Swaab, D. F., & Garcia-Falgueras, A. (2009). Sexual differentiation of the human brain in relation to gender identity and sexual orientation. *Functional Neurology, 24*(1), 17-28.

Swaab, D. F., Chung, W. C. J., Kruijver, F. P. M., Hofman, M. A., & Ishunina, T. A. (2001). Structural and functional sex differences in the human hypothalamus. *Hormones and Behavior, 40*(2), 93-98.

Sweeny, J. (2014). Undead statutes: The rise, fall and continuing uses of adultery and fornication criminal laws. *Loyola University Chicago Law Journal, 46*, 127-173. www.luc.edu/media/lucedu/law/students/publications/llj/pdfs/vol46/Sweeny.

Taylor, S. E., & Falcone, H. (1982). Cognitive bases of stereotyping: The relationship between categorization and prejudice. *Personality and Social Psychology Bulletin, 8*, 426-432.

Terburg, D., Aarts, H., & van Honk, J. (2012). Testosterone affects gaze aversion from angry faces outside of conscious awareness. *Psychological Science, 23*(5), 459-463.

Thomas, J. R., & French, K. E. (1985). Gender differences across age in motor performance: A meta-analysis. *Psychological Bulletin, 98*, 260-282.

Thompson, S. K. (1975). Gender labels and early sex-role development. *Child Development 46*, 339-347.

Time Magazine (2011). Complete List - Top Female Leaders Around the World. http://content.time.com/time/specials/packages/completelist/0,29569,2005455,00.html.

Todd, B. K., Fischer, R. A., Di Costa, S., Roestorf, A., Harbour, K., Hardiman, P., & Barry, J. A. (2017). Sex differences in children's toy preferences: A systematic review, meta-regression, and meta-analysis. *Infant and Child Development*, November 22.

Tomlinson, C., Macintyre, H., Dorrian, C. A., Ahmed, S. F., & Wallace, A. M. (2004). Testosterone measurements in early infancy. *Archives of Disease in Childhood - Fetal and Neonatal Edition, 89*, F558-F559.

Torjesen, P. A., & Sandnes, L. (2004). Serum testosterone in women as measured by an automated immuno-assay and a RIA. *Clinical Chemistry, 50*(3), 678; author reply 678-679. doi:10.1373/clinchem.2003.027565.

Trivers, R. (1972). Parental investment and sexual selection. In Campbell, B. (Ed.), *Sexual selection and the descent of man*. Chicago: Aldine-Atherton, pp. 136-179.

Turner, P. J., Gervai, J., & Hinde, R. A. (1993). Gender-typing in young children: Preferences, behavior and cultural differences. *British Journal of Developmental Psychology, 11*, 323-342.

U.N. Women (2011). Progress of the world's women: In pursuit of justice. www.unwomen.org/en/digital-library/publications/2011/7/progress-of-the-world-s-women-in-pursuit-of-justice.

United Nations Development Programme (2013). 2013 Human Development report. http://hdr.undp.org/en/2013-report.

United States Agency for International Development (2010). The DHS program: Demographic and Health Surveys. ww.dhsprogram.com/pubs/pdf/CR25/CR25.

United States Department of Justice (1997). An analysis of data on rape and sexual assault sex offenses and offenders. Office of Justice Programs. https://bjs.gov/content/pub/pdf/SOO.

United States Department of Labor (2014). Women's Bureau, Women and Families. .www.dol.gov/wb/stats/mother_families.htm. Retrieved January 4, 2018.

United States Department of Labor (2017). Women's Bureau, Data and Statistics. www.dol.gov/wb/stats/stats_data.htm. Retrieved January 4, 2018.

Vandello, J. A., & Bosson, J. K. (2013). Hard won and easily lost: A review and synthesis of theory and research on precarious manhood. *Psychology of Men & Masculinity, 14*(2), 101-113.

Vandello, J. A., Bosson, J. K., Cohen, D., Burnaford, R. M., & Weaver, J. R. (2008). Precarious manhood. *Journal of Personality and Social Psychology, 95*(6), 1325-1339.

Vonk, R., & Ashmore, R. D. (2003). Thinking about gender types: Cognitive organization of female and male types. *British Journal of Social Psychology, 42*(2), 257-280.

Wada, M. (2000). Undergraduates' feelings and behaviors in and after the dissolution of romantic relation-ships: An examination of sex differences and the intimacy of romantic relationships. *Japanese Journal of Experimental Social Psychology, 40*(1), 38-49.

Whiten, A., Goodall, J., McGrew, W. C., Nishida, T. A., Reynolds, V., Sugiyama, Y., Tutin, C. E. G., Wrangham, R. W., & Boesch, C. (1999). Cultures in chimpanzees. *Nature, 399*, 682-685.

Williams, J. E., & Best, D. L. (1990). *Cross-cultural research and methodology series, Vol. 13. Sex and psy-che: Gender and self viewed cross-culturally.* Newbury Park, CA: Sage Publications.

Wood, W., & Eagly, A. H. (2002). A cross-cultural analysis of the behavior of women and men: Implications for the origins of sex differences. *Psychological Bulletin, 128*, 699-727.

World Economic Forum (2017). The Global Gender Gap Report 2017. https://www.weforum.org/reports/the-global-gender-gap-report-2017. Retrieved January 8, 2018.

World Health Organization (2008). *Education material for teachers of midwifery: Midwifery education mod-ules* (2nd ed.). Geneva.

World Health Organization (2010). Maternal deaths worldwide drop by third. Report, September 15. Geneva/New York.

World Health Organization (2012). Understanding and addressing violence against women: Intimate partner vio-lence. https://apps.who.int/iris/bitstream/handle/10665/77432/WHO_RHR_12.36_eng.pdf?sequence=1.

World Health Organization (2017). Violence against women: Intimate partner and sexual violence against women. www.who.int/mediacentre/factsheets/fs239/en/. Retrieved January 6, 2018.

Yang, H. P., Wang, L., Han, L., & Wang, S. C. (2013). Nonsocial functions of hypothalamic oxytocin. *ISRN Neuroscience, 179272*. doi:10.1155/2013/179272.

Yeung, A. S., Craven, R. G., & Kaur, G. (2012). Gender differences in achievement motivation: Grade and cultural considerations. In McGeown, S. P. (Ed.), *Psychology of gender differences*. Hauppauge, NY: Nova Science Publishers, pp. 25-46.

Zak, P. J., Kurzban, R., & Matzner, W. T. (2005). Oxytocin is associated with human trustworthiness. *Hormones and Behavior, 48*, 522-527. http:// dx.doi.org/10.1016/j.yhbeh.2005.07.009.

Zerjal, T., Xue, Y., Bertorelle, G., et al. (2003). The genetic legacy of the Mongols. *American Journal of Human Genetics, 72*, 717-721. doi:10.1086/367774.

Zhou, J.-N., Hofman, M. A., Gooren, L. J. G., & Swaab, D. F. (1997). A sex difference in the human brain and its relation to transsexuality. *International Journal of Transgenderism, 1*(1).

Zucker, K. J., Wilson-Smith, D. N., Kurita, J. A., & Stern, A. (1995). Children's appraisals of sex-typed behavior in their peers. *Sex Roles, 33*(11-12), 703-725.

7 Global, Historical Sexism

Sexism Is Everywhere   161
Biological Differences: The Underpinnings of Sexism   162
   Physical Strength and Masculinity   162
   Reproductive Roles and Oppression   166
A Brief History of Sexism   168
Types of Sexism   171
How the Media Is Sexist   175
Heterosexism: Heterosexuality as Normative   177
Equality Around the World Today   179

INEQUALITIES AND INJUSTICES

Why Don't We Care about or Believe Women?

Global, Historical Sexism 155

Why don't we believe women when they say they were harassed, assaulted, or raped? Why don't we care? The current President of the United States, Donald Trump, has been accused by 19 women of sexual harassment, assault, or rape (Ford, 2017). Trump is heard on audiotape saying that he can "grab women by the pussy" (The New York Times, 2016). This audiotape was well publicized in October 2016, a month before the Presidential election. There are numerous other examples before, during, and after the election of Trump's hostile comments to women concerning their appearance, their gender, including calling women "slobs" and "dogs," and calling Hillary Clinton using the bathroom "disgusting" (O'Neil,

2017). He infamously made a comment about Fox News' Megyn Kelly having "blood coming out of her wherever" when he was unhappy with her questioning during a Presidential debate (Strum & Fears, 2015), again derogating women because they are female (see Chapter 8, "Inequalities and Injustices"). The President of the United States appears on video and audiotape attacking women verbally, and 19 women accuse him, including under oath, of sexual harassment or assault. And millions and millions of Americans still voted for him, regardless of his obviously heinous treatment of multiple women. Americans who voted for Trump are apparently willing to completely overlook all of this. They don't care how Trump talks about or treats women. Roy Moore, a former judge who was accused of child molestation and sexual assault, received millions of dollars in funding and huge popular support in his campaign for the United States Senate, including after the accusations were well publicized (Graham, 2017; Keneally & Parkinson, 2017; Savransky, 2017). Americans apparently do not care how women are treated. It is apparently acceptable to sexually harass and assault girls and women; people will still give you money and vote for you (although thankfully Roy Moore did lose, but only by a very slim margin; Alabama Secretary of State, 2017).

Examples of ignoring women or blaming women for their own assault, or simply not caring about the fate of women, abound, because the world is sexist. In a fortress in Kufstein, Austria, I read the history of a particular prisoner who was imprisoned in the fortress because he murdered his wife and several children with an axe. The story continued, blaming the savage murders on the man's melancholy over his lost love from an illicit affair. The story concludes that clearly, his young female lover, the seductress, the entire thing is her fault! If only she hadn't been a woman, so sexy! In May 2018, an 18-year-old man murdered two teachers and eight high school students in Santa Fe, Texas. Soon after, headlines appeared about how he committed the crimes because a girl at the school (the person he murdered first in his rampage) spurned his love and rejected him (Hennessy-Fiske, Pearce, & Jarvie, 2018). If only she hadn't broken his heart and hurt his ego, none of this would have happened. So just go out with him already, let's avoid all this murder, just give men their way. The message is clearly that men are not responsible for their bad behavior; women seduce, trick, deceive, and humiliate men, and as such men's physical violence is understandable, even acceptable (Dijkstra, 1996). The cases of Bill Cosby, Matt Lauer, and Harvey Weinstein are additional modern examples of multiple women accusing powerful men of sexual harassment, assault, and rape, with many people apparently being aware of such behavior, and it is covered up and ignored, so that men are never punished and additional women are victimized. This pattern of behavior by men against women is not uncommon, it is too frequent, and has been occurring since basically the dawn of time (Sell, Hone, & Pound, 2012). I know, this sounds extreme, an exaggeration. But it is not. The existence of these cases right now, in the 21st-century technologically evolved wealthy Western world, is proof of the utter indifference of a vast majority of people to the words and experiences of women.

CRITICAL THINKING

Is Everyone Sexist? Implicit Attitudes and Unconscious Bias

I am a sexist. I admit it. A sexist is a person who endorses sexist ideology (negative ideas about women) and engages in behaviors that subordinate individuals because of their sex. Now, men can be victims of sexism too, that's true. If a man doesn't get a job teaching kindergarten because of the hiring committee's beliefs about men not being "naturally" suited to caring for children, that is sexism. However, in our world, sexism toward women is so ingrained, so inculcated into cultures all over the world, that it has become implicit. Implicit ideas and processes are those that are so well-practiced or so commonly used that they have become automatic; that is, cognitive ideas and processes that are so frequently used they occur unintentionally and sometimes without conscious awareness (Greenwald & Banaji, 1995). Psychologically, implicit beliefs and attitudes are cognitive structures and processes that are so frequently and routinely used that they are automatically activated in response to particular stimuli. Walking and other well-learned motor behaviors are also implicit; they become so automatic that we don't have to consciously think about doing them, we just do them. It would be very difficult to unlearn how to walk. It is also difficult to unlearn very strong cognitive associations we have with ideas about women and men. Implicit thoughts and attitudes (evaluative beliefs) are automatically activated, in contrast to explicit thoughts and attitudes, which are fully conscious and consciously formulated. Explicit and implicit attitudes commonly do not match (Nosek et al., 2007), especially with regard to stereotypes about social groups. People with negative attitudes toward a social group are not likely to explicitly report those attitudes because of social desirability concerns (Green et al., 2007; Plant & Devine, 1998). For behavior toward social groups, implicit attitudes are actually more predictive of discriminatory behavior than explicit attitudes, again because people are less likely to reveal explicitly racist or sexist attitudes in self-report measures (Bargh & Chartrand, 1999).

As an example, I take a train daily to my campus, and many other campus people take the train as well. I was having a chat one day with a campus police officer, who said that his wife worked in a large hospital east of Los Angeles. In response, my automatic thoughts took over and I said, "Oh, she's a nurse." While saying it, I knew it was automatic, unthinking sexism, sometimes called unconscious bias (Moule, 2009). The female nurse prototype is so ingrained, so well-learned and overly used, it immediately came into my consciousness in response to the idea of a woman working in a hospital. The officer responded, "No, she's an orthopedic surgeon." Because societies have so effectively taught all of us what women are like and what men are like (stereotypes; see Chapter 5), all of us are indeed sexist to some degree because we possess and use ideas about women that are based on legitimizing myths, which reinforce ideas about women's inferiority relative to men. The challenge for each of us is to consciously recognize our overreliance and use of socially supplied stereotypes, to feel negatively about using such sexist ideas, and to consciously attempt every day to not use them (Devine, Monteith, Zuwerink, & Elliot, 1991). Overcoming prejudice against women that is based on negative stereotypes requires a conscious effort to disagree with legitimizing myths and to evaluate each individual person as just that, an individual person, not as a representation of negative stereotypical qualities.

While they are highly **accessible** and likely to be used in an automatic manner, implicit attitudes are not easy to observe or measure because they are not necessarily conscious (although people are often aware that they have implicit attitudes; Hahn, Judd, Hirsh, Holen, & Blair, 2014). Explicit attitudes are easily accessed and measured; you simply ask people what they think about X, in an open-ended format (e.g., *"What do you think about women?"*) or using carefully written questions to which participants give a response (e.g., *"Some people are just superior to others,"* 1 = *strongly disagree*, 5 = *strongly agree*). Researchers have developed a measure of various kinds of implicit attitudes called the **Implicit Association Test** (**IAT**; Greenwald, McGhee, & Schwartz, 1998). The IAT is based on the idea that people respond more quickly when two things are closely associated with each other. For example, when I say "fruit," you most likely think "apple" or "orange" or "banana." You are much more likely to quickly think one of those words than the word "China" or "gasoline" or "sunset" in response to the word "fruit." The score on the IAT is based on reaction time, how quickly participants respond to particular associations. Participants respond more quickly to associations that are automatic (implicit), and more slowly to associations that are not automatic (not implicit).

The typical task involves something like this. Participants sit in front of a computer or tablet screen and respond to pictures that appear on the screen using only two buttons. The task usually involves hitting one button (Button A) to represent certain categories (e.g., positive words, pictures of men) and a different button (Button B) to represent other or opposite categories (e.g., negative words, pictures of women). Positive words are words like *happy, enjoy, flower, beautiful*; negative words are *anger, suffer, death, ugly*. So in Condition 1, when a positive word or a man appears, participants hit the same button (A); when a negative word or a woman appears, participants hit the other button (B). In Condition 2, the categories are remixed, and participants hit A for positive words and pictures of women, and B for negative words and pictures of men. So in which condition do you think participants on average respond more quickly? When positive stimuli are associated with men and negative stimuli with women, or the opposite, when positive stimuli are associated with women, and negative stimuli with men? Research indicates that implicit attitudes toward women are more negative, with people responding more rapidly to the IAT when positive stimuli are associated with men, not with women (Nier & Gaertner, 2012). Such negative implicit attitudes toward women are predictive of negative discriminatory behavior toward women (Greenwald, Poehlman, Uhlmann, & Banaji, 2009). Researchers have used IAT measures of implicit attitudes toward homosexual people (Breen & Karpinski, 2013) and transgender people (Wang-Jones et al., 2017). While implicit attitudes may not be conscious, they can be made so by careful self-reflection and, with conscious effort, intentionally not used in social behavior (Monteith, 1993).

Global, Historical Sexism 159

BONUS BOX

#MeToo and #NotAllMen

The #MeToo movement began in 2017, and was started by women to express the wide-spread, rather common experience of sexual abuse and assault of girls and women in the United States and around the world. Statistics indicate that in the United States, one in three women has experienced some kind of sexual assault at some point in their lives (Smith et al., 2012); one in five women in the U.S. is raped (Black et al., 2011). Sexual assault is defined by the law as "any nonconsensual sexual act proscribed by Federal, tribal, or State law, including when the victim lacks capacity to consent" (United States Department of Justice, 2018); rape is defined as "the penetration, no matter how slight, of the vagina or anus with any body part or object, or oral penetration by a sex organ of another person, without the consent of the victim" (United States Department of Justice, 2017). Sexual harassment in the workplace is also rather commonplace for women, with 60% of women reporting being sexually harassed (Quinnipiac University, 2017). Nearly 80% of women report being verbally sexually harassed (Stop Street Harassment, 2018). The #MeToo movement is about the shared experience of being the smaller half of the human race that is under real threat every day from the other half of the human race. Men have greater size and strength than women and they have used that strength to physically control, dominate, threaten, and abuse women. Yes, men are victims of assault and abuse; one in six boys reports being the victim of sexual assault (Finkelhor, Hotaling, Lewis, & Smith, 1990), one in 71 men is raped (Black et al., 2011). Those perpetrators are also overwhelmingly likely to be men, not women (National Sexual Violence Resource Center, 2011). Of reported rapes (many rapes and sexual assaults are not reported to law enforcement; National Criminal Justice Reference Service, 2007), the vast majority, over 95%, of perpetrators are male (Uniform Crime Report, 2009). Men are perpetrators of rape so commonly that it is actually difficult to find statistics on rape perpetrator sex, because by default it is male. We address chronic, global violence toward women more closely in Chapter 11 (Aggression).

Women began using the #MeToo hashtag to share their experiences of being girls and women. It didn't take too long for the #NotAllMen hashtag to come into play. #NotAllMen is an expression of frustration from men who do not engage in sexual assault of women, a defense of themselves and a negative response to women's outcry about physical and sexual mistreatment of women by men. It is very clear that most men are not violent in any way toward women; good men abound and the hashtag is accurate, it is not all men. However, #MeToo doesn't say anything about all men; it's about women's shared experiences as targets, as victims, as survivors. It is important for women to speak out and make these discussions mainstream, out in the open, dragged into the sunlight instead of hidden in darkness. #NotAllMen (similar to "All Lives Matter") is an attempt to derail the conversation, to stop the subordinate group from talking, to control the situation. It is an attempt to edit, censor, and silence women. So regarding #MeToo, oppressors, please stop. Survivors and fighters, keep talking.

There are abundant cases of men, especially the wealthy and powerful, able to get away with assaulting women over and over again, engaging in illegal and immoral behaviors with many witnesses and bystanders aware of what is happening and enabling and ignoring it. Reporting sexual harassment is stressful for women and can cause health problems (Bergman, Lanhout, Palmieri, Cortina, & Fitzgerald, 2002; Hesson-McInnis & Fitzgerald, 1997). Legal decisions over centuries have not been kind to women who stand up and report their assaults and rapes; rape victims are still reluctant to come forward because they are not likely to be believed and are often blamed for their own rape (Felson & Palmore, 2018). The case of Brock Turner, the Stanford University swimming star who raped an unconscious woman behind a dumpster and was sentenced to six months in jail for it (he was released early after three months), is proof of the courts favoring perpetrators over victims. The President of the United States mocked the #MeToo movement in July 2018, saying that people have to do things "gently" now because of it (Merica, 2018), effectively mocking the fact that girls and women have been afraid to protest against their own victimization and have been shamed into silence for centuries. So yes, it is true that not all men use violence against or sexually harass women. It is also true that those who do engage in those behaviors are apparently likely to get away with it and to mock the victimization of girls and women. It is time for men to face the reality that it is indeed men who are much more likely to victimize women and children. Standing up and telling the truth is not a crime and men need to stop protesting when women speak the truth. The novelist Margaret Atwood famously said, *"Men are afraid that women will laugh at them. Women are afraid that men will kill them."* Indeed. Responsible, compassionate, egalitarian society must stop turning its face from men's victimization of girls and women. That's when we get to #TimesUp!

LEARN MORE

Sexist Science

If anything is run by human beings, it is likely to be sexist. Nearly every powerful social institution everywhere around the world and across time has been designed, created, and managed by men instead of women. Science is no exception. Science is actually a method; it is a set of rules for observing and discovering truth about the natural world. The methods of science are designed to be objective and unbiased. But because the methods of science are used by people, sexism comes into play. Scientists across the history of the world, including the United States, tend to be men (Jagsi et al., 2006; National Academy of Sciences, 2006; Xie & Shauman, 2003). Of all 923 Nobel Laureates (up to 2017), only 18 women have ever won a Nobel Prize in Science (Nobelprize.org, 2018). For centuries, science largely ignored women as objects of study. Other than sexual and reproductive functions and ideas about women as **hysterical** (suffering from extreme and irrational emotionality; derived from the Latin word for uterus), medical science largely ignored women (Green, 2008). Scholars within other disciplines are no different, studying and writing about and thinking about men to the exclusion of women. Within psychology, research participants up until the 1970s were nearly exclusively Euro-American privileged men; psychological science virtually ignored women and other ethnic groups for an entire century (Mays, 1988). Finally in the 1970s, psychologists decided that women, half the human race, might be of interest to scholarly research and might in fact be different from men and worthy of study. This bias against even caring about studying women, with a complete disregard by learned people of the experience of half of the human race, is proof of the implicit and **hostile sexism** our world has toward women in general. Women were so unimportant, so not of interest, to male-dominated science, that they weren't even considered as objects of study in psychology until the late 20th century, 100 years since the advent of psychological science. "Women's" issues and "women's" studies are still labeled as such within scholarly institutions and writings all over the world, while "men's" issues are apparently just "issues." These labels must be used as the bulk of knowledge that exists in the world today is descriptive of and reflective of the experience of men, not women.

Sexism Is Everywhere

The whole world is sexist and always has been. While some societies are more **egalitarian** than others (more oriented toward equality between the sexes), historians, anthropologists, and sociologists tend to agree that there has never been a truly **matriarchal** society in existence (Bamberger, 1974). Not one, not ever. It is true that particular social institutions within different cultures are matriarchal; for example, families within some cultures tend to follow a matriarchal structure, with mature women (mothers, grandmothers, aunts) making most of the major decisions within families (Solien, 1960). But no society has ever been entirely matriarchal, where women possess the majority of money, power, and status relative to men. To the contrary, human society has been consistently and thoroughly **patriarchal**, where men are in charge of most social institutions and maintain the majority of wealth, status, and power, including and importantly, decision-making power. Men create and control political, social, and cultural institutions in patriarchal societies; women are provided fewer opportunities to engage power and acquire wealth. The world's societies are currently, and have been in the past, patriarchal and **heteronormative** (where heterosexuality is considered normal and preferred).

This chapter focuses on sexism, which is a form of discrimination. **Sexism** refers to actions, attitudes, and institutional structures that subordinate a person because of her or his sex (Franzoi, 2006). In other words, because a person is X (female or male or other), they are treated differently than people who are not X. Sexism broadly involves behaviors, the way people are treated by individuals, groups, and social institutions. But what are the bases of sexism? People usually discriminate against a particular group because they have certain beliefs and feelings about the people in that group. Beliefs (**schemas**) about the traits, qualities, and attributes of broad social categories of people are called **stereotypes** (see Chapter 5). **Stereotypes** are the cognitive component of discrimination. Some stereotypes are so deeply learned that they become rather automatic and thus very likely to influence social judgments and behaviors because they are so easy to use (Bargh, Chen, & Burrows, 1996) (see "Critical Thinking"). Feelings about members of a particular social category involve **prejudice**. Usually when involved in discrimination, feelings about social groups are negative and involve fear, anger, even hatred. Some sexism

162   *Global, Historical Sexism*

involves a great deal of anger toward women, just as racism can involve a great deal of anger toward particular racial or ethnic groups. Prejudice can also be positive (e.g., feeling especially positive toward children versus feelings for adults); but sexism and feelings associated with it are typically negative rather than positive.

Sexism is unfair and harmful. Women suffer from discrimination based on sex, not just in terms of lower pay, fewer opportunities, and much less recognition of their work (Johns, 2013; Lips, 2003; Pew Research Center, 2018). Being treated in a negative manner simply because one is female is associated with negative physical (e.g., stress-related symptoms, pain) and psychological outcomes (depression, lower well-being and self-esteem) (Pascoe & Smart Richman, 2009; Schmitt, Branscombe, Postmes, & Garcia, 2014). Experiences with sexual objectification (ranging from body evaluation by others to sexual assault) are linked with substance abuse in women (Carr & Szymanski, 2011). Direct harassment or discrimination is not necessary; women who are merely exposed to sexist attitudes and behavior suffer lower psychological well-being than women not exposed (Glomb et al., 1997; Miner-Rubino & Cortina, 2007; Szymanski, Gupta, Carr, & Stewart, 2009). Among adolescents, girls within different ethnic groups suffer more suicidal thoughts, lower self-esteem, and greater depression relative to boys within those groups (Consolacion, Russell, & Sue, 2004). Stereotypes of women are negative; hearing negative information about one's own group, about your immutable characteristics, results in negative psychological outcomes, including internalization of negative stereotypes (Herek, 2007; Hurst & Beesley, 2013; Szymanski et al., 2009). Negative physical and psychological health outcomes associated with discrimination based on sex can be particularly pronounced among women of color (Beydoun et al., 2017; Chen & Li, 2015; Epstein, Blake, & González, 2017; Holley, Tavassoli, & Stromwall, 2016; Jang, Borenstein-Graves, Haley, Small, & Mortimer, 2003; Lewis et al., 2013; Walker, Wingate, Obasi & Joiner, 2008).

In this chapter we will discuss different forms of sexism and different explanations for sexism. But as we discuss sexism, try to keep this question in mind. Why do you think there have never been truly matriarchal societies? Is it because women are just inferior and can't do it? Because men are so much smarter and more capable than women? Is that why they are more powerful and have more money and always will have? Or is it because men, being significantly physically bigger and stronger, have consistently oppressed women, including with words, laws, religious edicts, and social norms for behavior, with their power to construct and use those things? So is half the human race completely inept and incapable of leading and governing, thus acquiring very little power; or has half the human race rather easily oppressed and controlled the other half, with muscles, force, money, laws, etc.? This is a rather simplistic question about something obviously myriad and very complex, but you get the idea, I hope.

Biological Differences: The Underpinnings of Sexism

Physical Strength and Masculinity

The average man has 50-80% greater upper body strength and 30-60% greater lower body strength than the average woman (Lassek & Gaulin, 2009). The effect sizes for throwing distance and for throwing velocity between women and men are around 2.00 (Thomas & French, 1985). That means that the average distance men can throw an object is two standard deviations higher than the average distance women can throw. That means that only 2.5% of women can throw farther than the average man; 97.5% of women cannot throw as far as the average man

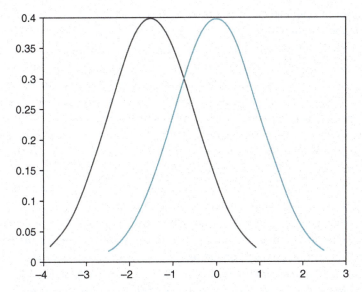

Figure 7.1 A two standard deviation difference between groups (Cohen's *d* = 2.00) representing overall differences in physical strength between women and men

(see Figure 7.1). That's a huge difference in strength (Cohen, 1988). These size and strength differences between female and male Homo Sapiens, which are most crucial for fighting ability among males, have existed since we first evolved in Africa around 200,000 years ago (Sell, Hone, & Pound, 2012). Men have other physical advantages that make them more effective at physically subduing and hurting others, including faster reaction times (Der & Deary, 2006), broader shoulders (Tanner, 1989), stronger bones (Schoenau, Neu, Rauch, & Manz, 2001; Wells, 2007), greater musculature (Loomba-Albrecht & Styne, 2009), higher metabolism (Garn & Clark, 1953), thicker skin (Shuster, Black, M& McVitie, 1975), greater lung capacity (Gursoy, 2010), and other physical advantages.

Let's agree to not be naïve; when there are two groups, and one group is substantially bigger, stronger, faster, and better fighters than the other group, the big and strong group is in charge. That's just the way it is. To think that men would somehow have more respect for the rights and dignity of women than to use brute force is a ridiculous idea (Sell et al., 2012). Yes, there are individual men who would never think of using force to coerce a woman to do something against her will. There were certainly such good men in the cave as well (although likely many fewer than today; Payne, 2004). But there are generations of other men who would do and have done just that, on a daily basis. Men have physically dominated women for centuries, and thus taken the bulk of power and wealth for themselves, for centuries. The ability to physically coerce another person is the essence of true power. When all else is stripped away, when other inequalities are diminished, the physical power difference remains. If women and men were exactly the same physical size, and equally as naturally muscular and strong, do you think that the inequalities we see between women and men around the world and throughout history would continue to exist?

When one group has all the power, they tend to like it and they will strive to keep it (Pratto & Walker, 2004). Because human beings are so clever, the powerful will develop mechanisms to maintain control, in addition to brute force, including religious ideology, formal laws, social norms (explicit and implicit rules for behavior within any particular situation), and customs (Hurrell, 2005; McAdams, 1997). For example, the Qu'ran asserts that men should take control of their wives and punish them for not obeying their husbands (4:34). The Bible has similar instructions to wives to submit to husbands (Colossians 3:18, Ephesians 5:22, 1 Peter 3:1), that husbands rule over wives (Genesis 3:16, Numbers 30:13). These religious texts have been the bases of kingdoms and governments around the world for thousands of years. Created by men, they are used by men to maintain power and control over all of society, especially women (Dobash & Dobash, 1979). There have been and still are laws all over the world that support a man's *right* to physically control his wife (Alfred, 2014; Olorunshola, 2016). So men, because they are men, are encouraged to use physical force, because darn those rascally women! When women "misbehave," men should punish and thus control them. In this way, men's physical domination is supported and reinforced by religious edicts, laws, and customs.

Women are simply and rather automatically viewed as being less competent than men, based on physical size differences and emotional brain (implicit) responding to them (Fiske, 2017). However, in addition to those implicit processes, we learn explicit beliefs about femaleness and we use those beliefs to process information about women as a group and as individuals. Groups with power develop legitimizing myths, false beliefs about a group that justify their continued oppression. Traditional gender role socialization requires that men dominate women to uphold patriarchal systems (Levant, Rankin, Williams, Hasan, & Smalley, 2010). So men in power develop ideas about why women should be dominated, why they should not have particular rights. So women cannot have sexual freedom, because that behavior is sinful, or dirty, or impure (Leviticus 21:14). Women cannot have dominion over their husbands, because God commands the opposite. Women cannot leave the house or travel without an escort because God commands it (*Fataawa al-Lajnah al-Daa'imah*, 17/339; Finnigan & Bingham, 2016). Women can't possibly be allowed to vote, they're too emotional and unreasonable (and not very bright; Smith & Stewart, 1983). Sexist legitimizing myths routinely portray women as stupid, as cognitively and morally deficient. Stereotypes of women all over the world today typically include the trait "unintelligent" or "stupid" (Fiske, 2017; Fiske, Cuddy, & Glick, 2007). Femininity is seen as immature and childlike (Nam, Lee, & Hwang, 2011; Powlishta, 2000; Smith & Stewart, 1983). False beliefs about rape called rape myths are used to justify men's sexual oppression, control, and abuse of women, including rape. Rape myths say that women should be raped if they get drunk on a date or at a party; they should get raped if they are promiscuous or dress too sexy (Burt, 1980). Clearly, there are many people who have real, genuine respect for women and think that they should be treated equally to men (those people are called feminists). For some people, particularly men who hold negative views of women, women are simply viewed as rather incapable of handling daily life, certainly not being a CEO, a judge, President of the United States, or their boss (Fiske et al., 2007; Pica at al., 2018). More common among men are ideas that sexism is not actually real and, if it is, it doesn't really have any effect on women (Olson et al., 2008). All of these beliefs are false and serve to maintain men's social dominance over women.

Because sexist legitimizing myths focus on women's weaknesses, weakness becomes anathema to sexist men. Physical weakness makes women inferior to men. Masculine ideals do not include weakness; physical weakness is inherently feminine. Women's greater emotionality than men (greater feeling of and expression of emotion than men; Brebner, 2003) is also portrayed as a weakness, an inferiority compared to men (see Chapter 9). Boys and men mock each other, with insults based on being "like a girl" ("you throw like a girl!" "you cry like a girl!" "you run like a girl!"). Men who are perceived as lacking in courage are described in derogatory terms that are inherently feminine, like "pussy" or "bitch." Men who show particular social weaknesses are called a "douche." Men who are devious or sneaky are called a "son of a bitch" (hey, what does his MOM have to do with it?). Men's perceptions of and enacting of masculinity reject femininity, especially in the United States (DiMuccio, Yost, & Helweg-Larsen, 2017).

Men react badly to being perceived as feminine and try to avoid it (Gallagher & Parrott, 2011; Pascoe, 2005). To be described as feminine is a particularly severe social punishment in cultures that are more conservative, less egalitarian, and more sexist (Gilmore, 1990). Men react strongly and negatively to being called feminine because it is threatening to their manhood (Vandello, Bosson, Cohen, Burnaford, & Weaver, 2008). Because of **precarious manhood** (masculinity that is easily threatened), men feel motivated to demonstrate and reassert masculinity to others (Vandello & Bosson, 2013). Being described as feminine or engaging in feminine tasks can cause men to feel anxiety (Dahl, Vescio, & Weaver, 2014) and to attempt to reassert masculinity in various ways, including greater risk-taking (Weaver, Vandello, & Bosson, 2013), showing greater prejudice toward women (Hunt & Gonsalkorale, 2014) and feminine men (Glick, Gangl, Gibb, Klumpner, & Weinberg, 2007), increased thoughts of physical aggression (Vandello et al., 2008), and increased actual aggression (Bosson, Vandello, Burnaford, Weaver, & Arzu Wasti, 2009; Cohn, Seibert, & Zeichner, 2009). Men also react aggressively toward women who act masculine (Reidy, Shirk, Sloan, & Zeichner, 2009). While it is important to note that these feelings, beliefs, and behaviors are most likely and are particularly pronounced among men termed "**hypermas-culine**" (extreme masculinity including endorsement of violence, callous sexual attitudes toward women, and risk-taking; Reidy et al., 2009), precarious manhood is not an uncommon or rare experience among men, including in the United States (Vandello & Bosson, 2013). The physical size and strength differences between women and men are central to men's assertions of masculinity through aggression and other demonstrations of physical strength and prowess (Vandello et al., 2008).

Perhaps the most egregious example of using physical force to overpower and control people who are smaller and physically weaker is the practice of child marriage across history and all over the world. Children cannot consent; the legal age of consent for sexual behavior and marriage varies around the world; in the United States it is 14 to 18 years old in most places (Waites, 2005). Child marriage currently occurs in many countries around the world, particularly in the Middle East and Africa. Over 700 million women around the world today were married before they were 18 years old, with 15 million children forced into marriage each year (UNICEF, 2017). Children forced into marriage are at huge psychological and physical risk, with their childhood gone and adult requirements, including sexuality, forced upon them. Children forced into marriage are most commonly girls (UNICEF, 2012). Children are forced into marriage and cannot possibly resist. How can a child resist a grown man, and her parents? In following a tradition, the parents become part of the coercion, the literal physical forcing into marriage. Child marriage is represented within religions, including Islam (Jamjoom, 2009; Spellberg, 1996). I acknowledge that girls did marry across cultures at much higher rates in the past, with a shorter lifespan and other considerations (Laiou, 1993). However, in the modern world, child marriage persists. Child marriage necessarily involves child rape, a horrifying situation for any child, rape by a grown man. The Supreme Court of India recently redefined rape to include any person under the age of 18 years, thereby attempting to protect child brides. Nevertheless, despite this ruling, the practice of child marriage persists in India (Meixler, 2017). Unfortunately, evangelical Christian groups in the United States are currently working to keep child marriage legal in some states (Sweeny, 2018).

166 *Global, Historical Sexism*

Reproductive Roles and Oppression

Biological differences in reproductive roles also underlie global, historical sexism. Men's oppression and ownership of women based on their sexual and reproductive capacities began in the cave (Lerner, 1986). In addition to physical weakness relative to men, women experience the vulnerability and life-threatening nature of pregnancy. Pregnancy can kill you; pregnancy and childbirth are among the leading causes of death for women, especially within countries that are still developing, and especially when high-quality health care is not available (World Health Organization, 2010; see Chapter 4). In addition, while pregnant, women cannot run as quickly, are more vulnerable to injury, and are more vulnerable to physical attack. Some research indicates that pregnant women are 35% more likely to experience any kind of violence compared to non-pregnant women (Gelles, 1988). These are additional physical weaknesses that lead women to be subordinate to bigger, stronger men who use their strength to subdue, intimidate, and control (Mosher & Sirkin, 1984; Willie, Khondkaryan, Callands, & Kershaw, 2018).

We can also see the oppression of women in the disparate duties of parenthood. Clearly, mothers are biologically structured to not only nurture children in utero, but after they are born through the production of milk (the perfect food for infants) and nursing. In this way, women's caretaking of infants is essential, especially before the advent of infant formula. Infants also form deep affectional and attachment ties to their mothers (**bonding**), because of experiences in utero, nursing, and other biochemical and psychological processes (Chess & Thomas, 1982). This early dependence on women's parenting, from both infants and fathers, cements the central role of women in the lives of children. That's all well and good, and very natural and beneficial to society, but women are then frankly stuck caring for children, and not obtaining education or employment or career opportunities. Mothering is largely unpaid around the world (although smart countries have long periods of maternity leave, including at 100% salary; Etehad & Lin, 2016). As women devote their day to childcare, they fall behind in terms of financial, occupational, educational, political, and social power. In addition, motherhood and childcare, the "stay-at-home" mom, is a largely unsung and derogated role in modern, technologically advanced cultures (Cuddy, Fiske, & Glick, 2004). Despite the veneration of the Virgin Mary and other famous mothers, staying at home and caring for children is not a high-status social role, another norm or label that men use to oppress women (Crittenden, 2001). If mothers were venerated, mothers would have more social power. But because they are not, there is a double whammy effect for women; they miss out on advancement and power opportunities while engaging in an essential yet derogated role.

Fathers are obviously central to children's healthy psychological development (Li & Meier, 2017); the role of fathers is more strongly valued around the world (Hossain & Juhari, 2015; Marsiglio & Hendricks, 2012; Moreno & Chuang, 2015; Nakazawa, 2015). A mother's care is essential and must happen; women who abandon their children are considered heartless, not real women (Rijken & Merz, 2014). Men's care of their offspring is largely viewed as optional; men can come and go, impregnating multiple women, and if they disappear from a child's life, there is no huge public outcry. In the modern world, especially in the United States, single mothers are blamed for many of society's ills, including criminality (Ford, 2017; Howell, 2015). Let's be clear here; single mothers have actually stayed with their children. There is apparently a sperm donor, even someone who considers himself a father, but what makes a single mother? A man who is not around, not interested in participating in the care and raising of his child(ren). Among young unwed mothers with children, one study found that over 50% of fathers never provided *any* monetary support (Rangarajan & Gleason, 1998). Of children of single mothers, over 50% rarely

Global, Historical Sexism 167

or never visit with their fathers (Seltzer, 1991). So men, who already make more money and have much greater social power, abandon women they've impregnated and the resulting children.

Reproductive roles are additionally linked to oppression as religious and governmental institutions around the world limit and attempt to limit women's access to safe, legal abortion. About 25% of all pregnancies around the world ended with abortion from 2010 to 2014; abortions are actually higher among married than among unmarried women (Guttmacher Institute, 2018a). About half of all pregnancies among women in the United States are unwanted (Guttmacher Institute, 2018b). Abortion is legal in 98% of the world's countries to save the life of the mother. However, abortion simply because you do not want to be pregnant is legal in only 27% of countries around the world (Berer, 2017). Since 2000, 33 countries have made abortions more allowable, under more and different circumstances (Guttmacher Institute, 2018a), although it is more or less illegal in many countries (Finer & Fine, 2013). Sixty-six percent of abortions occur before week 8 of pregnancy; 89% by week 12. Only 5% of abortions occur after 16 weeks, nearly always because of a complication that threatens the health of the mother or the viability of the fetus (Guttmacher Institute, 2018b). Legality of abortion is not linked to incidence of abortion; women have abortions regardless of whether it is legal or not. Unfortunately, illegal abortions are extremely dangerous and can cause permanent injury and death (Guttmacher Institute, 2018a).

Not allowing girls and women to abort unwanted fetuses is akin to threatening their lives (World Health Organization, 2010) and cutting off their futures, their goals, their dreams. If a girl or woman does not want a child, or cannot afford a child, or is endangered by pregnancy, the lack of access to safe, legal abortion is oppressive. Being forced to carry a fetus that is unwanted is a prison; women's bodies are turned into incubators, cocoons for something more important. A fetus is thus elevated to equal personhood with a girl or a woman. Yes, women can put unwanted children up for adoption, that is obvious. But adoption is not necessarily easily accomplished and can lead to additional **stigmatization** (social rejection and scorn). Family pressures are also a factor in decisions about adoption (Ellison, 2003; Klein et al., 2005). Some people assert that if girls and women do not want children, they should not have sex. This is just another form of **slut-shaming** (shaming women for their sexual behavior; see Chapter 7), and I assert that that is a ridiculous, unhealthy, sexist, and unscientific argument. Female human beings naturally want, desire, and engage in sexuality; their engaging in sexual behavior is not deserving of the punishment of 40 weeks of life-threatening pregnancy, not to mention that a child is not an appropriate punishment for anything. Men are never forced to risk their lives to bear a child, ever. Men also routinely walk away from parenthood and they always have; women, if denied access to modern medical abortion, cannot, at least for 40 life-threatening weeks. Safe, legal abortion saves women's lives (World Health Organization, 2010) and allows women to control their own destinies.

Girls and women who are forced to give birth to unwanted children will likely live in **poverty** for the rest of their lives (Hoffman, 2006). Given the lack of a second parent and the costs of childcare, young mothers are deprived of the ability to seek out education and employment (Bittman & Pixley, 1997; Craig, 2002; Gray & Chapman, 2001). A child born to a teenaged, unwed mother is nine times more likely to be poor across their life (U.S. Congress, Ways and Means Committee, 2004). Even if they are married, teenaged mothers are much more likely to live in poverty than people who don't marry and don't have children in their teens (Dahl, 2010). Ironically, especially in the United States, the same people who are "pro-life" (they oppose safe, legal abortion) are also opposed to government programs that aid women and children in poverty, including Head

168 *Global, Historical Sexism*

Start, the Children's Health Insurance Program (CHIP), WIC (food benefits for women with infant children), after school programs, and free school lunches. There is very clear evidence that these programs are a huge benefit to poor families, especially to children (Avruch & Cackley, 1995; Chatterji & Brooks-Gunn, 2004; Durlak, Weissberg, & Pachan, 2010; Lave et al., 1998). There are important long-term consequences of adequate health, nutrition, and education early in child-hood, consequences that affect society in the long run as children become productive (or not) adult members of society. Research on Head Start alone indicates a significant positive impact on adulthood outcomes, including graduating high school, income levels, and likelihood of arrest (Garces, Thomas, & Currie, 2002).

So the pro-lifers are not actually pro-life; a free lunch is life and nutrition for a poor child, CHIP is health care (which obviously can literally be life instead of death to a child), and Head Start is preschool. People who are "pro-life" are not pro-child; they are anti-woman. Forcing women to follow the religious beliefs of a few about the "sanctity of life" is a violation of the First and Fourteenth Amendments to the U.S. Constitution, hence the *Roe v. Wade* decision that made abortion legal in the United States. Nonetheless, the right to safe, legal abortion has always been and is especially currently under threat in the United States, with Supreme Court Justice Anthony Kennedy retiring in July 2018, and President Trump vowing to nominate Supreme Court Justices who are against abortion (Foran, 2018). Multiple states have rather recently passed near bans on abortion, banning them after just six or eight weeks of pregnancy, before most girls or women might even know they are pregnant. The freedoms, livelihoods, and safety of American girls and women hang in the balance as wealthy men in power decide what medical care women can receive to save their own lives. Women have the right to *life* (to not have their health and lives threatened by an unwanted pregnancy); *liberty* (freedom to pursue their own choices, to not be unfairly imprisoned or limited); and the *pursuit of happiness* (to pursue their goals and dreams). If you don't like abortion, don't have one, and don't impose your religious or other ideological beliefs on other people. Ironically, "pro-life" people also tend to be anti-birth control. Providing high-quality sex education and free condoms to every teen who wants them would prevent mil-lions and millions of dollars in costs to taxpayers and the life-ruining consequences of unwanted pregnancy (Hoffman, 2006; see Chapter 7). And by the way, the author of this book received free and reduced-cost lunches, being a kid with a single mom without much money. Thank you to the taxpayers of the great state of California for helping me be a strong kid who wasn't hungry at school, and became a healthy, productive adult.

A Brief History of Sexism

There are entire books and university courses on sexism, and given the around 10,000-year his-tory of human civilization and millions of years of hominid evolution before that, it is rather dif-ficult to summarize the breadth, depth, and impact of global, historical sexism. Women and men are and have been treated differently – with different expectations, roles, rights, rules for behav-ior – in every human culture that has ever existed (Marios & Hégy, 1998). I assert that sexism has affected every female human being who has ever lived; that there is not a single girl or woman on the planet living in the past or today who has not experienced sexism in some way. Every girl and woman has experienced some diminishment of herself simply because she is female and not male; some violation of her dignity or bodily autonomy; some unfair advantage given to male human beings. Sexism is inevitable given the size and strength differences between men and women; men dominate women because they can, and because they can, they always have. It is

Global, Historical Sexism   169

the challenge for reasonable, fair-minded, compassionate people today to bring an end to the broad historical acceptance of sexism and to instead push forward toward equality.

Not everyone agrees that women and men should be equal; individuals who follow traditional ideology will prefer men's higher status and power in the social hierarchy over women (Christopher & Mull, 2006). Individuals high in **social dominance orientation** (**SDO**) prefer inequality; those same people tend to already be on the top of the hierarchy. In other words, people of higher social status like it that way and thus legitimize and support system inequality (Vargas-Salfate, Paez, Liu, Pratto, & de Zúñiga, 2018). In a similar way, men and European Americans are higher in SDO than women and members of other ethnic groups, because they enjoy higher status already and legitimize it to keep it (Miller, Smith, & Mackie, 2004; Pratto, Sidanius, & Levin, 2006). Even many women are sexist and support patriarchal systems, even though they suffer negative outcomes because of the hierarchy. Psychologically, justifying the current system reduces uncertainty, makes the group feel stronger against external threats, and gives a sense of common purpose and shared fate with others (Friesen, Kay, Eibach, & Galisnky, 2014; Knight, Tobin, & Hornsey, 2014; Tullet, Kay, & Inzlicht, 2015). The belief that men should have more power and status and women should have less is in itself sexist ideology. It seems likely that sexism can never be eliminated, true equality never obtained, as long as there are real size and strength differences between women and men, and given the disproportionate share of wealth and power already possessed by men on the planet (Jacobs, 2018; Oxfam International, 2017; Tickamyer, 1981). But each of us, in our interpersonal behavior, our work, and our relationships, can choose (or not) to challenge sexism and work against it, a little bit at a time.

As we've already mentioned, religion as a social institution is very powerful in perpetuating myths that legitimize the oppression of women, and this has been true across history. The Creation myth includes the original sin of Eve, who disobeyed God and ate from the Tree of Knowledge. She then deceives and tricks Adam, so that forever after, humankind exists separately from God and Paradise is lost (Genesis 3:23-24). Eve is *only* a rib, a mere component of Adam (Genesis 2:21-22), and look what she did! The story of Abraham, in both the Bible and the Qu'ran, serves as the basis for specific religious traditions including Christianity, Judaism, and Islam. The people doing things in the Bible are male; men are the actors. Women and girls are rarely mentioned except in terms of how they might produce children. Boy children are worth more money than girl children (Leviticus 27:5). Abraham and other important Biblical characters are all **polygamous**, with many wives, so one particular woman is not really important. From Abraham the birth lineage to Jesus is established, but only for boys and men; no one cares apparently what happened to the daughters. Abraham and his son Isaac deceive other men and identify their wives (Sarah and Rebecca, respectively) as their sisters, and offer the women to men for sexual use (Genesis 12:10-20, 20:1-7). Lot similarly offers his virgin daughters to two strange men who show up at his house (Genesis 26:1-11). Powerful Biblical men typically not only had multiple wives, but many **concubines** (women living in common law with a man outside of marriage for sexual purposes), who were treated even worse than the wives, typically banished into the desert with their children when the men were finished with them (Genesis 21:8-14). The wise King Solomon had 700 wives and 300 concubines, all of whom are considered to be property (I Kings 10:14-29). King David, whom God called "a man after my own heart" (Acts 13:22), had many wives and concubines and murdered a man so he could steal his wife (2 Samuel 11:1-27). God commands soldiers to murder boys and women who have had sexual intercourse, but to keep all the virgins for themselves (Numbers 31:17-18). Islam is no different, calling for men to beat their wives (Qu'ran 4:34, 38:44), for women to cover themselves so that men are not tempted (Qu'ran 24:31,

170   *Global, Historical Sexism*

33:59), and asserting that a woman's word is worth only one-half of a man's by requiring two witnesses if they are female, only one if they are male (Qu'ran 2:282). I could go on, but that would be another book (a very sad, depressing book). The **misogyny** inherent in the world's religious traditions is appalling and, unfortunately, has helped shape attitudes toward women for centuries (Marios & Hégy, 1998; Wemple, 1992).

Women have been oppressed by men across the span of history around the world (hence the title of this chapter). Women in ancient Egypt were completely dominated by men, having no social, financial, or political power (Robins, 1993). Although Japan did have several female emperors (Tsurumi, 1981), the typical peasant woman in ancient Japan was subordinate to her father and husband (Ueno, 1987). Women in ancient Greece served as wives and mothers; husbands were expected to be more sexually attracted to their male lovers rather than wives (Lefkowitz & Flint, 1982). Women in ancient China, while sometimes powerful as queens and other nobility, were not at all equal to men and often excluded from positions of power and public life (Hinsch, 2018). In the Roman Republic, women were by and large considered property of men. If they were divorced by their husbands, they returned to their father and had no property rights at all. Women had no child custody rights and men could murder their children with impunity (Fergusen, 1993; Gardner, 1986). Women sometimes gained power by retaining the property of husbands who were killed in battle, although that property may go to a brother or sons instead (Balsdon, 1962). Whatever rights women gained were usually taken away at some later point when they became too powerful and men had to push them back down. Women had few rights and were considered fathers' and husbands' property throughout the Middle Ages (Martos, 1991). Women's low social status continued through the Renaissance and through to the modern era (Ozment, 1983), with their only reward from God for their obedience and submission to men. With the growth of intellectualism in Europe in the 18th and 19th centuries, women began expressing themselves more in literature and art, often using men's names to ensure their free expression (Coultrap-McQuin, 2000; Ezell, 1996; Shattock, 1993). Women began pursuing education and careers, including in America. World War II allowed American women to join the workforce in greater numbers, which established women's capability and motivation as workers (Anderson, 1981). Modern women have slowly over time challenged the tradition of their subjugation and oppression and have actively sought independence and freedom (Deckard, 1975).

In the United States, like everywhere else in the world since the dawn of time, sexism is inherent and ubiquitous. A famous event in women's movements toward equality (**feminism**) is a meeting among nearly 200 women at Seneca Falls, New York in the summer of 1848. This meeting is largely regarded as the beginning of the American women's **suffrage** movement (the movement toward the right to vote that continued as the women's movement) (DuBois & Dumenil, 2015). In 1848 in the United States, women could not vote. Married women were essentially legally dead, having no rights outside of their husband's rights. They were commonly not allowed to speak in public. Women had no say in any kind of formulation of laws or tax codes (taxation without representation), and they had no property rights. Husbands had legal authority and responsibility for their wives to the extent that they could imprison and beat them with impunity. Divorce and child custody laws favored men, giving no rights to women. Most occupations were closed to women and when women did work they were paid only a fraction of what men earned. Women were not allowed to enter professions such as medicine or law. No college or university would accept female students. With only a few exceptions, women were not allowed to participate in the affairs of the church. Essentially, women were given no opportunities to be independent of men at all. They literally had no rights. Women were forced to be totally dependent on men, destroying self-confidence and the ability to develop self-respect. These conditions are legitimized by beliefs that women are irrational, childlike, and half-witted. This is around 170 years ago, in the 10,000 plus years of human civilization. In 170 years, we have come a long way! Women earned the right to vote in 1920, to choose abortion in 1973, to have a credit card in 1974, to not be raped by husbands in 1976, and to not be fired for being or becoming pregnant in 1978 (see Table 7.1 for more about laws and women's rights in the United States).

Types of Sexism

Sexism is complex. As social institutions evolve, different forms of sexism appear. Basic sexism is old-fashioned sexism, beliefs that women are incapable and inferior to men, coupled with an open opposition to women's equality to men (Eagly, Karau, & Makhijani, 1995; Spence & Helmreich, 1972). These attitudes still exist, including of course in the United States, where many people consider women incapable of making decisions about their own medical care, their own bodies, let alone the important decisions required of an Army General, a CEO, a President of the United States (Eagly et al., 1995). Research indicates that people reporting higher levels of old-fashioned sexism also report racist attitudes and racial prejudice, negative attitudes toward LGBTQ individuals, religious intolerance, and negative attitudes toward the poor and the aged. Basically old-fashioned sexists hate everyone except younger to middle-aged white men. They also tend to be higher in acceptance of rape myths (Aosved & Long, 2006). Research indicates that traditional attitudes toward women and hostile attitudes toward women (hostile sexism) are accurate predictors of votes for Donald Trump for President in the 2016 U.S. Presidential election, even more than individual sex or political party affiliation (Bock, Byrd-Craven, & Burkley, 2017). In other words, hostility toward women is a better predictor of voting for Trump than being a Republican or a man. Trump voters do not like Hillary Clinton; they don't seem to like women in general.

As we just mentioned, old-fashioned sexism involves a hostility toward women called hostile sexism, which involves negative feelings accompanied by negative stereotypes of women and heterosexual hostility. The emotions experienced within hostile sexism are anger toward women, competitiveness, and fear, mainly a fear of being manipulated by women and losing masculinity (precarious manhood) (Cross, Overall, Hammond, & Fletcher, 2017). Men high in hostile sexism believe women are trying to overtake them, take away their power, and control them through feminist ideology or with sex (Lemonaki, Manstead, & Maio, 2015). Research indicates that thinking about nontraditional women, including the "career woman" and the feminist prototypes, triggers feelings of hostility toward women (Glick, Diebold, Bailey-Werner, & Zhu, 1997; Sibley & Wilson, 2004). Trump voters really do not like Hillary Clinton. In fact, if they are high in hostile sexism (Bock et al., 2017 suggest they are), they most likely want to see her "locked up" for her emails. Men high in hostile sexism are more aggressive toward women in general, including their intimate partners (Hammond & Overall, 2013; Overall, Sibley, & Tan, 2011), especially when they feel that they have low power in a relationship (Cross, Overall, Low, & McNulty, 2018).

The complexity of sexism is indicated perhaps most strongly by the concept of ambivalent sexism, the psychological co-existence of positive and negative attitudes toward women (Glick & Fiske, 1996; Glick et al., 1997) (see Table 7.1). Ambivalent sexism includes hostile sexism and benevolent sexism, paternalistic ideas that subordinate women. Benevolent sexism includes positive feelings of warmth, trust, and a desire for sexual and psychological intimacy with women. Women

172 Global, Historical Sexism

Table 7.1 A brief history of women's rights in the United States

- 1916: Margaret Sanger opens the first U.S. birth control clinic in Brooklyn, N.Y. Although the clinic is shut down 10 days later and Sanger is arrested, she eventually wins support through the courts and opens another clinic in NYC in 1923.
- 1920: The 19th Amendment granting women the right to vote is signed into law.
- 1936: Birth control literature is no longer classified as "obscene."
- 1960: The Food and Drug Administration approves birth control pills.
- 1964: Title VII of the Civil Rights Act bars discrimination in employment on the basis of race and sex. The EEOC is formed.
- 1965: In *Griswold v. Connecticut*, the Supreme Court strikes down the one remaining state law prohibiting the use of contraceptives by married couples.
- California becomes the first state with a "no fault" divorce law. Laws are also passed regarding the equal division of common property.
- 1972: In *Eisenstadt v. Baird* the Supreme Court rules that the right to privacy includes an unmarried person's right to use contraceptives.
- 1973: As a result of *Roe v. Wade*, the Supreme Court establishes a woman's right to safe and legal abortion, overriding the anti-abortion laws of many states.
- 1973: Title IX of the Education Act requires equal access to educational programs, including higher education, ending quotas limiting numbers of women in undergraduate and graduate programs at universities.
- 1974: The Equal Credit Opportunity Act prohibits discrimination in consumer credit practices on the basis of sex, race, marital status, religion, national origin, age, or receipt of public assistance. Most women were not permitted by banks to have credit cards until this passed.
- 1976: The first marital rape law is enacted in Nebraska, making it illegal for a husband to rape his wife.
- 1978: The Pregnancy Discrimination Act bans employment discrimination against pregnant women. Under the Act, a woman cannot be fired or denied a job or a promotion because she is or may become pregnant.
- 1986: *Meritor Savings Bank v. Vinson*: the Supreme Court finds that sexual harassment is a form of illegal job discrimination.
- 1994: The Violence Against Women Act tightens federal penalties for sex offenders, funds services for victims of rape and domestic violence, and provides for special training of police officers.

are idealized as pure and goddess-like, and as needing protection (see Table 7.2). These attitudes are triggered by thoughts of the **housewife/mother** prototype of women (Gaunt, 2013). Although motherhood is not strongly valued as a job (and as such is rarely if ever paid; Crittenden, 2001), the mother type is valued because we all have one and they are usually (hopefully) loving, understanding, caring, and helpful. What's not to love? Men prefer compliant, deferent women because of their dependence on women for caretaking and sex, and by treating women with benevolence (idealization, gratitude) and prescriptions for caretaking, they enforce women's subordinate role (Jackson, 1994). Racism in the United States is historically similar, with stereotypes of African Americans describing them as "happy-go-lucky," enslaved but not too bothered by it (Bayton, McAlister, & Hamer, 1956; Katz & Braly, 1933). **Communal** (cooperative, caretaking) behaviors are required of women precisely because they support patriarchy and men depend on women going along with that (Glick & Fiske, 1999).

The problem with benevolent sexist attitudes is that they subordinate women because of their sex. "Protecting" women can go a little far, including not letting them leave the house, not

Global, Historical Sexism 173

Table 7.2 Items from the Ambivalent Sexism Inventory

Benevolent sexism items:

1. No matter how accomplished he is, a man is not truly complete as a person unless he has the love of a woman.
2. In a disaster, women ought not necessarily to be rescued before men.*
3. People are often truly happy in life without being romantically involved with a member of the other sex.*
4. Many women have a quality of purity that few men possess.
5. Women should be cherished and protected by men.
6. Every man ought to have a woman whom he adores.
7. Men are complete without women.*
8. A good woman should be set on a pedestal by her man.
9. Women, compared to men, tend to have a superior moral sensibility.
10. Men should be willing to sacrifice their own well-being in order to provide financially for the women in their lives.
11. Women, as compared to men, tend to have a more refined sense of culture and good taste.

Hostile sexism items:

1. Many women are actually seeking special favors, such as hiring policies that favor them over men, under the guise of asking for "equality."
2. Most women interpret innocent remarks or acts as being sexist.
3. Women are too easily offended.
4. Feminists are not seeking for women to have more power than men.*
5. Most women fail to appreciate fully all that men do for them.
6. Women seek to gain power by getting control over men.
7. Women exaggerate problems they have at work.
8. Once a woman gets a man to commit to her, she usually tries to put him on a tight leash.
9. When women lose to men in a fair competition, they typically complain about being discriminated against.
10. There are actually very few women who get a kick out of teasing men by seeming sexually available and then refusing male advances.*
11. Feminists are making entirely reasonable demands of men.*

Items are answered using the following response-scale: 0 = *disagree strongly*; 1 = *disagree somewhat*; 2 = *disagree slightly*; 3 = *agree slightly*; 4 = *agree somewhat*; 5 = *agree strongly*.
*Item is reverse-scored (e.g., 0 = 5, 1 = 4, 2 = 3, 3 = 2, 4 = 1, 5 = 0).

Source: Glick, P., & Fiske, S. T. (1996). The ambivalent sexism inventory: Differentiating hostile and benevolent sexism. *Journal of Personality and Social Psychology, 70,* 491–512.

letting them vote or drive a car, **chastity belts**, **female genital mutilation** (**FGM**; see Chapter 8), and so on; and unfairly restricts women's freedoms. The experience of benevolent sexism is linked with poorer cognitive performance (Dardenne, Dumont, & Bollier, 2007), lower self-esteem, lower well-being, and greater self-doubt in women (Oswald, Baalbaki, & Kirkman, 2019). Further, although it would be nice to be seen as a goddess occasionally, women are entirely mortal and not perfect. Ideas of purity are unfair; they derogate women's sexual behaviors as dirty, immoral, harmful, none of which are true if sex is adult, consensual, and safe. Benevolent sexist beliefs are more socially accepted, more prevalent, endorsed equally by women and men (Glick & Fiske, 2001), and not necessarily recognized as sexist (Becker, 2010). Women who endorse benevolent sexist beliefs are also more likely to endorse hostile sexist beliefs, especially when they are high in **right-wing authoritarianism** (Sibley, Overall, & Duckitt, 2007). Research

174 *Global, Historical Sexism*

indicates that hostile sexism is predicted by higher social dominance orientation, greater right-wing authoritarianism, low **empathic concern** for others, and being male, while benevolent sexism is associated with greater religiosity and lower education level (Hellmer, Stenson, & Jylhä, 2018). While the emotions involved in benevolent sexism may be positive and socially desirable, why can't those feelings of admiration and honor be tied to women as independent, strong, capable, equal human beings? Men who describe themselves as feminists report positive emotions toward independent, feminist women (White & Gaines, 2006). Hopefully, greater numbers of women and men will come to identify with feminism, with the moral concerns of fairness, equality, and concern for the well-being of others, instead of fearing dominance by women (Precopio & Ramsey, 2017).

One study of ambivalent sexism examined perceptions of pregnant women in different roles. Hebl and colleagues (2007) asked female research **confederates** to wear a pregnancy prosthesis to look pregnant, and then either apply for a job or appear as a customer in a retail store (there were of course non-pregnant conditions as well). The results indicate that as a pregnant customer, women were treated with warmth and kindness, with sales associates touching the confederate and behaving in an overly friendly manner. As job applicants, however, confederates were treated more negatively by sales associates than non-pregnant applicants. Hostility toward a pregnant applicant was particularly likely when she was applying for a masculine-typed job. Cross-cultural research indicates that the experience of and endorsement of both hostile and benevolent sexist attitudes exist within women and men across cultures, especially in countries where there is greater gender inequality (Glick, 2006).

Yet another kind of sexism is called **modern sexism** (aka **neosexism**; Martínez & Paterna-Bleda, 2013), which refers to beliefs that women have already achieved equality, and that women who say otherwise are whining or trying to gain unfair advantage. Research suggests that modern sexism involves a set of beliefs that disavow women's current inequality (lack of equal pay, opportunities for power, etc.); that reject women's demands for equal economic and political power; and that disapprove of legislation and policies that promote gender equality (Swim, Aikin, Hall, & Hunter, 1995). Unfortunately, when people believe that sexism is not a problem anymore, that women are already equal and sexism is "a thing of the past" (Becker & Swim, 2012, p.128), they are more likely to blame women for inequality and less likely to challenge the existing status quo (Tougas, Brown, Beaton, & Joly, 1995). When women are exposed to modern sexist ideology (e.g., *"Women are already equal to men," "Sexism isn't really a problem"*), they experience anxiety. Unfortunately, modern sexist ideology appears to quell men's anxiety (Barreto & Ellemers, 2005), perhaps because a change in their superior status is not necessary if sexism does not actually exist. Research also suggests that modern sexism supports subtle forms of sexism, sexism that is not overtly discriminatory toward women but discriminatory nonetheless because it is built into social norms (Swim & Cohen, 1997). So for example, the notion that "boys will be boys" supports men's sexual assaulting of women and blaming women for being victimized. If men are incapable of controlling their strong sexual urges, being boys, it is clearly women's responsibility to serve as gatekeepers or regulators of men's sexuality (Weiss, 2009). It is this kind of implicit normative structure that is so very dangerous to women, because it is less likely to be explicitly recognized and challenged (Barreto & Ellemers, 2005). Men who endorse traditional masculine ideology are higher in modern sexism than men who do not (Martínez & Paterna-Bleda, 2013). Fortunately, when women and men are provided with accurate information about discrimination against women, they actually do become less sexist in their thinking and lower in modern sexism (Becker & Swim, 2012). This finding suggests that education is key; providing real evidence about

Global, Historical Sexism 175

sexism can cause people to rethink their beliefs and recognize the global, historical nature of sexism. See Table 7.1 for some facts about sexism and women's oppression in the United States.

How the Media Is Sexist

Like every social institution, the media in its various forms (news, magazines, advertising, television, movies, music, literature, etc.) is highly sexist. As you can probably already guess, given our discussions up to this point and your reading of Chapter 5, portrayals of girls and women in media are nearly always sexualized, with women's appearance and relationships with men emphasized (Scharrer, 2004). In an analysis of 1,699 American television commercials, one in four women are portrayed as sex objects (Coltrane & Messineo, 2000). Women's bodies are strongly emphasized, including individual body parts related to sexuality. Perception studies indicate that when people process sexualized visual images of women, they evaluate body parts individually in succession, rather than examining the image as a whole (Bernard, Gervais, Allen, Campomizzi, & Klein, 2012, 2015; Civile & Obhi, 2015). In advertisements, women are more commonly depicted as sexually desirable, in sexy clothing and sexual poses, than men (Conley & Ramsey, 2011; Lindner, 2004). Women depicted as sexual objects are particularly common in advertisements in magazines marketed to men (Baker, 2005; Stankiewicz & Rosselli, 2008), and in video games (Burgess, Stermer, & Burgess, 2007; Dill & Thill, 2007). Research indicates that women who are sexually objectified in media are perceived as less intelligent, less competent, and weaker and more passive (Cikara, Eberhardt, & Fiske, 2011; Heflick, Goldenberg, Cooper, & Puvia, 2011; Vaes, Paladino, & Puvia, 2011).

Girls' and women's personalities, intellects, abilities, careers, accomplishments, strength, and talents are rarely emphasized in most media (Long et al., 2010). Girls and women are often portrayed as dependent on men (Scharrer, 2004) or as damsels in distress in media (Dietz, 1998). Men and boys are more likely to be the stars or lead actors in television shows, movies, and video games, more so than women and girls (Braun & Giroux, 1989; Dill, Gentile, Richter, & Dill, 2005; Greenwood & Lippman, 2010). Even when women are lead characters engaged in more **agentic** behaviors, their physical appearance is still emphasized and will likely reflect ideal standards of beauty (Dietz, 1998; Mikula, 2003). LGBTQ characters are becoming more common in media (Gross, 2001), yet such representations tend to be stereotypical, unidimensional, and overly simplistic (McInroy & Craig, 2017).

Standards of beauty clearly vary across time and culture. In countries where food supplies are not abundant, women who are heavier are seen as more attractive than women who are thin (Marlowe & Wetsman, 2001). Modernly, there appears to be an obsession with the hourglass figure, a naturally impossible shape involving a size 10 at the bust, size 2 at the waist, and size 4 in the hips. Young adults exposed to idealized images of women are more likely to accept them as beauty ideals for women and more likely to endorse cosmetic surgery (Harrison, 2003). Both young women and men identify underweight women with accentuated waists as more attractive than other women (Kościński, 2013). Young men exposed to media ideals of female beauty find actual women whom they encounter less attractive compared to young men not exposed to such media images (Kenrick & Gutierres, 1980). Young women exposed to idealized attractive media images of women rate themselves as lower in attractiveness (Evans, 2003), desirability as a mate (Gutierres, Kenrick, & Partch, 1999), and report lower self-esteem (Fernandez & Pritchard, 2012; Rollero, 2013) and greater anxiety and depression (Jiménez-Cruz & Silva-Gutiérrez, 2008). Exposure to physical appearance ideals in the media is also linked with negative body image

176   *Global, Historical Sexism*

(Dohnt & Tiggemann, 2006; Grabe, Ward, & Hyde, 2008; Tiggemann & McGill, 2004) and disordered eating and dieting behaviors (Strahan, 2003; Thomsen, Weber, & Brown, 2002).

Media images of boys and men are likely to be **hypermasculine** (Ben-Zeev, Scharnetzki, Chan, & Dennehy, 2012; Messner, Dunbar, & Hunt, 2000), extreme masculinity involving danger, violence, and callous sexual attitudes toward women (Reidy et al., 2009). Young men exposed to hypermasculine, violent behavior in television shows are more accepting of and desiring of violence than young men exposed to nonviolent men's roles (Scharrer, 2004). Aggression portrayed in video games is also linked to boys' and men's greater feelings of aggression and aggressive behavior (Anderson et al., 2003; Anderson & Bushman, 2001; Anderson & Dill, 2000). Boys and young men exposed to idealized standards of male attractiveness that emphasize physical strength and stature report lower well-being (Halliwell, Dittmar, & Orsborn, 2007; Hobza & Rochlen, 2009; Rollero, 2013) and are more likely to engage in unhealthy behaviors including excessive exercise and use of harmful steroids (Smolak & Stein, 2006). Recent research suggests that greater exposure to television and movies, including sports programs, predicts greater endorsement of traditional masculinity among young men, which in turn is linked with their greater substance use, sexual risk-taking, and other self-destructive behaviors (Giaccardi, Ward, Seabrook, Manago, & Lippman, 2017). Women and men exposed to sexually objectified women in media are more likely to express sexist, negative attitudes toward women (Rollero, 2013; Swami et al., 2010) and greater acceptance of sexual harassment (Ward, 2002). Men exposed to portrayals of women as sex objects in advertising are more likely to endorse rape myths (Lanis & Covell, 1995). Greater exposure to sexualized media images of women is linked to women's self-objectification; that is, seeing themselves as merely sex objects with an emphasis on body and physical attractiveness (Fredrickson & Roberts, 1997). Women who self-objectify experience lower well-being, lower sexual satisfaction, and greater body shame than those who don't (Moradi & Huang, 2008).

Perhaps because they are "games," perhaps because the portrayals used are more cartoonish and less realistic, video games appear to get away with more violence toward women than any other medium except violent pornography. A popular series of video games in the late 1990s and 2000s was Grand Theft Auto (GTA). The men in the series are portrayed as hyperviolent and criminal (DeVane & Squire, 2008); they go through the game stealing cars and engaging in violence. Female characters in the game are prostitutes, who engage in sex with the male criminals. The male criminals can have sex with a prostitute, then kill her (Gibson, 2013). When the men beat the prostitutes, the women proclaim "I like it rough" (Dill & Thill, 2007, p. 853). This is just one example of the violent sexualization, essentially violent pornography (Brown, 2008), that is contained in popular video games. Exposure to violent pornography results in very harmful effects, including increased sexual aggression and acceptance of rape myths in men (Allen, Emmers, Gebhardt, & Giery, 1995; Malamuth, Addison, & Koss, 2000). Research indicates that exposure to violent pornography increases rape myth acceptance in women, especially when they are intoxicated (Davis, Norris, George, Martell, & Heiman, 2006). Given the billions of dollars earned by the video game industry (Entertainment Software Association, 2018) and other media each year, it seems doubtful that respect and concern for the well-being of women will outweigh the profits of selling women's victimization. It is up to the individual consumer to decide where to spend their money and to protect their children from sexist and violent media imagery.

One very interesting aspect of media images of women and men is the occurrence of **face-ism**, or the disproportionate display of men's faces and women's bodies in media images (Archer, Iritani, Kimes, & Barrios, 1983). In a classic series of studies, Dane Archer and his colleagues (1983) examined 1,700 magazine photographs, photographs and images in publications from

11 cultures, art and portraiture over six centuries, and amateur drawings of women and men. Their findings indicate that the faces of men are prominent in such images while the bodies of women are emphasized instead of their faces. Archer found that on average, the face takes up about 65% of a portrait of men, while the face takes up only about 45% of women's portraits. Other researchers have found that facial prominence is substantially lower for African Americans compared to European Americans, in American portrait paintings, pictures from European and American periodicals, even on American stamps created by Euro-American artists (Zuckerman & Kieffer, 1994). Research indicates that internet images of women and men are also disparate in terms of facial prominence and show face-ism in favor of men (Szillis & Stahlberg, 2007). So why does this matter? Consider how one judges the character of another person. Where are character, integrity, and competence located? In the body or in the mind? How is sexual attractiveness assessed in women, in their bodies or their faces? So the intellect and character of men are emphasized, while the bodies and sexual objectification of women are emphasized. Indeed, Archer et al. (1983) found that both women and men were judged to be higher in ambition, intelligence, warmth, and physical attractiveness when the face is displayed more prominently. More prominent faces are also associated with higher judgments of dominance (Zuckerman & Kieffer, 1994). These positive qualities have been emphasized for centuries in depictions of men, and de-emphasized for centuries in images of women. In this way, society creates another method to use to oppress women, portraying their bodies and ignoring their character and intellect.

Heterosexism: Heterosexuality as Normative

Sexual orientation involves romantic, emotional, and sexual attraction to people of certain gender(s), along with a sense of identity based on that attraction and related behaviors (American Psychological Association, 2008). There is no doubt that the world holds up **heterosexuality** (sexual attraction and activity between women and men) as **normative** (standard, typical, normal). **Sexual minority groups** include many different groups including anyone who does not identify as heterosexual (Sullivan, 2003). LGBTQ is one term used to refer to sexual minority groups (there are many genders in addition to sexualities; see Chapter 13). **Heterosexism** is an ideology valuing heterosexuality more than other sexualities. It is endorsed through institutional practices that work to advantage heterosexuals and disadvantage sexual minority groups (Herek, Gillis, & Cogan, 2009). Just as it is sexist, the world is heterosexist. Although **homosexuality** and **bisexuality** have been valued within various cultures in history (Lefkowitz & Flint, 1982; Weeks, 1999), at present religious and government institutions around the world condemn other sexualities and deprive people who are not heterosexual of equal rights. Christianity and Islam condemn homosexuality (Leviticus 18:22; Qu'ran 7:80-81, 29:28-29). The punishment for homosexual behavior in the Bible? Death (Leviticus 20:13). Homosexual behavior is a crime in 72 countries around the world today, and is punishable by death in eight countries, including Afghanistan, Pakistan, Saudi Arabia, Qatar, Iran, and Yemen (The Guardian, 2017). Although transgender people have always existed and have been culturally valued (the two-spirit persons in the Native American tradition; Jacobs, Thomas, & Lang, 1997), currently being **transgender** (having a gender identity different from the gender assigned at birth) is similarly criminalized and condemned around the world.

Being within a sexual minority group is **stigmatized** by society, defined as mental illness by the American Psychological Association until 1973 (Katz, 1995). There are no protections for LGBTQ employees from being fired for their sexual orientation in 15 states in the U.S. (Bellis, 2017a). The current U.S. Presidential Administration is opposed to LGBTQ rights (Bellis, 2017b). President

178 *Global, Historical Sexism*

Trump is attempting to discharge any military personnel who openly identify as transgender (Locker, 2017). The U.S. Supreme Court recently ruled that business owners can refuse service to LGBTQ people based on "deep and sincere religious beliefs" (*Masterpiece Cake Shop v. Colorado Civil Rights Commission*, 2018). The United States Department of Health and Human Services has instituted a new rule allowing health care providers to deny service to LGBTQ people and women seeking abortions or who have had abortions (Barasch, 2018). Hate crimes, including against LGBTQ individuals, have increased under President Trump (FBI Uniform Crime Report, 2016).

Some Americans are recently obsessed with public restrooms, claiming that transgender people are dangerous to children in restrooms (the same people think elementary school teachers should carry handguns). In arguing for a bill in the Texas Senate requiring transgender people to use the restroom corresponding to their gender assigned at birth, Republican Senator Lois Kolkhorst referred to "the God I believe in" (Steinmetz, 2017). Some Americans are against transgender people using public restrooms based on their gender identity because it makes them uncomfortable (Gelernter, 2017). You know what is really uncomfortable? Being excluded from using a toilet because of who you are. Being condemned by people because your identity doesn't fit with their personal magical beliefs. Sexual minority young people are already bullied at school without having to worry about which restroom to use (Birkett, Espelage, & Koenig, 2009; Kosciw, Greytak, & Diaz, 2009). LGBTQ youth report being negatively influenced by families, schools, and religious institutions in developing their identity (Rostosky, Danner, & Riggle, 2007), especially if their identity is prohibited and stigmatized within dominant cultural religions (Ream & Savin-Williams, 2005). Hostile prejudice, violence, and open discrimination are physically and psychologically harmful to sexual minority individuals (Bailey, 1999; Hatzenbuehler & Pachankis, 2016; Pachankis, Sullivan, Feinstein, & Newcomb, 2018). LGBTQ people are likely to hide their sexuality because of fear of stigmatization, violence, and discrimination (Ragins, Singh, & Cornwell, 2007).

In Chapter 8 we emphasize that **healthy sexuality** is adult, consensual, and safe (protecting against sexually transmitted diseases and unwanted pregnancy). Healthy sexuality of any kind is harmless and is in fact highly beneficial to the individuals involved (see Chapter 8). How then can it be regulated by the government, as if it is somehow harmful to people? Efforts to deprive Americans of equal protection under the law are unconstitutional; they violate the Fourteenth Amendment, which asserts that everyone is treated the same by the law. How could **equal protection** be applied if someone is not allowed to be married or serve in the military because of their sexuality or gender? What about the First Amendment, which asserts freedom of religion? Freedom of religion includes freedom *from* religion; no one can impose their religious beliefs onto another person, regardless of proclamations of the morality of that religion. Americans have the freedom to be atheists of course, to not believe in any supernatural event or being. How is it, then, that "sincerely held religious beliefs" are more important than freedom from religion, and the right to equal protection under the law? The same can be said for religious ideology about the "sanctity" of life, and false ideas that humanness begins at conception, being imposed on women seeking safe abortions. The primary prejudice against sexual minorities is religious, a religious condemnation of lust and **fornication** (see Chapter 8). Religion is a primary motivator in many hate crimes (Burke, 2017). Individual freedoms should not be stolen because of the magical beliefs of a few. And guess who is most likely to sexually assault children in restrooms? Heterosexual **cisgender** men, who are overwhelmingly most likely to commit all types of sexual assaults (FBI Uniform Crime Report, 2011; Robertiello & Terry, 2007; Tourigny & Baril, 2011). That has always been the case and always will be. Hypermasculine men tend to have the most negative, aggressive reactions to LGBTQ individuals (Parrott, 2009; Parrott, Peterson, Vincent, &

Bakeman, 2008; Talley & Bettencourt, 2008). Interestingly, heterosexual men who have the most negative reactions to homosexuality are also more likely to be physically sexually aroused by gay pornography (Adams, Wright, & Lohr, 1996). Hmmm, very interesting.

Equality Around the World Today

A male student once asked me, "So what's wrong with men having all the power?" What is wrong with global, historical sexism, the physical, financial, social, cultural oppression of one group by another? One-half of the human race, constantly oppressed by the other half, not allowed to pursue their full potential, denied equal status and equal access to opportunity, wealth, and power. What is wrong with that? It is actually rather difficult to answer such a question, as one assumes that fair-minded, kind, good people would support equality. On the other hand, it is easy to recognize that people with more power like to keep it, and will do so regardless of harm to groups with lower status. So how are women doing all over the world?

We have made some gains, with American women now making around 82% of what men make (Pew Research Center, 2018). Statistics from around the world are not so positive. U.S. News & World Report (2014) listed the ten worst countries in the world for gender equality as Jordan, Egypt, Indonesia, Turkey, Iran, Malaysia, Algeria, India, South Korea, and Saudi Arabia. All of these countries are in and around the Middle East, where Islam is prominent, including within governmental systems (Adib-Moghaddam, 2008; Eagleton, 1965; Ziring, 1984). Within these countries there are large occupational, financial, educational, and literacy gaps, with girls and women on the losing end. Within these countries, women have very few rights. They cannot divorce their husbands and cannot pass citizenship to their children. Spousal abuse and rape are not illegal, and there are extremely high sexual assault rates. Female genital mutilation is not uncommon and selective abortion is used for female fetuses because girls and women are devalued. Women are humiliated with virginity tests at marriage and women remain covered, either just the head and neck (the *hijab*) or the full body and face covering of the *burqa*, which limits perception, expression, communication, movement, body heat regulation, pretty much everything (see Figure 7.2). Not surprisingly, child marriage is also common in these countries (Jamjoon, 2009; World Economic Forum, 2016). Under extreme versions of Islamic law, women in these regions are stoned to death for being raped, being convicted of seducing their rapists (Pleasance, 2017). One case involved a 13-year-old girl who was raped by three men; she was convicted of adultery and stoned to death (United States Commission on International Religious Freedom, 2008). Stoning anyone to death is obviously inhumane and morally wrong; when they are being murdered because they were raped, the injustice is incomprehensible.

The World Economic Forum (2014) reports that the worst countries for women economically are Pakistan, Chad, and Yemen, with women making 18% of what men make in Pakistan; having a 28% literacy rate in Chad; and having only 26% labor force participation in Yemen. Obviously, low education, literacy, and labor force participation are associated with poverty, with many more women living in poverty around the world than men (Oxfam International, 2018). Women are much more likely to die from complications of pregnancy and childbirth in the developing world (239 deaths per 100,000 live births) than in developed nations (12 deaths per 100,000 live births), especially when they are younger than 15 years old. Although maternal mortality rates are declining worldwide, they are highest where poverty among women is high and where advanced, accessible health care is not available (the highest maternal mortality rates are in South Asia and sub-Saharan Africa) (World Health Organization, 2018).

Figure 7.2a A woman in a hijab
Source: Ridofranz/iStock Photo

Men control about 80% of political power around the globe (World Economic Forum, 2014; see Chapter 12). In the United States, women's political power is ridiculously low across the nation's history. At the time of this writing, there are 21 female U.S. Senators and 84 female members of the House of Representatives. Those 105 out of 535 seats in the U.S. Congress make up 19.6%; not 50%, not even 25%. There are currently five female governors of the 50 United States. Of the 112 U.S. Supreme Court Justices since 1789, only four have been women (Sandra Day O'Connor, Ruth Bader Ginsberg, Elena Kagan, Sonia Sotomayor). That's 3.6%; not 50%, not even 5%. And of course, the seat of world power has never been held by a woman. Not one single time. In 2016, former Secretary of State and U.S. Senator Hillary Clinton was defeated by a reality television star with no political experience and a history of sexual assault. Women are not equal in the United States; whether they ever will be is up to us, to you. It is true that women who confront sexism are often disliked by others and characterized as complainers, including by other women (Kaiser & Miller, 2004; Nicole & Stewart, 2004). Withstanding that legitimizing myth can be a personal battle for some of us. Thankfully, recent research indicates that angry confrontation of sexism is actually linked with improved well-being over time (Foster, 2013). Hopefully, with greater numbers of women achieving undergraduate and advanced degrees (Georgetown Center on Education and the Workforce, 2018), and with an increasing recognition of sexism and the importance of speaking out and activism toward fighting it (Foster, 2015), women's health, safety, happiness, and power will continue to increase all over the world.

Chapter Summary

Sexism is everywhere and has existed since Homo Sapiens has existed. Men are physically bigger and stronger than women; these physical differences enable men to oppress women at the most basic level. Women are also controlled and oppressed by men because of their reproductive

Figure 7.2b A woman in a burqa
Source: Richard Sowersby/Alamy Stock Photo

roles. Dependency and physical vulnerability during pregnancy and breastfeeding enables men to control women; men continue to control women worldwide through the denial of access to contraception and safe, legal abortion. Women have been considered property throughout history because of their sexual and reproductive capabilities. Men have created global and historical patriarchy through the use of physical force and legitimizing myths that are enforced through social and cultural institutions. Major world religions are particularly misogynistic and subordinate women because of their sex. Different types of sexism exist, most notably benevolent sexism, hostile sexism, and modern sexism. Hostile sexism is linked with hypermasculinity, which is in turn linked with negative attitudes about women and aggression toward women. The media is notoriously sexist, commonly sexually objectifying girls and women while making men the leaders and heroes. Media depictions of men emphasize their character and intellect, while women's bodies are emphasized instead of their character and skills. The world is also extremely heterosexist, with other sexual orientations persecuted and subordinated all over the world, including through criminalization. Religions also condemn any sexuality beyond marital heterosexuality for the purpose of reproduction. Sexism exists globally today in sexual assaults and physical attacks

182 *Global, Historical Sexism*

on women, and women's continued lower social status, incomes, opportunities, education, and literacy. Increasing activism, education, and political participation by women, and feminism by everyone, will continue the movement toward greater gender equality.

Thoughtful Questions

- Explain modern sexism. How does it work to maintain patriarchy?
- Explain the link between hypermasculinity, hostile sexism, and aggression.
- Discuss the Trump Administration's approach to LGBTQ equality.
- Explain heterosexism in terms of social dominance and legitimizing myths.
- Explain benevolent sexism. Why is it harmful to women?
- Explain the role of religion in patriarchy.
- Explain the difference between implicit and explicit attitudes. How is each measured?
- Why do you think people become angry about other people's sexual orientations and behaviors?
- Explain legitimizing myths and how they are used to oppress women.
- Explain the psychological effects of exposure to ideal beauty images.
- Describe how women are doing around the world today.

Glossary

#MeToo: started in 2017, a social media movement focused on speaking out truthfully and forcefully about men's widespread and common victimization of girls and women.

#NotAllMen: a social media response to the #MeToo movement emphasizing that not all men sexually victimize children and women.

#TimesUp: a social media movement calling for an end to tolerance of men's victimization of children and women.

Accessible: the degree to which a schema is easily retrieved and used for processing information. For sexists, gender stereotypes are highly accessible schemas.

Agentic: behaviors and qualities involving activity, strength, power, competence; a primary dimension of ideas about masculinity.

Ambivalent sexism: the psychological co-existence of positive and negative attitudes toward women, of benevolent and hostile sexism.

Attitude: an evaluative belief; thoughts and feelings about an attitude object.

Benevolent sexism: sexism involving warmth, trust, and desire for intimacy, along with paternalistic ideas that subordinate women.

Bisexuality: sexual attraction to and activity with persons of any sex.

Bonding: the formation of a deep affectional tie and attachment between infants and primary caregivers, commonly mother.

Career woman: a prototype (exemplar) of a type of woman, a women's role.

Chastity belt: a locking device worn over the genitals, usually female; used to prevent masturbation or sexual behavior among unmarried girls and women.

Cisgender: a person whose gender identity is the same as that assigned to them at birth.

Communal: emotions and behaviors motivated toward caring for the well-being of others; a primary dimension of ideas about femininity.

Global, Historical Sexism 183

Concubines: women living in common law with a man outside of marriage for sexual purposes. Throughout history, many concubines were involuntary, that is kidnapped and held prisoner for sexual use by men.

Confederate: a person working with researchers in a role to examine participant responses.

Discrimination: treating someone differently because of their group membership; any attitude, act, or institutional structure or process that subordinates a person because of their group membership.

Egalitarian: oriented toward equality. Egalitarian societies emphasize equality between women and men, ethnic and racial groups, sexual orientations, and other groups.

Emotional brain: the mid-brain structures (amygdala, hypothalamus, hippocampus) that respond automatically and implicitly to stimuli, including other people. The controlled brain (forebrain, processing and memory storage areas) processes information consciously and explicitly.

Empathic concern: feelings of empathy (understanding and feeling bad about another's plight) and concern for the well-being of others.

Equal protection: equal protection under the law, guaranteed in the Fourteenth Amendment to the United States Constitution.

Explicit attitudes: attitudes that are fully conscious and consciously formulated.

Female genital mutilation (FGM): mutilation of girls' and women's genitals for religious reasons. FGM is barbaric, dangerous, and leads to serious health, sexual, and psychological complications.

Feminism: advocating social, political, legal, and economic rights for women equal to those of men.

Feminists: people who have real, genuine respect for women and think that they should be treated equally to men.

Fornication: a negative term describing sexual relations between two people who are not married; or sexual behavior engaged in for pleasure, not for reproduction.

Healthy sexuality: sexuality that is adult, consensual, and safe (protecting against sexually transmitted diseases and unwanted pregnancy).

Heteronormative: when heterosexuality is considered normal and preferred in a society; the rules of sexuality are inherently heterosexual, to the neglect of other sexualities.

Heterosexism: an ideology embodied in institutional practices that work to the disadvantage of sexual minority groups.

Heterosexuality: sexual attraction to and activity with persons of the opposite sex.

Homosexuality: sexual attraction to and activity with persons of the same sex.

Hostile sexism: sexism involving negative feelings accompanied by negative stereotypes of women and heterosexual hostility.

Housewife/mother: a prototype (exemplar) of a type of woman, a women's role.

Hypermasculinity: extreme masculinity including endorsement of violence, callous sexual attitudes toward women, and risk-taking.

Hysterical: suffering from extreme and irrational emotionality; derived from the Latin word for uterus.

Implicit: cognitive ideas and processes that are so well-practiced or so commonly used that they have become automatic (occurring unintentionally and sometimes without conscious awareness).

Implicit attitudes: evaluative beliefs that are accessed and used automatically in response to external stimuli; may be used without conscious awareness.

184 *Global, Historical Sexism*

Implicit Association Test (IAT; Greenwald et al., 1998**):** a measure of implicit attitudes based on the idea that people respond more quickly when two things are closely associated with each other. When attitudes are implicit, people respond more quickly to them than when they are not implicit.

Legitimizing myths: false beliefs about a group that justify their continued oppression.

Matriarchal: a societal structure where women are in charge of all or most social institutions and maintain the majority of wealth, status, and power in society. A truly matriarchal society has never actually existed.

Misogyny: hatred of women. A **misogynist** is a person who hates women.

Modern sexism (aka **neosexism):** beliefs that women have already achieved equality, and that women who say otherwise are whining or trying to gain unfair advantage.

Normative: standard, typical, normal.

Old-fashioned sexism: beliefs that women are incapable and inferior to men, coupled with an open opposition to women's equality to men.

Patriarchy: a societal structure where men are in charge of all or most social institutions and maintain the majority of wealth, status, and power in society.

Polygamous: the condition where a man is married to more than one woman.

Poverty: lacking in material possessions and money, such that meeting basic needs (e.g., for food, shelter, medical care) is affected.

Precarious manhood: masculinity that is easily threatened. When men have precarious manhood, they react more negatively and aggressively to threats to self-concept.

Prejudice: negative feelings toward a broad social group and its members.

Rape myths: false beliefs about women and rape that men use to justify sexual aggression against women.

Right-wing authoritarianism (RWA): a very conservative belief system based on feelings of obedience to authority and respect for tradition and hierarchy. People high in RWA report hatred of unconventional people and people from outgroups.

Schema: a mental knowledge structure that contains everything a person knows about a particular topic or subject.

Science: a method; a set of rules for observing and discovering truth about the natural world.

Sexism: treating someone differently because of their sex; any attitude, act, or institutional structure or process that subordinates a person because of their sex.

Sexist: a person who endorses sexist ideology (negative ideas about women) and engages in behaviors that subordinate individuals because of their sex.

Sexual minority groups: many different groups including anyone who does not identify as heterosexual.

Sexual objectification: treating women only as sexual objects, ranging from body evaluation by others to sexual assault.

Sexual orientation: romantic, emotional, and sexual attraction to people of certain gender(s), along with a sense of identity based on that attraction and related behaviors.

Slut-shaming: shaming women for their sexual behavior.

Social dominance orientation (SDO): individual preference for inequality between groups. People higher in SDO prefer inequality and are usually already of higher status in the hierarchy.

Social dominance theory: an explanation of social hierarchies and oppression based on gender, sexuality, race/ethnicity, etc. People at the top of the hierarchy enjoy a disproportionate share of society's assets (power, wealth) and create **legitimizing myths** to maintain the hierarchy.

Social norms: explicit and implicit rules for behavior within any particular situation.

Stereotypes: beliefs (**schemas**) about the qualities, traits, and abilities of members of broad social categories.

Stigmatization: social rejection and scorn for an identifiable condition.

Suffrage: the right to vote. The women's suffrage movement in the United States evolved into the modern U.S. women's movement.

Transgender: having a gender identity different from the gender assigned at birth.

References

Adams, H. E., Wright, L. W., & Lohr, B. A. (1996). Is homophobia associated with homosexual arousal? *Journal of Abnormal Psychology, 105*(3), 440–445.

Adib-Moghaddam, A. (2008). *Iran in world politics: The question of the Islamic Republic.* London: Hurst & Co; New York: Columbia University Press.

Alabama Secretary of State (2017). U.S. Senate Special General Election 2017 Statewide Results. Retrieved December 18, 2017.

Alfred, C. (2014). These 20 countries have no law against domestic violence. *Huffington Post*, March 10. www. huffingtonpost.com/2014/03/08/countries-no-domestic-violence-law_n_4918784.html.

Allen, M., Emmers, T., Gebhardt, L., & Giery, M. A. (1995). Exposure to pornography and acceptance of rape myths. *Journal of Communication, 45*, 5–26.

American Psychological Association (2008). *Answers to your questions: For a better understanding of sexual orientation and homosexuality.* Washington, DC: APA. www.apa.org/topics/sorientation.

Anderson, C. A., & Bushman, B. J. (2001). Effects of violent video games on aggressive behavior, aggressive cognition, aggressive affect, physiological arousal, and prosocial behavior: A metaanalytic review of the scientific literature. *Psychological Science, 12*, 353–359.

Anderson, C. A., & Dill, K. E. (2000). Video games and aggressive thoughts, feelings, and behavior in the laboratory and in life. *Journal of Personality and Social Psychology, 78*, 772–790.

Anderson, C. A., Berkowitz, L., Donnerstein, E., Huesmann, L. R., Johnson, J., Linz, D., ... Wartella, E. (2003). The influence of media violence on youth. *Psychological Science in the Public Interest, 4*, 81–110.

Anderson, K. (1981). *Wartime women: Sex roles, family relations, and the status of women during World War II.* Westport, CT: Greenwood Press.

Aosved, A. C., & Long, P. J. (2006). Co-occurrence of rape myth acceptance, sexism, racism, homophobia, ageism, classism, and religious intolerance. *Sex Roles, 55*(7–8), 481–492.

Archer, D., Iritani, B., Kimes, D. D., & Barrios, M. (1983). Face-ism: Five studies of sex differences in facial prominence. *Journal of Personality and Social Psychology, 45*(4), 725–735.

Avruch, S., & A. P. Cackley (1995). Savings achieved by giving WIC benefits to women prenatally. *Public Health Reports, 110*(1), 27–34.

Bailey, J. M. (1999). Homosexuality and mental illness. *Archives of General Psychiatry, 56*(10): 883–884. doi:10.1001.

Baker, C. N. (2005). Images of women's sexuality in advertisements: A content analysis of Black- and White-oriented women's and men's magazines. *Sex Roles, 52*, 13–27. http://dx.doi.org/10.1007/s11199-005-1190-y.

Balsdon, J. P. V. D. (1962). *Roman women: Their history and habits.* London: Bodley Head.

Bamberger, J. (1974). The myth of matriarchy: Why men rule in primitive society. In Rosaldo, M. Z., & Lamphere, L. (Eds.), *Woman, culture, and society.* Stanford, CA: Stanford University Press, pp. 263–279.

Barasch, Alex (2018). HHS's new rule allows health care workers to discriminate against LGBTQ people and abortion seekers: This isn't just another form of Trumpian bigotry, which is why we should be even more nervous. *Slate.* https://slate.com/technology/2018/01/trumps-new-hhs-rule-is-a-license-to-discriminate-against-lgbtq-people-and-abortion-seekers.html.

Bargh, J. A., & Chartrand, T. (1999). The unbearable automaticity of being. *American Psychologist, 54*, 462–479.

Bargh, J. A., Chen, M., & Burrows, L. (1996). Automaticity of social behavior: Direct effects of trait construct and stereotype activation on action. *Journal of Personality and Social Psychology, 71*(2), 230–244.

Barreto, M., & Ellemers, N. (2005). The perils of political correctness: Men's and women's responses to old-fashioned and modern sexist views. *Social Psychology Quarterly, 68*(1), 75–88.

Bayton, J. A., McAlister, L. B., & Hamer, J. (1956). Race-class stereotypes. *The Journal of Negro Education, 25*(1), 75–78.

Becker, G. S. (2010). *The economics of discrimination*. Chicago: University of Chicago Press.

Becker, J. C., & Swim, J. K. (2012). Reducing endorsement of benevolent and modern sexist beliefs: Differential effects of addressing harm versus pervasiveness of benevolent sexism. *Social Psychology, 43*(3), 127-137. doi:10.1027/1864-9335/a000091.

Bellis, R. (2017a). Here's everywhere in the U.S. you can still get fired for being gay or trans. Fast Company. www.fastcompany.com/40456937/heres-everywhere-in-the-u-s-you-can-still-get-fired-for-being-gay-or-trans.

Bellis, R. (2017b). Jeff Sessions is making a mess in states like Florida that lack LGBT employment protections. Fast Company. www.fastcompany.com/40457541/jeff-sessions-is-making-a-mess-in-states-like-florida-that-lack-lgbt-employment-protections.

Ben-Zeev, A., Scharnetzki, L., Chan, L. K., & Dennehy, T. C. (2012). *Psychology of Popular Media Culture, 1*(1), 53-61.

Berer, M. (2017). Abortion law and policy around the world: In search of decriminalization. *Health and Human Rights, 19*(1), 13-27.

Bergman, M., Lanhout, R. D., Palmieri, P. A., Cortina, L. M., & Fitzgerald, L. F. (2002). The (un)reasonableness of reporting: Antecedents and consequences of reporting sexual harassment. *Journal of Applied Psychology, 87*, 230-242. doi:10.1037/0021-9010.87.2.230.

Bernard, P., Gervais, S. J., Allen, J., Campomizzi, S., & Klein, O. (2012). Integrating sexual objectification with object versus person recognition: The sexualized-body-inversion hypothesis. *Psychological Science, 23*, 469-471. http://dx.doi.org/10 .1177/0956797611434748.

Bernard, P., Gervais, S., Allen, J., Campomizzi, S., & Klein, O. (2015). Body parts reduction and self objectification in the objectification of sexualized bodies. *International Review of Social Psychology, 28*, 39-61.

Beydoun, M. A., Poggi-Burke, A., Zonderman, A. B., Rostant, O. S., Evans, M. K., & Crews, D. C. (2017). Perceived discrimination and longitudinal change in kidney function among urban adults. *Psychosomatic Medicine, 79*, 824-834.

Birkett, M., Espelage, D. L., & Koenig, B. (2009). LGB and questioning students in schools: The moderating effects of homophobic bullying and school climate on negative outcomes. *Journal of Adolescence, 38*, 989-1000.

Bittman, M., & Pixley, J. (1997). *The double life of the family: Myth, hope and experience*. Sydney: Allen & Unwin.

Black, M. C., Basile, K. C., Breiding, M. J., Smith, S. G., Walters, M. L., Merrick, M. T., & Stevens, M. R. (2011). The National Intimate Partner and Sexual Violence Survey (NISVS): 2010 summary report. Centers for Disease Control and Prevention, National Center for Injury Prevention and Control. www.cdc.gov/ViolencePrevention/pdf/NISVS_Report2010-a.

Bock, J., Byrd-Craven, J., & Burkley, M. (2017). The role of sexism in voting in the 2016 presidential election. *Personality and Individual Differences, 119*, 189-193. https://doi.org/10.1016/j.paid.2017.07.026.

Bosson, J. K., Vandello, J. A., Burnaford, R. M., Weaver, J. R., & Arzu Wasti, S. (2009). Precarious manhood and displays of physical aggression. *Personality and Social Psychology Bulletin, 35*, 623-634. http:// dx.doi.org/10.1177/0146167208331161 B.

Braun, C., & Giroux, J. (1989). Arcade video games: Proxemic, cognitive and content analyses. *Journal of Leisure Research, 21*, 92-105.

Brebner, J. (2003). Gender and emotions. *Personality and Individual Differences, 34*(3), 387-394.

Breen, A. B., & Karpinski, A. (2013). Implicit and explicit attitudes toward gay males and lesbians among heterosexual males and females. *The Journal of Social Psychology, 153*, 351-374. http://dx.doi.org/10.1080/00224545.2012.739581.

Brown, D. (2008). *Porn & Pong: How Grand Theft Auto, Tomb Raider and other sexy games changed our culture*. Port Townsend, WA: Feral House.

Burgess, M. C. R., Stermer, S. P., & Burgess, S. R. (2007). Sex, lies, and videogames: The portrayal of male and female characters on videogame covers. *Sex Roles, 57*, 419-433. http://dx.doi.org/10.1007/s11199-007-9250-0.

Burke, D. (2017). The four reasons people commit hate crimes. CNN Religion Editor, June 12. www.cnn.com/2017/06/02/us/who-commits-hate-crimes/index.html.

Burt, M. R. (1980). Cultural myths and supports for rape. *Journal of Personality and Social Psychology, 38*, 217-230.

Carr, E. R., & Szymanski, D. M. (2011). Sexual objectification and substance abuse in young adult women. *The Counseling Psychologist, 39*(1), 39-66. https://doi.org/10.1177/0011000010378449.

Chatterji, P., & Brooks-Gunn, J. (2004). WIC participation, breastfeeding practices, and well-child care among unmarried, low-income mothers. *American Journal of Public Health, 94*(8), 1324-1327. doi:10.2105/AJPH.94.8.1324.

Chen, L., & Li, C. I. (2015). Racial disparities in breast cancer diagnosis and treatment by hormone receptor and HER2 status. *Cancer Epidemiology, Biomarkers & Prevention, 24*, 1666-1672. doi:10.1158/1055-9965.epi-15-0293.

Christopher, A. N., & Mull, M. S. (2006). Conservative ideology and ambivalent sexism. *Psychology of Women Quarterly, 30*(2), 223-230.

Cikara, M., Eberhardt, J. L., & Fiske, S. T. (2011). From agents to objects: Sexist attitudes and neural responses to sexualized targets. *Journal of Cognitive Neuroscience, 23*, 540-551. http://dx.doi.org/ 10.1162/jocn.2010.21497.

Civile, C., & Obhi, S. S. (2015). Power, objectification, and recognition of sexualized women and men. *Psychology of Women Quarterly*. Advance online publication. http://dx.doi.org/10.1177/ 0361684315604820.

Cohen, J. (1988). *Statistical power analysis for the behavioral sciences* (2nd ed.). Hillsdale, NJ: Erlbaum.

Cohn, A. M., Seibert, L. A., & Zeichner, A. (2009). The role of restrictive emotionality, trait anger, and masculinity threat in men's perpetration of physical aggression. *Psychology of Men & Masculinity, 10*, 218-224. http://dx.doi.org/10.1037/a0015151.

Coltrane, S., & Messineo, M. (2000). The perpetuation of subtle prejudice: Race and gender imagery in 1990s television advertising. *Sex Roles, 42*(5-6), 363-389.

Conley, T. D., & Ramsey, L. R. (2011). Killing us softly? Investigating portrayals of women and men in contemporary magazine advertisements. *Psychology of Women Quarterly, 35*, 469-478. http:// dx.doi.org/10.1177/0361684311413383.

Consolacion, T. B., Russell, S. T., & Sue, S. (2004). Sex, race/ethnicity, and romantic attractions: Multiple minority status adolescents and mental health. *Cultural Diversity and Ethnic Minority Psychology, 10*(3), 200-214.

Coultrap-McQuin, S. (2000). *Doing literary business: American women writers in the nineteenth century.* Chapel Hill, NC: University of North Carolina Press.

Craig, L. (2002). Caring differently: A time-use analysis of the type and social context of child care performed by fathers and mothers. Social Policy Research Centre, University of New South Wales.

Crittenden, A. (2001). *The price of motherhood: Why the most important job in the world is still the least valued.* New York: Henry Holt.

Cross, E. J., Overall, N. C., Hammond, M. D., & Fletcher Garth, J. O. (2017). When does men's hostile sexism predict relationship aggression? The moderating role of partner commitment. *Social Psychological and Personality Science, 8*(3), 331-340.

Cross, E. J., Overall, N. C., Low, R. S. T., & McNulty, J. K. (2019). An interdependence account of sexism and power: Men's hostile sexism, biased perceptions of low power, and relationship aggression. *Journal of Personality and Social Psychology, 117*(2), 338-363. https://doi.org/10.1037/pspi0000167.

Cuddy, A. J.C., Fiske, S. T., & Glick, P. (2004). When professionals become mothers, warmth doesn't cut the ice. *Journal of Social Issues, 60*(4), 701-718. ttps://doi.org/10.1111/j.0022-4537.2004.00381.x.

Dahl, G. B. (2010). Early teen marriage and future poverty. *Demography, 47*, 689-718. doi:10.1353/dem.0.0120. PMC 3000061.

Dahl, J., Vescio, T., & Weaver, K. (2014). How threats to masculinity sequentially cause public discomfort, anger, and ideological dominance over women. *Social Psychology, 46*, 242-254. http://dx.doi.org/10.1027/1864-9335/a000248.

Dardenne, B., Dumont, M., & Bollier, T. (2007). Insidious dangers of benevolent sexism: Consequences for women's performance. *Journal of Personality and Social Psychology, 93*(5), 764-779. https://doi.org/10.1037/0022-3514.93.5.764.

Davis, K. C., Morris, J., George, W. H., Martell, J., & Heiman, J. R. (2006). Men's likelihood of sexual aggression: The influence of alcohol, sexual arousal, and violent pornography. *Aggressive Behavior, 32*(6), 581-589.

Deckard, B. S. (1975). *The women's movement: Political, socioeconomic, and philosophical issues.* New York: Harper and Row.

Der, G., & Deary, I. (2006). Age and sex differences in reaction time in adulthood: Results from the United Kingdom Health and Lifestyle Survey. *Psychology and Aging, 21*(1), 62-73.

DeVane, B., & Squire, K. D. (2008). The meaning of race and violence in Grand Theft Auto. *Games & Culture, 3*(3-4), 264-285. https://doi.org/10.1177/1555412008317308.

Devine, P. G., Monteith, M. J., Zuwerink, J. R., & Elliot, A. J. (1991). Prejudice with and without compunction. *Journal of Personality and Social Psychology, 60*(6), 817-830.

Dietz, T. L. (1998). An examination of violence and gender role portrayals in video games: Implications for gender socialization and aggressive behavior. *Sex Roles, 38*, 425-442.

Dijkstra, B. (1996). *Evil sisters: The threat of female sexuality and the cult of manhood.* New York: Knopf.

Dill, K. E., & Thill, K. P. (2007). Video game characters and the socialization of gender roles: Young people's perceptions mirror sexist media depictions. *Sex Roles, 57*, 851-864. http://dx.doi.org/10 .1007/s11199-007-9278-1.

Dill, K. E., Gentile, D. A., Richter, W. A., & Dill, J. C. (2005). Violence, sex, race, and age in popular video games: A content analysis. In Cole, E., & Daniel, J. H. (Eds.), *Featuring females: Feminist analyses of media.* Washington, DC: American Psychological Association, pp. 115-130.

DiMuccio, S. H., Yost, M. R., & Helweg-Larsen, M. (2017). A qualitative analysis of perceptions of precarious manhood in U.S. and Danish men. *Psychology of Men & Masculinity, 18*(4), 331-340.

Dobash, R. E., & Dobash, R. (1979). *Violence against wives: A case against the patriarchy.* New York: Free Press.

Dohnt, H., & Tiggemann, M. (2006). The contribution of peer and media influences to the development of body satisfaction and self-esteem in young girls: A prospective study. *Developmental Psychology, 42,* 929-936.

DuBois, E. C., & Dumenil, L. (2015). *Through women's eyes: An American history with documents* (4th ed.). New York: Bedford/St. Martin's.

Durlak, J. A., Weissberg, R. P., & Pachan, M. (2010). A meta-analysis of after-school programs that seek to promote personal and social skills in children and adolescents. *American Journal of Community Psychology, 45*(3-4), 294-309.

Eagleton, W. Jr. (1965). The Islamic Republic of Mauritania. *Middle East Journal, 19*(1), 45-53.

Eagly, A. H., Karau, S. J., & Makhijani, M. G. (1995). Gender and the effectiveness of leaders: A meta-analysis. *Psychological Bulletin, 117,* 125-145.

Ellison, M. A. (2003). Authoritative knowledge and single women's unintentional pregnancies, abortions, adoption, and single motherhood: Social stigma and structural violence. *Medical Anthropology Quarterly, 17*(3), 322-347. https://doi.org/10.1525/maq.2003.17.3.322.

Entertainment Software Association (2018). US video game industry revenue reaches $36 billion in 2017. Press Release. www.theesa.com/article/us-video-game-industry-revenue-reaches-36-billion-2017/.

Epstein, R., Blake, J., & González, T. (2017). Girlhood interrupted: The erasure of Black girls' childhood. Center on Poverty and Inequality. www.law.georgetown.edu/academics/centers-institutes/povertyinequality/upload/girlhood-interrupted.

Etehad, M., & Lin, J. C.F. (2016). The world is getting better at paid maternity leave. The U.S. is not. *The Washington Post,* August 13. www.washingtonpost.com/news/worldviews/wp/2016/08/13/the-world-is-getting-better-at-paid-maternity-leave-the-u-s-is-not/.

Evans, P. C. (2003). "If only I were thin like her, maybe I could be happy like her": The self implications of associating a thin female ideal with life success. *Psychology of Women Quarterly, 27,* 209-214.

Ezell, M. J. M (1996). *Writing women's literary history.* Baltimore, MD: Johns Hopkins University Press.

FBI Uniform Crime Report (2011). Crime in the U.S 2011; Table 66. https://ucr.fbi.gov/crime-in-the-u.s/2011/crime-in-the-u.s.-2011/tables/table_66_arrests_suburban_areas_by_sex_2011.

FBI Uniform Crime Report (2017). 2016 Hate Crime Statistics. https://ucr.fbi.gov/hate-crime/2016/topic-pages/incidentsandoffenses.

Felson, R. B., & Palmore, C. (2018). Biases in blaming victims of rape and other crime. *Psychology of Violence, 8*(3), 390-399.

Fergusen, E. (1993). *Backgrounds of early Christianity* (2nd ed.). Grand Rapids, MI: William B. Eerdmans.

Fernandez, S., & Pritchard, M. (2012). Relationships between self-esteem, media influence and drive for thinness. *Eating Behaviors, 13*(4), 321-325.

Finer, L., & Fine, J. B. (2013). Abortion law around the world: Progress and pushback. *American Journal of Public Health, 103*(4), 585-589. doi:10.2105/AJPH.2012.301197.

Finkelhor, D., Hotaling, G., Lewis, I. A., & Smith, C. (1990). Sexual abuse in a national survey of adult men and women: Prevalence, characteristics and risk factors. *Child Abuse & Neglect 14,* 19-28. doi:10.1016/0145-2134(90)90077-7.

Finnigan L., & Bingham, J. (2016). Women should not travel more than 48 miles without a male escort – Muslim group. *The Telegraph,* May 4. www.telegraph.co.uk/news/2016/05/04/women-should-not-travel-more-than-48-miles-without-a-male-escort/.

Fiske, S. T. (2017). Prejudices in cultural contexts: Shared stereotypes (gender, age) versus variable stereotypes (race, ethnicity, religion). *Perspectives on Psychological Science, 12*(5), 791-799.

Fiske, S. T., Cuddy, A. J.C., & Glick, P. (2007). Universal dimensions of social cognition: Warmth and competence. *Trends in Cognitive Sciences, 11*(2), 77-83.

Foran, C. (2018). The plan to overturn Roe v. Wade at the Supreme Court is already in motion. CNN Politics, June 29. www.cnn.com/2018/06/29/politics/abortion-roe-v-wade-supreme-court/index.html.

Ford, M. (2017). The 19 women who accused President Trump of sexual misconduct. *The Atlantic,* December 7.

Foster, M. D. (2013). Everyday confrontation of discrimination: The well-being costs and benefits to women over time. *Psychology Faculty Publications, 54.*

Foster, M. D. (2015). Tweeting about sexism: The well-being benefits of a social media collective action. *British Journal of Social Psychology, 54*(4), 629-647.

Franzoi, S. L. (2006). *Social psychology.* New York: McGraw Hill.

Fredrickson, B. L., & Roberts, T. (1997). Objectification theory: Toward understanding women's lived experiences and mental health risks. *Psychology of Women Quarterly, 21,* 173-206. http://dx.doi.org/10.1111/j.1471-6402.1997.tb00108.x.

Friesen, J. P., Kay, A. C., Eibach, R. P., & Galinsky, A. D. (2014). Seeking structure in social organization: Compensatory control and the psychological advantages of hierarchy. *Journal of Personality and Social Psychology, 106*, 590-609. doi:10.1037/ a0035620.

Gallagher, K. E., & Parrott, D. J. (2011). What accounts for men's hostile attitudes toward women? The influence of hegemonic male role norms and masculine gender role stress. *Violence Against Women, 17*, 568-583. http://dx.doi.org/10.1177/1077801211407296.

Garces, E., Thomas, D., & Currie, J. (2002). Longer-term effects of Head Start. *American Economic Review, 92*(4), 999-1012.

Gardner, J. F. (1986). *Women in Roman law and society*. Sydney: Croom Helm.

Garn, S., & Clark, L. (1953). The sex difference in the basal metabolic rate. *Child Development, 24*, 215-224.

Gaunt, R. (2013). Ambivalent sexism and the attribution of emotions to men and women. *Revue Internationale de Psychologie Sociale, 26*(2), 29-54.

Gelernter, J. (2016). A conservative defense of transgender rights. *National Review*, December 17.

Gelles, R. J. (1988). Violence and pregnancy: Are pregnant women at greater risk of abuse? *Journal of Marriage and Family, 50*(3), 841-847.

Georgetown Center on Education and the Workforce (2018). Women can't win. Georgetown University. https://cew.georgetown.edu/cew-reports/genderwagegap/.

Giaccardi, S., Ward, L. M., Seabrook, R. C., Manago, A., & Lippman, J. R. (2017). Media use and men's risk behaviors: Examining the role of masculinity ideology. *Sex Roles, 77*(9-10), 581-592.

Gibson, S. (2013). The history of Grand Theft Auto. IGN.com. May 6.

Gilmore, D. (1990). *Manhood in the making: Cultural concepts of masculinity*. New Haven, CT: Yale University Press.

Glick, P., & Fiske, S. T. (1996). The ambivalent sexism inventory: Differentiating hostile and benevolent sexism. *Journal of Personality and Social Psychology, 70*, 491-512. doi:10.1037/0022-3514. 70.3.491.

Glick, P., Diebold, J., Bailey-Werner, B., & Zhu, L. (1997). The two faces of Adam: Ambivalent sexism and polarized attitudes toward women. *Personality and Social Psychology Bulletin, 23*, 1323-1334. doi:10.1177/01461672972312009.

Glick, P., & Fiske, S. T. (1999). Sexism and other "isms": Independence, status, and the ambivalent content of stereotypes. In Swann, W. B., Jr., Langlois, J. H., & Gilbert, L. A. (Eds.), *Sexism and stereotypes in modern society: The gender science of Janet Taylor Spence* (pp. 193-221). Washington, DC: American Psychological Association. https://doi.org/10.1037/10277-008.

Glick, P., & Fiske, S. T. (2001). Ambivalent sexism. *Advances in Experimental Social Psychology, 33*, 115-188.

Glick, P., Gangl, C., Gibb, S., Klumpner, S., & Weinberg, E. (2007). Defensive reactions to masculinity threats: More negative affect toward effeminate (but not masculine) gay men. *Sex Roles, 57*, 55-59. http://dx.doi.org/10.1007/s11199-007-9195-3.

Glomb, T. M., Richman, W. L., Hulin, C. L., Drasgow, F., Schneider, K. T., & Fitzgerald, L. F. (1997). Ambient sexual harassment: An integrated model of antecedents and consequences. *Organizational Behavior and Human Decision Processes, 71*, 309-328. http://dx.doi.org/10.1006/obhd.1997.2728.

Grabe, S., Ward, L. M., & Hyde, J. S. (2008). The role of the media in body image concerns among women: A meta-analysis of experimental and correlational studies. *Psychological Bulletin, 134*(3), 460-476. http://dx.doi.org/10.1037/0033-2909.134.3.460.

Graham, M. (2017). Why Roy Moore is surging in Alabama. CBS News, December 5. www.cbsnews.com/news/commentary-why-roy-moore-is-surging-in-alabama/.

Gray, M., & Chapman, B. (2001). Foregone earnings from child rearing. *Family Matters, 58*, 4-9.

Green, A., Carney, D., Pallin, D., Ngo, L., Raymond, K., Iezzoni, L., & Banaji, M. (2007). Implicit bias among physicians and its prediction of thrombolysis decisions for Black and White patients. *Journal of General Internal Medicine, 22*, 1231-1238.

Green, M. H. (2008). *Making women's medicine masculine: The rise of male authority in pre-modern gynaecology*. Oxford: Oxford University Press.

Greenwald, A. G., & Banaji, M. R. (1995). Implicit social cognition: Attitudes, self-esteem, and stereotypes. *Psychological Review, 102*, 4-27. http://dx.doi.org/10.1037/0033-295X.102.1.4.

Greenwald, A. G., McGhee, D. E., & Schwartz, J. L. (1998). Measuring individual differences in implicit cognition: The Implicit Association Test. *Journal of Personality and Social Psychology, 74*, 1464-1480. http://dx.doi.org/10.1037/0022-3514.74.6.1464.

Greenwald, A. G., Poehlman, T. A., Uhlmann, E. L., & Banaji, M. R. (2009). Understanding and using the Implicit Association Test: III. Meta-analysis of predictive validity. *Journal of Personality and Social Psychology, 97*, 17- 41. http://dx.doi.org/10.1037/a0015575.

Greenwood, D. N., & Lippman, J. R. (2010). Gender and media: Content, uses, and impact. In Chrisler, J., & McCreary, D. (Eds.), *Handbook of gender research in psychology*. New York: Springer.

Gross, L. (2001). *Up from invisibility: Lesbians, gay men, and the media in America*. New York: Columbia University Press.

Guardian (2017). Gay relationships are still criminalised in 72 countries, report finds. *The Guardian*, July 27. www.theguardian.com/world/2017/jul/27/gay-relationships-still-criminalised-countries-report.

Gursoy, R. (2010). Sex differences in relations of muscle power, lung function, and reaction time in athletes. *Perceptual and Motor Skills, 110*(3), 714–720.

Gutierres, S. E., Kenrick, D. T., & Partch, J. J. (1999). Beauty, dominance, and the mating game: Contrast effects in selfassessment reflect gender differences in mate selection. *Personality and Social Psychology Bulletin, 25*, 1126–1134.

Guttmacher Institute (2018a). Induced abortion in the United States (January Fact Sheet). New York: Guttmacher Institute.

Guttmacher Institute (2018b). Induced abortion worldwide (March Fact Sheet). New York: Guttmacher Institute.

Hahn, A., Judd, C. M., Hirsh, H. K., & Blair, I. V. (2014). Awareness of implicit attitudes. *Journal of Experimental Psychology, 143*(3), 1369–1392.

Halliwell, E., Dittmar, H., & Orsborn, A. (2007). The effects of exposure to muscular male models among men: Exploring the moderating role of gym use and exercise motivation. *Body Image, 4*(3), 278–287. https://doi.org/10.1016/j.bodyim.2007.04.006.

Hammond, M. D., & Overall, N. C. (2013). Men's hostile sexism and biased perceptions of intimate partners: Fostering dissatisfaction and negative behavior in close relationships. *Personality and Social Psychology Bulletin, 39*, 1585–1599. doi:10.1177/ 0146167213499026.

Harrison, K. (2003). Television viewers' ideal body proportions: The case of the curvaceously thin woman. *Sex Roles, 48*, 255–264.

Hatzenbuehler, M. L., & Pachankis, J. E. (2016). Stigma and minority stress as social determinants of health among lesbian, gay, bisexual, and transgender youth: Research evidence and clinical implications. *Pediatric Clinics of North America, 63*, 985–997. doi:10.1016/j.pcl.2016.07.003.

Hebl, M. R., King, E. B., Glick, P., Singletary, S. L., & Kazama, S. (2007). Hostile and benevolent reactions toward pregnant women: Complementary interpersonal punishments and rewards that maintain traditional roles. *Journal of Applied Psychology, 92*(6), 1499–1511.

Heflick, N. A., Goldenberg, J. L., Cooper, D. P., & Puvia, E. (2011). From women to objects: Appearance focus, target gender, and perceptions of warmth, morality and competence. *Journal of Experimental Social Psychology, 47*, 572–581. http:// dx.doi.org/10.1016/j.jesp.2010.12.020.

Hellmer, K., Stenson, J. T., & Jylhä, K. M. (2018). What's (not) underpinning ambivalent sexism? Revisiting the roles of ideology, religiosity, personality, demographics, and men's facial hair in explaining hostile and benevolent sexism. *Personality and Individual Differences, 122*, 29–37. https://doi.org/10.1016/ j.paid.2017.10.001.

Hennessy-Fiske, M., Pearce, M., & Jarvie, J. (2018). Texas school shooter killed girl who turned down his advances and embarrassed him in class, her mother says. *The Los Angeles Times* , May 20. www.latimes. com/nation/la-na-texas-shooter-20180519-story.html.

Herek, G. M. (2007). Confronting sexual stigma and prejudice: Theory and practice. *Journal of Social Issues, 63*(4), 905–925. https://doi.org/10.1111/j.1540-4560.2007.00544.x.

Herek, G. M., Gillis, J. R., & Cogan, J. C. (2009). Internalized stigma among sexual minority adults: Insights from a social psychological perspective. *Journal of Counseling Psychology, 56*(1), 32–43. https://doi.org/ 10.1037/a0014672.

Hesson-McInnis, M. S., & Fitzgerald, L. F. (1997). Sexual harassment: A preliminary test of an integrative model. *Journal of Applied Social Psychology, 27*, 877–901. doi:10.1111/j.1559-1816.1997.tb00276.x.

Hinsch, B. (2018). *Women in Ancient China*. New York: Rowman & Littlefield.

Hobza, C. L., & Rochlen, A. B. (2009). Gender role conflict, drive for muscularity, and the impact of ideal media portrayals on men. *Psychology of Men & Masculinity, 10*(2), 120–130.

Hoffman, S. D. (2006). *By the numbers: The public costs of adolescent childbearing*. Washington, DC: The National Campaign to Prevent Teen Pregnancy.

Holley, L. C., Tavassoli, K. Y., & Stromwall, L. K. (2016). Mental illness discrimination in mental health treatment programs: Intersections of race, ethnicity, and sexual orientation. *Community Mental Health Journal, 52*(3), 311–322.

Hossain, Z., & Juhari, R. (2015). Fathers across Arab and non-Arab Islamic societies. In Roopnarine, J. L. (Ed.), *Fathers across cultures: The importance, roles, and diverse practices of dads*. Santa Barbara, CA: Praeger, pp. 368–387.

Howell, N. (2015). A link between single parent families and crime. Ed.D. Dissertations. https://digitalcommons.olivet.edu/edd_diss/79.

Hunt, C. J., & Gonsalkorale, K. (2014). "Who cares what she thinks, what does he say?" Links between masculinity, ingroup bonding and gender harassment. *Sex Roles, 70*, 14-27. http://dx.doi.org/10.1007/s11199-013-0324-x.

Hurrell, A. (2005). *Power in global governance.* New York: Cambridge University Press.

Hurst, R. J., & Beesley, D. (2013). Perceived sexism, self-silencing, and psychological distress in college women. *Sex Roles, 68*(5-6), 311-320.

Jackson, P. (1994). Black male advertising and the cultural politics of masculinity. *Gender, Place, & Culture, 1*, 49-59.

Jacobs, S. (2018). Just nine of the world's richest men have more combined wealth than the poorest 4 billion people: Jeff Bezos, Bill Gates and Warren Buffett lead the pack. *The Independent,* January 17.

Jacobs, S. E., Thomas, W., & Lang, S. (1997). *Two-spirit people: Native American gender identity, sexuality, and spirituality.* Champaign, IL: University of Illinois Press.

Jagsi, R., Guancial, E. A., Worobey, C. C., Henault, L. E., Chang, Y., Starr, R., Tarbell, N. J., & Hylek, E. M. (2006). The "Gender Gap" in authorship of academic medical literature – a 35-year perspective. *New England Journal of Medicine, 355*, 281-287. doi:10.1056/NEJMsa053910.

Jamjoom, M. (2009). Saudi judge refuses to annul 8-year-old's marriage. CNN, April 12. www.cnn.com/2009/WORLD/meast/04/12/saudi.child.marriage/.

Jang, Y., Borenstein-Graves, A., Haley, W. E., Small, B. J., & Mortimer, J. A. (2003). Determinants of a sense of mastery in African American and White older adults. *The Journals of Gerontology Series B, 58*, S221-S224.

Jiménez-Cruz, B. E., & Silva-Gutiérrez, C. (2008). Effects of a brief exposure to women's media images on levels of anxiety and depression of university women considering their body mass index and their attitudes towards weight and food. *Revista Mexicana de Psicología, 25*(1), 89-98.

Johns, M. L. (2013). Breaking the glass ceiling: Structural, cultural, and organizational barriers preventing women from achieving senior and executive positions. *Perspectives in Health Information Management, 10*, 1-11.

Kaiser, C. R., & Miller, C. T. (2004). A stress and coping perspective on confronting sexism. *Psychology of Women Quarterly Volume, 28*(2), 168-178.

Katz, D., & Braly, K. (1933). Racial stereotypes of one hundred college students. *The Journal of Abnormal and Social Psychology, 28*(3), 280-290. https://doi.org/10.1037/h0074049.

Katz, J. (1995). *Gay and American history: Lesbians and gay men in the United States.* New York: Thomas Crowell.

Keneally, M., & Parkinson, J. (2017). What Roy Moore's 8 accusers have said and his responses. ABC News. Retrieved November 16, 2017.

Kenrick, D. T., & Gutierres, S. E. (1980). Contrast effects and judgments of physical attractiveness: When beauty becomes a social problem. *Journal of Personality and Social Psychology, 38*, 131-140.

Klein, J. D., & Committee on Adolescence (2005). Adolescent pregnancy: Current trends and issues. *Pediatrics, 116*(1), 281-286.

Knight, C. G., Tobin, S. J., & Hornsey, M. J. (2014). From fighting the system to embracing it: Control loss promotes system justification among those high in psychological reactance. *Journal of Experimental Social Psychology, 54*, 139-146. doi:10.1016/j.jesp.2014.04.012.

Kościński, K. (2013). Attractiveness of women's body: Body mass index, waist-hip ratio, and their relative importance. *Behavioral Ecology, 24*(4), 914-925.

Kosciw, J., Greytak, E., & Diaz, E. (2009). Who, what, where, when, and why: Demographic and ecological factors contributing to hostile school climate for lesbian, gay, bisexual, and transgender youth. *Journal of Adolescence, 38*, 976-988.

Laiou, A. (1993). Coercion to sex and marriage in ancient and medieval societies. Washington, DC: Dumbarton Oaks Research Library and Collection, pp. 85-190.

Lanis, K., & Covell, K. (1995). Images of women in advertisements: Effects on attitudes related to sexual aggression. *Sex Roles, 32*, 639-649.

Lassek, W., & Gaulin, S. (2009). Costs and benefits of fat-free muscle mass in men: Relationship to mating success, dietary requirements and natural immunity. *Evolution and Human Behavior, 30*, 322-328.

Lave, J. R., Keane, C. R., Lin, C. J., Ricci, M., Amersbach, G., & LaVallee, C. P. (1998). Caring for the uninsured and underinsured: Impact of a children's health insurance program on newly enrolled children, *Journal of the American Medical Association, 279*(22), 1820-1825. doi:10.1001/jama.279.22.1820.

Lefkowitz M. R., & Flint, M. B. (1982). *Women's life in Greece and Rome.* Baltimore: Johns Hopkins University Press.

Lemonaki, E., Manstead, A. S. R., & Maio, G. R. (2015). Hostile sexism (de)motivates women's social competition intentions: The contradictory role of emotions. *British Journal of Social Psychology, 54*(3), 483-499.

Lerner, Gerda (1986). *The creation of patriarchy*. Oxford: Oxford University Press.

Levant, R., Rankin, T., Williams, C., Hasan, N., & Smalley, B. (2010). Evaluation of the factor structure and construct validity of scores on the Male Role Norms Inventory. *Psychology of Men & Masculinity, 11*, 25-37. doi:10.1037/a0017637.

Lewis, T. T., Troxel, W. M., Kravitz, H. M., Bromberger, J. T., Matthews, K. A., & Hall, M. H. (2013). Chronic exposure to everyday discrimination and sleep in a multiethnic sample of middle-aged women. *Health Psychology, 32*, 810-819. doi:10.1037/a0029938.

Li, X., & Meier, J. (2017). Father love and mother love: Contributions of parental acceptance to children's psychological adjustment. *Journal of Family Theory and Review, 9*(4), 459-490. https://doi.org/10.1111/jftr.12227.

Lindner, K. (2004). Images of women in general interest and fashion magazine advertisements from 1955 to 2002. *Sex Roles, 51*, 409-421. http://dx.doi.org/10.1023/B:SERS.0000049230 .86869.4d.

Lips, H. M. (2003). The gender pay gap: Concrete indicator of women's progress toward equality. *Analyses of Social Issues and Public Policy, 3*(1), 87-109.

Locker, M. (2017). Trump turns back on LGBT community with transgender military ban tweets. Fast Company, August 25. www.fastcompany.com/4045340/trump-turns-back-on-lgbt-community-with-transgender-military-ban-tweets.

Long, M., Steinke, J., Applegate, B., Knight Lapinski, M., Johnson, M. J., & Ghosh, S. (2010). Portrayals of male and female scientists in television programs popular among middle school-age children. *Science Communication, 32*(3), 356-382. https://doi.org/10.1177/1075547009357779.

Loomba-Albrecht, L., & Styne, D. M. (2009). Effect of puberty on body composition. *Current Opinion in Endocrinology Diabetes and Obesity, 16*, 10-15.

Malamuth, N. M., Addison, T., & Koss, M. (2000). Pornography and sexual aggression: Are there reliable effects and can we understand them? *Annual Review of Sexual Research, 11*, 26-91.

Marlowe, F., & Wetsman, A. (2001). Preferred waist-to-hip ratio and ecology. *Personality and Individual Differences, 30*, 481-489.

Marsiglio, W., & Hendricks, J. J. (2012). American fathers, children, and their educational experience. In Ho, H., & Hiatt-Michael, D.B. (Eds.), *Promising practices for fathers' involvement in children's education*. Charlotte, NC: Information Age Publishers, pp. 1-16.

Martínez, C., & Paterna-Bleda, C. (2013). Masculinity ideology and gender equality: Considering neo-sexism. *Anales De Psicología/Annals of Psychology, 29*(2), 558-564. https://doi.org/10.6018/analesps.29.2.141311.

Martos, J. (1991). *Doors to the sacred: A historical introduction to sacraments in the Catholic Church*. Liguori, MO: Triumph Books.

Martos, J., & Hégy, P. (1998). In Martos, J., & Hégy, P. (Eds.), *Equal at the Creation: Sexism, society, and Christian thought* (pp. v-vi). Toronto: University of Toronto Press.

Mays, V. M. (1988). Even the rat was white and male: Teaching the psychology of black women. In Bronstein, P., & Quina, K. (Eds.), *Teaching a psychology of people: Resource gender and sociocultural awareness*. Washington, DC: American Psychological Association, pp. 142-146.

McAdams, R. H. (1997). The origin, development, and regulation of norms. *Michigan Law Review, 96*(2), 338-433.

McInroy, L. B., & Craig, S. L. (2017). Perspectives of LGBTQ emerging adults on the depiction and impact of LGBTQ media representation. *Journal of Youth Studies, 20*(1), 32-46. doi:10.1080/13676261.2016.1184243.

Meixler, E. (2017). India's Supreme Court rules sex with child brides is rape. *Time Magazine*, October 12. http://time.com/4979039/india-child-bride-rape-court/.

Merica, D. (2018). Trump mocks #MeToo movement in riff on Elizabeth Warren's heritage during Montana rally. CNN, July 5. www.cnn.com/2018/07/05/politics/trump-montana-rally-pruitt-resigns/index.html.

Messner, M. A., Dunbar, M., & Hunt, D. (2000). The televised sports manhood formula. *Journal of Sport and Social Issues, 24*(4), 380-394. https://doi.org/10.1177/0193723500244006.

Mikula, J. (2003). Gender and videogames: The political valency of Lara Croft, continuum. *Journal of Media & Cultural Studies, 17*, 79-87.

Miller, D. A., Smith, E. R., & Mackie, D. M. (2004). Effects of intergroup contact and political predispositions on prejudice: Role of intergroup emotions. *Group Processes & Intergroup Relations, 7*, 221-237.

Miner-Rubino, K., & Cortina, L. M. (2007). Beyond targets: Consequences of vicarious exposure to misogyny at work. *Journal of Applied Psychology, 92*, 1254-1269. http://dx.doi.org/10.1037/0021-9010.92.5.1254.

Monteith, M. J. (1993). Self-regulation of prejudiced responses: Implications for progress in prejudice-reduction efforts. *Journal of Personality and Social Psychology, 65*(3), 469-485.

Moradi, B., & Huang, Y. (2008). Objectification theory and psychology of women: A decade of advances and future directions. *Psychology of Women Quarterly, 32,* 377-398. http://dx.doi.org/ 10.1111/j.1471-6402.2008.00452.x.

Moreno, R. P., & Chuang, S. S. (2015). Latino fathers: Myths, realities, and challenges. In Roopnarine, J. L. (Ed.), *Fathers across cultures: The importance, roles, and diverse practices of dads.* Santa Barbara, CA: Praeger, pp. 183-204.

Mosher, D. L., & Sirkin, M. (1984). Measuring a macho personality constellation. *Journal of Research in Personality, 18,* 150-163.

Moule, J. (2009). Understanding unconscious bias and unintentional racism. *Phi Delta Kappan, 90*(5), 320-326.

Nakawaza, J. (2015). Fathering in Japan. In Roopnarine, J. L. (Ed.), *Fathers across cultures: The importance, roles, and diverse practices of dads.* Santa Barbara, CA: Praeger, pp. 307-326.

Nam, K., Lee, G., & Hwang, J.-S. (2011). Gender stereotypes depicted by Western and Korean advertising models in Korean adolescent girls' magazines. *Sex Roles, 64*(3-4), 223-237.

National Academy of Sciences (2006). *Beyond bias and barriers: Fulfilling the potential of women in academic science and engineering.* Washington, DC: National Academy.

National Criminal Justice Reference Service (2007). Drug-facilitated, incapacitated, and forcible rape: A national study. NCJRS: 70. February. www.ncjrs.gov/. Retrieved July 2, 2018.

National Sexual Violence Resource Center (2011). Child sexual abuse prevention: Overview. www.nsvrc.org/sites/default/files/Publications_NSVRC_Overview_Child-sexual-abuse-prevention_0.

New York Times (2016). Transcript: Donald Trump's taped comments about women. October 8. www.nytimes.com/2016/10/08/us/donald-trump-tape-transcript.html.

Nicole, S. J., & Stewart, R. E. (2004). Confronting perpetrators of prejudice: The inhibitory effects of social costs. *Psychology of Women Quarterly, 28*(3), 215-223. https://doi.org/10.1111/j.1471-6402.2004.00138.x.

Nier, J. A., & Gaertner, S. L. (2012). The challenge of detecting contemporary forms of discrimination. *Journal of Social Issues, 68,* 207-220. http://dx.doi.org/10.1111/j.1540-4560.2012.01745.x.

Nobelprize.org (2018). Nobel Prize Awarded Women, Nobel Media, June 30. www.nobelprize.org/nobel_prizes/lists/women.html. Retrieved June 29, 2018.

Nosek, B. A., Smyth, F. L., Hansen, J. J., Devos, T., Lindner, N. M., Ranganath, K. A., Tucker Smith, C., Olson, K. R., Chugh, D., Greenwald, A. G., & Banaji, M. R. (2007). Pervasiveness and correlates of implicit attitudes and stereotypes. *European Review of Social Psychology, 18,* 36-88. https://doi.org/10.1080/10463280701489053.

Olorunshola, Y. (2016). Girls & women: 10 ridiculously sexist laws that have no place in the 21st century. GlobalCitizen.org, November 28.

Olson, L. N., Coffelt, T. A., Berlin Ray, E., Rudd, J., Botta, R., Ray, G., & Kopfman, J. E. (2008). I'm all for equal rights, but don't call me a feminist: Identity dilemmas in young adults' discursive representations of being a feminist. *Women's Studies in Communication, 31*(1), 104-132. https://doi.org/10.1080/07491409.2008.10162524.

O'Neil, L. (2017). From Megyn to Mika: A timeline of Trump's attacks on women's appearances. *The Hollywood Reporter,* June 30.

Oswald, D. L., Baalbaki, M., & Kirkman, M. (2019). Experiences with benevolent sexism: Scale development and associations with women's well-being. *Sex Roles, 80,* 362-380. https://doi.org/10.1007/s11199-018-0933-5.

Overall, N. C., Sibley, C. G., & Tan, R. (2011). The costs and benefits of sexism: Resistance to influence during relationship conflict. *Journal of Personality and Social Psychology, 101,* 271-290. doi:10.1037/a0022727.

Oxfam International (2017). Just 8 men own same wealth as half the world. January 16.

Oxfam International (2018). Why the majority of the world's poor are women. www.oxfam.org/en/even-it/why-majority-worlds-poor-are-women.

Ozment, S. (1983). *When fathers ruled: Family life in the Reformation.* Cambridge, MA: Harvard University Press.

Pachankis, J. E., Sullivan, T. J., Feinstein, B. A., & Newcomb, M. E. (2018). Young adult gay and bisexual men's stigma experiences and mental health: An 8-year longitudinal study. *Developmental Psychology, 54*(7), 1381-1393.

Parrott, D. J. (2009). Aggression toward gay men as gender role enforcement: Effects of male role norms, sexual prejudice, and masculine gender role stress. *Journal of Personality, 77,* 1137-1166. http://dx.doi.org/10.1111/j.1467-6494.2009.00577.x.

Parrott, D. J., Peterson, J. L., Vincent, W., & Bakeman, R. (2008). Correlates of anger in response to gay men: Effects of male gender role beliefs, sexual prejudice and masculine gender role stress. *Psychology of Men & Masculinity, 9,* 167-178. http://dx.doi.org/10.1037/1524-9220.9 .3.167.

194 *Global, Historical Sexism*

Pascoe, C. J. (2005). "Dude, you're a fag": Adolescent masculinity and the fag discourse. *Sexualities, 8*, 329–346. http://dx.doi.org/10.1177/ 1363460705053337.

Pascoe, E. A., & Smart Richman, L. (2009). Perceived discrimination and health: A meta-analytic review. *Psychological Bulletin, 135*, 531–554. doi:10.1037/a0016059.

Payne, J. L. (2004). *A history of force.* Sandpoint, ID: Lytton.

Pew Research Center (2018). The narrowing, but persistent, gender gap in pay. www.pewresearch.org/fact-tank/2018/04/09/gender-pay-gap-facts/.

Pica, G., Pierro, A., Pellegrini, V., De Cristofaro, V., Giannini, A., & Kruglanski, A. W. (2018). 'Keeping in mind the gender stereotype': The role of need for closure in the retrieval-induced forgetting of female managers' qualities. *Cognitive Processing*, May 19.

Plant, E. A., & Devine, P. G. (1998). Internal and external motivation to respond without prejudice. *Journal of Personality and Social Psychology, 75*, 811–832.

Pleasance, C. (2017). Woman, 19, is sentenced to death by stoning for adultery after she was 'raped at gunpoint by her cousin' in Pakistan. *Daily Mail*, May 30. www.dailymail.co.uk/news/article-4555734/Woman-19-sentenced-die-raped-Pakistan.html.

Powlishta, K. K. (2000). The effect of target age on the activation of gender stereotypes. *Sex Roles, 42*(3–4), 271–282.

Pratto, F., Sidanius, J., & Levin, S. (2006). Social dominance theory and the dynamics of intergroup relations: Taking stock and looking forward. *European Review of Social Psychology, 17*, 271–320.

Pratto, F., & Walker, A. (2004). The bases of gendered power. In Eagly, A. H., Beall, A. E., & Sternberg, R. J. (Eds.), *The psychology of gender.* New York: Guilford Press, pp. 242–268.

Precopio, R. F., & Ramsey, L. R. (2017). Dude looks like a feminist! Moral concerns and feminism among men. *Psychology of Men & Masculinity, 18*(1), 78–86.

Quinnipiac University (2017). 60% of U.S. women say they've been sexually harassed Quinnipiac University national poll finds; Trump job approval still stuck below 40%. https://poll.qu.edu/national/release-detail?ReleaseID=2502.

Ragins, B. R., Singh, R., & Cornwell, J. M. (2007). Making the invisible visible: Fear and disclosure of sexual orientation at work. *Journal of Applied Psychology, 92*(4), 1103–1118.

Rangarajan, A., & Gleason, P. (1998). Young unwed fathers of AFDC children: Do they provide support? *Demography, 35*(2), 175–186.

Ream, G., & Savin-Williams, R. (2005). Reconciling Christianity and positive nonheterosexual identity in adolescence, with implications for psychological wellbeing. *Journal of Gay and Lesbian Issues in Education, 2*, 19–36.

Reidy, D. E., Shirk, S. D., Sloan, C. A., & Zeichner, A. (2009). Men who aggress against women: Effects of feminine gender role violation on physical aggression in hypermasculine men. *Psychology of Men & Masculinity, 10*, 1–12. http://dx.doi.org/10.1037/a0014794.

Rijken, A. J., & Merz, E.-M. (2014). Double standards: Differences in norms on voluntary childlessness for men and women. *European Sociological Review, 30*(4), 470–482. https://doi.org/10.1093/esr/jcu051.

Robertiello, G., & Terry, K. J. (2007). Can we profile sex offenders? A review of sex offender typologies. *Aggression and Violent Behavior, 12*, 508–518.

Robins, G. (1993). *Women in Ancient Egypt.* Cambridge, MA: Harvard University Press.

Rollero, C. (2013). Men and women facing objectification: The effects of media models on well-being, self-esteem and ambivalent sexism. *Revista de Psicología Social, 28*(3), 373–382.

Rostosky, S., Danner, F., & Riggle, E. (2007). Is religiosity a protective factor against substance use in young adulthood? Only if you're straight! *Journal of Adolescent Health, 40*, 440–447.

Savransky, R. (2017). Roy Moore holds 10-point lead in poll taken after accusations. *The Hill*, November 13. http://thehill.com/homenews/senate/360121-poll-moore-leads-jones-by-10-points.

Scharrer, E. (2004). Virtual violence: Gender and aggression in video game advertisements. *Mass Communication and Society, 7*, 393–412.

Schmitt, M. T., Branscombe, N. R., Postmes, T., & Garcia, A. (2014). The consequences of perceived discrimination for psychological well-being: A meta-analytic review. *Psychological Bulletin, 140*, 921–948. doi:10.1037/ a0035754.

Schoenau, E., Neu, C., Rauch, F., & Manz, F. (2001). The development of bone strength at the proximal radius during childhood and adolescence. *The Journal of Clinical Endocrinology and Metabolism, 86*(2), 613–618.

Sell, A., Hone, L. S. E., & Pound, N. (2012). The importance of physical strength to human males. *Human Nature, 23*, 30–44. doi:10.1007/s12110-012-9131-2.

Seltzer, J. (1991). Relationships between fathers and children who live apart: The father's role after separation. *Journal of Marriage and the Family, 53*, 79–102.

Shattock, J. (1993). *The Oxford guide to British women writers*. Oxford/New York: Oxford University Press.

Shuster, S., Black, M., & McVitie, E. (1975). The influence of age and sex on skin thickness, skin collagen and density. *British Journal of Dermatology, 93*, 639–643.

Sibley, C. G., Overall, N. C. & Duckitt, J. (2007). When women become more hostilely sexist toward their gender: The system-justifying effect of benevolent sexism. *Sex Roles, 57*, 743. https://doi.org/10.1007/s11199-007-9306-1.

Sibley, C. G., & Wilson, M. S. (2004). Differentiating hostile and benevolent sexist attitudes toward positive and negative sexual female subtypes. *Sex Roles, 51*, 687–696. doi:10.1007/s11199-004-0718-x.

Smith, S. G., Chen, J., Basile, K. C., Gilbert, L. K., Merrick, M. T., Patel, N., Walling, M., & Jain, A. (2012). The National Intimate Partner and Sexual Violence Survey (NISVS): 2010–2012 state report. Centers for Disease Control and Prevention, National Center for Injury Prevention and Control. www.cdc.gov/violenceprevention/pdf/NISVS-StateReportBook.

Smith, A., & Stewart, A. J. (1983). Approaches to studying racism and sexism in Black women's lives. *Journal of Social Issues, 39*(3), 1–15.

Smolak, L., & Stein, J. (2006). The relationship of drive for muscularity to sociocultural factors, self-esteem, physical attributes gender role, and social comparison in middle school boys. *Body Image, 3*, 121–129.

Solien, N. L. (1960). Household and family in the Caribbean: Some definitions and concepts. *Social and Economic Studies, 9*(1), 101–106.

Spellberg, D. (1996), *Politics, gender, and the Islamic past: The legacy of 'A'isha Bint Abi Bakr*. New York: Columbia University Press.

Spence, J. T., & Helmreich, R. (1972). The Attitudes Toward Women Scale: An objective instrument to measure the rights and roles of women in contemporary society. *JSAS Catalog of Selected Documents in Psychology, 2*, 66.

Stankiewicz, J. M., & Rosselli, F. (2008). Women as sex objects and victims in print advertisements. *Sex Roles, 58*, 579–589. http://dx.doi.org/10.1007/ s11199-007-9359-1.

Steinmetz, K. (2017). Texas Senate approves controversial Bathroom Bill after five-hour debate. *Time Magazine*, March 14. http://time.com/4701658/texas-senate-bathroom-bill-sb6-transgender/.

Stop Street Harassment (2018). Study on sexual harassment and assault. www.stopstreetharassment.org/resources/2018-national-sexual-abuse-report/.

Strahan, E. J. (2003). Selling thinness: How media images increase importance of weight and beauty as a basis of women's self-esteem and decrease their body satisfaction and eating. Unpublished doctoral dissertation, University of Waterloo, Ontario, Canada.

Strum, B., & Fears, D. (2015). Trump: Megyn Kelly had 'blood coming out of her wherever'. *The New York Post*, August 8.

Sullivan, M. K. (2003). *Sexual minorities: Discrimination, challenges, and development in America*. Philadelphia: Haworth Social Work Practice Press.

Swami, V., Coles, R., & Wyrozumska, K. (2010). Oppressive beliefs at play: Associations among beauty ideals and practices and individual differences in sexism, objectification of others, and media exposure. *Psychology of Women Quarterly, 34*(3), 365–379. https://doi.org/10.1111/j.1471-6402.2010.01582.x.

Sweeny, J. (2018). Banning child marriage in America: An uphill fight against evangelical pressure. Kentucky's bill had to change to accommodate religious concerns. A similar bill is dying in Tennessee. Here's why. www.salon.com/2018/03/11/banning-child-marriage-in-america-an-uphill-fight-against-evangelical-pressure/.

Swim, J. K., Aikin, K. J., Hall, W. S., & Hunter, B. A. (1995). Sexism and racism: Old-fashioned and modern prejudices. *Journal of Personality and Social Psychology, 68*(2), 199–214.

Swim, J. K., & Cohen, L. L. (1997). Overt, covert, and subtle sexism: A comparison between the Attitudes Toward Women and Modern Sexism Scales. *Psychology of Women Quarterly, 21*(1), 103–118.

Szillis, U., & Stahlberg, D. (2007). The face-ism effect in the internet: Differences in facial prominence of women and men. *International Journal of Internet Science, 2*(1), 3–11.

Szymanski, D. M., Gupta, A., Carr, E. R., & Stewart, D. (2009). Internalized misogyny as a moderator of the link between sexist events and women's psychological distress. *Sex Roles, 61*(1-2), 101–109.

Talley, A. E., & Bettencourt, B. A. (2008). Evaluations and aggression directed at a gay male target: The role of threat and antigay prejudice. *Journal of Applied Social Psychology, 38*, 647–683. http://dx.doi.org/ 10.1111/j.1559-1816.2007.00321.x.

Tanner, J. M. (1989). *Foetus into man: Physical growth from conception to maturity* (2nd ed.). Ware, UK: Castlemead.

Thomas, J. R., & French, K. E. (1985). Gender differences across age in motor performance: A meta-analysis. *Psychological Bulletin, 98*, 260–282.

Thomsen, S. R., Weber, M. M., & Brown, L. B. (2002). The relationship between reading beauty and fashion magazines and the use of pathogenic dieting methods among adolescent females. *Adolescence, 37*(145), 1-18.

Tickamyer, A. R. (1981). Wealth and power: A comparison of men and women in the property elite. *Social Forces, 60*(2), 463-481.

Tiggemann, M., & McGill, B. (2004). The role of social comparison in the effect of magazine advertisements on women's mood and body dissatisfaction. *Journal of Social and Clinical Psychology, 23*, 23-44.

Tougas, F., Brown, R., Beaton, A. M., & Joly, S. (1995). Neosexism: Plus ca change, plus c'est pareil. *Personality and Social Psychology Bulletin, 21*, 842-849.

Tourigny, M., & Baril, K. (2011). Les agressions sexuelles durant l'enfance: Ampleur et facteurs de risque. In Hébert, M., Cyr, M., & Tourigny, M. (Eds.), *L'agression sexuelle envers les enfants, Tome 1* (pp. 7-42). Québec: Presses de l'Université du Québec. (Available in French only)

Tsurumi, E. P. (1981). Japan's early female emperors. *Historical Reflections/Réflexions Historiques, 8*(1), 41-49.

Tullet, A. M., Kay, A. C., & Inzlicht, M. (2015). Randomness increases self-reported anxiety and neurophysiological correlates of performance monitoring. *Social Cognitive and Affective Neuroscience, 10*, 628-635. doi:10.1093/scan/nsu097.

Ueno, C. (1987). The position of Japanese women reconsidered. *Current Anthropology, 28*(4), S75-S84.

UNICEF (2012). A note on child marriage. UNICEF.

UNICEF (2017). Child marriage in the Middle East and North Africa. UNICEF Middle East and North Africa Regional Office in collaboration with IRCW. www.icrw.org/publications/child-marriage-in-the-middle-east-and-north-africa/.

Uniform Crime Report (2009). Crime in the U.S. https://ucr.fbi.gov/crime-in-the-u.s/2009.

United States Commission on International Religious Freedom (2008). Somalia: USCIRF condemns stoning of 13-year-old girl. November 10. www.uscirf.gov/news-room/press-releases/somalia-uscirf-condemns-stoning-13-year-old-girl.

United States Department of Justice (2017). An updated definition of rape. www.justice.gov/archives/opa/blog/updated-definition-rape.

United States Department of Justice (2018). Sexual assault. www.justice.gov/ovw/sexual-assault.

U.S. Congress, Ways and Means Committee (2004). Steep decline in teen birth rate significantly responsible for reducing child poverty and single-parent families. (Issue Brief, April 23). Washington, DC: U.S. Congress.

U.S. News & World Report (2014). The 10 worst countries for gender equality, ranked by perception. www.usnews.com/news/best-countries/slideshows/the-10-worst-countries-for-gender-equality-ranked-by-perception.

Vaes, J., Paladino, M. P., & Puvia, E. (2011). Are sexualized females complete human beings? Why males and females dehumanize sexually objectified women. *European Journal of Social Psychology, 41*, 774-785.

Vandello, J. A., & Bosson, J. K. (2013). Hard won and easily lost: A review and synthesis of theory and research on precarious manhood. *Psychology of Men & Masculinity, 14*, 101-113. http://dx.doi.org/10 .1037/a0029826.

Vandello, J. A., Bosson, J. K., Cohen, D., Burnaford, R. M., & Weaver, J. R. (2008). Precarious manhood. *Journal of Personality and Social Psychology, 95*, 1325-1339. http://dx.doi.org/10.1037/a0012453.

Vargas-Salfate, S., Paez, D., Liu, J. H., Pratto, F., & de Zúñiga, H. G. (2018). A comparison of social dominance theory and system justification: The role of social status in 19 nations. *Personality and Social Psychology Bulletin, 44*(7), 1060-1076.

Waites, M. (2005). *The age of consent: Young people, sexuality and citizenship*. Basingstoke, UK: Palgrave Macmillan.

Walker R. L., Wingate L. R., Obasi, E. M., & Joiner, T. E. (2008). An empirical investigation of acculturative stress and ethnic identity as moderators for depression and suicidal ideation in college students. *Cultural Diversity and Ethnic Minority Psychology, 14*, 75-82.

Wang-Jones, T. 'T.' S., Alhassoon, O. M., Hattrup, K., Ferdman, B. M., & Lowman, R. L. (2017). Development of gender identity implicit association tests to assess attitudes toward transmen and transwomen. *Psychology of Sexual Orientation and Gender Diversity, 4*(2), 169-183.

Ward, L. M. (2002). Does television exposure affect emerging adults' attitudes and assumptions about sexual relationships? Correlational and experimental confirmation. *Journal of Youth and Adolescence, 31*(1), 1-15.

Weaver, J. R., Vandello, J. A., & Bosson, J. K. (2013). Intrepid, imprudent, or impetuous? The effects of gender threats on men's financial decisions. *Psychology of Men & Masculinity, 14*, 184-191. http://dx.doi.org/10 .1037/a0027087.

Weeks, J. (1999). Discourse, desire, and sexual deviance: Some problems in a history of homosexuality. In Aggleton, P., & Parker, R. (Eds.), *Culture, society and sexuality: A reader*. New York: Routledge, pp. 119-142.

Weiss, K. G. (2009). 'Boys will be boys' and other gendered accounts: An exploration of victims' excuses and justifications for unwanted sexual contact and coercion. *Violence Against Women, 15*(7), 810-834.

Wells, J. (2007). Sexual dimorphism of body composition. Best practice & research. *Clinical Endocrinology & Metabolism, 21*(3), 415–430.

Wemple, S. F. (1992). Women from the fifth to the tenth century. In Klapisch-Zuber, C. (Ed.), *Silences of the Middle Ages*, vol. II of *A history of women in the West*. Cambridge, MA: Harvard University Press, pp. 169–201.

White, A. M., & Gaines, S. O. Jr. (2006). 'You've got a friend': African American men's cross-sex feminist friendships and their influence on perceptions of masculinity and women. *Journal of Social and Personal Relationships, 23*(4), 523–542.

Willie, T. C., Khondkaryan, E., Callands, T., & Kershaw, T. (2018). "Think like a man": How sexual cultural scripting and masculinity influence changes in men's use of intimate partner violence. *American Journal of Community Psychology, 61*(1-2), 240–250. https://doi.org/10.1002/ajcp.12224

World Economic Forum (2014). The Global Gender Gap Report 2014. http://reports.weforum.org/global-gender-gap-report-2014/.

World Economic Forum (2016). These are the countries where child marriage is legal. www.weforum.org/agenda/2016/09/these-are-the-countries-where-child-marriage-is-legal/.

World Health Organization (2010). Maternal deaths worldwide drop by third. www.who.int/mediacentre/news/releases/2010/maternal_mortality_20100915/en/.

World Health Organization (2018). Maternal mortality. www.who.int/news-room/fact-sheets/detail/maternal-mortality.

Xie, Y., & Shauman, K. A. (2003). *Women in science: Career processes and outcomes*. Boston, MA: Harvard University Press.

Ziring, L. (1984). From Islamic republic to Islamic state in Pakistan. *Asian Survey, 24*(9), 931–946.

Zuckerman, M., & Kieffer, S. C. (1994). Race differences in face-ism: Does facial prominence imply dominance? *Journal of Personality and Social Psychology, 66*(1), 86–92.

8 Human Sexuality

Sexuality as a Biological Function, Regulated by Society	204
Development of Sexuality	206
First Sexual Experiences	208
Individual Qualities	208
Peer Influences	209
Family Influences	210
Social and Cultural Influences	212
Experiencing Sexuality: Adulthood Sexuality	216
Sexual Arousal	216
Sexual Attraction	217
Sexual Experiences	217
Hooking-Up	219
Orgasm	219
Self-Pleasuring	220
Social and Cultural Influences	221
Contraception and Reproductive Health	223
Controlling Sexuality	226

INEQUALITIES AND INJUSTICES

The Shaming of Women for Being Women

In any grocery or variety store, you will find an aisle labeled "feminine hygiene." In that aisle you will find products related to menstruation (tampons, pads) and different types of products related to having a vagina, including special soaps and douches. Girls and women report feeling ashamed or embarrassed when purchasing these products, not to mention the dads, boyfriends, and husbands who are sent to the store to buy them (Fahs, 2013). Research indicates that girls and women report being ashamed of their vaginas, including their appearance, secretions, and fragrance, and because of menstruation (Amann-Gainotti, 1994; Costos, Ackerman, & Paradis, 2002; Hensel, Fortenberry, & Orr, 2007; Roberts & Waters, 2004). Young men ridicule female genitals in their discussions with each

Figure 8.1 Do NOT put Lysol in your vagina!
Source: f8 archive/Alamy Stock Photo

other (Murnen, 2000). Why is having a vagina and menstruating embarrassing, and why do vaginas need special soap?

The vagina is presented as disgusting throughout Western media (Braun & Wilkinson, 2010; Hammers, 2010). Vaginas and menstruation are ridiculed within religion and have been for centuries. The Bible indicates that a woman should not be touched during menstruation (Leviticus 12:5) or after giving birth (especially to a female infant! Leviticus 12:2, 12:5). The Qu'ran contains similar verses (2:222, 65:4). Some cultures require that girls and women live in "menstrual huts" during menstruation, effectively separating them from everyone else and from their daily tasks, duties, and responsibilities (Guterman, Mehta, & Gibbs, 2008). Contraception that prevents menstruation is becoming more popular, with the never-menstruating woman preferable to women in their natural state (Johnston-Robledo, Barnack, & Wares, 2006; Rose, Chrisler, & Couture, 2008). Many products for "freshening" the vagina, from douches to Lysol, have been advertised regularly to women for decades (Levine, 2002; Rose, 2013) (see Figure 8.1), although douching is linked with development of vaginal infections and is not necessary (Ness et al., 2002). Douching is actually dangerous as it significantly increases the risk of HIV infection (Sewankambo et al., 1997), and douching with Lysol can be fatal (Pasulka, 2012). Vaginas do not need special soap; vaginas keep themselves quite clean, with no soap at all (National Health Service, 2015). Healthy vaginas smell like vaginas, not rose petals or Lysol. People who really like vaginas like how they smell.

So what gives? Every human being alive today and every person who has ever existed grew within a uterus of a woman, essentially feeding off of the bloody lining of the uterus which becomes the placenta during pregnancy. Most people are born coming out of a vagina. Heterosexual men think about sex a lot (Laumann, Gagnon, Michael, & Michaels, 1994), which presumably involves thinking about vaginas in a rather positive way. So why are vaginas seen as dirty, disgusting, and shamed as such, in media and culture? Why aren't they adored and venerated, especially considering their importance for producing every human being ever? I will let you answer that for yourself, but I would like to point out how dominant groups (in this case, men) create legitimizing myths that justify the oppression of less powerful groups (in this case, women) (Pratto & Walker, 2004). I think that men use ideas about shame and dirtiness to marginalize women, to separate them from men and condemn their natural being so that they are more easily oppressed. What do you think?

CRITICAL THINKING

Is Male Circumcision Genital Mutilation?

Male circumcision involves cutting off the foreskin of the penis, which is typically accomplished during the first month of life. When babies are born with a penis, the penis has a length of skin covering the top part of the penis that can be pulled back, a foreskin. The foreskin obviously evolved as a trait, and its function is to protect the glans penis, the sensitive tip of the penis that includes the urethral opening, because it is sensitive and can become infected. Removal of the foreskin is recorded as early as 5 BCE in Egypt, and is practiced today as a religious ritual in Judaism, Islam, and other groups, and for medical reasons (Aggleton, 2007). About 33% of the world's men are circumcised, the majority of whom (70%) are Muslim men (World Health Organization, 2007). Although rates fluctuate, between around 40 and 80% of American male babies are circumcised each year (Centers

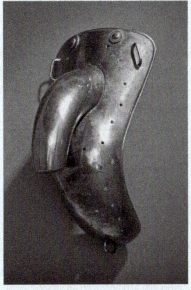

Figures 8.2a and 8.2b Devices designed and used to prevent masturbation

for Disease Control & Prevention, 2011). There are benefits of removing the foreskin. First, circumcision can protect against transmission of sexually transmitted diseases (STDs), especially HIV and AIDS. Implementation of millions of voluntary circumcisions of men and boys in Africa has helped reduce the spread of these in several regions (UNAIDS, 2007; World Health Organization, 2017a) (although truly safe sex requires use of a male condom). Second, it can protect against infections, including urinary tract and foreskin infections, and cancer of the penis. These conditions are rare and infections are easily treated. What are the cons of circumcision, which usually happens in the first month of life? Pain, mistakes that lead to serious negative outcomes (including mutilation or loss of the penis, blood loss, infections, even death; American Academy of Pediatrics, 2012), and loss of the benefits of the foreskin.

Male and female circumcision (more genuinely called female genital mutilation, or FGM, see below) increased in practice in the Western world during the late 19th and early 20th century, as a health practice that would prevent a myriad of negative outcomes for boys and girls (Gollaher, 2000) (although FGM was largely not adopted). Some scholars argue that because of the rise of negative beliefs about masturbation in the late 18th into the 19th century, including that it caused insanity, blindness, and stupidity (see Figure 8.2 for devices invented to prevent masturbation), genital circumcision was adopted in the West as a way to dull sexual pleasure and children's interest in masturbation (Darby, 2003). This apparently is not effective, as meta-analyses indicate that men with and without foreskins do not differ in their experience of sexual pleasure or satisfaction (Morris & Kreiger, 2013).

So what is the value of male circumcision? Again, it has been useful in reducing the spread of HIV and AIDS in Africa, reducing individual susceptibility by as much as 60% (Auvert et al., 2005; Bailey et al., 2007; Gray et al., 2007). But HIV and AIDS as risks are much higher in Africa than in the United States, Canada, Asia, and other regions. Is male circumcision necessary, for infant boys? For boys who when they become young men will hopefully have access to condoms and modern medicine? Problems with foreskins are rare, so why remove them? More and more people are asserting that there is little difference between male circumcision and female genital mutilation, that any kind of circumcision is *always* genital mutilation. There are pros and cons that parents must consider. Unfortunately, newborn baby boys cannot consent to their foreskin being removed, so the ethics of the procedure are always a question, it seems. Most important in deciding is that parents are provided with accurate information before and at the time of the decision (American Academy of Pediatrics, 2012).

BONUS BOX

Discrimination against Sexual Minorities

People who are attracted to others of the same sex (women attracted to women as lesbians, men attracted to men as gay), who are attracted to all sexes (bi- or multi-sexual), or who identify as multi-gendered or opposite-gendered (collectively referred to as LGBTQ individuals (lesbian, gay, bisexual, transgender, questioning or queer) or **sexual minorities**; Weeks, Heaphy, & Donovan, 2001) have been marginalized and oppressed in the United States for decades and around the world for centuries. Although homosexual relationships and bisexuality were lauded in ancient civilizations, including ancient Greece (Davidson, 2007), the influence of Judeo-Christianity on Western culture has led to prevailing negative attitudes toward non-heterosexuality (Adamczyk & Pitt, 2009; Fyfe, 1983). Although changes are certainly occurring, with young people around the world increasingly likely to have well-developed positive attitudes toward LGBTQ people (Donaldson, Handren, & Lac, 2017), current political trends toward extreme conservatism, even fascism in the West, are accompanied by increasing discrimination and violence toward LGBTQ people (Bahns & Branscombe, 2011; Dworkin & Yi, 2003; Wright, Bonita, & Mulick, 2011). Discrimination and violence against LGBTQ people has been documented around the world (Andrade-Rivas & Romero, 2017; Blanc, 2005; Ferfolja, 2013; Herek, 2008; Mujuzi, 2011; Schneeberger, Rauchfleisch, Battegay, & Schweizer, 2002). LGBTQ young people are susceptible to bullying by peers (Higa et al., 2012; Kelleher, 2009) and low family acceptance (Micucci, 2015; Yadegarfard, Meinhold-Bergmann, & Ho, 2014). Not surprisingly, LGBTQ youth and adults suffer higher rates of suicide and suicide attempts than heterosexuals (Hong, Espelage, & Kral, 2011; Katz-Wise, Ehrensaft, Vetters, Forcier, & Austin, 2018; Meyer, Dietrich, & Schwartz, 2008; Shearer et al., 2018). The stress of being a sexual minority is magnified among people of color (Meyer, 2010).

Sexuality is not a black and white, dichotomous quality; sexuality is complex (Klein, Sepekoff, & Wolf, 1985) and exists on a continuum, from totally completely heterosexual to totally completely homosexual, with every variation in between (Kinsey, Pomeroy, & Martin, 1948, 2003; Kinsey, Pomeroy, Martin, & Gebhard, 1953). Many people who identify as heterosexual have homosexual experiences (Peterson & Hyde, 2010); many people who identify as homosexual have heterosexual experiences (Bozett, 1982; Spitzer, 2003). Many people identify as bisexual (Gates, 2011). When it comes to negatively evaluating sexuality, or someone's identity, the real question in evaluating morality is *"is this behavior harmful to anyone?"* If sex is adult, consensual, and safe (i.e., prevents against STDs and unwanted pregnancy), I assert that it is not harmful to any of the participants. How does sexual activity between two or twelve consenting adults practicing safe sex harm anyone? Why is the personal sexual behavior of any adult relevant to or the business of anyone not involved in that behavior? What right does a government have in determining what sexual behavior between consenting adults is lawful (see *Lawrence v. Texas*, U.S. Supreme Court, 2003)? What right does a government have to impose religious ideology onto people who do not follow that ideology?

The current President of the United States has proposed banning transgender individuals from serving in the United States military (Block, Strangio, & Esseks, 2018). The Trump Administration has argued to the U.S. Supreme Court that discrimination against LGBTQ people is legal when not being heterosexual violates a person's religious beliefs (*Masterpiece Cakeshop v. Colorado Civil Rights Commission*, U.S. Supreme Court, 2018). The Trump Administration has created the Division of Conscience and Religious Freedom, a new federal office that will purportedly work to protect the religious liberties of health care providers (Lopez, 2018), including their choices to not provide care to LGBTQ people, women seeking **abortions**, and women who have previously had abortions. These discriminatory actions are occurring despite the First and Fourteenth Amendments of the U.S.

Constitution. How just or decent is it to disallow people from life, liberty, and the pursuit of happiness because they engage in a sexual behavior that some people don't like? These are questions each of us must consider if we are to be educated, informed, participative citizens who support democracy and human rights.

LEARN MORE

"Kinks": From Toys to Swinging

Does sex always have to be in bed, at night, with the lights off? Lots of adults have very few hang-ups about sexuality. Sex toys are used by approximately 40% of men and over 50% of women in the United States each year (Herbenick et al., 2009; Reece et al., 2009). Other people are into bondage (using restraints in sexual behavior), discipline (using dominance and punishment in sexual behavior), sadism (pleasure in causing pain), and masochism (pleasure in feeling pain), or BDSM (all of the above; Richters, De Visser, Rissel, Grulich, & Smith, 2008). Other people are in open relationships (committed relationships where each partner is free to engage sexually with others; Taormino, 2008) or in swinging (engaging as a couple with other people sexually; Jenks, 2001). There are sex clubs, places where people go to have sex with strangers, all over the United States (Schultz, 2006). While there is some risk, especially for gay men having sex in sex clubs and bathhouses (Faissol, Swann, Kolodziejski, Griffin, & Gift, 2007), use of condoms prevents STDs when they are used correctly (U.S. Food and Drug Administration, 2018). So-called "sex clubs" may also involve sex trafficking and abuse of women (Raymond & Hughes, 2001). But there are establishments where the only people having sex are consenting adults. I assert that healthy sexuality is adult, consensual, and safe (condoms and contraception are used). Outside those parameters, sexuality is a personal choice, and there are lots of choices out there!

Sexuality as a Biological Function, Regulated by Society

Sexuality is clearly a biological function, along with other functions such as hunger, thirst, waste elimination, and sleep. Nearly every species on earth reproduces through sexual behavior (more than 99% to be exact; Scudellari, 2014). Fungi, yeast, microscopic animals, insects, amphibians, reptiles, fish, birds, and mammals, all reproduce sexually. Several species, including yeast, fungi, and animals like insects, worms, snails, and even snakes and sharks, can also produce asexually (that is, without fertilization, as a singular organism, through processes such as budding and parthenogenesis; Booth et al., 2011; Chapman et al., 2007; Cosin, Novo, & Fernández, 2011; Pearcy, Aron, Doums, & Keller, 2004). Asexual reproduction results in a clone, a genetically identical offspring that adds genetic variability only through mutations (Hales et al., 2002); haploid offspring with half of the mother's genetic material (Pearcy, Aron, Doums, & Keller, 2004); or "half-cloning," whereby diploid offspring genes are 50% identical to mothers but have some gene differences due to **crossing over** that occurs during meiosis (Booth et al., 2011). Two genetically different species members who mate create a completely unique combination of genes that may result in characteristics which enhance survival within that particular environment. Sexual reproduction is more evolutionarily adaptive when living environments are diverse, crowded, and changing, because natural selection processes are enhanced when genetic variability is greater (Becks & Agrawal, 2012; Goddard, Godfray, & Burt, 2005; Ni et al., 2013). Sexual reproduction evolved because it greatly enhances genetic variability within a species.

Sexuality is an essential function for life, not just for reproduction but for exercising the sexual drive, a motivation that is evident across species (Toates, 2009). When people are considered as animals, their sexual behavior is comparable to that of other animals and understandable as such. Brain structures involved in sexual arousal and behavior include the **amygdala**, the **hippocampus**, and pleasure centers including the **hypothalamus** and **nucleus accumbens** (Baird, Wilson, Bladin, Saling, & Reutens, 2007; Georgiadis & Holstege, 2005); such brain structures and processes are similar across species (Rowland, 2006). Hormones involved in sexual arousal and behavior, regulated by the **pituitary gland**, are also similar across species (Demakis, 2006). As animals, human beings are motivated toward sexual behavior, not just for reproduction (although this may be a conscious motive during sex), but also for pleasure. Animals of various species, including humans, engage in sex for pleasure, recreation, social interaction, and mate bonding (Balcombe, 2006; Dubuc & Dixson, 2012; Packer & Pusey, 1987). From this biological perspective, sexuality becomes mundane, a normal healthy biologically-driven behavior that individual members of species engage in for health, pleasure, and reproduction. So what's all the fuss about? Why then is human sexual behavior currently and across history considered a rather salacious issue involving questions of morality (Miller, 2007), while the sexual behavior of animals is not? Dogs mating are not condemned; they are not shamed or ridiculed or imprisoned or stigmatized. Male sheep engaged in sexuality with each other are not excluded or rejected by the herd; the other sheep don't seem to mind it. **Bonobos** engaged in solo or group sexual activity are not seen as wicked or immoral, by other bonobos or by (most) humans. Only human sexuality is linked with morality in the human world. Why?

In answering this question, consider the results of unrestrained sexuality among people, especially without modern contraceptive technology and health care. Uncontrolled sexuality obviously leads to high rates of reproduction, resulting in greater competition for resources within any particular environment, within any particular species and between different species occupying that environment. Imbalances in ecosystems can result from uncontrolled reproduction within a species. For example, an increase in the number of white-tailed deer in North America has resulted in a reduction in various species of songbirds because the deer eat the shrubs where the birds like to nest (Chollet & Martin, 2012; deCalesta, 1994). Among human beings, uncontrolled sexuality not only results in more offspring competing for scarce resources, but in more children who are unwanted by either partner. Within any society, a child with two parents devoted to its welfare is more likely to be a healthy, successful, functioning adult who produces benefits for society through some kind of work. In contrast, **orphans** and "**bastards**" (a derogatory term for a child abandoned by its father) are not of benefit to a society; fatherless children result in a mother with few resources who must devote her time and energy to caring for those children on her own. Children without any providing parent become a burden to society and have poor long-term health and psychological outcomes (Campbell, Handa, Moroni, Odongo, & Palermo, 2010). In addition, when men are certain that children are indeed their offspring, property and wealth can be left behind and inherited by the "proper," genetically-related people (i.e., by **kin**). Human sexual behavior therefore must be controlled by social institutions so that children have two parents to support their development; so each parent (traditionally mothers) has resources to support them while they are engaged in childcare instead of other work; and so men (traditionally and still most of the time) can be assured of an heir for their wealth and property. Uncontrolled sexuality is also a public health issue. **Sexually transmitted diseases** (STDs) cause misery and negative physical and health outcomes. Without modern health care, STDs are very easily spread and can be debilitating and fatal (Centers for Disease Control and Prevention, 2017).

So how did earlier societies regulate and control sexuality, without modern medicine and tested, reliable, widely available contraception? First, early societies created **marriage**, the legal bonding of a woman and a man, to the exclusion of other sexual partners, so that any offspring that result must be the genetic kin of that woman and that man. Ensuring **paternity certainty**, men's certainty that offspring are genetically their own, is also enhanced by requiring female **virginity** at marriage. If a woman is a virgin at her marriage, any pregnancy is assured to be the child of her husband and no one else. Now of course this only works if women agree to follow the rules of marriage (e.g., **monogamy**, **fidelity**).

Behaviors that violate the marriage agreement, including premarital sex and adultery, are punished by society through social ridicule or **stigmatization**. Other punishments are also used to discourage sexuality outside of marriage, including formal punishments through laws around the world.

Rejecting people from the group is one way to stigmatize sexual behaviors that occur outside of marriage. One mechanism of stigmatizing sexual behavior is through religious prohibitions. Judeo-Christian religions, and others, eschew and condemn adultery and premarital sex, particularly by women (Dedek, 1980; Gatiss, 2005). Religions also condemn sexual desire (termed "lust"; Herbermann, 1913) and sex for its own sake, for pleasure, which is termed **fornication** (Witte, 2005). Fornication of course would include homosexual behavior, condemned by most religions, because it cannot result in offspring, the only reason for sexuality supported by most religions. Religious prohibitions against sexuality have been incorporated into laws around the world. Laws against **sodomy** (any sexual behavior other than penile-vaginal intercourse) existed in many U.S. states until the U.S. Supreme Court ruled that legal prohibitions on consensual adult sexual behavior are unconstitutional (*Lawrence v. Texas*, 2003). The word sodomy of course stems from the Biblical city of Sodom, whose people were wicked and destroyed by God (Genesis 13:13, 19:24). Religions also condemn **masturbation** or **self-pleasuring**, as it creates lust and leads one toward fornication (Payne, 1985). In this way, religion is used to regulate sexuality, threatening not just social rejection and stigma for sexual behavior, but deific condemnation, eternal damnation and separation from God, even death (Deuteronomy 22:22). Religion links sexuality to morality, to wickedness (Witte, 2005). This psychological and social link between moral goodness and sexuality is very powerful and affects the perception, interpretation, and experience of sexuality of every person, regardless of their culture or their own religiosity. Because every world religion condemns free and open sexuality to some degree, human sexual behavior is affected by emotions like fear, guilt, and shame. Sexual shame is unique to human beings and is yet another separation of us from the other animals.

Development of Sexuality

Although a great deal of sexuality development occurs during adolescence as **puberty** is occurring (see Chapter 4), the development of sexuality is a lifespan process that begins at birth and extends into old age. Infants and toddlers explore their worlds with touch, including their own bodies, and will touch their own genitals for comfort or pleasure (Bakwin, 1952; Chen, Knight, Tuxhorn, Shahid, & Lüders, 2015; Narchi, 2003). Toddlers up to about age 3 years are learning about the world through words, and so it is important for parents to identify their body parts, *all* of their parts, including genitals. Leaving genitals out of the conversation suggests to little kids that their genitals are strange, or weird, or a secret not to be discussed. Like a toe or a knee, a vulva or penis is a normal part of the body, important like everything else, and should be identified and properly labeled using real words, not baby talk (e.g., "wee wee") (Gartrell & Mosbacher, 1984). Toddlers also show curiosity about parents' bodies, including their genitals, as indicated by parental self-report (Schuhrke, 2000).

Children from about the ages of 3 to 6 years are learning about physical differences between the sexes and gender roles (ideas about what activities women and men typically engage in) (Fagot, 1995). They are learning what it means to be a boy and what it means to be a girl, usually by observing parents' behaviors and modeling after the same-sex parent. Gender roles include ideas about sexuality and the roles of women and men in sexual behaviors (Halpern & Perry-Jenkins, 2016). Gender roles in sexual behavior can be particularly challenging for children to learn about, because sex is hidden from children in most cultures and it is harder for them to learn about sex through observation (Gray & Anderson, 2010). Children as young as 3 or 4 years old will engage in "sex play" with peers (Montgomery, 2007; Thigpen, 2009). Children also engage in self-pleasuring before puberty (Campbell, Mallappa, Wisniewski, & Silovsky, 2013). Although there is an obvious question of consent regarding any sexual situation, and children are incapable of providing *any* form of consent, let alone informed consent (National Institutes of Health, 2016), peer sex play is normal and should not be considered alarming, as long as children are similar to each other in age and coercion is absent (Campbell et al., 2013; Okami, Olmstead, & Abramson, 1997). Larger age differences between children engaged sexually are more likely to involve coercion or deception and should not be tolerated by parents (Finkelhor, 1987).

The onset of puberty can begin as young as 10 years old or younger in girls and as young as 12 years old or younger for boys (Kail & Cavanaugh, 2010). During puberty, the development of more mature sexuality begins, paving the way for sexuality in adulthood. The development of sexuality during puberty is affected by many different factors, including biological, psychological, and social processes. Although already discussed to some degree in Chapter 4, let's remind ourselves about the physical changes occurring during puberty. The most important physical process related to sexual development and sexuality is the continuous interaction between the brain, the pituitary gland, and the gonads, and the sex hormones that result from it, that begins during puberty (called the hypothalamo-pituitary-gonadal axis; Charlton, 2008). As the brain signals the pituitary gland to stimulate the gonads to release estrogens (in girls) and testosterone (in boys), puberty begins. Girls begin to produce mature eggs and usually begin menstruating before the age of 17 years (Kail & Cavanaugh, 2010), while boys begin to produce mature sperm around the age of 13 years (Marieb, 2014). Secondary sex characteristics accompany these changes. In girls, body fat distribution changes, with the hips widening and breasts developing. Boys grow taller and their voice deepens. Both girls and boys develop greater body hair, especially boys on the face. These characteristics are evolutionary triggers of human desire (Fisher, 1930). As individual young people develop these qualities along with their peers, and continue to experience the regular release of sex hormones, sexual interest and attraction to others increases (McClintock & Herdt, 1996; Ponton, 2000).

First Sexual Experiences

Most adolescents in the United States engage in sexual intercourse for the first time around 17 years of age (Finer & Philbin, 2014). For American girls, around 71% have had sex by age 19 years old, while the same is true of 79% of boys (Hyde & Delamater, 1997). About one-third of American adolescents have had sexual intercourse by the age of 15 years old (Kaestle, Halpern, Miller, & Ford, 2005). Exploring sexual behavior is a normal part of development and is a positive aspect of adolescent health and well-being (Hawes, Wellings, & Stephenson, 2010; Heron et al., 2013). Unfortunately, sexual experiences that occur earlier in adolescence are associated with negative outcomes for young people, including increased risk for sexually transmitted diseases and infections (Kaestle et al., 2005), cervical cancer (Louie et al., 2009), and unwanted pregnancies (Ma et al., 2009). Younger adolescents having sex also have an increased likelihood of forcing someone to have sex (O'Donnell, O'Donnel, & Stueve, 2001). One study found that the main predictors of early intercourse for adolescents are being in a "steady" relationship, having sexually permissive attitudes, use of alcohol, and having delinquent peers (Whitbeck, Yoder, Hoyt & Conger, 1999). Endorsing gender stereotypes, traditional ideas about women and men, is also associated with having sex at a younger age and less effective use of contraceptives (Carpenter, 1998; Ward, 2002).

Risky sexual behaviors are sexual behaviors or practices that increase the risk of sexually transmitted diseases (STDs) and infections (STIs), unwanted pregnancies, abuse, and other harm to participants. Teens are of particular concern because they often don't know a lot about sex and are vulnerable to peer pressure and manipulation by adults. Risky sexual behaviors include unsafe sex, coerced sex, sex involving alcohol or drugs, having multiple sex partners, and low or unreliable use of birth control, all of which can have long-lasting consequences (Centers for Disease Control and Prevention, 2018a). Such consequences are not just for teens themselves, but for their families and future families, which is why it is so important for young people who are becoming sexual to learn the facts about safe and healthy sexuality. Teens have high rates of unprotected sex and as such are at high risk for unwanted pregnancies and STDs and STIs (American Association of World Health, 2001). Sexual victimization is also problematic particularly for teens. Many adolescents report that their first sexual experience was unwanted, especially girls (Abma, Driscoll, & Moore, 1998; Kellogg & Huston, 1995). Unwanted sex is less likely for male human beings over the entirety of the lifespan (Black et al., 2011; Finkelhor, Hotaling, Lewis, & Smith, 1990; Tjaden & Thoennes, 1998), both because they are typically bigger and stronger than most female human beings and have more power to coerce sex, and because male domination of sex is a cultural norm all over the world (Millett, 2016). Teens who identify as homosexual or bisexual (or who are in the process of doing so) are unfortunately more likely to engage in risky sexual behaviors, including heavier alcohol and drug use (Darwich, Hymel, & Waterhouse, 2012; Goldbach, Tanner-Smith, Bagwell, & Dunlap, 2014; Herrick, Marshal, Smith, Sucato, & Stall, 2011). Sexual minority teens are also more likely to be sexually victimized (Willoughby, Doty, & Malik, 2010) and are at greater risk for psychological difficulties than their heterosexual peers (Reuter, Sharp, Kalpakci, Choi, & Temple, 2016).

Individual Qualities

Researchers have identified several individual or personal qualities that are linked to sexuality development in adolescents. Onset of puberty and its accompanying physical changes is important for developing sexuality. For girls, development of secondary sex characteristics leads to sexualization by peers, which can result in sexual harassment (Lindberg, Grabe, & Hyde, 2007). Such early sexualization is linked with more negative outcomes for girls, including sexual advances from older boys and men, even sexual abuse (Boynton-Jarrett et al., 2013). Girls who develop early may feel insecure and self-conscious about their bodies (Lindberg et al., 2007), and are more likely to develop eating disorders (Adair & Gordon-Larsen, 2001), and other psychological difficulties (Kaltiala-Heino, Kosunen, & Rimpelä, 2003). Girls living in traditional cultures or in areas plagued by violence or war are even more likely to be sexually exploited during adolescence (United Nations Department of Economic and Social Affairs, 2004). Boys who are early maturers generally have a positive body image, being taller and more masculine at an earlier age compared to their peers. They are behaviorally independent and confident (Susman, Dorn, & Schiefelbein, 2003). Early maturing boys even show educational gains compared to their later maturing male peers (Daniel et al., 1982). They are however more likely to engage in sexual behavior earlier, including risky sexual behavior (Capaldi, Crosby, & Stoolmiller, 1996).

Personality traits are also important for sexual development during adolescence. Adolescents who are **introverted**, or quiet, withdrawn, and preferring solitary activities, may be more likely to experience difficulties in navigating sexuality, particularly in terms of feelings of anxiety and shame (Muris, Meesters, & Asseldonk, 2018). In contrast, **extraverted** adolescents, who are outgoing, sociable, talkative, and comfortable in group and social situations, are likely to be more successful at communicating about sexuality. Extraverted young men report earlier and more frequent sexual experiences than introverted young men (Schenk & Pfrang, 1986). Early research suggests that extraversion is related to sexual arousability (Harris, Yulis, & Lacoste, 1980). Extraverted young people are also higher in sensation-seeking and impulsivity, qualities not necessarily associated with the safest sexual behaviors (Kalichman, Hechman, & Kelly, 1996). One study found that teens higher in extraversion who identified themselves as sexual were more likely to present and consume sexual content online (Bobkowski, Shafer, & Ortiz, 2016). Young people who have conduct problems in general, including aggression and delinquency, are also more likely to engage in risky sexual behaviors compared to adolescents without conduct problems (Bryan & Stallings, 2002). Links between risky sexual behaviors and other risky behaviors are stronger among boys than among girls (Basen-Enquist, Edmundson, & Parcel, 1996) and in Euro-American samples than among other ethnic groups (Doljanac & Zimmerman, 1998).

Peer Influences

Communication with peers about sexuality is a common and frequently used source of information for most teens, especially when relationships with parents are lower quality (Boislard, Poulin, Kiesner, & Dishion, 2009; Sprecher, Harris, & Meyers, 2008). Young people are more likely to communicate with peers who are less conservative about sex and who communicate frequently about sex. Young women and older adolescents show higher quality communication about sex compared to young men and younger adolescents (Waterman, Wesche, & Lefkowitz, 2018). The sexual behaviors of older adolescents are more strongly influenced by peers than those of younger adolescents, who are more likely to be influenced by parents' attitudes about sexuality (Maguen & Armistead, 2006).

Adolescents express emotions and love through sexual behavior; many engage in sex with others for bonding and pleasure (Weisfeld & Woodward, 2004). Unfortunately, teens engage in sex for other reasons, including as a result of peer modeling and peer pressure to have sex (De

Gaston, Weed, & Jensen, 1996). The perception that close friends are having sex (Buhi & Goodson, 2007), having friends who actually are having sex (Wallace, Miller, & Forehand, 2008), and thinking that engaging in sex increases popularity among peers (Kinsman, Romer, Furstenberg, & Schwarz, 1998) are all strongly linked with adolescents engaging in sexual intercourse. Research indicates that the perceived number of sexually active friends is highly correlated with earlier sexual experiences and inconsistent use of contraception (Hampton, Jeffery, McWatters, & Smith, 2005; Kirby & Lepore, 2007). In other words, teens may feel pressured to have sex to "fit in" with everyone else or to follow perceived peer sexuality norms (Sneed, Tan, & Meyer, 2015). Among female adolescents, those with peers who engage in risky sexual behaviors are more likely to engage in such behaviors themselves (Bachanas et al., 2002). On the other hand, when peers discuss and endorse postponing sexual intercourse, earlier sexual experiences are less likely (Sieving, Eisenberg, Pettingell, & Skay, 2006).

Just as there is a double standard for adult sexuality, the same double standard exists for adolescents. The sexual **double standard** represents the inequality in social acceptance of sexuality for girls and women relative to that for boys and men (see "Controlling Sexuality" below). Sexual behavior in men is applauded and understood as a natural, healthy, normal behavior for them. Sexual behavior by women, in contrast, is viewed negatively, especially as it occurs outside of traditional marriage or monogamous relationships (Bordini & Sperb, 2013; Marks & Fraley, 2006). For adolescent girls, "making out" is associated with increases in acceptance by peers, while having sex is associated with decreases in peer acceptance over time. For adolescent boys, only making out is associated with decreases in peer acceptance, while having sex is associated with increases in peer acceptance (Kreager, Staff, Gauthier, Lefkowitz, & Feinberg, 2016). Sexual minority teens are the most challenged in terms of peer support, with many LGBTQ youth suffering lack of support and bullying by peers (Higa et al., 2012; Kelleher, 2009). Low peer acceptance is linked with risky sexual behaviors, substance use, and sexual victimization among these young people (Darwich et al., 2012; Dermody, Marshal, Burton, & Chisolm, 2016).

"**Sexting**" behavior between teens is a relatively new behavioral phenomenon that began with the widespread use of smartphones and texting (Cox Communications, 2009; Lenhart, 2012). Sexting can include sending images or sexual words to others through texting, online, or through social media (Drouin, Ross, & Tobin, 2015). Sexting behavior between teens is associated with earlier first sexual experiences, using drugs in association with sex, and having multiple sex partners two years later (Brinkley, Ackerman, Ehrenreich, & Underwood, 2017). The risks of sexual victimization increase with sexting behaviors (Moreno, Brockman, Wasserheit, & Christakis, 2012), including unintentional exposure to sexual content (Klettke, Hallford, & Mellor, 2014; Mitchell, Ybarra, & Korchmaros, 2014) and solicitations of sex (Baumgartner, Valkenburg, & Peter, 2010). Sexting and online victimization includes cyberbullying about sexuality and sexual orientation (Gruber & Fineran, 2008; Rinehart & Espelage, 2015).

Family Influences

A major factor influencing sexual development in adolescence is the family and its atmosphere. Parents are crucial sources of information about sexuality for teens (Dittus, Miller, Kotchick, & Forehand, 2004). Parental responsibilities consist of assisting adolescents in understanding their own sexuality (Jaccard, Dodge, & Dittus, 2002), providing accurate information about sex itself (Miller, Kotchick, Dorsey, Forehand, & Ham, 1998), and providing information about the risks, consequences, and responsibilities of sex (Dittus et al., 2004). Many studies have suggested that communication about sexuality with parents is relatively scarce (Rouvier, Campero, Walker, & Caballero, 2011; Wight, Williamson, & Henderson, 2006), particularly for boys (Leland & Barth, 1992; Swain, Ackerman, & Ackerman, 2006). Some studies have shown that a lack of communication between parents and adolescents stems from perceived discomfort during such topics and adolescents' perceptions that their parents are not competent concerning sexual matters and issues (Eisenberg, Sieving, Bearinger, Swain, & Resnick, 2006; O'Sullivan, Dolezal, Brackis-Cott, Traeger, & Mellins, 2005). Adolescents are less anxious and less avoidant when parents are more receptive, informal, composed, and informative during discussions about sex (Afifi, Joseph, & Aldeis, 2008).

Multiple studies indicate that frequent parent–child communication about sex is associated with less early sexual activity (Dittus et al., 2004; Huebner & Howell, 2003) and sexual risk-taking (Dilorio, Kelley, & Hockenberry-Eaton, 1999; Whitaker & Miller, 2000) among adolescents. However, other studies have determined that such communication may actually elevate risky sexual behaviors by adolescents depending on the nature and quality of parent–child relationships (Afifi et al., 2008) and the way the information about sex is conveyed (Fisher, 1986). More permissive maternal attitudes toward adolescent sexual activity are related to greater frequency of adolescent intercourse and a greater number of sexual partners during adolescence (Miller, Forehand, & Kotchick, 1999). Parents who express strong liberal views about sex (i.e., less restrictive and traditional) with their adolescent are more likely to have adolescents with more liberal sexual attitudes and behaviors (Fisher, 1986). Additionally, although greater communication with parents about sex has been linked to more accurate knowledge about contraceptives (Nadeem, Romo, & Sigman, 2006) and more consistent use of contraception (Bender & Kosunen, 2005), one study revealed that adolescent perceptions of parental approval for use of birth control were associated with increased tendency to use contraceptives while simultaneously increasing the risk for unplanned pregnancies through increased sexual activity (Jaccard & Dittus, 2000). Teens with parents who stress abstinence from sexual behavior are less likely to have earlier sexual experiences (Aspy et al., 2007; Dittus & Jaccard, 2000).

Research suggests that high-quality communication patterns with mothers in the home predict greater likelihood that parents will discuss sexuality and contraception with their children (Raffaelli, Bogenschneider, & Flood, 1998), and research has consistently shown that mothers take on a more proactive role in discussions about sex with their adolescents than do fathers (Miller et al., 1998). Adolescents are more likely to discuss sexual topics with mothers (Dilorio, Pluhar, & Belcher, 2003), perceive mothers as more effective communicators about sexual issues (Rosenthal, Senserrick, & Feldman, 2001), and report the most discomfort when discussing sex with fathers (Dilorio et al., 1999). Open communication with mothers about sexuality has been linked to positivity of relationships between Latina mothers and their adolescents (Romo, Lefkowitz, Sigman, & Au, 2002). Warm, supportive relationships with mothers in emerging adulthood include open, comfortable communications about sexuality, which are linked to features of sexual well-being of young adults (Riggio, Galaz, Garcia, & Matthies, 2014).

Other parenting behaviors are also meaningfully linked with risky sexual behavior among adolescents. Teens with parents who provide a great deal of support and monitoring, and who also exert parental control over children's behaviors, are less likely to engage in risky sexual behaviors (Price & Hyde, 2009). Higher levels of parental supervision, including of activities and relationships with peers, and explicit disapproval of risky sexual behaviors by parents, are associated with fewer risky sexual behaviors by teens (Boislard & Poulin, 2011; L'Engle & Jackson, 2008; Manlove, Logan, Moore, & Ikramullah, 2008). Teens who show poor quality of attachment to their

212   *Human Sexuality*

mothers show riskier sexual behaviors, likely because they lack closeness with, support from, and involvement with mothers (Udell, Sandfort, Reitz, Bos, & Dekovic, 2010). Sexual minority teens who lack family support, including for their identities, are most seriously at risk for sexual victimization and other risky sexual behaviors (Micucci, 2015; Willoughby et al., 2010; Yadegarfard et al., 2014).

Parents' personality qualities and psychological well-being are linked to risky sexual behavior in adolescents. Research indicates that parents who are low in **agreeableness** (a trait linked with nurturance, empathy, and tender-mindedness; Costa & McCrae, 1992) are less responsive to their children and are more likely to be harsh, critical, and coercive toward children (Clark, Kochanska, & Ready, 2000; Kochanska, Kim, & Nordling, 2012). Parents high in **neuroticism** are anxious, depressive, fearful, and tend toward anger (Costa & McCrae, 1992), qualities associated with lower quality parenting, including low support of autonomy, low control of their own behaviors, disorganization, and low warmth (Ellenbogen & Hodgins, 2004; Prinzie, Stams, Dekovic, Reijntjes, & Belsky, 2009). Low agreeableness and high neuroticism in parents are linked with risky sexual behaviors in teens (Nijjar, Ellenbogen, & Hodgins, 2016). Teens whose mothers suffer from poor mental health are more likely to engage in risky sexual behaviors (Hadley et al., 2011), likely because such mothers engage in less monitoring of teen behavior (Chang, Blasey, Steiner, & Ketter, 2001). High levels of family conflict are also linked with teens' risky sexual behaviors (Ary et al., 1999).

Social and Cultural Influences

At the broadest level of influence, sexuality and its development are obviously affected by multiple social and cultural factors surrounding us. Social institutions (government, education, religion, media) are particularly important in affecting sexual attitudes, beliefs, and behaviors. Social institutions provide so-called **sexual scripts** (Murray, 2018), the typical sequence of events each person follows during a sexual encounter. Scripts provide rules or **norms**, standards for particular behaviors adopted by social groups within a particular context. The sexual script provided by Western society is male-dominated; men initiate and control sex (Bowleg, Lucas, & Tschann, 2004; Rose & Frieze, 1989; Seabrook, Ward, Cortina, Giaccardi, & Lippman, 2017). Sex is heterosexual, involves only two people (who are married), occurs at night, in a bed, with the lights out. Sex toys are not involved in the typical sexual script, nor is doing it on the coffee table or in the garage. Norms for sexuality also involve punishments for violating rules, ranging from psychological guilt to ridicule to public shaming to death. Sexual scripts are used cognitively by individuals to guide their behaviors and feelings during sex (Gagnon & Simon, 1973; Simon & Gagnon, 1986). Sexual scripts operate within the psychology of the individual partners, which affects their interactions with each other. Sexual scripts operate at a societal level by telling us what are "normal" and what are "deviant" sexual behaviors.

Sexual scripts vary across cultures and subcultures within cultures, based on various cultural dimensions, including major religious, political, and family ideologies. Much research has compared Western romantic beliefs to Eastern or Asian beliefs about sexuality, and consistently shows that Eastern sexual beliefs and behaviors reflect greater conservatism or traditionality than Western sexuality. For example, one study found that Euro-Canadian women reported less sexual anxiety, more sexual knowledge, more liberal sexual attitudes, greater sexual desire and arousal, greater sexual pleasure, and more sexual experiences than Asian women who had immigrated to Canada. **Acculturation** (a process of blending between cultures, including at an individual psychological level) was linked with less conservative, more liberal sexual attitudes among the Asian women (Brotto, Chik, Ryder, Gorzalka, & Seal, 2005). Other studies show similar results, with Asian young people having first sex (or anticipating first sex) at older ages (Baldwin, Whiteley, & Baldwin, 1992; East, 1998; Huang & Uba, 1992), engaging in fewer sexual activities (Meston, Trapnell, & Gorzalka, 1996), and having fewer sexual partners than Euro-Canadian and Euro-American young people (Schuster, Bell, Nakajima, & Kanouse, 1998).

Among college students in the United States, Euro-American and Latinx-American students report similar sexual attitudes that are more liberal and more sexual experiences compared to Asian-American students. Asian-American students report lower frequency of sexual behaviors, later age at first sexual experience, and fewer sexual partners than Latinx- and Euro-American students. Greater acculturation among Latinx- and Asian-American students is linked with less conservative sexual attitudes and more sexual experiences (Ahrold & Meston, 2010; Meston & Ahrold, 2010). One study of American adolescents found that Latinx-American young people report greater sexual knowledge than African- and Euro-American youth (Davis & Niebes-Davis, 2010), although other research indicates lower sexual knowledge among Latinx-American youth (Centers for Disease Control and Prevention, 2008). Davis and Niebes-Davis (2010) also found that Euro-American youth were more conservative in their sexual attitudes than their African- and Latinx-American peers. Young people with less permissive sexual attitudes were more optimistic about their futures in terms of their health and whether they would attend college.

Mass media has a tremendous influence on sexuality. Body image is strongly affected by mass media. Everyone is exposed to a predominance of portrayals of women as sexualized beings. Women in media are generally quite beautiful and tending toward very thin (Greenberg, Eastin, Hofschire, Lachlan, & Brownell, 2003), and are portrayed in roles that are often dependent on men (Tuchman, 2000) and that involve the woman's romantic and sexual desirability (Johnson, 2010). Recent research indicates that sexualization of child and adult female characters is highly prevalent in television programming popular among U.S. Latina and Euro-American girls (McDade-Montez, Wallander, & Cameron, 2017). Girls exposed to such media depictions, in movies, on television, in print media, and in online images, are overwhelmed with an idealization of female beauty and sexuality. Adolescent girls and women with greater exposure to such images report lower self-esteem (Fernandez & Pritchard, 2012; Rollero, 2013), more negative body image (Grabe, Ward, & Hyde, 2008), more eating disorder symptoms (Strahan, 2003), more risky sexual behaviors (Peterson, Wingood, DiClemente, Harrington, & Davies, 2007), and are more likely to experience anxiety and depression (Jiménez-Cruz & Silva-Gutiérrez, 2008).

Portrayals of men in mass media, especially in the United States, are often **hypermasculine** (Ben-Zeev, Scharnetzki, Chan, & Dennehy, 2012; Mosher & Tomkins, 1988). Men in media are generally tall and handsome, with roles depicting them as strong, active, important (Scharrer, 2005), independent from women (Prentice & Carranza, 2002), and central to storylines and plots (Greenwood & Lippman, 2010). Exposure to these hypermasculine images can lower men's sense of well-being (Halliwell, Dittmar, & Orsborn, 2007; Hobza & Rochlen, 2009; Rollero, 2013). Men exposed to women objectified in media are more likely to express sexist, negative attitudes toward women (Rollero, 2013). Recent research suggests that greater exposure to television and movies, including sports programs, predicts greater endorsement of traditional masculinity among young men, which in turn is linked with their greater substance use, sexual risk-taking, and other self-destructive behaviors (Giaccardi, Ward, Seabrook, Manago, & Lippman, 2017).

Romantic love is a powerful cultural script that impacts sexual behavior (Lindholm, 1998). Romance novels are a particular kind of mass media to which girls and women are particularly attracted. Romance novels comprise 34% of the fiction book market in the United States (Nielsen BookScan, 2015); 84% of readers are female, and the majority are white and young (Nielsen Company, 2018). Romance novels are being increasingly marketed to teen girls and young adult women (Peterson, 2018). Unfortunately, the plots of romance novels are highly unrealistic, and often portray sexuality in a very male-dominated way. The typical plot of the romance novel is easy to discuss if you've ever read one. It usually consists of something like this: Heterosexual man and woman meet; they are white, American, and speak English. He is older, tall and handsome, she is younger, small, delicate, and beautiful. Man shows lack of interest or even negative emotions toward woman, because his instant desire for her disturbs him and he must avoid commitments. She feels intense dislike for him, but an unendurable physical longing for him that scares her. Eventually they come together in passionate embrace, introduced by him; she nearly faints and loses her head, swooning in his arms, her body has a will of its own, she has lost control! Eventually they end up in bed, although she has resisted previous attempts. During sex, he plays her like an instrument; she is putty in his hands and doesn't know much of what to do at all (he certainly does). Usually there is a happy ending, even if she was a bad girl and slept with him before the engagement or wedding itself. Her life is now complete, now that this man loves her (Christian-Smith, 2013). This script is common within romance novels published in the Western world across 20 years (Ménard & Cabrera, 2011). When romance novels involve teen romance, the boy similarly pursues the girl, usually not the other way around, and her parents protect her; her body in particular is precious and untouchable. Thus begins the negotiation for the girl's sexuality, between the parents, pastors, peers, and the boy (the girls is just in the middle of all the chaos) (Christian-Smith, 2013). All of this is male-dominated, men controlling, dictating, defining, and running sexuality, with women as passive and definitely not in charge. It is also heteronormative, presenting heterosexuality as normal and romantic and desirable. Homosexual romance novels are rare but are definitely increasing in availability (Crisp, 2009).

There are negative consequences of this kind of prototype of heterosexual experiences, in addition to the intentional and unfair exclusion of homosexual relationships from such storylines. First and foremost, such plots limit everyone's understanding of individual sexuality. If the typical romance plot is desired by women, or men, sexual behaviors will obviously be limited. While naturally sexually dominant to some degree because of testosterone and its link to men's sexuality, men can be sexual equals to women, and women can dominate sexuality as well, if and when they want to. Sex does not have to be in the bedroom, at night, with the lights off, with two people of the opposite sex. Sexual freedom from cultural scripts can be daunting or even frightening to people, but the script that is so common in our media is just one way. The predominance of male-dominated sexuality in mass media is a great disservice to women and men which limits women's sexual agency and healthy sexuality of women and men. It is designed to portray "appropriate" gender roles, where men have more power and women are sexually passive and dependent on men, including for their own sexuality. Research indicates that media consumption, including reading romance novels and watching television shows, is associated with greater endorsement of traditional, male-dominated sexual scripts, and women's lower sexual agency (Seabrook et al., 2017).

Sometimes sexual scripts of romance novels and other media (television shows, films) include what is called "**token resistance**," referring to women's false objections to sexual advances by men (sometimes called **scripted** or **token refusal**; Muehlenhard & Felts, 2011; Muehlenhard & McCoy, 1991). In other words, women resist men's advances, even when they really want to be sexual with men (Muehlenhard & Hollabaugh, 1988). Why do women engage in this behavior?

Most cultures around the world derogate women who desire sex. Women who are "lustful" are seen as likely to be promiscuous, lowering paternity certainty and increasing the likelihood of contracting an STI or STD (Buss, 1994). Because of negative views of women's sexuality, women may subdue their sexuality and explicitly deny it, even when they have sexual desire or interest. Men also engage in token resistance, especially in the United States (Sprecher, Hatfield, Cortese, Potapova, & Levitskaya, 2010). However, research indicates that when men do it, male and female partners tend to play a game about it and enjoy it (O'Sullivan & Allgeier, 1994). Research also indicates that the majority of refusals, from women and men, are intentional, explicit refusals of sex, nothing "token" about it (Muehlenhard & Rodgers, 1998).

When women do engage in token resistance or refusal, potential outcomes are more negative. Token resistance perpetuates male domination of sex and restricts women's power. If women pretend to not want sex, even when they do, men continue to decide where, when, and how sex occurs. Token resistance discourages honest communication about sex. Honest, open communication between sexual partners is associated with more psychologically and physically satisfying sexual experiences (Jones, Robinson, & Seedall, 2018). Further, token resistance teaches men that women's refusals are not important, to be ignored, because they are likely to be fake (Muehlenhard & McCoy, 1991; Osman & Davis, 1999). Women clearly engage in real resistance to men's advances. When men disregard resistance and the importance of consent, sexual assault becomes more likely. Token resistance perpetuates rape myths, or false beliefs about women and rape that men use to justify sexual aggression against women (see Chapter 11). Men who endorse rape myths believe that women enjoy forcible sex and find it sexually exciting (Burt, 1980). Rape myth beliefs are associated with sexism, traditional gender ideology, and low empathy for rape victims (Frese et al., 2004; Jimenez & Abreu, 2003; see Chapter 11). Heterosexual (but not homosexual) men are more likely to endorse rape myths than women are, and are likely to support and strengthen peers' rape myth beliefs (Bohner et al., 2006).

Another more specific negative consequence of romantic love as a cultural script involves the practice of safe sex and use of effective contraception. Romance novels and other mass media depictions of sexuality rarely show condom use (Braun-Courville & Rojas, 2009). Often within romance novels, films, and television shows, there is no discussion of preventing unwanted pregnancies or purchasing condoms or other contraceptives (Brown, Childers, & Waszak, 1990; Hust, Brown, & L'Engle, 2008). In one analysis of media content targeted to adolescents (in television, movies, magazines, music), only one-half of 1% included depictions of or information about healthy sexuality (Hust, Brown, & L'Engle, 2008). Research indicates that when characters in media do engage in discussion and use of contraception, attitudes toward contraception of consumers of that media are more positive (Diekman, McDonald, & Gardner, 2000). Avoidance of healthy sexuality messages hurts teens' understanding of safe and unsafe sexuality; positive, accurate, and healthy sexuality messages actually reduce teens' likelihood of having sex (Kirby, 2001). Avoiding safe sex information helps no one and is irrational and frankly asinine.

Pornography is another form of media that affects sexual development. Pornography is easily accessible to any person with a computer or smartphone and a link to the internet, so there seems to be no avoiding it (even if you wanted to). For adolescents, exposure to and regular use of pornography will obviously affect sexual development in a variety of ways, from allowing observation of various sexual activities to influencing ideas about the roles of women and men in sexual behavior. For many adolescents, exposure to pornographic material is unwanted or accidental (Wolak, Mitchell, & Finkelhor, 2007). A review of research examining adolescents and use of pornography indicates that boys more than girls use pornography during adolescence and

216 *Human Sexuality*

that age increases likelihood of use. Those adolescents who use pornography more frequently report more permissive sexual attitudes, greater sexual behavior, and higher rates of "casual" sex (e.g., hook-ups). Using pornography is linked to initiation of sexual behavior among adolescents (Collins et al., 2004). Unfortunately, pornography consumption is also linked to stronger and more traditional gender stereotypes about sexuality, greater sexual aggression, sexual perpetration, and sexual victimization (Peter & Valkenburg, 2016). Overtly pornographic material is not required to affect adolescents' sexuality. Exposure to highly sexual "mainstream" (i.e., non-pornographic) media is linked to increased likelihood of early sexual activity (Brown et al., 2006).

Because it is involved in regulating sexuality, religion is clearly informative of sexual scripts, across cultures. As we discussed at the beginning of this chapter, religious prohibitions against sexuality have existed for centuries, since religion began. Sex outside of marriage is risky, causes spread of disease, and produces unwanted children who may end up being abandoned by one or both parents. To control population growth, public health, and prevent poverty, religion was used by early societies to prevent sex outside of marriage by delineating it as sinful. Sexual desire and arousal become lustful and bad; sex not for reproduction is prohibited and punished, sometimes by death. Homosexuality is also forbidden, because it is lustful and encourages sexuality (Anderson & Koc, 2015; Herek & McLemore, 2013; Laythe, Finkel, & Kirkpatrick, 2001).

All major world religions, including Judaism, Christianity, Islam, Hinduism, and Buddhism, regulate sexuality in some way. For religious individuals, completely normal and natural feelings, sensations, and bodily responses become scary and threatening, one's own body becomes a threat to spirituality and connection to God. Religiosity unfortunately is linked to lower levels of sexual health (Efrati, 2019). Adolescents growing up in highly religious homes and cultures are likely to have more negative attitudes toward sex (Ahrold & Meston, 2010; Koenig, 2001; Taggart et al., 2018) and more negative sexual experiences (Efrati, 2019; Sheeran, Abrams, Abraham, & Spears, 1993) compared to adolescents with less religious backgrounds. Sadly, LGBTQ youth are particularly harmed by religious condemnation of their sexuality, and religious LGBTQ youth are significantly more likely to think about and attempt suicide compared to non-religious LGBTQ young people (Hong et al., 2011; Katz-Wise et al., 2018; Shearer et al., 2018). Suicidal ideation is also more common among heterosexual religious young people compared to the less religious when unwanted pregnancies occur (Chan et al., 2016).

Experiencing Sexuality: Adulthood Sexuality

Sexual Arousal

The adult experience of sexuality is obviously different from that of adolescents, if all goes well. Sexual desire involves being motivated toward sexual behavior, thinking about and wanting sex. Sexual desire motivates sex, it drives us to seek out sexual activity, either with ourselves or with others. Sexual desire is psychological. Sexual desire can be triggered by internal (thoughts, emotions) or external stimuli (pornography, seeing a partner, being touched). Sexual arousal is the physical, physiological response of the body to sexual desire, and it is essential for satisfying sexual activity. Sexual arousal occurs in anticipation of sexual activity. Sexual arousal is actually similar for women and men in terms of bodily processes. The heart beats faster, the body heats up, perspiration and respiration both also increase. Testosterone and estrogens are released into the bloodstream. For women, blood flows to the genitals, the vulva, vaginal walls, and the clitoris, engorging those tissues (vasocongestion). Vaginal lubrication occurs in preparation for intercourse. Blood flow to the nipples also increases. For men, blood flows to the penis, engorging it and resulting in an erection, also in preparation for intercourse (Rosen & Beck, 1988). Sexual arousal is an important feature of satisfying sex (Smith, Gallicchio, & Flaws, 2017). Sexual activity without real sexual arousal can not only be dissatisfying but also painful (Brauer, Le Kuile, Janssen, & Laan, 2007). Low sexual desire can be chronic and associated with lasting health issues (Hayes et al., 2007), especially for women. Approximately 40% of women in the United States report some kind of sexual dysfunction, especially low sexual arousal (Shifren, Monz, Russo, Segreti, & Johannes, 2008). About 33% of men in the United States experience erectile dysfunction on occasion after the age of 50 years (Bacon et al., 2003).

Sexual Attraction

Who are we attracted to sexually? Everyone seems to have their "type," body or facial features that trigger an initial attraction. Evolutionary theorists assert that sexual attraction is governed in a rather unconscious way by reproductive concerns (Buss & Schmitt, 1993). According to these explanations, men are biologically driven to produce as many offspring as possible. This means having sexual intercourse with as many women who are capable of conception and successful pregnancy as possible. As such, the main qualities men are looking for in a mate are youthfulness, health, and fertility, qualities that enhance the possibility of producing viable offspring. Older women are not fertile after a certain age (after menopause); women who are not healthy are less likely to be able to be successfully pregnant for nine months. In support of this explanation, much research indicates that heterosexual men all over the world report greater sexual attraction toward women who are younger and physically attractive (Buss et al., 1990; Chuang, 2002; Li et al., 2013). Men also show a preference for women with an hourglass type shape, argued to suggest successful childbirth likelihood (Singh, 1993; Zotto & Pegna, 2017). In contrast to men, who can hypothetically successfully fertilize women every day, resulting in many possibilities for viable offspring, women can only produce a few viable offspring over their lifetimes, due to the time and risks involved in pregnancy and the occurrence of menopause. Because of these physical limitations, women are more invested in the welfare and longevity of each individual offspring, and are therefore more concerned about the long-term caretaking of each child. These concerns drive women to seek out mates who are capable of providing for and supporting their offspring over longer periods of time. As such, heterosexual women seek out mates based on power and status concerns, including financial power (Buss et al., 1990; Buunk, Dijkstra, Fetchenhauer, & Kenrick, 2002; Shackelford, Schmitt, & Buss, 2005). Women also show a preference for tall men (Pawlowski, Dunbar, & Lipowicz, 2000), men with masculine facial features (Perrett et al., 1998), and older men (Kenrick & Keefe, 1992; Dunbar & Waynforth, 1995), all arguably rough indicators for power and status. While there is some evidence linking **fecundability** (current likelihood of pregnancy based on the menstrual cycle) to women's attraction to men with masculine facial features, research results are actually rather mixed (Welling & Burriss, 2019).

Sexual Experiences

Sexual health involves a positive and respectful approach to sexuality (World Health Organization, 2006). Healthy sex is adult, fully consensual (free of any type of coercion), and safe (protecting all participants from disease and unwanted pregnancy). Healthy adult sexuality is good for individuals and couples, and is an important feature of quality of life (Laumann, Paik, & Rosen, 1999).

Human beings have sex for pleasure, for reproduction, and for bonding (Penhollow, Young, & Denny, 2009; Young & Wang, 2004). **Bonding** refers to the development of a close affectional tie with another being; it is based on trust and concern for each other's welfare and well-being (Bowlby, 1969; Hazan & Shaver, 1987). Heterosexual married partners in the United States report having sex about five to seven times a month (Laumann, et al., 1994; Loewenstein, Krishnamurti, Kopsic, & McDonald, 2015). Younger adults have sex more often, about once a week (Blanchflower & Oswald, 2004). Research indicates that gay male couples have sex slightly more often and that lesbian couples have sex slightly less often than heterosexual couples (Blumstein & Schwartz, 1983). Healthy sexuality is an important feature of any positive, fulfilling intimate relationship. More frequent sex with a romantic partner results in greater relationship satisfaction and greater closeness to each other (Costa, Brody, Hess, & Weiss, 2011; Byers, 2005; Costa & Brody, 2007). Frequency of sex is associated in a positive, linear way to reports of life satisfaction (Amy Muise, Schimmack, & Impett, 2016). Research actually indicates that body fluids exchanged during sexual contact can have positive health benefits, including lower depression and better immune system functioning in women (Gallup, Burch, & Platek, 2002; Koelman et al., 2000). Of course, body fluids should only be exchanged between monogamous sexual partners who have been recently tested for STDs and who are practicing some other form of reliable birth control if needed. Condoms are essential for safe sex, especially for the experience of casual sex (Fielder & Carey, 2010; Maxwell, 2017; Planned Parenthood, 2018).

Although being involved in a committed relationship certainly has many benefits, including greater happiness (Stack & Eshleman, 1998), it is not necessary for sexual health. Sexuality of any form, with any number of people, simultaneously or sequentially, with or without accessories (see "Learn More") can be positive and healthy for adults who engage in consensual and safe sex. Healthy sexuality involves **sexual self-esteem**, involving emotionally positive feelings toward the self as a sexual being (Offman & Matheson, 2004). Positive sexual self-esteem is linked to more positive attitudes toward sex (including pornography and homosexual behavior), greater sexual satisfaction, and more frequent sexual behavior in the past month among American young adults (Riggio, Romero-Juarez, Rusk, & Umana, 2016). Sexual health is important across the lifespan (Penhollow et al., 2009). Among older adults with sexual partners, open sexual communication, partners' synchronous sexual desire, and sexual variety are linked with greater frequency of sexual behavior and greater sexual satisfaction (Gillespie, 2017).

Women and men are different sexually in many ways. Women and men differ in sexual activities and behaviors, in beliefs and attitudes about sex, in thoughts and feelings about sex, and in concerns and fears about sex. In terms of sexual activity, men show greater desire for activity and sexual variety (i.e., more different sexual partners) than women all over the world (Schmitt, 2003). Meta-analyses of studies on gender differences in sexuality indicate that men are more interested in and approving of casual sex, desire more sex partners, masturbate more, use more pornography, and have more heterosexual and homosexual sexual experiences than women. Women report more guilt, fear, and anxiety about sex than men (Oliver & Hyde, 1993; Petersen & Hyde, 2010). Men also think about sex more often than women, with over 50% of men saying they think about sex every day or several times a day, versus only 19% of women (Laumann et al., 1994). Studies indicate few differences between men and women in feelings of intimacy with sexual partners and reports of sexual satisfaction (Træen, Markovic, & Kvalem, 2016).

Body image is particularly relevant to sexuality, given the role of the body in all aspects of sexuality, including feelings of sexual self-esteem (Riggio et al., 2016). Body mass index (BMI; an indicator of body fat in adults) appears to be particularly relevant to feelings of satisfaction with one's body (Streeter, Milhausen, & Buchholz, 2012). Men tend to have a more positive image than women, and body image appears to be a greater factor in sexuality for women than for men (Træen et al., 2016). Among young women, positive body image and body satisfaction are linked to greater sexual self-esteem and sexual assertiveness (asserting individual sexual goals), fewer sexual problems, and lower sexual anxiety (Weaver & Byers, 2006). Some studies indicate that lower BMI is linked to a more positive body image, which is then linked with greater sexual satisfaction, especially for women (Træen et al., 2016). Other studies indicate that body image is highly subjective and actually affects sexual functioning independently of BMI and self-reported exercise (Weaver & Byers, 2006). While there does appear to be a relationship between BMI and women's positive sexual health, other factors appear to affect this link, including women's physical and psychological health and qualities of their sexual relationships (Ranjbar & Azmoude, 2018).

Hooking-Up

Human beings have sex with other human beings for various reasons. Sometimes, people just want sex for fun or pleasure or to feel a connection with someone, and for singles or people in so-called "open" relationships (Ramey, 1977), **hooking-up** is an option. **Hooking-up** is engaging sexually with a person (a friend or stranger), from kissing to intercourse, with no expectation of any further romantic behavior with each other (Snapp, Ryu, & Kerr, 2015). Casual sex is not uncommon and is becoming more normative in the United States, especially among young adults (Bogle, 2008; Garcia, Reiber, Massey, & Merriwether, 2012). Young people in particular are reporting greater rates of hooking-up, especially in college. Among American college students, as many as two-thirds to three-quarters are estimated to have had at least one casual sex encounter during college (England, Shafer, & Fogarty, 2008; Hamilton & Armstrong, 2009). Problems arise when alcohol or other substances are involved, which cloud ability to clearly give or not give consent and ability to interpret the consent messages of others (Abbey et al., 2002; Abbey, McAuslan, & Ross, 1998). Condom use is also problematic when alcohol or drugs are involved in hooking-up (Fielder & Carey, 2010). Problems are more likely to arise for women, just from the mere fact that the average man is physically larger and much stronger than the average woman, a fact that makes women more vulnerable to every kind of assault than men (Hollander, 2001; Parks, Romosz, Bradizza, & Hsieh, 2008; Stanko, 1987). Further, given the double standard, women are more subject to disapproval and stigmatization when they engage in casual sex. Casual sex is perceived as riskier for women because of these real social and physical dangers, so hooking-up is more commonly discouraged for women (Rudman et al., 2013).

Orgasm

The physical payoff for sexual activity is the **orgasm**, the sensation of intense pleasure that results from stimulation of the clitoris in women and stimulation of the penis in men. In men, orgasm generally includes **ejaculation**, the release of semen. Early research on orgasms indicated that women and men described the experience of orgasm in nearly identical ways, including a build up of pleasure throughout the sexual act, leading to a mounting feeling of tension throughout the body, ending with a climax of intense pleasure followed by a feeling of euphoria and release (Vance & Wagner, 1976). Later research suggests that women's orgasms are psychologically more complex and physically more intense than men's (Mah & Binik, 2001, 2002). In a national survey of Australian adults, Richters and colleagues (2006) found that men experienced an orgasm in 95% of recent sexual encounters, while women experienced orgasm in only 69% of recent sexual encounters. Women also tend to orgasm more frequently with a variety of sexual activities, especially when receiving oral sex. Women do not orgasm in every sexual encounter, as men typically do, and their experience of orgasm is more strongly determined by the quality of sexual experience a woman has had and the quality of the current sexual experience (Brody & Weiss, 2010; Puppo, 2011; Weiss & Brody, 2009). However, between 90 and 95% of women in Western nations report having experienced orgasm before, with nearly 90% indicating that they have experienced orgasm during intercourse (Lloyd, 2005). Multiple orgasms are also much more frequently reported by women than men (Darling, Davidson, & Cox, 1991; Masters & Johnson, 1966).

The male orgasm is obviously essential for conception to occur, and it often defines the sexual act of intercourse. The man's erection determines when penile-vaginal intercourse will begin, and the ejaculation signals the end, with most men experiencing a **refractory period** after ejaculation involving lack of interest in sex and inability to orgasm (Morrow, 2013). Some scholars argue that the female orgasm has evolved because it is linked to reproductive success. Puts, Dawood, and Welling (2012) assert that the female orgasm is more likely with male mates who are genetically superior or in other ways high-quality. Research indicates that women report having orgasms more quickly and more frequently during sex when their male partners are high in masculinity, facial attractiveness, and dominance (Puts, Welling, Burriss, & Dawood, 2012). Pollet and Nettle (2009) reported similar findings among a sample of Chinese women, who reported more frequent orgasms with male partners who made more money compared to women with partners who made less money. Sadly, some people are incapable of achieving orgasm, a condition called **anorgasmia** (Rowland et al., 2010).

Orgasms have health benefits. Some research indicates that regular masturbation is linked with lower incidence of prostate cancer in men (Giles et al., 2003). Other research indicates that orgasm is linked with lower blood pressure (Brody, 2006) and improvements in cardiovascular health (Graber, Balogh, Fitzpatrick, & Hendricks, 1991). Additional research indicates that orgasm is linked with longevity, with one study indicating that mortality risk was 50% lower in a group that reported high orgasm frequency compared to a group reporting few orgasms (Smith, Frankel, & Yarnell, 1997). Orgasms lead to release of hormones, including **prolactin**, which is calming and helps with sleep (Spiegel, Weibel, Gronfier, Brandenberger, & Follenius, 2009); and **dehydroepiandrosterone** (DHEA), a steroid hormone that promotes longevity (Mo, Lu, & Simon, 2006; Roberts, 1999). Longitudinal and other research indicates that frequency of orgasm is linked with youthfulness (Friedman & Martin, 2011; Weeks & James, 1998). Orgasms also cause the release of **oxytocin**, a hormone that promotes feelings of affection and bonding, especially in women (Insel, 1992), feelings which promote overall relationship satisfaction (Wudarczyk, Earp, Guastella, & Savulescu, 2013). Orgasms are clearly adaptive and have evolved because they promote successful reproduction and overall health and well-being.

Self-Pleasuring

Self-pleasuring is the modern, more positive term for **masturbation**, a word that has a more negative connotation (derived from the Latin word for *defilement*; Leung & Robson, 1993). Self-pleasuring, in case you didn't know, involves stimulating one's own genitals, usually to orgasm. As we've already discussed, orgasm is very good for the body, and as such, self-pleasuring is good for you. But these are rather modern conclusions. Traditionally, masturbation, especially in children, has been frowned upon in society, especially by religion, but also by medical practices informed by religion. Early American medical writers advised tying children's hands, putting a cage on the penis, and applying carbolic acid to the clitoris as effective treatments for masturbation in children (Kellogg, 1888). Some scholars assert that the increasing religious condemnation of self-pleasuring in the Western world at the end of the 19th century inspired the vast acceptance of male circumcision by medical practitioners (Darby, 2003) (see "Critical Thinking"). A website called howtostopmasturbation.com lists 23 negative "side effects" of masturbation, including reduced orgasm, loss of sex drive, increasing attraction to same-sex people, loss of motivation, memory loss, and suicidal thoughts. This list is false; there is no research linking self-pleasuring to any of these negative outcomes. Some people may report guilt or anxiety before or after they masturbate (Kelley, 1985); considering the historical and religious condemnation of self-pleasuring (Cornog, 2003), this is not surprising.

Meta-analyses indicate that women and men have similar attitudes toward self-pleasuring, although men report greater frequency of self-pleasuring (Oliver & Hyde, 1993; Petersen & Hyde, 2010). Laumann et al. (1994) found that 42% of women indicated that they engaged in self-pleasuring, compared to all men in their survey. Broadly speaking, self-pleasuring is good for you. Self-pleasuring helps maintain functionality of the genitals and reproductive systems (Levin, 2007). Frequency of self-pleasuring is linked with positive sexual outcomes, including greater sexual arousability, greater sexual desire, and greater likelihood of orgasm during sex, especially for women (Hurlbert & Whittaker, 1991). Greater frequency of self-pleasuring is also linked with body satisfaction and sexual empowerment among women (Bowman, 2014). Self-pleasuring information and instruction is widely used as a treatment method for sexual dysfunction, especially low sexual arousal and satisfaction (Both & Laan, 2009; Kay, 1992). Given the links between orgasm, positive health, and youthfulness discussed above, a daily dose of Vitamin M seems like a pretty good idea!

Social and Cultural Influences

The transition to adulthood obviously does not end the role of society and culture in affecting sexuality. Just as they influence adolescent sexual development, powerful social institutions continue to affect sexual thoughts, feelings, and behaviors among adults. Media sexualization and objectification of women negatively affect women's feelings about themselves (van den Berg et al., 2007; Vandenbosch, Muise, Eggermont, & Impett, 2015), their bodies (Grabe et al., 2008; Groesz, Levine, & Murnen, 2002), and their sexual behaviors (Brown, 2002). Media images of men as strong and virile are not positive for men's self-images either (Groesz et al., 2002), with negative effects for homosexual and heterosexual men (Duggan & McCreary, 2004). So why do we continue to create media like this? Who creates such advertisements, television shows, films? They are women and men, human beings who are likely not systematically different from consumers. The fact is, sex sells. People seek out sexualized images in advertising and story media (Blair, Stephenson, Hill, & Green, 2006; Sender, 2003). And such advertisements, shows, and films make money, the bottom line in a capitalistic society, often regardless of the human toll of capitalism's practices.

The question of sexualization of women and men then becomes, is it worth human beings' psychological health, to sell these products? We highly doubt that any CEOs of wealthy corporations are interested in making less money so that growing girls and women (and men) have healthier body image and self-esteem, although we wish they would be. A more efficient way to temper the effects of advertising and media images is through education. How can we educate children, adolescents, and adults better about what such advertisements are for and how they affect us? Teaching younger children about advertising and other media, that it generally presents current and popular ideals to consumers, not necessarily reality (even on so-called "reality" shows!), makes them informed consumers who are better able to cope with and interpret the constant barrage of sexualized, beautiful images. And if we think about sexy advertising as art, as an expression of humanity, an expression of a natural, quite beautiful human behavior, might we broaden our conceptualizations of what "sexy" is? Can we have people of all forms and features portrayed as sexy and sexual? Greater realism of human portrayals in advertising may perhaps prevent or even ameliorate some of the negative outcomes associated with media exposure (Ward, Day, & Epstein, 2006).

Pornography also affects adults and their sexuality, in positive and negative ways. Pornography obviously stimulates people sexually, in a perfectly natural way. You know how watching someone eat makes you feel hungry? The same goes for sex, through the operation of mirror neurons, brain cells responsible for a behavior that activate in response to watching others engaged in that behavior (Rizzolatti & Craighero, 2004). So when you see others eat, your brain cells that are involved in eating are activated (they "mirror" the activity that you see). When you see others having sex? The same thing happens, which is automatic, not easily consciously controlled, and perfectly healthy, normal, and natural. In this way, pornography can be a great stimulant for a sexual encounter or relationship, including obviously for self-pleasuring (Paasonen, 2009).

Among college men, 87% report viewing pornography, 20% on a daily or every other day basis. Thirty-one percent of college women reported using pornography (Carroll, Padilla-Walker, & Nelson, 2008). So what's the problem with porn? There is nothing morally wrong with pornography that portrays adult, consensual, and safe sexuality. Pornography is problematic when it violates any of these standards. Using pornography with a partner is associated with sexual benefits for women, including higher sexual quality (Poulsen, Busby, & Galovan, 2013) and greater sexual intimacy (Bridges & Morokoff, 2011). Those same studies however found negative sexual outcomes associated with male pornography use. In other words, among couples, women use pornography with their partner, which is beneficial for the relationship and their own sexuality. Men tend to use pornography for self-pleasuring, which can affect female partners' feelings about their sexual desirability (Stewart & Szymanski, 2012). Pornography that is violent is very dangerous (Malamuth & Ceniti, 1986; see Chapter 11, Aggression). Pornography that depicts rape or assault is harmful to men's ideas about women (Boeringer, 1994). Pornography that degrades or denigrates or humiliates women is harmful to viewers' perceptions of women (Demaré, Lips, & Briere, 1993; Hald, Malamuth, & Yuen, 2010) and to women's equality and dignity in the world. Role-playing is one thing, but depictions that indicate lack of consent teach people that lack of consent is okay, and it <u>never</u> is. So porn away, in a healthy, adult, balanced way that benefits your sexual partner(s) and yourself. Do not support pornography that is harmful to attitudes, sexuality, or people.

Religion is also obviously a presence in the lives of many adults and will thus affect their feelings, thoughts, and behaviors about sexuality. Research indicates that greater religiosity is associated with greater levels of self-reported sexual shame in adults (Riggio, Mendoza, Letona, & Gusha, 2018). Religious individuals can of course experience healthy, happy sexuality, there is no question of that. But because of its imposition of morality onto sexuality, religion can be a barrier to a healthy adult sex life. Among young adults, higher religiosity is linked with more negative attitudes toward sex in general, pornography, and homosexuality; and with lower sexual satisfaction (Riggio et al., 2016). Modernly, lower sexual health is associated with following traditional norms for sexuality and feeling shame about sex (Higgins, Mullinax, Trussell, Davidson, & Moore, 2011; Laumann et al., 1999; Masters & Johnson, 1979; Mereish & Poteat, 2015). Feelings of anxiety, guilt, and shame contribute to anorgasmia (Birnbaum, 2003). Mental health concerns, including depression and suicide, are particularly pronounced for LGBTQ individuals, who face stigma and discrimination related to their sexuality (Meyer, 2003; Meyer et al., 2008), largely due to prohibitions of religion against sexual behavior that is not heterosexual (Olson, Cadge, & Harrison, 2006).

Contraception and Reproductive Health

Thank goodness for modern medicine! Contraceptives have been around for a long time, pretty much since people discovered that children result from sexual intercourse. It is fairly certain that cave people were "pulling out" (practicing coitus interruptus or onanism), considering how pleasurable sex is for human beings and how difficult it is to bear and raise children. As we've already indicated, healthy sex is adult, consensual, and safe, meaning each person is protected from STIs, STDs, and from unwanted pregnancy. Contraception is thus essential to healthy sexuality (Planned Parenthood, 2018; World Health Organization, 2006). There are various contraceptive devices, including the male condom (essential for safe sex), the female condom, the intrauterine device (IUD), the diaphragm, vaginal rings and sponges, and female and male birth control pills and shots. Unfortunately, around the world contraception is feminized, meaning an undue burden for preventing unwanted pregnancies is placed on women (Kimport, 2018). Patriarchal society favors men's free sexuality but condemns women's sexuality, allowing men to be viewed as less responsible for pregnancy and contraception. The easiest way to prevent pregnancy is to control men's sperm, and condoms, vasectomy, and RISUG (see Bonus Box, Chapter 4) have many fewer side effects than female contraceptive methods. In the United States, abortion is legal and therefore safe (although not always accessible; see Chapter 7). Check the websites of the Centers for Disease Control and Prevention (www.cdc.gov/reproductivehealth/ contraception/index.htm) and Planned Parenthood (www.plannedparenthood.org/learn/birthcontrol) for more information (see also Chapter 4).

Sexually transmitted diseases (STDs) include dozens of different conditions that are spread from person to person through sexual contact, including vaginal or anal intercourse, oral sex, and petting (touching of genitalia with hands). STDs can obviously be prevented through abstinence; however, healthy sexual behavior is essential for well-being in adulthood and depriving or restricting healthy sexual behavior can result in pathologies surrounding sexuality (Costa et al., 2011). Many STDs can be prevented through correct use of the male condom (a flexible film made of latex or other material for placement over the penis during vaginal or anal intercourse). Engaging in sex only with people who have been tested and only with committed partners are other ways to prevent STDs. Unfortunately, approximately 20 million people in the United States are diagnosed with an STD each year, so safe sex is a modern imperative. Fortunately, all STDs can be treated with medication and many are entirely curable (Centers for Disease Control & Prevention, 2018b). Young people account for about half of all new STIs and STDs diagnosed in the United States (Centers for Disease Control & Prevention, 2013). STDs include gonorrhea, chlamydia, genital herpes, syphilis, Human Immunodeficiency Virus (HIV), Acquired Immunodeficiency Syndrome (AIDS), and others (see the CDC website, www.cdc.gov/std/ default.htm). If left untreated, some STDs can be fatal (especially AIDS and syphilis). HPV is linked

224   *Human Sexuality*

with the development of cervical, genital, and anal cancers. AIDS compromises the immune system, making people highly susceptible to infections and cancers. **Sexually transmitted infections (STIs)**, infections resulting from sexual contact, are also problematic and include **bacterial vaginosis**, which is the most common STI in women aged 15–44 in the United States (Centers for Disease Control & Prevention, 2015). Human papillomavirus (HPV) is the most common STI (Centers for Disease Control & Prevention, 2013). There are many other STDs and STIs; be sure to check the websites for the CDC and Planned Parenthood (www.plannedparenthood.org/learn/stds-hiv-safer-sex). Testing is easy and free or low-cost at Planned Parenthood and other clinics.

Unfortunately, not enough young people are practicing safe sex. STIs and STDs are increasing among young adults around the world (Brown et al., 2004; Fang, Oliver, Jayaraman & Wong, 2010), especially among gay and transgender young people (Clements-Nolle, Marx, Guzman, & Katz, 2001; Toibaro et al., 2009; Wolitski & Fenton, 2011). In the United States, half of all new STD infections affect young people between the ages of 15 and 24 years (Centers for Disease Control and Prevention, 2018b). Gay male youth and heterosexual girls who are ethnic minorities are especially at risk of HIV infection (Centers for Disease Control & Prevention, 2004; Valleroy et al., 2000). In the United States, approximately 800,000 adolescents become pregnant, many ending in abortion (Henshaw, 2004). In the United States in 2015, there were nearly 230,000 babies born to teen mothers (Centers for Disease Control & Prevention, 2017b). Girls who have children before age 19 years old suffer huge economic, social, psychological, and health detriments, for themselves and their children, over their entire lives. Unwanted children are a leading factor in poverty (Guttmacher Institute, 1994). Research suggests that young people do see condom use as consistent with romantic sexual scripts, but only for the prevention of pregnancy. Use of condoms to prevent STDs is not consistent with romantic scripts, and so if other contraception is in use (e.g., the birth control pill), condoms may not be used, thereby increasing risk of STIs and STDs (Flood, 2003; Kirkman, Rosenthal, & Smith, 1998). In a study of Canadian young adults, fewer than half of them between the ages of 18 and 24 years used a condom during their most recent sexual encounter (Milhausen et al., 2013).

So how do we increase the practice of safe sex? High-quality sex education is the answer. Sex education for adolescents is highly effective in increasing the safe sex behaviors and sexual health of young people all over the world. In a meta-analysis of 83 studies on safe sex curriculum in schools in Africa, the U.S., Europe, and Latin America, Kirby and colleagues (2007) found that sex education does not increase sexual behavior among young people. Sex education in fact may delay or decrease sexual behavior and does increase the practice of safe sex (using a male condom) and use of contraceptives. Positive effects of sex education are found across different groups of young people and cultures. Fisher and colleagues (1996) asserted that effective sex education messages involved three steps. First, young people need to be provided with accurate information about how STIs and STDs are transmitted. Second, effective messages increase young people's motivation to reduce their own risk of STDs and STIs. Teaching about the negative consequences of such conditions is a good start. Finally, effective sex education teaches young people specific skills and behaviors, including how to talk with doctors and parents about sex, how to purchase and use condoms and other contraception, and how to negotiate sexuality with partners.

For many years in the United States, the Bush Administration supported "abstinence-only" sex education, out of fears that educating young people about sexuality and safe sex would increase sexual activity in young people. The federal definition of abstinence-only education (see Table 8.1) states that sex within monogamous marriage is "the expected standard of human

Table 8.1 Federal definition of abstinence-only education*

A) has as its exclusive purpose teaching the social, psychological, and health gains to be realized by abstaining from sexual activity;

B) teaches abstinence from sexual activity outside marriage as the expected standard for all school-age children;

C) teaches that abstinence from sexual activity is the only certain way to avoid out-of-wedlock pregnancy, sexually transmitted diseases, and other associated health problems;

D) teaches that a mutually faithful monogamous relationship in the context of marriage is the expected standard of sexual activity;

E) teaches that sexual activity outside of the context of marriage is likely to have harmful psychological and physical effects;

F) teaches that bearing children out-of-wedlock is likely to have harmful consequences for the child, the child's parents, and society;

G) teaches young people how to reject sexual advances and how alcohol and drug use increase vulnerability to sexual advances, and

H) teaches the importance of attaining self-sufficiency before engaging in sexual activity.

* 1996 Title V of the Welfare Reform Act. https://ncac.org/resource/timeline-of-abstinence-only-education-in-u-s-classrooms (accessed June 25, 2018).

sexual activity"; and that sex outside of marriage is physically and psychologically "harmful" (Title V of the Welfare Reform Act, 1996). However, the majority of young Americans have sex before marriage (Abma, Martinez, Mosher, & Dawson, 2004). Young people are going to have sex; not providing them with accurate information about sexuality, disease prevention, and pregnancy prevention only increases disease and unwanted pregnancy, as indicated by national statistics about abstinence-only programs (Santelli et al., 2006). When young people hear more information about safe sex, they engage in safer sex, as evidenced by Kirby and colleagues (2007). Unfortunately, LGBTQ young people receive even less information about safe sex from school courses and educational websites, increasing their vulnerability to unsafe sex and STDs/STIs (Charest, Kleinplatz, & Lund, 2016). Not providing comprehensive sex education because of traditional and religious ideas about marriage and sexuality is not at all moral; it is threatening and harmful to the health, well-being, and futures of young people (Santelli et al., 2006).

Around the world, young people are not receiving enough sex education, and the spread of STDs, especially HIV and AIDS across entire nations in Africa, is evidence of that. Africa, especially the sub-Saharan region, is most affected by AIDS/HIV right now, especially among heterosexual young women. Of deaths from AIDS in the world, 70% occur in Africa. Approximately 26 million people in Africa have HIV; 2.3 million of them are children. Unfortunately, because HIV and AIDS are transmitted to infants by mothers, many children born in Africa contract them at birth. Of the world's children with HIV, 90% are from the sub-Saharan region of Africa (World Health Organization, 2017a). Death rates and new infections are declining, however, thanks to interventions by WHO and other agencies.

The World Health Organization (2017b) identifies several interrelated goals in Africa concerning sexual health. First, they strive to achieve universal access to sexual and reproductive health care, including contraception. To do this effectively, they need to challenge ideas that lead to restrictions on access to condoms and birth control, including ideas about morality that stem from religion. Related to this goal is an improvement in family planning. Second, they strive

226 *Human Sexuality*

for equity and human rights, especially for girls and women. This initiative addresses violence against women, restriction of women's sexual and sexual health rights, and child marriage (see Chapter 7). We can see traditional and religious ideology underlying a lack of equity in girls' and women's sexual health, including the practices of child marriage and female genital mutilation (FGM) (see below). Finally, WHO asserts that improvements must be made in accessibility and quality of sex education for adolescents and young adults. Ignorance is not helpful, not in any human endeavor, and sexuality should not be considered a taboo or forbidden topic in the modern world. STDs and unwanted pregnancies cause misery and pain; preventing them with reason and modern medical technology is relatively easy and extremely important.

Controlling Sexuality

The **double standard** refers to the fact that women's sexual behavior is subject to greater scrutiny, criticism, and control than that of men, with men's sexuality encouraged and women's sexuality discouraged. The double standard in sexual behavior occurs across cultures (Fugère, Escoto, Cousins, Riggs, & Haerich, 2008), and is especially likely to be strong and negative toward women in countries with more traditional cultures (McCarthy & Bodnar, 2005). Because of their greater control over resources and power across societies and the history of humankind, men have controlled women's sexuality through creation of religious ideology, laws, and scripts, and denial of women's equal sexual power, including in terms of controlling their own bodies. While linked somewhat to the different roles of women and men in reproduction and paternity certainty concerns, the double standard continues as a means of controlling and oppressing women, even in this modern age with easy and fast paternity testing (Rudman, Glick, Marquardt, & Fetterolf, 2017). College-aged men report viewing sex as a conquest, as something that they can persuade women into if they initially refuse, while college-aged women prioritize men's sexual needs over their own and hold traditional ideology that "good girls" don't have sex (Jozkowski, Marcantonio, & Hunt, 2017). Men receive sexual encouragement from peers (Rudman & Fetterolf, 2014) and from parents (Morgan et al., 2010), while women generally do not. Women hold a double standard against other women and themselves, especially in terms of having casual sex (Farvid, Braun, & Rowney, 2017).

The double standard promotes women's lack of **sexual agency** (ability to control and direct one's own sexual behaviors), which is linked with low sexual satisfaction and unsafe sex behaviors for women (Hynie, Schuller, & Couperthwaite, 2003; Sanchez, Phelan, Moss-Racusin, & Good, 2012; Williamson, Parkes, Wight, Petticrew, & Hart, 2009). Women who hold traditional standards that derogate their sexuality and subjugate it to men's, while at the same time trying to be a sexual adult, may experience negative psychological outcomes (Katz & Farrow, 2000). The double standard reinforces male sexual dominance and justifies sexual violence toward women (Krahé, Scheinberger-Olwig, & Kolpin, 2000; Warner, 2000). Men who endorse the double standard also tend to express **hostile sexism** (dominance-oriented, derogatory beliefs about women; Glick, Diebold, Bailey-Werner, & Zhu, 1997) toward women (Rudman, Fetterolf, & Sanchez, 2013).

Women's sexuality is derogated and controlled through everyday language. Sexual language is sexist; it promotes male dominance. Women are "screwed," "pounded," "banged," and "nailed." The word *"fuck"* is derived from a 16th-century German word (*fikken*) meaning "to strike." These words indicate that sex is aggressive, and because women are being entered or penetrated, it is men who are aggressing. Derogatory terms for the sexually active woman abound (e.g., slut, whore, bimbo, skank, dirty, just to name a few); terms for the sexually active man are actually quite positive (e.g., player, Casanova, stud). Socially attacking women and girls for presumed sexual activity is called "**slut-shaming**" (Armstrong, Hamilton, Armstrong, & Seeley, 2014) based on derogatory words used to publicly shame and hurt women. Scholars argue that because middle and high schools involve adolescents, sex education that emphasizes women as gatekeepers and men as naturally needing sex (Henry & Powell, 2014), and dress codes that target girls, who are again the gatekeepers and responsible for not arousing the boys (Dockterman, 2014), slut-shaming is more prevalent in these settings. Unfortunately, adolescence being the critical period for sexual development that it is, this means that youth are learning the sexual double standard first hand right up front, essentially learning frameworks for understanding later adult sexuality. In a study of college students, Murnen (2000) found that men use sexist language in their conversations about sex with other men. They objectified women, derogated them and their bodies, including their genitals, and expressed aggression when discussing sex. Sexist language reinforces negative views of women's sexuality, at individual psychological, dyadic, group, and societal levels. Men also use physical force to control women's sexuality; we discuss sexual assault, rape, and intimate partner violence in Chapter 11.

Religious ideology is a tool for controlling sexuality, particularly women's, as we've already discussed. But more than ideology, religion creates rituals as tools for oppression, including the barbaric practice of **female genital mutilation** (**FGM**; see also "Critical Thinking" regarding male circumcision). Usually practiced on girls aged 4 to 12 years, FGM is most common within countries of Islamic tradition, occurring in over 30 countries in Africa, Asia, and the Middle East (although it has been practiced in England, the United States, and other countries). The practice is thought to make girls more desirable brides, because when sexuality is obliterated, girls and women are more easily controlled and less likely to be sexually promiscuous or unfaithful after marriage. Girls who do not undergo FGM and remain intact are subject to social ridicule (Toubia & Sharief, 2003; UNICEF, 2016). According to the World Health Organization (2018), over 200 million women and girls worldwide have had their genitals mutilated in painful, often unhygienic procedures not conducted in medical settings (see Figure 8.3). FGM can involve **clitoridectomy**, which is a cutting off of the clitoris; **excision**, which involves removal of the clitoris and most of the inner vulva; and **infibulation**, sewing the vagina closed with only a small opening left for urine and menstrual fluid. These sutures have to be ripped out at sexual intercourse, on demand, by husbands (or rapists), and for childbirth. There are no health benefits of these procedures, ever, and many potential complications, including increased risk of HIV, chronic pelvic infections, urinary problems, childbirth complications, depression, and death from shock, blood loss, and infection. The World Health Organization makes a strong statement about FGM and what it involves; I agree with them and have reprinted it here:

> FGM is recognized internationally as a violation of the human rights of girls and women. It reflects deep-rooted inequality between the sexes, and constitutes an extreme form of discrimination against women. It is nearly always carried out on minors and is a violation of the rights of children. The practice also violates a person's rights to health, security and physical integrity, the right to be free from torture and cruel, inhuman or degrading treatment, and the right to life when the procedure results in death.
>
> (2018; www.who.int/news-room/fact-sheets/detail/female-genital-mutilation)

228 Human Sexuality

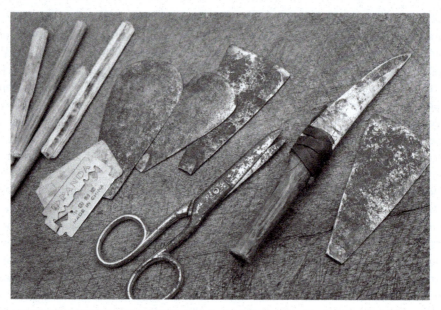

Figure 8.3 Tools used in female genital mutilation (FGM)
Source: Friedrich Stark/Alamy Stock Photo

Chapter Summary

Sexuality is a biological function that is essential for human health, happiness, and survival. Since human society began, sexuality has been rather stringently regulated, by laws, religion, and other social institutions. Sexuality begins at birth but advanced sexual development begins during puberty, in adolescence. There are many influences on the development of sexuality in young people, including peer, family, and social and cultural influences. Positive relationships with parents and open, honest communication about sex are healthy and important for understanding safe sex and avoiding risky sexual behaviors. First sexual experiences can be positive or negative for young people, with unwanted first sexual experiences more likely for girls than for boys. Mass media, including romantic scripts, pornography, and religion, can influence developing and adulthood sexuality. While most adults around the world report positive sexual experiences, with orgasm and sexual satisfaction linked to more positive psychological outcomes and romantic relationships, sexual dysfunction is not uncommon, especially among women. Self-pleasuring is common and normal and generally results in positive health and sexual benefits, again especially for women. Hooking-up or casual sex is becoming more common and socially acceptable, especially among young adults. Condom use is essential to safe sex and preventing the spread of sexually transmitted infections and diseases. Accessibility and correct use of contraception is essential to avoid unwanted pregnancy, which is a leading factor in keeping girls and women in poverty. Unfortunately, social institutions have been used to control sexuality, especially that of women, including religion and barbaric practices like female genital mutilation. Sexual and reproductive health is a human right; positive adult, consensual, and safe sexual behavior harms no one and is of great psychological and physical benefit to individuals and couples.

Thoughtful Questions

- Have you been tested for sexually transmitted diseases (STDs)? Consider and explain why you have or have not. If you have not, consider and explain why you should or should not be tested. (Hint: there are no reasons to not be tested, unless you have never had sexual contact.)
- Consider and explain the role of religious ideology in affecting sexuality.
- Consider and explain sexuality as a continuum of behaviors, including homosexual, bisexual, and heterosexual behaviors.
- Why do you think the majority of parents in the United States have their baby boys circumcised in infancy?
- Describe various methods of contraception and why contraception around the world is "feminized."
- Explain how and why men have controlled women's sexuality for centuries.
- Explain the practice of female genital mutilation (FGM) and its effects on girls and women.
- Why do you think hooking-up is most common among college students?
- Explain risky sexual behaviors. Why do you think LGBTQ young people are more likely to engage in risky sexual behaviors?
- Explain the effects of pornography on adolescent and adult sexuality.
- Explain the health benefits of self-pleasuring and orgasm.

Glossary

Abortion: various medical procedures that involve terminating a pregnancy.

Acculturation: a process of blending between cultures, including at an individual psychological level.

Agreeableness: a personality trait linked with nurturance, empathy, and tender-mindedness.

Amygdala: a brain structure in the mid-brain associated with pleasure and emotions; involved in sexual behavior across species. The amygdala is particularly important in experiences of fear and aggression.

Anal intercourse: insertion of the penis into the anus, usually until orgasm.

Bastard: a stigmatizing term used to describe children whose fathers have abandoned them.

BDSM: bondage (using restraints in sexual behavior), **discipline** (using dominance and punishment in sexual behavior), **sadism** (pleasure in causing pain), and **masochism** (pleasure in feeling pain).

Birth control pills (and shots): pills that are taken orally (or injections by a doctor) that affect hormones such that ovulation is prevented (in women) or production of viable sperm is prevented (in men).

Body image: one's subjective perception and liking of one's own body.

Bonding: the development of a close affectional tie with another being.

Bonobos (*Pan paniscus*): a species of primate, a great ape that is a type of chimpanzee. Bonobos are known for their rather constant sexual behavior.

230 *Human Sexuality*

Budding: a form of asexual reproduction where a new organism develops from a bud or growth from another organism; results from repeated mitotic cell division at one particular area on the "mother." Results in genetically identical offspring.

Clitoridectomy: cutting off of the clitoris in female genital mutilation.

Clone: a genetically identical offspring that results from asexual reproduction, especially budding but also parthenogenesis in some species.

Coitus interruptus (onanism): the practice of removing the penis from the vagina before ejaculation during vaginal intercourse; a primitive means of preventing pregnancy.

Contraception: a device or a method used in sexual intercourse to prevent pregnancy.

Crossing over: when sister chromatids (duplicated chromosomes) touch and exchange genetic material during synapse in meiosis. Results in unique combinations of genes on chromosomes, with sister chromatids no longer genetically identical.

Dehydroepiandrosterone (DHEA): an endogenous (naturally occurring) steroid hormone that promotes longevity.

Diaphragm: small cup or dome made of silicone or other material that is placed inside the vagina to prevent sperm from entering the cervix. Use of a spermicide is also required for greater protection against unwanted pregnancy.

Diploid: having a full number of chromosomes, one set from each parent in sexual reproduction (or one set from egg and polar body in **parthenogenesis**).

Double standard: the fact that all over the world, women's sexual behavior is subject to greater scrutiny, criticism, and control than that of men.

Excision: removal of the clitoris and most of the inner vulva during female genital mutilation.

Fecundability: a woman's current likelihood of pregnancy based on the menstrual cycle.

Female condom: an internal device made of latex that is inserted into the vagina that prevents sperm from entering the cervix to prevent unwanted pregnancies and transmission of infection and disease.

Female genital mutilation (FGM): mutilation of girls' and women's genitals for religious reasons. FGM is barbaric, dangerous, and leads to serious health, sexual, and psychological complications.

Fidelity: faithfulness, especially in terms of sexual faithfulness to a marriage partner.

Foreskin: a length of skin covering the top part of the penis that can be pulled back.

Fornication: a negative term describing sexual relations between two people who are not married; or sexual behavior engaged in for pleasure, not for reproduction.

Gender roles: ideas about the appropriate activities for women and men to engage in within a particular social context and culture. Includes ideas about sexuality and the roles of women and men in sexual behaviors.

Glans penis: the sensitive tip of the penis that includes the urethral opening.

Half-clone: an offspring with a diploid chromosomal number that is 50% genetically identical to the mother.

Haploid: having half the normal chromosomal number. Human gametes (sperm and egg) are haploid.

Hippocampus: a brain structure in the mid-brain associated with memory, pleasure, and emotions; involved in sexual behavior across species. The hippocampus is particularly important for the storage of new information into long-term memory.

Hooking-up: engaging sexually with a person (a friend or stranger), from kissing to intercourse, with no expectation of any further romantic behavior with each other.

Hypermasculinity: extreme masculinity including endorsement of violence, callous sexual attitudes toward women, and risk-taking.

Hypothalamus: a brain structure in the mid-brain associated with body regulation, thirst, hunger, sleep, pleasure, and emotions; involved in sexual behavior across species. The hypothalamus controls the pituitary gland.

Infibulation: sewing the vagina closed during female genital mutilation, with only a small opening left for urine and menstrual fluid. The sutures are removed for intercourse and childbirth.

Intrauterine device (IUD): a small device placed into the uterus that secretes hormones which prevents sperm from fertilizing eggs and prevents implantation of fertilized eggs in the uterus. IUDs are long-term contraceptive devices that can be removed at any time.

Kin: people who are genetically related to each other.

Legitimizing myths: false beliefs that justify the oppression of groups with less social power.

LGBTQ: lesbian, gay, bisexual, transgender, queer/questioning.

Male circumcision: cutting off the foreskin of the penis, which is typically accomplished during the first month of life.

Male condom: a flexible film made of latex or other material for placement over the penis during vaginal or anal intercourse. Condoms allow sperm to be captured and disposed of rather than ejaculated into another person. Condoms reduce the risk of pregnancies and prevent the transmission of sexually transmitted infections (STIs) and diseases (STDs).

Marriage: a legal agreement of commitment between two people.

Menopause: the cessation of menstruation in older age.

Monogamy: sexual relations between two people who are married to each other.

Neuroticism: a personality trait linked with being anxious, depressive, fearful, and tending toward anger.

Nucleus accumbens: a pleasure center in the brain located at the back of the forebrain that is important in the experience of pleasure; neurotransmitters like dopamine are released into the nucleus accumbens. Because it is involved in pleasure, the nucleus accumbens is involved in reward learning and motivated behavior.

Open relationships: committed relationships where each partner is free to engage sexually with others.

Oral sex: stimulating the genitals or anus with the mouth.

Orgasm: the sensation of intense pleasure that results from stimulation of the clitoris in women and stimulation of the penis in men.

Orphan: a child who is unsupported by either biological parent.

Oxytocin: a hormone that promotes feelings of affection and bonding, especially in women.

Parthenogenesis: development of a zygote from an unfertilized ovum (egg). Typically, part of an egg called a polar body acts as a sperm cell and fertilizes the egg, resulting in a half-clone (50% genetically identical to the mother) that has a diploid chromosomal number.

Paternity certainty: when a man can be certain that a child is actually his offspring, resulting from his genetic material. Paternity of an offspring is assured through virginity at marriage and monogamy (or modernly, using a DNA test).

Patriarchal: a society structured in a hierarchy with men enjoying a disproportionate share of political, economic, and social power. Women in such societies are oppressed and suffer a disproportionate share of society's shortcomings and disadvantages.

232   *Human Sexuality*

Petting: touching of another person's genitalia with one's hands.

Pituitary gland: the gland under the mid-brain that releases hormones and controls the release of hormones from other glands in the body (e.g., adrenal, thyroid, ovaries, testicles). Controlled by the hypothalamus.

Pornography: any media involving nudity and/or sexual activity.

Prolactin: a hormone released during sex that is calming and helps with sleep.

Rape myths: false beliefs about women and rape that men use to justify sexual aggression against women.

Refractory period: a period of time, from hours to days, after ejaculation involving men's lack of interest in sex and inability to orgasm.

Risky sexual behaviors: sexual behaviors or practices that increase the risk of STDs, STIs, unwanted pregnancies, abuse, and other harm to participants. Examples are unsafe sex, coerced sex, sex involving alcohol or drugs, having multiple sex partners, low or unreliable use of birth control.

RISUG (reversible inhibition of sperm under guidance): a contraceptive method involving injection of a polymer gel into the vas deferens, which reverses the ionization of sperm and shreds them when ejaculation occurs. Effective, safe, cheap, reversible; currently being researched in the U.S. as Vasalgel.

Self-pleasuring (masturbation): stimulation of one's own genitals, usually to orgasm.

Sexual agency: ability to control and direct one's own sexual behaviors.

Sexual arousal: the physical, physiological response of the body to sexual desire; essential for satisfying sexual activity.

Sexual desire: the motivation to engage in sexual behavior.

Sexual minorities: people who identify as gay, lesbian, bisexual, transgender, or queer (**LGBTQ**).

Sexually transmitted diseases (STDs): diseases transmitted from person to person through sexual behavior. Includes **gonorrhea, syphilis, herpes, chlamydia,** and **HIV,** the virus that causes **AIDS.**

Sexually transmitted infections (STIs): infections resulting from sexual contact; human papillomavirus (HPV) is the most common STI.

Slut-shaming: socially attacking and stigmatizing women and girls for presumed sexual activity.

Sodomy: a negative term used to refer to any sexual behavior other than penile-vaginal intercourse. Stems from the Biblical city of Sodom, which was destroyed by God because of the "sinful" sexual behavior of its inhabitants.

Stigmatization: social ridicule in response to an ascribed condition or proscribed behavior.

Swinging: engaging as a couple with other people sexually.

Token resistance (scripted or **token refusal):** women's false objections to sexual advances by men. Because of the double standard, women resist men's advances, even when they really want to be sexual with men.

Vaginal intercourse: insertion of the penis into the vagina, usually until orgasm.

Vaginal ring: a small ring of plastic placed into the vagina once a month to prevent unwanted pregnancy. The ring works much like the birth control hormone through affecting female hormones.

Vaginal sponge: a small sponge containing spermicide placed inside the vagina for birth control. The sponge also covers the cervix to prevent sperm from entering the uterus.

Vasocongestion: a sexual arousal response in women involving increased blood flow and engorgement of the female genitals, the vulva, vaginal walls, and clitoris.

Virginity: the state of never having engaged in sexual intercourse. Used traditionally as a social method to ensure paternity certainty.

References

Abbey, A., McAuslan, P., & Ross, L. T. (1998). Sexual assault perpetration by college men: The role of alcohol, misperception of sexual intent, and sexual beliefs and experiences. *Journal of Social and Clinical Psychology, 17*(2), 167-195.

Abbey, A., et al. (2002). How does alcohol contribute to sexual assault? Explanations from laboratory and survey data. *Alcoholism Clinical and Experimental Research, 26*(4).

Abma, J., Driscoll, A., & Moore, K. (1998). Young women's degree of control over first intercourse: An exploratory analysis. *Family Planning Perspectives, 30*(1), 12-18.

Abma, J., Martinez, G. M., Mosher, W., & Dawson, B. S. (2004). Teenagers in the United States: Sexual activity, contraceptive use, and childbearing. *Vital Health Statistics, 23*(24), 1-48.

Adair, L. S., & Gordon-Larsen, P. (2001). Maturational timing and overweight prevalence in US adolescent girls. *American Journal of Public Health, 91*(4), 642-644.

Adamczyk, A., & Pitt, C. (2009). Shaping attitudes about homosexuality: The role of religion and cultural context. *Social Science Research, 38*(2), 338-351.

Afifi, T. D., Joseph, A., & Aldeis, D. (2008). Why can't we just talk about it? An observational study of parents and adolescents' conversations about sex. *Journal of Adolescent Research, 23*, 689-721. doi:10.1177/0743558408323841.

Aggleton, P. (2007). "Just a Snip"? A social history of male circumcision. *Reproductive Health Matters, 15*(29), 15-21.

Ahrold, T. K., & Meston, C. M (2010). Ethnic, gender, and acculturation influences on sexual behaviors. *Archives of Sexual Behavior, 39*(1), 190-202.

Amann-Gainotti, M. (1994). Adolescent girls' internal body image. *International Journal of Adolescent Medicine and Health, 7*(1), 73-86.

American Academy of Pediatrics (2012). Task Force on Circumcision. http://pediatrics.aappublications.org/content/130/3/e756.full.html.

Anderson, J., & Koc, Y. (2015). Exploring patterns of explicit and implicit anti-gay attitudes in Muslims and atheists. *European Journal of Social Psychology, 45*, 687-701.

Andrade-Rivas, F., & Romero, M. (2017). Misinformation about HIV and negative attitudes toward homosexuality and same-sex couples' rights: The case of Colombia. *International Journal of Public Opinion Research, 29*(3), 426-448.

Armstrong, E. A., Hamilton, L. T., Armstrong, E. M., & Seeley, J. T. (2014). Good girls: Gender, social class, and slut discourse on campus. *Social Psychology Quarterly, 77*, 100-122. doi:10.1177 /0190272514521220.

Ary, D. V., Duncan, T. E., Biglan, A., Metzler, C. W., Noell, J. W., & Smolkowski, K. (1999). Development of adolescent problem behavior. *Journal of Abnormal Child Psychology, 27*, 141-150. doi:10. 1023/A:1021963531607.

Aspy, C. B., Vesely, S. K., Oman, R. F., Rodine, S., Marshall, L., & McLeroyd, K. (2007). Parental communication and youth sexual behaviour. *Journal of Adolescence, 30*(3), 449-466. https://doi.org/10.1016/j.adolescence.2006.04.007.

Auvert, B., Taljaard, D., Lagarde, E., Sobngwi-Tambekou, J., Sitta, R., & Puren, A. (2005). Randomized, controlled intervention trial of male circumcision for reduction of HIV infection risk: The ANRS 1265 Trial. *PLoS Med, 2*(11), e298.

Bachanas, P. J., Morris, M. K., Lewis-Gess, J. K., Sarett-Cuasay, E. J., Flores, A. L., Sirl, K. S., & Sawyer, M. K. (2002). Psychological adjustment, substance use, HIV knowledge, and risky sexual behavior in at-risk minority females: Developmental differences during adolescence. *Journal of Pediatric Psychology, 27*, 373-384.

Bacon, C. G., Mittleman, M. A., Kawachi, I., Giovannucci, E., Glasser, D. B., & Rimm, E. B. (2003). Sexual function in men older than 50 years of age: Results from the Health Professionals Follow-up Study. *Annals of Internal Medicine, 139*(3), 161-168. doi:10.7326/0003-4819-139-3-200308050-00005.

Bahns, A. J., & Branscombe, N. R. (2011). Effects of legitimizing discrimination against homosexuals on gay bashing. *European Journal of Social Psychology, 41*(3), 388-396.

Bailey, R. C., Moses, S., Parker, C. B., Agot, K., Maclean, I., Krieger, J. N., Williams, C. F., Campbell, R. T., & Ndinya-Achola, J. O. (2007). Male circumcision for HIV prevention in young men in Kisumu, Kenya: A randomised controlled trial. *Lancet., 369*(9562), 643-656.

Baird, A. D., Wilson, S. J., Bladin, P. F, Saling, M. M., & Reutens, D. C. (2007). Neurological control of sexual behaviour: Insights from lesion studies. *Journal of Neurology, Neurosurgery & Psychiatry, 78*, 1042-1049.

Bakwin, H. B. (1952). Masturbation in infants. *The Journal of Pediatrics, 40*, 675-678.

Balcombe, J. (2006). *Pleasurable kingdom: Animals and the nature of feeling good.* Basingstoke: Palgrave Macmillan.

Baldwin, J. D., Whiteley, S., & Baldwin, J. I. (1992). The effect of ethnic group on sexual activities related to contraception and STDs. *Journal of Sex Research, 29*(2), 189-205.

Basen-Engquist, K., Edmundson, E. W., & Parcel, G. S. (1996). Structure of health risk behavior among high school students. *Journal of Consulting and Clinical Psychology, 64*, 764-775.

Baumgartner, S. E., Valkenburg, P. M., & Peter, J. (2010). Unwanted online sexual solicitation and risky sexual online behavior across the lifespan. *Journal of Applied Developmental Psychology, 31*, 439-447. http://dx.doi.org/10.1016/j.appdev.2010.07.005.

Becks, L., & Agrawal, A. F (2012). The evolution of sex is favoured during adaptation to new environments. *PLOS Biology, 10*, e1001317.

Bender, S. S., & Kosunen, E. (2005). Teenage contraceptive use in Iceland: A gender perspective. *Public Health Nursing, 22*, 17-26. doi:10.1111/j.0737-1209.2005.22104.x.

Ben-Zeev, A., Scharnetzki, L., Chan, L. K., & Dennehy, T. C. (2012). *Psychology of Popular Media Culture, 1*(1), 53-61.

Birnbaum, G. E. (2003). The meaning of heterosexual intercourse among women with female orgasmic disorder. *Archives of Sexual Behavior, 32*, 61-71.

Black, M. C., Basile, K. C., Breiding, M. J., Smith, S. G., Walters, M. L., Merrick, M. T., ..., Stevens, M. R. (2011). The National Intimate Partner and Sexual Violence Survey: 2010 summary report. Centers for Disease Control and Prevention, National Center for Injury Prevention and Control. www.cdc.gov/ViolencePrevention/pdf/NISVS_Report2010-a.

Blair, J. D., Stephenson, J. D., Hill, K. L., & Green, J. S. (2006). Ethics in advertising: Sex sells, but should it? *Journal of Legal, Ethical and Regulatory Issues, 9*(1/2), 109-118.

Blanc, M.-E. (2005). Social construction of male homosexualities in Vietnam. Some keys to understanding discrimination and implications for HIV prevention strategy. *International Social Science Journal, 57*(186), 661-673.

Blanchflower, D. G., & Oswald, A. J. (2004). Money, sex and happiness: An empirical study. *Scandinavian Journal of Economics, 106*, 393-415. doi:10.1111/j.1467-9442.2004.00369.x.

Block, J., Strangio, C., & Esseks, J. (2018). Breaking down Trump's trans military ban. March 30. American Civil Liberties Union. www.aclu.org/blog/lgbt-rights/transgender-rights/breaking-down-trumps-trans-military-ban.

Blumstein, P., & Schwartz, P. (1983). *American couples.* New York: Pocket Books.

Bobkowski, P. S., Shafer, A., & Ortiz, R. R. (2016). Sexual intensity of adolescents' online self-presentations: Joint contribution of identity, media consumption, and extraversion. *Computers in Human Behavior, 58*, 64-74.

Boeringer, S. B. (1994). Pornography and sexual aggression: Associations of violent and nonviolent depictions with rape and rape proclivity. *Deviant Behavior, 15*(3), 289-304. |https://doi.org/10.1080/01639625.1994.9967974.

Bogle, K. (2008). *Hooking up: Sex, dating, and relationships on campus.* New York: New York University Press.

Bohner, G., Siebler, F., & Schmelcher, J. (2006). Social norms and the likelihood of raping: Perceived rape myth acceptance of others affects men's rape proclivity. *Personality and Social Psychology Bulletin, 32*(3), 286-297. https://doi.org/10.1177/0146167205280912.

Boislard, P. M., & Poulin, F. (2011). Individual, familial, friends-related and contextual predictors of early sexual intercourse. *Journal of Adolescence, 34*(2), 289-300.

Boislard, P. M. A., Poulin, F., Kiesner, J., & Dishion, T. J. (2009). A longitudinal examination of risky sexual behaviors among Canadian and Italian adolescents: Considering individual, parental, and friend characteristics. *International Journal of Behavioral Development, 33*(3), 265-276.

Booth, W., Million, L., Reynolds, R. G., Burghardt, G. M., Vargo, E. L., Schal, C., Tzika, A. C., & Schuett, G.W. (2011). Consecutive virgin births in the New World Boid Snake, the Colombian Rainbow Boa, Epicrates maurus. *Journal of Heredity, 102*(6), 759-763. doi:10.1093/jhered/esr080.

Bordini, G. S., & Sperb, T.M. (2013). Sexual double standard: A review of the literature between 2001 and 2010. *Sexuality & Culture, 17*, 686-704. https://doi.org/10.1007/s12119-012-9163-0.

Both, S., & Laan, E. (2009). Directed masturbation: A treatment of female orgasmic disorder. In O'Donohue, W. T., & Fisher, J. E. (Eds.), *General principles and empirically supported techniques of cognitive behavior therapy.* Hoboken, NJ: John Wiley, pp. 256-264.

Bowlby, J. (1969). *Attachment and loss.* New York: Basic Books.

Bowleg, L., Lucas, K. J., & Tschann, J. M. (2004). "The ball was always in his court": An exploratory analysis of relationship scripts, sexual scripts, and condom use among African American women. *Psychology of Women Quarterly*, *28*(1), 70-82. https://doi.org/10.1111/j.1471-6402.2004.00124.x.

Bowman, C. P. (2014). Women's masturbation: Experiences of sexual empowerment in a primarily sex-positive sample. *Psychology of Women Quarterly*, *38*(3), 363-378.

Boynton-Jarrett, R., Wright, R. J., Putnam, F. W., Hibert, E. L., Michels, K. B., Forman, M. R., & Rich-Edwards, J. (2013). Childhood abuse and age at menarche. *Journal of Adolescent Health*, *52*(2), 241-247.

Bozett, F. W. (1982). Heterogenous couples in heterosexual marriages: Gay men and straight women. *Journal of Marital and Family Therapy*, *8*(1), 81-89. https://doi.org/10.1111/j.1752-0606.1982.tb01424.x.

Brauer, M., Le Kuile, M. M., Janssen, S. A., & Laan, E. (2007). The effect of pain-related fear on sexual arousal in women with superficial dyspareunia. *European Journal of Pain*, *11*(7), 788-798. https://doi.org/10.1016/j.ejpain.2006.12.006.

Braun, V., & Wilkinson, S. (2001). Socio-cultural representations of the vagina. *Journal of Reproductive and Infant Psychology 19*(1), 17-32. https://doi.org/10.1080/02646830020032374.

Braun-Courville, D. K., & Rojas, M. (2009). Exposure to sexually explicit web sites and adolescent sexual attitudes and behaviors. *Journal of Adolescent Health*, *45*(2), 156-162.

Bridges, A. J., & Morokoff, P. J. (2011). Sexual media use and relational satisfaction in heterosexual couples. *Personal Relationships*, *18*(4), 562-585.

Brinkley, D. Y., Ackerman, R. A., Ehrenreich, S. E., & Underwood, M. K. (2017). Sending and receiving text messages with sexual content: Relations with early sexual activity and borderline personality features in late adolescence. *Computers in Human Behavior*, *70*, 119-130.

Brody, S. (2006). Blood pressure reactivity to stress is better for people who recently had penile-vaginal intercourse than for people who had other or no sexual activity. *Biological Psychology*, *71*(2), 214-222. doi:10.1016/j.biopsycho.2005.03.005. PMID 15961213.

Brody, S., & Weiss, P. (2010). Vaginal orgasm is associated with vaginal (not clitoral) sex education, focusing mental attention on vaginal sensations, intercourse duration, and a preference for a longer penis. *Journal of Sexual Medicine*, *7*, 2774-2781.

Brotto, L. A., Chik, H. M., Ryder, A. G., Gorzalka, B. B., & Seal, B. N. (2005). Acculturation and sexual function in Asian women. *Archives of Sexual Behavior*, *34*(6), 613-626.

Brown, A. E., Sadler, K. E., Tomkins, S. E., McGarrigle, C. A., LaMontagne, D. S., Goldberg, D., ..., Fenton, K. A. (2004). Recent trends in HIV and other STIs in the United Kingdom: Data to the end of 2002. *Sexually Transmitted Infections*, *80*, 159-166. http://dx.doi.org/10.1136/sti.2004.009571.

Brown, J. D. (2002). Mass media influences on sexuality. *Journal of Sex Research*. *39*(1), 42-45. https://doi.org/10.1080/00224490209552118.

Brown, J. D., Childers, K. W., & Waszak, C. S. (1990). Television and adolescent sexuality. *Journal of Adolescent Health*, *11*(1), 62-70. doi:https://doi.org/10.1016/0197-0070(90)90131-K.

Brown, J. D., L'Engle, K. L., Pardun, C. J., Guo, G., Kenneavy, K, & Jaskson, C. (2006). Sexy media matter: Exposure to sexual content in music, movies, television, and magazines predicts black and white adolescents' sexual behavior. *Pediatrics*, *117*, 1018-1027.

Bryan, A., & Stallings, M. C. (2002). A case control study of adolescent risky sexual behavior and its relationship to personality dimensions, conduct disorder, and substance use. *Journal of Youth and Adolescence*, *31*(5), 387-396.

Buhi, E. R., & Goodson, P. (2007). Predictors of adolescent sexual behavior and intention: A theory-guided systematic review. *Journal of Adolescent Health*, *40*, 4-21.

Burt, M. R. (1980). Cultural myths and supports for rape. *Journal of Personality and Social Psychology*, *38*, 217-230.

Buss, D. M. (1994). *The evolution of desire*. New York: Basic Books.

Buss, D. M., Abbott, M., Angleitner, A., Asherian, A., Biaggio, A., Blanco-Villasenor, A.,...., Yang, K.-S. (1990). International preferences in selecting mates: A study of 37 cultures. *Journal of Cross-Cultural Psychology*, *21*, 5- 47. doi:10.1177/0022022190211001.

Buss, D. M., & Schmitt, D. P. (1993). Sexual strategies theory: An evolutionary perspective on human mating. *Psychological Review*, *100*, 204-232. doi:10.1037/0033-295X.100.2.204.

Buunk, B. P., Dijkstra, P., Fetchenhauer, D., & Kenrick, D. T. (2002). Age and gender differences in mate selection criteria for various involvement levels. *Personal Relationships*, *9*(3), 271-278. https://doi.org/10.1111/1475-6811.00018.

Byers, E. S. (2005). Relationship satisfaction and sexual satisfaction: A longitudinal study of individuals in long-term relationships. *Journal of Sex Research*, *42*, 113-118. doi:10.1080/00224490509552264.

Campbell, C., Mallappa, A., Wisniewski, A. B., & Silovsky, J. F. (2013). Sexual behavior of prepubertal children. In Bromberg, D. S., & O'Donohue, W. T. (Eds.), *Handbook of child and adolescent sexuality: Developmental and forensic psychology*. San Diego: Elsevier Academic Press, pp. 145-170.

Campbell, P., Handa, S., Moroni, M., Odongo, S., & Palermo, T. (2010). Assessing the 'orphan effect' in determining development outcomes for children in 11 eastern and southern African countries. *Vulnerable Children and Youth Studies, 5*(1), 12-32.

Capaldi, D. M., Crosby, L., & Stoolmiller, M. (1996). Predicting the timing of first sexual intercourse for at-risk adolescent males. *Child Development, 67*(2), 344-359.

Carpenter, L. M. (1998). From girls into women: Scripts for sexuality and romance in Seventeen magazine, 1974-1994. *Journal of Sex Research, 35*, 158-168.

Carroll, J., Padilla-Walker, L. M., & Nelson, L. J. (2008). Generation XXX: Pornography acceptance and use among emerging adults. *J Adoles Res.,23*, 6-30.

Centers for Disease Control and Prevention (2008). Youth risk behavior surveillance: United States, 2005. Atlanta, GA: U.S. Department of Health and Human Services. www.cdc.gov/mmwr/preview/mmwrhtml/ss5505a1.htm.

Centers for Disease Control and Prevention (2013). Incidence, prevalence, and cost of sexually transmitted infections in the United States. www.cdc.gov/std/stats/STI-Estimates-Fact-Sheet-Feb-2013.

Centers for Disease Control and Prevention (2017). Information for teens: Staying healthy and preventing STDs. www.cdc.gov/std/life-stages-populations/stdfact-teens.htm, Retrieved June 19, 2018.

Centers for Disease Control and Prevention (2018a). Sexual risk behaviors: HIV, STD, & teen pregnancy prevention. www.cdc.gov/healthyyouth/sexualbehaviors/. Retrieved June 20, 2018.

Centers for Disease Control & Prevention (2018b). Sexually transmitted diseases. www.cdc.gov/std/default.htm. Retrieved June 24, 2018.

Chan, L. F., Mohamad A. B., Norazlin, K. N., Siti Haida, M. I., Lee, V. Y., Norazura, A. W., Ek Zakuan, K., & Tan, S. M. K. (2016). Suicidal ideation among single, pregnant adolescents: The role of sexual and religious knowledge, attitudes and practices. *Journal of Adolescence, 52*, 162-169.

Chang, K. D., Blasey, C., Steiner, H., & Ketter, T. A. (2001). Family environment of children and adolescents with bipolar parents. *Bipolar Disorders, 3*, 68-72.

Chapman, D. D., Shivji, M. S., Louis, E., Sommer, J., Fletcher, H., & Prodöhl, P. A. (2007). Virgin birth in a hammerhead shark. *Biology Letters, 3*(4), 425-427. doi:10.1098/rsbl.2007.0189.

Charest, M., Kleinplatz, P. J., & Lund, J. I. (2016). Sexual health information disparities between heterosexual and LGBTQ+ young adults: Implications for sexual health. *The Canadian Journal of Human Sexuality, 25*(2), 74-85.

Charlton, H. (2008). Hypothalamic control of anterior pituitary function: A history. *Journal of Neuroendocrinology, 20*(6), 641-646. doi:10.1111/j.1365-2826.2008.01718.x.

Chen, L., Knight, E. M. P., Tuxhorn, I., Shahid, A., & Lüders, H. O. (2015). Paroxysmal non-epileptic events in infants and toddlers: A phenomenologic analysis. *Psychiatry and Clinical Neurosciences, 69*(6), 351-359.

Chollet, S., & Martin, J. (2012). Declining woodland birds in North America: Should we blame Bambi? *Diversity and Distributions.* doi:10.1111/ddi.12003.

Christian-Smith, L. K. (2013). Sweet dreams: Gender and desire in teen romance novels. In Christian-Smith, L. K. (Ed.), *Texts of desire: Essays of fiction, femininity and schooling.* New York: Routledge, pp. 45-68.

Chuang, Y.-C. (2002). Sex differences in mate selection preference and sexual strategy: Tests for evolutionary hypotheses. *Chinese Journal of Psychology, 44*(1), 75-93.

Clark, L. A., Kochanksa, G., & Ready, R. (2000). Mothers' personality and its interaction with child temperament as predictors of parenting behavior. *Journal of Personality and Social Psychology, 79*, 274-285. doi:10.1037/0022-3514.79.2.274.

Clements-Nolle, K., Marx, R., Guzman, R., & Katz, M. (2001). HIV, prevalence, risk behaviors, health care use, and mental health status of transgender persons: Implications for public health intervention. *American Journal of Public Health, 91*(6), 915-921.

Collins, R. L., Elliott, M. N., Berry, S. H., Kanouse, D. E., Kunkel, D., Hunter, S. B., & Miu, A. (2004). Watching sex on television predicts adolescent initiation of sexual behavior. *Pediatrics, 114*, 280-289.

Cornog, M. (2003). *The big book of masturbation: From angst to zeal.* San Francisco: Down There Press.

Cosín, D. J. D., Novo, M., & Fernández, R. (2011). Reproduction of earthworms: Sexual selection and parthenogenesis. In Karaca, A. (Ed.), *Biology of earthworms.* Berlin, Heidelberg: Springer.

Costa, P. T., & McCrae, R. R. (1992). *Revised NEO Personality Inventory (NEO PI-R): Professional manual.* Odessa: Psychological Assessment Resources.

Costa, R. M., & Brody, S. (2007). Women's relationship quality is associated with specifically penile-vaginal intercourse orgasm and frequency. *Journal of Sex & Marital Therapy, 33*(4), 319-327.

Costa, R. M., Brody, S., Hess, U., & Weiss, P. (2011). Vaginal orgasm is related to better mental health and is relevant to evolutionary psychology: A response to Zietsch et al. *Journal of Sexual Medicine, 8*(12), 3523-3525.

Costos, D., Ackerman, R., & Paradis, L. (2002), Recollections of menarche: Communication between mothers and daughters regarding menstruation. *Sex Roles, 46*(2), 49-59.

Cox Communications (2009). Teen online & wireless safety survey: Cyberbullying, sexting, and parental controls. Atlanta, GA: Cox Communications, National Center for Missing & Exploited Children. http://ww2.cox.com/ wcm/en/aboutus/datasheet/sandiego/internetsafety.

Crisp, T. (2009). From romance to magical realism: Limits and possibilities in gay adolescent fiction. *Children's Literature in Education, 40,* 333.

Daniel, A. Jr., Duke, P. M., Carlsmith, J. M., Jennings, D., Martin, J. A., Dornbusch, S. M., Gross, R. T., & Siegel-Gorelick, B. (1982). Educational correlates of early and late sexual maturation in adolescence. *Journal of Pediatrics, 100*(4), 633-637.

Darby, R. (2003). The masturbation taboo and the rise of routine male circumcision: A review of the historiography. *Journal of Social History, 36*(3), 737-757.

Darling, C. A., Davidson, J. K., & Cox, R. P. (1991). Female sexual response and the timing of partner orgasm. *Journal of Sex and Marital Therapy, 17,* 3-21.

Darwich, L., Hymel, S., & Waterhouse, T. (2012). School avoidance and substance use among lesbian, gay, bisexual, and questioning youths: The impact of peer victimization and adult support. *Journal of Educational Psychology, 104,* 381-392.

Davidson, J. (2007). *The Greeks and Greek love: A radical reappraisal of homosexuality in ancient Greece.* London: Weidenfeld & Nicolson.

Davis, M. J., & Niebes-Davis, A. J. (2010). Ethnic differences and influence of perceived future certainty on adolescent and young adult sexual knowledge and attitudes. *Health, Risk & Society, 12*(2), 149-167. https://doi.org/10.1080/13698571003632452.

De Gaston, J. F., Weed, S., & Jensen, L. (1996). Understanding gender differences in adolescent sexuality. *Adolescence, 31*(121), 217-231.

deCalesta, D. S. (1994). Effect of white-tailed deer on songbirds within managed forests in Pennsylvania. *Journal of Wildlife Management, 58*(4), 711-718.

Dedek, J. F. (1980). Premarital sex: The theological argument from Peter Lombard to Durand. *Theological Studies, 41*(4), 643-667. doi:10.1177/004056398004100401.

Demakis, G. J. (2006). Sex and the brain. In McAnulty, R. D., & Burnette, M. M. (Eds.), *Sex and sexuality: Sexual function and dysfunction* (pp. 19-36). Westport, CT: Greenwood Publishing Group.

Demaré, D., Lips, H. M., & Briere, J. (1993). Sexually violent pornography, anti-women attitudes, and sexual aggression: A structural equation model. *Journal of Research in Personality, 27*(3), 285-300. https://doi.org/10.1006/jrpe.1993.1020.

Dermody, S. S.. Marshal, M. P., Burton, C. M., & Chisolm, D. J. (2016). Risk of heavy drinking among sexual minority adolescents: Indirect pathways through sexual orientation-related victimization and affiliation with substance-using peers. *Addiction, 111*(9), 1599-1606.

Diekman, A. B., McDonald, M., & Gardner, W. L. (2000). Love means never having to be careful: The relationship between reading romance novels and safe sex behavior. *Psychology of Women Quarterly, 24*(2), 179-188.

Dilorio, C., Kelley, M., & Hockenberry-Eaton, M. (1999). Communication about sexual issues: Mothers, fathers, and friends. *Journal of Adolescent Health, 24,* 181-189. doi:10.1016/S1054-139X(98)00115-3.

Dilorio, C., Pluhar, E., & Belcher, L. (2003). Parent-child communication about sexuality: A review of the literature from 1980-2002. *Journal of HIV/AIDS Prevention & Education for Adolescents & Children, 5,* 7-32. doi:10.1300/J129v05n03 02.

Dittus, P., Miller, K. S., Kotchick, B. A., & Forehand, R. (2004). Why parents matter! The conceptual basis for a community based HIV prevention program for the parents of African American youth. *Journal of Child and Family Studies, 13,* 5-20. doi:10.1023/B:JCFS.0000010487.46007.08.

Dockterman, E. (2014). Schools are still slut-shaming girls while enforcing dress code. Time.com, 1.

Doljanac, R. F., and Zimmerman, M. A. (1998). Psychosocial factors and high-risk sexual behavior: Race differences among urban adolescents. *Journal of Behavioral Medicine, 21,* 451-467.

Donaldson, C. D., Handren, L. M., & Lac, A. (2017). Applying multilevel modeling to understand individual and cross-cultural variations in attitudes toward homosexual people across 28 European countries. *Journal of Cross-Cultural Psychology, 48*(1), 93-112.

Drouin, M., Ross, J., & Tobin, E. (2015). Sexting: A new, digital vehicle for intimate partner aggression? *Computers In Human Behavior, 50,* 197-204. http:// dx.doi.org/10.1016/j.chb.2015.04.001.

Dubuc, C., & Dixson, A. F. (2012). Primate sexuality: Comparative studies of the prosimians, monkeys, apes, and humans. *International Journal of Primatology, 34,* 216-218. doi:10.1007/s10764-012-9648-6.

Duggan, S. J., & McCreary, D. R. (2004). Body image, eating disorders, and the drive for muscularity in gay and heterosexual men. *Journal of Homosexuality, 47*(3-4), 45-58. |https://doi.org/10.1300/J082v47n03_03.

Dunbar, R. I.M., & Waynforth, D. (1995). Conditional mate choice strategies in humans: Evidence from 'lonely hearts' advertisements. *Behaviour, 132*(9-10), 755-779. https://doi.org/10.1163/156853995X00135.

Dworkin, S. H., & Yi, H. (2003). LGBT identity, violence, and social justice: The psychological is political. *International Journal for the Advancement of Counselling 25*(4), 269-279.

East, P. L. (1998). Racial and ethnic differences in girls' sexual, marital, and birth expectations. *Journal of Marriage and the Family, 60*(1), 150-162.

Efrati, Y. (2019). God, I can't stop thinking about sex! The rebound effect in unsuccessful suppression of sexual thoughts among religious adolescents. *Journal of Sex Research, 56*(2), 146-155. doi:10.1080/00224499.2018.1461796.

Eisenberg, M. E., Sieving, R. E., Bearinger, L. H., Swain, C., & Resnick, M. D. (2006). Parents' communication with adolescents about sexual behavior: A missed opportunity for prevention? *Journal of Youth Adolescence, 35*, 893-902. doi:10.1007/s10964-006-9093-y.

Ellenbogen, M. A., & Hodgins, S. (2009). Structure provided by parents in middle childhood predicts cortisol reactivity in adolescence among the offspring of parents with bipolar disorder and controls. *Psychoneuroendocrinology, 34*, 773-785.

England, P., Shafer, E. F., & Fogarty, A. C. K. (2008). *The gendered society reader: Hooking up and forming romantic relationships on today's college campuses.* New York: Oxford University Press.

Fagot, B. I. (1985). Beyond the reinforcement principle: Another step toward understanding sex roles. *Developmental Psychology, 21*, 1097-1104.

Fahs, B. (2013). Raising bloody hell: Inciting menstrual panics through campus and community activism. In Fahs, B., Dudy, M. L., & Stage, S. (Eds.), *The moral panics of sexuality.* London: Palgrave Macmillan, pp. 77-91.

Faissol, D., Swann, J. L., Kolodziejski, B., Griffin, P., & Gift, T. (2007). The role of bathhouses and sex clubs in HIV transmission: Findings from a mathematic model. *Journal of Acquired Immune Deficiency Syndromes, 44*(4), 386-394. doi:10.1097/QAI.0b013e31803220dd.

Fang, L., Oliver, A., Jayaraman, G. C., & Wong, T. (2010). Trends in age disparities between younger and middle-age adults among reported rates of chlamydia, gonorrhea, and infectious syphilis infections in Canada: Findings from 1997 to 2007. *Sexually Transmitted Diseases, 37*(1), 18-25. http://dx.doi.org/10.1097/.

Farvid, P., Braun, V., & Rowney, C. (2017). 'No girl wants to be called a slut!': Women, heterosexual casual sex and the sexual double standard. *Journal of Gender Studies, 26*(5), 544-560.

Ferfolja, T. (2013). Sexual diversity, discrimination and 'homosexuality policy' in New South Wales' government schools. *Sex Education, 13*(2), 159-171. doi:10.1080/14681811.2012.697858.

Fernandez, S., & Pritchard, M. (2012). Relationships between self-esteem, media influence and drive for thinness. *Eating Behaviors, 13*(4), 321-325.

Fielder, R. L., & Carey, M. P. (2010). Prevalence and characteristics of sexual hookups among first-semester female college students. *Journal of Sex & Marital Therapy, 36*(4), 346-359. doi:10.1080/0092623x.2010.488118.

Finer, L. B., & Philbin, J. M. (2024). Trends in ages at key reproductive transitions in the United States, 1951-2010. *Women's Health Issues, 24*(3), e271-e279. doi:10.1016/j.whi.2014.02.002.

Finkelhor, D. (1987). The sexual abuse of children: Current research reviewed. *Psychiatric Annals, 17*(4), 233-241.

Finkelhor, D., Hotaling, G., Lewis, I. A., & Smith, C. (1990). Sexual abuse in a national survey of adult men and women: Prevalence, characteristics, and risk factors. *Child Abuse & Neglect, 14*(1), 19-28. https://doi.org/10.1016/0145-2134(90)90077-7.

Fisher, J. D., Fisher, W. A., Misovich, S. J., Kimble, D. L., & Malloy, T. E. (1996). Changing AIDS risk behavior: Effects of an intervention emphasizing AIDS risk reduction information, motivation, and behavioral skills in a college student population. *Health Psychology, 15*(2), 114-123.

Fisher, R. (1930). *The genetical theory of natural selection.* Oxford: Clarendon Press.

Fisher, T. D. (1986). Parent-child communication and adolescents' sexual knowledge and attitudes. *Adolescence, 21*, 517-527. doi:10.1177/019251398019003005.

Flood, M. (2003). Lust, trust and latex: Why young heterosexual men do not use condoms. *Culture, Health & Sexuality, 5*(4), 353-369. |https://doi.org/10.1080/1369105011000028273.

Frese, B., Moya, M., & Megías, J. L. (2004). Social perception of rape: How rape myth acceptance modulates the influence of situational factors. *Journal of Interpersonal Violence, 19*(2), 143-161. https://doi.org/10.1177/0886260503260245.

Friedman, Howard S. and Martin, Leslie R.. (2011). *The longevity project: Surprising discoveries for health and long life from the landmark eight-decade study.* New York: Hudson Street Press/Penguin.

Fugère, M. A., Escoto, C., Cousins, A. J., Riggs, M. L., & Haerich, P. (2008). Sexual attitudes and double standards: A literature review focusing on participant gender and ethnic background. *Sexuality & Culture, 12*(3), 169-182.

Fyfe, B. (1983). "Homophobia" or homosexual bias reconsidered. *Archives of Sexual Behavior, 12*(6), 549-554.

Gagnon, J. H., & Simon, W. (1973). *Sexual conduct*. Chicago: Aldine.

Gallup, G. G. Jr., Burch, R. L., & Platek, S. M. (2002). Does semen have antidepressant properties? *Archives of Sexual Behavior, 31*(3), 289-293.

Garcia, J. R., Reiber, C., Massey, S. G., & Merriwether, A. M. (2012). Sexual hookup culture: A review. *Review of General Psychology, 16*(2), 161-176. https://doi.org/10.1037/a0027911.

Gartrell, N., & Mosbacher, D. (1984). Sex differences in the naming of children's genitalia. *Sex Roles, 10*(11-12), 869-876.

Gates, G. J. (2011). How many people are lesbian, gay, bisexual and transgender? UCLA: The Williams Institute. https://escholarship.org/uc/item/09h684X2.

Gatiss, L. (2005). The issue of pre-marital sex. *The Theologian*. www.theologian.org.uk/pastoralia/premaritalsex.html.

Georgiadis, J., & Holstege, G. (2005). Human brain activation during stimulation of the penis. *Journal of Comparative Neurology, 493*, 33-38.

Giaccardi, S., Ward, L. M., & Seabrook, R. C., Manago, A., & Lippman, J. R. (2017). Media use and men's risk behaviors: Examining the role of masculinity ideology. *Sex Roles, 77*(9-10), 581-592.

Giles, G. G., Severi, G., English, D. R., McCredie, M. R. E., Borland, R., Boyle, P., & Hopper, J. L. (2003). Sexual factors and prostate cancer. *BJU International, 92*(3), 211-216. doi:10.1046/j.1464-410X.2003.04319.x.

Gillespie, B. J. (2017). Correlates of sex frequency and sexual satisfaction among partnered older adults. *Journal of Sex & Marital Therapy, 43*(5), 403-423.

Glick, P., Diebold, J., Bailey-Werner, B., & Zhu, L. (1997). The two faces of Adam: Ambivalent sexism and polarized attitudes toward women. *Personality and Social Psychology Bulletin, 23*(12), 1323-1334. https://doi.org/10.1177/01461672972312009.

Goddard, M. R., Godfray, H. C. J., & Burt, A. M. R. (2005). Sex increases the efficacy of natural selection in experimental yeast populations. *Nature, 434*, 636-640.

Goldbach, J. T., Tanner-Smith, E. E., Bagwell, M., & Dunlap, S. (2014). Minority stress and substance use in sexual minority adolescents: A meta-analysis. *Prevention Science, 15*, 350-363.

Gollaher, D. (2000). *Circumcision*. New York: Basic Books.

Grabe, S., Ward, L. M., & Hyde, J. S. (2008). The role of the media in body image concerns among women: A meta-analysis of experimental and correlational studies. *Psychological Bulletin, 134*(3), 460-476. http://dx.doi.org/10.1037/0033-2909.134.3.460.

Graber, B., Balogh, S., Fitzpatrick, D., & Hendricks, S. (1991). Cardiovascular changes associated with sexual arousal and orgasm in men. *Sexual Abuse, 4*(2), 151-165. doi:10.1007/BF00851611.

Gray, P. B., & Anderson, K. G. (2010). *Fatherhood: Evolution and human paternal behavior*. Cambridge, MA: Harvard University Press.

Gray, R. H., Kigozi, G., Serwadda, D., Makumbi, F., Watya, S., Nalugoda, F., Kiwanuka, N., Moulton, L. H., Chaudhary, M. A., Chen, M. Z., et al. (2007). Male circumcision for HIV prevention in men in Rakai, Uganda: A randomised trial. *Lancet, 369*(9562), 657-666.

Greenberg, B. S., Eastin, M., Hofschire, L., Lachlan, K., & Brownell, K. D. (2003). Portrayals of overweight and obese individuals on commercial television. *American Journal of Public Health, 93*, 1342-1348. https://doi.org/10.2105/AJPH.93.8.1342.

Greenwood, D. N., & Lippman, J. R. (2010). Gender and media: Content, uses, and impact. In Chrisler, J., & McCreary, D. (Eds.), *Handbook of gender research in psychology*. New York: Springer.

Groesz, L. M., Levine, M. P., & Murnen, S. K. (2002). The effect of experimental presentation of thin media images on body satisfaction: A meta-analytic review. *International Journal of eating disorders, 31*(1), 1-16. https://doi.org/10.1002/eat.10005.

Gruber, J., & Fineran, S. (2008). Comparing the impact of bullying and sexual harassment victimization on the mental and physical health of adolescents. *Sex Roles, 59*, 1-13.

Guterman, M. A., Mehta, P., & Gibbs, M. S. (2008). Menstrual taboos among major religions. *The Internet Journal of World Health and Societal Politics, 5*(2).

Guttmacher Institute (1994). *Sex and America's teenagers*. New York and Washington, DC: The Alan Guttmacher Institute.

Hadley, W., Hunter, H. L., Tolou-Shams, M., Lescano, C., Brown, L. K., Thompson, A., Donenberg, G., DiClemente, R., & Project STYLE Study Group (2011). Monitoring challenges: A closer look at parental monitoring, maternal psychopathology, and adolescent sexual risk. *Journal of Family Psychology, 25*, 319-323.

Hald, G. M., Malamuth, N. M., & Yuen, C. (2010). Pornography and attitudes supporting violence against women: Revisiting the relationship in nonexperimental studies. *Aggressive Behavior, 36*, 14-20.

Hales, D. F., Wilson, A. C. C., Sloane, M. A., Simon, J.-C., Legallic, J.-F., & Sunnucks, P. (2002). Lack of detectable genetic recombination on the X chromosome during the parthenogenetic production of female and male aphids. *Genetics Research, 79*(3), 203-209. doi:10.1017/S0016672302005657.

Halliwell, E., Dittmar, H., & Orsborn, A. (2007). The effects of exposure to muscular male models among men: Exploring the moderating role of gym use and exercise motivation. *Body Image, 4*(3), 278-287. https://doi.org/10.1016/j.bodyim.2007.04.006.

Halpern, H. P., & Perry-Jenkins, M. (2016). Parents' gender ideology and gendered behavior as predictors of children's gender-role attitudes: A longitudinal exploration. *Sex Roles, 74*(11-12), 527-542.

Hamilton, L., & Armstrong, E. A. (2009). Gendered sexuality in young adulthood: Double binds and flawed options. *Gender & Society, 23*(5), 589-616. doi:10.1177/0891243209345829.

Hammers, M. L. (2010). Talking about "down there": The politics of publicizing the female body through *The Vagina Monologues*. *Women's Studies in Communication, 29*(2), 220-243. doi:10.1080/07491409.2006.10162499.

Hampton, M. R., Jeffery, B., McWatters, B., & Smith, P. (2005). Influence of teens' perceptions of parental disapproval and peer behavior on their initiation of sexual intercourse. *The Canadian Journal of Human Sexuality, 14*(3-4), 105-121.

Harris, R., Yulis, S., & Lacoste, D. (1980). Relationships among sexual arousability, imagery ability, and introversion-extraversion. *Journal of Sex Research, 16*(1), 72-86.

Hawes, Z. C., Wellings, K., & Stephenson, J. (2010). First heterosexual intercourse in the United Kingdom: A review of the literature. *Journal of Sex Research, 47*, 137-152.

Hayes, R. D., Dennerstein, L., Bennett, C. M., Koochaki, P. E., Leiblum, S. R., & Graziottin, A. (2007). Relationship between hypoactive sexual desire disorder and aging. *Fertility and Sterility, 87*(1), 107-112. https://doi.org/10.1016/j.fertnstert.2006.05.071.

Hazan, C., & Shaver, P. R. (1987). Romantic love conceptualized as an attachment process. *Journal of Personality and Social Psychology, 52*(3), 511-524. doi:10.1037/0022-3514.52.3.511.

Henry, N., & Powell, A. (Eds.) (2014). *Preventing sexual violence: Interdisciplinary approaches to overcoming a rape culture*. New York: Palgrave Macmillan.

Hensel, D. J., Fortenberry, J. D., & Orr, D. P. (2007). Variation in coital and non-coital sexual repertoire among adolescent women. *Journal of Adolescent Health, 40*(2), Suppl, S1. https://doi.org/10.1016/j.jadohealth.2006.11.007.

Henshaw, S. K. (2004). U.S. teenager pregnancy statistics with comparative statistics for women aged 20-24. New York: The Alan Guttmacher Institute.

Herbenick, D., Reece, M., Sanders, S., Dodge, B., Ghassemi, A., and Fortenberry, J. D. (2009). Prevalence and characteristics of vibrator use by women in the United States: Results from a nationally representative study. *Journal of Sexual Medicine, 6*, 1857-1866.

Herbermann, C. (Ed.) (1913). Lust. In *Catholic encyclopedia*. New York: Robert Appleton Company.

Herek, G. M. (2008). Hate crimes and stigma-related experiences among sexual minority adults in the United States: Prevalence estimates from a national probability sample. *Journal of Interpersonal Violence, 24*(1), 54-74. https://doi.org/10.1177/0886260508316477.

Herek G. M., & McLemore, K. A. (2013). Sexual prejudice. *Annual Review of Psychology, 64*, 309-333.

Heron, J., Low, N., Lewis, G., Macleod, J., Ness, A., & Waylen, A. (2013). Social factors associated with readiness for sexual activity in adolescents: A population-based cohort study. *Archives of Sexual Behavior, 27*, 669-678.

Herrick, A. L., Marshal, M. P., Smith, H. A., Sucato, G., & Stall, R. D. (2011). Sex while intoxicated: A meta-analysis comparing heterosexual and sexual minority youth. *Journal of Adolescent Health, 48*(3), 306-309. http://dx.doi.org/10.1016/j.jadohealth.2010.07.008.

Higa, D., Hoppe, M. J., Lindhorst, T., Mincer, S., Beadnell, B., Morrison, D. M., Wells, E. A., Todd, A., & Mountz, S. (2012). Negative and positive factors associated with the well-being of lesbian, gay, bisexual, transgender, queer, and questioning (LGBTQ) youth. *Youth & Society, 46*(5), 663-687. https://doi.org/10.1177/0044118X12449630.

Higgins, J. A., Mullinax, M., Trussell, J., Davidson, J. K. Sr., & Moore, N. B. (2011). Sexual satisfaction and sexual health among university students in the United States. *American Journal of Public Health, 101*(9), 1643-1654.

Hobza, C. L., & Rochlen, A. B. (2009). Gender role conflict, drive for muscularity, and the impact of ideal media portrayals on men. *Psychology of Men & Masculinity, 10*(2), 120-130.

Hollander, J. A. (2001). Vulnerability and dangerousness: The construction of gender through conversation about violence. *Gender and Society, 15*(1), 83-109. https://doi.org/10.1177/089124301015001005.

Hong, J. S., Espelage, D. L., & Kral, M. J. (2011). Understanding suicide among sexual minority youth in America: An ecological systems analysis. *Journal of Adolescence, 34*, 885-894.

Huang, K., & Uba, L. (1992). Premarital sexual behavior among Chinese college students in the United States. *Archives of Sexual Behavior, 21*(3), 227-240.

Huebner, A. J., & Howell, L. W. (2003). Examining the relationship between adolescent sexual risk-taking and perceptions of monitoring, communication, and parenting styles. *Journal of Adolescent Health, 33*, 71-78. doi:10.1016/S1054-139X(03)00141-1.

Hurlbert, D. F., & Whittaker, K. E. (1991). The role of masturbation in marital and sexual satisfaction: A comparative study of female masturbators and nonmasturbators. *Journal of Sex Education & Therapy, 17*(4), 272-282.

Hust, S. J. T., Brown, J. D., & L'Engle, K. L. (2008). Boys will be boys and girls better be prepared: An analysis of the rare sexual health messages in young adolescents' media. *Mass Communication and Society, 11*(1), 3-23. https://doi.org/10.1080/15205430701668139.

Hyde, J. S., & Delamater, J. (1997). *Understanding human sexuality* (6th ed.). New York: McGraw Hill.

Hynie, M., Schuller, R. A., & Couperthwaite, L. (2003). Perceptions of sexual intent: The impact of condom possession. *Psychology of Women Quarterly, 27*, 75-79. doi:10.1111/1471-6402.t01-2-00009.

Insel, T. R. (1992). Oxytocin - A neuropeptide for affiliation: Evidence from behavioral, receptor autoradiographic, and comparative studies. *Psychoneuroendocrinology, 17*(1), 3-35. doi:https://doi.org/10.1016/0306-4530(92)90073-G.

Jaccard, J., & Dittus, P. (2000). Adolescent perceptions of maternal approval of birth control and sexual risk behavior. *American Journal of Public Health, 90*, 1426-1430. doi:10.2105/AJPH.90.9.1426.

Jaccard, J., Dodge, T., & Dittus, P. (2002). Parent–adolescent communication about sex and birth control: A conceptual framework. *New Directions for Child and Adolescent Development, 97*, 9-41. doi:10.1002/cd.48.

Jenks, R. (2001). The lifestyle: A look at the erotic rites of swingers, by Terry Gould. *Journal of Sex Research, 38*, 171-173.

Jimenez, J. A., & Abreu, J. M. (2003). Race and sex effects on attitudinal perceptions of acquaintance rape. *Journal of Counseling Psychology, 50*(2), 252-256. https://doi.org/10.1037/0022-0167.50.2.252.

Jiménez-Cruz, B. E., & Silva-Gutiérrez, C. (2008). Effects of a brief exposure to women's media images on levels of anxiety and depression of university women considering their body mass index and their attitudes towards weight and food. *Revista Mexicana de Psicología, 25*(1), 89-98.

Johnston-Robledo, I., Barnack, J., & Wares, S. (2006). "Kiss your period good-bye": Menstrual suppression in the popular press. *Sex Roles, 54*, 353. https://doi.org/10.1007/s11199-006-9007-1.

Jones, A. C., Robinson, W. D., & Seedall, R. B. (2018). The role of sexual communication in couples' sexual outcomes: A dyadic path analysis. *Journal of Marital and Family Therapy, 44*(4), 606-623.

Jozkowski, K. N., Marcantonio, T. L., & Hunt, M. E. (2017). College students' sexual consent communication and perceptions of sexual double standards: A qualitative investigation. *Perspectives on Sexual and Reproductive Health, 49*(4), 237-244.

Kaestle, C. E., Halpern, C. T., Miller, W. C., & Ford, C. A. (2005). Young age at first sexual intercourse and sexually transmitted infections in adolescents and young adults. *American Journal of Epidemiology, 161*(8), 774-780. https://doi.org/10.1093/aje/kwi095.

Kail, R. V., & Cavanaugh, J. C. (2010). *Human development: A lifespan view* (5th ed.). Belmont, CA: Cengage Learning.

Kalichman, S. C., Hechman, T., & Kelly, J. A. (1996). Sensation seeking as an explanation for the association between substance use and HIV-related risky sexual behavior. *Archives of Sexual Behavior, 25*, 141-154.

Kaltiala-Heino, R., Kosunen, E., & Rimpelä, M. (2003). Pubertal timing, sexual behaviour and self-reported depression in middle adolescence. *Journal of Adolescence, 26*(5), 531-545. https://doi.org/10.1016/S0140-1971(03)00053-8.

Katz-Wise, S. L., Ehrensaft, D., Vetters, R., Forcier, M., & Austin, S. B. (2018). Family functioning and mental health of transgender and gender-nonconforming youth in the trans teen and family narratives project. *Journal of Sex Research, 55*(4-5), 582-590.

Kay, D. S. G. (1992). Masturbation and mental health - uses and abuses. *Sexual and Marital Therapy, 7*(1), 97-107.

Kelleher, C. (2009). Minority stress and health: Implications for lesbian, gay, bisexual, transgender, and questioning (LGBTQ) young people. *Counselling Psychology Quarterly, 22*(4), 373-379. doi:10.1080/09515070903334995.

Kelley, K. (1985). Sex, sex guilt, and authoritarianism: Differences in responses to explicit heterosexual and masturbatory slides. *Journal of Sex Research, 21*(1), 68-85.

Kellogg, J. H. (1888). *Plain facts for young and old: Embracing the natural history of hygiene and organic life* (2nd ed.). Burlington, IA: I. F. Segner, pp. 294-296.

Kellogg, N. D., & Huston, R. L. (1995). Unwanted sexual experiences in adolescents: Patterns of disclosure. *Clinical Pediatrics, 34*(6), 306-312. https://doi.org/10.1177/000992289503400603.

Kenrick, D. T., and Keefe, R. C. (1992). Age preferences in mates reflect sex differences in reproductive strategies. *Behavioral and Brain Sciences, 15*, 75-133.

Kimport, K. (2018). Talking about male body-based contraceptives: The counseling visit and the feminization of contraception. *Social Science & Medicine, 201*, 44-50.

Kinsey, A. C., Pomeroy, W. B., & Martin, C. E. (1948/2003). Sexual behavior in the human male. *American Journal of Public Health, 93*(6), 894-898. doi:10.2105/AJPH.93.6.894 (originally published in 1948).

Kinsey, A. C., Pomeroy, W. B., Martin, C. E., & Gebhard, P. H. (1953). *Sexual behavior in the human female.* Philadelphia: W. B. Saunders.

Kinsman, S. B., Romer, D., Furstenberg, F. F., & Schwarz, D. F. (1998). Early sexual initiation: The role of peer norms. *Pediatrics, 102*(5).

Kirby, D. (2001). Emerging answers: Research findings on programs to reduce teen pregnancy (summary). *American Journal of Health Education, 32*(6), 348-355. doi:10.1080/19325037.2001.10603497.

Kirby, D., & Lepore, G. (2007). Sexual risk and protective factors: Factors affecting teen sexual behavior, pregnancy, childbearing, and sexually transmitted disease: Which are important? Which can you change? Washington, DC: National Campaign to Prevent Teen Pregnancy.

Kirby, D. B., Laris, B. A., & Rolleri, L. A. (2007). Sex and HIV education programs: Their impact on sexual behaviors of young people throughout the world. *Journal of Adolescent Health, 40*(3), 206-217. doi:https://doi.org/10.1016/j.jadohealth.2006.11.143.

Kirkman, M., Rosenthal, D., & Smith, A. M. A. (1998). Adolescent sex and the romantic narrative: Why some young heterosexuals use condoms to prevent pregnancy but not disease. *Psychology, Health & Medicine, 3*(4), 355-370.

Klein, F., Sepekoff, B., & Wolf, T. J. (1985). Sexual orientation: A multi-variable dynamic process. *Journal of Homosexuality, 11*(1-2), 35-49. | https://doi.org/10.1300/J082v11n01_04.

Klettke, B., Hallford, D. J., & Mellor, D. J. (2014). Sexting prevalence and correlates: A systematic literature review. *Clinical Psychology Review, 34*, 44-53. http://dx.doi.org/ 10.1016/j.cpr.2013.10.007.

Kochanska, G., Kim, S., & Nordling, J. K. (2012). Challenging circumstances moderate the links between mothers' personality traits and their parenting in low-income families with young children. *Journal of Personality and Social Psychology, 103*, 1040-1049. doi:10.1037/a0030386.

Koelman, C. A., Coumans, A. B.C., Nijman, H. W., Doxiadis, I. I. N., Dekker, G. A., & Claas, F. H. J. (2000). Correlation between oral sex and a low incidence of preeclampsia: A role for soluble HLA in seminal fluid? *Journal of Reproductive Immunology 46*, 155-166.

Koenig, H. G. (2001). Religion and medicine II: Religion, mental health, and related behaviors. *International Journal of Psychiatry in Medicine, 31*, 97-109.

Krahé, B., Scheinberger-Olwig, R., & Kolpin, S. (2000). Ambiguous communication of sexual intentions as a risk marker of sexual aggression. *Sex Roles, 42*, 313-337.

Kreager, D. A., Staff, J., Gauthier, R., Lefkowitz, E. S., & Feinberg, M. E. (2016). The double standard at sexual debut: Gender, sexual behavior and adolescent peer acceptance. *Sex Roles, 75*(7-8), 377-392.

Laumann, E. O., Gagnon, H. J., Michael, R. T., & Michaels, S. (1994). *The social organization of sexuality: Sexual practices in the United States.* Chicago: University of Chicago Press.

Laumann, E. O., Paik, A., & Rosen, R. C. (1999). Sexual dysfunction in the United States: Prevalence and predictors. *Journal of the American Medical Association, 281*(6), 537-544.

Laythe, B., Finkel, D., & Kirkpatrick, L. A. (2001). Predicting prejudice from religious fundamentalism and right-wing authoritarianism: A multiple-regression approach. *Journal for the Scientific Study of Religion, 40*, 1-10.

Leland, N. L., & Barth, R. P. (1992). Gender differences in knowledge, intentions, and behaviors concerning pregnancy and sexually transmitted disease prevention among adolescents. *Journal of Adolescent Health, 13*, 589-599. doi:10.1016/1054-139X(92)90373-J.

L'Engle, K. L., & Jackson, C. (2008). Socialization influences on early adolescents' cognitive susceptibility and transition to sexual intercourse. *Journal of Research on Adolescence 18*(2), 353-378.

Lenhart, A. (2012). Teens, smartphones, & texting: Texting volume is up while the frequency of voice calling is down. About one in four teens say they own smartphones. http://pewinternet.org/~/media//Files/Reports/2012/ PIP_Teens_Smartphones_and_Texting.

Leung, A. K.C., & Robson, L. M. (1993). Childhood masturbation. *Clinical Pediatrics, 32*(4), 238-241. https://doi.org/10.1177/000992289303200410.

Levin, R. J. (2007). Sexual activity, health and well-being – the beneficial roles of coitus and masturbation. *Sexual and Relationship Therapy, 22*(1), 135-148. https://doi.org/10.1080/14681990601149197.

Levine, E. (2002). "Having a female body doesn't make you feminine": Feminine hygiene advertising and 1970s television. *The Velvet Light Trap – A Critical Journal of Film and Television, 50*, 36-47.

Li, N. P., Yong, J. C., Tov, W., Sng, O., Fletcher, G. J. O., Valentine, K. A., Jiang, Y. F., & Balliet, D. (2013). Mate preferences do predict attraction and choices in the early stages of mate selection. *Journal of Personality and Social Psychology, 105*(5), 757-776.

Lindberg, S. M., Grabe, S., & Hyde, J. S. (2007). Gender, pubertal development, and peer sexual harassment predict objectified body consciousness in early adolescence. *Journal of Research on Adolescence, 17*(4), 723-742. https://doi.org/10.1111/j.1532-7795.2007.00544.x.

Lloyd, E. A. (2005). *The case of the female orgasm: Bias in the science of evolution.* Cambridge, MA: Harvard University Press.

Loewenstein, G., Krishnamurti, T., Kopsic, J., & McDonald, D. (2015). Does increased sexual frequency enhance happiness? *Journal of Economic Behavior & Organization, 116*, 206-218.

Lopez, G. (2018). Trump promised to be LGBTQ-friendly. His first year in office proved it was a giant con: From Trump's ban on transgender military service to his failure to acknowledge Pride Month, his administration now has a long anti-LGBTQ record. Lopez@germanrlopezgerman.lopez@vox.com, January 22, 2018. www.vox.com/identities/2018/1/22/16905658/trump-lgbtq-anniversary.

Louie, K. S., de Sanjose, S., Diaz, M., Castellsagué, X., Herrero, R., Meijer, C. J., Shah, K., Franceschi, S., Muñoz, N., & Bosch, F. X. (2009). Early age at first sexual intercourse and early pregnancy are risk factors for cervical cancer in developing countries. *British Journal of Cancer, 100*, 1191-1197.

Ma, Q., Ono-Kihara, M., Cong, L., Xu, G., Pan, X., Zamani, S., ..., Kihara, M. (2009). Early initiation of sexual activity: A risk factor for sexually transmitted diseases, HIV infection, and unwanted pregnancy among university students in China. *BMC Public Health, 9*, 111. https://doi.org/10.1186/1471-2458-9-111.

Maguen, S., & Armistead, L. (2006). Abstinence among female adolescents: Do parents matter above and beyond the influence of peers? *American Journal of Orthopsychiatry, 76*(2), 260-264. https://doi.org/10.1037/0002-9432.76.2.260.

Mah, K., & Binik, Y. M. (2001). The nature of human orgasm: A critical review of major trends. *Clinical Psychology Review, 21*, 823-856.

Mah, K., & Binik, Y. M. (2002). Do all orgasms feel alike? Evaluating a two-dimensional model of the orgasm experience across gender and sexual context. *Journal of Sex Research, 39*, 104-113.

Malamuth, N. M., & Ceniti, J. (1986). Repeated exposure to violent and nonviolent pornography: Likelihood of raping ratings and laboratory aggression against women. *Aggressive Behavior, 12*(2), 129-137.

Manlove, J., Logan, C., Moore, K. A., & Ikramullah, E. (2008). Pathways from family religiosity to adolescent sexual activity and contraceptive use. *Perspectives on Sexual and Reproductive Health, 40*(2), 105-117.

Marieb, E. N. (2014). *Essentials of human anatomy and physiology* (11th ed.). Boston, MA: Pearson.

Marks, M. J., & Fraley, R. C. (2006). Confirmation bias and the sexual double standard. *Sex Roles, 54*, 19-26. https://doi.org/10.1007/s11199-006-8866-9.

Masters, W. H., & Johnson, V. E. (1966). *Human sexual response.* Boston, MA: Little, Brown.

Masters, W. H., Johnson, V. E., & Kolodny, L. (1979). *Textbook of sexual medicine.* Boston, MA: Little, Brown.

Maxwell, K. (2017). Yes, you should be wearing a condom every time: Let's talk about (safe) sex, baby. North Carolina State University. https://spoonuniversity.com/healthier/condom-importance-for-safe-sex.

McCarthy, B. W., & Bodnar, L. E. (2005). The equity model of sexuality: Navigating and negotiating the similarities and differences between men and women in sexual behaviour, roles and values. *Sexual and Relationship Therapy, 20*(2), 225-235.

McClintock, M. K., & Herdt, G. (1996). Rethinking puberty: The development of sexual attraction. *Current Directions in Psychological Science, 5*(6), 178-183.

McDade-Montez, E., Wallander, J., & Cameron, L. (2017). Sexualization in U.S. Latina and white girls' preferred children's television programs. *Sex Roles, 77*(1-2), 1-15.

Ménard, A. D., & Cabrera, C. (2011). 'Whatever the approach, Tab B still fits into Slot A': Twenty years of sex scripts in romance novels. *Sexuality & Culture, 15*(3), 240-255.

Mereish, E. H., & Poteat, V. P. (2015). A relational model of sexual minority mental and physical health: The negative effects of shame on relationships, loneliness, and health. *Journal of Counseling Psychology, 62*(3), 425-437.

Meston, C. M., & Ahrold, T. (2010). Ethnic, gender, and acculturation influences on sexual behaviors. *Archives of Sexual Behavior, 39*(1), 179-189.

Meston, C. M., Trapnell, P. D., & Gorzalka, B. B. (1998). Ethnic, gender, and length-of-residency influences on sexual knowledge and attitudes. *Journal of Sex Research, 35*(2), 176-188.

Meyer, I. H. (2003). Prejudice, social stress, and mental health in lesbian, gay, and bisexual populations: Conceptual issues and research evidence. *Psychological Bulletin, 129*, 674-697.

Meyer, I. H. (2010). Identity, stress, and resilience in lesbians, gay men, and bisexuals of color. *Counseling Psychology, 38*(3), 442-454. https://doi.org/10.1177/0011000009351601.

Meyer, I. H., Dietrich, J., & Schwartz, S. (2008). Lifetime prevalence of mental disorders and suicide attempts in diverse lesbian, gay, and bisexual populations. *American Journal of Public Health, 98,* 1004-1006. http://dx.doi.org/10.2105/AJPH.2006.096826.

Micucci, J. A. (2015). Working with families of lesbian, gay, and bisexual adolescents. In Browning, S., & Pasley, K. (Eds.), *Contemporary families: Translating research into practice.* New York: Routledge, pp. 213-228.

Milhausen, R. R., McKay, A., Graham, C. A., Crosby, R. A., Yarber, W. L., & Sanders, S. A. (2013). Prevalence and predictors of condom use in a national sample of Canadian university students. *Canadian Journal of Human Sexuality, 22*(3), 142-151. http://dx.doi.org/10.3138/cjhs.2316.

Miller, G. F. (2007). Sexual selection for moral virtues. *The Quarterly Review of Biology, 82*(2), 97-125.

Miller, K. S., Forehand, R., & Kotchick, B. A. (1999). Adolescent sexual behavior in two ethnic minority samples: The role of family variables. *Journal of Marriage and the Family, 61,* 85-98. doi:10.2307/353885.

Miller, K. S., Kotchick, B. A., Dorsey, S., Forehand, R., & Ham, A. Y. (1998). Family communication about sex: What are parents saying and are their adolescents listening? *Family Planning Perspectives, 30,* 218-223. doi:10.2307/2991607.

Millett, K. (2016), *Sexual politics.* New York: Columbia University Press.

Mitchell, K. J., Ybarra, M. L., & Korchmaros, J. D. (2014). Sexual harassment among adolescents of different sexual orientations and gender identities. *Child Abuse and Neglect, 38,* 280-295. http://dx.doi.org/10.1016/j.chiabu.2013.09.008.

Mo, Q., Lu, S. F., & Simon, N. G. (2006). Dehydroepiandrosterone and its metabolites: Differential effects on androgen receptor trafficking and transcriptional activity. *The Journal of Steroid Biochemistry and Molecular Biology, 99*(1), 50-58. doi:10.1016/j.jsbmb.2005.11.011.

Montgomery, H. (2007). Child sexual abuse: An anthropological perspective. In Rousseau, G. (Ed.), *Children and sexuality: From the Greeks to the great war* (pp. 319-347). New York: Palgrave Macmillan.

Moreno, M. A., Brockman, L. N., Wasserheit, J. N., & Christakis, D. A. (2012). A pilot evaluation of older adolescents' sexual reference displays on Facebook. *Journal of Sex Research, 49*(4), 390-399. http://dx.doi.org/10.1080/ 00224499.2011.642903.

Morgan, E. M., Thorne, A., & Zurbriggen, E. L. (2010). A longitudinal study of conversations with parents about sex and dating during college. *Developmental Psychology, 46*(1), 139-150. https://doi.org/10.1037/a0016931.

Morris, B. J., & Krieger, J. N. (2013). Does male circumcision affect sexual function, sensitivity, or satisfaction? - A systematic review. *Journal of Sexual Medicine, 10*(11), 2644-2657.

Morrow, R. (2013). *Sex research and sex therapy: A sociological analysis of Masters and Johnson.* London: Routledge.

Mosher, D. L., & Tomkins, S. S. (1988). Scripting the macho man: Hypermasculine socialization and enculturation. *The Journal of Sex Research, 25*(1), 60-84. | https://doi.org/10.1080/00224498809551445.

Muehlenhard, C. L., & Felts, A. S. (2011). The sexual beliefs scale. In Fisher, T. D., Davis, C. M., Yarber, W. L., Bauserman, R., Schreer, G. E., & Davis, S. L. (Eds.), *Handbook of sexuality-related measures* (3rd ed., pp. 127-129). Philadelphia: Taylor & Francis.

Muehlenhard, C. L., & Hollabaugh, L. C. (1988). Do women sometimes say no when they mean yes? The prevalence and correlates of women's token resistance to sex. *Journal of Personality and Social Psychology, 54,* 872-879. doi:10.1037/ 0022-3514.54.5.872.

Muehlenhard, C. L., & McCoy, M. L. (1991). Double standard/double bind: The sexual double standard and women's communication about sex. *Psychology of Women Quarterly, 15,* 447-461. doi:10.1111/j.1471-6402.1991.tb00420.x.

Muehlenhard, C. L., & Rodgers, C. S. (1998). Token resistance to sex: New perspectives on an old stereotype. *Psychology of Women Quarterly, 22*(3), 443-463.

Muise, A., Schimmack, U., & Impett, E. A. (2016). Sexual frequency predicts greater well-being, but more is not always better. *Social Psychological and Personality Science, 7*(4), 295-302.

Mujuzi, J. D. (2011). Discrimination against homosexuals in Malawi: Lessons from the recent developments. *International Journal of Discrimination and the Law, 11*(3), 150-160.

Muris, P., Meesters, C., & Asseldonk, M. (2018). Shame on me! Self-conscious emotions and big five personality traits and their relations to anxiety disorders symptoms in young, non-clinical adolescents. *Child Psychiatry and Human Development, 49,* 268-278. https://doi.org/10.1007/s10578-017-0747-7.

Murnen, S. K. (2000). Gender and the use of sexually degrading language. *Psychology of Women Quarterly, 24*(4), 319-327. https://doi.org/10.1111/j.1471-6402.2000.tb00214.x.

Murray, S. H. (2018). Heterosexual men's sexual desire: Supported by, or deviating from, traditional masculinity norms and sexual scripts? *Sex Roles, 78*(1-2), 130-141.

Nadeem, E., Romo, L. F., & Sigman, M. (2006). Knowledge about condoms among low-income pregnant Latina adolescents in relation to explicit maternal discussion of contraceptives. *Journal of Adolescent Health, 39,* e9–e15. doi:10.1016/j.jadohealth.2005. 09.012.

Narchi, H. (2003). Infantile masturbation mimicking paroxysmal disorders. *Journal of Pediatric Neurology, 1*(1), 43–45.

National Health Service (2015). Sexual health. www.nhs.uk/live-well/sexual-health/keeping-your-vagina-clean-and-healthy./ Retrieved June 25, 2018.

National Institutes of Health (2016). Research involving children. https://humansubjects.nih.gov/children1.

Ness, R. B., Hillier, S. L, Richter, H. E., Soper, D. E., Stamm, C., McGregor, J., ..., Rice, P. (2002). Douching in relation to bacterial vaginosis, lactobacilli, and facultative bacteria in the vagina. *Obstetrics & Gynecology, 100*(4), 765–772. https://doi.org/10.1016/S0029-7844(02)02184-1.

Ni, M., Feretzaki, M., Li, W., Floyd-Averette, A., Mieczkowski, P., Dietrich, F. S., & Heitman, J. (2013). Unisexual and heterosexual meiotic reproduction generate aneuploidy and phenotypic diversity de novo in the yeast Cryptococcus neoformans. *PLOS Biology, 11,* e1001653. https://doi.org/10.1371/journal.pbio.1001653.

Nielsen BookScan (2015). 2015 U.S. book industry year-end review. www.nielsen.com/us/en/insights/reports/2016/2015-us-book-industry-year-end-review.html.

Nielsen Company (2018). Romance readers by the numbers. www.nielsen.com/us/en/insights/news/2016/romance-readers-by-the-numbers.html.

Nijjar, R., Ellenbogen, M. A., & Hodgins, S. (2016). Sexual risk behaviors in the adolescent offspring of parents with bipolar disorder: Prospective associations with parents' personality and externalizing behavior in childhood. *Journal of Abnormal Child Psychology, 44*(7), 1347–1359.

O'Donnell, L., O'Donnell, C. R., & Stueve, A. (2001). Early sexual initiation and subsequent sex-related risks among urban minority youth: The Reach for Health Study. *Family Planning Perspectives, 33*(6), 268–275.

Offman, A., & Matheson, K. (2004). The sexual self-perceptions of young women experiencing abuse in dating relationships. *Sex Roles, 51,* 551–560. doi:10.1007/s11199-004-5465.

Okami, P., Olmstead, R., & Abramson, P. R. (1997). Sexual experiences in early childhood: 18-year longitudinal data from the UCLA family lifestyles project. *Journal of Sex Research, 34,* 339–347. doi:10.1080/00224499709551902.

Oliver, M. B., & Hyde, J. S. (1993). Gender differences in sexuality: A meta-analysis. *Psychological Bulletin, 114*(1), 29–51.

Olson, L. R., Cadge, W., & Harrison, J. T. (2006). Religion and public opinion about same-sex marriage. *Social Science Quarterly, 87*(2), 340–360. https://doi.org/10.1111/j.1540-6237.2006.00384.x.

Osman, S. L., & Davis, C. M. (1999). Belief in token resistance and type of resistance as predictors of men's perceptions of date rape. *Journal of Sex Education & Therapy, 24*(3), 189–196.

O'Sullivan, L. F., Dolezal, C., Brackis-Cott, E., Traeger, L., & Mellins, C. A. (2005). Communication about HIV and risk behaviors among mothers living with HIV and their early adolescent children. *Journal of Early Adolescence, 25,* 148–167. doi:10.1177/0272431604274176.

Paasonen, S. (2009). Healthy sex and pop porn: Pornography, feminism and the Finnish context. *Sexualities, 12*(5), 586–604. https://doi.org/10.1177/1363460709340369.

Parks, K. A., Romosz, A. M., Bradizza, C. M., & Hsieh, Y. (2008). A dangerous transition: Women's drinking and related victimization from high school to the first-year at college. *Journal of Studies on Alcohol and Drugs, 69,* 65–74.

Pasulka, N. (2012). When women used Lysol as birth control: A look back at shocking ads for the popular, dangerous, and ineffective antiseptic douche. Mother Jones, March 8. www.motherjones.com/media/2012/03/when-women-used-lysol-birth-control/.

Pawlowski, B., Dunbar, R. I. M., & Lipowicz, A. (2000). Evolutionary fitness: Tall men have more reproductive success. *Nature, 403,* 156.

Payne, F. E., Jr. (1985). *Biblical/medical ethics: The Christian and the practice of medicine.* Milford, MI: Mott Media, Inc.

Pearcy, M., Aron, S., Doums, C., & Keller, L. (2004). Conditional use of sex and parthenogenesis for worker and queen production in ants. *Science, 306* (5702), 1780–1783. doi:10.1126/science.1105453. PMID 15576621.

Penhollow, T. M., Young, M., & Denny, G. (2009). Predictors of quality of life, sexual intercourse, and sexual satisfaction among active older adults. *American Journal of Health Education, 40*(1), 14–22.

Perrett, D., Lee, K., Penton-Voak, I., Rowland, D., Yoshikawa, S., Burt, D., ... Akamatsu, S. (1998). Effects of sexual dimorphism on facial attractiveness. *Nature, 394,* 884–887.

Peter, J., & Valkenburg, P. M. (2016). Adolescents and pornography: A review of 20 years of research. *Journal of Sex Research, 53*(4–5), 509–531.

Petersen, J. L., & Hyde, J. S. (2010). A meta-analytic review of research on gender differences in sexuality, 1993–2007. *Psychological Bulletin, 136*(1), 21–38. https://doi.org/10.1037/a0017504.

Peterson, S. H., Wingood, G. M., DiClemente, R. J., Harrington, K., & Davies, S. (2007). Images of sexual stereotypes in rap videos and the health of African American female adolescents. *Journal of Women's Health, 16*(8), 1157-1164. https://doi.org/10.1089/jwh.2007.0429.

Peterson, V. (2018). Young adult and new adult book markets: Facts and figures to know. www.thebalancecareers.com/the-young-adult-book-market-2799954.

Planned Parenthood (2018). Safer sex. www.plannedparenthood.org/learn/stds-hiv-safer-sex/safer-sex. Retrieved June 24, 2018.

Pollet, T. V., & Nettle, D. (2009). Partner wealth predicts self-reported orgasm frequency in a sample of Chinese women. *Evolution and Human Behavior, 30*(2), 146-151. https://doi.org/10.1016/j.evolhumbehav.2008.11.002.

Ponton, L. (2000). *The sex lives of teenagers.* New York: Dutton.

Poulsen, F. O., Busby, D. M., & Galovan, A. M. (2013). Pornography use: Who uses it and how it is associated with couple outcomes. *The Journal of Sex Research, 50*(1), 72-83. doi:10.1080/00224499.2011.648027.

Pratto, F., & Walker, A. (2004). The bases of gendered power. In Eagly, A. H., Beall, A. E., & Sternberg, R. J. (Eds.), *The psychology of gender* (pp. 242-268). New York: Guilford Press.

Prentice, D. A., & Carranza, E. E. (2002). What women and men should be, shouldn't be, are allowed to be, and don't have to be: The contents of prescriptive gender stereotypes. *Psychology of Women Quarterly, 26,* 269-281. doi:10.1111/ 1471-6402.t01-1-00066.

Price, M. N., & Hyde, J. S. (2009). When two isn't better than one: Predictors of early sexual activity in adolescence using a cumulative risk model. *Journal of Youth and Adolescence, 38,* 1059-1071. https://doi.org/10.1007/s10964-008-9351-2.

Prinzie, P., Stams, G. J., Dekovic, M., Reijntjes, A. H., & Belsky, J. (2009). The relations between parents' big five personality factors and parenting: A meta-analytic review. *Journal of Personality and Social Psychology, 97,* 351-362. doi:10.1037/a0015823.

Puppo, V. (2011). Embryology and anatomy of the vulva: The female orgasm and women's sexual health. *European Journal of Obstetrics, Gynecology, and Reproductive Biology, 154,* 3-8.

Packer, C., & Pusey, A. E. (1987). The evolution of sex-biased dispersal in lions. *Behaviour, 101*(4), 275-310. https://doi.org/10.1163/156853987X00026.

Puts, D. A., Dawood, K., & Welling, L. L.M. (2012). Why women have orgasms: An evolutionary analysis. *Archives of Sexual Behavior, 41,* 1127-1143. doi:10.1007/s10508-012-9967-x.

Puts, D. A., Welling, L. L.M., Burriss, R. P., & Dawood, K. (2012). Men's masculinity and attractiveness predict their female partners' reported orgasm frequency and timing. *Evolution and Human Behavior, 33*(1), 1-9. https://doi.org/10.1016/j.evolhumbehav.2011.03.003.

Raffaelli, M., Bogenschneider, K., & Flood, M. F. (1998). Parent-teen communication about sexual topics. *Journal of Family Issues, 19,* 315-333. doi:10.1177/019251398019003005.

Ramey, J. W. (1977). The sexual bond: Alternative life styles. *Society, 14*(5), 43-47. doi:10.1007/BF02700827.

Ranjbar, H., & Azmoude, E. (2018). The relationship between body mass index and sexual dysfunction among women: A meta-analysis. *Shiraz E-Medical Journal, 19*(2), e14409. doi:10.5812/semj.14409.

Reece, M., Herbenick, D., Sanders, S. A., Dodge, B., Ghassemi, A., & Fortenberry, J. D. (2009). Prevalence and characteristics of vibrator use by men in the United States. *Journal of Sexual Medicine, 6,* 1867-1874.

Reuter, T. R., Sharp, C., Kalpakci, A. H., Choi, H. J., & Temple, J. R. (2016). Sexual orientation and borderline personality disorder features in a community sample of adolescents *Journal of Personality Disorders, 30*(5), 694-707.

Richters, J., de Visser, R., Rissel, C., & Smith, A. (2006). Sexual practices at last heterosexual encounter and occurrence of orgasm in a national survey. *The Journal of Sex Research, 43*(3), 217-226. https://doi.org/10.1080/00224490609552320.

Richters, J., de Visser, R. O., Rissel, C. E., Grulich, A. E., & Smith, A. M.A. (2008). Demographic and psychosocial features of participants in bondage and discipline, "sadomasochism" or dominance and submission (BDSM): Data from a national survey. *Journal of Sexual Medicine, 5*(7), 1660-1668. https://doi.org/10.1111/j.1743-6109.2008.00795.x.

Riggio, H. R., Galaz, B., Garcia, A. L., & Matthies, B. K. (2014). Contraceptive attitudes and sexual self-esteem among young adults: Communication and quality of relationships with mothers. *International Journal of Sexual Health, 26,* 268-281. doi:10.1080/19317611.2014.885924.

Riggio, H. R., Mendoza, J., Letona, C., & Gusha, H. (2018). The measurement of sexual shame. Poster presented at the annual meeting of the Western Psychological Association, April, Portland, OR.

Riggio, H. R., Romero-Juarez, M., Rusk, J., & Umana, V. (2016). Sexual self-esteem: Links with religiosity and sexual satisfaction. Poster presented at the annual meeting of the Western Psychological Association, April, Long Beach, CA.

Rinehart, S. J., & Espelage, D. L. (2015). Psychology of violence: A multilevel analysis of school climate homophobic name calling, and sexual harassment victimization/perpetration among middle school youth. *Psychology of Violence, 6,* 1-10. http://dx.doi.org/10.1037/a0039095.

Rizzolatti, G., & Craighero, L. (2004). The mirror-neuron system. *Annual Review of Neuroscience, 27*(1), 169-192. doi:10.1146/annurev.neuro.27.070203.144230.

Roberts, E. (1999). The importance of being dehydroepiandrosterone sulfate (in the blood of primates):A longer and healthier life? *Biochemical Pharmacology, 57*(4), 329-346. doi:10.1016/S0006-2952(98)00246-9.

Roberts, T.-A., & Waters, P. L. (2004). Self-objectification and that "not so fresh feeling":Feminist therapeutic interventions for healthy female embodiment. *Women & Therapy, 27*(3-4), 5-21.

Rollero, C. (2013), Men and women facing objectification: The effects of media models on well-being, self-esteem and ambivalent sexism. *Revista de Psicología Social, 28*(3), 373-382.

Romo, L. F., Lefkowitz, E. A., Sigman, M., & Au, T. K. (2002). A longitudinal study of maternal messages about dating and sexuality and their influence on Latino adolescents. *Journal of Adolescent Health, 31*, 59-69. doi:10.1016/S1054-139X(01)00402-5.

Rose, E. (2013). Lysol's vintage ads subtly pushed women to use its disinfectant as birth control. smithsonianmag.com. Retrieved February 2, 2015.

Rose, J. G., Chrisler, J. C., & Couture, S. (2008). Young women's attitudes toward continuous use of oral contraceptives:The effect of priming positive attitudes toward menstruation on women's willingness to suppress menstruation. *Health Care for Women International, 29*(7), 688-701. doi:10.1080/07399330802188925.

Rose, S., & Frieze, I. H. (1989). Young singles' scripts for a first date. *Gender & Society, 3*(2), 258-268. https://doi.org/10.1177/089124389003002006.

Rosen, R. C., & Beck, J. G. (1988). *Patterns of sexual arousal:Psychophysiological processes and clinical application.* New York:Guilford Press.

Rosenthal, D., Senserrick, T., & Feldman, S. (2001). A typology approach to describing parents as communicators about sexuality. *Archives of Sexual Behavior, 30*, 463-482. doi:10.1023/A:1010235116609.

Rouvier, M., Campero, L., Walker, D., & Caballero, M. (2011). Factors that influence communication about sexuality between parents and adolescents in the cultural context of Mexican families. *Sex Education, 11*, 175-191. doi:10.1080/14681811.2011.558425.

Rowland, D. L. (2006). The psychobiology of sexual arousal and response:Physical and psychological factors that control our sexuality. In McAnulty, R. D., & Burnette, M. M. (Eds.), *Sex and sexuality: Sexual function and dysfunction* (pp. 37-66). Westport, CT:Greenwood Publishing Group.

Rowland, D., McMahon, C. G., Abdo, C., Chen, J., Jannini, E., Waldinger, M. D., Ahn, T. Y. (2010). Disorders of orgasm and ejaculation in men. *Journal of Sexual Medicine, 7*, 1668-1686. https://doi.org/10.1111/j.1743-6109.2010.01782.x.

Rudman, L. A., Fetterolf, J. C., & Sanchez, D. T. (2013). What motivates the sexual double standard? More support for male versus female control theory. *Personality and Social Psychology Bulletin, 39*, 251-263. doi:10.1177/0146167212472375.

Rudman, L. A., Glick, P., Marquardt, T., & Fetterolf, J. C. (2017). When women are urged to have casual sex more than men are: Perceived risk moderates the sexual advice double standard. *Sex Roles, 77*(5-6), 409-418.

Sanchez, D., Phelan, J. E., Moss-Racusin, C. A., & Good, J. J. (2012). The gender role motivation model of women's sexually submissive behavior and satisfaction in heterosexual couples. *Personality and Social Psychology Bulletin, 38*, 528-539. doi:10.1177/0146167211430088.

Santelli, J., Ott, M. A., Lyon, M., Rogers, J., Summers, D., & Schleifer, R. (2006). Abstinence and abstinence-only education: A review of U.S. policies and programs. *Journal of Adolescent Health, 38*(1), 72-81.

Scharrer, E. (2005). Hypermasculinity, aggression, and television violence:An experiment. *Media Psychology, 7*(4), 353-376. doi:10.1207/S1532785XMEP0704_3.

Schenk, J., & Pfrang, H. (1986). Extraversion, neuroticism, and sexual behavior:Interrelationships in a sample of young men. *Archives of Sexual Behavior, 15*(6), 449-455.

Schmitt, D. P. (2003). Universal sex differences in the desire for sexual variety: Tests from 52 nations, 6 continents, and 13 islands. International Sexuality Description Project. *Journal of Personality and Social Psychology, 85*(1), 85-104.

Schneeberger, A., Rauchfleisch, U., & Battegay, R. (2002). Psychosomatic consequences and phenomena of discrimination at work against people with homosexual orientation. *Schweizer Archiv für Neurologie und Psychiatrie, 153*(3), 137-143.

Schuhrke, B. (2000). Young children's curiosity about other people's genitals. *Journal of Psychology & Human Sexuality, 12*(1-2), 27-48. doi:10.1300/J056v12n01_03.

Schultz, G. (2006). Legal swingers clubs fuel growth in Canadian group sex activity. *LifeSiteNews,* May 16.

Schuster, M. A., Bell, R. M., Nakajima, G. A., & Kanouse, D. E. (1998). The sexual practices of Asian and Pacific Islander high school students. *Journal of Adolescent Health, 23*(4), 221-231.

Scudellari, M. (2014). The sex paradox. Birds do it. Bees do it. We do it. But not without a physical, biochemical, and genetic price. How did the costly practice of sex become so commonplace? *The Scientist,* July, cover story.

248 *Human Sexuality*

Seabrook, R. C., Ward, L. M., Cortina, L. M., Giaccardi, S., & Lippman, J. R. (2017). Girl power or powerless girl? Television, sexual scripts, and sexual agency in sexually active young women. *Psychology of Women Quarterly, 41*(2), 240-253.

Sender, K. (2003). Sex sells: Sex, taste, and class in commercial gay and lesbian media. *GLQ: A Journal of Lesbian and Gay Studies, 9*(3), 331-365.

Sewankambo, N., Gray, R. H., Wawer, M. J., Paxton, L., McNairn, D., Wabwire-Mangen, F., ..., Konde-Lule, J. (1997). HIV-1 infection associated with abnormal vaginal flora morphology and bacterial vaginosis, *Lancet, 350*(9077), 546-550. https://doi.org/10.1016/S0140-6736(97)01063-5.

Shackelford, T. K., Schmitt, D. P., & Buss, D. M. (2005). Universal dimensions of human mate preferences. *Personality and Individual Differences, 39*, 447-458. doi:10.1016/j.paid.2005.01.023.

Shearer, A., Russon, J., Herres, J., Wong, A., Jacobs, C., Diamond, G. M., & Diamond, G. S. (2018). Religion, sexual orientation, and suicide attempts among a sample of suicidal adolescents. *Suicide and Life-Threatening Behavior, 48*(4), 431-437.

Sheeran, P., Abrams, D., Abraham, C., & Spears, R. (1993). Religiosity and adolescents' premarital sexual attitudes and behaviour: An empirical study of conceptual issues. *European Journal of Social Psychology, 23*(1), 39-52.

Shifren, J. L., Monz, B. U., Russo, P. A., Segreti, A., & Johannes, C. B. (2008). Sexual problems and distress in United States women: Prevalence and correlates. *Obstetrics & Gynecology: 112* (5), 970-978. doi:10.1097/AOG.0b013e3181898cdb.

Sieving, R. E., Eisenberg, M. E., Pettingell, S., & Skay, C. (2006). Friends' influence on adolescents' first sexual intercourse. *Perspectives on Sexual and Reproductive Health, 38*(1), 13-19.

Simon, W., & Gagnon, J. H. (1986). Sexual scripts: Permanence and change. *Archives of Sexual Behavior, 15*, 97-120. doi:10.1007/ BF01542219.

Singh, D. (1993). Adaptive significance of female physical attractiveness: Role of waist-to-hip ratio. *Journal of Personality and Social Psychology, 65*, 293-307. doi:10.1037/0022-3514.65.2.293.

Smith, D. G., Frankel, S., & Yarnell, J. (1997). Sex and death: Are they related? Findings from the Caerphilly Cohort Study. *British Medical Journal, 315*(7123), 1641-1644.

Smith, R. L., Gallicchio, L., & Flaws, J. A. (2017). Factors affecting sexual function in midlife women: Results from the Midlife Women's Health Study. *Journal of Women's Health, 26*(9), 923-932.

Snapp, S., Ryu, E., & Kerr, J. (2015). The upside to hooking up: College students' positive hookup experiences. *International Journal of Sexual Health, 27*(1), 43-56. https://doi.org/10.1080/19317611.2014.939247.

Sneed, C. D., Tan, H. P., & Meyer, J. C. (2015). The influence of parental communication and perception of peers on adolescent sexual behavior. *Journal of Health Communication, 20*, 888-892. doi:10.1080/10810730.2015.1018584.

Spiegel, K., Weibel, L., Gronfier, C., Brandenberger, G., & Follenius, M. (2009). Twenty-four-hour prolactin profiles in night workers. *Chronobiology International, 13*(4), 283-293. doi:10.3109/07420529609020908.

Spitzer, R. L. (2003). Can some gay men and lesbians change their sexual orientation? 200 participants reporting a change from homosexual to heterosexual orientation. *Archives of Sexual Behavior, 32*(5), 403-417. https://doi.org/10.1023/A:1025647527010.

Sprecher, S., Harris, G., & Meyers, A. (2008). Perceptions of sources of sex education and targets of sex communication: Sociodemographic and cohort effects. *Journal of Sex Research, 45*(1), 17-26. http://dx.doi.org/10.1080/00224490701629522.

Sprecher, S., Hatfield, E., Cortese, A., Potapova, E., & Levitskaya, A. (2010). Token resistance to sexual intercourse and consent to unwanted sexual intercourse: College students' dating experiences in three countries. *Journal of Sex Research, 31*(2), 125-132. doi:10.1080/00224499409551739.

Stack, S., & Eshleman, J. R. (1998). Marital status and happiness: A 17-nation study. *Journal of Marriage and the Family, 60*(2), 527-536.

Stanko, E. A. (1987). Typical violence, normal precaution: Men, women and interpersonal violence in England, Wales, Scotland and the USA. In Hanmer, J., & Maynard, M. (Eds.), *Women, violence and social control. Explorations in sociology* (British Sociological Association conference volume series). London: Palgrave Macmillan.

Stewart, D.N., & Szymanski, D.M. (2012). Young adult women's reports of their male romantic partner's pornography use as a correlate of their self-esteem, relationship quality, and sexual satisfaction. *Sex Roles, 67*(5-6), 257-271. https://doi.org/10.1007/s11199-012-0164-0.

Strahan, E. J. (2003). Selling thinness: How media images increase importance of weight and beauty as a basis of women's self-esteem and decrease their body satisfaction and eating. Unpublished doctoral dissertation, University of Waterloo, Ontario, Canada.

Streeter, V. M., Milhausen, R. R., & Buchholz, A. C. (2012). Body image, body mass index, and body composition in young adults. *Canadian Journal of Dietetic Practice and Research, 73*(2), 78-83.

Susman, E. J., Dorn, L. D., & Schiefelbein, V. L. (2003). Puberty, sexuality, and health. In Lerner, R. M., Easterbrooks, M. A., & Mistry, J. (Eds.), *Handbook of psychology: Developmental psychology*, Vol. 6. New York: John Wiley & Sons, pp. 295-324.

Swain, C. R., Ackerman, L. K., & Ackerman, M. A. (2006). The influence of individual characteristics and contraceptive beliefs on parent-teen sexual communications: A structural model. *Journal of Adolescent Health, 38*, 753.e9-e18. doi:10.1016/j.jadohealth.2005.08.015.

Taggart, T., Gottfredson, N., Powell, W., Ennett, S., Chatters, L. M., Carter-Edwards, L., & Eng, E. (2018). The role of religious socialization and religiosity in African American and Caribbean black adolescents' sexual initiation. *Journal of Religion and Health, 57*, 1889-1904. https://doi.org/10.1007/s10943-018-0605-3.

Taormino, T. (2008). *Opening up: A guide to creating and sustaining open relationships*. Jersey City, NJ: Cleis Press.

Thigpen, J. W. (2009). Early sexual behavior in a sample of low-income, African American children. *Journal of Sex Research, 46*, 67-79. doi:10. 1080/00224490802645286.

Tjaden, P., & Thoennes, N. (1998). Prevalence, incidence, and consequences of violence against women: Findings from the National Violence against Women Survey. Research in Brief. Department of Justice, Washington, DC. National Institute of Justice, Centers for Disease Control and Prevention (DHHS/PHS), Atlanta, GA.

Toates, F. (2009). An integrative theoretical framework for understanding sexual motivation, arousal, and behavior. *Journal of Sex Research, 46*(2-3), 168-193. https://doi.org/10.1080/00224490902747768.

Toibaro, J. J., Ebensrtejin, J. E., Parlante, A., Burgoa, P., Freyre, A., Romero, M., & Losso, M. H. (2009). Sexually transmitted infections among transgender individuals and other sexual identities. *Medicina, 69*(3), 327-330.

Toubia, N. F., & Sharief, E. H. (2003). Female genital mutilation: Have we made progress? *Journal of Gynecology and Obstetrics, 82*(3), 251-261. https://doi.org/10.1016/S0020-7292(03)00229-7.

Træen, B., Markovic, A., & Kvalem, I. L. (2016). Sexual satisfaction and body image: A cross-sectional study among Norwegian young adults. *Sexual and Relationship Therapy, 31*(2), 123-137.

Tuchman, G. (2000). The symbolic annihilation of women by the mass media. In Crothers, L., & Lockhart, C. (Eds.), *Culture and politics*. New York: Palgrave Macmillan, pp. 150-174.

Udell, W., Sandfort, T., Reitz, E., Bos, H., & Dekovic, M. (2010). The relationship between early sexual debut and psychosocial outcomes: A longitudinal study of Dutch adolescents. *Archives of Sexual Behavior, 39*, 1133-1145. doi:10.1007/s10508-009-9590-7.

UN Department of Economic and Social Affairs (2004). *World Youth Report 2003: The global situation of young people*. New York: UN.

UNAIDS (2007). WHO and UNAIDS announce recommendations from expert meeting on male circumcision for HIV prevention. Press release March 28. http://data.unaids.org/pub/pressrelease/2007/20070328_pr_mc_recommendations_en.

UNICEF (2016). Female genital mutilation/cutting: A global concern. New York: UNICEF.

U.S. Food and Drug Administration (2018). Condoms and sexually transmitted diseases. www.fda.gov/forpatients/illness/hivaids/ucm126372.htm. Retrieved June 24, 2018.

Valleroy, L. A., MacKellar, D. A., Karon, J. M., Rosen, D. H., McFarland, W., Shehan, D. A., ..., Janssen, R. S., for the Young Men's Survey Study Group (2000). HIV prevalence and associated risks in young men who have sex with men. *Journal of the American Medical Association, 284*(2), 198-204. doi:10.1001/jama.284.2.198.

Vance, E. B., & Wagner, N. N. (1976). Written descriptions of orgasm: A study of sex differences. *Archives of Sexual Behavior, 5*(1), 87-98. https://doi.org/10.1007/BF01542242.

van den Berg, P., Paxton, S. J., Keery, H., Wall, M., Guo, J., & Neumark-Sztainera, D. (2007). Body dissatisfaction and body comparison with media images in males and females. *Body Image, 4*(3), 257-268.

Vandenbosch, L., Muise, A., Eggermont, S., & Impett, E. A. (2015). Sexualizing reality television: Associations with trait and state self-objectification. *Body Image, 13*, 62-66.

Wallace, S. A., Miller, K. S., & Forehand, R. (2008). Perceived peer norms and sexual intentions among African American preadolescents. *AIDS Education & Prevention, 20*, 360-369.

Ward, L. M. (2002). Does television exposure affect emerging adults' attitudes and assumptions about sexual relationships? Correlational and experimental confirmation. *Journal of Youth and Adolescence, 31*(1), 1-15.

Ward, L. M., Day, K. M., & Epstein, M. (2006). Uncommonly good: Exploring how mass media may be a positive influence on young women's sexual health and development. *New Directions for Child and Adolescent Development, 112*, 57-70.

Warner, K. (2000). Sentencing in cases of marital rape: Towards changing the male imagination. *Legal Studies, 20*, 592-611.

Waterman, E. A., Wesche, R., & Lefkowitz, E. S. (2018). Longitudinal correlates of peer sexual communication quality in late adolescence. *Sexuality Research & Social Policy, 15*, 421-432. https://doi.org/10.1007/s13178-017-0315-8.

Weaver, A. D., & Byers, E. S. (2006). The relationships among body image, body mass index, exercise, and sexual functioning in heterosexual women. *Psychology of Women Quarterly, 30*(4), 333-339. https://doi.org/10.1111/j.1471-6402.2006.00308.x.

Weeks, D. J., & James, J. (1998). *Secrets of the superyoung: The scientific reasons some people look ten years younger than they really are - and how you can, too.* New York: Villard Books.

Weeks, J., Heaphy, B., & Donovan, C. (2001). *Same sex intimacies: Families of choice and other life experiments.* New York: Routledge.

Weisfeld, G. E., & Woodward, L. (2004). Current evolutionary perspectives on adolescent romantic relations and sexuality. *Journal of the American Academy of Child & Adolescent Psychiatry, 43*(1), 11-19.

Weiss, P., & Brody, S. (2009). Women's partnered orgasm consistency is associated with greater duration of penile-vaginal intercourse but not of foreplay. *Journal of Sexual Medicine, 6,* 135-141.

Welling, L. L. M., & Burriss, R. P. (2019). Investigating the ovulatory cycle: An overview of research and methods. In Welling, L. L. M., & Shackelford, T. K. (Eds.), *The Oxford handbook of evolutionary psychology and behavioral endocrinology.* New York: Oxford University Press, pp. 1-28.

Whitaker, D. J., & Miller, K. S. (2000). Parent-adolescent discussions about sex and condoms: Impact on peer influences of sexual risk behavior. *Journal of Adolescent Research, 15,* 251-273. doi:10.1177/0743558400152004.

Whitbeck, L. B., Yoder, K. A., Hoyt, D. R., & Conger, R. D. (1999). Early adolescent sexual activity: A developmental study. *Journal of Marriage and Family, 61*(4), 934-946.

Wight, D., Williamson, L., & Henderson, M. (2006). Parental influences on young people's sexual behavior: A longitudinal analysis. *Journal of Adolescence, 29,* 473-494. doi:10.1016/j.adolescence.2005.08.007.

Williamson, L. M., Parkes, A., Wight, D., Petticrew, M., & Hart, G. J. (2009). Limits to modern contraceptive use among young women in developing countries: A systematic review of qualitative research. *Reproductive Health, 6,* 1-12. doi:10.1186/1742-4755-6-3.

Willoughby, B. L., Doty, N. D., & Malik, N. M. (2010). Victimization, family rejection, and outcomes of gay, lesbian, and bisexual young people: The role of negative GLB identity. *J GLBT Fam Stud, 6,* 403-424.

Witte, J. (2005). *Sex, marriage, and family in John Calvin's Geneva: Courtship, engagement, and marriage.* Grand Rapids, MI: Eerdmans.

Wolak, J., Mitchell, K., & Finkelhor, D. (2007). Unwanted and wanted exposure to online pornography in a national sample of youth internet users. *Pediatrics, 119,* 247-257. doi:10.1542/peds.2006-1891.

Wolitski, R. J., & Fenton, K. A. (2011). Sexual health, HIV, and sexually transmitted infections among gay, bisexual, and other men who have sex with men in the United States. *AIDS and Behavior, 15*(1 Suppl 1), S9-S17. http://dx.doi.org/10.1007/s10461-011-9901-6.

World Health Organization (2006). Defining sexual health: Report of a technical consultation on sexual health, 28-31 January 2002. Geneva. www.who.int/reproductivehealth/publications/sexual_health/defining_sh/en/.

World Health Organization (2007). Male circumcision: Global trends and determinants of prevalence, safety and acceptability.

World Health Organization (2017a). HIV/AIDS. www.afro.who.int/health-topics/hivaids. Retrieved June 24, 2018.

World Health Organization (2017b). Regional consultation on universal access to sexual and reproductive health. www.afro.who.int/news/regional-consultation-universal-access-sexual-and-reproductive-health. Retrieved June 24, 2018.

World Health Organization (2018). Female genital mutilation. www.who.int/news-room/fact-sheets/detail/female-genital-mutilation. Retrieved June 21, 2018.

Wright, L. W. Jr., Bonita, A. G., & Mulick, P. S. (2011). An update and reflections on fear of and discrimination against bisexuals, homosexuals, and individuals with AIDS. *Journal of Bisexuality, 11*(4), 458-464.

Wudarczyk, O. A., Earp, B. D., Guastella, A., & Savulescu, J. (2013). Could intranasal oxytocin be used to enhance relationships? Research imperatives, clinical policy, and ethical considerations. *Current Opin Psychiatry, 26*(5), 474-484. doi:10.1097/YCO.0b013e3283642e10.

Yadegarfard, M., Meinhold-Bergmann, M. E., & Ho, R. (2014). Family rejection, social isolation, and loneliness as predictors of negative health outcomes (depression, suicidal ideation, and sexual risk behavior) among Thai male-to-female transgender adolescents. *Journal of LGBT Youth, 11*(4), 347-363.

Young, L. J., & Wang, Z. (2004). The neurobiology of pair bonding. *Nature Neuroscience, 7*(10), 1048-1054.

Zotto, M., & Pegna, A. J. (2017). Electrophysiological evidence of perceived sexual attractiveness for human female bodies varying in waist-to-hip ratio. *Cognitive, Affective & Behavioral Neuroscience, 17*(3), 577-591.

9 Personality, Emotions, and Health

Defining Personality	256
The Five Factor Model of Personality	259
Biological Bases of Personality	261
Hormones, Emotions, and Personality	263
Behavioral Genetics: Understanding Genes and Behavior	267
The Environment and Socialization of Personality	268
Gender Differences in Personality and Emotions	272
Gender Differences in Cognitive Abilities	275
Gender and Physical and Mental Health	276

INEQUALITIES AND INJUSTICES

Disparities in Health Care around the World

The World Health Organization (WHO) is sounding the alarm on a global health care crisis, particularly among refugees and migrants, and particularly female refugees and migrants (2017a, 2018b). Migrant women are themselves often care workers, caring for children, the sick, and the elderly, including in public health care settings; however they also have few labor and social protections, face barriers to accessing care, and are frequently exposed to health risks. Barriers to accessing health care that migrants and poor people of minority ethnic status face are myriad and can be tied to high costs of health care, culturally insensitive or uninformed services, lack of health and health care awareness, administrative complexities, lack of flexibility in access, low social support, low access to information, discrimination, and many other factors (World Health Organization, 2017b). Especially vulnerable populations in terms of health care disparities, including among migrant groups and ethnic minority groups, are poor women, unemployed men, and families headed by women (Witter, Govender, Ravindran, & Yates, 2017).

In their 1948 Constitution, the World Health Organization asserts that every human being, everyone, has a right "to enjoy the highest attainable standard of physical and mental health" (World Health Organization, 2018b, www.who.int/migrants/en). The World Health Organization (2017b, p.13) asserts that "equity is the absence of avoidable, unfair or

Personality, Emotions, and Health

remediable differences among groups of people, whether those groups are defined socially, economically, demographically or geographically, or by other means of stratification" (also see World Health Organization, 2017b). They also assert that moving toward global **universal health care** coverage, providing health care and financial protection from health care costs to all or nearly all of a country's people (2018c), is the strongest remedy for inequity in health care around the world (2017b). Increasing equity is also accomplished through interventions in models of care that help overcome barriers faced by migrant and ethnic minority groups, including free and low-cost services, gender- and culturally-sensitive providers, longer consultation hours, bilingual staff and use of interpreters, outreach services, and free transportation to appointments (Joshi et al., 2013).

The debate over health care in the United States is at a high point (Sanders, 2017). The Republican Party is strongly against the universal health care urged by the World Health Organization (RepublicanViews.org, 2014). The Republican Party voted over 50 times to repeal the Affordable Care Act (ACA), which benefited millions of Americans and families, allowing them access to affordable health care (Berenson, 2017). Why? Nearly 45,000 Americans die each year from preventable causes because they are uninsured, with uninsured Americans of working age having a death rate 40 times higher than their insured counterparts (Wilper et al., 2009). The U.S. Constitution provides for the right of every American to *life*; essential to this is access to quality health care, regardless of income. As a right to every American, enough money can never be a requirement; rights exist regardless of circumstances, privileges, or other individual qualities. Universal health care is the standard in every other developed country around the world, whose citizens enjoy good health and longevity without being burdened by overpriced, inflated medical costs (Organisation for Economic Cooperation and Development, 2016). Why not in the United States? Why the emphasis on wealth and individual achievement over the well-being of the group? The Republican Party seems to support and care about the profits of insurance companies and CEO salaries rather than the health and well-being of all Americans. Yes, the ideals of **individualism** are strongly entrenched in American culture, but in this case unfortunately to the detriment of the well-being of the collective. Perhaps it is time that Americans consider how the well-being of everyone benefits each of us, regardless of individual effort or achievement. Individual achievement is important, but is meaningless when it is surrounded by suffering, poor health, and poverty. The wealth of a few should never outweigh the well-being of all in a democratic, humane, sophisticated, reasonable society.

LEARN MORE

Freud's Psychodynamic Theory of Personality

Sigmund Freud (1856-1939) is arguably the most famous "psychologist" the average person would identify. Freud was not a psychologist (he was a neurologist) and his theorizing is not based on the highly structured methods of research followed by most scientists. He

was a practitioner, however, and clearly a very important one, given his emphases on the *talking cure* (Freud, 1917) and psychoanalytic therapy as a *cure of love* (Haynal, 1994, p.24). Freud is largely responsible for the general acceptance and utility of so-called **talk therapy** today around the world (me too, I have a great therapist). Freud is also an extremely important theorist within modern psychology, particularly in terms of his explanations of the development of personality.

Freud's approach to personality is **intrapsychic** (inside the mind), is focused on the operations and activities of the mind (hence the title **psychodynamic**), and begins in infancy. **Libido**, life energy, is fixed at birth, no more can be gained. Libido must be used to successfully manage successive challenges and obstacles through childhood. If issues remain unresolved or unsuccessfully managed, some libido is trapped at that stage of development, libido is **fixated** at that stage, and a **neurosis** may result. A person with a neurosis will always be irrational, anxious, and preoccupied with the unresolved issue into adulthood. The only way to ameliorate a neurosis is to discover it through **psychoanalytic therapy**. Much of what is contained in the mind, including troubling emotions and sources of neurosis, is relegated to the **unconscious** part of the mind; the person is totally or mostly unaware of the contents of the unconscious mind. Once a child attains some conscious control over the mind, troubling events and feelings will be intentionally put into the unconscious using **defense mechanisms** (e.g., denial, rationalization, projection).

According to Freud, infants at birth are all **Id**; they are wanting, insatiable, hungry little animals with no self-control. Ids operate on the **pleasure principle**; that's all the Id cares about. They are completely helpless, entirely dependent on the exterior world and the people in it. The physical focus is the mouth (the Oral Stage), because that is where pleasure is obtained, and the psychological themes are trust and dependence. In the Anal Stage, the child learns about self-control and obedience. The ultimate in self-control is the ability to control one's eliminative functions (truly the bedrock of civilization). The Ego emerges here to deal with increasing demands for self-control from the external world. The Ego is consciousness, the self. It is our conscious self, managing our daily lives, trying to reach compromises between pleasure, practicality, and morality (the Superego, which emerges in the Phallic Stage, the internalized parent). The Ego operates on the rationality principle ("what works here?"), the Superego on morality. Various personality qualities reveal if the person's Ego is healthy and able to reach positive, fulfilling compromises, or if the Ego is weak because of fixated libido (Freud, 1917). The healthy person has plenty of libido and puts energy into pursuing creativity, productivity, and adult sexuality. The unhealthy person's libido is fixated and unavailable for mature, adult, positive pursuits. Freud's approach to personality is not highly popular among personality researchers for various reasons (e.g., poor operational definitions; how do you measure libido?), but it remains a fascinating and predictive model of personality that has provided many useful concepts and ideas to psychology research, theory, and practice.

CRITICAL THINKING

Maternal Mortality in the U.S.: What's Going on?

Maternal mortality refers to the rates of women who die from complications during childbirth, and soon after childbirth (Beck et al., 2010). The World Health Organization (2015a) reports that maternal mortality rates (MMR) have fallen substantially around the world over the past 25 years, an overall very substantial decrease of 44%. The current worldwide average MMR is 216 maternal deaths per 100,000 live births. The vast majority of maternal deaths occur in developing regions, especially sub-Saharan Africa, which has an MMR of 545 per 100,000 live births. Sierra Leone is highest worldwide in MMR at 1,360 deaths per 100,000. Multiple government and public organizations around the world recognize a particular national condition called a fragile state. The Organisation for Economic Cooperation and Development (OECD) defines fragile states as countries where the government is weak and ineffective, unwilling or unable to perform necessary basic functions for security, social services, and the rule of law (OECD, 2018). These countries are poor with few protections for the people. In fragile state regions, MMR is high at 1 in 54 women dying from childbirth complications. India and Nigeria accounted for nearly one-third of all maternal deaths worldwide in 2015 (World Health Organization, 2015a).

Please note that these numbers do not include the hundreds of thousands of women every year around the world who die from pregnancy complications, without ever reaching childbirth, including around 700 women per year in the United States (Centers for Disease Control & Prevention, 2018a). Around the world each year, around 300,000 women die from largely preventable causes related to pregnancy and childbirth (World Health Organization, 2018a).

While maternal mortality rates are dramatically decreasing around the world, especially in developing regions because of greater accessibility and quality of health care available to girls and women, the MMR increased in the United States from 1990 to 2015 (World Health Organization, 2015a). The U.S. MMR is rather low at 12 deaths per 100,000 live births in 2015; but with nearly four million live births each year, that's several hundred women each year (Centers for Disease Control & Prevention, 2018b). The U.S. rate is higher than it was in 1990 and it is higher than that of all other developed nations, including all of Europe, Australia and New Zealand, and many other countries including South Korea, Qatar, and Saudi Arabia (World Health Organization, 2015a).

So what's going on? Why is the MMR in the United States increasing instead of falling with advancements in medical technology? One reason is obvious; American women are experiencing a decrease in access to prenatal care and medical services essential to safe childbirth. Why is such access decreasing? First, health care costs are increasing (Clemens, 2017). Second, poor women are receiving less in public assistance (Moffitt, Ribar, & Wilhelm, 1998; Semuels, 2016). Third, federal and state government actions are limiting women's access to essential reproductive health care offered through organizations like Planned Parenthood (Alonso-Zaldivar & Crary, 2018; Vestal, 2017). Many states have passed legislation limiting government funding for Planned Parenthood and women's health care in the battle to restrict girls' and women's options for contraception and abortion. Such actions are based on assertions that life is sacred, that life begins at conception, that women are supposed to expect to reproduce when they have sex, that unwanted pregnancies are some kind of magical gift from a supernatural force or a punishment for having sex for pleasure. These beliefs are based on religious ideology; outside of religious ideas, these assertions have no weight, are not based on evidence, and are actually false. Unfortunately, such patriarchal, archaic, mystical beliefs are affecting the health and well-being of millions of women, especially poor women, as religiously motivated politicians make decisions about women's bodies and choices. The modern Republican Party in the United States opposes contraception and abortion (RepublicanViews.org, 2014).

So why are the religious beliefs of a few being imposed on everyone, including women and girls who don't share or care about someone else's religious beliefs? I assert, once again, that such ideas are myths that legitimize women's oppression. Requiring women to be merely "two-legged wombs" (Atwood, 1986), against a woman's own will for her own life, is patriarchal at best, life-threatening at worst. Every American is guaranteed freedom of (or from) religion in the First Amendment of the U.S. Constitution. Every American is also guaranteed the rights to life, liberty, and the pursuit of happiness. As such, I and every American have a right to ignore any religious beliefs in my own decisions (First Amendment), a right to not be unfairly restricted by the government (liberty), a right to not endanger my life through pregnancy (life), and a right to pursue my own goals, my own desires (pursuit of happiness). Politicians, mainly wealthy white men, are continuing to restrict the rights of women for their own interests, which obviously includes their continued domination over half the human race.

BONUS BOX

The Safety of Children's Athletics

Professional and amateur sports programs generate billions and billions of dollars all over the world. And part of being an athlete or playing a sport is taking risks, especially physical risks. Race car drivers (is that a sport?), boxers, skiers, for example, literally put their lives in danger for their sport, to compete at the highest levels. In return, some professional athletes earn millions and millions of dollars for the talent they have cultivated over entire lifetimes. Is all of this money, this thrill and excitement, worth the physical dangers, the potential for long-term damage, even the possibility of death? Certainly there are professional athletes who would argue that not following their passion is akin to death, that they would rather die doing something they love than live without it. But what about children? Like for all humans, there are numerous positive benefits to children and adolescents from engaging in athletic activities, including improved cardiovascular health, lower body fat, decreased anxiety and depression, positive self-concept, and improved academic performance (Strong et al., 2005). Yet to become a professional athlete, one must begin the sport in earnest during childhood, probably the earlier the better to really develop talent. How much choice and power do children have to decide for themselves whether or not to engage in sports that are dangerous, especially to their developing bodies and minds?

Research on children's football indicates that football is a leading cause of sports-related childhood injuries (Shankar et al., 2007). Children who play soccer are also at high risk for head injuries, broken bones, and permanent injuries (Yard et al., 2008). Gymnastics is particularly damaging to the back and spine and may disturb physical growth (Maffulli, Longo, Gougoulias, Loppini, & Denaro, 2010; Theintz, Howald, Allemann, & Sizonenko, 1989). Children suffer long-term injuries from sports (Maffulli, Longo, Spiezia, & Denaro, 2015). It is extremely important for parents to be informed about the dangers of children's sports. Fortunately, more parents and adolescent athletes are paying attention to the realities of concussions and other injuries, especially younger child athletes and parents who use the internet more frequently (Bloodgood et al., 2013). While recognizing the benefits of professional sports (money, entertainment, fame), individuals, parents, and society as a whole must weight those benefits against the real costs of children's athletics. Sadly, today in Western, highly individualistic cultures, it seems that money and profits trump almost everything, including our children's psychological and physical well-being.

Defining Personality

Personality is difficult to define, and personality theorists have disagreed about the nature of personality for decades. There are many theoretical and philosophical approaches to understanding personality, including dispositional (trait), biological, intrapsychic (inside the mind), and adjustment (health) approaches (see Table 9.1). Scholars also disagree about the best ways to study personality. Some argue for an idiographic approach that emphasizes individual uniqueness and

Table 9.1 Approaches to understanding personality

Dispositional Approach ("trait approach"): focuses on "individual differences." A central goal is to identify and measure the most important ways in which individual personalities differ.

Biological Approach: focuses on biological and physiological processes in affecting human personality. Three major areas of interest within this approach include behavioral genetics; physiological psychology and neuroscience; and evolutionary psychology.

Intrapsychic Approach: focuses on mental mechanisms of personality, including those occurring outside of consciousness. Freud's approach is intrapsychic, emphasizing psychic conflict and structures (Id, Ego, Superego).

Cognitive-Experiential Approach: focuses on cognitive processes and subjective experiences in determining personality. Individual phenomenology is important.

Social and Cultural Approach: focuses on cultural influences and socialization in the development of personality.

Adjustment Approach: focuses on the role of personality in psychological health, coping, happiness.

---

complexity. Methodology is rather qualitative, taking a holistic approach to understanding each person in-depth. Methods include diary studies, interviews, review of personal records, examination of living spaces, and so on. These kinds of approaches spend a long time investigating each individual person. Other scholars argue for a nomothetic approach to understanding human personality, which involves applying quantitative measurements to examine individual differences across large groups of people. A quantitative approach is a numerical approach; participants complete various measures of personality (questionnaires, behavioral tasks, etc.) and a score is applied to their responses. For example, many people are asked the same question, "I care about being on time," using the same response scale (e.g., 1 = *not at all like me*; 2 = *somewhat like me*; 3 = *moderately like me*; 4 = *very much like me*). A person's responses across many different items are then averaged to indicate an average item response. This approach examines many people at once using quantitative measures.

The oldest and most productive approach to understanding personality is the dispositional or trait approach. Modernly, most personality scholars study traits using a quantitative, nomothetic approach. Some scholars who take a trait approach argue for a multifaceted approach to personality that involves many different individual traits and qualities. Others assert that there are only a few major dimensions of personality that are responsible for most individual differences in qualities, traits, and abilities.

A simple definition of personality for our purposes is each individual person's unique and characteristic ways of thinking, behaving, and feeling (Funder, 1997). This definition emphasizes the uniqueness of individual personality (each person is genuinely unique) and also that personality is characteristic (a person can be described in ways they consistently or characteristically behave, across situations and across time).

Personality scholars today tend to agree that there are a few major personality traits that can account for a multitude of differences between people in terms of their characteristic thoughts, behaviors, and feelings. Traits are words that describe how people are different; although there are many words that we can use to describe people, words that describe similar qualities (e.g., orderly, organized, hard-working, responsible; anxious, depressed, fearful, stressed) can be clustered into larger categories that reflect broader, more important traits. These major traits are the underlying forces within a person that are responsible for many different behaviors they may

Personality, Emotions, and Health

Table 9.2 Cattell's 16 basic source traits (1966)

1. Outgoing – Reserved
2. More intelligent – Less intelligent
3. High ego strength – Low ego strength
4. Assertive – Humble
5. Happy-go-lucky – Sober
6. Strong conscience–Lack of internal standards
7. Adventuresome – Shy
8. Tough-minded – Tender-minded
9. Trusting – Suspicious
10. Imaginative – Practical
11. Shrewd – Forthright
12. Apprehensive – Self-assured
13. Experimental – Conservative
14. Group-dependent – Self-sufficient
15. Casual – Controlled
16. Relaxed – Tense

display. It is helpful here to differentiate between what are called **surface traits** and what are called **source traits**. **Surface traits** are behavioral manifestations of major personality dimensions; they are behaviors that are driven by major personality dimensions. For example, making your bed in the morning, paying your bills on time, turning in work by assigned deadlines, cleaning up after yourself are all behavioral manifestations of the same major trait. The major trait is the **source trait**, the underlying, latent force within the person that is responsible for all of those behaviors. Raymond Cattell was the first personality theorist to point out this distinction (Cattell, Cattell, & Rhymer, 1947). Cattell asserted that to describe Dave as being lazy because he is lazy is circular (tautological) reasoning; the argument and the evidence to support it are the same thing. Instead, Cattell said Dave's behavior is lazy because he is low in **Ego Strength** (psychosocial maturity and adjustment; Gfellner & Armstrong, 2012), one of 16 major dimensions of personality identified by Cattell (1943; see Table 9.2).

A primary research method used to identify major dimensions of personality may also be attributed to Cattell and his colleague, Charles Spearman, the method of **factor analysis** (Cattell, 1945). Factor analysis is a statistical technique based on correlation. Responses to many self-report items assessing personality traits (e.g., "I like to go to social events"; "I feel anxious when I am late"; "I am a responsible person") are examined in terms of how they are correlated with each other. Items that are highly correlated with each other represent a cluster of related responses; the responses are reflective of the same thing, the same underlying quality. These correlated responses (assessments of surface traits) are hypothesized to represent an underlying latent dimension of personality, a source trait. Items that are not correlated with each other are surface representations of different underlying dimensions. For example, any individual person's responses to multiple questions about being anxious, fearful, and emotional, are likely to be similar to each other. Their responses to questions about making their bed daily and paying their bills on time will not be correlated with questions about being anxious and emotional (see Table 9.3). Dimensions represented by clusters of responses are then named by the researcher, depending on their content. For example, the factor representing responses to questions about being anxious and emotional could be called **Emotional Stability**; the factor representing responses to questions about being orderly and on time could be called **Conscientiousness**. In fact, these two

Table 9.3 Sample correlation matrix reflecting clusters of related responses (factors).

	I make my bed	I pay bills on time	I am responsible	I am anxious	I am fearful
I pay my bills on time	.41***				
I am responsible	.48***	.50***			
I am anxious	.05	.04	-.02		
I am fearful	.02	-.01	.03	.57***	
I am emotional	-.03	.05	.04	.46***	.61***

***p < .001.

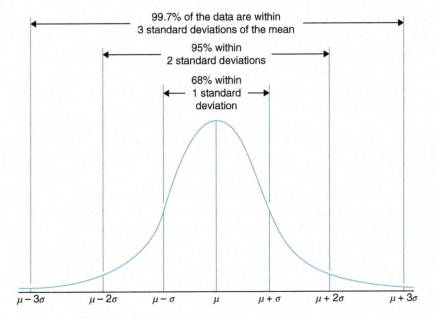

Figure 9.1 The normal distribution

major dimensions of personality and three others have been identified by personality scientists as capturing most of the individual differences we see in thoughts, feelings, and behavior, among most people around the world.

The Five Factor Model of Personality

The **Five Factor Model** (FFM, aka the Big Five; McCrae & Costa, 1987) of personality is the major trait approach to understanding human personality in Psychology today. The Big Five factors were identified through repeated studies using factor analysis revealing the same five personality dimensions. Each of the five major dimensions is represented by six behavioral facets of the trait (Costa & McCrae, 1992). The five dimensions are indeed dimensions; they are normally distributed in the population, with rather few people being very high or very low on any particular trait, and most people possessing a moderate amount of any trait (Cobb-Clark & Schurer, 2012) (see Figure 9.1). The five traits can easily be remembered using the word OCEAN; the traits are

260 *Personality, Emotions, and Health*

Openness to Experience, Conscientiousness, Extraversion, Agreeableness, and **Neuroticism** (now more commonly referred to as **Emotional Stability**, but that ruins the OCEAN thing).

The trait of **Extraversion** largely represents sociability and social energy; the six facets are warmth, gregariousness, assertiveness, activity, excitement-seeking, and positive emotions. People who are high on extraversion are active, positive, cheerful, energetic, and enjoy social interactions and activities. People who are lower on extraversion are called **introverted**; they are quieter, withdrawn, and cautious. They prefer solitary activities. Extraverts are confident, enthusiastic, happy, and optimistic (Bono & Judge, 2004). Scholars assert that "compared to introverts, extraverts view themselves as more effectively and pleasurably engaged in various aspects of their lives" (Lee & Clark, 1997, p. 767).

The trait of **Agreeableness** can largely be thought of as friendliness, with facets involving trust, straightforwardness, altruism, compliance, modesty, and tender-mindedness. Highly agreeable people are forthright, trusting, not arrogant, high in empathy, and compassionate. People lower on this trait are **disagreeable**; they are suspicious, mistrusting of others, low in compassion, not helpful, and not cooperative. Children higher in agreeableness earn higher grades and have fewer behavior problems than children low in agreeableness. Adults lower in agreeableness are more likely to be arrested, to be depressed, and to suffer from alcoholism than adults higher in agreeableness (Laursen, Pulkkinen, & Adams, 2002).

The major trait of **Conscientiousness** is the degree to which a person is hard-working and responsible. The six facets for conscientiousness are competence, order, dutifulness, achievement striving, self-discipline, deliberation. People high in conscientiousness are high achievers; they work hard, meet their obligations, care about achieving, and are thoughtful and careful in their actions. People low in this trait are unreliable; they are not high achievers, have job difficulties, and are not motivated toward achievement. Low conscientiousness is linked with procrastination (Watson, 2001), while high conscientiousness is positively predictive of achievement motivation and grades earned in college (Komarraju, Karau, & Schmeck, 2009), career success (Gelissen & Graaf, 2006; Schmidt & Hunter, 1992), healthy behaviors and lifestyle (Bogg & Roberts, 2004), and longevity (Kern et al., 2009).

The major trait of **Emotional Stability** (aka **Neuroticism**) is about stability of one's emotions over the day and in response to stress. The term neuroticism has a negative connotation, being derived from Freud's conceptualization of neuroses (fixations of psychological energy on unresolved needs in childhood; Freud, 1918). People high in neuroticism are highly emotional. The six facets here are anxiety, angry hostility, depression, self-consciousness, impulsiveness, and vulnerability. People high in this trait act impulsively based on their very strong emotions, especially in response to stress. They are anxious and fearful and can react with anger when stressed or afraid. They are prone to depression and are easily hurt (**vulnerable**). They are high in private **self-consciousness**, which is a tendency to look inward at the self as an object of attention and focus (Carver & Scheier, 1981). Such inward focus often leads to **rumination**, a dwelling on one's emotions that can amplify emotional distress (Newman & Nezlek, 2019). In contrast, people higher in emotional stability are low on all of these facets; they are even-tempered, laid back, not easily stressed with few highly emotional responses to anything. This dimension could just as easily be called Emotionally Cold versus Emotionally Hot, which would have a more positive connotation toward being higher in Emotional Hotness!

Finally, the trait of **Openness** involves just that, one's openness to different experiences in terms of fantasy, aesthetics, feelings, actions, ideas, and values. People who are always seeking new experiences, open to all kinds of art and music, politically and ideologically open-minded,

Personality, Emotions, and Health 261

with an imaginative, sophisticated way of thinking are high in openness (McCrae, 1987). Openness to experience is linked with intelligence and some theorists assert that they are virtually the same (McCrae & Costa, 1997). People who are more down-to-earth, more interested in stability and habits and doing the same things again and again? They are lower in openness. As your author, I will reveal that I am rather low on this trait. I am very open-minded and enjoy intellectual activities, but when I'm having Mexican food, it's the number 7 every time (beef taco, cheese enchilada). <u>Every single time</u>. People lower on openness are not as open to new experiences, sometimes because they really want what they already like.

The Big Five dimensions have been identified around the world, across cultures (McCrae & Allik, 2002). In other words, these five qualities are universal dimensions of human behavior. The expression and distribution of such traits will certainly vary across cultures (McCrae et al., 2005); but they exist to characterize the behavior of most people most of the time around the world. The Big Five traits have even been identified in non-human primates, chimpanzees to be precise, along with a sixth personality dimension of dominance (King, Weiss, & Farmer, 2005). A newer approach to personality indicates the same five major traits as the FFM, but includes a sixth dimension reflecting **Honesty-Humility**. This is the **HEXACO** model, indicating major traits of Honesty-Humility (H), Emotionality (E), Extraversion (X), Agreeableness (A), Conscientiousness (C), and Openness (O). The Honesty-Humility dimension describes qualities involving lower and higher degrees of modesty, sincerity, and fairness (Lee & Ashton, 2004). The HEXACO model is based on a **lexical process** where thousands of adjectives describing human traits, qualities, and attributes in multiple languages are grouped into larger, meaningful categories (Ashton et al., 2004; Ashton, Lee, & Goldberg, 2004). This model is useful in examining major personality traits (de Vries & van Gelder, 2015; Rolison, Hanoch, & Gummerum, 2013).

Biological Bases of Personality

Another trait approach to personality is extremely important because it links biologically-based, physiological processes to major personality traits. A notable practitioner and personality scholar, Hans Eysenck (1947, 1958, 1983), asserted in his **biosocial approach** to personality that much of personality is determined by essential biological processes involving arousal. Eysenck built on the work of ancient philosophers and physicians, including Hippocrates (from around 450 BCE) and Galen (130–200 CE). Both of these physicians asserted that human personality is controlled by the **body humors** of blood, phlegm, yellow bile, and black bile, each of which was believed to be associated with particular qualities and emotions. A person's personality was thought to be dominated by whichever body humor was most prevalent throughout the body. Galen indicated that a person with a predominance of blood was **sanguine** in character, cheerful, hearty, happy. A person with a predominance of phlegm is called **phlegmatic**, a person who is thoughtful, quiet, analytical. Someone with a predominance of yellow bile is called **choleric**, which means hot-tempered, irascible, irritable. Those with a predominance of black bile are **melancholic**, sad, depressive, with low energy.

Eysenck also relied on the early work of Wilhelm Wundt, who asserted that dimensions of arousal related to **changeability** (changes in excitation in the body, physical and cognitive arousal) and **emotionality** (how easily emotionally aroused a person is, emotional arousal) are the forces behind human personality (see Figure 9.2). Eysenck agreed, and he asserted that the major trait of Extraversion is largely determined by activity of the entire **central nervous system** (**CNS**), but particularly CNS structures related to overall arousal. Eysenck identified the

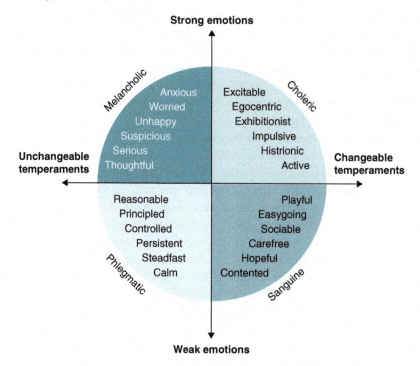

Figure 9.2 Eysenck's model of Extraversion (changeability) and Neuroticism (emotionality) as dimensions

brain structure called the **reticular formation** and its associated structures which comprise the **ascending reticular activating system** (**ARAS**). The ARAS controls overall excitation and arousal of the body. It controls consciousness and as such is important for sleep and attention. The ARAS determines how much excitation is allowed within the body at any one time. During sleep, the ARAS is activated and shutting off nearly all excitation of the body. During periods of peak energy, the ARAS is allowing high excitation into the brain from the body and sensory stimulation. This physiological process is not readily subject to conscious control; there is a baseline functioning of the ARAS that is unique to each person. Eysenck argued that this baseline functioning of the ARAS is responsible for the individual differences we see in the major trait of Extraversion.

Now here's the tricky part (sort of). Eysenck stated that individuals who are high in Extraversion (they show sociability, high activity, liveliness, impulsivity) have an ARAS that has strong inhibitory mechanisms (it actively prevents too much excitation), and weak excitatory mechanisms (the ARAS is not easily excited). The Extravert is actually suffering a rather low level of baseline arousal and needs much stimulation to increase excitation. Because their ARAS is preventing excitation from within, the Extravert seeks stimulation from the environment. Extraverts want the volume up, the top down, smoking a cigarette and drinking coffee while driving to Las Vegas to gamble and party. They are often higher in **sensation-seeking**, a quality involving seeking out a variety of new experiences that are high in complexity and intensity (Bone & Montgomery, 1970; Zuckerman, 2009). People lower in Extraversion, the Introverts, have an ARAS with opposite qualities; it has weak inhibitory mechanisms and strong excitatory mechanisms. Introverts are already cognitively and physically aroused, inside. They are easily overwhelmed by too much

Personality, Emotions, and Health   263

stimulation and thus must actively, in their conscious behavior, protect themselves and limit the amount of stimulation they receive from the environment. They show a stronger preference for quiet, solitary activities, because they're doing just fine thank you, and no, they don't need to hang out.

Eysenck also focused on individual differences in emotionality in describing personality and biological and physiological processes involved in the experience of emotions. Eysenck suggested that the **visceral brain**, the **limbic system**, mid-brain structures involved in regulating needs (thirst, hunger, sex) and emotions, are responsible for the major trait of Neuroticism. Specific mid-brain structures involved in regulating emotions are the **amygdala** (important for anger and fear, fight-or-flight responses) and the **hypothalamus** (controls hormone release, needs, emotions). According to Eysenck, some persons are born with mid-brain structures that are very sensitive, very easily aroused, easily activated. These individuals are thus likely to experience emotions more frequently and more intensely. Other people have mid-brain structures that are comparatively less sensitive, not easily activated, not easily aroused. The person with sensitive, arousable mid-brain structures is thus higher in Neuroticism and has lower Emotional Stability. The person with a not easily aroused mid-brain is low key, easygoing, not readily upset or emotionally aroused (see Figures 9.3a and 9.3b).

Eysenck (1983) argued for the existence of a third major trait of personality, that of **Psychoticism**. Individuals high in Psychoticism are emotionally cold, tough-minded, unempathic. They are egocentric, impersonal, aggressive, even antisocial. People who are low on Psychoticism are not like this. Eysenck asserted that unlike the major traits of Extraversion and Neuroticism, Psychoticism is not normally distributed in the population, but is positively skewed, with most people scoring rather low on Psychoticism (see Figure 9.4). Psychoticism is a rather frightening quality, and it can be seen as overlapping to some degree with **Antisocial Personality Disorder**, which involves a persistent pattern of behavior involving rule-breaking, criminality, deceitfulness, aggressiveness, irresponsibility, and disregard for the feelings of others (Berg et al., 2013). People with Antisocial Personality Disorder (which occurs more commonly in men; Cale & Lilienfeld, 2002) have little remorse for hurting others. The Honesty-Humility dimension of the HEXACO model can be seen as involving similar qualities, with low scores on H linked with criminality (Rolison et al., 2013), self-control (de Vries & van Gelder, 2015), counterproductive academic behavior (Schwager, Hülsheger, & Lang, 2016), dishonesty (Hilbig & Zettler, 2015), and risk-taking (Burtaverde, Chraif, Anitei, & Dumitru, 2017). Eysenck (1983) suggested that the influence of **androgens** (male hormones) may be important for this trait, especially in terms of aggressiveness. Men around the world are higher in Psychoticism than women (Lynn & Martin, 1997).

Hormones, Emotions, and Personality

Are hormones linked with aggression? The answer is very clearly yes. Although we discuss more about this link in Chapter 11, it bears repeating, that naturalistic and laboratory studies support a causal link between the male hormone **testosterone** and aggressive behavior. Experimental studies using animals and injecting them with testosterone indicate that increasing blood levels of testosterone increases aggressive behavior (Allee, Collias, & Lutherman, 1939; Beeman, 1947; Ewing et al., 1979). Experimental studies injecting human beings with testosterone show similar results, with aggressive behavior increasing along with testosterone (Bos, Panksepp, Bluthé, & van Honk, 2012). With men on average having about seven to eight times the blood testosterone of women (Torjesen & Sandnes, 2004), there is an obvious difference in aggressive behavior

Figures 9.3a and 9.3b People lower in Neuroticism are higher in emotional stability and show more positive emotions (top) than people higher in Neuroticism (bottom)
Source: AntonioGuillem/iStock Photo and Petko Ninov/iStock Photo

associated with this physically and psychologically important hormone. Individuals with higher than average levels of testosterone, whether naturally or because of ingesting it, will characteristically behave more aggressively, showing a more aggressive personality (see Figure 9.5). If this higher level is stable or continues over time, the person will be seen as having an aggressive personality, high in Psychoticism.

Another hormone that is critical for human behavior is **oxytocin**. Oxytocin is a hormone that is involved in female and male sexuality, childbirth, and breastfeeding. Oxytocin is essentially the

Personality, Emotions, and Health 265

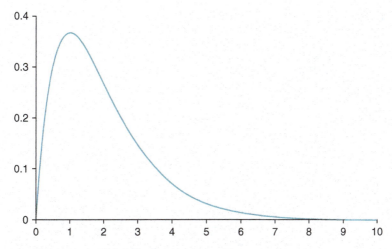

Figure 9.4 A positively skewed distribution

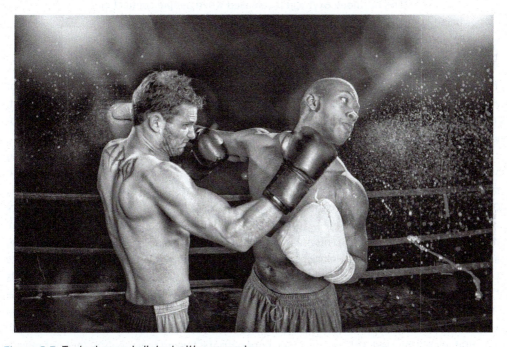

Figure 9.5 Testosterone is linked with aggression
Source: Owen Price/iStock Photo

physiological foundation of the emotions involved in **bonding**, the development of a close affectional tie with another being (Ainsworth, 1978; Bowlby, 1969, 1973). Bonding is based on trust and concern for each other's welfare and well-being (Maud, Ryan, McIntosh, & Olsson, 2018). Oxytocin is released by the pituitary gland, controlled by the hypothalamus. It is released during orgasm for both sexes (Carmichael et al., 1987; Carmichael, Warburton, Dixen, & Davidson, 1994), and is essential to childbirth and breastfeeding (World Health Organization, 2009). And because nature is miraculous, childbirth and breastfeeding promote bonding with the baby.

266 *Personality, Emotions, and Health*

Figure 9.6 The bonding hormone oxytocin is released when people connect closely with another being
Source: Fotografixx/iStock Photo

A healthy bond with a primary caregiver is essential for the psychological health and wellness of every human being (Bowlby, 1980; Chaffin et al., 2006; Donnellan, Trzesniewski, Robins, Moffitt, & Caspi, 2005; Passmore, Fogarty, Bourke, & Baker-Evans, 2005) (see Chapter 10). Oxytocin promotes this essential foundation for self-esteem, trust in others, and self-love.

When people are in close intimate interaction with someone they trust, it feels good. Hugging someone you love is pleasurable. Having an orgasm with another person also feels good. Oxytocin makes it feel good, that's why it is now popularly referred to as the "love hormone" (Grillon et al., 2013) (see Figure 9.6). Oxytocin underlies feelings of trust, affection, empathy, and generosity toward others (Cardoso, Ellenbogen, Serravalle, & Linnen, 2013; Lane et al., 2013; Sheng, Liu, Zhou, Zhou, & Han, 2013; Zak, Stanton, & Ahmadi, 2007), whether they are close intimates (e.g., partners, children, best friends; Heinrichs, Baumgartner, Kirschbaum, & Ehlert, 2003) or members of a larger social group (Shalvi & De Dreu, 2014). Dogs and their owners show increased levels of oxytocin in the blood after engaging in petting, play, and other bonding behaviors (Odendaal & Meintjes, 2003). People engaged in nurturing behaviors produce oxytocin, especially women (Jankowski et al., 2004; Kendrick, 2004; van Leengoed, Kerker, & Swanson, 1987). Research indicates that people injected with oxytocin feel more patriotic toward their country (but not toward other countries) (Ma et al., 2014). Oxytocin increases protective behaviors toward one's ingroup, especially during conflict (De Dreu, Shalvi, Greer, Van Kleef, & Handgraaf, 2012); and modulates feelings of fear and anxiety (Kirsch et al., 2005; McCarthy, 1995; Theodoridou, Penton-Voak, & Rowe, 2013). Oxytocin appears to have anti-depressive effects as well (Matsuzaki, Matsushita, Tomizawa, & Matsui, 2012).

Estrogens stimulate the production of oxytocin (Lischke et al., 2012), and testosterone suppresses oxytocin (Okabe, Kitano, Nagasawa, Mogi, & Kikusui, 2013), so women produce more and have more oxytocin in their blood than men. As such, women are physiologically primed to be higher in emotions and behaviors involved in trust, nurturance, empathy, and generosity. Because estrogens increase the effects of oxytocin (Fahrbach, Morrell, & Pfaff, 1985; McCarthy,

Personality, Emotions, and Health   267

1995), women and men respond differently to oxytocin. When women and men are given oxytocin, women respond more quickly to social bonding behaviors than men (Lischke et al., 2012; Theodoridou et al., 2013). Women who are administered oxytocin show a greater amygdala response to fearful stimuli; this response is not found in men. Testosterone decreases oxytocin (Okabe et al., 2013), which some argue is evolutionarily adaptive as it decreases empathy and makes aggression against others (primarily other males over sexual access) easier for men and more likely to be successful (Hurlemann et al., 2010). Differences in the genes that encode for oxytocin production are linked with aggressive (Malik, Zai, Abu, Nowrouzi, & Beitchman, 2012) and antisocial behavior (Smearman, Winiarski, Brennan, & Naj, 2015).

Behavioral Genetics: Understanding Genes and Behavior

Behavioral genetics is a scientific discipline which examines the heritability of behavioral qualities and characteristics. Heritability refers to the degree to which traits can be attributed to the operation of genes inherited from parents (see Chapter 3). Do you look like your mother or father? Is your nose more like your mom's or your dad's? People readily acknowledge that physical qualities, how tall we are, hair and eye color, face and body shapes, and so on, are determined by the operation of genes, the molecular units of heredity. But what about behavioral qualities? What about the way you respond to the pain of other people, the way you deal with disagreements, the anxiety (or lack thereof) that you feel when you're faced with challenges, the degree to which you enjoy social gatherings, how many friends you have, how you feel when someone rejects you, whether you make your bed and organize your closet? Are these ways of thinking, behaving, and feeling heritable, or influenced by your genes?

If body structures (like the ARAS and the mid-brain) and hormones (like oxytocin and testosterone) have an influence on personality, that suggests a role of genes. Parents and children may be similar to each other in their emotionality because they share genes that affect morphology and function of mid-brain structures. Similarly, at birth, if the ARAS has particularly inhibitory and excitatory mechanisms, that would also suggest a role of genes. Behavioral geneticists have concluded that genes are linked with personality and many other behavioral qualities, using family studies and the twin design. The basic assertion is that people with greater genetic similarity will be more similar in personality than those with fewer shared genes. Parents and children are 50% genetically similar, as are first-degree siblings (same two biological parents). Grandparents and grandchildren share 25% of their genes. Adoptive relatives share 0 genes. Monozygotic twins (one egg, one sperm; MZ) are 100% genetically identical; dizygotic twins (two eggs, two sperm; DZ) are just like first-degree siblings genetically (50%) but are the same age, can be the same sex, and they are "twinny" (treated like twins). By examining different living arrangements of people of differing degrees of genetic relatedness, behavioral geneticists can partial out the roles of genes (G) and the environment (E) in accounting for personality.

A typical family is genetically related and lives together in the same environment, a complete confounding of G and E together, making it nearly impossible to separate them out. So behavioral geneticists have tried other designs. Adoption designs examine adoptive relatives living together (all E, no G) and biological relatives (parents and offspring, twins) adopted apart (all G, no E). Most notable are studies examining identical (MZ) twins who were adopted apart at birth. These twins, who have never known each other, are highly similar in many qualities including personality (Tellegen et al., 1988). Another method is called the twin method, and involves comparing trait similarities between MZ and DZ twins. If MZ twins are more similar to each other on a trait than

DZ twins, those similarities must be caused by genes, particularly given the similarities in how twin pairs are treated.

Using these methods, behavioral geneticists have concluded that personality and many other behavioral qualities are indeed heritable. The major traits of personality (the Big Five) are each about 40-50% attributable to genes we inherited from our parents. In other words, about 40-50% of the variability in these traits across individuals can be attributed to the operations of our genes; they are 40-50% heritable (Henderson, 1982; Jang, Livesley, & Vemon, 1996; Plomin, De-Fries, McClearn, & Rutter, 2008) (see Chapter 3). Psychoticism is also about 40-50% heritable (Fulker, 1981; Martin & Jardine, 1986; Young, Eaves, & Eysenck, 1980), which also supports the rather high heritability of aggression and criminal behavior (although shared environment is also very important for these traits) (Coccaro, Bergeman, Kavoussi, & Seroczynski, 1997). Even conservatism and traditionalism have been found to be at least 50% heritable (Bouchard et al., 2003). Mental health problems and alcoholism also have genetic components (McGuffin, Katz, Watkins, & Rutherford, 1996; Sartor et al., 2012; Verhulst, Neale, & Kendler, 2015). Based on the clear evidence supporting genetic contributions to personality, evolutionary theorists assert that various identifiable human personality qualities have evolved over time because they enhance the ability of our species to survive and reproduce (Buss, 2009).

The Environment and Socialization of Personality

While most scholars acknowledge the role of genes and their biological and physiological out-comes in affecting personality, the role of socialization and one's living environment from birth until death has a huge impact on personality. Remember, Eysenck's model was called **biosocial**, because he recognized the equally powerful impacts of biological and social processes. One cannot overestimate the importance of money in affecting well-being in today's world. **Poverty** is the experience of daily deprivation because of a lack of personal money required for basic needs in a society. The **poverty threshold** (the "poverty line," an annual income below which one is considered poor) in the U.S. is currently around $15,000.00 per year for a single person of working age. Over 43 million Americans are currently poor, most of them single women with children, elderly, and disabled (Semega, Fotenot, & Kollar, 2017). Of those people, 18.5 million are living in **deep poverty** (annual income is below 50% of poverty threshold) (Lei, 2013). Over 750 million people around the world are living in poverty (Atkinson, 2016) (see Figures 9.7a and 9.7b). Poverty has powerful, myriad, negative effects for everyone, and is exceedingly harmful to child development. Poor children are malnourished; food and water quality are much lower in poor neighborhoods in developed countries, everywhere in undeveloped regions of the world. Poor children experience lower quality education (if they even get an opportunity for education) and lower quality health care (again, if any). Their environments are full of dangers; cheap construction, pestilence and poisons, higher crime rates, adults who abuse substances and abuse the kids. All of this contributes over time to making poor children exponentially more at risk for poor physical, cognitive, and emotional development, and poor physical, cognitive, and emotional outcomes in adulthood (Evans, 2004).

Cultural influences are also important for personality development, as children learn and observe others behaving (Triandis & Suh, 2002). The living environment, including its ecology (climate, terrain, natural resources, etc.) and primary economic structures (means of production, subsistence patterns), affect childrearing practices and socialization patterns and practices (Bond & Smith, 1996; Maccoby, 2000; O'Kelly & Carney, 1986; Triandis, 1996; Van de

Figures 9.7a and 9.7b **Images of poverty**
Source: Kaetana/iStock Photo and Mazzzur/iStock Photo

Vliert, Schwartz, Huismans, Hofstede, & Daan, 1999). The cultural dimension of **individualism-collectivism** is linked with various features of personality (Triandis & Suh, 2002). For example, people from individualistic cultures (which emphasize individual achievement and success) are more likely to describe themselves as assertive, pleasure-seeking, and independent compared to individuals from more collectivistic cultures (which emphasize group goals and harmony) (Grimm, Church, Katigbak, & Reyes, 1999). People from collectivistic cultures report less optimism (Lee & Seligman, 1997) and lower self-esteem (Heine, Lehman, Markus, & Kitayama, 1999) than those from individualistic cultures, who also report greater subjective well-being (Suh, 2000). The positive emotions of people in individualistic cultures are more about the self (e.g., feeling proud, superior), while people in collectivistic cultures report more frequent positive emotions in terms of relationships with others (e.g., feeling close with others, feeling respect for others) (Kitayama, Markus, & Kurokawa, 2000). Approval from others is predictive of life satisfaction among people from collectivistic cultures, while positive emotions (personal happiness) are more predictive of life satisfaction for people from individualistic cultures (Suh et al., 1998).

Parenting beginning in early childhood is crucial for children's psychological outcomes, especially for **attachment** and children's sense of trust (Ainsworth, 1978). If parents are loving, kind, and responsive to their children, providing for their basic needs, the child's healthy personality development will be supported. A basic premise of **social learning/cognitive theory** is that children learn through observation, particularly of parents and other important role models (Bandura, 1997, 2001). Children develop qualities they observe in their parents' behaviors, including characteristic ways of thinking, feeling, and behaving. Research generally indicates that when parents behave in ways that are loving, kind, accepting, and affectionate toward the child and others, children develop positive, moderate personality qualities, including sociability, high self-esteem, emotional stability, and a positive view of others and the world. When parents are hostile, abusive, and unresponsive to their children, children's personality development is impaired and traits like hostility, aggression, immaturity, low self-esteem, and a negative view of others and the world are more likely (Rohner, 1986, 1999). All children need love and real acceptance from their parents, only one reason why it is so critical to be a *wanted* child (Safonova & Leparsky, 1998). The children of women who are single, young, poor, and who have few warm, positive feelings toward their children are at much greater risk for physical abuse, sexual abuse, and neglect than children born to mothers who want them and are financially and emotionally ready to be mothers (Brown, Cohen, Johnson, & Salinger, 1998).

Developmental theories of gender, like **gender schema theory**, emphasize the socialization of femininity and masculinity, beginning before birth as parents prepare the child's room, clothing, toys, and books. Gender schema formation begins early in life, in infancy, as we have seen in studies showing infant ability to distinguish between genders (Leinbach & Fagot, 1993) and infant gaze preference for gender-congruent toys (Campbell et al., 2000; Lauer et al., 2015). Young children show clear knowledge of gender stereotypes within their culture and emphasize gender in describing people (Berk, 2009; Gelman, Taylor, & Nguyen, 2004). Parents begin to socialize children as their assigned gender at birth, modifying their behaviors and environments to emphasize the child's gender (Clearfield & Nelson, 2006; Pomerleau et al., 1990). Parents emphasize gender-congruent toys and play activities (Caldera, Huston, and O'Brien, 1989; Idle, Wood, & Desmarais, 1993), which inform gender stereotypes, roles, and norms for children (Bem, 1984; Martin & Halverson, 1981). Parents implicitly and explicitly, behaviorally, emotionally, and verbally, instruct children on expectations for their behavior along gender lines (Bulanda, 2004). More traditional parents engage in family roles clearly delineated by gender, with mothers engaged in caretaking and fathers engaged in decision-making (Turner & Gervai, 1995). Parents who are highly traditional in their gender roles are likely to encourage children's development of traditional gender ideology (Kane, 2009; Riggio & Desrochers, 2006). Requiring children and young people to follow rigid gender stereotypes for the sake of tradition (aka maintaining **patriarchy**) can cause long-lasting damage, including negative feelings about the self and one's abilities, poor social development, and limitations on educational and career aspirations (Liben, Bigler, & Krogh, 2002; Rainey & Rust, 1999). Parents who demonstrate equality and egalitarian values within the family and society teach their children that women and men are equally valuable and important. They demonstrate **egalitarianism** by showing that their family and social roles are interchangeable, equally valued, and not determined by gender (Perrone-McGovern, Wright, Howell, & Barnum, 2014).

Media portrayals of women and men are highly stereotypical, emphasizing women's physical attractiveness and bodies (Bernard, Gervais, Allen, Campomizzi, & Klein, 2012, 2015; Coltrane & Messineo, 2000; Conley & Ramsey, 2011), men's accomplishments, strengths, characters, and faces (Archer et al., 1983). Of interest here is the media socialization of femininity and masculinity, especially the contrast between passive, weak, submissive women and active, strong, dominant men. Women who are sexually objectified in media, which is more common than not, are perceived as less intelligent, less competent, and weaker and more passive (Cikara, Eberhardt, & Fiske, 2011; Heflick, Goldenberg, Cooper, & Puvia, 2011; Vaes, Paladino, & Puvia, 2011). Men are commonly portrayed as forceful, decisive, active leaders and heroes (Ben-Zeev, Scharnetzki, Chan, & Dennehy, 2012; Sparks, 1996), while women are portrayed as passive (Lithgow, 2000) and less competent than men (Serini, Powers, & Johnson, 1998; Gidengil & Everitt, 1999; Scharrer, 2002). Women's starring roles often emphasize their relationships with men, not themselves in their own right (Scharrer, 2004). Women in historically accurate films are of course portrayed as passive, weak, and subordinate much of the time, as those behaviors have been expected of and prescribed for women across history (Prentice & Carranza, 2002).

Religion is another powerful socialization agent affecting women's roles and power in society across thousands of years. Judeo-Christianity portrays women as not just characteristically submissive (1 Peter 3:4), but as required to be submissive to men (1 Peter 3:5). Women are ordered, multiple times in the Bible, to submit, obey, be silent (1 Corinthians 14:34; 1 Timothy 2:12; Ephesians 5:22-24). Why? God doesn't like women speaking? The idea that an omnipotent supernatural being who created the universe would favor one gender over the other is quite powerful and has been used quite effectively in silencing and oppressing women. Men are more like God, made in his image from dust (1 Corinthians 11:7), while woman came directly from a rather insignificant part of man, his rib (Genesis 2:22), specifically to be his helper (Genesis 2:16-18). As woman came from man, she is inferior to him (1 Corinthians 11:8). Women are also described as unclean, immoral, untrustworthy, manipulative, and deceitful (Ecclesiastes 7:26; Leviticus 15:19; Proverbs 5-7; Proverbs 11:22; Psalm 140:2), more reasons for them to be oppressed by superior males (there are too many verses to list here). Biblereasons.com asserts that "evil women" are "greedy, rebellious, unsubmissive, wicked, adulterous, gossiping, slandering, and sexually immoral" (https://biblereasons.com/evil-women-and-bad-wives/). Another website exclaims, "A Christian Wife is to Obey Her Husband in EVERY THING!" and "Feminism is Evil!" (www.jesus-is-savior.com/Evils%20 in%20America/Feminism/everything.htm). A website called *The Interactive Bible* (www.bible.ca) has this to say about the Bible and its role in affecting women's and men's behavior: "Culture has never been a factor as to whether a woman must submit to her husband in the Bible. Modern

272 *Personality, Emotions, and Health*

times of woman's liberation are irrelevant. God gives us His reasons why women must submit to her husband" (www.bible.ca/marriage/submission-independent-of-culture.htm).

Along the exact same lines designed to allow men to maintain power and control over half the human race, Islam also demands silence and obedience from women, the religious requirement of submission to men, and encourages men to beat women who do not submit (Qu'ran 2:222, 2:228, 33:33, 33:59, 38:44, 66:5). Many hadith in Islam also command women to submit to men, describe women as sinful and as sexual property, and support men beating their wives into submission (Bukhari 2:28, 6:321, 58:125, 62:81, 72:715). **Religiosity** (one's identification of the self as a religious person) is thus obviously linked with endorsement of traditional gender ideology, and the hostile and benevolent sexism that go along with that (Glick, Lameiras, & Castro, 2002; Taşdemir & Sakallı-Uğurlu, 2010). Religiosity is also linked with rape myth acceptance among men and women (Riggio, Groskopf, Dennem-Tigner, & Garcia, 2015). Demanding that girls and women be a certain way, or else God (or husbands, uncles, fathers, brothers, sons) will punish them, is obviously abusive, threatening, and coercive. Religious tools of social dominance are especially effective in controlling people who are poor and less educated (Albrecht & Heaton, 1984; Arias-Vazquez, 2012; Paul, 2009). The role of education is vital in opening the minds of the world's children to the realities of religious domination and discrimination against the world's girls and women. Encouraging children to critically examine the supernatural claims and misogynistic mandates of religion is essential for ending religious oppression of girls and women around the world.

Gender Differences in Personality and Emotions

Based on our discussion thus far, do you think there are gender differences in personality? Are girls and boys, women and men, different in their characteristic ways of thinking, behaving, and feeling? How different are they? Do these differences occur universally, all over the world? The answer is to these questions is yes. Multiple studies (including **meta-analyses**) indicate that across cultures, for younger and older adults, women and men describe themselves differently and are described differently by others. Women describe themselves, more than men do, as higher in qualities related to Agreeableness and Neuroticism. In particular, women are more likely to describe themselves as tender-minded, trusting, fearful, and anxious; men are more likely to describe themselves as assertive and risk-taking (Brody & Hall, 2000; Byrnes, Miller, & Schafer, 1999; Feingold, 1994; Kring & Gordon, 1998; Lynn & Martin, 1997; McCrae, 2002). Women across cultures also describe themselves as high in Extraversion, especially **warmth** (although other studies find men higher in Extraversion; Schmitt, Realo, Voracek, &, Jüri, 2008) and Openness to Feelings, compared to men. Men describe themselves as higher in Openness to Ideas compared to women (Costa, Terracciano, & McCrae, 2001; Schmitt et al., 2008). Women describe themselves as higher in Conscientiousness, particularly order, than men (Feingold, 1994; Schmitt et al., 2008). Gender differences in personality begin in adolescence, with girls showing gender-congruent traits earlier than boys, a pattern that is found across cultures (De Bolle et al., 2015).

The same differences found using self-descriptions are found all over the world in descriptions provided by others, with reports by others indicating that women are seen as higher in tender-mindedness, anxiety, and openness to feelings, and men are seen as higher in assertiveness and excitement-seeking (McCrae et al., 2005). Similar differences in infant **temperament** support a substantial biological component to personality and gender differences in personality

Personality, Emotions, and Health 273

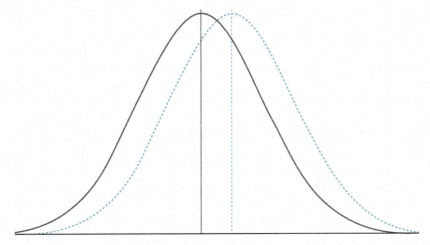

Figure 9.8 Differences among women and men are greater than differences between women and men

(Else-Quest, Hyde, Goldsmith, & Van Hulle, 2006; Laursen et al., 2002; Wilgenbusch & Merrell, 1999). These personality qualities are reliably linked to women's and men's different activities, occupational preferences, lifestyles, and physical and mental health outcomes (Browne, 1998; Lippa, 2005). Gender differences in self-descriptions are stable from young to older adulthood (Feingold, 1994; McCrae & Costa, 1984). While personality differences between women and men are actually fewer than among women and among men (Costa et al., 2001) (see Figure 9.8), the same differences are found consistently all over the world and are larger than gender differences in other important qualities, including self-esteem and cognitive abilities (Else-Quest et al., 2006; Hyde, 2005).

While personality differences between women and men are found all over the world, the sizes of the differences do vary by culture (McCrae et al., 2005). In an expansive study of the Big Five personality traits across 55 cultures, Schmitt and colleagues (2008) found larger gender differences in personality in wealthier countries offering more equal access to education compared to poorer, less developed countries. The authors assert that greater wealth and equality allows women and men to be less constrained in their personality traits, allowing everyone to be more like their "innate personality," leading to a greater **sexual dimorphism** in personality (Schmitt et al., 2008, p. 168). Other scholars argue that cultures in less-developed, poorer countries will be more traditional and more **collectivistic** because of limitations on individual independence. People living in collectivistic cultures act according to qualities related to and valued by the group, including their own specific roles within the group (Costa et al., 2001). In collectivistic cultures, cultural norms are more important than gender role norms; as such, individual expression of personality, including individual femininity or masculinity, is not highly emphasized (Fischer & Manstead, 2000; Markus & Kitayama, 1991). Individualistic cultures emphasize individual expression much more than collectivistic cultures, thus individual personalities and differences between them, including strong emphases on masculinity versus femininity, become more evident (Markus & Kitayama, 1991; Triandis, 1989). People in individualistic cultures also focus more on the individual rather than the role, and thus focus more on individual traits in describing people (Valchev, van de Vijver, Nel, Rothmann, & Meiring, 2013). This difference in perspective, focusing on situations and context more than on individuals or vice versa, is associated with

274 Personality, Emotions, and Health

many differences in social cognitive processes between individuals from collectivistic and individualistic cultures (Fiske & Taylor, 2013).

In addition to the Big Five personality traits, women and men around the world are different in the traits of Femininity and Masculinity, which essentially encompass gender stereotypes. The trait of Femininity involves qualities typically associated with women, including gentleness, warmth, and gullibility. Masculinity involves qualities typically associated with men, including ambitiousness, strength, assertiveness, and independence. The qualities are not mutually exclusive and most people possess both qualities to some degree (Bem, Martyna, & Watson, 1976). The Bem Sex Role Inventory is an important measure of these qualities (Bem, 1974). An individual's degree of androgyny refers to their possession of both feminine and masculine qualities (Heilbrun & Schwartz, 1982). As we discussed in Chapters 5 and 6, women tend to be more feminine in their characteristic ways of behaving, thinking, and feeling, while men tend to be more masculine in personality, personality differences that correspond to the reproductive roles and traditional division of labor between women and men (Eagly, 1987). Evolutionary theorists assert that masculine qualities of risk-taking and social dominance are adaptive for men and linked with their lesser investment in parenting, while women evolved qualities of nurturance and cautiousness because of their greater role and investment in parenting each offspring (Buss, 1997; Campbell, 2002). Indeed, the largest gender differences in personality appear to be in anxiety; tender-mindedness, feeling empathy and care toward others which motivates nurturing behaviors; and assertiveness, the assertion of one's will in interpersonal and social interactions (McCrae et al., 2005; Schmitt et al., 2008).

In the modern world, gender roles are changing for women and men. Women entered higher education and the workforce in increasing numbers during the 1970s and thereafter (Davis & Robinson, 1988). Meta-analyses indicate that from 1973 to 2012, American women became more androgynous over time as their masculinity scores increased, and men became slightly more feminine up until the 1990s; after that until now, masculinity and femininity have declined among women and men (Donnelly & Twenge, 2017). The authors assert that neither trait is particularly relevant to individual psychology anymore due to the blurring of gender roles in modern society, with traditional gender roles less common in American society. Individual androgyny is linked with positive psychological and social outcomes, while being either highly feminine or highly masculine is not (Green & Kenrick, 1994; O'Heron & Orlofsky, 1990). Some scholars argue for a new type of femininity that is based on bodily power, with women's bodies representing their femininity as self-control, self-discipline, and social standing (Gill, 2007; Smolak, Murnen, & Myers, 2014). In addition, highly feminine qualities are associated with individual and social weakness, qualities that are devalued in many social and professional contexts (Fiske, Cuddy, Glick, & Xu, 2002; Twenge, Konrath, Foster, Campbell, & Bushman, 2008). Roles are changing as more men are contributing to work in the home and caring for children (Livingston, 2014). However, men are not becoming more feminine (Donnelly & Twenge, 2017) and women remain primarily responsible for household and childcare work in the home (Wall & Arnold, 2007; see Chapter 12).

Women and men are also different around the world in terms of their experience and expression of emotions. Women are higher overall in emotionality, describing themselves and being described by others as higher in anxiety than men (Brody & Hall, 2000; McCrae et al., 2005). One feature of anxiety is fearfulness. Given that women are physically weaker and so much more vulnerable to physical attack and assault by the other half of the human race, it makes much evolutionary sense that women would be higher in fear (Buss, 1997). Emotional expression is much more culturally discouraged for men than for women (Avila & Avila, 1995; Liu & Iwamoto, 2006; Sue & Sue, 2008; Wester, 2008). Masculinity traditionally involves notions of physical and emotional strength, and emotionality is associated with perceptions of weakness and dependence on others. Traditional ideals of masculinity include restrictions on emotionality (Levant, 1995) and notions of **stoicism**, the suppression of expression of pain, grief, and other vulnerable or tender feelings (Jansz, 2000). Boys learn from an early age that showing emotion, especially fear, sadness, and hurt, is not masculine (Mahalik, Pierre, & Wan, 2003; Newberger, 1999). Indeed, men all over the world report experiencing less intense and less frequent emotions than women. Brebner (2003) asked 6,500 adults from 41 countries how frequently and intensely they experience eight fundamental emotions (joy, contentment, pride, affection, fear, anger, sadness, guilt). In line with expected differences based on gender stereotypes, except for pride and guilt, women from all countries reported more frequent and intense experiences of emotions than men. Many studies indicate that women are more expressive of emotions that they experience than men as well (Brody & Hall, 1993).

Gender Differences in Cognitive Abilities

There are differences in cognitive abilities between girls and boys, women and men, but they are consistently found to be small, smaller than differences in major traits of personality (Hyde, 2005). In terms of mathematics performance, meta-analyses indicate a lack of overall difference based on gender. Girls show slightly better performance during elementary school and middle school in computational skills, while boys outperform girls slightly in mathematical problem-solving in high school and college. Gender differences in math performance have also been steadily declining over the years (Hyde, Fennema, & Lamon, 1990). There appears to be a substantial socialization component in development of math skills, with boys more strongly encouraged in their math performance than girls (Ai, 2002). Gender differences in math performance and attitude are smaller in countries with gender equity in school enrollment, and women's increasing representation as researchers and politicians (Else-Quest, Hyde, & Linn, 2010). Gender differences in spatial skills are larger than those in math, but dependent on the type of skill being assessed. Meta-analyses indicate that boys and men score significantly better on spatial skills of **mental rotation** and spatial perception, with gender differences increasing across age groups (Voyer, Voyer, & Bryden, 1995). Differences in skill at mental rotation tasks between boys and girls have been observed in infants, strongly suggesting innate sex differences in such skills (Moore & Johnson, 2008). Evolutionary theorists suggest that mental rotation skills are highly evolved in men because of their adaptive roles as fighters and hunters (Sell, Hone, & Pound, 2012). However, other research indicates that cultural practices and education, powerful socialization agents, account for a large part of gender differences in spatial abilities (Hoffman, Gneezy, & List, 2011).

Meta-analyses of gender differences in verbal ability are similar to those of math ability, indicating very small gender differences, with girls scoring higher than boys at different ages. These differences are so small and insubstantial for any particular verbal skill that researchers argue it is counterproductive to continue speculating about gender differences in verbal ability (Hyde & Linn, 1988). There are no gender differences in general intelligence (Halpern & LaMay, 2000). The lack of systematic differences in cognitive abilities by gender suggests that stereotypes of such differences are **legitimizing myths**, false beliefs that justify gender segregation in different activities, fields, and professions. Legitimizing myths make men feel justified in treating women like an inferior group and they operate on women's self-concepts and consciousness in affecting behavior, in a process known as **stereotype threat** (see Chapter 5). Women exposed to stereotypical information about women's inferior math abilities perform poorly on a difficult math test, while women not exposed to such information perform significantly better. In a similar test of spatial skills involving mental rotation, women exposed to a negative stereotype perform more poorly than men, while those exposed but who use **self-affirmation** (thinking positively about the self, one's valuable qualities, one's social groups) perform just as well as men (Martens, Johns, Greenberg, & Schimel, 2006). The same process of stereotype threat operates on the self-concepts of other groups oppressed by heteronormative white patriarchy, including African Americans (Aronson, Fried, & Good, 2002; Aronson, Quinn, & Spencer, 1998), the poor (Croizet & Claire, 1998), and LGBTQ individuals (Bosson, Haymovitz, & Pinel, 2004).

Gender and Physical and Mental Health

There are numerous physical differences between women and men, with many physical and physiological processes favoring male strength, stamina, and skill in fighting and hunting (Sell et al., 2012). Women are obviously solely at risk for death due to pregnancy and childbirth, leading causes of death in many countries (Beck et al., 2010; see "Critical Thinking"). Men show greater cardiorespiratory and physical endurance than women, although differences are smaller as people are more rigorously physically trained (Dada, Anderson, Grier, Alemany, & Jones, 2017). Men tend to have higher **mortality** rates (Singh-Manoux, 2008), while some research indicates that women experience higher **morbidity** (the experience of symptoms, chronic illness, disability) (Austad & Fischer, 2016; Carmel & Bernstein, 2003; Mendoza-Sassi & Béria, 2007). Some scholars assert that the difference in morbidity is caused by women's greater tendency to self-disclose and seek help, including medical and mental health services (Mendoza-Sassi & Béria, 2007). Others find no gender differences in morbidity (Macintyre, Ford, & Hunt, 1999; Singh-Manoux, 2008). The health benefits associated with being married are greatest for men (Kiecolt-Glaser & Newton, 2001; Robles, Slatcher, Trombello, & McGinn, 2014; Wanic & Kulik, 2011), including greater longevity (Burman & Margolin, 1992).

There are gender differences in mental health that have been documented around the world. The World Health Organization (2015b) asserts that gender predicts misdiagnoses of mental health disorders, with women being more likely than men to be diagnosed as depressed, and men more likely to be diagnosed as alcoholic. This is unfortunate for depressed men and alcoholic women, who are likely to be misdiagnosed and not offered appropriate and helpful treatments. Similarly, research indicates that women are significantly more likely than men to be diagnosed with depression and anxiety, and that mental illness in men is associated with unemployment and physical illness (Vázquez-Barquero et al., 1992). In a recent study of American military veterans, female veterans were found to have a greater lifetime prevalence of post-traumatic stress, lifetime prevalence of and current major depression, and lifetime histories of migraines and arthritis. Male veterans were higher in substance abuse disorders, including nicotine and alcohol dependence. Men were also at greater risk of high blood pressure, heart attacks, and diabetes (Ziobrowski, Sartor, Tsai, & Pietrzak, 2017).

Unfortunately, men are less likely to seek mental health counseling than women (Addis & Mahalik, 2003). A growing literature indicates that men view mental health problems as stigmatizing and violating masculine gender norms. Men view seeking help for such problems as

Personality, Emotions, and Health 277

not masculine, which decreases their help-seeking behaviors (Hammer, Vogel, & Heimerdinger-Edwards, 2013). Men also mask depression with substance abuse (Cochran & Rabinowitz, 2000) and may develop behaviors that restrict expression of typical depression symptoms that themselves become associated with depression (Addis, 2008; Leimkühler, Heller, & Paulus, 2007). Men are more likely to **ruminate** and distance themselves from others during depression (Nolen-Hoeksema, 2002). Although women attempt suicide more often than men, men are much more likely to die from suicide (Moscicki, 1997; Oquendo et al., 2001).

Gender role stress (stress caused by pressures to conform to expected gender roles) appears to be a critical variable in affecting mental health outcomes, particularly among boys and men (D'Augelli, Grossman, & Starks, 2006; Rieger & Savin-Williams, 2012). Scholars describe **masculine discrepancy stress** (**MDS**) as stress boys and men experience caused by fear of being perceived as not masculine; Pleck, 1995; Reidy, Brookmeyer, Gentile, Berke, & Zeichner, 2016b). Social punishments for feminine behavior by boys and men are obvious, including bullying, physical attacks, peer and parental rejection (Bosson, Prewitt-Freilino, & Taylor, 2005; Bosson, Taylor, & Prewitt-Freilino, 2006; D'Augelli et al., 2006; Kann et al., 2016; Reisner, Greytak, Parsons, & Ybarra, 2015; Toomey, Ryan, Diaz, Card, & Russell, 2010). Because of the social pressures to be masculine and not feminine that boys experience over time, they develop feelings of anxiety about being perceived as not masculine, and may act in hyper-masculine, dominant, and aggressive ways to demonstrate masculinity (Reidy et al., 2016b). These anxious feelings are particularly likely when manhood is **precarious** (easily threatened; Vandello & Bosson, 2013) and when men are hypermasculine (Reidy, Shirk, Sloan, & Zeichner, 2009). In response to threats to masculinity, such men are likely to engage in risky sexual behaviors, intimate partner violence (IPV), and other violent behavior (Reidy, Berke, Gentile, & Zeichner, 2014; Reidy et al., 2016b; Reidy, Berke, Gentile, & Zeichner, 2016a). MDS is associated with multiple indicators of maladjustment in adolescent boys, including substance use, mood disorder symptoms, feelings of hopelessness, and violent behavior (Reidy, Smith-Darden, Vivolo-Kantor, Malone, & Kernsmith, 2018).

Is womanhood also precarious? Do women experience feminine discrepancy stress? Vandello and Bosson (2013) suggest that womanhood is ascribed, that it does not have to be earned the way masculinity does, it just happens. As such, it is not easily threatened; femaleness just is. Others disagree, and assert that femininity is not ascribed to all women because traditional notions of it rely on physical beauty and motherhood, which not all women have. As such, women who are not beautiful or not mothers are excluded from womanhood (Chrisler, 2013). Women are also subject to the dichotomy of **benevolent** and **hostile sexism**, where women are either idealized and protected as pure and fragile, or hated and rejected because they are too assertive, sexual, demanding, manipulative (Glick & Fiske, 1996). **Female gender role stress** (**FGRS**) involves stress in response to threats associated with being female. Researchers have identified multiple fear experiences associated with FGRS: fear of victimization, of not being nurturant, of behaving assertively, of being unattractive, and of experiencing unemotional relationships (Gillespie & Eisler, 1992). Women who report greater FGRS experience greater depression, psychological distress, and eating disorder symptoms than women with less FGRS (Gillespie & Eisler, 1992; Martz, Handley, & Eisler, 1995; Tang & Tang, 2001).

Minority stress also affects people belonging to racial and sexual minorities. Minority stress refers to the fact that it is inordinately stressful to belong to a minority group that is subject to negative stereotypes, prejudice, and discrimination. Racial inequality is linked with greater psychological distress and depressive symptoms among racial minority groups (especially African Americans) from adolescence into young adulthood (Brown, Meadows, & Elder, 2007). The intersectionality of race, gender, class, and sexual orientation is critical to understanding role stress, as belonging to multiple minority groups can compound negative outcomes (Lehavot & Simoni, 2011). Negative mental health outcomes from sexual assault are amplified for poor and minority women (Bryant-Davis, Chung, & Tillman, 2009). Women in minority racial groups who are poor are particularly vulnerable to mental health problems (Belle, 1990; Catz, Gore-Felton, & McClure, 2002). Minority stress is linked with poor mental health outcomes among LGBTQ individuals, especially among those with internalized homonegativity and lack of family support (Kuyper & Fokkema, 2011), especially among women (Balsam & Szymanski, 2005; Lehavot & Simoni, 2011) and transgender people (Steele et al., 2017). People who are intersectional are more likely to experience mental health problems and not receive treatment for those problems because of lack of needed social support, lack of money, and systemic discrimination in health care and other social institutions (Alvidrez, 1999; Chow, Jaffee, & Snowden, 2003; Steele et al., 2017). Society's constructed expectations of gender, race, and sexuality so powerfully affect individual psychology that they affect the individual experience of mental health, help-seeking for problems, one's experience of treatment by and support from others, and operations within social institutions. Reconsidering gender, racial, and sexuality constructions, and addressing poverty, can only be accomplished through widespread education, open dialogue, and acceptance of each other as human beings.

Chapter Summary

Personality comprises individual differences in characteristic ways of thinking, behaving, and feeling. Multiple theoretical approaches to personality exist, with dispositional or trait approaches being oldest and most popular. The most popular current model (the Five Factor Model) identifies five major traits of personality (Openness to Experience, Conscientiousness, Extraversion, Agreeableness, Neuroticism). There is a substantial biological basis to personality, as indicated by research examining excitability and arousal, hormones and emotion, and behavioral genetics. Personality development is strongly influenced by living environments and socialization forces, including parents, the media, and religion, all of which emphasize activity and strength in boys and men, passivity and submissiveness in girls and women. There are gender differences in personality that are found consistently all over the world, although differences are smaller within various cultures. Across cultures, women describe themselves and are described as higher in emotionality (Neuroticism, especially anxiety), Agreeableness (especially tender-mindedness), warmth (part of Extraversion), and Openness to Feelings. Men in contrast describe themselves and are described as higher in assertiveness (part of Extraversion) and Openness to Ideas. There are few if any gender differences in cognitive abilities, the largest difference being in spatial reasoning tasks, especially mental rotation, favoring men. These differences appear to be affected by genetic and socialization forces. Men around the world generally have higher mortality rates while women have higher morbidity rates. Women are more likely to be diagnosed as depressed or anxious, but less likely than men to be diagnosed as alcoholic. Men experience significant gender role stress surrounding psychological problems, which may affect their display of depression symptoms and decrease their help-seeking behaviors. Gender role and minority stress affect psychological and social outcomes among men, women, members of racial minority groups, and LGBTQ individuals.

Thoughtful Questions

- How do you think culture is linked with personality? Explain the dimension of individualism-collectivism and how it might account for differences in characteristic emotions.
- Do you think Cattell's 16 personality factors (see Table 9.2) can be clustered into the Big Five traits? How about Eysenck's three major personality traits? The HEXACO traits?
- Explain Eysenck's biosocial model of personality.
- How are hormones linked to personality characteristics?
- Explain the results of the research by behavioral geneticists on the heritability of personality traits.
- Explain each of the major traits of personality as described by the Five Factor Model.
- Explain how the major world religions of Judeo-Christianity and Islam view women.
- Describe the research findings on gender differences in personality around the world.
- Explain stoicism, gender stereotypes, and gender differences in emotions and emotional expression.
- Explain the research on gender differences in cognitive abilities.
- Discuss how gender role stress is linked to mental health of women, men, and LGBTQ individuals.
- Explain how poverty affects child development and the experience of mental health problems in adulthood.

Glossary

Agreeablenesss: a major personality trait that involves trust, straightforwardness, altruism, compliance, modesty, and tender-mindedness.

Amygdala: a mid-brain structure that is important for anger and fear, fight-or-flight responses.

Androgens: male hormones, including testosterone.

Androgyny: the degree to which a person possesses both feminine and masculine qualities. The person who possesses equal degrees of feminine and masculine qualities is called androgynous.

Antisocial Personality Disorder: a personality disorder that involves a persistent pattern of behavior involving rule-breaking, criminality, deceitfulness, aggressiveness, irresponsibility, and disregard for the feelings and rights of others.

Anxiety: an aspect of Neuroticism, fearfulness.

Ascending reticular activating system (ARAS): the system of brain structures that control overall excitation and arousal of the body. It controls consciousness and as such is important for sleep and attention. The reticular formation at the top of the brain stem is central to the system.

Assertiveness: an aspect of Extraversion, the assertion of one's will in interpersonal and social interactions.

Attachment: the close affectional tie infants develop with their primary caregiver.

Behavioral genetics: a scientific discipline which examines the heritability of behavioral qualities and characteristics.

280 *Personality, Emotions, and Health*

Benevolent sexism: sexism involving warmth, trust, and desire for intimacy, along with paternalistic ideas that subordinate women.

Biosocial: theories that consider the interaction of biological and social forces in determining personality.

Body humors: bodily fluids, namely blood, phlegm, yellow bile, and black bile.

Bonding: the development of a close affectional tie with another being.

Central nervous system (CNS): the brain and the spinal cord, which control thought, movement, and regulation of the body. A central part of Eysenck's approach.

Changeability: changes in excitation in the body, changes in an individual's physical and cognitive arousal. A personality dimension originally developed by Wundt that is linked with **Extraversion**.

Characteristic: a person's behavior that is typical of them, across time and across situations.

Choleric: a person who is hot-tempered, irascible, irritable, based on a predominance of yellow bile in the body.

Conscientiousness: a major personality trait that involves competence, order, dutifulness, achievement striving, self-discipline, deliberation.

Deep poverty: when a person's annual income is below 50% of the poverty threshold.

Defense mechanisms: unconscious mechanisms the Ego uses to defend itself against threatening feelings and memories.

Disagreeable: people who are suspicious, mistrusting of others, low in compassion, not helpful, and not cooperative.

Dispositional approach ("trait approach"): focuses on individual differences; seeks to identify and measure the most important ways in which individual personalities differ (major traits).

Dizygotic: twins or multiple births that result from two (or more) eggs, two (or more) sperm (two or more zygotes); offspring are 50% genetically similar.

Egalitarianism: a philosophical valuing of equality between all people, with all people having the same rights and opportunities.

Ego: Freud's conceptualization of the conscious mind, responsible for reaching a compromise between needs and wants, morals, and practical, rational considerations.

Ego Strength: a personality trait involving psychosocial maturity and adjustment.

Emotional Stability (aka **Neuroticism**): a major personality trait that involves anxiety, angry hostility, depression, self-consciousness, impulsiveness, and vulnerability.

Emotionality: how easily emotionally aroused a person is, changes in an individual's emotional arousal. A personality dimension originally developed by Wundt that is linked with **Neuroticism**.

Evolutionary psychology: the area of psychology that focuses on the evolution of human behavior, thoughts, and emotions over time as adaptations (qualities and characteristics that enhance ability to survive and reproduce in a particular environment).

Extraversion: a major personality trait that involves sociability and social energy; the six facets are warmth, gregariousness, assertiveness, activity, excitement-seeking, and positive emotions.

Factor analysis: a statistical technique based on correlation. Items that are highly correlated with each other represent a cluster of related responses; the responses are reflective of the same thing, the same underlying quality or factor.

Family studies: examination of relatives of different degrees of relatedness to determine heritability of traits. For example, the adoption design examines trait similarity in identical twins reared apart or other biological relatives separated through adoption (e.g., parents and adopted away children).

Female gender role stress (FGRS): stress in response to threats associated with being female (fear of victimization, of not being nurturant, of behaving assertively, of being unattractive, and of unemotional relationships).

Femininity: qualities typically associated with women, including gentleness, warmth, submissiveness, gullibility.

Five Factor Model: a dispositional approach to personality that identifies five major personality traits (Openness, Conscientiousness, Extraversion, Agreeableness, Neuroticism).

Fixation: when mental energy becomes stuck on an unresolved issue from earlier in personality development; fixated libido cannot be used for growth and activity in the current stage because of neuroses.

Fragile states: countries where the government is weak and ineffective, unwilling or unable to perform necessary basic functions for security, social services, and the rule of law.

Gender role stress: stress caused by pressures to conform to expected gender roles.

Gender schema theory: emphasizes the importance of learning about gender and development of schemas representing ideas about women and femininity, men and masculinity, in developing gender identity.

Gender stereotypes: cognitive schemas for women and men that include the traits, qualities, and abilities typically associated with women and men.

Genes: the molecular units of heredity; genes provide the recipe for protein production at the cellular level, thus influencing morphology and physiology.

Heritability: the degree to which traits can be attributed to the operation of genes inherited from parents.

HEXACO: a model of major traits of personality including Honesty-Humility (H), Emotionality (E), Extraversion (X), Agreeableness (A), Conscientiousness (C), and Openness (O).

Honesty-Humility: qualities involving lower and higher degrees of modesty, sincerity, and fairness.

Hostile sexism: sexism involving negative feelings accompanied by negative stereotypes of women and heterosexual hostility.

Hypermasculinity: extreme masculinity including endorsement of violence, callous sexual attitudes toward women, and risk-taking.

Hypothalamus: a mid-brain structure that controls hormone release, needs, emotions, and pleasure.

Id: Freud's conceptualization of the infantile, animalistic mind that is pleasure-seeking, irrational, and largely unconscious.

Idiographic approach: a scholarly approach to personality that emphasizes individual uniqueness and complexity.

Individual differences: ways in which people differ on traits of personality; exemplified by the normal distribution.

Individualism-collectivism: a cultural dimension involving greater valuation of individual goals and achievements or group goals and group harmony.

282 *Personality, Emotions, and Health*

Internalized homonegativity: holding negative attitudes toward sexual minority groups that have been internalized, resulting in negative self-attitudes among LGBTQ individuals.

Intersectionality: the experience of more than one minority group membership, including race, gender, class, and sexual orientation groups. Intersectionality increases the negative effects of **minority stress**.

Legitimizing myths: false beliefs about women that legitimize their oppression by men.

Lexical process: identifying major traits of personality through the analysis of language, where thousands of adjectives describing human traits, qualities, and attributes in multiple languages are grouped into larger, meaningful categories.

Libido: mental, life energy, in Freud's model of personality.

Masculine discrepancy stress (MDS): stress boys and men experience caused by fear of being perceived as not masculine.

Masculinity: qualities typically associated with men, including ambitiousness, strength, assertiveness, and independence.

Maternal mortality: rates of women who die from complications during childbirth, and soon after childbirth.

Melancholic: a person who is sad, depressive, with low energy, based on a predominance of black bile in the body.

Mental rotation: cognitive abilities involved in mentally rotating the visual representation of a physical object.

Meta-analysis: a higher order analysis; a scientific investigation involving the examination of the results of many different studies, how results vary by study design or measurement techniques (or other features), and estimations of an overall relationship between variables.

Minority stress: the inordinate and chronic stress experienced by members of minority groups associated with subjection to negative stereotypes, prejudice, and discrimination.

Monozygotic: twins or multiple births resulting from one egg, one sperm (one zygote); offspring are 100% genetically identical.

Morality principle: followed by the Superego, which seeks the most morally appropriate behavior.

Morbidity: the experience of medical or psychological symptoms, chronic illness, disability.

Mortality: the likelihood of death.

Neuroscience: the subdiscipline of psychology that is concerned with operations and structures of the brain.

Neurosis: fundamental preoccupation, anxiety, and irrationality focused on an issue left unresolved in childhood.

Nomothetic approach: a scholarly approach to personality which involves examining personality differences among large groups of people.

Openness to Experience: a major personality trait that involves openness to different experiences in terms of fantasy, aesthetics, feelings, actions, ideas, and values.

Oxytocin: a hormone involved in female and male sexuality, childbirth, and breastfeeding. It is essential for human bonding.

Patriarchy: a hierarchical structure where men hold the majority of financial, political, and social power.

Personality: each person's unique and characteristic ways of thinking, behaving, and feeling.

Phenomenology: individual, ongoing, subjective awareness and experience of reality.

Phlegmatic: a person who is thoughtful, quiet, analytical, based on a predominance of phlegm in the body.

Physiological psychology: a subdiscipline of psychology that focuses on behavioral effects of physiology (daily bodily functions and neural processes).

Pleasure principle: followed by the Id, focused on obtaining pleasure.

Poverty: the experience of daily deprivation because of a lack of personal money required for basic needs in a society.

Poverty threshold: the "poverty line," an annual income below which one is considered poor.

Precarious manhood: when masculinity is easily threatened, resulting in psychological stress and reassertion of masculinity.

Psychic conflict: part of Freud's psychodynamic approach to personality; the conflict that is inherent and ongoing between different parts of the mind (needs and desires, morality, practicality).

Psychoanalytic therapy: Freud's approach to therapy, an analysis of the unconscious mind.

Psychodynamic: movement of the mind; Freud's approach to personality.

Psychoticism: a major personality trait involving emotional sensitivity to others. Individuals high in this trait are emotionally cold, tough-minded, unempathic, egocentric, impersonal, aggressive, antisocial.

Qualitative: refers to research methodology that is focused on an in-depth, holistic approach to understanding each person's uniqueness. Qualitative methods include diary studies, interviews, review of personal records, examination of living spaces, and so on.

Quantitative: refers to research methodology that takes a numerical approach. For example, large groups of people complete various measures of personality (questionnaires, behavioral tasks, etc.) and a score is applied to their responses.

Rationality principle: followed by the Ego, which seeks a practical, sensible compromise between itself, the Id, and the Superego.

Religiosity: one's identification of the self as a religious person.

Rumination: dwelling on one's emotions that can amplify emotional distress.

Sanguine: a person who is cheerful, hearty, happy; taken from the idea of a predominance of blood in the body.

Self-affirmation: mentally affirming positive aspects of the self in terms of valuable characteristics, positive outcomes, and social group memberships. Can ameliorate the negative effects of stereotype threat.

Self-consciousness: an aspect of Neuroticism, a tendency to look psychologically inward at the self as an object of attention and focus.

Sensation-seeking: a personality trait involving seeking out a variety of new experiences that are high in complexity, intensity, and novelty.

Sexual dimorphism: difference in forms between the sexes. Greater dimorphism reflects greater sex differences.

Social cognition: processes by which people process new social information based on stored representations of past experience.

Social learning/cognitive theory: the explanation for socialization that children learn through observation, particularly of parents and other important role models.

Source traits: underlying, latent forces within the person that are responsible for surface behaviors.

284 *Personality, Emotions, and Health*

Stereotype threat: detriments in performance that result from exposure to a negative group stereotype.

Stoicism: the suppression of expression of pain, grief, and other vulnerable or tender feelings.

Superego: Freud's conceptualization of the part of the mind concerned with morality and expectations of others.

Surface traits: behavioral manifestations of major personality dimensions.

Talk therapy: therapy models based on talking with therapists, alone, in families, or in groups.

Temperament: emotionality, activity, and reactivity of an infant; the precursor to later personality.

Tender-mindedness: an aspect of Agreeableness, feeling empathy and care toward others which motivates nurturing behaviors.

Testosterone: a male hormone (androgen) associated with male sexual development, sexual behavior, and aggression.

Twin design: a research design used by behavioral geneticists that involves the comparison of monozygotic and dizygotic twins. If monozygotic twins are more similar on a trait than dizygotic twins, the trait is more heritable.

Unconscious: the part of the mind that exists outside of conscious awareness. Includes the **Id**, most of the **Superego**, and part of the **Ego. Defense mechanisms** may be used by the Ego without conscious awareness.

Uniqueness: an aspect of personality, with each person being genuinely unique, even identical twins.

Universal health care: providing health care and financial protection from health care costs to all or nearly all of a country's people.

Visceral brain: structures in the middle of the brain, also called the **limbic system**; mid-brain structures involved in regulating needs (thirst, hunger, sex) and emotions.

Vulnerable: an aspect of Neuroticism, when a person is easily hurt.

Warmth: an aspect of Extraversion, being interpersonally warm, friendly, accepting.

References

Addis, M. E. (2008). Gender and depression in men. *Clinical Psychology Science and Practice, 15*(3), 153-168. https://doi.org/10.1111/j.1468-2850.2008.00125.x.

Addis, M. E., & Mahalik, J. R. (2003). Men, masculinity, and the contexts of help-seeking. *American Psychologist. 58*, 5-14.

Ai, X. (2002). Gender differences in growth in mathematics achievement: Three-level longitudinal and multi-level analyses of individual, home, and school influences. *Mathematical Thinking and Learning, 4*(1), 1-22. https://doi.org/10.1207/S15327833MTL0401_1.

Ainsworth, M. D. S. (1978). The Bowlby-Ainsworth attachment theory. *Behavioral and Brain Sciences, 1*(3), 436-438.

Albrecht, S. L., & Heaton, T. B. (1984). Secularization, higher education, and religiosity. *Review of Religious Research, 26*(1), 43-58.

Allee, W. C., Collias, N. E., & Lutherman, C. Z. (1939). Modification of the social order in flocks of hens by injection of testosterone propionate. *Physiological Zoology, 12*, 412-440.

Alonso-Zaldivar, R., & Crary, D. (2018). Trump remaking federal policy on women's reproductive health. Associated Press, May 30. https://apnews.com/0a165e54c0a94600871539472ba82ba1/Trump-remaking-federal-policy-on-women's-reproductive-health. Retrieved August 8, 2018.

Alvidrez, J. (1999). Ethnic variations in mental health attitudes and service use among low-income African American, Latina, and European American young women. *Community Mental Health Journal, 35*, 515-530.

Archer, D., Iritani, B., Kimes, D. D., & Barrios, M. (1983). Face-ism: Five studies of sex differences in facial prominence. *Journal of Personality and Social Psychology, 45*(4), 725-735.

Arias-Vazquez, F. J. (2012). A note on the effect of education on religiosity. *Economics Letters*, *117*(3), 895-897. https://doi.org/10.1016/j.econlet.2012.07.005.

Aronson, J., Fried, C. B., & Good, C. (2002). Reducing effects of stereotype threat on African American college students by shaping theories of intelligence. *Journal of Experimental Social Psychology*, *37*, 1-13.

Aronson, J., Quinn, D. M., & Spencer, S. J. (1998). Stereotype threat and the academic underperformance of minorities and women. In Swimm, J. K., & Stangor, C. (Eds.), *Prejudice: The target's perspective*. San Diego: Academic Press, pp. 83-103.

Ashton, M. C., Lee, K., & Goldberg, L. R. (2004). A hierarchical analysis of 1,710 English personality-descriptive adjectives. *Journal of Personality and Social Psychology*, *87*(5), 707-721.

Atkinson, A. (2016). Monitoring global poverty. Report of the Commission on Global Poverty. Washington, DC: World Bank Group. https://openknowledge.worldbank.org/.

Atwood, M. (1986). *The handmaid's tale*. New York: Penguin Random House.

Austad, S. N., & Fischer, K. E. (2016). Sex differences in lifespan. *Cell Metabolism*, *23*(6), 1022-1033. doi:10.1016/j.cmet.2016.05.019.

Avila, D. L., & Avila, A. L. (1995). Mexican-Americans. In Vacc, N. A., DeVaney, S. B., & Wittmer, J. (Eds.), *Experiencing and counseling multicultural and diverse populations*. Bristol, PA: Accelerated Development, pp. 119-146.

Balsam, K. F., & Szymanski, D. M. (2005). Relationship quality and domestic violence in women's same-sex relationships: The role of minority stress. *Psychology of Women Quarterly*, *29*, 258-269. doi:10.1111/j.1471-6402.2005.00220.x.

Bandura A. (1997). *Social learning theory*. New York: Prentice-Hall.

Bandura, A. (2001). Social cognitive theory: An agentic perspective. *Annual Review of Psychology*, *52*, 1-26.

Beck, S., Wojdyla, D., Say, L., Betran, A. P., Merialdi, M., Requejo, J. H., ..., Van Look, P. F. A. (2010). The worldwide incidence of preterm birth: A systematic review of maternal mortality and morbidity. *Bulletin of the World Health Organization*, *88*, 31-38, doi:10.2471/BLT.08.062554.

Beeman, A. E. (1947). The effect of male hormone on aggressive behavior in mice. *Physiological Zoology*, *20*, 373-405.

Belle, D. (1990). Poverty and women's mental health. *American Psychologist*, *45*(3), 385-389.

Bem, S. L. (1974). The measurement of psychological androgyny. *Journal of Consulting and Clinical Psychology*, *42*(2), 155-162.

Bem, S. L. (1984). Androgyny and gender schema theory: A conceptual and empirical investigation. *Nebraska Symposium on Motivation*, *32*, 179-226.

Bem, S. L., Martyna, W., & Watson, C. (1976). Sex typing and androgyny: Further explorations of the expressive domain. *Journal of Personality and Social Psychology*, *34*, 1016-1023.

Ben-Zeev, A., Scharnetzki, L., Chan, L. K., & Dennehy, T. C. (2012). Hypermasculinity in the media: When men "walk into the fog" to avoid affective communication. *Psychology of Popular Media Culture*, *1*(1), 53-61.

Berenson, T. (2017). Reminder: The House voted to repeal Obamacare more than 50 times. *Time Magazine*, March 24. http://time.com/4712725/ahca-house-repeal-votes-obamacare/.

Berg, J. M., Smith, S. F., Watts, A. L., Ammirati, R., Green, S. E., & Lilienfeld, S. O. (2013). Misconceptions regarding psychopathic personality: Implications for clinical practice and research. *Neuropsychiatry*, *3*, 63-74. http://dx.doi.org/10.2217/npy.12.69.

Berk, L. E. (2009). *Child development* (8th ed.). Boston, MA: Pearson.

Bernard, P., Gervais, S., Allen, J., Campomizzi, S., & Klein, O. (2015). Body parts reduction and self objectification in the objectification of sexualized bodies. *International Review of Social Psychology*, *28*, 39-61.

Bloodgood, B., Inokuchi, D., Shawverb, W., Olson, K., Hoffman, R., Cohen, E., ..., Muthuswamy, K. (2013). Exploration of awareness, knowledge, and perceptions of traumatic brain injury among American youth athletes and their parents. *Journal of Adolescent Health*, *53*(1), 34-39. https://doi.org/10.1016/j.jadohealth.2013.01.022.

Bogg, T., & Roberts, B.W. (2004). Conscientiousness and health-related behaviors: A meta-analysis of the leading behavioral contributors to mortality. *Psychological Bulletin*, *130*, 887-919.

Bond, R., & Smith, P. B. (1996). Culture and conformity: A meta-analysis of studies using Asch's (1952b, 1956). line judgment task. *Psychological Bulletin*, *119*, 111-137.

Bone, R. N., & Montgomery, D. D. (1970). Extraversion, neuroticism, and sensation seeking. *Psychological Reports*, *26*(3), 974.

Bos, P. A., Panksepp, J., Bluthé, R.-M., & van Honk, J. (2012). Acute effects of steroid hormones and neuropeptides on human social-emotional behavior: A review of single administration studies. *Frontiers in Neuroendocrinology*, *33*(1), 17-35. doi.org/10.1016/j.yfrne.2011.01.002.

Bosson, J. K., Haymovitz, E. L., & Pinel, E. C. (2004). When saying and doing diverge: The effects of stereotype threat on self-reported versus non-verbal anxiety. *Journal of Experimental Social Psychology*, *40*(2), 247-255. doi:10.1016/s0022-1031(03)00099-4.

Bosson, J. K., Prewitt-Freilino, J. L., & Taylor, J. N. (2005). Role rigidity: A problem of identity misclassification? *Journal of Personality and Social Psychology, 89*, 552-565. http://dx.doi.org/10.1037/0022-3514.

Bosson, J. K., Taylor, J. N., & Prewitt-Freilino, J. L. (2006). Gender role violations and identity misclassification: The roles of audience and actor variables. *Sex Roles, 55*, 13-24. http://dx.doi.org/10.1007/s11199-006-9056-5.

Bouchard, T. J. Jr., Segal, N. L., Tellegen, A., McGue, M., Keyes, M., & Krueger, R. (2003). Evidence for the construct validity and heritability of the Wilson–Patterson conservatism scale: A reared-apart twins study of social attitudes. *Personality and Individual Differences, 34*(6), 959-969. https://doi.org/10.1016/S0191-8869(02)00080-6.

Bowlby, J. (1969). *Attachment and loss, Vol. 1: Attachment*. New York: Basic Books.

Bowlby, J. (1973). *Attachment and loss, Vol. 2: Separation: Anxiety and anger*. New York: Basic Books.

Bowlby, J. (1980). *Attachment and loss, Vol. 3: Loss, sadness and depression*. New York: Basic Books.

Brebner, J. (2003). Gender and emotions. *Personality and Individual Differences, 34*(3), 387-394.

Brody, L. R., & Hall, J. A. (1993). Gender and emotion. In Lewis, M., & Haviland, J. M. (Eds.), *Handbook of emotions*. New York: Guilford Press, pp. 447-460.

Brody, L. R., & Hall, J. A. (2000). Gender, emotion, and expression. In Lewis, M., & Haviland-Jones, J. M. (Eds.), *Handbook of emotions: Part IV: Social/personality issues* (2nd ed.). New York: Guilford Press, pp. 325-414.

Brown, J., Cohen, P., Johnson, J. G., & Salzinger, S. (1998). A longitudinal analysis of risk factors for child maltreatment: Findings of a 17-year prospective study of officially recorded and self-reported child abuse and neglect. *Child Abuse & Neglect, 22*(11), 1065-1078. https://doi.org/10.1016/S0145-2134(98)00087-8.

Brown, J. S., Meadows, S. O., & Elder, G. H. Jr. (2007). Race-ethnic inequality and psychological distress: Depressive symptoms from adolescence to young adulthood. *Developmental Psychology, 43*(6), 1295-1311.

Browne, K. (1998). *Divided labours*. New Haven, CT: Yale University Press.

Bryant-Davis, T., Chung, H., & Tillman, S. (2009). From the margins to the center: Ethnic minority women and the mental health effects of sexual assault. *Trauma, Violence, & Abuse, 10*(4), 330-357. https://doi.org/10.1177/1524838009339755.

Bulanda, R. E. (2004). Paternal involvement with children: The influence of gender ideologies. *Journal of Marriage and Family, 66*(1), 40-45. https://doi.org/10.1111/j.0022-2455.2004.00003.x.

Burman, B., & Margolin, G. (1992). Analysis of the association between marital relationships and health problems: An interactional perspective. *Psychological Bulletin, 112*, 39-63.

Burtaverde, V., Chraif, M., Aniţei, M., & Dumitru, D. (2017). The HEXACO model of personality and risky driving behavior. *Psychological Reports, 120*(2), 255-270. doi.org/10.1177/0033294116688890.

Buss, D. M. (1997). Evolutionary foundations of personality. In Hogan, R. (Ed.), *Handbook of personality psychology* . London: Academic Press, pp. 317-344.

Buss, D. M. (2009). How can evolutionary psychology successfully explain personality and individual differences? *Perspectives on Psychological Science, 4*(4), 359-366.

Byrnes, J. P., Miller, D. C., & Schafer, W. D. (1999). Gender differences in risk-taking: A meta-analysis. *Psychological Bulletin, 125*, 367-383.

Caldera, Y. M., Huston, A. C., & O'Brien, M. (1989). Social interactions and play patterns of parents and toddlers with feminine, masculine, and neutral toys. *Child Development, 60*(1), 70-76.

Cale, E. M., & Lilienfeld, S. O. (2002). Sex differences in psychopathy and antisocial personality disorder: A review and integration. *Clinical Psychology Review, 22*(8), 1179-1207.

Campbell, A. (2002). *A mind of her own: The evolutionary psychology of women*. New York: Oxford University Press.

Campbell, A., Shirley, L., Heywood, C., & Crook, C. (2000). Infants' visual preference for sex-congruent babies, children, toys and activities: A longitudinal study. *British Journal of Developmental Psychology, 18*(4), 479-498. doi.org/10.1348/026151000165814.

Cardoso, C., Ellenbogen, M. A., Serravalle, L., & Linnen, A. M. (2013). Stress-induced negative mood moderates the relation between oxytocin administration and trust: Evidence for the tend-and-befriend response to stress? *Psychoneuroendocrinology, 38*(11), 2800-2804. doi:10.1016/j.psyneuen.2013.05.006.

Carmel, S., & Bernstein, J. H. (2003). Gender differences in physical health and psychosocial well being among four age-groups of elderly people in Israel. *International Journal of Aging and Human Development, 56*(2), 113-131.

Carmichael, M. S., Humbert, R., Dixen, J., Palmisano, G., Greenleaf, W., & Davidson, J. M. (1987). Plasma oxytocin increases in the human sexual response. *Journal of Clinical Endocrinology and Metabolism, 64*, 27-31.

Carmichael, M. S., Warburton, V. L., Dixen, J., & Davidson, J. M. (1994). Relationship among cardiovascular, muscular, and oxytocin responses during human sexual activity. *Archives of Sexual Behavior, 23*, 59-79.

Cattell, R. B. (1943). The description of personality: Basic traits resolved into clusters. *The Journal of Abnormal and Social Psychology, 38*(4), 476–506.

Cattell, R. B. (1945). The description of personality: Principles and findings in a factor analysis. *The American Journal of Psychology, 58*(1), 69–90.

Cattell, R. B., Cattell, A. K. S., & Rhymer, R. M. (1947). P-technique demonstrated in determining psychophysiological source traits in a normal individual. *Psychometrika, 12*(4), 267–288.

Catz, S. L., Gore-Felton, C., & McClure, J. B. (2002). Psychological distress among minority and low-income women living with HIV. *Journal of Behavioral Medicine, 28*(2), 53–60.

Centers for Disease Control & Prevention (2018a). Pregnancy Mortality Surveillance System. www.cdc.gov/reproductivehealth/maternalinfanthealth/pregnancy-mortality-surveillance-system.htm.

Centers for Disease Control & Prevention (2018b). Birth data. www.cdc.gov/nchs/nvss/births.htm.

Chaffin, M., Hanson, R., Saunders, B. E., Nichols, T., Barnett, D., Zeanah, C., ..., Miller-Perrin, C. (2006). Report of the APSAC Task Force on Attachment Therapy, Reactive Attachment Disorder, and Attachment Problems. *Child Maltreatment, 11*(1), 76–89. https://doi.org/10.1177/1077559505283699.

Chow, J. C.-C., Jaffee, K., & Snowden, L. (2003). Racial/ethnic disparities in the use of mental health services in poverty areas. *American Journal of Public Health, 93*(5), 792–797. doi:10.2105/AJPH.93.5.792.

Chrisler, J. C. (2013). Womanhood is not as easy as it seems: Femininity requires both achievement and restraint. *Psychology of Men & Masculinity, 14*(2), 117–120.

Cikara, M., Eberhardt, J. L., & Fiske, S. T. (2011). From agents to objects: Sexist attitudes and neural responses to sexualized targets. *Journal of Cognitive Neuroscience, 23,* 540–551. http://dx.doi.org/ 10.1162/jocn.2010.21497.

Clearfield, M. W., & Nelson, N. M. (2006). Sex differences in mothers' speech and play behavior with 6-, 9-, and 14-month-old infants. *Sex Roles, 54*: 127–137. https://doi.org/10.1007/s11199-005-8874-1.

Clemens, M., (2017). Technology and rising health care costs. Forbes, October 26. www.forbes.com/sites/forbestechcouncil/2017/10/26/technology-and-rising-health-care-costs/#27811a95766b. Retrieved August 8, 2018.

Cobb-Clark, D. A., & Schurer, S. (2012). The stability of big-five personality traits. *Economics Letters, 115*(1), 11–15.

Coccaro, E. F., Bergeman, C. S., Kavoussi, R. J., & Seroczynski, A. D. (1997). Heritability of aggression and irritability: A twin study of the Buss-Durkee aggression scales in adult male subjects. *Biological Psychiatry, 41*(3), 273–284. https://doi.org/10.1016/S0006-3223(96)00257-0.

Cochran, S. V., & Rabinowitz, F. E. (2000). *Men and depression: Clinical and empirical perspectives.* San Diego: Academic Press.

Coltrane, S., & Messineo, M. (2000). The perpetuation of subtle prejudice: Race and gender imagery in 1990s television advertising, *Sex Roles, 42*(5–6), 363–389.

Conley, T. D., & Ramsey, L. R. (2011). Killing us softly? Investigating portrayals of women and men in contemporary magazine advertisements. *Psychology of Women Quarterly, 35,* 469–478. http:// dx.doi.org/10.1177/0361684311413383.

Costa, P. T. Jr., & McRae, R. R. (1992). *Revised NEO Personality Inventory (NEO-PI-R) and NEO Five-Factor Inventory (NEO-FFI) professional manual* . Odessa, FL: Psychological Assessment Center.

Costa P. T. Jr., Terracciano, A., & McCrae, R. R. (2001). Gender differences in personality traits across cultures: Robust and surprising findings. *Journal of Personality and Social Psychology, 81*(2), 322–331.

Croizet, J., & Claire, T. (1998). Extending the concept of stereotype threat to social class: The intellectual underperformance of students from low socioeconomic backgrounds. *Personality and Social Psychology Bulletin, 24,* 588–594.

Dada, E. O., Anderson, M. K., Grier, T., Alemany, J. A., & Jones, B. H. (2027). Sex and age differences in physical performance: A comparison of Army basic training and operational populations. *Journal of Science and Medicine in Sport, 20*(Suppl 4), S68–S73.

D'Augelli, A. R., Grossman, A. H., & Starks, M. T. (2006). Childhood gender atypicality, victimization, and PTSD among lesbian, gay, and bisexual youth. *Journal of Interpersonal Violence, 21,* 1462–1482. http://dx.doi.org/10.1177/0886260506293482.

Davis, N. J., & Robinson, R. V. (1988). Class identification of men and women in the 1970s and 1980s. *American Sociological Review, 53*(1), 103–112.

De Bolle, M., De Fruyt, F., McCrae, R. R., Löckenhoff, C. E., Costa, P. T. Jr., Aguilar-Vafaie, M. E., ..., Terracciano, A. (2015). The emergence of sex differences in personality traits in early adolescence: A cross-sectional, cross-cultural study. *Journal of Personality and Social Psychology, 108*(1), 171–185.

De Dreu, C. K., Shalvi, S., Greer, L. L., Van Kleef, G. A., & Handgraaf, M. J. (2012). Oxytocin motivates non-cooperation in intergroup conflict to protect vulnerable in-group members. *PLoS ONE, 7*(11): e46751. doi:10.1371/journal.pone.0046751.

De Vries, R. E., & van Gelder, J.-L. (2015). Explaining workplace delinquency: The role of Honesty–Humility, ethical culture, and employee surveillance. *Personality and Individual Differences, 86*, 112–116. doi.org/10.1016/j.paid.2015.06.008.

Donnellan, M. B., Trzesniewski, K. H., Robins, R. W., Moffitt, T. E., & Caspi, A. (2005). Low self-esteem is related to aggression, antisocial behavior, and delinquency. *Psychological Science, 16*(4), 328–335. https://doi.org/10.1111/j.0956-7976.2005.01535.x.

Donnelly, K., & Twenge, J. M. (2017). Masculine and feminine traits on the Bem Sex-Role Inventory, 1993–2012: A cross-temporal meta-analysis. *Sex Roles, 76*(9–10), 556–565. https://doi.org/10.1007/s11199-016-0625-y.

Eagly, A. H. (1987). *Sex differences in social behavior: A social role interpretation* . Hillsdale, NJ: Erlbaum.

Else-Quest, N. M., Hyde, J. S., Goldsmith, H. H., & Van Hulle, C. A. (2006). Gender differences in temperament: A meta-analysis. *Psychological Bulletin, 132*, 33–72.

Else-Quest, N. M., Hyde, J. S., & Linn, M. C. (2010). Cross-national patterns of gender differences in mathematics: A meta-analysis. *Psychological Bulletin, 136*(1), 103–127.

Evans, G. W. (2004). The environment of childhood poverty. *American Psychologist, 59*(2), 77–92.

Ewing, L. L., Gorski, R. A., Sbordone, R. J., Tyler, J. V., Desjardins, C., & Robaire, B. (1979). Testosterone-estradiol filled polydimethylsiloxane subdermal implants: Effect on fertility and masculine sexual and aggressive behavior of male rats. *Biology of Reproduction, 21*(4), 765–772. https://doi.org/10.1095/biolreprod21.4.765.

Eysenck, H. J. (1947). *Dimensions of personality: A record of research carried out in collaboration with H.T. Himmelweit [and others]* . London: Kegan Paul, Trench, Trubner.

Eysenck, H. J. (1958). A short questionnaire for the measurement of two dimensions of personality. *Journal of Applied Psychology, 42*(1), 14–17.

Eysenck, H. J. (1983). Psychophysiology and personality: Extraversion, Neuroticism, and Psychoticism. In Gale, A., & Edwards, J. A. (Eds.), *Physiological correlates of human behaviour, Vol. 3, Individual differences and psychopathology* (pp. 13–30). London: Elsevier.

Fahrbach S. E., Morrell, J. I., & Pfaff, D. W. (1985). Possible role for endogenous oxytocin in estrogen-facilitated maternal behavior in rats. *Neuroendocrinology, 40*, 526–532. https://doi.org/10.1159/000124125.

Feingold, A. (1994). Gender differences in personality: A meta-analysis. *Psychological Bulletin, 116*, 429–456.

Fischer, A. H., & Manstead, A. S. R. (2000). The relation between gender and emotions in different cultures. In Fischer, A. (Ed.), *Gender and emotion: Social psychological perspectives* . Cambridge: Cambridge University Press, pp. 71–165.

Fiske, S. T., Cuddy, A. J., Glick, P., & Xu, J. (2002). A model of (often mixed) stereotype content: Competence and warmth respectively follow from perceived status and competition. *Journal of Personality and Social Psychology, 82*(6), 878–902. doi:10.1037//0022-3514.82.6.878.

Fiske, S. T., & Taylor, S. E. (2013). *Social cognition: From brains to culture*. Thousand Oaks, CA: Sage.

Freud, S. (1917). *Vorlesungen zur Einführung in die Psychoanalyse mit drei Teilen: Fehlleistung – Traum – Allgemeine Neurosenlehre, Nachdruck des Originals von 1920* . Norderstedt, Germany: Books on Demand, 2012.

Freud, S. (1918). From the history of an infantile neurosis. In *The standard edition of the complete psychological works of Sigmund Freud* (J. Strachey, Ed.). New York: Macmillan, 1964.

Fulker, D. W. (1981). The genetic architecture of psychoticism, extraversion and neuroticism. In Eysenck, H. J. (Ed.), *A model for personality*. New York: Springer-Verlag, pp. 99–122.

Funder, D. (1997). *The personality puzzle*. New York: Norton.

Gelissen, J., & Graaf, P. M. (2006). Personality, social background, and occupational career success. *Social Science Research, 35*, 702–726. https://doi.org/10.1016/j.ssresearch.2005.06.005.

Gelman, S. A., Taylor, M. G., & Nguyen, S. P. (2004). Mother-child conversations about gender: Understanding the acquisition of essentialist beliefs. *Monographs of the Society for Research in Child Development, 69*, 1–14. doi:10.1111/j.1540 5834.2004.06901002.x.

Gfellner, B. M., & Armstrong, H. D. (2012). Ego development, ego strengths, and ethnic identity among First Nation adolescents. *Journal of Research on Adolescence, 22*, 225–234. http://dx.doi.org/10.1111/j.1532-7795.2011.00769.x.

Gidengil, E., & Everitt, J. (1999). Metaphors and misrepresentation: Gendered mediation in news coverage of the 1993 Canadian leaders' debates. *Harvard International Journal of Press/Politics, 4*(1), 48–65. doi.org/10.1177/1081180X99004001005.

Gill, R. (2007). Postfeminist media culture: Elements of a sensibility. *European Journal of Cultural Studies, 10*, 147–166. doi:10.1177/1367549407075898.

Gillespie, B. L., & Eisler, R. M. (1992). Development of the Feminine Gender Role Stress Scale: A cognitive-behavioral measure of stress, appraisal, and coping for women. *Behavior Modification, 16*(3), 426–438. https://doi.org/10.1177/01454455920163008.

Glick, P., & Fiske, S. T. (1996). The ambivalent sexism inventory: Differentiating hostile and benevolent sexism. *Journal of Personality and Social Psychology, 70*, 491-512. doi:10.1037/0022-3514. 70.3.491.

Glick, P., Lameiras, M., & Castro, Y. R. (2002). Education and Catholic religiosity as predictors of hostile and benevolent sexism toward women and men. *Sex Roles, 47*(9-10), 433-441.

Green, B. L., & Kenrick, D. T. (1994). The attractiveness of gender-typed traits at different relationship levels: Androgynous characteristics may be desirable after all. *Personality and Social Psychology Bulletin, 20*, 244-253. doi:10.1177/0146167294203002.

Grillon, C., Krimsky, M., Charney, D. R., Vytal, K., Ernst, M, & Cornwell, B. (2013). Oxytocin increases anxiety to unpredictable threat. *Molecular Psychiatry, 18*(9), 958-960. doi:10.1038/mp.2012.156. PMC 3930442.

Grimm, S. D., Church, A. T., Katigbak, M. S., & Reyes, J. A. (1999). Self-described traits, values, and moods associated with individualism and collectivism: Testing I-C theory in an individualistic (U.S.) and a collectivistic (Philippine) culture. *Journal of Cross-Cultural Psychology, 30*, 466-500.

Halpern, D. F., & LaMay, M. L. (2000). The smarter sex: A critical review of sex differences in intelligence. *Educational Psychology Review, 12*(2), 229-246.

Hammer, J. H., Vogel, D. L., & Heimerdinger-Edwards, S. R. (2013). Men's help seeking: Examination of differences across community size, education, and income. *Psychology of Men & Masculinity, 14*(1), 65-75.

Haynal, A. (1994). *100 years of psychoanalysis: Contributions to the history of psychoanalysis.* Sterling, VA: Stylus Publishing.

Heflick, N. A., Goldenberg, J. L., Cooper, D. P., & Puvia, E. (2011). From women to objects: Appearance focus, target gender, and perceptions of warmth, morality and competence. *Journal of Experimental Social Psychology, 47*, 572-581. http:// dx.doi.org/10.1016/j.jesp.2010.12.020.

Heilbrun, A. B., & Schwartz, H. L. (1982). Sex-gender differences in level of androgyny. *Sex Roles, 8*, 201-214. https://doi.org/10.1007/BF00287923.

Heine, S. J., Lehman, D. R., Markus, H. R., & Kitayama, S. (1999). Is there a universal need for positive self-regard? *Psychological Review, 106*, 766-794.

Heinrichs, M., Baumgartner, T., Kirschbaum, C., & Ehlert, U. (2003). Social support and oxytocin interact to suppress cortisol and subjective responses to psychosocial stress. *Biological Psychiatry, 54*(12), 1389-1398.

Henderson, N. D. (1982). Human behavior genetics. *Annual Review of Psychology, 33*, 403-440.

Hilbig, B. E., & Zettler, I. (2015). When the cat's away, some mice will play: A basic trait account of dishonest behavior. *Journal of Research in Personality, 57*, 72-88.

Hoffman, M., Gneezy, U., & List, J. A. (2011). Nurture affects gender differences in spatial abilities. *Proceedings of the National Academy of Sciences of the United States of America, 108*(36), 14786-14788. doi:10.1073/pnas.1015182108.

Hurlemann, R., Patin, A., Onur, O. A., Cohen, M. X., Baumgartner, T., Metzler, S., ..., Kendrick, K. M. (2010). Oxytocin enhances amygdala-dependent, socially reinforced learning and emotional empathy in humans. *The Journal of Neuroscience, 30*(14), 4999-5007. doi:10.1523/JNEUROSCI.5538-09.2010.

Hyde, J. S. (2005). The gender similarities hypothesis. *American Psychologist, 60*, 581-592.

Hyde, J. S., Fennema, E., & Lamon, S. J. (1990). Gender differences in mathematics performance: A meta-analysis. *Psychological Bulletin, 107*(2), 139-155.

Hyde, J. S., & Linn, M. C. (1988). Gender differences in verbal ability: A meta-analysis. *Psychological Bulletin, 104*(1), 53-69.

Idle, T., Wood, E., & Desmarais, S. (1993). Gender role socialization in toy play situations: Mothers and fathers with their sons and daughters. *Gender Roles, 28*, 679-691.

Jankowski, M., Danalache, B., Wang, D., Bhat, P., Hajjar, F., Marcinkiewicz, M., ..., Gutkowska, J. (2004). Oxytocin in cardiac ontogeny. *Proceedings of the National Academy of Sciences of the United States of America, 101*(35), 13074-13079.

Jansz, J. (2000). Masculine identity and restrictive emotionality. In Fischer, A. (Ed.), *Gender and emotion: Social psychological perspectives* . Cambridge: Cambridge University Press, pp. 166-186.

Joshi, C., Russell, G., Cheng, I. H., Kay, M., Pottie, K., Alston, M., Smith, M., et al. (2013). A narrative synthesis of the impact of primary health care delivery models for refugees in resettlement countries on access, quality and coordination. *International Journal for Equity in Health, 12*, 88.

Kane, E. W. (2009). Policing gender boundaries: Parental monitoring of preschool children's gender nonconformity. In Nelson, M. K., & Garey, A. I. (Eds.), *Who's watching? Daily practices of surveillance among contemporary families* . Nashville: Vanderbilt University Press, pp. 239-259.

Kann, L., Olsen, E. O'M., McManus, T., Harris, W. A., Shanklin, S. L., Flint, K. H., ..., Zaza, S. (2016). Sexual identity, sex of sexual contacts, and health-related behaviors among students in grades 9-12 - United States and selected sites, 2015. *MMWR. Surveillance Summaries, 65*, 1-202. http://dx.doi.org/10.15585/mmwr.ss6509a1.

Kendrick, K. M. (2004). The neurobiology of social bonds. *Journal of Neuroendocrinology, 16*, 1007–1008.

Kern, M. L., Friedman, H. S., Martin, L. R., Reynolds, C. A., & Luong, G. (2009). Conscientiousness, career success, and longevity: A lifespan analysis. *Annals of Behavioral Medicine, 37*(2), 154–163. doi.org/10.1007/s12160-009-9095-6.

Kerry, L. J., Livesley, W. J., & Vemon, P. A. (1996). Heritability of the Big Five personality dimensions and their facets: A twin study. *Journal of Personality, 64*(3), 577–592.

Kiecolt-Glaser, J. K., & Newton, T. (2001). Marriage and health: His and hers. *Psychological Bulletin, 127*, 472–503.

King, J. E., Weiss, A., & Farmer, K. H. (2005). A chimpanzee (Pan troglodytes) analogue of cross-national generalization of personality structure: Zoological parks and an African sanctuary. *Journal of Personality, 73*(2), 389–410. https://doi.org/10.1111/j.1467-6494.2005.00313.x.

Kirsch, P., Esslinger, C., Chen, Q., Mier, D., Lis, S., Siddhanti, S., …, Meyer-Lindenberg, A. (2005). Oxytocin modulates neural circuitry for social cognition and fear in humans. *The Journal of Neuroscience, 25*(49), 11489–11493. doi:10.1523/JNEUROSCI.3984-05.2005.

Kitayama, S., Markus, H. R., & Kurokawa, M. (2000). Culture, emotion, and well-being: Good feelings in Japan and the United States. *Cognition & Emotion, 14*, 93–124.

Komarraju, M., Karau, S. J., & Schmeck, R. R. (2009). Role of the Big Five personality traits in predicting college students' academic motivation and achievement. *Learning and Individual Differences, 19*(1), 47–52. https://doi.org/10.1016/j.lindif.2008.07.001.

Kring, A. M., & Gordon, A. H. (1998). Sex differences in emotion: Expression, experience, and physiology. *Journal of Personality and Social Psychology, 74*, 686–703.

Kuyper, L., & Fokkema, T. (2011). Minority stress and mental health among Dutch LGBs: Examination of differences between sex and sexual orientation. *Journal of Counseling Psychology, 58*(2), 222–233.

Lane, A., Luminet, O., Rimé, B., Gross, J. J., de Timary, P., & Mikolajczak, M. (2013). Oxytocin increases willingness to socially share one's emotions. *International Journal of Psychology, 48*(4), 676–681. doi:10.1080/00207594.2012.677540.

Lauer, J. E., Ilksoy, S. D., & Lourenco, S. F. (2018). Developmental stability in gender-typed preferences between infancy and preschool age. *Developmental Psychology, 54*(4), 613–620. https://doi.org/10.1037/dev0000468.

Laursen, B., Pulkkinen, L., & Adams, R. (2002). The antecedents and correlates of agreeableness in adulthood. *Developmental Psychology, 38*(4), 591–603.

Lee, D. W., & Clark, A. (1997). Extraversion and its positive emotional core. In Hogan, R., Johnson, J., & Briggs, S. (Eds.), *Handbook of personality psychology* . Cambridge, MA: Academic Press, pp. 767–793.

Lee, K., & Ashton, M. C. (2004). Psychometric properties of the HEXACO personality inventory. *Multivariate Behavioral Research, 39*(2), 329–358.

Lee, Y.-T., & Seligman, M. E. P. (1997). Are Americans more optimistic than the Chinese? *Personality and Social Psychology Bulletin, 23*, 32–40.

Lehavot, K., & Simoni, J. M. (2011). The impact of minority stress on mental health and substance use among sexual minority women. *Journal of Consulting and Clinical Psychology, 79*(2), 159–170.

Lei, S. (2013). *The unwaged war on deep poverty* . Washington, DC: The Urban Institute.

Leimkühler, A.-M. M., Heller, J., & Paulus, N.-C. (2007). Subjective well-being and "male depression" in male adolescents. *Journal of Affective Disorders, 98*, 65–72.

Leinbach, M. D., & Fagot, B. I. (1993). Categorical habituation to male and female faces: Gender schematic processing in infancy. *Infant Behavior & Development, 16*(3), 317–332.

Levant, R. F. (1995). Toward the reconstruction of masculinity. In Levant, R. F., & Pollack, W. S. (Eds.), *A new psychology of men* (pp. 229–251). New York: Basic Books. (Reprinted in modified form from *Journal of Family Psychology, 5*(3/4), 1992, 379–402.)

Liben, L. S., Bigler, R. S., & Krogh, H. R. (2002). Language at work: Children's gendered interpretations of occupational titles. *Child Development, 73*, 810–823. doi:10.1111/1467-8624.00440.

Lippa, R. A. (2005). *Gender, nature, and nurture* . Mahwah, NJ: Erlbaum.

Lischke, A., Gamer, M., Berger, C., Grossmann, A., Hauenstein, K., Heinrichs, M., …, Domes, G. (2012). Oxytocin increases amygdala reactivity to threatening scenes in females. *Psychoneuroendocrinology, 37*(9), 1431–1438. doi:10.1016/j.psyneuen.2012.01.011.

Lithgow, L. (2000). A question of relativity: The role of the news media in shaping the view of women in Asian political dynasties. The Joan Shorenstein Center on the Press, Politics and Public Policy, Harvard University, Working Papers. http://www.hks.harvard.edu/presspol/research_publications/ papers/working_papers/2000_13.PDF. Retrieved April 27, 2010.

Liu, W. M., & Iwamoto, D. K. (2006). Asian American men's gender role conflict: The role of Asian values, self-esteem, and psychological distress. *Psychology of Men & Masculinity, 7*(3), 153–164. https://doi.org/10.1037/1524-9220.7.3.153.

Livingston, G. (2014). Growing number of dads home with the kids: Biggest increase among those caring for family. www.pewresearch.org.

Lynn, R., & Martin, T. (1997). Gender differences in extraversion, neuroticism, and psychoticism in 37 countries. *Journal of Social Psychology, 137*, 369-373.

Ma, X., Luo, L., Geng, Y., Zhao, W., Zhang, Q., & Kendrick, K. M. (2014). Oxytocin increases liking for a country's people and national flag but not for other cultural symbols or consumer products. *Frontiers in Behavioral Neuroscience, 8*, 266. doi:10.3389/fnbeh.2014.00266.

Maccoby, E. E. (2000). Parenting and its effects on children: On reading and misreading behavior genetics. *Annual Review of Psychology, 51*, 1-27.

Macintyre, S., Ford, G., & Hunt, K. (1999). Do women 'over-report' morbidity? Men's and women's responses to structured prompting on a standard question on long standing illness. *Social Science and Medicine, 48*(1), 89-98.

Maffulli, N., Longo, U. G., Gougoulias, N., Loppini, M., & Denaro, V. (2010). Long-term health outcomes of youth sports injuries. *British Journal of Sports Medicine, 44*, 21-25.

Maffulli, N., Longo, U. G., Spiezia, F., & Denaro, V. (2015). Sports injuries in young athletes: Long-term outcome and prevention strategies. *The Physician and sportsmedicine, 38*(2), 29-34.

Mahalik, J. R., Pierre, M. R., & Wan, S. S. C. (2006). Examining racial identity and masculinity as correlates of self-esteem and psychological distress in Black men. *Journal of Multicultural Counseling and Development, 34*, 94-104.

Malik, A. I., Zai, C. C., Abu, Z., Nowrouzi, B., & Beitchman, J. H. (2012). The role of oxytocin and oxytocin receptor gene variants in childhood-onset aggression. *Genes, Brain, and Behavior, 11*(5), 545-551. doi:10.1111/j.1601-183X.2012.00776.x.

Markus, H. R., & Kitayama, S. (1991). Culture and the self: Implications for cognition, emotion, and motivation. *Psychological Review, 98*(2), 224-253.

Martens, A., Johns, M., Greenberg, J., & Schimel, J. (2006). Combating stereotype threat: The effect of self-affirmation on women's intellectual performance. *Journal of Experimental Social Psychology, 42*(2), 236-243.

Martin, C. L., & Halverson, C. F. (1981). A schematic processing model of sex typing and stereotyping in children. *Child Development, 52*(4), 1119-1134.

Martin, N. G., & Jardine, R. (1986). Eysenck's contribution to behavior genetics. In Modgil, S., & Modgil, C. (Eds.), *Hans Eysenck: Consensus and controversy* . London: Falmer Press, pp. 13-62.

Martz, D. M., Handley, K. B., & Eisler, R. M. (1995). The relationship between feminine gender role stress, body image, and eating disorders. *Psychology of Women Quarterly, 19*(4), 493-508. https://doi.org/10.1111/j.1471-6402.1995.tb00088.x.

Matsuzaki, M., Matsushita, H., Tomizawa, K., & Matsui, H. (2012). Oxytocin: A therapeutic target for mental disorders. *The Journal of Physiological Sciences, 62*(6), 441-444. doi:10.1007/s12576-012-0232-9.

Maud, C., Ryan, J., McIntosh, J. E., & Olsson, C. A. (2018). The role of oxytocin receptor gene (OXTR) DNA methylation (DNAm) in human social and emotional functioning: A systematic narrative review. *BMC Psychiatry, 18*, 154.

McCarthy, M. M. (1995). Estrogen modulation of oxytocin and its relation to behavior. *Advances in Experimental Medicine and Biology, 395*, 235-245.

McCrae, R. R. (1987). Creativity, divergent thinking, and openness to experience. *Journal of Personality and Social Psychology, 52*(6), 1258-1265.

McCrae, R. R. (2002). NEO-PI-R data from 36 cultures: Further intercultural comparisons. In McCrae, R. R., & Allik, J. (Eds.), *The Five-Factor Model of personality across cultures*. New York: Kluwer Academic/Plenum, pp. 105-125.

McCrae, R. R., & Allik, J. (Eds.) (2002). *The Five-Factor Model of personality across cultures*. New York: Kluwer Academic/Plenum.

McCrae, R. R., & Costa, P. T. (1984). *Emerging lives, enduring dispositions* . Glenview, IL: Scott Foresman.

McCrae, R. R., & Costa, P. T. (1987). Validation of the five-factor model of personality across instruments and observers. *Journal of Personality and Social Psychology, 52*(1), 81-90.

McCrae, R. R., & Costa, P. T., Jr. (1997). Conceptions and correlates of openness to experience. In Hogan, R., Johnson, J. A., & Briggs, S. R. (Eds.), *Handbook of personality psychology* (pp. 825-847). Cambridge, MA: Academic Press. https://doi.org/10.1016/B978-012134645-4/50032-9.

McCrae, R. R., Terracciano, A., & Personality Profiles of Cultures Project (2005). Personality profiles of cultures: Aggregate personality traits. *Journal of Personality and Social Psychology, 89*(3), 407-425. https://doi.org/10.1037/0022-3514.89.3.407.

McGuffin, P., Katz, R., Watkins, S., & Rutherford, J. (1996). A hospital-based twin register of the heritability of DSM-IV unipolar depression. *Archives of General Psychiatry, 53*(2), 129-136. doi:10.1001/archpsyc.1996.01830020047006.

Mendoza-Sassi, R. A., & Béria, J. U. (2007). Gender differences in self-reported morbidity: Evidence from a population-based study in southern Brazil. *Cadernos de Saúde Pública* (Rio de Janeiro), *23*(2). http://dx.doi.org/10.1590/S0102-311X2007000200010.

Moffitt, R., Ribar, D., & Wilhelm, M. (1998). The decline of welfare benefits in the U.S.: The role of wage inequality. *Journal of Public Economics, 68,* 3, 421-452. doi:10.1016/S0047- 2727(98)00017-6.

Moore, D. S., & Johnson, S. P. (2008). Mental rotation in human infants: A sex difference. *Psychological Science, 19*(11), 1063-1066. https://doi.org/10.1111/j.1467-9280.2008.02200.x.

Moscicki, E. K. (1997). Identification of suicide risk factors using epidemiologic studies. *Psychiatric Clinics of North America, 20,* 499-517.

Newberger, E. H. (1999). *The men they will become: The nature and nurture of male character.* Cambridge, MA: De Capo Press.

Newman, D. B., & Nezlek, J. B. (2019). Private self-consciousness in daily life: Relationships between rumination and reflection and well-being, and meaning in daily life. *Personality and Individual Differences, 136,* 184-189.

Nolen-Hoeksema, S. (2002). Gender differences in depression. In Gotlib. I. H., & Hammen, C. L. (Eds.), *Handbook of depression* (pp. 492-509). New York: Guilford Press.

Odendaal, J. S., & Meintjes, R. A. (2003). Neurophysiological correlates of affiliative behaviour between humans and dogs. *Veterinary Journal* (London), *165*(3), 296-301. doi:10.1016/S1090-0233(02)00237-X.

O'Heron, C. A., & Orlofsky, J. L. (1990). Stereotypic and nonstereotypic sex role trait and behavior orientations, gender identity, and psychological adjustment. *Journal of Personality and Social Psychology, 58,* 134-143. doi:10.1037/0022-3514.

Okabe, S., Kitano, K., Nagasawa, M., Mogi, K., & Kikusui, T. (2013). Testosterone inhibits facilitating effects of parenting experience on parental behavior and the oxytocin neural system in mice. *Physiology & Behavior, 118,* 159-164. doi:10.1016/j.physbeh.2013.05.017.

O'Kelly, C. G., & Carney, L. S. (1986). *Women and men in society* (2nd ed.). Belmont, CA: Wadsworth.

Oquendo, M. A., Ellis, S. P., Greenwald, S., Malone, K. M., Weissman, M. M., & Mann, J. J. (2001). Ethnic and sex differences in suicide rates relative to major depression in the United States. *American Journal of Psychiatry, 158,* 1652-1658.

Organisation for Economic Cooperation and Development (OECD) (2016). Universal health coverage and health outcomes. www.oecd.org/els/health-systems/Universal-Health-Coverage-and-Health-Outcomes-OECD-G7-Health-Ministerial-2016.

Organisation for Economic Cooperation and Development (OECD) (2018). States of fragility report. www.oecd.org/dac/conflict-fragility-resilience/listofstateoffragilityreports.htm.

Passmore, N. L., Fogarty, G. J., Bourke, C. J., & Baker-Evans, S. F. (2005). Parental bonding and identity style as correlates of self-esteem among adult adoptees and nonadoptees. *Family Relations, 54*(4), 523-534. https://doi.org/10.1111/j.1741-3729.2005.00338.x.

Paul, G. (2009). The chronic dependence of popular religiosity upon dysfunctional psychosociological conditions. *Evolutionary Psychology, 7*(3). https://doi.org/10.1177/147470490900700305.

Perrone-McGovern, K. M., Wright, S. L., Howell, D. S., & Barnum, E. L. (2014). Contextual influences on work and family roles: Gender, culture, and socioeconomic factors. *The Career Development Quarterly, 62,* 21-28. doi:10.1002/ j.2161-0045.2014.00067.x.

Pleck, J. H. (1995). The gender role strain paradigm: An update. In Levant, R. F., & Pollack, W. S. (Eds.), *A new psychology of men* (pp. 11-32). New York: Basic Books.

Plomin, R., DeFries, J. C., McClearn, G. E., & Rutter, M. (2008). *Behavioral genetics* (4th ed.). New York: Freeman.

Pomerleau, A., Bolduc, D., Malcuit, G., & Cossette, L. (1990). Pink or blue: Environmental gender stereotypes in the first two years of life. *Sex Roles, 22*(5-6), 359-367. https://doi.org/10.1007/BF0028833.

Prentice, D. A., & Carranza, E. E. (2002). What women and men should be, shouldn't be, are allowed to be, and don't have to be: The contents of prescriptive gender stereotypes. *Psychology of Women Quarterly, 26,* 269-281. doi:10.1111/ 1471-6402.t01-1-00066.

Rainey, A. B., & Rust, J. O. (1999). Reducing gender stereotyping in kindergartners. *Early Child Development and Care, 150,* 33-42. doi:10.1080/0300443991500103.

Reidy, D. E., Berke, D. S., Gentile, B., & Zeichner, A. (2014). Man enough? Masculine discrepancy stress and intimate partner violence. *Personality and Individual Differences, 68,* 160-164. http://dx.doi.org/10.1016/j.paid.2014.04.021.

Reidy, D. E., Berke, D. S., Gentile, B., & Zeichner, A. (2016a). Masculine discrepancy stress, substance use, assault and injury in a survey of U.S. men. *Injury Prevention, 22,* 370 -374. http://dx.doi.org/10.1136/injuryprev-2015-041599.

Reidy, D. E., Brookmeyer, K. A., Gentile, B., Berke, D. S., & Zeichner, A. (2016b). Gender role discrepancy stress, high-risk sexual behavior, and sexually transmitted disease. *Archives of Sexual Behavior, 45,* 459-465. http://dx.doi.org/10.1007/s10508-014-0413-0.

Reidy, D. E., Shirk, S. D., Sloan, C. A., & Zeichner, A. (2009). Men who aggress against women: Effects of feminine gender role violation on physical aggression in hypermasculine men. *Psychology of Men & Masculinity, 10,* 1-12. http://dx.doi.org/10.1037/a0014794.

Reidy, D. E., Smith-Darden, J. P., Vivolo-Kantor, A. M., Malone, C. A., & Kernsmith, P. D. (2018). Masculine discrepancy stress and psychosocial maladjustment: Implications for behavioral and mental health of adolescent boys. Psychology of Men & Masculinity, 19(4), 560-569. https://doi.org/10.1037/.

Reisner, S. L., Greytak, E. A., Parsons, J. T., & Ybarra, M. L. (2015). Gender minority social stress in adolescence: Disparities in adolescent bullying and substance use by gender identity. *Journal of Sex Research, 52,* 243-256. http://dx.doi.org/10.1080/00224499.2014.886321.

RepublicanViews.org. (2014). Republican views on health care. November 25. www.republicanviews.org/republican-views-on-health-care/.

Rieger, G., & Savin-Williams, R. C. (2012). Gender nonconformity, sexual orientation, and psychological well-being. *Archives of Sexual Behavior, 41,* 611-621. http://dx.doi.org/10.1007/s10508-011-9738-0.

Riggio, H. R., & Desrochers, S. J. (2006). Maternal employment: Relations with young adults' work and family expectations and self-efficacy. *American Behavioral Scientist, 49*(10), 1328-1353.

Riggio, H. R., Groskopf, C., Dennem-Tigner, J., & Garcia, A. (2015). Religiosity and rape myth acceptance: Mediating role of traditional gender ideology. Paper presented at the annual meeting of the Western Psychological Association, Las Vegas, NV, April.

Robles, T. F., Slatcher, R. B., Trombello, J. M., & McGinn, M. M. (2014). Marital quality and health: A meta-analytic review. *Psychological Bulletin, 140,* 140-187.

Rohner, R. P. (1986). *The warmth dimension: Foundations of parental acceptance rejection theory.* Newbury Park, CA: Sage.

Rohner, R.P. (1999). Acceptance and rejection. In Levinson, D., Ponzetti, J., & Jorgensen, P. (Eds.), *Encyclopedia of human emotions,* vol. 1. New York: Macmillan, pp. 6-14.

Rolison, J. J., Hanoch, Y., & Gummerum, M. (2013). Characteristics of offenders: The HEXACO model of personality as a framework for studying offenders' personality. *Journal of Forensic Psychiatry & Psychology, 24*(1), 71-82.

Safonova T., & Leparsky, E. A. (1998). The unwanted child. *Child Abuse and Neglect, 22*(2), 155-157.

Sanders, B. (2017). Health care is a right, not a privilege. Huff Post, December 6. www.huffingtonpost.com/rep-bernie-sanders/health-care-is-a-right-no_b_212770.html.

Sartor, C. E., Grant, J. D., Lynskey, M. T., McCutcheon, V. V., Waldron, M., Statham, D. J., ..., Nelson, E. C. (2012). Common heritable contributions to low-risk trauma, high-risk trauma, posttraumatic stress disorder, and major depression. *Archives of General Psychiatry, 69*(3), 293-299.

Scharrer, E. (2002). Third-person perception and television violence: The role of out-group stereotyping in perceptions of susceptibility to effects. *Communication Research, 29*(6), 681-704. doi.org/10.1177/009365002237832.

Scharrer, E. (2004). Virtual violence: Gender and aggression in video game advertisements. *Mass Communication and Society, 7,* 393-412.

Schmidt, F. L., & Hunter, J. E. (1992). Development of a causal model of processes determining job performance. *Current Directions in Psychological Science, 1,* 89-92 https://doi.org/10.1111/1467-8721.ep10768758.

Schmitt, D. P., Realo, A., Voracek, M., & Allik, J. (2008). Why can't a man be more like a woman? Sex differences in Big Five personality traits across 55 cultures. *Journal of Personality and Social Psychology, 94*(1), 168-182.

Schwager, I. T. L., Hülsheger, U. R., & Lang, J. W. B. (2016). Be aware to be on the square: Mindfulness and counterproductive academic behavior. *Personality and Individual Differences, 93,* 74-79.

Sell, A., Hone, L. S. E., & Pound, N. (2012). The importance of physical strength to human males. *Human Nature, 23,* 30-44. doi:10.1007/s12110-012-9131-2.

Semega, J., Fotenot, K. R., & Kollar, M. A. (2017). Income and poverty in the United States: 2016. Census Bureau. University of California Davis. https://poverty.ucdavis.edu/faq/what-current-poverty-rate-united-states.

Semuels, A. (2016). The end of welfare as we know it: America's once-robust safety net is no more. *The Atlantic,* April 1. www.theatlantic.com/business/archive/2016/04/the-end-of-welfare-as-we-know-it/476322/. Retrieved August 8, 2018.

Serini, S., Powers, A., & Johnson, S. (1998). Of horse race and policy issues: A study of gender in coverage of a gubernatorial election by two major metropolitan newspapers. *Journalism Quarterly, 75,* 194-204.

Shalvi, S., & De Dreu, C. K. (2014). Oxytocin promotes group-serving dishonesty. *Proceedings of the National Academy of Sciences of the United States of America, 111*(15), 5503-5507. doi:10.1073/pnas.1400724111.

Shankar, P. R., Fields, S. K., Collins, C. L., Dick, R. W., & Comstock, R. D. (2007). Epidemiology of high school and collegiate football injuries in the United States, 2005-2006. *The American Journal of Sports Medicine, 35*(8), 1295-1303.

Sheng, F., Liu, Y., Zhou, B., Zhou, W., & Han, S. (2013). Oxytocin modulates the racial bias in neural responses to others' suffering. *Biological Psychology, 92*(2), 380-386. doi:10.1016/j.biopsycho.2012.11.018.

Singh-Manoux, A., Guéguen, A., Ferrie, J., Shipley, M., Martikainen, P., Bonenfant, S., ..., Marmot, M. (2008). Gender differences in the association between morbidity and mortality among middle-aged men and women. *American Journal of Public Health, 98*, 2251-2257. https://doi.org/10.2105/AJPH.2006.107912.

Smearman, E. L. D., Winiarski, A., Brennan, P. A., & Naj, J. (2015). Social stress and the oxytocin receptor gene interact to predict antisocial behavior in an at-risk cohort. *Development and Psychopathology, 27*(1), 309-318.

Smolak, L., Murnen, S. K., & Myers, T. A. (2014). Sexualizing the self: What college women and men think about and do to be 'sexy'. *Psychology of Women Quarterly, 38*(3), 379-397. doi:10.1177/0361684314524168.

Sparks, R. (1996). Masculinity and heroism in the Hollywood 'blockbuster': The culture industry and contemporary images of crime and law enforcement. *The British Journal of Criminology, 36*(3), 348-360. https://doi.org/10.1093/oxfordjournals.bjc.a014099.

Steele, L. S., Daley, A., Curling, D., Gibson, M. F., Green, D. C., Williams, C. C., & Ross, L. E. (2027). LGBT identity, untreated depression, and unmet need for mental health services by sexual minority women and trans-identified people. *Journal of Women's Health, 26*(2), 116-127.

Strong, W. B., Malina, R. M., Blimkie, C. J. R., Daniels, S. R., Dishman, R. K., Gutin, B., ..., Trudeau, F. (2005). Evidence based physical activity for school-age youth. *The Journal of Pediatrics, 146*(6), 732-737.

Sue, D., & Sue, D. M. (2008). *Foundations of counseling and psychotherapy: Evidence-based practices for a diverse society* . Hoboken, NJ: John Wiley & Sons.

Suh, E. M. (2000). Self, the hyphen between culture and subjective well-being. In Diener, E., & Suh, E. M. (Eds.), *Culture and subjective well-being* . Cambridge, MA: MIT Press, pp. 63-87.

Suh, E., Diener, E., Oishi, S., & Triandis, H. (1998). The shifting basis of life satisfaction judgements across cultures: Emotions versus norms. *Journal of Personality and Social Psychology, 74*, 482-493.

Tang, T. N., & Tang, C. S. (2001). Gender role internalization, multiple roles, and Chinese women's mental health. *Psychology of Women Quarterly, 25*(3), 181-196. https://doi.org/10.1111/1471-6402.00020.

Taşdemir, N., & Sakallı-Uğurlu, N. (2010). The relationships between ambivalent sexism and religiosity among Turkish university students. *Sex Roles, 62*(7-8), 420-426.

Tellegen, A., Lykken, D. T., Bouchard, T. I., Wilcox, K. J., Segal, N. L., & Rich, S. (1988). Personality similarity in twins reared apart and together. *Journal of Personality and Social Psychology, 54*, 1031-1039.

Theintz, G. E., Howald, H., Allemann, Y., & Sizonenko, P. C. (1989). Growth and pubertal development of young female gymnasts and swimmers: A correlation with parental data. *International Journal of Sports Medicine, 10*(2), 87-91. doi:10.1055/s-2007-1024880.

Theodoridou, A., Penton-Voak, I. S., & Rowe, A. C. (2013). A direct examination of the effect of intranasal administration of oxytocin on approach-avoidance motor responses to emotional stimuli. *PLoS ONE, 8*(2), e58113. doi:10.1371/journal.pone.0058113.

Toomey, R. B., Ryan, C., Diaz, R. M., Card, N. A., & Russell, S. T. (2010). Gender-nonconforming lesbian, gay, bisexual, and transgender youth: School victimization and young adult psychosocial adjustment. *Developmental Psychology, 46*, 1580-1589. http://dx.doi.org/10.1037/a0020705.

Torjesen, P. A., & Sandnes, L. (2004). Serum testosterone in women as measured by an automated immunoassay and a RIA. *Clinical Chemistry, 50*(3), 678; author reply 678-679. doi:10.1373/clinchem.2003.027565.

Triandis, H. C. (1989). The self and social behavior in differing cultural contexts. *Psychological Review, 96*(3), 506-520.

Triandis, H. C. (1996). The psychological measurement of cultural syndromes. *American Psychologist, 51*, 407-415.

Triandis, H. C., & Suh, E. M. (2002). Cultural influences on personality. *Annual Review of Psychology, 53*, 133-160. https://doi.org/10.1146/annurev.psych.53.100901.135200.

Turner, P. J., & Gervai, J. (1995). A multidimensional study of gender typing in preschool children and their parents: Personality, attitudes, preferences, behavior, and cultural differences. *Developmental Psychology, 31*, 759-772. doi:10.1037/0012-1649.31.5.759.

Twenge, J. M., Konrath, S., Foster, J. D., Campbell, W. K., & Bushman, B. J. (2008). Egos inflating over time: A cross-temporal meta-analysis of the Narcissistic Personality Inventory. *Journal of Personality, 76*, 875-902.

Vaes, J., Paladino, M. P., & Puvia, E. (2011). Are sexualized females complete human beings? Why males and females dehumanize sexually objectified women. *European Journal of Social Psychology, 41*, 774-785.

Valchev, V. H. van de Vijver, F. J. R., Nel, J. A., Rothmann, S., Meiring, D. (2013). The use of traits and contextual information in free personality descriptions across ethnocultural groups in South Africa. *Journal of Personality and Social Psychology, 104*(6), 1077-1091.

Van de Vliert, E., Schwartz, S. H., Huismans, S. E., Hofstede, G., & Daan, S. (1999). Temperature, cultural masculinity, and domestic political violence: A cross-national study. *Journal of Cross-Cultural Psychology, 30*, 291-314.

van Leengoed, E., Kerker, E., & Swanson, H. H. (1987). Inhibition of post-partum maternal behaviour in the rat by injecting an oxytocin antagonist into the cerebral ventricles. *The Journal of Endocrinology, 112*(2), 275-282. doi:10.1677/joe.0.1120275.

Vandello, J. A., & Bosson, J. K. (2013). Hard won and easily lost: A review and synthesis of theory and research on precarious manhood. *Psychology of Men & Masculinity, 14*, 101-113. http://dx.doi.org/10 .1037/a0029826.

Vázquez-Barquero, J. L., Diez-Manrique, J. F., Muñoz, J., Menendez Arango, J., Gaite, L., Herrera, S., & Der, G. J. (1992). Sex differences in mental illness: A community study of the influence of physical health and sociodemographic factors. *Social Psychiatry and Psychiatric Epidemiology, 27*(2), 62-68.

Verhulst, B., Neale, M. C., & Kendler, K. S. (2015). The heritability of alcohol use disorders: A meta-analysis of twin and adoption studies. *Psychological Medicine, 45*(5), 1061-1072.

Vestal, C. (2017). How states are fighting over women's access to health care. *Politics,* July 25. Public Broadcasting Service (PBS). www.pbs.org/newshour/politics/states-fighting-womens-access-health-care. Retrieved August 8, 2018.

Voyer, D., Voyer, S., & Bryden, M. P. (1995). Magnitude of sex differences in spatial abilities: A meta-analysis and consideration of critical variables. *Psychological Bulletin, 117*(2), 250-270.

Wall, G., & Arnold, S. (2007). How involved is involved fathering? An exploration of the contemporary culture of fatherhood. *Gender & Society, 21*(4), 508-527. https://doi.org/10.1177/0891243207304973.

Wanic, R., & Kulik, J. (2011). Toward an understanding of gender differences in the impact of marital conflict on health. *Sex Roles, 65*, 297-312.

Watson, D. C. (2001). Procrastination and the five-factor model: A facet level analysis. *Personality and Individual Differences, 30*(1), 149-158.

Wester, S. R. (2008). Male gender role conflict and multiculturalism: Implications for counseling psychology. *The Counseling Psychologist, 36*, 294-324. doi:10.1177/0011000006286341.

Wilgenbusch, T., & Merrell, K. W. (1999). Gender differences in self concept among children and adolescents: A meta-analysis of multidimensional studies. *School Psychology Quarterly, 14*, 101-120.

Wilper, A. P., Woolhandler, S., Lasser, K. E., McCormick, D., Bor, D. H., & Himmelstein, D. U. (2009). Health insurance and mortality in US adults. *American Journal of Public Health, 99*(12), 2289-2295. doi:10.2105/AJPH.2008.157685.

Witter, S., Govender, V., Ravindran, T. K. S., & Yates, R. (2017). Minding the gaps: Health financing, universal health coverage and gender. *Health Policy Plan,* 1-9. (https://doi.org/10.1093/heapol/czx063).

World Health Organization (2009). Infant and young child feeding: Model chapter for textbooks for medical students and allied health professionals. 2 The physiological basis of breastfeeding. www.who.int/nutrition/publications/infantfeeding/9789241597494/en/.

World Health Organization (2015a). Trends in maternal mortality: 1990 to 2015 estimates by WHO, UNICEF, UNFPA, World Bank Group and the United Nations Population Division Executive Summary. http://apps.who.int/iris/bitstream/handle/10665/193994/WHO_RHR_15.23_eng.pdf; jsessionid=20200FE75FF7724F2F7DAAAE4A82A6B0?sequence=1.

World Health Organization (2015b). Integrating equity, gender, human rights and social determinants into the work of WHO Roadmap for Action (2014-2019). www.who.int/gender-equity-rights/knowledge/webroadmap.pdf?ua=1.

World Health Organization (2017a). Women on the move: Migration, care work and health. www.who.int/gender-equity-rights/knowledge/women-on-the-move/en/.

World Health Organization (2017b). Beyond the barriers: Framing evidence on health system strengthening to improve the health of migrants experiencing poverty and social exclusion. www.who.int/gender-equity-rights/knowledge/beyond-barriers/en/.

World Health Organization (2017c). Regional consultation on universal access to sexual and reproductive health. www.afro.who.int/news/regional-consultation-universal-access-sexual-and-reproductive-health. Retrieved June 24, 2018.

World Health Organization (2018a). Maternal mortality. www.who.int/news-room/fact-sheets/detail/maternal-mortality.

World Health Organization (2018b). Refugee and migrant health. www.who.int/migrants/en/.

World Health Organization (2018c). Universal health coverage. www.who.int/healthsystems/universal_health_coverage/en/.

Young, P. A., Eaves, L. J., & Eysenck, H. J. (1980). Intergenerational stability and change in the causes of variation in personality. *Personality and Individual Differences, 1*, 35-55.

Zak, P., Stanton, A., & Ahmadi, S. (2007). Oxytocin increases generosity in humans. *PLoS ONE, 2*, e1128.

Ziobrowski, H., Sartor, C. E., Tsai, J., & Pietrzak, R. H. (2017). Gender differences in mental and physical health conditions in U.S. veterans: Results from the National Health and Resilience in Veterans Study. *Journal of Psychosomatic Research, 101*, 110-113. https://doi.org/10.1016/j.jpsychores.2017.08.011.

Zuckerman, M. (2009). Sensation seeking. In Leary, M. R., & Hoyle, R. H. (Eds.), *Handbook of individual differences in social behavior*. New York: The Guilford Press, pp. 455-465.

10 Intimacy and Interpersonal Relationships

Attachment in Infancy	303
Attachment in Adulthood	306
Parenting Differences for Girls and Boys	308
Parenting Is Gendered	309
Family Relationships	311
Gender Differences in Social Interaction and Communication	313
Friendships across the Lifespan	315
Love and Intimate Relationships	316
Attraction	316
The Experience of Love	318
Marriage, Divorce, Widowhood	321

INEQUALITIES AND INJUSTICES

Coming out and Identity Formation: The Struggle for LGBTQ Young People

LGBTQ youth in our world are at risk. In a study of LGBTQ young people in all 50 United States, the Human Rights Campaign (2018) reports that nearly 80% of LGBTQ youth report feeling depressed, including feelings of worthlessness and hopelessness, in the past week. Sixty-seven percent of them have heard relatives make negative comments about LGBTQ people and nearly all of them report trouble sleeping. LGBTQ youth report lower self-esteem, greater substance use, and greater anxiety compared to heterosexual young people (Birkett, Newcomb, & Mustanski, 2014), and they are five times more likely to attempt suicide (Centers for Disease Control & Prevention, 2016). Despite increasing tolerance toward LGBTQ people around the world (especially in secular and wealthy countries; Pew Research Center, 2013), nearly all current societies have a history of negative social attitudes toward any sexuality that is not strictly heterosexual, prohibitions that are linked with religiosity (Pew Research Center, 2018). Being not heterosexual is a stigma that subjects people to social ridicule and rejection, and violent hate crimes (Dashow, 2017; Mays & Cochran, 2001; Meyer, Schwartz, & Frost, 2008). The worst form of rejection it seems for LGBTQ youth is rejection by their own family members, with approximately 3% of LGBTQ youth completely expelled from the family after coming out (Herdt & Boxer, 1993).

Coming out involves revealing **sexual orientation** and/or **gender identity** to important people, including friends, teachers, and family members. While heterosexual or **cisgender** youth do not typically "come out" to anyone (because heterosexuality is **normative**), coming out is an important facet of identity formation, a primary developmental task in adolescence and young adulthood (Erikson, 1963). Coming out is a highly selective process, with young people coming out over time only to certain, obviously trusted individuals. LGBTQ youth are most likely to be out to friends, especially LGBTQ friends (Human Rights Campaign, 2018). For LGBTQ young people, identity formation is especially complicated by social negativity and difficulties involved in forming a positive LGBTQ identity in a **heteronormative**, oppressive world (Human Rights Campaign, 2018; Troiden, 1989). LGBTQ young people are likely to feel isolated within heterosexual majority groups, including at school (Human Rights Campaign, 2018). They may have little access to identity-affirming social support and resources, including interaction with other LGBTQ youth and adults (Greene, 1994).

LGBTQ youth fear parental rejection and so may avoid coming out to their families (Hersch, 1991). Descriptive research indicates that typical parents may have several different reactions to their child's coming out, including loving acceptance (Muller, 1987). LGBTQ youth with abusive parents may engage in withdrawal or escape behaviors, including drug use, running away from home, prostitution, and sadly, suicide (Savin-Williams, 1994). Parents' rejection of their LGBTQ child is typically associated with parents expressing **homonegativity** (Robinson & Walters, 1987), endorsing traditional values, and following traditional religions, documented across many cultures (Newman & Muzzonigro, 1993). LGBTQ youth who are members of ethnic minority groups may come from more traditional and religious families, and as such are at greater risk for parental rejection and imposition of religious condemnation than white LGBTQ youth (Higa et al., 2014; Ream & Savin-Williams, 2005; Savin-Williams, 1996b). LGBTQ youth who are not white suffer racial prejudice and discrimination on a regular basis, unlike Euro-American youth, which compounds the struggles involved in forming a positive identity during adolescence (Human Rights Campaign, 2018).

Despite the risks involved, developing a positive identity and coming out is associated with positive outcomes for LGBTQ youth, including higher **self-esteem**, less **depression** and anxiety, and higher academic performance (Russell & Fish, 2016). Similarly, the Human Rights Campaign (2018) found that when LGBTQ youth expressed a positive identity, coming out resulted in more positive outcomes for their well-being. It is important for LGBTQ youth service and school programs to address issues involved in developing a positive identity and coming out, with coming out more likely to be positive and successful when young people have additional **social supports** (D'Augelli, 1994). Because school is such an important environment for adolescents, impacting their overall health and well-being, it is particularly important for educators and schools to implement positive support programs for LGBTQ students (Zewditu, Rasberry, Steiner, Brener, & McManus, 2018).

Intimacy and Interpersonal Relationships 299

BONUS BOX

The Blurring of Paternity in Tribal Groups

In several parts of this book, we discuss the idea of paternity certainty, a man's certainty (or lack thereof) that a child is indeed his offspring. A mother always knows whether a child is genetically hers because she would bear such a child (except in cases of implantation of another woman's egg). In modern times, anyone can quite quickly determine paternity and genetic relationships with others with a home kit. Before modern DNA testing became available, however, paternity was more of a mystery sometimes for men (or made into a mystery by men who wanted to walk away from unwanted children and their mothers). Paternity certainty underlies the historical, multicultural emphasis on female virginity at marriage. If a man's wife has only had intercourse with him, any children that result must be his, as long as she is chaste at marriage and faithful to him. Evolutionary theorists argue that establishing paternity certainty is important for men because it would be disadvantageous to devote time, energy, and resources to a child that is not genetically related, not actually one's child. Because of this motivation, evolutionary theorists have commonly asserted that the nuclear family (one heterosexual couple with children) is the evolutionary ideal. It ensures paternity certainty for men, and ensures resources provided to offspring for women.

Evidence from anthropologists studying more primitive groups in the Amazon rainforest in South America suggests that the nuclear family may not be the family arrangement that is most evolutionarily adaptive. In multiple tribes (from other areas of the world as well), the practice of partible or shared paternity is practiced. That is, women are free to have sex with any man they choose, in addition to their husband. If a child results, or if sex occurs during pregnancy, each of those men is considered a possible father to the child. As such, paternity is blurred and a child has multiple men on whom to rely for resources while growing up (Beckerman et al., 1998; Beckerman & Valentine, 2002; Crocker & Crocker, 1994). The saying *"it takes a village"* takes on new meaning here. In this way, every child is likely to have at least one father; if not their biological father, then a man considered as father. For children, this situation seems more ideal, with no child suffering the deprivation that comes from having one (or two) missing parents. What do you think? Is the nuclear family the modern ideal? How do ideas of morality derived from religious prohibitions on sexuality come into play here?

CRITICAL THINKING

Single Mothers, Missing Fathers

Over 26% of all American children live in poverty. A primary mechanism for poverty for any adult person is having children (Grall, 2016; Hoffman, 1998). In the United States and around the world, there are clear inequalities between women and men in terms of taking responsibility for living with and supporting children. Everywhere, including in the U.S., more women live in poverty than men in every age group (United Nations, 2010; United States Census Bureau, 2014). In the U.S., about 62% of people living in the worst poverty are single women with four or more children. Childcare is expensive, and one low-wage job is not sufficient to pay for childcare and other living expenses, not with that number of children. Custodial mothers with full-time jobs or a Bachelor's degree are less likely to live in poverty. Women comprise about 84% of unmarried people with custody of their children, approximately 11 million U.S. women. Of those women, 31% live in poverty. Only 17.5% of single-parent households are headed by single fathers, who are much less likely to live in poverty than single mothers. Racial minority children are especially likely to live in poverty, with nearly one-half (48%) of African American children and nearly 30% of Latinx children living in one-parent households. Of single parents entitled to child support, mainly women, less than one-half receive the full payment regularly.

Children with so-called **absent fathers** (noncustodial fathers who rarely visit and provide little if any financial support) suffer many negative outcomes that children with responsible, loving fathers do not. Daughters and sons of absent fathers may be impulsive, including engaging in risky sexual behaviors, and gambling and substance use (Cherlin et al., 1991; James, Ellis, Schlomer, & Garber, 2012; Sheppard, Garcia, & Sear, 2014). Children and adolescents with absent fathers are at greater risk of delinquency and aggressive behaviors, especially sons (Bereczkei & Csanaky, 1996; D'Onofrio et al., 2005; Ember & Ember, 2001; Hetherington, 1972). In contrast, greater involvement and financial support by noncustodial fathers are predictive of higher academic and social competence and well-being in children (Geary, 2010; Sarkadi, Kristiansson, Oberklaid, & Bremberg, 2008).

Girls and women who are denied comprehensive sex education are obviously more likely to experience an unwanted pregnancy as they lack knowledge of reproduction, sexuality, and contraception (Saito, 1998); and they are more likely to engage in unsafe sex, which is associated with poverty for both women and men around the world (World Health Organization, 2004). But why are men, in this modern world, abandoning their children? And why does society decry the wretched single mother and her poor choices, with nary a word about the missing father and what he had done to put that woman and her child into poverty through his lack of responsibility and conscience? The same people who oppose accurate, comprehensive sex education for adolescents in public schools also oppose safe, legal abortion for women (www.catholicparents.org/ten-good-reasons-oppose-public-school-sex-education/), and they tend to view women as the gatekeepers of sexuality, with men somehow less responsible for their risky sexual behavior and resulting unwanted pregnancies (Abbott, Harris, & Mollen, 2016). Boys and men are equally responsible for unwanted pregnancies, and if they're not going to spend a few bucks and wear a condom, they need to be held equally accountable as parents and providers in the long run, whether they like it or not.

LEARN MORE

Child Abuse and Neglect: The Intergenerational Poverty Trap

Approximately 700,000 children in the United States are reported as abused in some way each year, with infants and young children most at risk (U.S. Administration for Children & Families, 2014). In approximately 80% of all cases, abusers are the parents or other relatives of the children. Naturally, abusers are bigger and stronger than their victims, so it is adults and older relatives who victimize children. Fathers are the most common parent abuser, followed by mothers, and stepfathers or male partners of mothers (CAADA, 2014; United States Department of Health and Human Services, 2005). When children live with adults who are unrelated to them, the risk of abuse is 50 times greater, is more likely to be severe, and is more likely to be fatal (Schnitzer & Ewigman, 2005; Yampolskaya, Greenbaum, & Berson, 2009). There are various types of child abuse, although each type rarely occurs in isolation (Thornberry, Knight, & Lovegrove, 2012). In the United States, the Child Abuse Prevention and Treatment Act (CAPTA) defines child abuse as "any recent act or failure to act on the part of a parent or caretaker, which results in death, serious physical or emotional harm, sexual abuse, or exploitation, or an act or failure to act which presents an imminent risk of serious harm." Abuse includes physical, sexual, and emotional abuse; neglect is the most common form of child abuse (U.S. Administration for Children & Families, 2014). Abuse affects girls and boys at fairly equal rates, although girls are more likely to be the victims of sexual abuse (Centers for Disease Control & Prevention, 1997). According to the World Health Organization (2002), 57,000 children under the age of 15 years from around the world are murdered by parents or caretakers each year. Child abuse is an epidemic, a public health emergency that everyone should be concerned about.

Poverty is a major factor involved in the abuse of children, with poor parents lacking resources and social support, constantly living with the daily stress of being poor (Evans, 2004; Frias-Armenta & McCloskey, 1998; Hadi, 2000; Hunter, Jain, Sadowski, & Sanhueza, 2000; National Research Council, 1993). The greatest proportion of poor people in the United States are single mothers and their children (United States Census Bureau, 2017). Adding a child to a situation of little money, opportunity, and support leads to negative outcomes for everyone, but particularly the child. Children are expensive and poverty is obviously associated with children's poor nutrition and health care (Evans, 2004). Children living in poverty are especially likely to be neglected (Slack, Holl, McDaniel, Yoo, & Bolger, 2004).

What happens to these people in adulthood, these victimized, abused children who grew up with nothing? Abused children become troubled adults suffering from mental disorders, depression, substance abuse, risky sexual behavior, and suicide (Beitchman et al., 1992; Norman et al., 2012).

People who grow up poor and neglected have poorer physical health in adulthood (Case, Lubotsky, & Paxson, 2002; Drossman, Talley, Leserman, et al., 1995; Fuller-Thomson, Bottoms, Brennenstuhl, & Hurd, 2011; Leventhal & Newman, 2010). They are more likely than other people to suffer from depression (Bareis & Mezuk, 2016), **post-traumatic stress disorder** (**PTSD**; Nikulina, Widom, & Czaja, 2011), and to abuse substances, including alcohol and drugs (Widom & White, 1997). They are more likely to be arrested as adults (Nikulina et al., 2011; Widom & White, 1997). Children in poverty experience poor quality education (Evans, 2004), and as such, as adults they are not well-prepared to be productive, successful workers (Nikulina et al., 2011). As adults, they are likely to be poor themselves, a result of the intergenerational transmission of poverty (Bird, 2013). As poverty continues, it affects the well-being of every individual within society. Individuals belonging to racial minority groups are more likely to be poor than European Americans because of historical and systemic racism and lack of opportunity (Adler & Rehkopf, 2008; Macartney, 2011).

This is how poverty becomes entrenched in a country, and people in growing numbers are sleeping on the streets. Punishing the poor for being poor (especially accusing them of being lazy; Katz & Hass, 1988) is the apparent preferred approach of many politicians in the United States. Social benefits that are designed to lift people out of poverty are being cut (Parrott et al., 2018), while politicians cut taxes for the super-wealthy (your private jet is a tax deduction; Delk, 2017). Resources for education and programs that really help poor children, like free meals, Head Start, and after-school programs, are always in danger. Funding for public higher education is under constant attack (Mitchell, Leachman, & Masterson, 2017). A healthy body and solid education are forces for use in adulthood and are part of every American's pursuit of life and happiness. In addition, politicians, a preponderance of wealthy white men in the U.S., are seemingly always working feverishly to control women's bodies, to force women to have pregnancies and give birth against their will. How is a poor woman, especially a young woman, supposed to successfully parent a child when 1) they have no or little money or resources, and 2) the boy or man does not want to be a parent (or is a rapist)? Unwanted children are not an effective punishment against girls and women for having sex, and they contribute to poverty around the world. A major factor in women's financial independence and success around the world is access to reproductive health care, including contraceptives and safe abortion (Chronic Poverty Research Centre, 2010).

Intimacy and Interpersonal Relationships 303

Attachment in Infancy

An infant's experience of the world is mainly limited to bodily sensations, including feelings of hunger, pleasure in **sucking** (an inborn instinct), physical effects of the external world on the body (e.g., temperature, noises), all of the comforts and discomforts of the body. These bodily sensations, particularly how pleasant or unpleasant they are, are largely determined by the adults surrounding the infant, who is completely helpless to meet her own needs. The infant's early ongoing experience of the world is recorded in the brain through neural pathways that affect later learning and expectations about people and the world (Greenough, Black, & Wallace, 1987; Shore, 1997). Early bonds with caretakers (or lack thereof) affect the brain's foundational development of neural pathways related to formation of social relationships (Numan & Young, 2016; Perry, 2002). Such neural pathways include cognitive representational or **working models** of the self and others, primary views of the self and others as lovable and trustworthy, or not, that the infant develops through relationships with parents (Bowlby, 1969). In addition, neuroscience research indicates that malleable infant neurotransmitter and stress response systems adjust rather quickly and somewhat permanently based on caregiving they receive, with early **attachment** having foundational and long-term effects on the brain and body's habitual physiological responses to stress (Francis, Diorio, Liu, & Meaney, 1999; Hertsgaard, Gunnar, Erickson, & Nachmias, 1995; Nemeroff, 1996).

When parents have the capabilities (money, knowledge, maturity) and motivation (the child is wanted and loved) to care for their infant, they respond with emotional warmth and responsiveness, and they do so with regularity, in response to the child's expression of needs (e.g., crying, fussing) (Brown, Cohen, Johnson, & Salinger, 1998). Over time, with repetition, the child begins to recognize that their discomforts or unmet needs do not last long; a nice warm adult will come and speak soothingly, will hold her close and treat her with affection, and the unmet need will be recognized and eventually satisfied. Being loved and cared for affects rudimentary beliefs about the self and others; that the self is worthy of love and care, that others are loving. When the child's needs are not met, when discomforts last and cries are ignored, the child learns a different lesson over time; that the world is cold and undependable, that adults do not respond with love and care. The child will likely develop a feeling of being unlovable, a painful feeling that affects attitudes toward the self, or **self-esteem**, in the long term if mistreatment of the child continues. A child who is not properly cared for will become a person who doesn't love herself, a negative and painful feeling that will affect every aspect of her life, including her relationships with other people (Perry, 2002; Winston & Chicot, 2016).

Attachment to parents, especially mother, begins in utero, as the fetus in later months can hear the mother's voice and other external noises. Newborn infants recognize and prefer their mother's voice (Hepper, Scott, & Shahidullah, 1993), and scent (Porter, 1998), which promotes bonding between mothers and infants. **Bonding** is a strong, primitive feeling of connection between mother and infant that begins at birth, and it is the foundation of attachment, a feeling of closeness and trust between two people, a preference for one person over others (Bowlby, 1969). Bonding is viewed as originating in mothers, who feel bonded to their infant (Myers, 1984). Bonding is supported by early physical contact between the newborn and its mother, including "skin-to-skin" contact and breastfeeding (Klaus & Kennell, 1976). Hormones associated with childbirth, most notably **oxytocin**, promote bonding (Feldman, Weller, Zagoory-Sharon, & Levine, 2007), although healthy bonding does not require such postpartum hormones (i.e., not only biological mothers experience a bond toward a new infant)

(Singer, Brodzinsky, Ramsay, Steir, & Waters, 1985). Fathers who engage in higher amounts of physical contact with their newborns show greater oxytocin levels than fathers who are less engaged (Feldman, Gordon, Schneiderman, Weisman, & Zagoory-Sharon, 2010), supporting the cyclical nature of such hormones (hormones promote contact, contact promotes hormones; Pryce, 1992; Rosenblatt & Siegel, 1981).

Bonding occurs between newborns and their parents; attachment develops a bit later in the child (between 6 and 12 months of age) and is reflected in the baby's desire for closeness with mother (or another primary caregiver) and a strong preference for mother over all other people (Bowlby, 1969). Infants who are securely attached to their mothers cry in protest when she leaves (they show **separation distress**); securely attached infants show **stranger anxiety**, a turning away from strangers to the familiar, desirable arms of mother (Ainsworth, Blehar, Waters, & Wall, 1978). Evolutionary theorists argue that attachment to parents is adaptive as it keeps children close to stronger, more capable adults who can protect them from predators and other dangers (Bowlby, 1969; Simpson, 1999). The primary determinant of **secure**, healthy attachment between infants and their primary caregivers is emotional sensitivity and warm, positive responsiveness of caregivers to infant signals and needs (Bell & Ainsworth, 1972; Richter, 2004).

Mary Ainsworth developed a measure of infant attachment called the *Strange Situation* (Ainsworth, 1978; Ainsworth et al., 1978) (see Figure 10.1). The Strange Situation involves a mother (or other caregiver) and her infant visiting a laboratory room that is full of colorful toys that are attractive to babies and toddlers. Babies must be ambulatory (capable of movement)

Figure 10.1 Securely attached babies show a preference for their mother over other adults
Source: Weekend Images Inc./iStock Photo

Intimacy and Interpersonal Relationships 305

to be assessed. The mother puts the baby down in the room and stays nearby. At some point, the mother leaves the situation, leaving the baby there. The mother then returns after a brief period. During all of these actions, the baby's responses are observed and recorded. Based on her research, Ainsworth determined that infants showed three primary forms of attachment, each one characterized by different responses from babies in the Strange Situation. First, many babies are securely attached, approximately 55% in the general population (van Ijzendoorn, Schuengel, & Bakermans-Kranenburg, 1999). In the Strange Situation, securely-attached babies arrive comfortably in mother's arms; they are not anxious upon arrival. The babies are attracted to the toys, and when mother puts them down, they usually explore the environment by crawling or toddling. However, they usually keep track of where their mothers are, making sure she is in close proximity, called **secure base** behaviors (Waters & Cummings, 2000). When mother leaves the situation, the securely-attached baby becomes distressed and will cry until mother returns. When mother returns, she re-establishes connection with the baby, picking him up, and the baby is easily soothed by mother, becoming calm rather quickly because mother has returned. The child may again show interest in the toys, but will continue with secure base behaviors.

Infants who are not securely attached react differently to the Strange Situation. Infants who display anxious or **anxious-ambivalent attachment** (about 8% of infants; van Ijzendoorn et al., 1999) show anxiety and fear in the Strange Situation. They tend to cling to their mothers, hiding their faces and showing little interest in the toys or surroundings. When the mother can disentangle herself from the baby and leave, the baby cries loudly in protest. When mother returns and attempts reconnection, the child is not easily soothed, and continues crying, perhaps struggling in mother's arms as she attempts comfort. Unlike the securely-attached baby, this baby shows ambivalence toward mother, distress at separation, anxiety, and preference for mother all at the same time. Mothers of these infants tend to show inconsistency in their emotional responsiveness to infants (Ainsworth et al., 1978) and high parenting stress (Scher & Mayseless, 2000). A third type of infant attachment is called **avoidant** (about 23% of infants; van Ijzendoorn et al., 1999). Avoidantly-attached babies show low to no preference for their mothers; they do not protest when she leaves the Strange Situation and have little reaction upon her return. These babies may show a preference for people in the Strange Situation (e.g., researchers) rather than stranger anxiety. Infants develop such avoidant behaviors as a defense against the anxiety and fear they have experienced concerning their mother's lack of emotional responsiveness (Bowlby, 1969; Carlson & Sroufe, 1995).

Main and Solomon (1990) identified a fourth type of attachment in babies called **disorganized** or **disoriented**. Children with disorganized attachment show a variety of different attachment behaviors, including anxiety, indifference, and more disturbing behaviors including anger and aggression (Lyons-Ruth, Melnick, Bronfman, Sherry, & Llanas, 2004), dissociation (Carlson, 1998), and bizarre or strange behaviors (Jacobvitz & Hazan, 1999). This type of attachment is often seen in babies who are severely abused, neglected, or depressed (Carlson, Cicchetti, Barnett, & Braunwald, 1989; van Ijzendoorn et al., 1999). Contradictory emotional behaviors by mothers, low maternal involvement, maternal psychosocial problems, and frightening or bizarre behaviors by parents are linked with disorganized infant attachment (Lyons-Ruth, Bronfman, & Parsons, 1999; Main, 1991; van Ijzendoorn et al., 1999). Over 80% of infants at high risk (e.g., abusive, chaotic, neglectful, impoverished homes; Shaw & Vondra, 1995) likely experience disorganized attachment (van Ijzendoorn et al., 1999).

306 *Intimacy and Interpersonal Relationships*

Infant attachment is linked with multiple outcomes later in childhood and adulthood. Poor quality attachment with parents affects self-esteem and one's ability to cope with stress. Loving relationships with parents are a protective factor against developmental risks, a safe haven from threats in the environment, including psychological and social threats. Longitudinal research indicates that infants with poor attachment to parents are at greater risk for emotional and social maladjustment (Cooper, Shaver, & Collins, 1998; Egeland & Hiester, 1995; van IJzendoorn, Sagi, & Lambermon, 1992). Disorganized attachment is predictive of particularly poor outcomes for children, including serious psychopathology and mental illness (Boris, Fueyo, & Zeanah, 1997; Carlson, 1998; Green & Goldwyn, 2002), aggressive behavior (Solomon, George, & De Jong, 1995; Speltz, Greenberg, & Deklyen, 1990), high vulnerability to stress (Greenberg, Speltz, & DeKlyen, 1993; Splanger & Grossmann, 1993), depression (Solomon et al., 1995), poor peer relationships and social difficulties (Moss, Rousseau, Parent, St-Laurent, & Saintonge, 1998), dissociation (Carlson, 1998), and academic difficulties (Green & Goldwyn, 2002; Moss et al., 1998). Disorganized attachment is consistently linked with psychopathology and behavioral problems in young adulthood (Carlson, 1998; Jacobsen, Edelstein, & Hofmann, 1994), including **dissociation** (a mental experience of disconnection between feelings, thoughts, identity, actions, and/or the external world) (Hesse & van Ijzendoorn, 1998).

Attachment in Adulthood

Given the powerful effects of poor attachment on outcomes in childhood, it is not surprising that research indicates links between attachment to parents in infancy and childhood and psychological and social outcomes in adulthood. Similar to outcomes for children, adults who report more secure attachments to mothers and fathers show greater satisfaction with life and lower overall distress (Kumar & Mattanah, 2016), and higher self-esteem (Frederick, Sandhu, Morse, & Swami, 2016). Insecure attachment is linked with anxiety and mood disorders in adulthood (Mickelson, Kessler, & Shaver, 1997) and with physical symptomology, including sleep disturbance, autonomic nervous system reactions to stress, and disease (Caplan, Maunder, Stempak, Silverberg, & Hart, 2014; Maunder, Lancee, Nolan, Hunter, & Tannenbaum, 2006; Maunder, Hunter, & Lancee, 2011). Research suggests that childhood trauma and abuse are linked to problems in adulthood, including substance abuse (Kassel, Wardle, & Roberts, 2007; Le, Mann, Levitan, George, & Maunder, 2017), mental health problems (Sheinbaum et al. 2015; Tasca et al. 2013), and risky sexual behavior (Ahrens, Ciechanowski, & Katon, 2012; Craig, Gray, & Snowden, 2013), because childhood trauma creates insecure, dysfunctional attachment and low self-esteem (see Figure 10.2).

Sex differences in adult attachment style are apparent, with anxious attachment more common in women and avoidant attachment more common in men. Evolutionary theorists assert that these differences are adaptive because they are linked with sex differences in **parental investment** (Blanchard & Lyons, 2016). Women, who are more invested in any particular child they may have, show greater levels of anxious attachment because it promotes heightened awareness of potential abandonment by male partners and loss of resources to support offspring (Schmitt, 2003; Schmitt & Jonason, 2014). Avoidant attachment involves lack of emotional connection to mates, facilitating a greater number of sexual partners (and viable offspring) for men. Problems in attachment to mothers and fathers appear to be linked to different negative outcomes for women and men. Research indicates that women with anxious attachment report fathers who were absent in childhood or difficult relationships with fathers (Hazan & Shaver, 1987), including in relation to mental health problems in adulthood (Boyd, Ashcraft, & Belgrave, 2006). For men,

Figure 10.2 The experience of abuse in childhood is associated with numerous negative outcomes in adulthood, including abuse of substances
Source: Sturti/iStock Photo

Table 10.1 Attachment styles

Attachment style descriptions

1. I find it relatively easy to get close to others and am comfortable depending on them and having them depend on me. I don't often worry about being abandoned or about someone getting too close to me. (**Secure**)
2. I am somewhat uncomfortable being close to others; I find it difficult to trust them completely, difficult to allow myself to depend on them. I am nervous when anyone gets too close, and often, love partners want me to be more intimate than I feel comfortable being. (**Avoidant**)
3. I find that others are reluctant to get as close as I would like. I often worry that my partner doesn't really love me or won't want to stay with me. I want to merge completely with another person, and this desire sometimes scares people away. (**Anxious/Ambivalent**)

Source: Hazan & Shaver, 1987.

mental health problems in adulthood are linked with avoidant attachment and reports of uncaring, controlling mothers (Blanchard & Lyons, 2016).

Attachment is particularly important to the experience of relationships in adulthood, including romantic relationships. In 1987, social psychologists Hazan and Shaver placed advertisements in local newspapers. They asked readers to characterize themselves as one of three descriptions (see Table 10.1). Securely-attached adults describe themselves as comfortable with dependency; they feel safe depending on others and having others depend on them. They describe their romantic relationships as satisfying and close and describe positive childhood experiences with parents, including loving, supportive relationships. Adults who are anxiously-attached are anxious to establish closeness and anxious about losing closeness. They may want more closeness than most of their partners and may try to develop closeness quickly. They describe frequent experiences of "love at first sight" and are often fearful of being cheated on or abandoned. These adults describe difficult, conflicted relationships with parents in childhood. Finally, adults who are avoidantly-attached describe discomfort with closeness and dependency. They distance themselves from people and avoid intimacy. They describe cold, rejecting relationships with parents in childhood and adulthood. Hazan and Shaver (1987) conclude that attachment with parents sets a deep psychological template for approaching and understanding relationships, including into adulthood; that this template involves prototypical ideas (**"working models"**) about the self and others in relationships; that frequencies of attachment styles are similar among adults and children; and that attachment styles are linked to predictable outcomes in romantic relationships.

Research supports the importance of attachment to parents in affecting social relationships in adulthood. Some research indicates that insecure attachment is related to greater experiences of loneliness through links with poorer social skills and lower social competence (DiTommaso, Brannen-McNulty, Ross, & Burgess, 2003). One study found that avoidant attachment is linked to poor motivation in relationships through lower feelings of self-efficacy (competence) as a relationship partner (Hocker & Riggio, 2018). Other research indicates that experiences of parental conflict and family violence are predictive of relationship violence and attachment anxiety, both of which are linked to low relationship satisfaction (Godbout et al., 2017). Additional research supports the relevance of attachment style to adults' experiences within romantic relationships and relationship outcomes, with secure attachment style associated with greater romantic relationship satisfaction and commitment, and lower relationship conflict (Diamond, Brimhall, & Elliott, 2018; Etcheverry, Le, Wu, & Wei, 2013; Nelson, Peleg-Koriat, & Ben-Ari, 2018). Secure attachment is also predictive of greater sexual satisfaction in relationships, with more securely attached individuals less anxious about and avoidant of sexual communication with partners (Goldsmith, Dunkley, Dang, & Gorzalka, 2016).

Other models of attachment within psychology yield similar results and indicate the importance of fundamental experiences of anxiety and avoidance in insecure attachment (Brennan, Clark, & Shaver, 1998). Other models are similarly useful in approaching and understanding how attachment with parents influences adult relationship behaviors, dyadic processes, and outcomes (Bartholomew, 1990). Links between attachment style based on relationships with parents and outcomes in adult romantic relationships have been found for LGBTQ individuals (Cook, Valera, Calebs, & Wilson, 2017; Guzmán-González et al., 2016; Nematy & Oloomi, 2016) and across cultures (Guzmán-González et al., 2016; Mota & Martins, 2018; Nelson et al., 2018; Nematy & Oloomi, 2016; Wang, Han, Bai, & Li, 2019; Yokoyama et al., 2017), making attachment theory a powerful approach to understanding human psychology about dependency and intimacy in relationships.

Parenting Differences for Girls and Boys

Throughout this book, I have emphasized the importance of the parenting one receives for all aspects of individual psychology, including **self-esteem, self-concept, gender identity, sexuality**. It is very clear that parents treat little girls and boys differently, typically around the world emphasizing rather traditional gender roles and expectations for girls and for boys. All over the world, there are strong proscriptions for unladylike, assertive behaviors by girls, and strong proscriptions against feminine behavior by boys. Girls are expected to be polite, sweet, tidy, not rambunctious, definitely not sexual. In very traditional gender ideology, girls and women are helpers to boys and men; they are sidekicks, supporters, they care for the home and offspring while men hunt, fight, build, lead. Boys are discouraged from being emotional, tender, or vulnerable, all of which are seen as feminine, because emotionality is weak; it violates masculine expectations of strength, courage, and independence. As such, historically and globally, parents treat girls like "girls," and boys like "boys," whatever those ideas (stereotypes) entail in any particular culture.

Recall from Chapter 6 (Theories of Gender) the explanations provided by social role theory (Eagly, 1987; Eagly & Wood, 1999), which asserts primarily that biological and physical differences between the sexes are reflected in social roles for women and men. Women are physically smaller and much weaker than men (Sell, Hone, & Pound, 2012), thus they are subject to physical control by men. Of course they are then helpers; men have the physical power to coerce and control women and so that is what they do. Women are also physically vulnerable because of pregnancy and childbirth, and thus are dependent on others to a much greater degree than any man. Feeding and caring for infants and children is no small task either, with dependency again increased because of lactation and protecting children. Being much physically stronger on average, men are more well-suited to work that requires physical strength (fighting, building, hunting). That is their burden, the fact of their greater physical size and strength.

People are then raised in this world, with these real differences and corresponding differing social roles and behaviors by women and men. Through observation, as explained by social learning theory (Bandura, 1977) (aka social cognitive theory; Bandura, 1986), children learn about what women and men do, what girls and boys do. Parents serve as role models to children, including for gender and gender roles. Children develop stereotypes of women and girls, men and boys, stereotypes that encompass real differences in social roles. They develop expectations of women as dependent, caretakers of others, and as such loving, kind, engaged in domestic activities. They develop expectations of men as being in charge, strong, providing resources to the family. Exposure to explicit messages about gender (e.g., "boys are tough and girls are sweet") and implicit information about girls and boys (e.g., surrounding girls with pink and flowers, boys with blue and cars), women and men (e.g., the prevalence of women in some professions, men in others), also affects children's learning of gender roles and stereotypes (Bigler & Liben, 2006). Over time, these expectations come to operate at an implicit level cognitively, automatically affecting psychological processing of individual women and men (Greenwald & Banaji, 1995). In the modern world, although size and strength are much less required in modern work, we still have expectations for teachers to be female and Presidents to be male, and heavily gendered ideas about women and men, girls and boys.

Parenting Is Gendered

Gender differences in parenting evolved over time because they are functional and adaptive, enhancing the ability of humans to survive and reproduce on the planet (Geary, 2010; Möller, Majdandžić, de Vente, & Bögels, 2013). Because of the biological differences between women and men in pregnancy, childbirth, and lactation, mothers are more involved in all aspects of caring for infants and children than fathers are, beginning at birth of the child, and during young years, but continuing by and large through childhood (Lawson & Mace, 2009; Sayer, Bianchi, & Robinson, 2004). Further, as we've discussed in other chapters and according to evolutionary approaches, men are less invested in any particular child because they have the ability to produce multiple

310 *Intimacy and Interpersonal Relationships*

pregnancies each day with access to fertile women. So men are invested in mating. Parental certainty is obviously not an issue for mothers, but it can be for fathers, especially before modern technology allowed easy determination of paternity. This also affects men's motivation to invest in any child (Geary, 2000). In contrast, women are more invested in each individual offspring, because of the dangers and difficulties of reproducing when one is female (Clutton-Brock, 1991). Modernly, most men who are married to the mother of their children are involved in the regular lives of their children (Cabrera, Tamis-LeMonda, Bradley, Hofferth, & Lamb, 2000) (although see "Inequalities and Injustices").

Because of their greater investment in each child, mothers are very protective of and nurturing toward them, with research supporting that mothers are more likely than fathers to engage in basic caregiving (feeding, cleaning; Best, House, Barnard, & Spicker, 1994) and protection of children (Eckel & Grossman, 2008; Verhoeven, Bögels, & Van der Bruggen, 2011). Mothers report closer, more intimate relationships with their children and teens than fathers, and they provide greater support and warmth to their children (McKinney & Renk, 2008; Simons & Conger, 2007; Winsler, Madigan, & Aquilino, 2005). Mothers are commonly found to be more emotionally responsive to children in interactions compared to fathers (Barnett, Deng, Mills-Koonce, Willoughby, & Cox, 2008; Lewis & Lamb, 2003), although other studies indicate that mothers and fathers are equally sensitive and responsive to children (Malmberg et al., 2007; Tamis-LeMonda, Shannon, Cabrera, & Lamb, 2004). Fathers are more likely to be figures of power and authority in directing children, while mothers are more likely to use nurturing and reasoning to parent (Bentley & Fox, 1991). Fathers are more likely to engage in play behaviors with their children than mothers (Bonney, Kelley, & Levant, 1999; Levey & Fagot, 1997; Lewis & Lamb, 2003), particularly rough-and-tumble play and play that encourages risk-taking, adventure, responsibility, and movement (Block, 1983; Carson, Burks, & Parke, 1993; Keren, Feldman, Namdari-Weinbaum, Spitzer, & Tyano, 2005; Paquette, 2004). Notably, fathers are more risk-averse and protective in play with daughters (Kindleberger & Kuebli, 2007; Lindsey & Mize, 2001). In this way, fathers teach their children (especially their sons) about using physical strength and prowess and engaging in competition, evolutionary requirements for men (Power, McGrath, Hughes, & Manire, 1994). Mothers' play with children tends to emphasize relationships and perspective taking, including pretend play (e.g., playing house or school) (Bergen, 2002; Lindsey & Mize, 2001; Youngblade & Dunn, 1995), modeling the functional importance of social competence and communality (Power et al., 1994). These parenting behaviors vary predictably by child gender, with girls treated more protectively by parents with emphasis on relationships, and boys encouraged to engage in greater risk-taking (Lytton & Romney, 1991).

It is clear that parents treat their daughters and their sons differently. Children are reinforced by parents and others for gender-congruent behavior (behavior deemed acceptable by a particular culture for one's identified gender) and punished or not rewarded for gender-incongruent behavior (behavior of the opposite sex deemed not acceptable by a particular culture). Children are treated according to their gender beginning at birth (Laflamme, Pomerleau, & Malcuit, 2002); their rooms are decorated and furnished based on **gender stereotypes** (Pomerleau, Bolduc, Malcuit, & Cossette, 1990). Infant girls are talked to more by mothers than infant boys (Clearfield & Nelson, 2006), and fathers engage in more physical play behaviors with boys than with girls, beginning around age 7-8 months (MacDonald & Parke, 1986; Power & Parke, 1983). Observations of parents indicate that they are most engaged and excited when playing with their infants with gender-congruent toys, compared to their play with neutral or incongruent toys (Caldera, Huston, & O'Brien, 1989). Parents are more likely to choose gender-congruent than incongruent

Intimacy and Interpersonal Relationships 311

toys for toddlers (Idle, Wood, & Desmarais, 1993). Parents are more likely to read to girls (Baker & Milligan, 2016) and engage in relationship play (e.g., with dolls) with girls (Caldera & Sciaraffa, 1998) and to engage in rough-and-tumble play with boys (Jacklin, DiPietro, & Maccoby, 1984). Boys are discouraged from crying and emotional behaviors by parents, while girls' emotionality and expression is encouraged (Bronstein, 2006). Gender-congruent toys are very heavily marketed to children (Fine & Rush, 2018), and television shows and films geared to children show children in highly stereotypical roles (Hust & Brown, 2008). Babies show preferences for gender-congruent toys (Snow, Jacklin, & Maccoby, 1983) and children show strong preferences for same-sex playmates (Maccoby, 1990). Society rewards girls for being girls and boys for being boys, and that fact is quite evident early in life. Boys (Lauer, Ilksoy, & Lourenco, 2018) and men (Gal & Wilkie, 2010) show particular preferences for gender-congruent behaviors.

Modernly, some people are trying to de-emphasize gender in their parenting and socialization of children. A preschool in Sweden ("The Egalia School") made headlines in its expansive attempt to eliminate ideas of gender (Hebblethwaite, 2011). Although all of the children are aware of their biological sex, social constructions of gender are avoided in the school. There are many kinds of toys, none of them segregated, all grouped together, dolls with trucks and cars with dress-up clothes. The books for the children are gender neutral. The children are called by their name, or they are called "friend" or *hen*, a Finnish pronoun that is gender neutral. The Swedish education system includes so-called "gender advisers" for students in schools and anti-discrimination is a theme in curricula. Some parents decide to not reveal the biological sex of their babies to most people and adopt gender-neutral names for their child, preventing the child from being treated in a gender-typed way and allowing the child to decide their gender (which most children do by around age 4 to 7 years; Kohlberg & Ullian, 1974). Some people react very negatively to nontraditional approaches to gender like that of this little preschool. Typically, the people who get most upset about nontraditional or liberal ideas are people who are already higher in the social hierarchy because of their ascribed or socially constructed qualities (e.g., white skin, male sex, Christian), and who are motivated to maintain their social dominance over others (Pratto & Walker, 2004).

Family Relationships

Research indicates that there are other differences in the way parents relate to their daughters and sons, and how their children respond. Although some theorists argue that mothers are predisposed to greater intimacy with daughters (Gilligan, 1996), research indicates that mothers show similar responsiveness, sensitivity, and concern toward infant and toddler daughters and sons (Leaper, 2002; Lytton & Romney, 1991), and that mother-child mutual responsiveness is similar in mother-daughter and mother-son dyads in childhood (Maccoby, 1998). When children are asked about their mothers, girls and boys do not differ in descriptions of their mothers as responsive and warm (Oppenheim, Emde, & Warren, 1997; Solomonica-Levi, Yirmiya, Erel, Samet, & Oppenheim, 2001). Other research does indicate dyadic differences in relationship closeness, with *mutual* concern and responsiveness greater in mother-daughter and father-daughter dyads than in parental relationships with sons (Butler & Shalit-Naggar, 2008). While concern of parents toward children does not tend to vary by child sex, it seems that relationships with daughters are more mutually responsive, likely because girls and women are socialized to be relational and tend to show more interpersonal concern in all types of relationships (Eisenberg & Fabes, 1998; Maccoby, 1990). Although some studies show greater closeness and influence in opposite-sex

(Xie & Hultgren, 1994) or same-sex parent–child dyads (Li, Delvecchio, Miconi, Salcuni, & Di Riso, 2014; Niu, Chen, Wang, & Zhang, 2004), other studies indicate that mothers and fathers feel closer to daughters than to sons (Driscoll & Pianta, 2011; Liu, Li, Lv, & Li, 2013; Xu, Liu, Li, Liu, & Huntsinger, 2018).

Closeness with both parents is important in childhood. In preschool, girls who are closer to their mothers show fewer behavior problems and greater social skills, while conflict with fathers is predictive of more behavior problems and poorer social skills for boys (Xu et al., 2018). Additional studies show links between expression of emotions by children and their parents during play and children's social competence. In one study of children from kindergarten to first grade, expression of positive emotions by mothers and fathers during play is linked with greater expression of positive emotions by daughters and sons, with similar mutuality in expression of negative emotions. Moreover, parental expression of positive affect is linked with lower aggression and disruptiveness, and more prosocial behavior (sharing, helping), as indicated by ratings from peers and teachers, for girls and boys (Isley, O'Neil, Clatfelter, & Parke, 1999). Parents' sensitivity to their children and positive stimulation of children (cognitive stimulation through reading, learning toys, play) are linked with children's academic competence and positive school adjustment (Pianta & Harbers, 1996). Children with poor relationships with parents show greater anxiety, which hampers learning, school adjustment, and relationships with peers (Wood, 2007). Warm, loving, involved parents have children who relate positively and warmly to others, including peers (Cohn, 1990; Hastings & Rubin, 1999; McDonald & Parke, 1984), and who relate warmly to themselves with feelings of positive self-esteem (Bàmaca, Umana-Taylor, Shin, & Alfaro, 2005). Parental marital conflict is disruptive to all relationships in the family, particularly for children who are totally or somewhat helpless at all ages. Parental marital conflict is predictive of low emotional responsiveness toward children, harsh, inconsistent parenting, and less effective use of discipline (Bradley & Corwyn, 2004; Simons, Whitbeck, Melby, & Wu, 1994). Marital unhappiness affects the total family environment as a major disruption to the family system and to a positive family atmosphere (emotional tone of relationships within the family; Ansbacher & Ansbacher, 1964) (Cox & Paley, 1997; Cummings, Davies, & Campbell, 2000).

Relationships with parents continue to be important for adult children's outcomes (Steele & McKinney, 2019), especially in young adulthood when parents are often primary sources of social support, including financial support (Aquilino, 2006; Umberson, 1992). Chronic conflict between parents in the family of origin is linked with long-term psychological and relationship difficulties for offspring in adulthood (Amato & Booth, 1991; Booth & Edwards, 1990). Young adults from high-conflict homes report feelings of low trust and closeness in their relationships with parents (Afifi & Schrodt, 2004; Amato & Afifi, 2006; Richardson & McCabe, 2001). Young adults' recollections of high parental conflict are associated with feelings of anxiety in personal relationships; and lower warmth, emotional support, and facilitation of independence in relationships with parents (Riggio, 2004).

Parental divorce is also associated with poorer outcomes in relationships with parents, but particularly relationships with fathers (Amato & Booth, 1991; Riggio, 2004; Riggio & Valenzuela, 2010). In the great majority of divorces, it is fathers who leave the home, with children remaining in the primary physical custody of mothers in over 80% of divorces (Grall, 2016; Seltzer, 1991). Even when noncustodial fathers maintain a relationship with their children, daily contact is greatly diminished (Cooney, 1994). In over 40% of divorce cases, fathers' contact with children decreases, and sometimes they essentially disappear, providing little financial and emotional support and rarely visiting with children, if ever (Manning & Smock, 1999; see "Inequalities and

Injustices"). Because men decide to eschew their parental responsibilities and abandon their children, many young adults from divorced families report negative feelings toward their fathers and very low-quality relationships with them (Riggio, 2004). Young adults generally describe more positive relationships (greater warmth, closeness, support) with their mothers than with fathers, with women reporting particularly positive relationships with mothers (Lindell, Campione-Barr, & Killoren, 2017; Riggio, 2004). Relationships with mothers are sometimes closer in divorced families, especially if marital conflict was low, a kind of drawing-together process that happens with single mothers and their kids (Riggio, 2004; Riggio & Valenzuela, 2010).

The sibling relationship is often the longest relationship of one's lifetime, beginning at birth of the younger sibling and ending at death. Siblings play a large part in the development of interpersonal and social skills, conflict management and resolution skills, and maintenance of social support networks (Cicirelli, 1995; Lamb & Sutton-Smith, 1982). Siblings in childhood have a positive influence on children's cognitive and social development (Brody, Stoneman, & MacKinnon, 1982; Dunn & Kendrick, 1982). High-quality sibling relationships serve a protective role for individual children, ameliorating the negative impact of parental conflict (Davies, Parry, Bascoe, Martin, & Cummings, 2018) and of parental divorce (Huntley & Phelps, 1990). Sibling relationships in families characterized by divorce and high conflict are generally of poorer quality, however, especially if divorce occurred later in childhood or in adolescence (Brody, Stoneman, & McCoy, 1994; MacKinnon, 1989). When parental divorce occurs in earlier childhood, sibling relationships are of similar quality to those in married families (Wallerstein, 1984; Wallerstein & Kelly, 1980). Among young adults, some research indicates an increased warmth and closeness among siblings whose parents divorced in their early childhood, again reflecting a drawing-together effect, where individuals rely more on each other, when parental divorce occurs (Riggio, 2001).

There is a "female present" effect for warmth and closeness in sibling relationships as in other personal relationships. Among children, sisters are closest across childhood and into adolescence, and sister-brother dyads are close as well, especially when sisters are older than brothers (Dunn, Slomkowski, & Beardsall, 1994). Research on siblings across adulthood indicates that sibling dyads that include at least one sister tend to be closer and more supportive than brother dyads (Riggio, 2000, 2006; Wilson, Calsyn, & Orlofsky, 1994). In later adulthood, daughters are more likely to provide care for elderly parents than sons. While daughters provide more care overall to elderly parents, when sons provide care it is more often to their fathers than their mothers (Grigoryeva, 2017).

Gender Differences in Social Interaction and Communication

Evolutionary theory predicts that women more strongly rely on social competence and **communal**, caregiving behaviors in general, because of their likelihood of having to join non-kin groups through marriage (Geary & Flinn, 2001); and because of their greater parental investment and hence greater dependency on the support of others, including other women (Geary, Byrd-Craven, Hoard, Vigil, & Numtee, 2003; Taylor et al., 2000). Women are said to have evolved a "tend-and-befriend" response in stressful situations (Hall, 2011, p. 726). In contrast, men in the past tended to stay in kin groups rather than join new non-kin groups. Intergroup competition, including for sexual access to women, and social dominance are more important motivations for men. As such, men's behavior is characterized by **agentic**, power-seeking activities (Wilson & Daly, 1985) and competitiveness (Van Vugt, De Cremer, & Janssen, 2007). Around the world, women are socialized to be dependent and interrelational in their behavior, while men are encouraged to be

Figures 10.3a and 10.3b Children and young adults show a preference for same-sex friends
Source: CHBD/iStock Photo and Ridofranz /iStock Photo

independent, emotionally isolated, acting without regard to feelings, reflecting these evolutionary imperatives (Geary, 2010). Through the operation of genes, hormones, **socialization**, and **social dominance**, children develop predictable and gendered behaviors which affect their communication and relationship behaviors.

Intimacy and Interpersonal Relationships   315

Early in life, children show a preference for same-sex companions and playmates, that is spontaneous (Eisenhart & Holland, 1983; Maccoby, 1988) (see Figures 10.3a and 10.3b). Girls and boys differ in their play activities to some degree. Boys show a preference for active, rough-and-tumble, outdoor play, while girls tend to prefer quieter activities indoors and toys like dolls (Blurton Jones & Konner, 1973; Eaton & Enns, 1986; Liss, 1981). Boys choose friends based on shared preferences in activities (Humphreys & Smith, 1987), while girls' friendships are based on closeness, trust, and sharing secrets (Kraft & Vraa, 1975). Boys' play groups are usually larger than those of girls, who prefer interacting with one or two close peers (Erwin, 1985). Some scholars assert that little girls prefer not to interact with boys for several reasons. First, some girls find rough-and-tumble play aversive or do not prefer it to more relational, quieter activities (Maccoby, 1988; Maccoby & Jacklin, 1987). Second, boys are less responsive to the verbal communications of girls. In preschool and kindergarten, girls and boys begin to influence playmates so as to engage in coordinated play. In attempting influence, girls tend to use suggestions while boys tend to be demanding and more assertive (Sachs, 1987; Serbin, Sprafkin, Elman, & Doyle, 1984). Boys are less likely to respond to the suggestions of girls than to demands of boys. Scholars explain that this occurs through socialization, through rewarding boys' communications and responses to other boys, but not their communications with girls (Fagot, 1985).

As children get older, their communication styles continue to diverge, with boys interrupting others more, making more demands, disagreeing and boasting more, refusing to comply with others, and giving information and commands. Boys' interactions are more likely to include conflict and negative reciprocity than girls' (Miller, Danaher, & Forbes, 1986). Boys' communications are about establishing strength in the group (Maccoby, 1990). In all-girl groups, girls are polite, supportive, and generous to each other. They tend not to interrupt, they encourage others to communicate, they acknowledge good points, and they express agreement with others (Maltz & Borker, 1983). They are not passive and do assert themselves, but in a way that maintains positive feelings and group harmony (Sheldon, 1992). Maccoby (1990, p. 516) says conversation among girls is a "socially binding process." Across contexts, girls show more prosocial behaviors, greater empathy for others, and more interpersonal responsibility than boys (Eisenberg & Fabes, 1998; Maccoby, 1998).

As children move into adolescence and adulthood, interactive and communication patterns in same-sex dyads and groups are similar to those observed in children, with gendered communication patterns reinforced (Carli, 1989; Cowan, Drinkard, & MacGavin, 1984). In adulthood, men are less influenced by other people in groups and are more assertive and influential of others than women (Lockheed, 1985; Pugh & Wahrman, 1983; Shackelford, Wood, & Worchel, 1996). In groups, women tend to engage in more behaviors that promote positive relationships and group atmosphere, while men's behavior tends to be more task-oriented (Eagly, 1987). In same-sex friendships in adulthood, women focus more on maintaining relationship harmony and mutuality than men (Burke & Fuqua, 1987; Wright, 1982). In heterosexual relationships, women show greater sensitivity and active listening than men (Fishman, 1983; Tannen, 1993). Women are said to bear the "emotional labor" in heterosexual relationships, with men engaging in less self-disclosure, sensitive communication, and relationship maintenance than their female partners (Bartky, 1990).

Friendships across the Lifespan

Like family relationships, friendships are an important part of overall social and psychological well-being (Tesch, 1983). Research indicates that friendships involving mutual support, intimacy, companionship, and **reciprocity** are experienced as more satisfying (Hays, 1988; Rook, 1987; Walster, Walster, & Berscheid, 1978). Important qualities of friendships include loyalty, **intimacy** and **self-disclosure** (sharing of personal information), feelings of closeness, and self-esteem support (Berndt, 2002). Among children, stable friendships that last over a few years (i.e., "best" friends) are linked with better mental health and academic performance in middle school (Ng-Knight et al., 2018). When children are bullied in school (a not uncommon experience, sadly), having a group of good friends is associated with better emotional well-being among targets (Bayer et al., 2018). In adolescence, having at least one close friendship is linked with positive psychosocial adjustment and psychological health, including greater feelings of happiness (Bukowski, Newcomb, & Hartup, 1996; Wilkinson, 2010). During this critical time of identity formation, close friendships help adolescents feel unique (Demir, Simsek, & Procsal, 2012), and are linked with greater self-awareness and more advanced identity development (Larson et al., 2007). Close friendships are also linked with academic motivation and performance in adolescence (Crosnoe, 2000; Larson et al., 2007). **Longitudinal** studies indicate that adolescents who report closer friendships tend to have lower anxiety and depression, and more positive self-worth, in young adulthood (Narr, Allen, Tan, & Loeb, 2019). In adulthood, friendships are similarly linked with psychological adjustment and mental health (King & Terrance, 2008).

Just as we find in other relationships, there are gender differences in the experiences of friendships. Communal behaviors, including emotional availability and self-disclosure on both sides, are particularly important in friendships (Wright, 1988). Girls more highly value intimacy with friends than boys do (Bigelow & La Gaipa, 1980; La Gaipa, 1987), and women report greater intimacy in adult same-sex friendships than men (Reis, 1998). Girls and women are more likely than boys and men to use emotional support received from friends to cope with stress (Tamres, Janicki, & Helgeson, 2002). In a **meta-analysis** examining 37 studies, Hall (2011) found that girls and women have higher expectations of friendships than boys and men. Girls and women expect greater loyalty, commitment, trust, self-disclosure, and intimacy in same-sex friendships than do boys and men, with smaller gender differences in expectations for companionship and mutual activities. In further support of evolutionary theory's predictions, agentic features of friendships (e.g., physical fitness and status of same-sex friends) are more highly valued by boys and men, less so by girls and women. Additional research indicates that women's same-sex friendships are more supportive (Hays, 1988), involve greater acceptance, attachment, caring, and intimacy (Peretti & Venton, 1986), and greater openness and relationship maintenance behaviors (Oswald, Clark, & Kelly, 2004) compared to men's same-sex friendships. Although men recognize the kinds of behaviors that establish intimacy in relationships (most notably self-disclosure; Reis, 2017), men are less likely to engage in those types of communal, expressive behaviors in same-sex friendships than women (Fehr, 2004; Parker & de Vries, 1993).

Love and Intimate Relationships

Attraction

Attraction is primary to establishing any kind of romantic relationship (Rubin, 1973). **Attraction** can be defined as a feeling of interest in a person, feeling drawn to them, both physically and psychologically. Some attraction is more physical (i.e., sexual), while other attraction is psychological (we desire to know the person, to spend time with them). Social psychologists have documented multiple factors involved in attraction, including features and characteristics of people that make

Intimacy and Interpersonal Relationships 317

them attractive to us. Physical attraction is obviously important in the development of romantic and sexual relationships; people are attracted to particular physical features, including features that indicate overall good health (Nedelec & Beaver, 2014). While overall **physical attractiveness** is important in determining who people are drawn to or who they enjoy looking at (Eagly, Ashmore, Makhijani, & Longo, 1991; Walster, Aronson, Abrahams, & Rottman, 1966), most individuals make attractiveness judgments and decisions to approach potential lovers in terms of how the person matches oneself in terms of attractiveness (Berscheid, Dion, Walster, & Walster, 1971). In other words, the perfect 10 on our own individual attractiveness scale is lovely to look at, but the average 5 is not likely to approach her/him as a love object. Instead, we are likely to seek out as partners people who are similar to us in level of attractiveness. We prefer as friends and mates people who are **similar** to us in general, including in terms of background, age, even facial features and other physical characteristics (Penton-Voak, Perrett, & Peirce, 1999). We also like people who we expect will like us, especially when we think we are similar to them (Condon & Crano, 1988). While most people do simply **reciprocate** liking, regardless of similarity (i.e., if someone expresses liking and is kind, most people reciprocate those positive emotions; Montoya & Horton, 2012), in forming romantic partnerships, attitude similarity is rather important, particularly for religious and political ideologies (Finkel & Baumeister, 2010; Finkel & Eastwick, 2015).

Importantly in terms of evolutionary success as a species, human beings grow in liking for each other. That is, liking may increase over time through repeated exposure, mainly because we become familiar with the person and get to know them (Priest & Sawyer, 1967). People respond to familiarity with positivity in general. We like familiar things, like our own homes, our own people, our own patterned ways of doing things, our routines. We build familiarity around us, intentionally, because it increases predictability and order in our lives. We depend on it. Consumers prefer familiar brand names because they feel predictable, it feels like if it's a brand we recognize, we know what we're getting (Bogart & Lehman, 1973). We watch the same movies again and again and eat the same beef taco/cheese enchilada combo plate every time because we are assured of enjoyment, with little risk of disappointment. The personality trait of **Openness to Experience** is important here, with people high in Openness less inclined to the familiar than those lower in Openness (see Chapter 9; McCrae, 1987). The major personality trait of **Extraversion** is also important for preference for familiarity because Extraverts engage in high levels of **sensation-seeking**, which involves seeking out and engaging in novel and stimulating activities (Zuckerman, 2009). Regardless of these individual differences in individual traits, however, familiarity operates on an almost automatic level in people, with people showing greater liking for repeatedly seen foreign language ideographs and other rather meaningless stimuli, an effect called **mere exposure** (Zajonc, 1968).

Evolutionary explanations for attraction are of course based on functionality and how forming sexual, **monogamous** relationships may support survival of the species. Evolutionary theorists assert that human beings select mates (people with whom to have sex and possibly reproduce) based on, once again, differences in parental investment. Because of their greater investment in any particular child, women are seeking mates who have power and resources to devote to their offspring. As such, women should seek men who are older, who are of higher social status, and before modern times, men who were bigger and stronger to protect offspring. Human beings have formed family units based on monogamous sexual bonds so that men can be assured of paternity certainty and women can be assured of resources for children (Buss, 1998). Multiple studies indicate that women are more strongly attracted to physical (muscularity, height, masculine voice and facial features; Feinberg et al., 2006; Little, Jones, & Burriss, 2007; Pawlowski & Jasienska, 2005; Roney, Simmons, & Gray, 2011) and behavioral (social dominance behaviors;

318   *Intimacy and Interpersonal Relationships*

Gangestad, Garver-Apgar, Simpson, & Cousins, 2007) features of masculinity on **high-fertility days** (days when women are ovulating and most fertile) than on low-fertility days in the menstrual cycle. Such masculine features are cues that are implicitly linked with assessment of male strength, power, and overall fitness to provide, as well as genetic fitness (Larson, Pillsworth, & Haselton, 2012).

Monogamy, especially continuing provision of resources, requires a man's **fidelity** as well, to one female mate, which may be difficult to attain because of men's evolutionary imperative. Because of their lesser investment in any particular child, men are seeking healthy women who are likely to be fertile and capable of surviving pregnancy and childbirth and actually producing a child. As such, men seek mates who are young and healthy, often signaled by physical attractiveness (Buss, 1998). Research evidence supports these predictions, with women valuing earning potential in mates and men valuing physical attractiveness more in potential mates (Feingold, 1990, 1991, 1992; Sprecher, Sullivan, & Hatfield, 1994), including across cultures (Buss et al., 1990). Men also seek out domestic skills in female mates, supporting **social role theory** explanations of mate selection. In their reanalysis of Buss et al.'s (1990) data from 37 countries, Eagly and Wood (1999) found that the largest sex differences in desirable mate qualities were for *good earning capacity* (more desired by women), *good housekeeper and cook* (more desired by men), and *physical attractiveness* (more desired by men). Interestingly, across cultures, as women's economic and social equality increases, men's earning capacity and older age become significantly less important to women looking for male romantic partners.

In further support of evolutionary ideas about paternity certainty and parental investment, multiple studies of the experience of **jealousy** indicate that women experience greater feelings of jealousy in response to thoughts about male partners' **emotional infidelity** (e.g., falling in love with another woman), while men experience greater jealousy in response to thinking about sexual infidelity of female partners (Buss, Larsen, Westen, & Semmelroth, 1992; Buunk, Angleitner, Oubaid, & Buss, 1996). Men's overt concern with women's sexual behavior around the world and across history is also reflected in paternalistic, heteronormative social structures that shame and control women's sexuality, namely religion (Dedek, 1980; Gatiss, 2005). Men control women directly with physical force, with men more likely to commit and be a repeated committer of **intimate partner violence** (IPV; Dobash, Dobash, Wilson, & Daly, 1992) (see Chapter 11). Rape and sexual assault are also most likely to be committed by men against women, particularly women they know (Rennison, 2002; Uniform Crime Report, 2011).

The Experience of Love

We have already discussed one major approach to understanding love relationships, attachment theory. Another approach to understanding love and romantic relationships is Sternberg's descriptive, triangular model of love (Sternberg, 1986). Sternberg asserts that there are three primary components of love relationships: intimacy, passion, and commitment. **Intimacy** involves feelings of trust, warmth, closeness, and connection with another person. It is essentially emotional, a feeling of caring and love for the other person and for the relationship itself. **Passion** involves intense feelings of physical and sexual attraction to another person. Passion is about the anticipation and experience of physical pleasure in the relationship. **Commitment** is rather cognitive; it involves an active, conscious decision to maintain the relationship in the long term. Commitment does not necessarily arise from intimacy and passion; it can be rather empty and

Intimacy and Interpersonal Relationships   319

Table 10.2 Sternberg's taxonomy of kinds of love

Kind of love	Intimacy	Passion	Commitment
Nonlove	-	-	-
Liking	+	-	-
Infatuated love	-	+	-
Empty love	-	-	+
Fatuous love	-	+	+
Romantic love	+	+	-
Companionate love	+	-	+
Consummate love	+	+	+

Note: + = component present; - = component absent.
Source: Sternberg, 1986.

based on family obligations or financial considerations. Commitment is rather cold in relation to the warmth of intimacy and the hotness of passion.

According to Sternberg, true love, or **consummate love**, involves all three components; deep trust, companionship, physical passion, and commitment to each other. In addition, other forms of relationships can be understood based on the presence or absence of the three components (see Table 10.2). For instance, **liking** is based on intimacy; we feel liking and warmth toward friends that we trust. There is no passion or necessarily a commitment involved in friendships. **Infatuated love**, on the other hand, is based on passion only, a sexual relationship devoid of intimacy or commitment. Sternberg's model describes **romantic love** as involving passion and intimacy; romantic love is typical of the beginning stages of a monogamous relationship. **Companionate love** is more typical of couples who have been together over long periods of time, a relationship based on trust, intimacy, and companionship more than passion (Hatfield, 1988).

Social psychologists examining love relationships have also examined **love schemas**, or cognitive representations and understandings of what love is and what romantic relationships are expected to be like (Hatfield & Rapson, 1996; Sternberg, 1998). Love schemas are likely to vary by gender, mainly because of gender stereotypes and expectations of how women and men are supposed to act in interaction with each other. As you likely already know from reading other chapters in this book, women in relationships are expected to be loving, patient, caring, emotionally expressive, and communal. Men are expected to be none of these things, especially in the **hypermasculine** United States. Men are expected to be emotionally less available, less **interdependent** with partners, more independent and not expressive (Fabes & Martin, 1991; Mirowsky & Ross, 1995). Internalized gender stereotypes result in different interaction patterns and development of different skills in relating to others, creating gender differences in relationship behaviors (Moir & Jessel, 1993; Shields, 2002). Women are more expressive of positive emotions and love than men, including within romantic relationships (Blier & Blier-Wilson, 1989; Floyd, 1997). Women are more expressive of negative emotions than men as well (Lewis, 1992; Nolen-Hoeksema & Girgus, 1994). Research indicates that women expect negative outcomes of not expressing positive emotions toward others, while men do not expect any type of consequence for failing to express positive emotions, also likely to affect expressiveness in relationships (Stoppard & Grunn Gruchy, 1993).

Research indicates that among young adults, men are more likely to report an **erotic love style** (a desire for affective and sexual intimacy; Lee, 1977), to be more permissive about casual

320 Intimacy and Interpersonal Relationships

Table 10.3 Lee's (1977) styles of love

Style	Love is based on	Combination?	Description
Ludus	Conquest	A primary love style	Love is a game, "winning" means you make a partner love you but do not love them back. The goal is not love, but to win.
Storge	Friendship	A primary love style	Love that grows slowly out of friendship, based on familiarity and commitment rather than passion.
Eros	Romance	A primary love style	Passionate romantic love that is based on a strong physical attraction.
Agape	Selflessness	Eros + Storge	An unconditional, selfless love that is based on strong commitment.
Pragma	Practicality	Ludos + Storge	Practical, realistic love that is based on a cost-benefit analysis and long-term outcomes.
Mania	Obsession	Eros + Ludos	Possessive, jealous love that is based on feelings of insecurity.

Source: Lee, J. A. (1977). A typology of styles of loving. *Personality and Social Psychology Bulletin, 3,* 173-182.

sex and have a greater number of sexual partners (Petersen & Hyde, 2010), and to be less aware of affectional needs of partners in relationships (Remshard, 1999). Romantic relationships tend to be of higher quality for women when their male partners have secure attachment style (i.e., they are comfortable with dependency and closeness), while men report higher quality relationships with women who are more anxious in attachment (Collins & Read, 1990). Men are more likely than women to prefer a **ludus love style** (Lee, 1977), so-called game-playing characterized by variety of sexual partners and dating multiple people at once (Canary, Emmers-Sommer, & Faulkner, 1997; Hendrick & Hendrick, 1995). For men, a ludus love style is linked with greater life satisfaction; the opposite is true for women (Yancey & Eastman, 1995). Having companionate love with a male partner is linked to life satisfaction for women, less so for men in relationships with women (Hendrick & Hendrick, 1995) (see Table 10.3 for more **love styles**).

Comparatively little research has examined romantic relationships among LGBTQ individuals, for various reasons associated with the stigma attached to anything but heterosexual sex (Alvarez, 2006; Meyer et al., 2008). It is additionally difficult to study LGBTQ youth because of stigma and teens' fears about coming out (Human Rights Campaign, 2018; see Bonus Box). Further, again because of stigma imposed by society, and the social ridicule and hostility that it entails, LGBTQ young people have additional difficulties in pursuing, establishing, and maintaining same-sex relationships compared to heterosexual youth (Bogle, 2008; Diamond, 2003; Diamond, Savin-Williams, & Dube, 1999; Savin-Williams, 1996a). There are also different expectations associated with men in **homosexual** and heterosexual relationships. Gay men or men having sex with men are often expected to be very sexually active and not involved in a heteronormative-type monogamous relationship. However, research indicates that gay men do pursue romantic, long-term commitments with male partners (Eyre, Arnold, Peterson, & Strong, 2007; Mutchler, 2000). Research also indicates that heterosexual, **cisgender** men prefer monogamous, longer lasting relationships more than LGBTQ men (Meier, Hull, & Ortyl, 2009). One study found little difference between LGBTQ individuals and cisgender, heterosexual individuals in terms of love attitudes, attachment styles in romantic relationships, sexuality, and links of such with relationship satisfaction (Couperthwaite, 2015). Another study finds similar love experiences for lesbian and heterosexual women, with intimacy and passion strongly linked to relationship satisfaction similarly for both groups (Cusack, Hughes, & Cook, 2012). Additional studies indicate no differences in romantic relationship satisfaction, experiences of love, or evaluations of important relationship qualities between LGBTQ and heterosexual individuals (Peplau 1991; Savin-Williams & Esterberg, 2000). In spite of negative stigma and subsequent lower opportunity to establish love relationships for LGBTQ individuals compared to heterosexuals (Barrios & Lundquist, 2012), it appears that LGBTQ individuals enjoy love relationships that are as passionate, intimate, committed, and fulfilling as those of heterosexual, cisgender people.

Marriage, Divorce, Widowhood

Gender is linked with **marital timing**, or when marriage typically occurs in the average person's life. Marital timing is important as it impacts everything about a person's life, including where a person lives, employment, access to resources, and having children. These concerns are obviously more impactful for women around the world, who globally and historically have and have had fewer opportunities to possess and earn financial and social power than men (Dorius & Firebaugh, 2010). The average age at marriage is older for men all over the world, in 114 countries observed by the United Nations (2011). Women marry at younger ages, on average about 3.3 years earlier than men as a group. Age gaps are higher in areas of the world that practice child marriage, that are less affluent, and where educational opportunities are disparate by gender. For example, the average gap in marital timing is 6.6 years in Western Africa, but much lower in the U.S., Canada, and northern Europe at about 2 years (Ortega, 2014). The average age at marriage for women in the U.S. is around 27 years, for men it is around 29 years, a bit higher for both in Canada (worldatlas.com, 2018).

As you might expect, evolutionary and social role theorists have something to say about marriage, and research supports their explanations. According to Becker (1981), women marry at a younger age because they need the resources and support of the husband for children and because they are less likely to be financially independent. When such opportunities for education, wealth, and power are more abundant to women, in countries that are affluent and technologically advanced, women are less in need of marriage, may delay marriage, and may not marry at all. While some research supports this explanation, indicating that gender differences in marital timing are explained nearly entirely by education and employment (Shafer & James, 2013), other research indicates that marital timing age differences remain, even when socioeconomic characteristics are considered (Sassler & Schoen, 1999; South, 2011). Additional research indicates that cultural values about traditional gender roles are also important in marital timing, with more traditional gender ideology not highly valuing women's education and professional advancement, but the domestic roles of wife and mother (Allendorf & Thornton, 2015; Carlson, McLanahan, & England, 2004; Jennings, Axinn, & Ghimire, 2012). In egalitarian countries, for example the Scandinavian countries, where professional accomplishments of women and men are equally valued with equal opportunities emphasized, age at first marriage is older on average (approaching 35 years), with less of a difference between women and men (Jalovaara, 2012; worldatlas.com, 2018).

Marriage is beneficial to people, as long as the marriage is of higher quality and low in stressful interactions and conflict (Kiecolt-Glaser & Newton, 2001) (see Figure 10.4). Married people

Figures 10.4a and 10.4b Happy marriage is associated with positive psychological and health outcomes
Source: Rawpixel/iStock Photo and Freemixer/iStock Photo

Intimacy and Interpersonal Relationships 323

report greater income, more positive mental health and well-being, and have better physical health than unmarried people (Waite & Gallagher, 2000). There is a primary financial benefit to marriage, with two people living more cheaply together than as individuals. As such, married people enjoy a higher standard of living, with access to higher quality housing, services, food, and greater opportunities (Ross, Mirowsky, & Goldsteen, 1990). People who are married are at less risk for smoking, obesity, and high blood pressure than people who are unmarried (House, Landis, & Umberson, 1988). **Mortality** rates are higher for unmarried people than married people (Chandra, Szklo, Goldberg, & Tonascia, 1983; Gordon & Rosenthal, 1995; House et al., 1988). Individuals who have experienced divorce show significantly higher levels of psychological problems and substance abuse compared to married individuals, especially during dissolution (Horwitz, White, & Howell-White, 1996; Ross, Mirowsky, & Goldstein, 1990; Waite, 1995). **Cohabiting** relationships are less beneficial than marriages (Cherlin, 2013; Stack & Eshleman, 1998), perhaps because they lack greater relationship commitment (Cherlin, 2009). Marriages are equally beneficial to same-sex couples, and cohabiting is more beneficial for same-sex than opposite-sex couples (Cherlin, 2013). The health benefits of marriage for men are much greater than those for women (Ross, Mirowsky, & Goldsteen, 1990), with women more promotive of health-related behaviors in relationships than men (Umberson, 1992). Wives are also likely to serve as primary and even sole providers of social support for husbands, whereas women are likely to have broader social support networks, within and outside of marriage (Phillipson, 1997). Similarly, while divorce and spousal loss through death are linked with poorer health outcomes than marriage, marital disruption is more detrimental to the physical health of men than of women (House et al., 1988). Research on wives' and husbands' depression indicates that for men, depression predicts problems with marital adjustment, whereas the opposite is true for women (who become depressed because of marital problems) (Fincham, Beach, Harold, & Osborne, 1997).

Chapter Summary

Attachment to parents in infancy and childhood has a profound and lasting effect on beliefs about the self and others in relationships (working models). Individuals with secure attachment feel comfortable depending on others and having others depend on them; individuals with insecure attachment feel anxious in relationships and may avoid them because of that anxiety. Disorganized attachment is associated with the poorest outcomes for individuals, including into adulthood. Parenting is gendered from the start, with little girls treated differently from little boys, with gender-congruent behaviors and attitudes rewarded and gender-incongruent behaviors discouraged. Mothers and fathers have different relationships with their children, with mothers generally reporting greater closeness with their children. Parental marital conflict and divorce are more likely to negatively affect relationships with fathers, including into adulthood. Sibling relationships with sisters tend to involve greater closeness; daughters are more likely to care for elderly parents; and women in general are more likely to provide emotional labor in relationships. Same-sex peers and friends are preferred early in life, with girls' and women's friendships characterized by greater trust, loyalty, and closeness than those of boys and men. Women are more likely to show anxious attachment in adulthood romantic relationships, while men tend to show more avoidant attachment (with secure attachment most common for both). LGBTQ romantic relationships are similar in qualities of satisfaction, passion, and commitment to those of heterosexual, cisgender adults. Men are likely to benefit from

324 *Intimacy and Interpersonal Relationships*

marriage physically and psychologically to a greater degree compared to women, although marriage is associated with psychological and physical health benefits for both women and men, heterosexual and LGBTQ couples.

Thoughtful Questions

- Explain the Strange Situation and how it reveals infant attachment.
- Explain how infant attachment influences quality of romantic relationships in adulthood.
- Explain parenting differences of women and men, including evolutionary explanations for those differences.
- What are the research findings on relationships with mothers and siblings in divorced families?
- How does parental divorce affect the quality of relationships with fathers, especially in young adulthood?
- How does parental investment influence ideas about parenting? About mate selection?
- Explain the nature of gender differences in relationship experiences.
- Explain differences in friendships between girls and boys, women and men.
- Explain the effects of father absence on children (see "Injustices and Inequalities").
- Explain Sternberg's triangular theory of love.
- How does marital timing relate to opportunities for women around the world?
- Explain differences in experiences of love for women and men, heterosexual and LGBTQ individuals.
- Explain sex differences in benefits of marriage and why theorists think they exist.

Glossary

Absent fathers: noncustodial fathers who rarely visit and provide little if any financial support.

Agentic: behaviors that are active, powerful, effective. A primary dimension of masculinity stereotypes.

Ambulatory: capable of movement.

Anxious-ambivalent attachment: the experience of anxiety and approach-avoidance responses in intimate relationships. In infancy, associated with anxiety and difficulty soothing. In adulthood, associated with anxiety, emotional extremes, and fear of abandonment in relationships.

Ascribed: qualities that one is born with, in contrast to achieved qualities which are developed, gained, or earned.

Attachment: feeling of closeness and trust between two people, a preference for one person over others. Develops in infancy around age 6–12 months.

Avoidant attachment: the experience of anxiety and discomfort with dependency and closeness in relationships. In infancy, associated with lack of response to primary caregivers. In adulthood, associated with avoidance of closeness and intimacy and relationships in general.

Bonding: a strong, primitive feeling of connection between mother and infant that begins at birth, and is the foundation of attachment.

Chaste: the state of virginity, of never having engaged in any type of sexual behavior. Associated with ideas of female purity.

Intimacy and Interpersonal Relationships 325

Child abuse: "any recent act or failure to act on the part of a parent or caretaker, which results in death, serious physical or emotional harm, sexual abuse, or exploitation, or an act or failure to act which presents an imminent risk of serious harm" (Child Abuse Prevention and Treatment Act, CAPTA).

Cisgender: a person whose gender identity is the same as their biological sex.

Cohabiting: unmarried people living together in a romantic relationship, with or without children.

Coming out: an important part of identity formation in adolescence that involves revealing sexual orientation and/or gender identity to important people.

Commitment: an active, conscious decision to maintain a romantic relationship in the long term.

Communal: behaviors that are caretaking, generative, nurturing, empathic toward others; behaviors that maintain the positivity and harmony of the group. A primary dimension of femininity stereotypes.

Companionate love: love that involves feelings of trust, intimacy, and companionship, more typical of couples who have been together over long periods of time.

Consummate love: love that involves all three components of love; deep trust, companionship, physical passion, and commitment to each other.

Depression: a mood disorder involving feelings of hopelessness, sadness, and negative feelings about the self and the future. Serious depression causes serious impairment of a person's life.

Disorganized or disoriented attachment: children with disorganized attachment show a variety of different attachment behaviors, including anxiety, indifference, and more disturbing behaviors including anger and aggression. Associated with social and behavioral difficulties in childhood and adulthood.

Emotional labor: refers to women's greater burden in maintaining positivity and emotional health in relationships than men.

Erotic love style: a style of romantic activity that involves desire for affective and sexual intimacy.

Extraversion: a major personality trait that involves sociability and social energy; the six facets are warmth, gregariousness, assertiveness, activity, excitement-seeking, and positive emotions.

Family atmosphere: the emotional tone of relationships within the family, an Adlerian concept.

Family system: the view of the family as a complex social system involving multiple members in relationship to each other. Disruptions to one part of the system affect the entire system.

Fidelity: faithfulness to a commitment to another person. Sexual fidelity requires committing to sex with only one mate.

Gender identity: an individual's identification as a particular gender (female, male, neither, both, or something else).

Gender-congruent behavior: behavior deemed acceptable by a particular culture for one's identified gender.

Gender-incongruent behavior: behavior of the opposite sex deemed not acceptable by a particular culture.

Hen: a Finnish pronoun that is gender neutral.

Heteronormative: a society that favors heterosexual sexuality over other orientations; societal beliefs, norms, practices, and social structures that favor heterosexuality over other sexualities.

326 *Intimacy and Interpersonal Relationships*

Heterosexual: feelings of sexual and romantic attraction to people of a different sex, typically the opposite sex using a female-male binary.

High-fertility days: days when women are ovulating and most fertile.

Homonegativity: negative attitudes toward people who are not heterosexual.

Homosexual: feelings of sexual and romantic attraction to people of the same sex.

Hypermasculinity: extreme masculinity including endorsement of violence, callous sexual attitudes toward women, and risk-taking.

Infatuated love: love that is based on passion only, a sexual relationship devoid of intimacy or commitment.

Interdependent: when love partners' goals are intertwined.

Intimacy: psychological closeness and trust with another person.

LGBTQ: Lesbian, Gay, Bisexual, Transgender, Queer/Questioning; an abbreviation used to refer to people who are not exclusively heterosexual or **cisgender**.

Liberal: open-minded, tolerant of differences; openness in thought and ideas; interested in different ways of being, thinking, and feeling.

Liking: a feeling of attraction and warm emotions toward another person.

Longitudinal: a research design involving following the same group of people over time. Generally used to examine developmental processes and predictability of future outcomes.

Love schemas: cognitive representations and understandings of what love is and what romantic relationships are expected to be like.

Ludus love style: a style of romantic activity that involves so-called game-playing characterized by variety of sexual partners and dating multiple people at once.

Marital timing: when marriage typically occurs in the average person's life.

Mere exposure: increased liking for symbols, objects, ideas, and people based on increasing familiarity that comes through repeated exposure.

Meta-analysis: a research design involving statistical analyses of effect sizes gathered from multiple studies. Allows determination of the overall strength and direction of relationships between variables and if any study characteristics are associated with variations in effects.

Monogamous: a pair bond involving two people who are emotionally and sexually faithful to each other.

Mortality rates: rates of death for different groups of people (e.g., women versus men, married people versus unmarried people).

Nontraditional: ideas, practices, behaviors that do not conform to traditional gender ideology or any traditional ideology.

Normative: a practice or behavior that characterizes most people; a practice, belief, or behavior that is socially sanctioned, promoted, and preferred by most people over alternative practices, beliefs, and behaviors.

Openness to Experience: a major personality trait that involves openness to different experiences in terms of fantasy, aesthetics, feelings, actions, ideas, and values.

Oxytocin: a hormone involved in bonding, produced during pregnancy, childbirth, and intimate interactions with others.

Parental investment: the degree to which a parent is invested in the long-term well-being of any particular child. Because reproduction is so difficult and dangerous for women, every individual offspring is of particular value and parental investment will be high. Because men could possibly begin a pregnancy every day, evolutionarily they are less interested and committed to any one particular offspring.

Passion: intense feelings of physical and sexual attraction to another person.

Paternity certainty: a man's certainty (or lack thereof) that a child is indeed his offspring.

Post-traumatic stress disorder (PTSD): a disorder that develops after a person has experienced a traumatic (shocking, dangerous, scary) event. Involves various symptoms including anxiety, depression, night terrors, fearfulness, and flashbacks.

Reciprocity: a behavioral norm involving giving and receiving, with equality in sharing preferred, expected, and socially rewarded.

Romantic love: love that involves passion and intimacy; romantic love is typical of the beginning stages of a monogamous relationship.

Secure attachment: comfort with intimacy and dependency on others; a lack of anxiety in relationships and a feeling of security (without fear of abandonment).

Self-concept: individual thoughts, feelings, and beliefs about the self; includes self-esteem, an overall evaluation of the self as good, bad, or mediocre.

Self-disclosure: sharing of personal information with another person. Self-disclosure underlies intimacy in relationships.

Self-esteem: one's self-attitude; the overall positive, negative, and neutral feelings one has about the self as a person.

Sensation-seeking: a personality trait involving seeking out a variety of new experiences that are high in complexity, intensity, and novelty.

Separation distress: emotional distress (e.g., crying) immediately shown by infants when separated from their mothers.

Sexual orientation: one's feelings of sexual attraction to a particular gender(s).

Sexual self-esteem: positive or negative evaluations about the sexual self, one's sexual behaviors and qualities.

Sexuality: a broad term that refers to all aspects of a person's sexual feelings, thoughts, and behaviors. Includes sexual orientation, sexual behavior, sexual self-esteem, and ideas about sex.

Social dominance: power over others within the social hierarchy and being oriented toward it. Men, white people, and those who follow traditional ideologies are higher in social dominance and social dominance orientation than women, people of color, and the nontraditional.

Social learning theory (aka **social cognitive theory**): the explanation for gender identity that focuses on how children learn about gender through observation of important role models (adults the child models after or imitates, especially parents).

Social support: the perception that one is cared for by others; emotional and other kinds of support provided by people (family, friends, co-workers, bosses, other relatives, clergy, counselors, etc.).

Socialization: the process of learning cultural and social norms, practices, and other expectations for behavior. A lifelong process that begins in utero.

Stereotypes: schemas for the characteristics, traits, and abilities that are typical of a broad social group. For example, **gender stereotypes** of women typically involve feminine traits and qualities (e.g., weak, dependent, emotional, passive), while those of men typically involve masculine traits and qualities (e.g., strong, agentic, independent, not emotional).

Strange Situation: a laboratory paradigm used to examine infant attachment.

Stranger anxiety: securely attached infants turn away from strangers, showing anxiety and a preference for mother or the primary caretaker.

Sucking: an instinctive behavior in infants that is present at birth.

Working models: primary cognitive representations of the self and others as lovable and trustworthy, or not, that the infant develops through relationships with parents.

References

Abbott, D. M., Harris, J. E., & Mollen, D. (2016). The impact of religious commitment on women's sexual self-esteem. *Sexuality & Culture*, 20(4), 1063-1082.

Adler, N. E., & Rehkopf, D. H. (2008). U.S. disparities in health: Descriptions, causes, and mechanisms. *Annual Review of Public Health*, 29, 235-252. doi.org/10.1146/annurev.publhealth.29.020907.090852.

Afifi, T. D., & Schrodt, P. (2004). Adolescents' and young adults' feelings of being caught between their parents in divorced and non-divorced households. *Communication Monographs*, 70, 142-173.

Ahrens, K. R., Ciechanowski, P., & Katon, W. (2012). Associations between adult attachment style and health risk behaviors in an adult female primary care population. *Journal of Psychosomatic Research*, 72, 364-370.

Ainsworth, M. D. S. (1978). The Bowlby-Ainsworth attachment theory. *Behavioral and Brain Sciences*, 1(3), 436-438.

Ainsworth, M. D. S., Blehar, M. C., Waters, E., & Wall, S. (1978). *Patterns of attachment: A psychological study of the Strange Situation*. Hillsdale, NJ: Erlbaum.

Allendorf, K., & Thornton, A. (2015). Caste and choice: The influence of developmental idealism on marriage behavior. *American Journal of Sociology*, 121, 243-287. https://doi.org/10.1086/ 681968.

Alvarez, P. (2006). "Adolescents can't be gay": Perceptions on youth, sexual diversity, and the case of Mexico. *Journal of Gay and Lesbian Issues in Education*, 3(2/3), 141-145.

Amato, P. R., & Afifi, T. D. (2006). Feeling caught between parents: Adult children's relations with parents and subjective well-being. *Journal of Marriage and Family*, 68, 222-235.

Amato, P. R., & Booth, A. (1991). Consequences of parental divorce and marital unhappiness for adult well-being. *Social Forces*, 69, 895-914.

Ansbacher, H. L., & Ansbacher, R. R. (Eds.) (1964). *The individual psychology of Alfred Adler: A systematic presentation in selections from his writings*. New York: Harper & Row.

Aquilino, W. S. (2006). Family relationships and support systems in emerging adulthood. In Arnett, J. J., & Tanner, J. L. (Eds.), *Emerging adults in America: Coming of age in the 21st century*. Washington, DC: American Psychological Association, pp. 193-217.

Baker, M., & Milligan, K. (2016). Boy-girl differences in parental time investments: Evidence from three countries. *Journal of Human Capital*, 10(4), 399-441.

Bàmaca, M. Y., Umana-Taylor, A. J., Shin, N., & Alfaro, E. C. (2005). Latino adolescents' perception of parenting behaviors and self-esteem: Examining the role of neighborhood risk. *Family Relations*, 54, 621-632.

Bandura A. (1986). *Social foundations of thought and action: A social cognitive theory*. New York: Prentice-Hall.

Bandura A. (1997). *Social learning theory*. New York: Prentice-Hall.

Bareis, N., & Mezuk, B. (2016). The relationship between childhood poverty, military service, and later life depression among men: Evidence from the Health and Retirement Study. *Journal of Affective Disorders*, 206, 1-7.

Barnett, M. A., Deng, M., Mills-Koonce, W. R., Willoughby, M., & Cox, M. (2008). Interdependence of parenting of mothers and fathers of infants. *Journal of Family Psychology*, 22, 561-573. http://dx.doi.org/10.1037/ 0893- 3200.22.3.561.

Barrios, R. J., & Lundquist, J. H. (2012). Boys just want to have fun? Masculinity, sexual behaviors, and romantic intentions of gay and straight males in college. *Journal of LGBT Youth*, 9(4), 271-296.

Bartholomew, K. (1990). Avoidance of intimacy: An attachment perspective. *Journal of Social and Personal Relationships*, 7, 147-178.

Bartky, S. L. (1990). Feeding egos and tending wounds: Deference and disaffection in women's emotional labor. In Bartky, S. L. (Ed.), *Femininity and domination: Studies in the phenomenology of oppression*. New York: Routledge, pp. 99-119.

Bayer, J. K., Mundy, L., Stokes, I., Hearps, S., Allen, N., & Patton, G. (2018). Bullying, mental health and friendship in Australian primary school children. *Child and Adolescent Mental Health*, 23(4), 334-340.

Beckerman, S., Lizarralde, R., Ballew, C., Schroeder, S., Fingelton, C., Garrison, A., & Smith, H. (1998). The Barí Partible Paternity Project: Preliminary results. *Current Anthropology*, 39(1), 164-168.

Beckerman, S., & Valentine, P. (2002). *Cultures of multiple fathers: The theory and practice of partible paternity in lowland South America*. Gainesville, FL: University Press of Florida.

Beitchman, J. H., Zucker, K. J., Hood, J. E., DaCosta, G. A., Akman, D., & Cassavia, E. (1992). A review of the long-term effects of child sexual abuse. *Child Abuse & Neglect*, 16(1), 101-118. https://doi.org/10.1016/ 0145-2134(92)90011-F.

Bell, S. M., & Ainsworth, M. D. (1972). Infant crying and maternal responsiveness. *Child Development*, 43, 1171-1190.

Bentley, K. S., & Fox, R. A. (1991). Mothers and fathers of young children: Comparison of parenting styles. *Psychological Reports, 69*, 320-322.

Bereczkei, T., & Csanaky, A. (1996). Evolutionary pathway of child development: Lifestyles of adolescents and adults from father-absent families. *Human Nature – an Interdisciplinary Biosocial Perspective, 7*(3), 257-280.

Bergen, D. (2002). The role of pretend play in children's cognitive development. *Early Childhood Research and Practice, 4*(1). www.ecrp.uiuc.edu/v4n1/bergen.html.

Berndt, T. J. (2002). Friendship quality and social development. *Current Directions in Psychological Science, 11*, 7-10. https://doi.org/10.1111/1467-8721.00157.

Berscheid, E., Dion, K., Walster, E., & Walster, G. W. (1971). Physical attractiveness and dating choice: A test of the matching hypothesis. *Journal of Experimental Social Psychology, 7*(2), 173-189. https://doi.org/10.1016/0022-1031(71)90065-5.

Best, D. L., House, A. S., Barnard, A. E., & Spicker, B. S. (1994). Parent-child interactions in France, Germany, and Italy; the effects of gender and culture. *Journal of Cross-Cultural Psychology, 25*, 181-193. http://dx.doi.org/10.1177/0022022194252002.

Bigelow, B. J., & La Gaipa, J. J. (1980). The development of friendship values and choice. In Foot, H. C., Chapman, A. J., & Smith, J. R. (Eds.), *Friendship and social relations in children* (pp. 15-44). New York: John Wiley & Sons.

Bigler, R. S., & Liben, L. S. (2006). A developmental intergroup theory of social stereotypes and prejudice. *Advances in Child Development and Behavior 34*, 39-89.

Bird, K. (2013). The intergenerational transmission of poverty: An overview. In Shepherd, A., & Brunt, J. (Eds.), *Chronic poverty*. Rethinking International Development Series. London: Palgrave Macmillan.

Birkett, M., Newcomb, M. E., & Mustanski, B. (2014). Does it get better? A longitudinal analysis of psychological distress and victimization in lesbian, gay, bisexual, transgender and questioning youth. *Journal of Adolescent Health, 56*(3), 280-285.

Blanchard, A., & Lyons, M. (2016). Sex differences between primary and secondary psychopathy, parental bonding, and attachment style. *Evolutionary Behavioral Sciences, 10*(1), 56-63. http://dx.doi.org/10.1037/ebs0000065.

Blier, M., & Blier-Wilson, L. (1989). Gender differences in self-rated emotional expressiveness. *Sex Roles, 21*, 287-295.

Block, J. H. (1983). Differential premises arising from differential socialization of the sexes: Some conjectures. *Child Development, 54*, 1335-1354. http://dx.doi.org/10.2307/1129799.

Blurton Jones, N. G., & Konner, M. (1973). Sex differences in behavior of two to five year olds in London and among the Kalahari Desert Bushmen. In Michael, R. P., & Crook, J. H. (Eds.), *Comparative ecology and behavior of primates*. London: Academic Press.

Bogart, L., & Lehman, C. (1973). What makes a brand name familiar? *Journal of Marketing Research, 10*(1), 17-22.

Bogle, K. (2008). *Hooking up: Sex, dating, and relationships on campus*. New York: New York University Press.

Bonney, J. F., Kelley, M. L., & Levant, R. F. (1999). A model of fathers' behavioral involvement in child care in dual earner families. *Journal of Family Psychology, 13*, 401-415. http://dx.doi.org/10.1037/0893-3200.13.3.401.

Booth, A., & Edwards, J. N. (1990). The transmission of marital and family quality over the generations: The effects of parental divorce and unhappiness. *Journal of Divorce, 13*, 41-58.

Boris, N. W., Fueyo, M., & Zeanah, C. H. (1997). Clinical assessment of attachment in children under five. *Journal of the American Academy of Child & Adolescent Psychiatry, 36*, 291-293.

Bowlby, J. (1969). *Attachment and loss*. New York: Basic Books.

Boyd, K., Ashcraft, A., & Belgrave, F. Z. (2006). The impact of mother-daughter and father-daughter relationships on drug refusal self-efficacy among African American adolescent girls in urban communities. *Journal of Black Psychology, 32*, 29-42. http://dx.doi.org/10.1177/0095798405280387.

Bradley, R. H., & Corwyn, R. F. (2004). Life satisfaction among European American, African American, Chinese American, Mexican American, and Dominican American adolescents. *International Journal of Behavioral Development, 28*(5), 385-400.

Brennan, K. A., Clark, C. L., & Shaver, P. R. (1998). Self-report measurement of adult attachment: An integrative overview. In Simpson, J. A., & Rholes, W. S. (Eds.), *Attachment theory and close relationships*. New York: Guilford Press, pp. 46-76.

Brody, G. H., Stoneman, Z., & MacKinnon, C. E. (1982). Role asymmetries in interactions among school-aged children, their younger siblings, and their friends. *Child Development, 53*, 1364-1370.

Brody, G. H., Stoneman, Z., & McCoy, J. K. (1994). Contributions of family relationships and child temperaments to longitudinal variations in sibling relationship quality and sibling relationship styles. *Journal of Family Psychology, 8*, 274-286.

330　*Intimacy and Interpersonal Relationships*

Bronstein, P. (2006). The family environment: Where gender role socialization begins. In Worell, J., & Goodheart, C. D. (Eds.), *Handbook of girls' and women's psychological health: Gender and well-being across the lifespan.* New York: Oxford University Press, pp. 262-271.

Brown, J., Cohen, P., Johnson, J. G., & Salzinger, S. (1998). A longitudinal analysis of risk factors for child maltreatment: Findings of a 17-year prospective study of officially recorded and self-reported child abuse and neglect. *Child Abuse & Neglect, 22*(11), 1065-1078. https://doi.org/10.1016/S0145-2134(98)00087-8.

Bukowski, W. M., Newcomb, A. F., & Hartup, W. W. (Eds.) (1996). *The company they keep: Friendship in childhood and adolescence.* Cambridge: Cambridge University Press.

Burke, R. A., & Fuqua, D. R. (1987). Sex differences in same and cross-sex supportive relationships. *Sex Roles, 17,* 339-352.

Buss, D. M. (1998). The psychology of human mate selection: Exploring the complexity of the strategic repertoire. In Crawford, C., & Krebs, D. L. (Eds.), *Handbook of evolutionary psychology: Ideas, issues, and applications* (pp. 405-429). Mahwah, NJ: Erlbaum.

Buss, D. M., Abbott, M., Angleitner, A., Asherian, A., Biaggio, A., Blanco-Villasenor, A.,...., Yang, K.-S. (1990). International preferences in selecting mates: A study of 37 cultures. *Journal of Cross-Cultural Psychology, 21,* 5- 47. doi:10.1177/0022022190211001.

Buss, D. M., Larsen. R. J., Westen, D., & Semmelroth, J. (1992). Sex differences in jealousy: Evolution, physiology, and psychology. *Psychological Science, 3,* 251-255.

Butler, R., & Shalit-Naggar, R. (2008). Gender and patterns of concerned responsiveness in representations of the mother-daughter and mother-son relationship. *Child Development, 79*(4), 836-851.

Buunk, B. P., Angleitner, A., Oubaid, V., & Buss, D. M. (1996). Sex differences in jealousy in evolutionary and cultural perspective: Tests from the Netherlands, Germany, and the United States. *Psychological Science, 7*(6), 359-363.

CAADA Research Report (2014). In plain sight: The evidence from children exposed to domestic abuse. Coordinated Action Against Domestic Abuse. www.caada.org.uk/documents/In_plain_sight_the_evidence_from_children_exposed_to_domestic_abuse.

Cabrera, N., Tamis-LeMonda, C. S., Bradley, R. H., Hofferth, S., & Lamb, M. E. (2000). Fatherhood in the twenty-first century. *Child Development, 71*(1), 127-136. https://doi.org/10.1111/1467-8624.00126.

Caldera, Y. M., & Sciaraffa, M. A. (1998). Parent-toddler play with feminine toys: Are all dolls the same? *Sex Roles, 39*(9-10), 657-668.

Canary, D. J., Emmers-Sommer, T. M., & Faulkner, S. (1997). *Sex and gender: Differences in personal relationships.* New York: Guilford Press.

Caplan, R. A., Maunder, R. G., Stempak, J. M., Silverberg, M. S., & Hart, T. L. (2014). Attachment, childhood abuse, and IBD-related quality of life and disease activity outcomes. *Inflammatory Bowel Disease, 20,* 909-915.

Carli, L. L. (1989). Gender differences in interaction style and influence. *Journal of Personality and Social Psychology, 56,* 565-576.

Carlson, E. A. (1998). A prospective longitudinal study of attachment disorganization/disorientation. *Child Development, 69*(4), 1107-1128.

Carlson, E. A., & Sroufe, L. A. (1995). The contribution of attachment theory to developmental psychopathology. In Cicchetti, D., & Cohen, D. (Eds.), *Developmental processes and psychopathology: Vol. 1. Theoretical perspectives and methodological approaches* (pp. 581-617). New York: Cambridge University Press.

Carlson, M., McLanahan, S., & England, P. (2004). Union formation in fragile families. *Demography, 41,* 237-261. https://doi.org/10.1353/dem.2004 .0012.

Carlson, V., Cicchetti, D., Barnett, D., & Braunwald, K. (1989). Disorganized/disoriented attachment relationships in maltreated infants. *Developmental Psychology, 25*(4), 525-531. http://dx.doi.org/10.1037/0012-1649.25.4.525.

Carson, J., Burks, V., & Parke, R. D. (1993). Parent-child physical play: Determinants and consequences. In MacDonald, K. (Ed.), *Parent-child play: Descriptions and implications.* Albany: State University of New York Press.

Case, A., Lubotsky, D., & Paxson, C. (2002). Economic status and health in childhood: The origins of the gradient. *American Economic Review, 92*(5), 1308-1334.

Centers for Disease Control & Prevention (1997). Adverse Childhood Experiences Study. www.cdc.gov/nccd-php/ace/prevalence.htm.

Centers for Disease Control & Prevention (2016). Gay and bisexual men's health, suicide and violence prevention. www.cdc.gov/msmhealth/suicide-violence-prevention.htm.

Chandra, V., Szklo, M., Goldberg, R., & Tonascia, J. (1983). The impact of marital status on survival after an acute myocardial infarction: A population-based study. *American Journal of Epidemiology, 117,* 320-325.

Cherlin, A. (2009). *Marriage, divorce, remarriage.* Cambridge, MA: Harvard University Press.

Cherlin, A. J. (2013). Health, marriage, and same-sex partnerships. *Journal of Health and Social Behavior, 54*(1), 64–66.

Cherlin, A. J., Furstenberg, F. F., Chase-Lansdale, P. L., Kiernan, K. E., Robins, P. K., Morrison, D. R., & Teitler, J. O. (1991). Longitudinal studies of effects of divorce on children in Great Britain and the United States. *Science, 252*(5011), 1386–1389. doi:10.1126/science.2047851.

Chronic Poverty Research Centre (2010). Stemming girls' chronic poverty: Catalysing development change by building just social institutions. Chronic Poverty Research Centre. www.chronicpoverty.org/uploads/assets/files/reports/Full_report.

Cicirelli, V. G. (1995). *Sibling relationships across the life span.* New York: Plenum.

Clearfield, M. W., & Nelson, N. M. (2006). Sex differences in mothers' speech and play behavior with 6-, 9-, and 14-month-old infants. *Sex Roles, 54*: 127–137. https://doi.org/10.1007/s11199-005-8874-1.

Clutton-Brock, T. H. (1991). *The evolution of parental care.* Princeton, NJ: Princeton University Press.

Cohn, D. A. (1990). Child-mother attachment of six-year-olds and social competence at school. *Child Development, 61*, 152–162.

Collins, N. L., & Read, S. J. (1990). Adult attachment, working models, and relationship quality in dating couples. *Journal of Personality and Social Psychology, 58*, 644–663.

Condon, J. W., & Crano, W. D. (1988). Inferred evaluation and the relation between attitude similarity and interpersonal attraction. *Journal of Personality and Social Psychology, 54*(5), 789–797.

Cook, S. H., Valera, P., Calebs, B. J., & Wilson, P. A. (2017). Adult attachment as a moderator of the association between childhood traumatic experiences and depression symptoms among young Black gay and bisexual men. *Cultural Diversity and Ethnic Minority Psychology, 23*(3), 388–397.

Cooney, T. M. (1994). Young adults' relations with parents: The influence of recent parental divorce. *Journal of Marriage and the Family, 56*, 45–56.

Cooper, M. L., Shaver, P. R., & Collins, N. L. (1998). Attachment styles, emotion regulation, and adjustment in adolescence. *Journal of Personality and Social Psychology, 74*, 1380–1397.

Couperthwaite, L. M. Z. (2015). Relationship satisfaction among individuals of diverse sexual orientations and gender identities: The role of love and attachment styles. *Dissertation Abstracts International: Section B: The Sciences and Engineering, 75*(11-B)(E).

Cowan, C., Drinkard, J., & MacGavin, L. (1984). The effects of target, age and gender on use of power strategies. *Journal of Personality and Social Psychology, 47*, 1391–1398.

Cox, M. J., & Paley, B. (1997). Families as systems. *Annual Review of Psychology, 48*, 243–267. https://doi.org/10.1146/annurev.psych.48.1.243.

Craig, R. L., Gray, N. S., & Snowden, R. J. (2013). Recalled parental bonding, current attachment, and the triarchic conceptualisation of psychopathy. *Personality and Individual Differences, 55*, 345–350. http://dx.doi.org/10.1016/j.paid.2013.03.012.

Crocker, W.H., & Crocker, J. (1994). *The Canela: Bonding through kinship, ritual, and sex.* Fort Worth, TX: Harcourt College Publishers.

Crosnoe, R. (2000). Friendships in childhood and adolescence: The life course and new directions. *Social Psychology Quarterly, 63*, 377–391.

Cummings, E. M., Davies, P. T., & Campbell, S. B. (2000). *Developmental psychology and family processes.* New York: Guilford.

Cusack, C. E., Hughes, J. L., & Cook, R. E. (2012). Components of love and relationship satisfaction: Lesbians and heterosexual women. *Psi Chi Journal of Psychological Research, 17*(4), 171–179.

Dashow, J. (2017). New FBI data shows increased reported incidents of anti-LGBTQ hate crimes in 2016. www.hrc.org/blog/new-fbi-data-shows-increased-reported-incidents-of-anti-lgbtq-hate-crimes-i.

D'Augelli, A. R. (1994). Lesbian and gay male development: Steps toward an analysis of lesbians' and gay men's lives. In Greene, B., & Herek, G. M. (Eds.), *Psychological perspectives on lesbian and gay issues: Vol 1. Lesbian and gay psychology: Theory, research, and clinical applications.* Thousand Oaks, CA: Sage.

Davies, P. T., Parry, L. Q., Bascoe, S. M., Martin, M. J., & Cummings, E. M. (2018). Children's vulnerability to interparental conflict: The protective role of sibling relationship quality. *Child Development, 90*(6), 2118–2134.

Dedek, J. F. (1980). Premarital sex: The theological argument from Peter Lombard to Durand. *Theological Studies, 41*(4), 643–667. doi:10.1177/004056398004100401.

Delk, J. (2017). Senate bill clarifies tax law for private jet companies. The Hill, November 16. https://thehill.com/blogs/blog-briefing-room/360785-senate-tax-bill-includes-tax-break-for-private-jets.

Demir, M., Simsek, O. F., & Procsal, A. D. (2012). I am so happy 'cause my best friend makes me feel unique: Friendship, personal sense of uniqueness and happiness. *Journal of Happiness Studies, 14*, 1201–1224.

Diamond, L. (2003). Love matters: Romantic relationships among sexual-minority adolescents. In Florsheim, P. (Ed.), *Adolescent romantic relations and sexual behavior: Theory, research, and practice implications.* Mahwah, NJ: Erlbaum, pp. 85–107.

Diamond, L., Savin-Williams, R., & Dube, E. (1999). Sex, dating, passionate friendships, and romance: Intimate peer relations among lesbian, gay, and bisexual adolescents. In Furman, W., Brown, B., & Feiring, C. (Eds.), *The development of romantic relationships in adolescence* (Cambridge: Cambridge University Press, pp. 175-210.

Diamond, R. M., Brimhall, A. S., & Elliott, M. (2018). Attachment and relationship satisfaction among first married, remarried, and post-divorce relationships. *Journal of Family Therapy, 40*(Suppl 1), S111-S127.

DiTommaso, E., Brannen-McNulty, C., Ross, L., & Burgess, M. (2003). Attachment styles, social skills and loneliness in young adults. *Personality and Individual Differences, 35*(2), 303-312. https://doi.org/10.1016/S0191-8869(02)00190-3.

Dobash, R. P., Dobash, R. E., Wilson, M., & Daly, M. (1992). The myth of sexual symmetry in marital violence. *Social Problems, 39,* 71-91.

D'Onofrio, B. M., Turkheimer, E., Emery, R. E., Slutske, W. S., Heath, A. C., Madden, P. A., & Martin, N. G. (2005). A genetically informed study of marital instability and its association with offspring psychopathology. *Journal of Abnormal Psychology, 114*(4), 570-586. doi:10.1037/0021-843X.114.4.570.

Dorius, S. F., & Firebaugh, G. (2010). Trends in global gender inequality. *Social Forces, 88*(5), 1941-1968. https://doi.org/10.1353/sof.2010.0040.

Driscoll, K., & Pianta, R. C. (2011). Mothers' and fathers' perceptions of conflict and closeness in parent-child relationships during early childhood. *Journal of Early Childhood and Infant Psychology, 7,* 1-24.

Drossman, D. A., Talley, N. J., Leserman, J., Olden, K. W., & Barreiro, M. A. (1995). Sexual and physical abuse and gastrointestinal illness: Review and recommendations. *Annals of Internal Medicine, 123*(10), 782-794. doi:10.7326/0003-4819-123-10-199511150-00007.

Dunn, J., & Kendrick, S. (1982). *Siblings: Love, envy and understanding.* Cambridge, MA: Harvard University Press.

Dunn, J., Slomkowski, C., & Beardsall, L. (1994). Sibling relationships from the preschool period through middle childhood and early adolescence. *Developmental Psychology, 30*(3), 315-324.

Eagly, A. H. (1987). *Sex differences in social behavior: A social role interpretation.* Hillsdale, NJ: Erlbaum.

Eagly, A. H., Ashmore, R. D., Makhijani, M. G., & Longo, L. C. (1991). What is beautiful is good, but...: A meta-analytic review of research on the physical attractiveness stereotype. *Psychological Bulletin, 110*(1), 109-128.

Eagly, A. H., & Wood, W. (1999). The origins of sex differences in human behavior: Evolved dispositions versus social roles. *American Psychologist, 54,* 408-423.

Eaton, W. O., & Enns, L. R. (1986). Sex differences in human motor activity level. *Psychological Bulletin, 100,* 19-28.

Eckel, C. C., & Grossman, P. J. (2008). Men, women and risk aversion: Experimental evidence. In Plott, C., & Smith, V. (Eds.), *Handbook of experimental economics results.* Amsterdam: Elsevier, pp. 1061-1073. http://dx.doi.org/10.1016/S1574-0722(07)00113-8.

Egeland, B., & Hiester, M. (1995). The long-term consequences of infant day-care and mother-infant attachment. *Child Development, 66,* 474-485.

Eisenberg, N., & Fabes, R. A. (1998). Prosocial development. In Damon, W., & Eisenberg, N. (Eds.), *Handbook of child psychology: Vol. 3. Social, emotional, and personality development* (5th ed., pp. 702-778). New York: Wiley.

Eisenhart, M. A., & Holland, D. C. (1983). Learning gender from peers: The role of peer group in the cultural transmission of gender. *Human Organization, 42,* 321-332.

Ember, C. R., & Ember, M. (2001). Father absence and male aggression. A re-examination of the comparative evidence. *Ethos: Journal of the Society of Psychological Anthropology, 29*(3), 296-314. https://doi.org/10.1525/eth.2001.29.3.296.

Erikson, E. H. (1963). *Youth: Change and challenge.* New York: Basic Books.

Erwin, P. (1985). Similarity of attitudes and constructs in children's friendships. *Journal of Experimental Child Psychology, 40,* 470-485.

Etcheverry, P. E., Le, B., Wu, T.-F., & Wei, M. (2013). Attachment and the investment model: Predictors of relationship commitment, maintenance, and persistence. *Personal Relationships, 20*(3), 546-567.

Evans, G. W. (2004). The environment of childhood poverty. *American Psychologist, 59*(2), 77-92.

Eyre, S., Arnold, E., Peterson, E., & Strong, T. (2007). Romantic relationships and their social context among gay/bisexual male youth in the Castro district of San Francisco. *Journal of Gayity, 53*(4), 1-29.

Fabes, R. A., & Martin, C. L. (1991). Gender and age stereotypes of emotionality. *Personality and Social Psychology Bulletin, 17,* 532-544.

Fagot, B. I. (1985). Beyond the reinforcement principle: Another step toward understanding sex roles. *Developmental Psychology, 21,* 1097-1104.

Fehr, B. (2004). Intimacy expectations in same-sex friendships: A prototypical interaction-pattern model. *Journal of Personality and Social Psychology, 86,* 265-284. doi:10.1037/0022-3514.86.2.265.

Feinberg, D. R., Jones, B. C., Law Smith, M. J., Moore, F. R., DeBruine, L. M., et al. (2006). Menstrual cycle, trait estrogen level, and masculinity preferences in the human voice. *Hormones and Behavior, 49,* 215-222.

Feingold, A. (1990). Gender differences in effects of physical attractiveness on romantic attraction: A comparison across five research paradigms. *Journal of Personality and Social Psychology, 59,* 981-993.

Feingold, A. (1991). Sex differences in the effects of similarity and physical attractiveness on opposite-sex attraction. *Basic and Applied Social Psychology, 12,* 357-367.

Feingold, A. (1992). Gender differences in mate selection preferences: A test of the parental investment model. *Psychological Bulletin, 112,* 125-139.

Feldman, R., Gordon, I., Schneiderman, I., Weisman, O., & Zagoory-Sharon, O. (2010). Natural variations in maternal and paternal care are associated with systematic changes in oxytocin following parent-infant contact. *Psychoneuroendocrinology, 35*(8), 1133-1141. https://doi.org/10.1016/j.psyneuen.2010.01.013.

Feldman, R., Weller, A., Zagoory-Sharon, O., & Levine, A. (2007). Evidence for a neuroendocrinological foundation of human affiliation: Plasma oxytocin levels across pregnancy and the postpartum period predict mother-infant bonding. *Psychological Science, 18*(11), 965-970. https://doi.org/10.1111/j.1467-9280.2007.02010.x.

Fincham, F. D., Beach, S. R. H., Harold, G. T., & Osborne, L. N. (1997). Marital satisfaction and depression: Different causal relationships for men and women? *Psychological Science, 8,* 351-357.

Fine, C., & Rush, E. (2018). 'Why does all the girls have to buy pink stuff?' The ethics and science of the gendered toy marketing debate. *Journal of Business Ethics, 149,* 769-784. https://doi.org/10.1007/s10551-016-3080-3.

Finkel, E. J., & Baumeister, R. F. (2010). Attraction and rejection. In Baumeister, R. F., & Finkel, E. J. (Eds.), *Advanced social psychology: The state of the science.* New York: Oxford University Press, pp. 419- 459.

Finkel, E. J., & Eastwick, P. E. (2015). Interpersonal attraction: In search of a theoretical Rosetta stone. In Simpson, J. A., & Dovidio, J. F. (Eds.), *Handbook of personality and social psychology: Interpersonal relationships and group processes.* Washington, DC: American Psychological Association, pp. 179- 210.

Fishman, P. M. (1983). Interaction: The work women do. In Thorne, B., Kramerae, C., & Henley, N. (Eds.), *Language, gender and society* (pp. 89-101). Cambridge, MA: Newbury House.

Floyd, K. (1997). Communicating affection in dyadic relationships: An assessment of behavior and expectancies. *Communication Quarterly, 45,* 68-80.

Francis, D., Diorio, J., Liu, D., & Meaney, M. J. (1999). Nongenomic transmission across generations of maternal behavior and stress responses in the rat. *Science, 286*(5442), 1155-1158. doi:10.1126/science.286.5442.1155.

Frederick, D. A., Sandhu, G., Morse, P. J., & Swami, V. (2016). Correlates of appearance and weight satisfaction in a U.S. national sample: Personality, attachment style, television viewing, self-esteem, and life satisfaction. *Body Image, 17,* 191-203.

Frias-Armenta, M., & McCloskey, L. A. (1998). Determinants of harsh parenting in Mexico. *Journal of Abnormal Child Psychology, 26,* 129-139.

Fuller-Thomson, E., Bottoms, J., Brennenstuhl, S., & Hurd, M. (2011). Is childhood physical abuse associated with peptic ulcer disease? Findings from a population-based study. *Journal of Interpersonal Violence, 26*(16), 3225-3247. https://doi.org/10.1177/0886260510393007.

Gal, D., & Wilkie, J. (2010). Real men don't eat quiche: Regulation of gender-expressive choices by men. *Social Psychological and Personality Science, 1*(4), 291-301.

Gangestad, S. W., Garver-Apgar, C. E., Simpson, J. A., & Cousins, A. J. (2007). Changes in women's mate preferences across the ovulatory cycle. *Journal of Personality and Social Psychology, 92,* 151-163.

Gatiss, L. (2005). The issue of pre-marital sex. *The Theologian.* www.theologian.org.uk/pastoralia/premaritalsex.html.

Geary, D. C. (2000). Evolution and proximate expression of human paternal investment. *Psychological Bulletin, 126,* 55-77. http://dx.doi.org/10.1037/0033-2909.126.1.55.

Geary, D. C. (2010). *Male, female: The evolution of human sex differences* (2nd ed.). Washington, DC: American Psychological Association. http://dx.doi.org/10.1037/12072-000.

Geary, D. C., Byrd-Craven, J., Hoard, M. K., Vigil, J., & Numtee, C. (2003). Evolution and development of boys' social behavior. *Developmental Review, 23,* 444-470.

Geary, D. C., & Flinn, M. V. (2001). Evolution of human parental behavior and the human family. *Parenting: Science and Practice, 1,* 5-61.

Gilligan, C. (1996). The centrality of relationship in human development: A puzzle, some evidence, and a theory. In Noam, G. G., & Fischer, K. W. (Eds.), *Development and vulnerability in close relationships* (pp. 237-261). Hillsdale, NJ: Erlbaum.

Godbout, N., Daspe, M.-È., Lussier, Y., Sabourin, S., Dutton, D., & Hébert, M. (2017). Early exposure to violence, relationship violence, and relationship satisfaction in adolescents and emerging adults: The role of romantic attachment. *Psychological Trauma: Theory, Research, Practice, and Policy, 9*(2), 127-137.

Goldsmith, K. M., Dunkley, C. R., Dang, S. S., & Gorzalka, B. B. (2016). Sexuality and romantic relationships: Investigating the relation between attachment style and sexual satisfaction. *Sexual and Relationship Therapy, 31*(2), 190-206. http://dx.doi.org/10.1080/14681994.2016.1158804.

Gordon, H. S., & Rosenthal, G. E. (1995). Impact of marital status on outcomes in hospitalized patients. *Archives of Internal Medicine, 155*, 2465-2471.

Grall, T. (2016). Custodial mothers and fathers and their child support: 2013. Current population reports, issued January 2016. www.census.gov/content/dam/Census/library/publications/2016/demo/P60-255.

Greene, B. (1994). Lesbian women of color: Triple jeopardy. In Comas-Diaz, L., & Greene, B. (Eds.), *Women of color: Integrating ethnic and gender identities in psychotherapy* (pp. 389-427). New York: Guilford Press.

Green, J., & Goldwyn, R. (2002). Annotation: Attachment disorganisation and psychopathology: New findings in attachment research and their potential implications for developmental psychopathology in childhood. *Journal of Child Psychology and Psychiatry, 43*, 835-846.

Greenberg, M. T., Speltz, M. L., & DeKlyen, M. (1993). The role of attachment in the early development of disruptive behavior problems. *Development and Psychopathology, 3*, 413-430.

Greenough, W. T., Black, J. E., & Wallace, C. S. (1987). Experience and brain development. *Child Development, 58*, 539-559. doi:10.2307/1130197.

Greenwald, A. G., & Banaji, M. R. (1995). Implicit social cognition: Attitudes, self-esteem, and stereotypes. *Psychological Review, 102*, 4-27. http://dx.doi.org/10.1037/0033-295X.102.1.4.

Grigoryeva, A. (2017). Own gender, sibling's gender, parent's gender: The division of elderly parent care among adult children. *American Sociological Review, 82*(1), 116-146.

Guzmán-González, M., Barrientos, J., Cárdenas, M., Espinoza, M. F., Quijada, P., Rivera, C., & Tapia, P. (2016). Romantic attachment and life satisfaction in a sample of gay men and lesbians in Chile. *International Journal of Sexual Health, 28*(2), 141-150.

Hadi, A. (2000). Child abuse among working children in rural Bangladesh: Prevalence and determinants. *Public Health, 114*, 380-384.

Hall, J. A. (2011). Sex differences in friendship expectations: A meta-analysis. *Journal of Social and Personal Relationships, 28*(6), 723-747.

Hastings, P. D., & Rubin, K. H. (1999). Predicting mothers' beliefs about preschool-aged children's social behavior: Evidence for maternal attitudes moderating child effects. *Child Development, 70*, 722-741.

Hatfield, E. (1988). Passionate and companionate love In Sternberg, R. J., & Barnes, M. L. (Eds.), *The psychology of love*. New Haven, CT: Yale University Press, pp. 191-217.

Hatfield, E., & Rapson, R. L. (1996). *Love and sex: Cross-cultural perspectives*. Needham Heights, MA: Allyn & Bacon.

Hays, R. B. (1988). Friendship. In Duck, S., Hay, D. F., Hobfoll, S. E., Ickes, W., & Montgomery, B. M. (Eds.), *Handbook of personal relationships: Theory, research and interventions*. Hoboken, NJ: John Wiley, pp. 391-408.

Hazan, C., & Shaver, P. R. (1987). Romantic love conceptualized as an attachment process. *Journal of Personality and Social Psychology, 52*(3), 511-524. doi:10.1037/0022-3514.52.3.511.

Hebblethwaite, C. (2011). Sweden's 'gender-neutral' pre-school. BBC News, July 8. www.bbc.com/news/world-europe-14038419.

Hendrick, S. S., & Hendrick, C. (1995). Gender differences and similarities in sex and love. *Personal Relationships, 2*(1), 55-65. doi:10.1111/j.1475-6811.1995.tb00077.x.

Hepper, P. G., Scott, D., & Shahidullah, S. (1993). Newborn and fetal response to maternal voice. *Journal of Reproductive and Infant Psychology, 11*(3), 147-153.

Herdt, G., & Boxer, A. (1993). *Children of horizons: How gay and lesbian teens are leading a new way out of the closet*. Boston: Beacon Press.

Hersch, P. (1991). Secret lives: Lesbian and gay teens in fear of discovery. *The Family Therapy Networker*, 36-39, 41-43.

Hertsgaard, L., Gunnar, M., Erickson, M. F., & Nachmias, M. (1995). Adrenocortical responses to the Strange Situation in infants with disorganized/disoriented attachment relationships. *Child Development, 66*(4), 1100-1106. https://doi.org/10.1111/j.1467-8624.1995.tb00925.x.

Hessem, E., & van IJzendoornm, M. H. (1998). Parental loss of close family members and propensities towards absorption in offspring. *Developmental Science, 1*, 299-305.

Hetherington, E. M. (1972). The effects of father absence on personality development in adolescent daughters. *Developmental Psychology, 3*, 313-326.

Higa, D., Hoppe, M. J., Lindhorst, T., Mincer, S., Beadnell, B., Morrison, D. M., ..., Mountz, S. (2014). Negative and positive factors associated with the well-being of lesbian, gay, bisexual, transgender, queer, and questioning (LGBTQ) youth. *Youth & Society, 46*(5), 663-687. doi:[10.1177/0044118X12449630].

Hocker, L., & Riggio, H. R. (2018). Relationship motivations: Links with attachment and relationship self-efficacy. Poster presented at the annual meeting of the Western Psychological Association, Portland, OR, April.

Hoffman, S. D. (1998). Teenage childbearing is not so bad after all ... or is it? A review of the literature. *Family Planning Perspectives, 30*(5): 236-239, 243.

Horwitz, A. V., White, H. R., & Howell-White, S. (1996). The use of multiple outcomes in stress research: A case study of gender differences in responses to marital dissolution. *Journal of Health and Social Behavior, 37*(3), 278-291.

House, J. S., Landis, K. R., & Umberson, D. (1988). Social relationships and health. *Science, 241*, 540-545.

Human Rights Campaign (2018). 2018 LGBTQ Youth Report. www.hrc.org/resources/2018-lgbtq-youth-report.

Humphreys, A. P., & Smith, P. K. (1987). Rough and tumble friendship and dominance in school children: Evidence for continuity and change with age in middle childhood. *Child Development, 58*, 201-212.

Hunter, W. M., Jain, D., Sadowski, L. S., & Sanhueza, A. I. (2000). Risk factors for severe child discipline practices in rural India. *Journal of Pediatric Psychology, 25*(6), 435-447. https://doi.org/10.1093/jpepsy/25.6.435.

Huntley, D. K., & Phelps, R. E. (1990). Depression and social contacts of children from one-parent families. *Journal of Community Psychology, 18*, 66-72.

Hust, S. J. T., & Brown, J. D. (2008). Gender, media use, and effects. In Calvert, S. L., & Wilson, B. J. (Eds.), *The handbook of children, media, and development*. Malden: Blackwell Publishing, pp. 98-120.

Idle, T., Wood, E., & Desmarais, S. (1993). Gender role socialization in toy play situations: Mothers and fathers with their sons and daughters. *Gender Roles, 28*, 679-691.

Isley, S. L., O'Neil, R., Clatfelter, D., & Parke, R. D. (1999). Parent and child expressed affect and children's social competence: Modeling direct and indirect pathways. *Developmental Psychology, 35*(2), 547-560.

Jacklin, C. N., DiPietro, J. A., & Maccoby, E. E. (1984). Sex-typing behavior and sex-typing pressure in child/parent interaction. *Archives of Sexual Behavior, 13*(5), 413-425.

Jacobsen, T., Edelstein, W., & Hofmann, V. (1994). A longitudinal study of the relation between representations of attachment in childhood and cognitive functioning in childhood and adolescence. *Developmental Psychology, 30*, 112-124.

Jacobvitz, D., & Hazan, N. (1999). Developmental pathways from infant disorganization to childhood peer relationships. In Solomon, J., & George, C. (Eds.), *Attachment Disorganization*. New York: Guilford Press.

Jalovaara, M. (2012). Socio-economic resources and first-union formation in Ginland, cohorts born 1969-81. *Population Studies, 66*, 69-85. https:// doi.org/10.1080/00324728.2011.641720.

James, J., Ellis, B. J., Schlomer, G. L., & Garber, J. (2012). Sex-specific pathways to early puberty, sexual debut, and sexual risk taking: Tests of an integrated evolutionary-developmental model. *Developmental Psychology, 48*(3), 687.

Jennings, E. A., Axinn, W. G., & Ghimire, D. J. (2012). The effect of parents' attitudes on sons' marriage timing. *American Sociological Review, 77*, 923-945. https://doi.org/10.1177/ 0003122412464041.

Kassel, J. D., Wardle M., & Roberts J. E. (2007). Adult attachment security and college student substance use. *Addictive Behaviors, 32*, 1164-1176.

Katz, I., & Hass, R. G. (1988). Racial ambivalence and American value conflict: Correlational and prime studies of dual cognitive structures. *Journal of Personality and Social Psychology, 55*, 893-905.

Keren, M., Feldman, R., Namdari-Weinbaum, I., Spitzer, S., & Tyano, S. (2005). Relations between parents interactive in dyadic and triadic play and toddlers' symbolic capacity. *American Journal of Orthopsychiatry, 75*, 599-604. http://dx.doi.org/10.1037/0002-9432.75.4.599.

Kiecolt-Glaser, J. K., & Newton, T. (2001). Marriage and health: His and hers. *Psychological Bulletin, 127*, 472-503.

Kindleberger, L., & Kuebli, J. (2007). Mothers' and fathers' socialization of preschoolers' physical risk-taking. *Journal of Applied Developmental Psychology, 28*, 2-14. http://dx.doi.org/10.1016/j.appdev.2006.10.007.

King, A. R., & Terrance, C. (2008). Best friendship qualities and mental health symptomatology among young adults. *Journal of Adult Development, 15*(1), 25-34.

Klaus, M. H., & Kennell, J. H. (1976). *Maternal-infant bonding*. St. Louis: Mosby.

Kohlberg, L., & Ullian, D. Z. (1974). Stages in the development of psychosexual concepts and attitudes. In Friedman, R. C., Richart, R. M., Vande Wiele, R. L., & Stern, L. O. (Eds.), *Sex differences in behavior*. Oxford: John Wiley & Sons.

Kraft, L. W., & Vraa, C. W. (1975). Sex composition of groups and pattern of self-disclosure by high school females. *Psychological Reports, 37*, 733-734.

Kumar, S. A., & Mattanah, J. F. (2016). Parental attachment, romantic competence, relationship satisfaction, and psychosocial adjustment in emerging adulthood. *Personal Relationships, 23,* 801-817.

Laflamme, D., Pomerleau, A., & Malcuit, G. A. (2002). Comparison of fathers' and mothers' involvement in childcare and stimulation behaviors during free-play with their infants at 9 and 15 months. *Sex Roles, 47,* 507-518. https://doi.org/10.1023/A:1022069720776.

La Gaipa, J. J. (1987). Friendship expectations. In Burnett, R., McGhee, P., & Clarke, D. (Eds.), *Accounting for relationships: Explanation, representation and knowledge* (pp. 134-157). London: Methuen.

Lamb, M. E., & Sutton-Smith, B. (1982). *Sibling relationships: Their nature and significance across the life span.* Hillsdale, NJ: Erlbaum.

Larson, C. M., Pillsworth, E. G., & Haselton, M. G. (2012). Ovulatory shifts in women's attractions to primary partners and other men: Further evidence of the importance of primary partner sexual attractiveness. *PLoS ONE, 7*(9), e44456.

Larson, J. J., Whitton, S. W., Hauser, S. T., & Allen, J. P. (2007). Being close and being social: Peer ratings of distinct aspects of young adult social competence. *Journal of Personality Assessment, 89,* 136-148. https://doi.org/10.1080/00223890701468501.

Lauer, J. E., Ilksoy, S. D., & Lourenco, S. F. (2017). Developmental stability in gender-typed preferences between infancy and preschool age. *Developmental Psychology, 54*(4), 613-620. https://doi.org/10.1037/dev0000468.

Lawson, D. W., & Mace, R. (2009). Trade-offs in modern parenting: A longitudinal study of sibling competition for parental care. *Evolution and Human Behavior, 30,* 170-183. http://dx.doi.org/10.1016/j.evolhumbehav.2008.12.001.

Le, T. L., Mann, R. E., Levitan, R. D., George, T. P., & Maunder, R. G. (2017). Sex differences in the relationships between childhood adversity, attachment anxiety and current smoking. *Addiction Research & Theory, 25*(2), 146-153. http://dx.doi.org/10.1080/16066359.2016.1233968.

Leaper, C. (2002). Parenting girls and boys. In Bornstein, M. H. (Ed.), *Handbook of parenting: Vol. 1: Children and parenting* (pp. 189-225). Mahwah, NJ: Erlbaum.

Lee, J. A. (1977). A typology of styles of loving. *Personality and Social Psychology Bulletin, 3,* 173-182.

Leventhal, T., & Newman, S. (2010). Housing and child development. *Children and Youth Services Review, 32*(9), 1165-1174. https://doi.org/10.1016/j.childyouth.2010.03.008.

Levey, L., & Fagot, B. (1997). Gender-role socialization and discipline processes in one- and two-parent families. *Sex Roles, 36,* 1-21. http://dx.doi.org/10.1007/BF02766236.

Lewis, C., & Lamb, M. E. (2003). Fathers' influences on children's development: The evidence from two-parent families. *European Journal of Psychology of Education, 18,* 211-228. http://dx.doi.org/10.1007/BF03173485

Lewis, M. (1992). *Shame: The exposed self.* New York: Free Press.

Li, J. B., Delvecchio, E., Miconi, D., Salcuni, S., & Di Riso, D. (2014). Parental attachment among Chinese, Italian, and Costa Rican adolescents: A cross-cultural study. *Personality and Individual Differences, 71,* 118-123.

Lindell, A. K., Campione-Barr, N., & Killoren, S. E. (2017). Implications of parent–child relationships for emerging adults' subjective feelings about adulthood. *Journal of Family Psychology, 31*(7), 810-820.

Lindsey, E. W., & Mize, J. (2001). Contextual differences in parent-child play: Implications for gender role development. *Sex Roles, 44,* 155-176. http://dx.doi.org/10.1023/A:1010950919451.

Liss, M. B. (1981). Patterns of toy play: An analysis of sex differences. *Sex Roles, 7,* 1143-1150.

Little, A. C., Jones, B. C., & Burriss, R. P. (2007). Preferences for masculinity in male bodies change across the menstrual cycle. *Hormones and Behavior, 52,* 633-639.

Liu, L. S., Li, Y. F., Lv, Y., & Li, Y. W. (2013). The effects of father's involvement and parenting on children's early social skills [in Chinese]. *Psychological Development and Education, 29,* 49-56.

Lockheed, M. E. (1985). Sex and social influence: A meta-analysis guided by theory. In Berger, J., & Zelditch, M., Jr. (Eds.), *Status, rewards, and influence: How expectancies organize behavior* (pp. 406-429). San Francisco: Jossey-Bass.

Lyons-Ruth, K., Bronfman, E., & Parsons, E. (1999). Maternal frightened, frightening, or atypical behavior and disorganized infant attachment patterns. *Monographs of the Society for Research in Child Development, 64*(3), 67-96. https://doi.org/10.1111/1540-5834.00034.

Lyons-Ruth, K., Melnick, S., Bronfman, E., Sherry, S., & Llanas, L. (2004). Hostile-helpless relational models and disorganized attachment patterns between parents and their young children: Review of research and implications for clinical work. In Atkinson, L., & Goldberg, S. (Eds.), *Attachment issues in psychopathology and intervention* (p. 65-94). Mahwah, NJ: Erlbaum.

Lytton, H., & Romney, D. M. (1991). Parents' differential socialization of boys and girls: A meta-analysis. *Psychological Bulletin, 109,* 267-296. http://dx.doi.org/10.1037/0033-2909.109.2.267.

Maccoby, E. E. (1988). Gender as a social category. *Developmental Psychology, 26,* 755-765.

Maccoby, E. E. (1990). Gender and relationships: A developmental account. *American Psychologist, 45*(4), 513-520.

Maccoby, E. E. (1998). *The two sexes: Growing up apart, coming together.* Cambridge, MA: Harvard University Press.

Maccoby, E. E., & Jacklin, C. M. (1987). Gender segregation in childhood. *Advances in Child Development and Behavior, 20,* 239-287.

MacDonald, K., & Parke, R. D. (1986). Parent-child physical play: The effects of sex and age of children and parents. *Sex Roles, 15,* 367-378.

MacKinnon, C. E. (1989). An observational investigation of sibling interactions in married and divorced families. *Developmental Psychology, 25,* 36-44.

Main, M. (1991). Metacognitive knowledge, metacognitive monitoring, and singular (coherent) vs. multiple (incoherent) models of attachment. In Parkes, C. M., Stevenson-Hinde, J., & Marris, P. (Eds.), *Attachment across the life cycle.* London: Routledge, pp. 127-159.

Main, M., & Solomon, J. (1990). Procedures for identifying infants as disorganized/disoriented during the Ainsworth Strange Situation. In Greenberg, M. T., Cicchetti, D., & Cummings, E. M. (Eds.), *Attachment in the preschool years: Theory, research, and intervention.* Chicago: University of Chicago Press, pp. 121-160.

Malmberg, L.-E., Stein, A., West, A., Lewis, S., Barnes, J., Leach, P., & Sylva, K. (2007). Parent-child interaction: A growth model approach. *Infant Behavior and Development, 30,* 615-630. http://dx.doi.org/10.1016/j.infbeh.2007.03.007.

Maltz, D. N., & Borker, R. A. (1983). A cultural approach to male-female miscommunication. In Gumperz, J. A. (Ed.), *Language and social identity* (pp. 195-216). New York: Cambridge University Press.

Manning, W. D., & Smock, P. J. (1999). New families and nonresident father-child visitation. *Social Forces, 78,* 87-116.

Maunder, R. G., Hunter, J. J., & Lancee, W. J. (2011). The impact of attachment insecurity and sleep disturbance on symptoms and sick days in hospital-based health-care workers. *Journal of Psychosomatic Research, 70,* 11-17.

Maunder, R. G., Lancee, W. J., Nolan, R. P., Hunter, J. J., & Tannenbaum, D. W. (2006). The relationship of attachment insecurity to subjective stress and autonomic function during standardized acute stress in healthy adults. *Journal of Psychosomatic Research, 60,* 283-290.

Mays, V. M., & Cochran, S. D. (2001). Mental health correlates of perceived discrimination among lesbian, gay, and bisexual adults in the United States. *American Journal of Public Health, 91,* 1869-1876. http://dx.doi.org/10.2105/AJPH.91.11.1869.

McCrae, R. R. (1987). Creativity, divergent thinking, and openness to experience. *Journal of Personality and Social Psychology, 52*(6), 1258-1265.

McDonald, K. B., & Parke, R. D. (1984). Bridging the gap: Parent-child play interaction and interactive competence. *Child Development, 55,* 1265-1277.

McKinney, C., & Renk, K. (2008). Differential parenting between mothers and fathers. Implications for late adolescents. *Journal of Family Issues, 29,* 806-827. http://dx.doi.org/10.1177/0192513X07311222.

Meier, A., Hull, K. E., & Ortyl, T. A. (2009). Young adult relations values at the intersection of gender and sexuality. *Journal of Marriage and Family, 71*(3), 510-525. doi:10.1111/j.1741-3737.2009.00616.x.

Meyer, I. H., Schwartz, S., & Frost, D. M. (2008). Social patterning of stress and coping: Does disadvantaged social statuses confer more stress and fewer coping resources? *Social Science & Medicine, 67,* 368-379. http://dx.doi.org/10.1016/j.socscimed.2008.03.012.

Mickelson, K. D., Kessler, R. C., & Shaver, P. R. (1997). Adult attachment in a nationally representative sample. *Journal of Personality and Social Psychology, 73,* 1092-1106.

Miller, P., Danaher, D., & Forbes, D. (1986). Sex-related strategies for coping with interpersonal conflict in children aged five and seven. *Developmental Psychology, 22,* 543-548.

Mitchell, M., Leachman, M., & Masterson, K. (2017). A lost decade in higher education funding: State cuts have driven up tuition and reduced quality. *Education Week,* August 23. www.cbpp.org/research/state-budget-and-tax/a-lost-decade-in-higher-education-funding.

Moir, A., & Jessel, D. (1993). *Brain sex.* Warszawa: PIW (Polish edition).

Möller, E., Majdandžić, L., de Vente, M. W., & Bögels, S. M. (2013). The evolutionary basis of sex differences in parenting and its relationship with child anxiety in Western societies. *Journal of Experimental Psychopathology, 4*(2), 88-117. http://dx.doi.org.mimas.calstatela.edu/10.5127/jep.026912.

Montoya, R. M., & Horton, R. S. (2012). The reciprocity of liking effect. In Paludi, M. A. (Ed.), *The psychology of love,* Vols. 1-4. Santa Barbara, CA: Praeger/ABC-CLIO, pp. 39-57.

Moss, E., Rousseau, D., Parent, S., St-Laurent, D., & Saintonge, J. (1998). Correlates of attachment at school age: Maternal reported stress, mother-child interaction, and behavior problems. *Child Development, 69*, 1390-1405.

Mota, C. P., & Martins, C. (2018). Vinculação aos pais e relação amorosa: Papel mediador dos conflitos interparentais em jovens adultos. (Attachment to parents and romantic relationship: Mediational role of interparental conflicts in young adults). *Psicologia: Revista da Associação Portuguesa Psicologia, 32*(1), 1-14.

Muller, A. (1987). *Parents matter: Parents' relationships with lesbian daughters and gay sons.* Tallahassee, FL: Naiad Press.

Mutchler, M. (2000). Seeking sexual lives: Gay youth and masculinity tensions. In Nardi, P. (Ed.), *Gay masculinities*. London: Sage, pp. 12-43.

Myers, B. J. (1984). Mother-infant bonding: The status of this critical-period hypothesis. *Developmental Review, 4*, 240-274.

Narr, R. K., Allen, J. P., Tan, J. S., & Loeb, E. L. (2017). Close friendship strength and broader peer group desirability as differential predictors of adult mental health. *Child Development, 90*(1), 298-313. https://doi.org/10.1111/cdev.12905.

National Research Council (1993). *Understanding child abuse and neglect.* Washington, DC: National Academy of Sciences Press.

Nedelec, J. L., & Beaver, K. M. (2014). Physical attractiveness as a phenotypic marker of health: An assessment using a nationally representative sample of American adults. *Evolution and Human Behavior, 35*(6), 456-463.

Nelson, N., Peleg-Koriat, I., & Ben-Ari, R. (2018). Perceived procedural justice and conflict management in intimate relationships: The moderating effects of anxious attachment and personal power. *Couple and Family Psychology: Research and Practice, 7*(1), 34-46.

Nematy, A., & Oloomi, M. (2016). The comparison of attachment styles among Iranian lesbian, gay, and bisexual and heterosexual people. *Journal of Gay & Lesbian Social Services: The Quarterly Journal of Community & Clinical Practice, 28*(4), 369-378.

Nemeroff, C. (1996). The corticotropin-releasing factor (CRF) hypothesis of depression: New findings and new directions. *Molecular Psychiatry, 1*, 336-342.

Newman, B. S., & Muzzonigro, P. G. (1993). The effects of traditional family values on the coming out process of gay male adolescents. *Adolescence, 28*, 213-226.

Ng-Knight, T., Shelton, K. H., Riglin, L., Frederickson, N., McManus, I. C., & Rice, F. (2018). 'Best friends forever'? Friendship stability across school transition and associations with mental health and educational attainment. *British Journal of Educational Psychology, 89*(4), 585-599. https://doi.org/10.1111/bjep.12246.

Nikulina, V., Widom, C. S., & Czaja, S. (2011). The role of childhood neglect and childhood poverty in predicting mental health, academic achievement and crime in adulthood. *American Journal of Community Psychology, 48*(3-4), 309-321.

Niu, Z., Chen, H. C., Wang, L., & Zhang, H. X. (2004). Behavioral representations of 7-year-old children in helping situation and its relationship with parenting style [in Chinese]. *Psychological Development and Education, 20*, 17-21.

Nolen-Hoeksema, S., & Girgus, J. S. (1994). The emergence of gender differences in depression during adolescence. *Psychological Bulletin, 115*, 424-443.

Norman, R. E., Byambaa, M., De, R., Butchart, A., Scott, J., & Vos, T. (2012). The long-term health consequences of child physical abuse, emotional abuse, and neglect: A systematic review and meta-analysis. *PLoS Medicine, 98*(11), e1001349.1-e1001349.31. https://doi.org/10.1371/journal.pmed.1001349.

Numan, M., & Young, L. J. (2016). Neural mechanisms of mother-infant bonding and pair bonding: Similarities, differences, and broader implications. *Hormones and Behavior, 77*, 98-112. https://doi.org/10.1016/j.yhbeh.2015.05.015.

Oppenheim, D., Emde, R. N., & Warren, S. (1997). Children's narrative representations of mothers: Their development and associations with child and mother adaptation. *Child Development, 68*, 127-138.

Ortega, J. A. (2014). A characterization of world union patterns at the national and regional level. *Population Research and Policy Review, 33*, 161-188. https://doi.org/10.1007/s11113-013- 9301-x.

Oswald, D. L., Clark, E. M., & Kelly, C. M. (2004). Friendship maintenance: An analysis of individual and dyad behaviors. *Journal of Social and Clinical Psychology, 23*, 413-441. doi:10.1521/jscp.23.3.413.35460.

Paquette, D. (2004). Theorizing the father-child relationship: Mechanisms and developmental outcomes. *Human Development, 47*, 193-219. http://dx.doi.org/10.1159/000078723.

Parker, S., & de Vries, B. (1993). Patterns of friendship for women and men in same and cross-sex relationships. *Journal of Social and Personal Relationships, 10*, 617-626. doi:10.1177/0265407593104010.

Parrott, S., Aron-Dine, A., Rosenbaum, D., Rice, D., Floyd, I., & Romig, K. (2018). Trump budget deeply cuts health, housing, other assistance for low-and moderate-income families. Center on Budget and Policy Priorities. www.cbpp.org/research/federal-budget/trump-budget-deeply-cuts-health-housing-other-assistance-for-low-and.

Pawlowski, B., & Jasienska, G. (2005). Women's preferences for sexual dimorphism in height depend on menstrual cycle phase and expected duration of relationship. *Biological Psychology, 70*, 38–43.

Penton-Voak, I. S., Perrett, D. I., & Peirce, J. W. (1999). Computer graphic studies of the role of facial similarity in judgements of attractiveness. *Current Psychology: Developmental, Learning, Personality, Social, 18*(1), 104–117.

Peplau, L. A. (1991). Lesbian and gay relationships. In Gonsiorek, J. C., & Weinrich, J. D. (Eds.), *Homosexuality: Research implications for public policy*. Newbury Park, CA: Sage, pp. 177–196.

Peretti, P. O., & Venton, W. C. (1986). The influence of functional components of reciprocity of maintaining and sustaining closest friendship. *Journal of Psychological Researches, 30*, 83–87.

Perry, B. D. (2002). Childhood experience and the expression of genetic potential: What childhood neglect tells us about nature and nurture. *Brain and Mind, 3*, 79–100.

Pew Research Center (2013). Modern parenthood, social & demographic trends. March 4. www.pewsocialtrends.org/2013/03/14/modern-parenthood-roles-of-moms-and-dads-converge-as-they-balance-work-and-family/. Retrieved January 4, 2018.

Pew Research Center (2018). The narrowing, but persistent, gender gap in pay. www.pewresearch.org/fact-tank/2018/04/09/gender-pay-gap-facts/.

Phillipson, C. (1997). Social relationships in later life: A review of the research literature. *International Journal of Geriatric Psychiatry, 12*, 505–512.

Pianta, R. C., & Harbers, K. L. (1996). Observing mother and child behavior in a problem-solving situation at school entry: Relations with academic achievement. *Journal of School Psychology, 34*, 307–322.

Pomerleau, A., Bolduc, D., Malcuit, G., & Cossette, L. (1990). Pink or blue: Environmental gender stereotypes in the first two years of life. *Sex Roles, 22*(5–6), 359–367. https://doi.org/10.1007/BF0028833.

Porter, R. H. (1998). Olfaction and human kin recognition. *Genetica, 104*(3), 259–263.

Power, T. G., McGrath, M. P., Hughes, S. O., & Manire, S. H. (1994). Compliance and self-assertion: Young children's responses to mothers versus fathers. *Developmental Psychology, 30*, 980–989. http://dx.doi.org/10.1037/0012-1649.30.6.980.

Power, T. G., & Parke, R. D. (1983). Patterns of mother and father play with their 8-month-old infant: A multiple analyses approach. *Infant Behavior and Development, 6*, 453–459.

Pratto, F., & Walker, A. (2004). The bases of gendered power. In Eagly, A. H., Beall, A. E., & Sternberg, R. J. (Eds.), *The psychology of gender*. New York: Guilford Press, pp. 242–268.

Pryce, C. R. (1992). A comparative systems model of the regulation of maternal motivation in mammals. *Animal Behaviour, 43*(3), 417–441. https://doi.org/10.1016/S0003-3472(05)80102-2.

Pugh, M. D., & Wahrman, R. (1983). Neutralizing sexism in mixed sex group: Do women have to be better than men? *American Journal of Sociology, 88*, 746–761.

Ream, G., & Savin-Williams, R. (2005). Reconciling Christianity and positive nonheterosexual identity in adolescence, with implications for psychological wellbeing. *Journal of Gay and Lesbian Issues in Education, 2*, 19–36.

Reis, H. T. (1998). Sex differences in intimacy and related behaviors: Context and process. In Canary, D. J., & Dindia, K. (Eds.), *Sex differences and similarities in communication* (pp. 203–231). Mahwah, NJ: Erlbaum.

Reis, H. T. (2017). The interpersonal process model of intimacy: Maintaining intimacy through self-disclosure and responsiveness. In Fitzgerald, J. (Ed.), *Foundations for couples' therapy: Research for the real world*. London: Routledge, pp. 216–225.

Remshard, M. E. (1999). Adult attachment styles, love styles, sexual attitudes, and sexual behaviors of college students. *Dissertation Abstracts International: Section B: The Sciences and Engineering, 59*(10-B), 5622.

Rennison, C. M. (2002). Rape and sexual assault: Reporting to police and medical attention, 1992-2000 [NCJ194530]. U.S. Department of Justice, Office of Justice Programs, Bureau of Justice Statistics. www.bjs.gov/content/pub/pdf/rsarp00.

Richardson, S., & McCabe, M. (2001). Parental divorce during adolescence and adjustment in early adulthood. *Adolescence, 36*, 467–489.

Richter, L. (2004). *The importance of caregiver-child interactions for the survival and healthy development of young children: A review*. Geneva: World Health Organization, Department of Child and Adolescent Health and Development.

Riggio, H. R. (2000). Measuring attitudes toward adult sibling relationships: The Lifespan Sibling Relationship Scale. *Journal of Social and Personal Relationships, 17*, 707–728.

Riggio, H. R. (2001). Relations between parental divorce and the quality of adult sibling relationships. *Journal of Divorce and Remarriage, 36,* 67-82.

Riggio, H. R. (2004). Parental marital conflict and divorce, parent-child relationships, social support, and relationship anxiety in young adulthood. *Personal Relationships, 11,* 99-114.

Riggio, H. R. (2006). Structural features of sibling dyads and attitudes toward sibling relationships in young adulthood. *Journal of Family Issues, 27,* 1233-1254.

Riggio, H. R., & Valenzuela, A. M. (2010). Parental conflict, divorce, parent-child relationships, and social support among Latino-American young adults. *Personal Relationships, 18,* 392-409.

Robinson, B., & Walters, L. (1987). The AIDS epidemic hits home. *Psychology Today* (April), 48-52.

Roney, J. R., Simmons, Z. L., & Gray, P. B. (2011). Changes in estradiol predict within-women shifts in attraction to facial cues of men's testosterone. *Psychoneuroendocrinology, 36,* 742-749.

Rook, K. S. (1987). Social support versus companionship: Effects on life stress, loneliness, and evaluations by others. *Journal of Personality and Social Psychology, 52*(6), 1132-1147.

Rosenblatt, J. S., & Siegel, H. I. (1981). Factors governing the onset and maintenance of maternal behavior among nonprimate mammals: The role of hormonal and nonhormonal factors. In Gubemick, D. J., & Klopfer, P. H. (Eds.), *Parental care in mammals.* New York: Plenum.

Ross, G. E., Mirowsky, J., & Goldsteen, K. (1990). The impact of the family on health: The decade in review. *Journal of Marriage and the Family, 55,* 1059-1078.

Rubin, Z. (1973). *Liking and loving: An invitation to social psychology.* Oxford: Holt, Rinehart & Winston.

Russell, S., & Fish, J. N. (2016). Mental health in lesbian, gay, bisexual, and transgender (LGBT) youth. *Annual Review of Clinical Psychology, 12,* 465-487.

Sachs, J. (1987). Preschool boys' and girls' language use in pretend play. In Phillips, S. U., Steele, S., & Tanz, C. (Eds.), *Language, gender and sex in comparative perspective* (pp. 178-188). Cambridge: Cambridge University Press.

Saito, M. (1998). Sex education in school: Preventing unwanted pregnancy in adolescents. *International Journal of Gynecology & Obstetrics, 63*(Suppl 1), S157-S160.

Sarkadi, A., Kristiansson, R., Oberklaid, F., & Bremberg, S. (2008). Fathers' involvement and children's developmental outcomes: A systematic review of longitudinal studies. *Acta Paediatrica, 97,* 153-158. http://dx.doi.org/10.1111/j.1651-2227.2007.00572.x.

Sassler, S., & Schoen, R. (1999). The effect of attitudes and economic activity on marriage. *Journal of Marriage and the Family, 61,* 147-159. https:// doi.org/10.2307/353890.

Savin-Williams, R. C. (1994). Verbal and physical abuse as stressors in the lives of lesbian, gay male and bisexual youths: Associations with school problems, running away, substance abuse, prostitution, and suicide. *Journal of Consulting and Clinical Psychology, 62,* 261-269.

Savin-Williams, R. (1996a). Dating and romantic relationships among gay, lesbian, and bisexual youths. In Savin-Williams, R., & Cohen, K. (Eds.), *The lives of lesbians, gays, and bisexuals: Children to adults.* Forth Worth, TX: Harcourt Brace, pp. 166-180.

Savin-Williams, R. C. (1996b). Ethnic- and sexual-minority youth. In Savin-Williams, R. C., & Cohen, C. M. (Eds.), *The lives of lesbians, gays, and bisexuals: Children to adults.* Forth Worth, TX: Harcourt Brace, pp. 152-165.

Savin-Williams, R. C., & Esterberg, K. G. (2000). Lesbian, gay, and bisexual families. In Demo, D. H., Allen, K. R., & Fine, M. A. (Eds.), *Handbook of family diversity.* New York: Oxford University Press, pp. 197-215.

Sayer, L. C., Bianchi, S. M., & Robinson, P. (2004). Are parents investing less in children? Trends in mothers' and fathers' time with children. *American Journal of Sociology, 10,* 1-43. http://dx.doi.org/10.1086/386270.

Scher, A., & Mayseless, O. (2000). Mothers of anxious/ambivalent infants: Maternal characteristics and childcare context. *Child Development, 71*(6), 1629-1639.

Schmitt, D. P. (2003). Universal sex differences in the desire for sexual variety: Tests from 52 nations, 6 continents, and 13 islands. International Sexuality Description Project. *Journal of Personality and Social Psychology, 85*(1), 85-104.

Schmitt, D. P., & Jonason, P. K. (2014). Attachment and sexual permissiveness: Exploring differential associations across sexes, cultures, and facets of short-term mating. *Journal of Cross-Cultural Psychology, 46*(1), 119-133. https://doi.org/10.1177/0022022114551052.

Schnitzer, P. G., & Ewigman, B. G. (2005). Child deaths resulting from inflicted injuries: Household risk factors and perpetrator characteristics. *Pediatrics, 116* (5), 687-693.

Sell, A., Hone, L. S. E., & Pound, N. (2012). The importance of physical strength to human males. *Human Nature, 23,* 30-44. doi 10.1007/s12110-012-9131-2.

Seltzer, J. (1991). Relationships between fathers and children who live apart: The father's role after separation. *Journal of Marriage and the Family, 53,* 79-102.

Serbin, L. A., Sprafkin, C., Elman, M., & Doyle, A. (1984). The early development of sex ditL*x~tiated patterns of social influence. *Canadian Journal of Social Science, 14*, 350-363.

Shackelford, S., Wood, W., & Worchel, S. (1996). Behavioral styles and the influence of women in mixed-sex groups. *Social Psychology Quarterly, 59*(3), 284-293. http://dx.doi.org.mimas.calstatela.edu/10.2307/2787024.

Shafer, K., & James, S. L. (2013). Gender and socioeconomic status differences in first and second marriage formation. *Journal of Marriage and Family, 75*, 544-564. https://doi.org/10.1111/jomf .12024.

Shaw, D. S., & Vondra, J. I. (1995). Infant attachment security and maternal predictors of early behavior problems: A longitudinal study of low-income families. *Journal of Abnormal Child Psychology, 23*, 335-357.

Sheinbaum, T., Bifulco, A., Biful Ballespi, S., Mitjavila, M., Kwapil, T. R., & Barrantes-Vidal, N. (2015). Interview investigation of insecure attachment styles as mediators between poor childhood care and schizophrenia-spectrum phenomenology. *PLoS ONE, 10*, e0135150.

Sheldon, A. (1992). Conflict talk: Sociolinguistic challenges to self-assertion and how young girls meet them. *Merrill-Palmer Quarterly, 38*(1), 95-117.

Sheppard, P., Garcia, J. R., & Sear, R. (2014). A not-so-grim tale: How childhood family structure influences reproductive and risk-taking outcomes in a historical US population. *PLoS ONE, 9*(3), e89539. https://doi.org/10.1371/journal.pone.0089539.

Shields, S. A. (2002). *Speaking from the heart: Gender and the social meaning of emotion*. Kraków: Wydawnictwo Literackie (Polish translation).

Shore, R. (1997). *Rethinking the brain*. New York: Families and Work Institute.

Simons, L. G., & Conger, R. D. (2007). Linking mother-father differences in parenting to a typology of family parenting styles and adolescent outcomes. *Journal of Family Issues, 28*, 212-241. http://dx.doi.org/10.1177/0192513X06294593.

Simons, R. L., Whitbeck, L. B., Melby, J. N., & Wu, C. (1994). Economic pressure and harsh parenting. In Conger, R. D., & Elder, G. H., Jr. (Eds.), *Families in troubled times: Adapting to change in rural America*. New York: Aldine, pp. 207-222.

Simpson, J. A. (1999). Attachment theory in modern evolutionary perspective. In Cassidy, J., & Shaver, P. R. (Eds.), *Handbook of attachment: Theory, research, and clinical applications*. New York: Guilford Press, pp. 115-140.

Singer, L. M., Brodzinsky, D. M., Ramsay, D., Steir, M., & Waters, E. (1985). Mother-infant attachment in adoptive families. *Child Development, 56*(6), 1543-1551.

Slack, K. S., Holl, J. L., McDaniel, M., Yoo, J., & Bolger, K. (2004). Understanding the risks of child neglect: An exploration of poverty and parenting characteristics. *Child Maltreatment, 9*(4), 395-408. https://doi.org/10.1177/1077559504269193.

Snow, M. E., Jacklin, C. N., & Maccoby, E. E. (1983). Sex-of-child differences in father-child interaction at one year of age. *Child Development, 54*(1), 227-232.

Solomon, J., George, C., & De Jong, A. (1995). Children classified as controlling at age six: Evidence of disorganized representational strategies and aggression at home and at school. *Development and Psychopathology, 7*, 447-463.

Solomonica-Levi, D., Yirmiya, N., Erel, O., Samet, I., & Oppenheim, D. (2001). The associations between observed maternal behavior, children's narrative representations of mothers, and children's behavior problems. *Journal of Social and Personal Relationships, 18*, 673-690.

South, S. J. (2001). The variable effects of family background on the timing of first marriage: United States, 1969-1993. *Social Science Research, 30*, 606-626. https://doi.org/10.1006/ssre.2001.0714.

Speltz, M. L., Greenberg, M. T., & Deklyen, M. (1990). Attachment in preschoolers with disruptive behavior: A comparison of clinic-referred and nonproblem children. *Development and Psychopathology, 2*, 31-46.

Splanger, G., & Grossmann, K. E. (1993). Biobehavioral organization in securely and insecurely attached infants. *Child Development, 64*, 1439-1450.

Sprecher, S., Sullivan, Q., & Hatfield, E. (1994). Mate selection preferences: Gender differences examined in a national sample. *Journal of Personality and Social Psychology, 66*, 1074-1080.

Stack, S., & Eshleman, J. R. (1998). Marital status and happiness: A 17-nation study. *Journal of Marriage and the Family, 60*(2), 527-536.

Steele, E. H., & McKinney, C. (2018). Emerging adult psychological problems and parenting style: Moderation by parent-child relationship quality. *Personality and Individual Differences, 146*, 201-208.

Sternberg, R. J. (1986). A triangular theory of love. *Psychological Review, 93*(2), 119-135.

Sternberg, R. J. (1998). *Love is a story*. Oxford: Oxford University Press.

Stoppard, J. M., & Grunn Gruchy, C. D. (1993). Gender, context and expression of positive emotion. *Personality and Social Psychology Bulletin, 19*, 143-156.

Tamis-LeMonda, C. S., Shannon, J. D., Cabrera, N. J., & Lamb, M. E. (2004). Fathers and mothers at play with their 2- and 3-year-olds: Contributions to language and cognitive development. *Child Development, 75,* 1806-1820. http://dx.doi.org/10.1111/j.1467-8624.2004.00818.x.

Tamres, L. K., Janicki, D., & Helgeson, V. S. (2002). Sex differences in coping behavior: A meta-analytic review and an examination of relative coping. *Personality and Social Psychology Review, 6,* 2-30.

Tannen, D. (1993). *Gender and conversational interaction.* New York: Oxford University Press.

Tasca, G. A., Ritchie, K., Zachariades, F., Proulx, G., Trinneer, A, Balfour, L., ..., Bissada, H. (2013). Attachment insecurity mediates the relationship between childhood trauma and eating disorder psychopathology in a clinical sample: A structural equation model. *Child Abuse & Neglect, 37,* 926-933.

Taylor, S. E., Klein, L. C., Lewis, B. P., Gruenewald, T. L., Gurung, R. A. R., & Updegraff, J. A. (2000). Biobehavioral responses to stress in females: Tend-and-befriend, not fight-or-flight. *Psychological Review, 107*(3), 411-429. https://doi.org/10.1037/0033-295X.107.3.411.

Tesch, S. A. (1983). Review of friendship development across the life span. *Human Development, 26*(5), 266-276.

Thornberry, T. P., Knight, K. E., & Lovegrove, P. J. (2012). Does maltreatment beget maltreatment? A systematic review of the intergenerational literature. *Trauma Violence Abuse, 13*(3), 135-152.

Troiden, R. (1989). *Gay and lesbian identity: A sociological analysis.* Dix Hills, NY: General Hall, Inc.

Umberson, D. (1992). Gender, marital status and the social control of health behavior. *Social Science and Medicine, 24,* 907-917.

Uniform Crime Report (2011). Crime in the U.S., Table 66. https://ucr.fbi.gov/crime-in-the-u.s/2011/crime-in-the-u.s.-2011/tables/table_66_arrests_suburban_areas_by_sex_2011.xls.

United Nations (2010). https://unstats.un.org/unsd/demographic-social/products/worldswomen/documents/Poverty.

United Nations (2011). World marriage patterns. www.un.org/en/ development/desa/population/publications/pdf/ popfacts/PopFacts_2011-1.

United States Census Bureau (2014). Income and poverty in the United States: 2014 Current population reports. www.census.gov/content/dam/Census/library/publications/2015/demo/p60-252.

United States Census Bureau (2017). Income and poverty in the United States: 2016 Current population reports. www.census.gov/library/publications/2017/demo/p60-259.html.

U.S. Administration for Children & Families (2014). Child maltreatment. www.acf.hhs.gov/cb/resource/child-maltreatment-2014.

United States Department of Health and Human Services (2005). Male perpetrators of child maltreatment: Findings from NCANDS. New York: Office of the Assistant Secretary for Planning and Evaluation.

Van Ijzendoorn, M. H., Sagi, A., & Lambermon, M. W. E. (1992). The multiple caretaker paradox: Data from Holland and Israel. In Pianta, R. C. (Ed.), *New Directions for Child Development, No. 57. Beyond the parent: The role of other adults in children's lives.* San Francisco: Jossey-Bass, pp. 5-24.

Van Ijzendoorn, M. H., Schuengel, C., & Bakermans-Kranenburg, M. J. (1999). Disorganized attachment in early childhood: Meta-analysis of precursors, concomitants, and sequelae. *Development and Psychopathology, 11,* 225-249.

Van Vugt, M., De Cremer, D., & Janssen, D. P. (2007). Gender differences in cooperation and competition. The male-warrior hypothesis. *Psychological Science, 18,* 19-23. http://dx.doi.org/10.1111/j.1467-9280.2007.01842.x.

Verhoeven, M., Bögels, S. M., & Van der Bruggen, C. O. (2011). Unique roles of mothering and fathering in child anxiety: Moderation of child's age and gender. *Journal of Child and Family Studies, 21,* 331-343. http://dx.doi.org/10.1007/s10826-011-9483-y.

Waite, L. J. (1995). Does marriage matter? *Demography, 32*(4), 483-507.

Waite, L. J., & Gallagher, M. (2000). *The case for marriage: Why married people are happier, healthier and better off financially.* New York: Doubleday.

Wallerstein, J. S. (1984). Children of divorce: Preliminary report of a ten-year follow-up of young children. *American Journal of Orthopsychiatry, 54,* 444-458.

Wallerstein, J. S., & Kelly, J. B. (1980). *Surviving the breakup: How children and parents cope with divorce.* New York: Basic Books.

Walster, E., Aronson, V., Abrahams, D., & Rottman, L. (1966). Importance of physical attractiveness in dating behavior. *Journal of Personality and Social Psychology, 4*(5), 508-516.

Walster, E., Walster, G. W., & Berscheid, E. (1978). *Equity: Theory and research.* Boston: Allyn and Bacon.

Wang, H., Han, Z. R., Bai, L., & Li, X. (2019). Attachment experience and cortisol recovery from romantic conflict among young Chinese couples: A dyadic analysis. *International Journal of Psychology, 47*(1), 3994-4000.

Waters, E., & Cummings, E. M. (2000). A secure base from which to explore close relationships. *Child Development, 71,* 164-172.

Widom, C. S., & White, H. R. (1997). Problem behaviours in abused and neglected children grown up: Prevalence and co-occurrence of substance abuse, crime and violence. *Criminal Behavior and Mental Health*, 7(4), 287-310. https://doi.org/10.1002/cbm.191.

Wilkinson, R. B. (2010). Best friend attachment versus peer attachment in the prediction of adolescent psychological adjustment. *Journal of Adolescence*, 33(5), 709-717. doi.org/10.1016/j.adolescence.2009.10.013Get.

Wilson, J. G., Calsyn, R. J., & Orlofsky, J. L. (1994). Impact of sibling relationships on social support and morale in the elderly. *Journal of Gerontological Social Work*, 22, 157-170.

Wilson, M., & Daly, M. (1985). Competitiveness, risk-taking, and violence: The young male syndrome. *Ethnology and Sociobiology*, 6, 59-73. http://dx.doi.org/10.1016/0162-3095(85)90041-X.

Winsler, A., Madigan, A. L., & Aquilino, S. A. (2005). Correspondence between maternal and paternal parenting styles in early childhood. *Early Childhood Research Quarterly*, 20, 1-12. http://dx.doi.org/10.1016/j.ecresq.2005.01.007.

Winston, R., & Chicot, R. (2016). The importance of early bonding on the long-term mental health and resilience of children. *London Journal of Primary Care*, 8(1), 12-14. doi:[10.1080/17571472.2015.1133012].

Wood, J. J. (2007). Academic competence in preschool: Exploring the role of close relationships and anxiety. *Early Education and Development*, 18, 223-242.

World Health Organization (2002). World report on violence and health. http://apps.who.int/iris/bitstream/handle/10665/42495/9241545615_eng.pdf?sequence=1.

World Health Organization (2004). Poverty: Assessing the distribution of health risks by socioeconomic position at national and local levels. www.who.int/quantifying_ehimpacts/publications/en/ebd10.

worldatlas.com (2018). The nations of Europe by the average age at first marriage. WorldAtlas. www.worldatlas.com/articles/the-nations-of-europe-by-the-average-age-at-first-marriage.html. Retrieved April 10, 2018.

Wright, P. H. (1982). Men's friendships, women's friendships, and the alleged inferiority of the latter. *Sex Roles*, 8, 1-20.

Wright, P. H. (1988). Interpreting research on gender differences in friendship: A case for moderation and a plea for caution. *Journal of Social and Personal Relationships*, 5, 367-373.

Xie, Q., & Hultgren, F. (1994). Urban Chinese parents' perceptions of their strengths and needs in rearing "only" sons and daughters. *Home Economics Research Journal*, 22, 340-356.

Xu, L., Liu, L., Li, Y., Liu, L., & Huntsinger, C. S. (2018). Parent-child relationships and Chinese children's social adaptations: Gender difference in parent-child dyads. *Personal Relationships*, 25(4), 462-479.

Yampolskaya, S., Greenbaum, P. E., & Berson, I. R. (2009). Profiles of child maltreatment perpetrators and risk for fatal assault: A latent class analysis. *Journal of Family Violence*, 24(5), 337-348. http://dx.doi.org/10.1007/s10896-009-9233-8.

Yancey, G. B., & Eastman, R. L. (1995). Comparison of undergraduates with older adults on love styles and life satisfaction. *Psychological Repodsddrts*, 76(3), 1211.

Yokoyama, K., Shirakawa, K., Hirao, T., Nakatsu, M., YodadFe, T., Suzuki, H., ..., Shirakami, G. (2017). Sex differences in attachment to spouses among older Japanese couples. *Geriatrics & Gerontology International*, 17(5), 834-838.

Youngblade, L. M., & Dunn, J. (1995). Individual differences in young children's pretend play with mother and sibling: Links to relationships and understanding of other people's feelings and beliefs. *Child Development*, 66, 1472-1492. http://dx.doi.org/10.2307/1131658.

Zajonc, R. B. (1968). Attitudinal effects of mere exposure. *Journal of Personality and Social Psychology*, 9(2, Pt. 2), 1-27.

Zewditu, D., Rasberry, C., Steiner, R., Brener, N., & McManus, T. (2018). Trends in secondary schools' practices to support lesbian, gay, bisexual, transgender, and questioning students, 2008-2014. *American Journal of Public Health*, 108(4), 557-564.

Zuckerman, M. (2009). Sensation seeking. In Leary, M. R., & Hoyle, R. H. (Eds.), *Handbook of individual differences in social behavior*. New York: The Guilford Press, pp. 455-465.

11 Aggression

Biological Underpinnings: Evolved to Fight	348
Socialization of Aggression	350
Media Violence	351
Parenting and Aggression in Offspring	355
Religion and Aggression against Women	357
Gender Roles and Aggression	359
Physical and Verbal Aggression in Children and Adults	362
Intimate Partner Violence (IPV)	362
Rape and Sexual Assault	365
Violent Pornography	368

INEQUALITIES AND INJUSTICES

Rewarding Male Aggression

Aggressive behavior is masculine. Masculinity is another term for the stereotype of what it means to be male, or the traits, qualities, and attributes that we associate with men as a social group (see Chapter 5). Masculinity involves ideas we have about men in general and feelings about the self as masculine (Schwalbe & Wolkomir, 2001). Aggression is a part of this personality trait (Huddy & Terkildsen, 1993). Femininity represents stereotypical ideas about what it means to be female; the traits, qualities, and attributes we associate with women as a social group. Femininity also involves feelings about the self as feminine and definitely does not involve aggression (Prentice & Carranza, 2002; Reidy, Sloan, & Zeichner, 2009). It is clear that aggressive behavior and qualities have evolved because there is survival value in them; aggression increases access to resources, including fertile women (Buss & Shackleford, 1997). Men who are bigger and stronger have more aggressive power against others, including women, children, and smaller men. Aggression today is valued in warfare, in professional and amateur sports, and in entertainment. Media all over the world is extremely violent and that violence nearly always involves many more men than women (Anderson et al., 2010; Bushman & Huesmann, 2006; Slater, Henry, Swaim, & Anderson, 2003). Many professional sports focus on endurance and other athletic skills, but physical strength and aggression are often necessary and highly valued, especially in aggressive sports like football, boxing, ultimate fighting, and others. Boys are encouraged to display aggressive behaviors, including in play and in interactions with peers (Ruble & Martin, 1997).

Male aggression is valued to some degree all over the world. However, Western cultures, which are highly focused on individual achievements and strengths (individualism), highly value male aggression, to a greater degree than Eastern, more collectivistic cultures (Cuddy et al., 2015; Forbes et al., 2009). Men in Western cultures display aggression in everyday behaviors, especially as a way to confirm their masculinity if it has been somehow challenged (Bosson, Vandello, Burnaford, Weaver, & Wasti, 2009). Precarious manhood refers to the idea that manhood and masculinity are considered difficult to achieve yet easily threatened or lost (Vandello & Bosson, 2013). Men view some events as emasculating, especially failure in a manly endeavor or being called feminine (Vandello, Bosson, Cohen, Burnaford, & Weaver, 2008). Men who are hypermasculine are high in aggression; they are easily threatened and think violence is desirable and an appropriate response to personal slights (Reidy, Shirk, Sloan, & Zeichner, 2009). In contrast, little girls are strongly discouraged from aggressive behaviors all over the world (Carlo, Raffaelli, Laible, & Meyer, 1999; Ruble & Martin, 1997). Because of the biologically-based motherhood role, women across cultures are expected to possess qualities that promote good mothering, such as gentleness, kindness, cooperative and caretaking behaviors (Eagly & Wood, 1999; Wood & Eagly, 2002). Aggressive behavior suggests a bad or immoral woman who violates feminine ideals (Löckenhoff et al., 2014; Prentice & Carranza, 2002). Even assertive behavior by women (asserting one's goals to others) is viewed in a generally negative way, especially by men (Butler & Geis, 1990; Homer, 1972; Porter & Geis, 1981).

With men raised to be aggressive and women raised to not be, physical size and strength differences between the sexes are reinforced by beliefs about the desirable qualities of women and men (stereotypes, see Chapter 5). I assert that these beliefs (which derive from expectations of social roles; Wood & Eagly, 2002) not only help people process social information in a rather quick and automatic manner, the main reason why stereotypes and other schemas exist (Fiske & Taylor, 1991), they also function to legitimize men's physical control over women, a key factor in establishing patriarchy and oppression of girls and women (Pratto & Walker, 2004). Society highly prizes male aggression and encourages it in boys and men, to continue patriarchal control.

CRITICAL THINKING

Blaming the Victim: Why?

Blaming the victim is a psychological process that involves blaming victims of crime rather than perpetrators of crime. The author had an experience with a beloved family member who, in a discussion of a 13-year-old girl who was gang raped after accepting a ride from a young man she knew, exclaimed, "Well, she asked for it." Why would someone think that the rape of a 13-year-old is her own fault, that she is more responsible than the four older teens who raped her? They raped her, in a brutal physical attack. Why are they excused and she is blamed? First, a 13-year-old is a child who cannot legally consent to anything. Second, rape is intentional; it is a physical attack, forcible and based on physically attacking and overcoming a person. Those teenage rapists are expected then to have no control, no respect, they can violate anyone who is stupid enough to trust them? Anyone who happens to be outside after dark, or is wearing a sexy blouse, or is just a girl? Trusting another person and accepting a ride is not an invitation to rape and it is not an offense punishable by rape. Trust is actually a lovely quality and should never be used to blame a person for anything.

Why do people blame girls and women for their own victimization? Why would anyone do that? There are several explanations provided by social psychology. First, people form explanations about events, including the behavior of others, called **attributions** (Weiner, 1980). One feature of attributions is how much control a person is thought to have over an outcome or their own behavior. Out at night? That's controllable. Accepting a ride? Also controllable. That young girl could have said no and not gotten into the car. When people are seen as controlling negative events, including negative events that happen to themselves, they are seen as culpable, accountable, and the resulting emotion of the person forming the explanation is likely to be anger ((Weiner, Perry, & Magnusson, 1988). For example, if someone intentionally stepped on your foot and caused pain, you would be angry at that person (they controlled that behavior). If someone accidentally stepped on your foot in a crowded bus, you might feel frustrated but not angry at the person; their behavior was uncontrolled, caused by the bus and the crowd. People also blame victims because it makes them feel safer. If going outside is why you got raped, that controllable behavior is amenable to change, so I can prevent my rape by not going out at night. People may also have what is called a **belief in a just world**, the idea that the world is just, that good things happen to good people and bad things happen to bad people. If the world is just, and someone is raped, it must be their fault (Furnham, 2003). Finally, people blame victims, especially women who are sexually harassed or assaulted or raped, because of social, cultural endorsement and reinforcement of **rape myths**, false beliefs that legitimize raping women. In this way, women are controlled through sexual assault and patriarchy is maintained (Peterson & Muehlenhard, 2004). Consider these explanations the next time you feel an urge to blame someone for their own negative outcomes; you might be surprised how your feelings change when you consider **situational factors** (circumstances, features of the external environment and the immediate situation, including violent, selfish men) and how they impact individual behavior.

BONUS BOX

Gay Men and Masculine Gender Norms

As we discuss in "Inequalities and Injustices" in this chapter, **masculinity** is highly valued around the world, especially in Western cultures that emphasize individual strength, ability, and achievement (Forbes et al., 2009). Masculine ideals include men as physically strong, tall, courageous, decisive, and tough (Reidy et al., 2009). Masculinity in the West is decidedly not **feminine**, which includes qualities of emotionality, gentleness, caretaking, and fearfulness (see Chapter 5). Feminine qualities are seen as indicating weakness, especially in men (Blair & Hoskin, 2015; Rudman, Moss-Racusin, Phelan, & Nauts, 2012). People who identify as LGBTQ are less likely as a group to strongly endorse traditional gender role norms compared to people who identify as heterosexual (Warriner, Nagoshi, & Nagoshi, 2013), and gay men are particularly likely to be perceived as or stereotyped as possessing feminine qualities (Minton, 1986). However, because masculinity is so strongly valued and emphasized to girls and boys through socialization, gay men in particular may struggle to accommodate identities as gay and as male. A study by Sánchez, Westefeld, Liu, and Vilain (2010) examined the responses of several hundred gay men to self-report measures of gender role conflict, gay identity, and ratings of the importance of masculinity. Their results indicate that the majority of the gay men in their sample strongly valued the public display of masculinity and wished to be more masculine than they thought they were. Positively valuing ideal masculine qualities was linked with negative feelings about oneself being gay. Additional research indicates that traditional attitudes and conservatism among LGBTQ and heterosexual people are linked with negative attitudes toward LGBTQ people (Nagoshi et al., 2008; Polimeni, Hardie, & Buzwell, 2000; Szymanski, 2005; Warriner et al., 2013). Intimate partner violence (IPV) among same-sex couples is linked with internalized homonegativity, or negative feelings about the self as homosexual (Balsam & Szymanski, 2005; Edwards & Sylaska, 2013; Pepper & Sand, 2015).

These studies provide further empirical evidence of how social institutions and their messages, including those of religion, government, and media, can affect individual psychological outcomes such as feelings of self-esteem and competence. Religious condemnation of homosexuality (Leviticus 18:22, 20:13) and ridicule of women (Leviticus 12:2, 12:5; 1 Timothy 2:11-12) supports negative attitudes toward LGBTQ people and femininity. Recent government actions include banning transgender individuals from military service (Block, Strangio, & Esseks, 2018) and cutting funding to global health initiatives and services that include any mention of abortion services (Elbagir, Leposo, & Mackintosh, 2018). Such actions are designed to marginalize the rights and eliminate the freedoms of LGBTQ people and women, and add further emphasis to a social condemnation of being anything but heterosexual male. Challenging and changing social institutions and their messages seems to be the most powerful, lasting, impactful way to combat such negative outcomes. Challenging traditional religious ideology and civil rights violations by the government can involve activism. Challenging traditional and gendered media portrayals is strongly enabled through incorporation of realistic LGBTQ characters, strong female characters, and realistic portrayals of men as still valuable, good men while being emotional, tender, or gay.

LEARN MORE

Men as Victims of Intimate Partner Violence (IPV)

Men are definitely victims of intimate partner violence (IPV), with perpetrators against them both female and male (Archer, 2002; Tjaden, Thoennes, & Allison, 1999). Fourteen percent of men in the United States report experiencing severe physical violence from an intimate partner (Centers for Disease Control & Prevention, 2015). Most research indicates that when perpetrators against men are women, aggressive acts against male partners are unlikely to result in serious injury (Archer, 2000; Carmo, Grams, & Magalhães, 2011) and are likely to involve kicking, punching, slapping, biting, or throwing objects (Archer, 2002). Within typical romantic couples, married or dating, so-called "common couple conflict" is not necessarily rare or unusual (Johnson, 1995). Within such couples, there are few or small sex differences in physical and verbal aggression toward partners (Muñoz-Rivas et al., 2007). Some studies indicate that women more frequently commit acts of physical aggression toward male partners (Allen et al., 2009; Straus, 2008). However, within intimate relationships men are much more likely to use sexual aggression, coercion, stalking, and very violent aggression than women (Swan et al., 2008). Multiple studies indicate that women's aggression in intimate relationships often occurs while they are receiving aggression from male partners or in self-defense (DeKeseredy, Saunders, Schwartz, & Alvi, 1997; Johnson & Ferraro, 2000; Saunders, 1986; Swan, Gambone, Caldwell, Sullivan, & Snow, 2008). Women are also more likely to suffer serious injuries and negative consequences as victims of IPV compared to men (Archer, 2000). Research indicates that men's aggression toward partners is more typically motivated by control needs, while women's aggression is more likely to involve fear (Swan et al., 2008). There are serious IPV offenses by women toward male victims. There are common risk factors associated with female perpetrators of IPV against men, including substance abuse, mental illness, and the experience of childhood abuse (Dutton, Nicholls, & Spidel, 2005; Hines, Brown, & Dunning, 2007; Swan et al., 2008).

Unfortunately, physical and sexual intimate partner violence occurs at much higher rates for homosexual and bisexual men than heterosexual men, at similar rates to heterosexual women (Messinger, 2011; Tjaden, Thoennes, & Allison, 1999). Researchers Finneran and colleagues (Finneran, Chard, Sineath, Sullivan, & Stephenson, 2012) conducted a study in six countries, recruiting gay men over the age of 18 years old through ads on Facebook. The researchers asked over 2,300 men to report recent experiences of physical and sexual violence as victims, and recent perpetration of physical violence against a male partner. Participants also completed several self-report measures, including the Gay Identity Scale, which assesses a person's acceptance of their homosexuality (Williamson et al., 2008). Low scores indicated internalized homonegativity, or negative feelings toward one's homosexuality. Participants also indicated their experiences of discrimination because of being homosexual, such as being made fun of as a child; and experiences of heteronormative social pressure (e.g., people pressuring one to get married, have children). The results indicated that experiences of internalized homonegativity, discrimination, and heteronormativity are linked to IPV between gay men. Increasing social acceptance of LGBTQ people, including through actively condemning bigotry and promoting equality and value of all people, at individual and group levels, can reduce violence in gay intimate relationships.

Biological Underpinnings: Evolved to Fight

There are sex differences in frequency and intensity of aggressive behavior, and they are linked to physical, biological differences between girls and boys, women and men. Aggression is an intentional act that is intended to cause psychological or physical harm to another person (Coie

& Dodge, 1998). Sex differences in aggression have evolved over time with the human species, favoring aggressive behavior by men in competition with each other for sexual access to women and other forms of power in primitive groups. Scholars argue that fighting ability in humans and in other animals evolved because it underlies dominance and status within groups, relations between predators and prey, aggressive communication, sexual dimorphism, and mating competition (Sell, Hone, & Pound, 2012). Part of fighting ability is size and strength, which human males developed differentially over evolution compared to women precisely because of the relations indicated above. As we have discussed several times already (see Chapters 1 and 7), there are substantial differences in physical size and strength between women and men. The average man has 50–80% greater upper body strength and 30–60% greater lower body strength than the average woman (Lassek & Gaulin, 2009). The effect sizes for throwing distance and for throwing velocity between women and men are around 2.00 (Thomas & French, 1985). That means that the average distance men can throw an object is two standard deviations higher than the average distance women can throw. That means that only 2.5% of women can throw farther than the average man; 97.5% of women cannot throw as far as the average man. That's a huge difference in strength (Cohen, 1988). Men have other physical advantages that make them more effective at physically subduing and hurting others, including faster reaction times (Der & Deary, 2006), broader shoulders (Tanner, 1989), stronger bones (Schoenau, Neu, Rauch, & Manz, 2001; Wells, 2007), greater musculature (Loomba-Albrecht & Styne, 2009), higher metabolism (Garn & Clark, 1953), thicker skin (Shuster, Black, M& McVitie, 1975), greater lung capacity (Gursoy, 2010), and other physical advantages. Because they have a greater capacity for aggression, including a greater ability to subdue and harm others, men are higher in aggression than women, in all areas of life, across the lifespan.

There are hormonal differences between women and men that are also linked to sex differences in aggression, mainly differences in the male hormone (androgen) called **testosterone**. Much research substantiates that across animal species, males are substantially higher in testosterone than females, differences that are greatest beginning at the time of sexual maturity, where testosterone is linked to sexual development, the production of mature sperm, and increasing competition with other males for access to potential mates (Archer, 1988). Sexual competition within species tends to be most intense in young adulthood; correspondingly, studies indicating that young adult males in many species, including *Homo Sapiens*, are highest in levels of physical aggression and killing members of the same sex, than other sex and age groups (Archer, 2004; Daly & Wilson, 1988). Males fight and kill other males for sexual access to females, the evolutionary imperative (Archer, 2006). Men's testosterone levels decrease after entering into committed relationships and after having children (Burnham et al., 2003), substantiating the role of the hormone in competition and mating behaviors. Experimental studies using animals and injecting them with testosterone substantiate natural observations and indicate that increasing blood levels of testosterone increases aggressive behavior (Allee, Collias, & Lutherman, 1939; Beeman, 1947; Ewing et al., 1979). Experimental studies injecting human beings with testosterone show similar results, with aggressive behavior increasing along with testosterone (Bos, Panksepp, Bluthé, & van Honk, 2012). With men on average having about seven to eight times the blood testosterone of women (Torjesen & Sandnes, 2004), there is an obvious difference in aggressive behavior associated with this physically and psychologically important hormone.

Women and men are clearly biologically different, and these differences affect our perceptions and understandings of what it means to be female and what it means to be male. Women are biologically structured to bear and feed babies; it is their primary reproductive function. Because potential motherhood is a key feature of women as a group, this function leads to the valuing of qualities that are recognizably positive for infant outcomes, namely being a loving, kind, nurturing, gentle caretaker. Men in contrast, biologically structured to be strong, to hunt, build, and fight, should in an idealization of that role be physically strong, tough, definitely not weak. These desirable qualities come to be associated with each gender and expected from each gender, as explained by **social role theory** (Eagly & Wood, 1999; Wood & Eagly, 2002). Women and men are expected to have qualities associated with biological roles, even when they are not engaged in any behavior related to motherhood or to hunting, fighting, and building. As such, even childless women or women who are not pregnant or caring for children are expected to be gentle, kind, cooperative, caretaking. Men who are not hunting, fighting, or building are expected to be strong and fit. As I assert in "Inequalities and Injustices," qualities associated with social roles are then used to legitimize primitive roles that are based more on biological functions, so as to reinforce and maintain men's **social dominance** over women (Pratto & Walker, 2004). **Legitimizing myths** are transmitted through social institutions created by men which are used to maintain men's dominance within the social hierarchy in multiple ways beyond transmission of gender norms.

Socialization of Aggression

In addition to biological and physiological differences between the sexes and links with aggressive behavior, social processes clearly influence the development of aggressive behavior. Cultural institutions, which provide psychological frameworks for understanding the world through ideologies, norms, and habits, encourage features of gendered behavior. Around the world, all types of cultural and social institutions value male action and dominance, including aggressive behavior. Masculinity involves a rejection of feminine behavior as weak, dependent, submissive, childlike; such qualities are taboo to traditional ideas of maleness (Prentice & Carranza, 2002). As such, cultures and social institutions value and encourage masculinity in boys and men (see "Inequalities & Injustices"; Huddy & Terkildsen, 1993). Eastern and many other cultures are more **collectivistic**; that is, they highly value group outcomes, with individual needs and goals subsumed to those of the group (Hofstede, 1983). Within Eastern cultures, public interpersonal aggressive behaviors are not appropriate and are considered selfish, damaging to the group, and shameful. Individuals from Eastern cultures report substantially lower motivation to interpersonally aggress than those from Western cultures, including when the aggression target is at fault or aggressed first (Kornadt, 1991). Aggression is valued in sports but only in so far that it is related to winning or excelling; petty aggression is highly devalued in Eastern cultures (Forbes, Zhang, Doroszewicz, & Haas, 2009; Kim, Pan, & Park, 1998). If cultures are collectivistic but highly traditional, however, as is the case in Latin America, Africa, and Southeast Asia, aggression toward women is encouraged as a means of patriarchal control (Centers for Disease Control and Prevention, 2012; Kumagai & Straus, 1983; Morley, 1994; Shamim, 1992; Schuler, Hashemi, Riley, & Akhter, 1996). Western cultures are **individualistic**, and emphasize individual strengths and achievements, with personal outcomes and goals elevated over those of the group or larger society (Triandis, 1995). Research indicates that aggression is substantially lower in collectivistic cultures which value moral discipline, egalitarianism, and values associated with Confucianism (Bergeron & Schneider, 2005).

Media Violence

Portrayals of aggression through various media, including television, movies, music, and video games, are highly violent and highly traditional in terms of female and male roles and behaviors (Anderson, 2004; Anderson & Bushman, 2001; Comstock & Scharrer, 2007; Gentile, 2003; Gentile, Saleem, & Anderson, 2007; Kirsh, 2006; Singer & Singer, 2001). Research very strongly and conclusively indicates that exposure to media violence increases the likelihood of aggressive behavior in children and adults, both in the short and long term (Anderson & Bushman, 2002; Anderson et al., 2003; Paik & Comstock, 1994). Government health agencies from all over the world and groups of health professionals strongly agree that exposure to media violence is dangerous and harmful to children (Gentile et al., 2007). Many people enjoy violent media; viewing violent media (and engaging in it through video games; Anderson, Gentile, & Buckley, 2007) increases various features of physiological arousal, which can create a sense of euphoria, especially among people who are already aggressive (Berkowitz, 1993; Geen & O'Neal, 1969). Because violence sells, creators and purveyors of violent media produce billions of dollars in revenue every year around the world (Bushman & Anderson, 2001; Entertainment Software Association, 2018). Because of such "positive outcomes" of media violence, people sometimes choose to ignore, minimize, or disbelieve the evidence linking media violence to harmful effects on children. But like all addictions, short-term experiences of pleasure lead to psychological, interpersonal, and societal costs, including long-term costs. Addictions to violence, money, and power, that are so prevalent in humankind across time, history, and geography, lead to long-term widespread costs that are incalculable.

As accurately described by Bandura's social learning theory (1997), observation of violent behavior leads to learning of violent behavior (**observational learning**). Children at a very young age imitate the behaviors of others whom they observe; this tendency is clearly adaptive and appears to be innate (Meltzoff & Moore, 2000). Imitation is enabled and made essential by so-called **mirror neurons** in the brain (neurons associated with a certain behavior that activate while observing others engaged in that behavior) (Rizzolatti, Fadiga, Gallese, & Fogassi, 1996). Observational learning plays a crucial role in the construction of schematic frameworks used to understand the world. Such **schemas** are developed over time through experience and are used to guide behavior and processing of new information (Chaiken, Liberman, & Eagly, 1989). In schema development, two primary processes become evident, as described by Piaget (1976). The first is **assimilation**, where new information is altered to fit with pre-existing schemas. For example, a child forming a schema for animals may view a cow not as new or different, but as just like a dog, in keeping with her beginning schema. Similarly, a woman may be perceived as being more similar to traditional female gender roles than she actually is. This process does not require much effort; "all of them are the same" is the judgment and the schema remains relatively unchallenged and unchanged.

A second, more effortful process involves changing schemas in response to new information (**accommodation**). Accommodation is cognitively difficult because it involves more effortful examination of the new information and cognitive processing of how the new information does and does not fit with the existing schema. If the child engaged in accommodation of the cow, she would notice how the cow was different (in size, body structures, behavior, typical use and setting); this would lend greater complexity to her animal schema and may even lead to a new subcategorization (*farm animals* versus *pets*). Similarly, a powerful, accomplished woman who challenges one's schema about women may lead one to change one's ideas about women and include professional achievement and power in one's gender stereotype. Because accommodation is a more effortful process, the person must be motivated and able to engage in it for it to occur. That is, children must be interested in the topic (animals) and able (not sick, sleepy, hungry) for them to engage in the hard work of complex schema development. Adults must be motivated and able to change their traditional, automatic stereotypes about women and men. Assimilation requires little effort and is not based on thorough processing (**elaboration**) of the evidence; as such, it is a biased process that does not promote learning and healthy schema development.

Childhood is particularly important for schema development. When children observe violent behavior, they encode such behaviors within their schemas which are used to guide behavior in interpersonal and social situations. Exposure to media violence over long periods of time leads to long-term permanent effects on behavior, as violence is encoded into cognitive frameworks and may be used rather automatically in guiding behavior (Bargh & Pietromonaco, 1982). Children exposed to violence develop beliefs that the world is dangerous and that people are hostile. As such, they learn to rather automatically assume anger and hostility on the part of others and are thus more likely to behave with anger and hostility themselves (Dodge, 1985; Dodge, Pettit, & Bates, 1995; Gerbner, Gross, Morgan, & Signorielli, 1994). Repeated exposures to media violence also result in **desensitization** to violence. The shock and horror of observing violence dramatically decreases when violence is repeatedly observed (Cline, Croft, & Courrier, 1973; Thomas, Horton, Lippincott, & Drabman, 1977). Exposure to pretend violence in video games can decrease physiological reactions (e.g., heart-rate, perspiration, respiration) to actual real-life violence (Carnagey, Anderson, & Bushman, 2007). Long-term exposure to media violence (as indicated by long-term media consumption habits) affects long-term thoughts, emotions, and behaviors. As such, children are particularly vulnerable to schematic effects of media violence and as exposure increases over long periods of time, violence is more widely and deeply incorporated into cognitive frameworks used to guide emotional responses, interpersonal behaviors, and understanding of the world (Bushman & Huesmann, 2006).

Viewing media aggression has short-term effects on behavior as well. In the short term, viewing aggression makes children and adults feel aggressive emotions (Yukawa & Yoshida, 1999) and may **prime** (activate) developing or already existing schemas (**scripts**) for aggressive behavior (Berkowitz & LePage, 1967). Modeling and imitation of aggressive behavior is another short-term effect of exposure to media violence. Children exposed to aggressive models engage in mimicking of that behavior, especially when such behavior is rewarded (Bandura, Ross, & Ross, 1963). Children's media can be excessively violent, depicting interpersonal violence and use of weapons (Road Runner, anyone?) (National Television Violence Study, 1996, 1997, 1998; Wilson et al., 2002). Adults are actually not much different from children in terms of short-term effects of exposure to media violence. Viewing violent behavior primes use of violent scripts and negative feelings of anger and aggression. The short-term effects of media violence exposure on adults are actually stronger than they are for children, as adults have well-developed schemas that are easily (and sometimes automatically) accessible into consciousness as a guide for behavior compared to children. When adults possess schemas for aggressive behavior that are well-learned and repeatedly used, aggressive interpretations of social experiences and aggressive behaviors become easily triggered, even habitual (Bushman & Huesmann, 2006; Huesmann, 1998). With repeated practice and activation, including through video game play that essentially requires aggressive thoughts, aggressive thoughts and feelings can become chronically activated, even beyond the person's conscious control. Aggression thus becomes part of a person's personality, their characteristic thoughts, feelings, and behaviors across situations (Bartholow, Sestir, & Davis, 2005; Strack & Deutsch, 2004; Wegner & Bargh, 1998).

There are literally thousands of studies on exposure to media violence and aggressive behavior. Because there are so many studies, meta-analyses of research on aggressive behavior are common. A **meta-analysis** is a higher order analysis; it is a scientific investigation involving the examination of the results of many different studies, how results vary by study design or measurement techniques, and estimations of the overall relationship between variables (Rosenthal,

1991). Recent decades have seen increases in studies of violent video games and how they affect aggression in children and adults. One meta-analysis examined over 130 studies of video game playing and exposure and several different cognitive, emotional, and behavioral outcomes, including studies from Western and Eastern cultures (mainly Japan) (Anderson et al., 2010). The results indicated a strong causal influence of violent video games on aggressive behaviors, cognitions, and emotions, and physiological arousal, with greater aggression and arousal with greater exposure. Results also indicated strong causal effects of violent video games on desensitization to violence; individuals exposed to violent video games show lower sensitivity to violence, lower feelings of empathy, and are less likely to engage in prosocial behaviors. These results occurred regardless of culture and regardless of sex (i.e., girls and boys, women and men are equally susceptible to the causal influence of violent video games on aggressive thoughts, behaviors, and feelings). Although some scholars argue that the negative effects of violent video games on children and adults are exaggerated and that such games actually have some positive effects (Ferguson, 2007a, 2007b), the research evidence is strong and clear. Exposure to media violence, including through video games, is a cause of increased aggressive behaviors, feelings and thoughts, and decreased feelings of empathy and behaviors directed toward caring for others. While such games may be fun to play, long-term use can lead to serious negative outcomes for individuals, families, and society as a whole.

As we discussed in Chapter 7, men and boys are commonly portrayed as aggressive in all types of media (Anderson et al., 2010; Bushman & Huesmann, 2006; Slater et al., 2003). Media portrayals of girls and women are much more likely to include victimization of some kind, while portrayals of male victims are less frequent (Stankiewicz & Rosselli, 2008). Women are typically portrayed as dependent on men (Scharrer, 2004; Ward, 1995) or as damsels in distress (Dietz, 1998). Even when women are lead characters engaged in more agentic behavior, their physical appearance is still emphasized and will likely reflect ideal standards of beauty (Dietz, 1998; Mikula, 2003). Women are sexually objectified in media; print images of women are often processed in terms of individual body parts, rather than as whole human beings (Bernard et al., 2012, 2015; Civile & Obhi, 2015). Some media depictions of women, especially in video games, involve exaggerated and sexualized body parts (e.g., naturally impossible body shapes, overly large breasts and behinds; Dill & Thill, 2007). Overly sexualized images of women result in perceptions of women as interchangeable, meaning one is as good as the other based on their bodies (Gervais, Vescio, & Allen, 2012) (see Figure 11.1).

Portraying women as sex objects and victims is harmful and dangerous to women. Research indicates that women who are sexually objectified in media are perceived as less intelligent, less competent, and weaker and more passive (Cikara et al., 2011; Heflick et al., 2011; Vaes et al., 2011). Sexualized media images of women reinforce traditional views of women, gender roles, and sexual roles (Peter & Valkenburg, 2007; Ward, 2003). Such ideas about women are stereotypical, negative, false, and they serve to legitimize women's oppression. A large body of research indicates that exposure to media portrayals of women as sex objects, including in video games, music videos, magazines, and television, has a causal influence on attitudes and beliefs about women. Greater exposure to sexual objectification of women in media is linked with lower acceptance of feminism, greater acceptance of interpersonal violence, greater gender role stereotyping, and greater feelings of **benevolent sexism** (Kalof, 1999; MacKay & Covell, 1997; Milburn, Mather, & Conrad, 2000; Stermer & Burkley, 2015). Women and men exposed to women sexually objectified in media are more likely to express sexist, negative attitudes toward women (Rollero, 2013; Swami et al., 2010) and greater acceptance of sexual harassment (Ward, 2002). Women and men

Aggression 355

Figure 11.1 Sexual objectification of women is common in popular media
Source: Frazer Harrison/Getty Images

exposed to sexualized depictions of women are more likely to blame women for their own victimization than people not exposed to such images (Bernard, Legrand, & Klein, 2018). Men exposed to portrayals of women as sex objects in advertising are more likely to endorse **rape myths** (Lanis & Covell, 1995). Multiple studies link violent pornography to violence against women (more later in this chapter; DeKeseredy & Schwartz, 1998; Malamuth, 1984). Unfortunately, the portrayal of women as victims in art reflects reality. Violence toward girls and women is widespread around the world, and they are much more likely to be the victims of sexual violence and **intimate partner violence** (IPV) than men (Centers for Disease Control and Prevention, 2012).

Parenting and Aggression in Offspring

Parents and parental figures are an important and powerful source of socialization for every person, beginning during in utero development and possibly extending across the lifespan. Across cultures, children learn about gender beginning within the family context. Parents inform children verbally, behaviorally, and emotionally about their beliefs and feelings about gender, including women's and men's typical roles, behaviors, and activities and how valued and important those

356 Aggression

are (Bulanda, 2004). More traditional parents model more traditional roles for their children, with mothers viewed as more capable of caretaking responsibilities for the family and fathers as more capable of decision- and money-making (Turner & Gervai, 1995). Parents also teach their children about aggressive behavior, both in the ideology and preferences they share with their children, and in their behaviors toward each other (the marital relationship) and the children in the family. Physical aggression is more strongly associated with the male gender role than the female gender role, and this distinction is directly and indirectly taught to children (Maccoby & Jacklin, 1974). Parents treat daughters and sons differently. Girls are taught to be nurturing and kind, and to engage in quiet indoor activities. Boys are taught to be strong, tough, and assertive, and to engage in rough-and-tumble play, competitive sports, and outdoor activities (Gilligan, 1982; Maccoby & Martin, 1983; Ruble & Martin, 1997). As a result, boys are more aggressive than girls and, in the long run, men are far more aggressive than women, especially physically (Coie & Dodge, 1998; Crick & Grotpeter, 1995).

Parents directly model and teach scripts for expectations of behaviors from others and from the world. Parents with a **hostile attribution bias** believe that others are generally hostile in their intentions and feelings; as such, these people experience hostility themselves and are more likely to behave aggressively toward others (Orobio De Castro, Veerman, Koops, Bosch, & Monshouwer, 2002). Parents who continually show this hostility bias will have children with the same scripts and expectations of the behavior of others. Similarly, parents who see goodness in others and who have empathy and compassion toward others will teach their children empathy and prosocial behavior (Eron, 1986). Parents teach their children about aggression in their relationships with their children, particularly their use of discipline. Longitudinal research using data from multiple countries indicates that harsh emotional and physical punishment is linked with aggressive behavior by both female and male offspring. Excessive punishment and rejection by parents is linked with aggression in childhood and adolescence among boys, while for girls, harsh parental punishment is linked with aggressive behavior toward intimates (partners, spouses, children, friends) in adulthood (Eron, Huesmann, & Zelli, 1991).

It is estimated that over 10 million American children are witness to IPV between their parents each year (Bender, 2004). Some research indicates that observation of aggression between parents is not directly linked to aggression by children. For example, Holmes (2013) found that parental IPV is linked with poor maternal mental health, which is in turn linked with psychological and physical abuse of children in the family. This abuse and low warmth from mothers are directly linked with more aggressive behaviors among children (Holmes, 2013). Other studies indicate direct links between observation of parental IPV and aggressive behavior toward same- and opposite-sex peers among boys and girls (McCloskey & Lichter, 2003; Moretti, Obsuth, Odgers, & Reebye, 2006; Nowakowski Sims, Dodd, & Tejeda, 2006). Aggression against same-sex peers was especially likely with observations of aggression by the same-sex parent in parental IPV (Moretti et al., 2006). The observation of parental IPV is more strongly linked to depression and other internalizing behaviors among girls (e.g., depression) and to externalizing behaviors (e.g., interpersonal aggression) among boys (McCloskey & Lichter, 2003). Although direct links between parental IPV and aggression in childhood and adulthood are not always found, there does appear to be an intergenerational transmission of IPV. It appears that witnessing IPV as a child is associated with family chaos and violence in general. As such, witnessing IPV is associated with experiencing psychological and physical abuse as a child and suffering from psychological disorders, including post-traumatic stress disorder (PTSD), in adulthood. Such psychological disorders are associated with increased perpetration of IPV among men, and increased perpetration and experience of IPV among women (Bensley, Van Eenwyk, & Wynkoop Simmons, 2003; Bevan & Higgins, 2002; Cannon, Bonomi, Anderson, & Rivara, 2009; Ernst et al., 2007; Renner & Slack, 2006).

Exposure to violence in one's neighborhood and community is also associated with aggressive behavior, especially when it occurs in childhood, affecting the development of schemas for understanding others and the world. One study of several thousand children living in urban neighborhoods found that witnessing violence affected beliefs about aggression (with fewer inhibition norms) and increased aggressive behavior. The authors suggest that the witnessing of community violence leads both to imitation of aggressive behaviors by children and effects on their cognitive understandings of violence, especially as children get older (Guerra, Huesmann, & Spindler, 2003). Witnessing of community violence is not only linked with aggressive behavior, but with a host of other problems including substance use, anxiety, and depression (Boney-McCoy & Finkelhor, 1995; Campbell & Schwarz, 1996; Cooley-Ouille, Turner, & Beidel, 1995; Gorman-Smith & Tolan, 1998; Osofsky, Wewers, Hann, & Fick, 1993; Schwab-Stone et al., 1995). Although some sex differences are found in these negative effects (Gorman-Smith & Tolan, 1998; Schwab-Stone et al., 1995), results overall indicate negative effects of witnessing violence for both girls and boys, including long-term negative outcomes.

Religion and Aggression against Women

As we have discussed in other chapters and in other areas of this chapter, religious doctrine, through the enforcement of religious norms and edicts, is linked to attitudes and behaviors toward women all over the world and across history. The Abrahamic religions (originating with the story of the Creation and of Abraham and his offspring) are three of the world's major religions, Christianity, Islam, and Judaism. The Bible, the Torah, and the Qu'ran have very powerful and impactful messages about the worth of women and how to treat them. And as you can guess, those messages are not good. In all of these religions, women are worth less than and subordinate to men (Marios & Hégy, 1998; Wemple, 1992). Their behavior is regulated by men based on the fact of their being female. Orthodox Judaism involves separation of women and men, in the Temple and everywhere else (Goldman, 2001). Wives cover their heads with wigs and scarves, a sign of modesty and unavailability (Bronner, 1993). Sex is highly regulated, with men making sexual decisions and women sexually passive (Anderson, 1992; Boyarin, 1992). Women are marginalized because of the biological functions of menstruation, pregnancy, and childbirth (Weissler, 1992). Men are superior to women, holding superior status in all walks of life (Goldman, 2001). Islam indicates that a woman's word is only worth half of that of a man, with two female witnesses required to equal the strength of one male witness (Qu'ran 2:282). Women are encouraged to cover themselves (Qu'ran 24:31, 33:59), including with the *burqa* which severely limits movement, perception, communication, and can be dangerous in extremely hot environments (see Figure 11.2). Christianity similarly indicates that women are to submit to men, to be silent in church, and to not hold positions of authority (1 Peter 3:5; 1 Corinthians 14:34; 1 Timothy 2:11-12). Women are ridiculed and condemned as unclean because of menstruation and childbirth (Leviticus 12:2, 12:5).

Even worse than these proclamations of women's inferiority and subordinate status to men are religious texts and norms encouraging violence against women (Gassin, 2015; Starkey, 2015). Judaism prescribes physical control of women (Fortune, 2001). The Bible Old Testament demands the stoning to death of women who are not virgins at marriage (Deuteronomy 22:20-21), and

358 *Aggression*

Figure 11.2 The burqa, required only of women, never of men
Source: iStock Photo

those who are raped but do not protest loudly enough (Deuteronomy 22:23-27). The Bible provides that soldiers should take all the virgin women and girls for themselves, while killing everyone else including married women and mothers (Numbers 31:17-18). Although the practice of religion and religious ideals may be used by intimate partners as a way to reduce or cope with intimate partner violence (IPV) (Choi, 2015; Goldberg-Looney, Perrin, Snipes, & Calton, 2016; Sullivan, Weiss, Price, Pugh, & Hansen, 2018), because of links with patriarchal attitudes, endorsement of traditional religious ideology can be linked with increased intimate partner violence (Ross, 2014; St. Lawrence & Joyner, 1991), including among LGBTQ couples (Pepper & Sand, 2015).

Rape is common in Islamic countries (although underreported) and women are often punished for being raped (Akbar, 2013). Women in Islamic countries have been stoned to death or otherwise murdered for adultery and marrying against family wishes (British Broadcasting Corporation, 2014, 2015), and for being raped which is viewed as a form of adultery (Pleasance, 2017; Sadowa, 2015; Tiwari & Mehrotra, 2016). In several Islamic countries there are no laws making marital rape illegal (Kheetan, 2017), and laws requiring female victims to marry their male rapists exist across the Middle East (Sengupta, 2017). **Shari'a law**, which exists in some form in most Islamic nations (Abiad, 2008), fairly commands and commends the murder of women, through proclamations of stoning women to death for sex or pregnancy outside of marriage (Poonwala, 2007). Women who are raped in Islamic countries may bring shame to their families and are sometimes murdered by relatives to avoid this stigma to the men in the family for not maintaining female relatives' purity (Mercy, Abdel Megid, Salem, & Lotfi, 1993). Men are given nearly complete control over all women in their lives under Shari'a law, including whether women can drive a car, vote, or even leave the house (Abedi, 2016). Such restrictions are obviously oppressive of women and designed to be so, in my assertion, by men so that men can maintain their disproportionate share of power and resources. Religion is clearly personally important to many people, and it is clearly a personal and private decision whether one will follow any particular religion(s) in one's own life. That is not what this is about. This is about religion as a historical, global power in the abuse and oppression of women, in the perpetration of misogyny. How such knowledge plays into individual choices about religion remains to be seen, but this violent oppression of women cannot be allowed to continue. The only force capable of defeating violent religious ideology is individuals who value peace and equality and who are brave enough to stand up for it.

Gender Roles and Aggression

As we have already discussed, including in other chapters (e.g., Chapters 5 and 7), social norms for masculinity are associated with dominance and aggression (Huddy & Terkildsen, 1993) (see Figures 11.3a and 11.3b). Aggressive behavior by men is rewarded and applauded, including in violent media portrayals (Anderson et al., 2010; Bushman & Huesmann, 2006; Ruble & Martin, 1997; Slater et al., 2003) (see Figure 11.4). Idealizations of masculinity can involve portrayals of hypermasculinity, extreme masculinity including endorsement of violence, callous sexual attitudes toward women, and risk-taking (Reidy et al., 2009). Men who are hypermasculine have a tendency to be aggressive, as a way of demonstrating masculinity and maintaining dominance over others, including women (Mosher & Sirkin, 1984). Hypermasculine men admit to more physical aggression toward women and behave more aggressively toward women in laboratory settings compared to men who are not hypermasculine (Parrott & Zeichner, 2003). Hypermasculine men are particularly sensitive to violation of traditional gender roles and norms; such violations make hypermasculine men angry and aggressive toward role violators (Herek, 1986). Using an experimental design involving supposed (but not actual) aggression against a female confederate, Reidy and colleagues (2009) found that hypermasculine men were more aggressive in administering electrical shocks to a female confederate than men who were not hypermasculine (a main effect); and that hypermasculine men were particularly aggressive toward women who were less feminine. In other words, hypermasculine men are aggressive to establish dominance over women. In addition, hypermasculine men are especially likely to aggress when women violate traditional gender roles and act in ways that are more masculine. Hypermasculine men are also aggressive toward gay men in laboratory research, especially after they witness or engage in violations of masculine gender roles (Parrott & Zeichner, 2008).

Recent research suggests that personality traits involving traditionality and authoritarianism (a personality trait involving strong obedience to traditional authorities; see Chapters 6, 7, and 13) underlie hypermasculine aggression (Duncan, Peterson, & Winter, 1997). As such, hypermasculine men become angry and then use aggression as a method of maintaining the traditional status quo and social hierarchy, where heterosexual men are idealized and receive a disproportionate share of society's wealth, power, and other resources (Goodnight, Cook, Parrott, & Peterson, 2014). Highly traditional, role-conforming, hyperfeminine women display a similar

Figures 11.3a and 11.3b Sports activities for girls tend to be not or less aggressive compared to those of boys
Source: Amysuem/iStock Photo and Ebstock/iStock Photo

Figure 11.4 Male characters in media are commonly portrayed as hypermasculine
Source: Pictorial Press Ltd/Alamy Stock Photo

anger and obedience to tradition in their behavior toward individuals who violate gender norms. Such women are more aggressive toward women who violate traditional standards of feminine behavior than women who behave femininely (Reidy, Sloan, & Zeichner, 2009). Hyperfeminine women become angrier after exposure to nontraditional (e.g., same-sex female) sexual behavior than do women who are not hyperfeminine (Parrott & Gallagher, 2008). As such, this aggression by women toward other women is also in service of maintaining the patriarchal status quo, behavior that stems from anger toward nontraditional behavior and a desire to be obedient and maintain the status quo.

Traditionality and other traits related to conservatism are also linked to **sexual prejudice** and aggressive behavior toward LGBTQ individuals, among both women and men but especially among men (Nagoshi et al., 2008; Polimeni et al., 2000; Stevenson & Medler, 1995). Women are less likely to feel aggressive toward LGBTQ individuals than men, even if they show negative sexual prejudice toward LGBTQ people. Further, women who are higher in **egalitarianism** (attitudes favoring social and economic equality between groups) are less likely to show prejudice against LGBTQ people (Theodore & Basow, 2000). Scholars assert that men experience greater anxiety in response to male homosexuality than women, especially because men perceive homosexual men to be feminine, a violation of gender role norms (Parrott, Adams, & Zeichner, 2002; Patel, Long, McCammon, & Wuensch, 1995; Sinn, 1997). In this way, gay men and their feminine behavior are threats to the masculine identity of men, a theoretical approach (**threat theory**) that fits with evidence concerning **precarious manhood** (the precarious nature of the masculine identity; Vandello & Bosson, 2013). Hypermasculine men with insecure masculinity feel negative feelings toward women and LGBTQ people, especially when they violate expected and traditional standards of behavior that maintain patriarchy, because they threaten the social power of

362 *Aggression*

men (Warriner et al., 2013). The association of feminine behaviors with masculinity and women who disobey role expectations are threats to the norms that support male patriarchy (Norton, 1997). The experience of threat is negative and results in anger and aggressive behavior that is designed to maintain dominance in the social hierarchy.

Physical and Verbal Aggression in Children and Adults

As I have already indicated in our discussions thus far, at all ages, boys and men are more aggressive physically than girls and women (Cairns, Cairns, Neckerman, Ferguson, & Gariepy, 1989; Eagly, 1987; Eagly & Steffen, 1986; Hyde, 1984; Knight, Fabes, & Wilson, 1996; Tapper & Boulton, 2004). In meta-analyses of studies of children's aggression, Hyde (1984, 1986) and Knight, Fabes, and Higgins (1996) found that boys are higher in physical and verbal aggression than girls across age groups, with moderate to large **effect sizes** (Cohen's *d* of .91 for physical aggression, .46 for verbal aggression). These results are true whether individual studies use self-reports of aggression or direct observations of children's behavior. Crime statistics show a similar sex difference, with boys and men more likely to commit serious violent crimes and more likely to be arrested and incarcerated for aggression than girls and women (United States Department of Justice, 1995). Studies of children indicate that girls are higher in sympathy than boys (Eisenberg & Lennon, 1983) and that parental support and parental monitoring are important in reducing aggression in both girls and boys (Lamborn, Mounts, Steinberg & Dornbusch, 1991; Carlo, Raffaelli, Laible, & Meyer, 1999). Children from disadvantaged neighborhoods are also more likely to behave aggressively (Chang, Wang, & Tsai, 2016). In a meta-analysis of studies examining sex differences in aggression in individuals aged 14 years and older, Eagly and Steffan (1986) similarly found reliable sex differences in physical and verbal aggression, with men higher in aggression than women. Their findings also indicate that women are more likely to report experiencing anxiety, guilt, and fear of consequences after engaging in aggression than men. Other meta-analyses indicate that men are more likely to use serious physical aggression than women (Archer, 2004). When violent cues or provocation are involved, sex differences in aggression are much smaller. In other words, when women are directly and seriously provoked, they can be just as physically and verbally aggressive as men, but men as a group are still more aggressive than women (Bettencourt & Kernahan, 1997).

Intimate Partner Violence (IPV)

Although there are many scholars from across many disciplines who are interested in understanding and helping to prevent IPV, there are two primary and important theoretical perspectives in understanding IPV (Archer, 2000). One perspective is a **feminist** one, which focuses on male perpetration of violence against women because of their greater physical size and strength and as a way to maintain patriarchy through physical oppression of women (Dobash, Dobash, Wilson, & Daly, 1992). This perspective is also based on **social dominance** (Pratto & Walker, 2004) and **evolutionary theories** (Buss & Shackleford, 1997; Smuts, 1995). I have primarily taken this perspective in my writing about aggression against women in this book. There is however what is called "**common couple violence**," which is IPV that occurs between couples, is not highly injurious to either, and is not based on coercion or oppression. This type of IPV is based on anger and loss of control by either or both partners in the relationship (Johnson, 1995). Researchers examining this kind of family violence do not view IPV as a means of coercive male control of women, but rather as a not necessarily unusual relationship behavior.

Because the level of violence is key to understanding either perspective, each of these approaches generally targets different groups of people in trying to understand IPV (Straus, 1999). A feminist approach focuses more on severe violence and usually targets men who are known to be high in violence (e.g., men seeking treatment or who have been arrested for violence) (Claes & Rosenthal, 1990), their female victims (Mooney, 1994), or surveys about crime (Dobash & Dobash, 1980; Schwartz, 1987). In contrast, researchers taking a family conflict perspective are likely to study young people involved in romantic relationships and married couples from communities, people who are not selected to participate in research because they are high in violence (Magdol et al., 1997; Morse, 1995; Straus & Gelles, 1988). Obviously, different types of people will report different kinds of violence happening in their intimate relationships, so research within each perspective yields different results. There is also a distinction between the terms *aggression* and *violence* within these areas of scholarship. Physical aggression is used to refer to physical acts and behaviors that are aggressive, regardless of their harm or outcome. In this way, not all aggressive acts result in real harm. Violence is used to refer to the outcomes of physical aggression between intimate partners, typically in terms of physical injury or outcome severity (Archer, 1994, 2000).

Scholars studying common couple violence assert that there are actually few gender differences in perpetration of and victimization within IPV. Some argue that there is no "consensus" among researchers and that whether men perpetrate more IPV than women is "under dispute" (Chan, 2011, p.167). Research using nonclinical samples of married partners (i.e., people not seeking treatment for IPV) does indeed indicate that female partners can be perpetrators of IPV, with male partners as victims, with few if any differences in perpetration of IPV by gender (Straus, 1990; Vivian & Langhinrichsen-Rohling, 1994). While it may be true that many couples have never experienced IPV or that there are few gender differences in typical or "common" couples, I strongly disagree with the idea that there is any confusion about who is more likely to be victimized by IPV and who is more likely to be IPV perpetrators. Across all people, all intimate partnerships all over the world and across time, it is abundantly clear that men are much more likely to be IPV perpetrators, that female partners are much more likely to be victims, and that female partners are much more likely to be seriously injured or dead as a result of IPV than men. Even with regard to common couple violence, meta-analyses indicate that while frequency of IPV between partners shows few gender differences, types of aggressive acts committed do vary, with men more likely to beat up their female partner or strangle her, and women more likely to slap, punch, kick, and throw objects (Archer, 2002). Meta-analytic results also indicate that 62% of partners injured by IPV are female (Archer, 2000). While some argue that these results indicate "gender-symmetry" in IPV (Chan, 2011, p.169), I argue from the feminist perspective that while common couple violence may reveal few or small gender differences, the occurrence and damage of IPV taken as a whole around the world reveals a systematic, widespread, and consistent use of violence by men against female intimate partners (Heise & Garcia Moreno, 2002; Heise, Ellsberg, & Gottemoeller, 1999).

Global statistics indicate that IPV against women, perpetrated by men, is a global public health emergency, with one in three women around the world experiencing physical and/or sexual IPV in her lifetime (Garcia-Moreno, Jansen, Ellsberg, Heise, & Watts, 2006; World Health Organization, 2010). The National Health Resource Center on Domestic Violence asserts that in the United States, IPV affects more women than diabetes and breast cancer combined (Futures Without Violence, 2018). Twenty-seven percent of women and 11% of men in the U.S. have experienced IPV (Smith et al., 2012), but again, the injuries and costs are much greater for girls and women (Black, 2011; Silverman, Raj, Mucci, & Hathaway, 2001). Women are much more likely to be injured by IPV and suffer more severe forms of violence than male victims of IPV (Tjaden & Thoennes, 2000).

364 *Aggression*

Table 11.1 Intimate partner violence: stalking

Stalking: A pattern of repeated, unwanted, attention and contact that causes fear or concern for one's own safety or the safety of someone else (e.g., family member, close friend).

Stalking acts by a perpetrator can include, but are not limited to:
- Repeated and unwanted phone calls, voice messages, text messages, pages, and hang-ups
- Repeated and unwanted emails, instant messages, or messages through websites (e.g., Facebook)
- Leaving cards, letters, flowers, or presents when the victim doesn't want them
- Watching or following from a distance
- Spying with a listening device, camera, or global positioning system (GPS)
- Approaching or showing up in places (e.g., home, work, school) when the victim does not want to see them
- Leaving strange or potentially threatening items for the victim to find
- Sneaking into the victim's home or car and doing things to scare the victim by letting them know they (perpetrator) had been there
- Damaging the victim's personal property, pets or belongings
- Harming or threatening to harm the victim's pet
- Making threats to physically harm the victim

Criteria for stalking victimization:
Victim must have experienced:
- multiple stalking tactics or a single stalking tactic multiple times by the same perpetrator and:
- felt fearful or
- believed that they or someone close to them would be harmed or killed as a result of the perpetrator's behavior.

Source: Centers for Disease Control & Prevention (2015). Intimate partner violence surveillance uniform definitions and recommended data elements. Available at: www.cdc.gov/violenceprevention/pdf/ipv/intimatepartnerviolence.

Female victims of IPV experience psychological trauma and report various psychiatric disorders (e.g., depression, anxiety, PTSD, suicidality) (Campbell, 2002; Hellmuth, Jaquier, Swan, & Sullivan, 2014). IPV is also associated with substance abuse (Ashare, Weinberger, McKee, & Sullivan, 2011; Sullivan, Cavanaugh, Buckner, & Edmondson, 2009; Yoshihama, Horrocks, & Bybee, 2010).

IPV is associated with numerous and long-term negative physical health outcomes for women (Black, 2011; Breiding, Black, & Ryan, 2005). The health costs and costs due to work absenteeism because of IPV are billions of dollars all over the world every year (Centers for Disease Control & Prevention, 2003; Duvvury, Callan, Carney, & Raghavendra, 2013). IPV is a leading cause of death for pregnant women (Horon & Cheng, 2001) and a leading cause of injury to women aged 15 to 44 years in the United States (Barrier, 1998). Of all women murdered in the United States each year, over 50% are killed by a male intimate partner or ex-partner (Catalano, Smith, Snyder, & Rand, 2009). For men in the U.S. who are murdered each year, only 4% are killed by female partners or ex-partners (Fox & Zawitz, 1999). Men are also more likely to engage in **stalking** of female partners or ex-partners, and women are more likely to be stalked than men (Spitzberg & Cupach, 2006; Tjaden & Thoennes, 1998; see Table 11.1).

Some women are at higher risk for IPV than others. Poor women (Daoud et al., 2012; Heise & Garcia Moreno, 2002), women low in education (Daoud et al., 2012; Heise & Garcia Moreno, 2002; James, Brody, & Hamilton, 2013), and women who are unemployed (Charles & Perreira, 2007; Heise & Garcia Moreno, 2002) are all at greater risk for IPV than other women. Younger women, especially when pregnant, are also at greater risk (Daoud et al., 2012; Saltzman, Johnson, Gilbert, & Goodwin, 2003). Women in very traditional societies are particularly at risk for IPV, with traditional conceptions of male dominance and control encouraging use of violence in the family. Beating a wife is seen as a culturally and religiously justified practice to discipline her (Armstrong, 1998; Gonzalez, 1998; Michau, 1998; Osakue & Hilber, 1998; Schuler, Hashemi, Riley, & Akhter, 1996; Yilo & Straus, 1984; Zimmerman, 1995). Women in traditional cultures may endorse their husbands' beating of them as well, following the same cultural and family norms of patriarchy as their parents (Bawah et al., 1999; David & Chin, 1998; El-Zanaty et al., 1995). Women living in rural areas are more isolated and have fewer social supports and other resources and thus are more likely to be victims of IPV (El-Zanaty et al., 1995; Peek-Asa et al., 2011). Being a victim of childhood sexual abuse and a witness to IPV between parents are also risk factors for IPV for female victims (Abramsky et al., 2011; Heise & Garcia Moreno, 2002; World Health Organization, 2010). Risk factors for men as perpetrators of IPV have been identified from studies all over the world, including young age, low income, low academic achievement (Moffitt & Caspi, 1999); alcohol abuse (Ellsberg, Peña, Herrera, Liljestrand, & Winkvist, 2000; Jewkes, Penn-Kekana, Levin, Ratsaka, & Schrieber, 2001; Moreno, 1999; Nelson & Zimmerman, 1996; Rodgers, 1994); and experiencing or witnessing violence during childhood, including fathers perpetrating IPV toward mothers (Ellsberg, Peña, Herrera, Liljestrand, & Winkvist, 1999; Hakimi, Hayati, Marlinawati, Winkvist, & Ellsberg, 2001; Johnson, 1996; Larrain, 1994; Moreno, 1999; Nelson & Zimmerman, 1996).

Research indicates that men's traditionality and expectations of women's gender roles in the relationship and in the family are important factors underlying IPV. Traditional, hypermasculine men are more likely than men low in these qualities to experience what is called **masculine gender role stress**, feelings of intense pressure to fulfill traditional norms of masculinity (Eisler, 1995). It turns out that such men also react badly to women who do not abide by traditional norms of femininity. Men who are high in gender role stress react with greater anger and aggression to female intimate partners whose behavior somehow threatens male masculinity (Eisler, Franchina, Moore, Honeycutt, & Rhatigan, 2000; Franchina, Eisler, & Moore, 2001; Moore & Stuart, 2004). Men who are high in perpetration of IPV explain their violence toward female partners as resulting from women not fulfilling household responsibilities, including cooking and cleaning (Dobash & Dobash, 1979). Studies from developing and industrialized countries yield very similar results in terms of men's stated reasons for perpetrating IPV against female partners, including her disobedience, not having meals prepared on time, not caring for the home or children properly, going somewhere without the man's permission, arguing back to the man, questioning the man about money or his activities, suspicions of infidelity, and refusing sex (Armstrong, 1998; Gonzalez, 1998; Michau, 1998; Osakue & Hilber, 1998; Schuler et al., 1996; Zimmerman, 1995). Men who endorse traditional, patriarchal gender norms respond violently to women who violate prescribed gender roles (Websdale & Chesney-Lind, 1998). Gender role conflict and female partners' increasing independence are commonalities identified in cases where men murder their wives (Stark & Flitcraft, 1996). These common reasons for men battering (and murdering) their female partners strongly support the assertion that IPV is used as a method of control and oppression of women, literally physically forcing women to be submissive and subordinate, following men's orders.

Rape and Sexual Assault

Similar to the global public health crisis of intimate partner violence against women, rape and sexual assault are epidemics affecting women every day all over the world. **Rape** is legally defined in the United States as "The penetration, no matter how slight, of the vagina or anus with any body part or object, or oral penetration by a sex organ of another person, without the consent of the victim" (United States Department of Justice, 2012). The definition of **sexual assault** in the U.S. is more inclusive, defined as "any nonconsensual sexual act proscribed by Federal, tribal, or State law, including when the victim lacks capacity to consent" (United States Department of Justice, 2018).

Women are overwhelmingly the victims of rape and sexual assault (91%; Rennison, 2002), and men are overwhelmingly the perpetrators (99% of the time; Uniform Crime Report, 2011). Research in the United States indicates that at some point in their lives, one in five women and one in 71 men will be raped (Black et al., 2011). The experience of any kind of sexual violence is obviously more common, affecting one in three women and one in six men (Smith et al., 2012). Most rapes of women are by intimate partners or acquaintances, while the majority of rapes of men involve an acquaintance (Black et al., 2011). Overall, approximately 80% of rapists are acquainted with their victims (Miller, Cohen, & Wiersema, 1996). Women and girls who belong to racial minority groups and poor women are particularly vulnerable to rape and sexual assault (Bureau of Justice Statistics, 2016). Nearly half of multiracial women and Native American women in the U.S. experience some kind of sexual violence (Smith et al., 2012).

Rape is the most seriously underreported crime (American Medical Association, 1995; U.N. Women, 2011). Rape is especially underreported in highly traditional countries emphasizing male dominance over women and male entitlement to sex (Ariffin, 1997; Bennett, Manderson, & Astbury, 2000; Wood & Jewkes, 2001). In some highly traditional countries, women can be executed for being raped in so-called **honor killings**. In such countries, being raped brings dishonor onto a girl's or woman's family; the victim of rape is blamed, the shame is to her family, the perpetrator and his family are off limits (Pleasance, 2017; Sadowa, 2015; Tiwari & Mehrotra, 2016). This thinking about women goes right along with covering women from head to toe so that men are not aroused or inflamed. Rape statistics from around the world indicate that in some countries nearly 25% of women experience sexual violence (Ellsberg, 1997; Hakimi et al., 2001; Mooney, 1993). Around the world, nearly one-third of adolescent girls describe their first sexual experiences as forced and unwanted (Buga, Amoko, Ncayiyana, 1996; Jewkes, Vundule, Maforah, & Jordaan, 2001; Matasha et al., 1998). Rape is particularly high in countries that are less developed, poorer, more traditional, and less egalitarian (United Nations Office on Drugs and Crime, 2018). Women in poorer countries have even less power, including to report rape and be believed and protected (World Health Organization, 2002). In many highly traditional countries, there are no clear legal definitions of rape, which makes it much more difficult to prosecute rapists, another reason for women's silence (Amnesty International, 2008).

Men are also the victims of rape and sexual assault, usually by other men. Nearly 90% of male rape victims report a male perpetrator (Smith et al., 2012). Research in the United States indicates that approximately 3 to 4% of men experience a sexual assault in adulthood (Elliott, Mok, & Briere, 2004; Pimlott-Kubiak & Cortina, 2003). Studies from other countries report rates as high as 8% of men in adulthood (Coxell, King, Mezey, & Kell, 2000) and 11% of boys being sexually victimized (Plant, Plant, & Miller, 2005). Men are particularly unlikely to report being raped or sexually assaulted because of the stigma of sexual victimization and the threats to masculinity involved in being attacked (Davies, 2002; McLean, Balding, & White, 2005). The fact of male perpetration of rape on male victims is also demonstrated in the high rates of sexual assault reported by gay and bisexual men (Krahe, Schutze, Fritscher, & Waizenhofer, 2000). Gay and bisexual men are overrepresented among male rape victims (Keane, Young, Boyle, & Curry, 1995). Among men who are raped, over 60% report also being sexually victimized in childhood (Elliot et al., 2004).

Aggression 367

Table 11.2 Measurement of rape myths: the Rape Myth Acceptance Scale

1. A woman who goes to the home or apartment of a man on their first date implies that she is willing to have sex.
2. Any female can get raped.
3. One reason that women falsely report a rape is that they frequently have a need to call attention to themselves.
4. Any healthy woman can successfully resist a rapist if she really wants to.
5. When women go around braless or wearing short skirts and tight tops, they are just asking for trouble.
6. In the majority of rapes, the victim is promiscuous or has a bad reputation.
7. If a girl engages in necking or petting and she lets things get out of hand, it is her own fault if her partner forces sex on her.
8. Women who get raped while hitchhiking get what they deserve.
9. A woman who is stuck-up and thinks she is too good to talk to guys on the street deserves to be taught a lesson.
10. Many women have an unconscious wish to be raped, and may then unconsciously set up a situation in which they are likely to be attacked.
11. If a woman gets drunk at a party and has intercourse with a man she's just met there, she should be considered "fair game" to other males at the party who want to have sex with her too, whether she wants to or not.

Respondents indicate degree of agreement with each item using the following scale: 1 = *strongly disagree*; 2 = *moderately disagree*; 3 = *slightly disagree*; 4 = *neutral*; 5 = *slightly agree*; 6 = *moderately agree*; 7 = *strongly agree*. Higher scores indicate greater rape myth acceptance.

Source: Burt, M. R. (1980). Cultural myths and supports for rape. *Journal of Personality and Social Psychology, 38*(2), 217–230.

Traditional gender norms emphasize male dominance of women and their sexuality, in a sense giving men entitlement to sex on demand (Ariffin, 1997; Bennett, Manderson, & Astbury, 2000; Wood & Jewkes, 2001). This entitlement is particularly strong regarding wives' sexuality in traditional cultures, with women having no right to refuse marital sex (Sen, 1999). Men raised to be aggressive and dominant and to believe that they have sexual authority over women are high in **hypermasculinity**, extreme masculinity that includes endorsement of violence, negative and sexist attitudes toward women, and callous sexual attitudes toward women (Mosher & Sirkin, 1984). Rape proclivity among men involves hypermasculinity, hostile sexism, and heavy reliance on traditional gender stereotypes of women (Murnen, Wright, Kaluzny, 2002; Stotzer & MacCartney, 2016). Hypermasculine men surround themselves with other hypermasculine men, who are sexually aggressive, view women as sexual objects and conquests, and endorse **rape myths**, false beliefs about women and rape that justify rape (see Table 11.2) (Kilmartin, 2000; Riggio, Groskopf, Dennem-Tigner, & Garcia, 2015; Rozee & Koss, 2001).

Consumption of and sexual arousal in response to violent pornography are also associated with rape proclivity, rape callousness, and physical abuse of women (DeKeseredy & Schwartz, 1998; Malamuth, Hald, & Koss, 2012). Men who admit raping women show a strong preference for violent pornography, including simulated rapes (Carr & Van Deusen, 2004). Sexually aggressive men are also likely to abuse alcohol, using it as an excuse or motivator for sexual assault (Abbey, 1991, 2002; Berkowitz, 1992; Larimer, Lydum, Anderson, & Turner, 1999). Such men are also likely to use alcohol with victims in the hopes of incapacitating them or making sex more likely (Abbey, McAuslan, & Ross, 1998). Some scholars assert that college campuses, centers of higher learning, are particularly likely to create a **rape culture**, where hypermasculine men form peer groups

368 *Aggression*

that encourage hostile sexism, rape callousness, victim blaming, and alcohol abuse (Carr & Van Deusen, 2004; Sanday, 1996; Stotzer & MacCartney, 2016). One study of college-aged men found that one out of three indicated that they would rape someone if it were certain that they would not be caught (Stotzer & MacCartney, 2016).

Some men express concerns about false reports of rape, that women lie about being raped to cover up their promiscuity or because they regret a sexual encounter after the fact. Let's be clear about this: rape is seriously underreported (Rennison, 2002), and exaggerated claims of false reporting are another false belief promulgated by men to justify men's sexual assault and rape of women (Belknap, 2010). Men's claims of false reporting of rape are often based on the fact that women may delay reporting sexual assault for a variety of reasons (Archambault & Lonsway, 2006). A delay in filing a report is not unusual and is not evidence of a false claim. False reports of rape are actually very unlikely, occurring in about 2% of reports of rape (Heenan & Murray, 2006).

Violent Pornography

Violent pornography is just plain harmful. Violent pornography is not really about "rough" sex between consenting partners. Violent pornography depicts real physical and sexual abuse of women, the causing of pain, sometimes with women's apparent (dramatic or actual) lack of consent. Violent pornography is not just dangerous for men who are already aggressive. A classic laboratory paradigm exposes men to various kinds of films in an **experiment** (an experiment is the only research design allowing identification of causal relationships between **variables**). The men are first asked to write an essay, which is then later criticized by a female **confederate**. The men are then **randomly assigned** to view a neutral film (not sexual, not violent); a nonviolent pornographic film; or a violent pornographic film that may include simulated rape. After the film, the men engage in another task involving their administering electric shocks to that same insulting female confederate, the intensity and frequency of which the men control. Men exposed to the violent (but not the nonviolent) pornographic film administer significantly more and more intense electric shocks to the confederate (Donnerstein & Berkowitz, 1981). Exposure to violent pornography is also linked to increased acceptance of rape myths (Intons-Peterson, Roskos-Ewoldsen, Thomas, Shirley, & Blut, 1989; Malamuth & Check, 1981) and men's fantasizing about rape (Malamuth, 1981).

Other studies of violent pornography, including those involving exposure over longer periods of time on repeated occasions, show no effects on men's attitudes toward women, rape myth acceptance, or fantasizing about rape (Donnerstein, 1984; Linz, Donnerstein, & Penrod, 1988; Malamuth & Ceniti, 1986). However, an additional factor in the negative effects of violent pornography exposure is alcohol. Men who are intoxicated and exposed to violent pornography with expressions of pleasure by women report greater sexual arousal. Beliefs that women who are drinking are sexually vulnerable are also linked with sexual arousal in response to violent pornography (Davis et al., 2006a). Similar results are found with women who are intoxicated. Intoxicated women exposed to violent pornography were less likely to label depictions in the film as rape and reported greater rape myth acceptance than not intoxicated women (Davis et al., 2006b). Intoxication and alcohol abuse are linked with perpetration of sexual assault and being victimized sexually (Miczek et al., 1993).

Figures 11.5a and 11.5b Serial predators of women Ted Bundy (left) and Kenneth Bianchi (right)
Source: Everett Collection Inc/Alamy Stock Photo and Bettmann/Getty Images

Very violent men who repeatedly seek out women and children to victimize are called **serial sexual predators**. They are predators of women children. Well-known cases include those of Ted Bundy and the Hillside Stranglers, Kenneth Bianchi and Angelo Buono (see Figures 11.5a and 11.5b). These men identified women in public situations and, using deception and their greater physical strength (Bianchi and Buono worked together, two men versus one woman or girl), would abduct them, incapacitate them (through blows to the head, suffocation, strangling, binding), and take them elsewhere, to a place where they could sadistically torture her and rape her before murdering her. Ted Bundy enjoyed sexually stimulating himself using the mouths of the decapitated heads of his victims (that he kept in his basement refrigerator) (Rule, 2008). These behaviors are unbelievable to normal, caring human beings. These men, and many others like them, were sexually stimulated by violence. At some crucial developmental point, they formed an association between violence and sexual arousal and pleasure. Ted Bundy reportedly enjoyed "True Detective" magazine as a boy, a magazine that often portrayed women as sexy and afraid, threatened with violence, bound with rope on the cover. Richard Ramirez, the Night Stalker, who terrorized Southern California by breaking into homes, murdering men and then raping women (before usually murdering them as well), was exposed to graphic photographs of rape of women alive and dead by his cousin returning from the war in Vietnam (Carlo, 2016). The common tie among these sadistic serial killers is an exposure in childhood and adolescence to violent pornography, a linking of violence with sexual arousal. Children should never be exposed to violence tied to sexuality.

370 *Aggression*

Chapter Summary

Aggression is any act that is intended to cause physical or psychological harm to another person, and it has evolved within the human species because it serves adaptive purposes. Aggression has evolved in particular because it aids human beings in hunting and it aids men's sexual access to women. Biologically, men are evolved to fight; they are substantially larger and stronger than women and have evolved other physical features that make them more adept at fighting with and subduing others, particularly women who are substantially smaller and physically weaker. Men also possess a much larger quantity of testosterone on a daily basis, a hormone linked with aggressive behavior in humans and animals. Because of women's roles in reproduction (pregnancy, caring for infants) and men's evolution of size and strength, people associate qualities and traits that aid those roles with women and men in general. These ideas about social roles are then promulgated through numerous social institutions, including the media, religion, and parenting, promoting social dominance of men over women in cultures all over the world. Social institutions promote and reward male aggression while discouraging female aggression. Men's aggression toward women is particularly rewarded through religion and violent media including violent pornography. Men are higher in physical and verbal aggression than women at all ages, beginning in early childhood. Men are higher in intimate partner violence (IPV) perpetration and rape and sexual assault perpetration all over the world. Indeed, violence against girls and women is a global public health epidemic endangering lives. Men who are highest in physical and sexual aggression tend to be highly traditional, virulently sexist, and hypermasculine, a masculinity that endorses interpersonal violence, hostility toward women, and sexual callousness. Rape cultures emphasize male dominance and control of female sexuality, derogate women's sexuality, and endorse rape myths, false beliefs that justify sexual victimization of women.

Thoughtful Questions

- Explain the research findings on exposure to media violence and aggressive behavior in children and adults.
- Explain how sexual objectification of women in media is linked with aggression toward women.
- What are the short-term and long-term effects of exposure to media violence on aggression?
- What roles do parents play in socializing aggressive behavior?
- How are hypermasculinity and hyperfemininity linked with aggression?
- Explain the intergenerational transmission of IPV.
- Compare and contrast feminist and family conflict explanations of IPV.
- Explain how men's traditionality and gender role stress underlie IPV.
- What are risk factors for women as victims of IPV and men as perpetrators of IPV? Why do you think these are risk factors?
- Explain how traditional religions are linked with misogyny.
- Explain hypermasculinity and rape proclivity.
- Explain how violent pornography is linked to violence against women.
- Explain the idea of a rape culture, both in terms of cultural ideology defining a particular country and social norms that arise in groups of men on college campuses.

Glossary

Abrahamic religions: religions based on the Creation story of Adam and Eve and the story of Abraham and his offspring; includes Judaism, Christianity, and Islam.

Accommodation: a cognitive process where existing schemas are changed in response to new information that does not fit with the initial schema. For example, changing one's traditional ideas about women in response to a woman who does not fit traditional ideas or roles. Requires cognitive effort.

Aggression: any act that is intended to cause physical or psychological harm to another person.

Assimilation: a cognitive process where new stimuli or information are altered to fit with pre-existing schemas. For example, a woman may be perceived as being more similar to traditional female gender roles than she actually is. A low effort process.

Attributions: explanations for the causes of events that people form to enhance feelings of understanding; explanations formed to make sense of the world.

Belief in a just world: the idea that the world is just, that good things happen to good people and bad things happen to bad people.

Benevolent sexism: warm feelings toward women that involve beliefs about women as weak, inferior, childlike, and in need of men's protection. Benevolent sexism involves protective paternalism (fatherly, protective feelings toward women).

Blaming the victim: a cognitive bias (a cognitive habit or preference) that involves blaming victims of crime rather than perpetrators of crime.

Collectivism: a cultural dimension involving valuing group outcomes over individual outcomes; individual needs and goals are subsumed to those of the group (contrasted with individualism). Eastern cultures are highly collectivistic.

"Common couple violence": intimate partner violence (IPV) that occurs between married or committed couples that is not highly injurious to either and is not based on coercion or oppression.

Confederate: a person working with a researcher who is pretending to be a research participant.

Desensitization: the decrease in arousal and empathic feelings in response to violence that occurs after repeated exposure to violence.

Effect size: an indicator of the strength of the relationship between variables. Cohen's d is an indicator of effect size, representing the difference between group means in standard deviation units. A Cohen's d of .20 is considered small; .50 is considered moderate; .80 is considered large.

Egalitarian: oriented toward equality. Egalitarian societies emphasize equality between women and men, ethnic and racial groups, sexual orientations, and other groups.

Elaboration: deep cognitive processing of information; understanding new information by comparing it to existing information; thorough, effortful, careful, deliberate cognitive processing.

Evolutionary theories: theories that emphasize the evolution of human qualities over time as they serve to maximize the ability to survive and reproduce in a particular environment. For example, evolutionary theories explain intimate partner violence (IPV) as resulting from men's need to dominate and control women for sexual access.

Experiment: a method of research where an experimenter systematically alters one or more variables to determine whether such changes affect some aspect of behavior; the only research design allowing determination of cause and effect relationships between variables.

372   *Aggression*

Family conflict perspective: a perspective on intimate partner violence (IPV) that considers IPV to be not unusual between couples, symmetrical by gender, and low in violence.

Femininity: the **stereotype** of what it means to be female; the traits, qualities, and attributes that we associate with women as a social group. Traditional qualities include emotional, understanding, gentle, tender-hearted, submissive.

Feminist theories of IPV: explanations for intimate partner violence which focus on male perpetration of violence against women because of their greater physical size and strength and as a way to maintain patriarchy through physical oppression of women. **Feminism** seeks and promotes equality between women and men.

Heteronormative social pressure: social pressures to comply with **heteronormativity** (heterosexuality as normal and preferred). For example, when homosexual people are pressured to marry someone of the opposite sex or have children.

Homonegativity: negative feelings toward people who are homosexual or not heterosexual.

Honor killings: killing female relatives who are suspected of having sex before marriage, committing adultery, or who are raped, which involves sex without marriage. In highly traditional cultures, women who have sex outside of marriage, even by rape, bring shame and dishonor to her family; killing her is believed to restore honor to the family.

Hostile attribution bias: a cognitive tendency to believe that other people feel hostility toward oneself and are acting with hostile intent. Individuals with hostile attribution bias are interpersonally hostile and aggressive.

Hostile sexism: competitive, angry, and fearful feelings toward women that involve beliefs about women as promiscuous, manipulative, and attempting to control men, especially through sex or promoting women as equal (**feminism**).

Hyperfemininity: extreme femininity involving endorsement of traditional female qualities (submissiveness to men, quietness, passivity, caretaking of others).

Hypermasculinity: extreme masculinity including endorsement of violence, callous sexual attitudes toward women, and risk-taking.

Individualism: a cultural dimension involving valuing personal achievement and strengths; individual needs and goals are elevated and valued more than those of the group (contrasted with **collectivism**). Western cultures are highly individualistic.

Internalized homonegativity: negative feelings about the self for being homosexual or not heterosexual.

Intimate partner violence (IPV): violence that occurs between intimate partners (aka **domestic violence**). Includes physical, psychological, emotional, and sexual abuse, as well as behaviors like stalking.

Legitimizing myths: false beliefs about a group that justify their continued oppression.

Masculine gender role stress: feelings of intense pressure to fulfill traditional norms of masculinity that some men experience.

Masculinity: the **stereotype** of what it means to be male; the traits, qualities, and attributes that we associate with men as a social group. Traditional qualities include dominant, decisive, tough, strong, powerful, unemotional.

Meta-analysis: a higher order analysis; a scientific investigation involving the examination of the results of many different studies, how results vary by study design or measurement techniques, and estimations of an overall relationship between variables.

Mirror neurons: neurons that fire when watching others engaged in particular behaviors. For example, mirror neurons make one feel hungry when watching other people eat.

Misogyny: hatred of women. A **misogynist** is a person who hates women.

Observational learning: learning through observation of other people behaving; imitative learning.

Patriarchy: a societal structure where men are in charge of all or most social institutions and maintain the majority of wealth, status, and power in society.

Precarious manhood: masculinity that is easily threatened. When men have precarious manhood, they react more negatively and aggressively to threats to self-concept.

Priming: the activation of a behavior through exposure to related stimuli. For example, aggressive behavior may be primed or activated by observing aggressive objects (e.g., guns) or other people behaving aggressively.

Random assignment: assigning participants to treatment and control groups such that each participant has an equal likelihood of being assigned to either condition. Random assignment creates equivalent groups and is the defining feature of experimentation.

Rape: "The penetration, no matter how slight, of the vagina or anus with any body part or object, or oral penetration by a sex organ of another person, without the consent of the victim" (United States Department of Justice, 2012).

Rape culture: a social environment promoting male dominance of women, violence toward women, hostile sexism, sexual callousness, and rape myth acceptance.

Rape myths: false beliefs about women and rape that men use to justify sexual aggression against women.

Schemas: repeatedly accessed patterns of thought about some stimulus that are built up from experience and that guide the processing of new information. **Stereotypes** and **scripts** are types of schemas.

Scripts: schemas for particular sequences of events (e.g., the first date script).

Serial sexual predators: very violent men who repeatedly seek out women, men, and children to victimize.

Sexual assault: "any nonconsensual sexual act proscribed by Federal, tribal, or State law, including when the victim lacks capacity to consent" (United States Department of Justice, 2018).

Sexual prejudice: negative emotions (anger, hatred, fear) directed toward people who are not heterosexual or people who are transgender.

Shari'a law: set of religious principles involved in Islamic culture. Shari'a law is highly **patriarchal**.

Situational factors: circumstances, features of the external environment and the immediate situation that may affect individual behavior.

Social dominance theory: an explanation for social inequality and injustice that focuses on how the powerful use legitimizing myths to maintain their disproportionate share of society's resources by oppressing subordinate groups. For example, according to this approach, men use their greater physical size and strength, and false beliefs about women's inferiority, to maintain patriarchal social structures.

Social role theory: an explanation for gender roles, norms, and stereotypes that emphasizes physical differences and differences in reproductive roles for women and men evolving into psychological expectations for typical and desirable qualities of women and men.

Stalking: A pattern of repeated, unwanted attention and contact that causes fear or concern for one's own safety or the safety of someone else (e.g., family member, close friend).

Stereotypes: schemas (mental knowledge structures) containing ideas about the typical traits, qualities, and attributes of members of a social group (e.g., **femininity** is a stereotype of what women are like, **masculinity** is a stereotype of what men are like).

Testosterone: a male hormone (androgen) associated with male sexual development, sexual behavior, and aggression.

Threat theory: an explanation of male aggression and violence that focuses on nontraditional gender behaviors as threatening to male dominance and superiority.

Variable: any measurable characteristic that can take on more than one value.

References

Abbey, A. (1991). Acquaintance rape and alcohol consumption on college campuses: How are they linked? *Journal of American College Health, 39*, 165-169.

Abbey, A. (2002). Alcohol-related sexual assault: A common problem among college students. *Journal of Studies on Alcohol* (Suppl 14), 118-128.

Abbey, A., McAuslan, P., & Ross, L. T. (1998). Sexual assault perpetration by college men: The role of alcohol, misperception of sexual intent, and sexual beliefs and experiences. *Journal of Social and Clinical Psychology, 17*(2), 167-195.

Abedi, D. (2016). As long as there is sharia law, women will not have human rights. Huff Post, September 12. www.huffingtonpost.in/deeba-abedi/as-long-as-there-is-sharia-law-women-will-not-have-human-rights_a_21620496/.

Abiad N. (2008). *Sharia, Muslim states and international human rights treaty obligations.* London: British Institute of International and Comparative Law.

Abramsky, T., Watts, C. H., Garcia-Moreno, C., Devries, K., Kiss, L., Ellsberg, M., ..., Heise, L. (2011). What factors are associated with recent intimate partner violence? Findings from the WHO multi-country study on women's health and domestic violence. *BMC Public Health 11*, 109. https://doi.org/10.1186/1471-2458-11-109.

Akbar, N. (2013). No justice for rape victims in Afghanistan. *UN Dispatch*, July 26. www.undispatch.com/no-justice-for-rape-victims-in-afghanistan/.

Allee, W. C., Collias, N. E., & Lutherman, C. Z. (1939). Modification of the social order in flocks of hens by injection of testosterone propionate. *Physiological Zoology, 12*, 412-440.

Allen, C. T., Swan, S. C., & Raghavan, C. (2009). Gender symmetry, sexism, and intimate partner violence. *Journal of Interpersonal Violence, 24*(11), 1816-1834. doi.org/10.1177/0886260508325496.

American Medical Association (1995). *Sexual assault in America.* Chicago: AMA.

Amnesty International (2008). *Rape and sexual violence human rights law and standards in the International Criminal Court.* London: Amnesty International Publications. www.amnesty.org/download/Documents/32000/ior530012011en.

Anderson, C. A. (2004). An update on the effects of violent video games. *Journal of Adolescence, 27*, 113-122.

Anderson, C. A., Berkowitz, L., Donnerstein, E., Huesmann, L. R., Johnson, J., Linz, D., ..., Wartella, E. (2003). The influence of media violence on youth. *Psychological Science in the Public Interest, 4*, 81-110.

Anderson, C. A., & Bushman, B. J. (2001). Effects of violent video games on aggressive behavior, aggressive cognition, aggressive affect, physiological arousal, and prosocial behavior: A metaanalytic review of the scientific literature. *Psychological Science, 12*, 353-359.

Anderson, C. A., & Bushman, B. J. (2002). The effects of media violence on society. *Science, 295*(5564), 2377-2379. doi:10.1126/science.1070765.

Anderson, C. A., Gentile, D. A., & Buckley, K. E. (2007). *Violent video game effects on children and adolescents: Theory, research, and public policy.* New York: Oxford University Press.

Anderson, C. A., Shibuya, A., Ihori, N., Swing, E. L., Bushman, B. J., Sakamoto, A., ..., Saleem, M. (2010). Violent video game effects on aggression, empathy, and prosocial behavior in Eastern and Western countries: A meta-analytic review. *Psychological Bulletin, 136*(2), 151-173.

Anderson, G. (1992). The Garden of Eden and sexuality in early Judaism. In Eilberg-Schwartz, H. (Ed.), *People of the body: Jews and Judaism from an embodied perspective* (pp. 47-68). New York: State University of New York Press.

Archambault, J., & Lonsway, K. A. (2006). *Dynamics of sexual assault: What does sexual assault really look like?* (Rev. ed. 2008). End Violence Against Women International's On-Line Training Institute. http://evaw-intl.org/onlinetraining.aspx.

Archer, J. (1988). *The behavioural biology of aggression*. Cambridge: Cambridge University Press.

Archer, J. (1994). Introduction. In Archer, J. (Ed.), *Male violence* (pp. 1-20). London and New York: Routledge.

Archer, J. (2000). Sex differences in aggression between heterosexual partners: A meta-analytic review. *Psychological Bulletin* 126(5), 651-680. doi:10.1037MJ033-2909.I26.5.651.

Archer, J. (2002). Sex differences in physically aggressive acts between heterosexual partners: A meta-analytic review. *Aggression and Violent Behavior, 7*(4), 313-351.

Archer, J. (2004). Sex differences in aggression in real-world settings: A meta-analytic review. *Review of General Psychology, 8*, 291÷322.

Archer, J. (2006). Testosterone and human aggression: An evaluation of the challenge hypothesis. *Neuroscience and Biobehavioral Reviews, 30*(3), 319-345. doi:10.1016/j.neubiorev.2004.12.007.

Ariffin, R. E. (1997). *Shame, secrecy and silence: Study of rape in Penang*. Penang: Women's Crisis Centre.

Armstrong, A. (1998). *Culture and choice: Lessons from survivors of gender violence in Zimbabwe*. Harare: Violence Against Women in Zimbabwe Research Project.

Ashare, R. L., Weinberger, A. H., McKee, S. A., & Sullivan, T. P. (2011). The role of smoking expectancies in the relationship between PTSD symptoms and smoking behavior among women exposed to intimate partner violence. *Addictive Behaviors, 36*, 1333-1336. http://dx.doi.org/10.1016/j.addbeh.2011.07.022.

Balsam, K. F., & Szymanski, D. M. (2005). Relationship quality and domestic violence in women's same-sex relationships: The role of minority stress. *Psychology of Women Quarterly, 29*, 258-269. doi:10.1111/j.1471-6402.2005.00220.x.

Bandura, A. (1997). *Social learning theory*. New York: Prentice-Hall.

Bandura, A., Ross, D., & Ross, S. A. (1963). Imitation of film-mediated aggressive models. *Journal of Abnormal and Social Psychology, 66*, 3-11.

Bargh, J. A., & Pietromonaco, P. (1982). Automatic information processing and social perception: The influence of trait information presented outside of conscious awareness on impression formation. *Journal of Personality and Social Psychology, 43*(3), 437-449.

Barrier, P. A. (1998). Domestic violence. *Mayo Clinic Proceedings, 73*, 271-274.

Bawah, A. A. et al. (1999). Women's fears and men's anxieties: The impact of family planning on gender relations in northern Ghana. *Studies in Family Planning, 30*, 54-66.

Beeman, A. E. (1947). The effect of male hormone on aggressive behavior in mice. *Physiological Zoology, 20*, 373-405.

Belknap, J. (2010). Rape: Too hard to report and too easy to discredit victims. *Violence Against Women, 16*, 1335-1344. doi:10.1177/1077801210387749.

Bender, E. (2004). PTSD, other disorders evident in kids who witness domestic violence. *Psychiatric News, 39*, 14-15.

Bennett, L., Manderson, L., & Astbury, J. (2000). *Mapping a global pandemic: Review of current literature on rape, sexual assault and sexual harassment of women*. Melbourne: University of Melbourne.

Bensley, I., Van Eenwyk, J., & Wynkoop Simmons, K. (2003). Childhood family violence history and women's risk for intimate partner violence and poor health. *American Journal of Preventative Medicine, 25*, 38-44.

Bergeron, N., & Schneider, B. H. (2005). Explaining cross-national differences in peer-directed aggression: A quantitative synthesis. *Aggressive Behavior, 31*, 116-137.

Berkowitz, A. (1992). College men as perpetrators of acquaintance rape and sexual assault: A review of recent research. *Journal of American College Health, 40*, 175-181.

Berkowitz, L. (1993). *Aggression: Its causes, consequences, and control*. Boston: McGraw-Hill.

Berkowitz, L., & LePage, A. (1967). Weapons as aggression-eliciting stimuli. *Journal of Personality and Social Psychology, 7*, 202-207.

Bernard, P., Gervais, S. J., Allen, J., Campomizzi, S., & Klein, O. (2012). Integrating sexual objectification with object versus person recognition: The sexualized-body-inversion hypothesis. *Psychological Science, 23*, 469-471. http://dx.doi.org/10 .1177/0956797611434748.

Bernard, P., Gervais, S., Allen, J., Campomizzi, S., & Klein, O. (2015). Body parts reduction and self objectification in the objectification of sexualized bodies. *International Review of Social Psychology, 28*, 39-61.

Bernard, P., Legrand, S., & Klein, O. (2018). From bodies to blame: Exposure to sexually objectifying media increases tolerance toward sexual harassment. *Psychology of Popular Media Culture, 7*(2), 99-112. https://doi.org/10.1037/ppm0000114.

Bettencourt, A. A., & Kernahan, C. (1997). A meta-analysis of aggression in the presence of violent cues: Effects of gender differences and aversive provocations. *Aggressive Behavior, 23*, 447-456.

Bevan, F., & Higgins, D. J. (2002). Is domestic violence learned? The contribution of five forms of child maltreatment to men's violence and adjustment. *Journal of Family Violence, 17*, 223-245.

Black, M. C. (2011). Intimate partner violence and adverse health consequences: Implications for clinicians. *American Journal of Lifestyle Medicine, 5*(5), 428-439.

Black, M. C., Basile, K. C., Breiding, M. J., Smith, S. G., Walters, M. L., Merrick, M. T., & Stevens, M. R. (2011). The National Intimate Partner and Sexual Violence Survey (NISVS): 2010 summary report. Centers for Disease Control and Prevention, National Center for Injury Prevention and Control. www.cdc.gov/ViolencePrevention/pdf/NISVS_Report2010-a.

Blair, K. L., & Hoskin, R. A. (2015). Experiences of femme identity: Coming out, invisibility and femmephobia. *Psychology & Sexuality, 6*(3), 229-244. |https://doi.org/10.1080/19419899.2014.921860.

Block, J., Strangio, C., & Esseks, J. (2018). Breaking down Trump's trans military ban. March 30. www.aclu.org/blog/lgbt-rights/transgender-rights/breaking-down-trumps-trans-military-ban.

Boney-McCoy, S., and Finkelhor, D. (1995). Psychosocial sequelae of violent victimization in a national youth sample. *Journal of Consulting and Clinical Psychology, 63*, 726-736.

Bos, P. A., Panksepp, J., Bluthé, R.-M., & van Honk, J. (2012). Acute effects of steroid hormones and neuropeptides on human social-emotional behavior: A review of single administration studies. *Frontiers in Neuroendocrinology, 33*(1), 17-35.

Bosson, J. K., Vandello, J. A., Burnaford, R. M., Weaver, J. R., & Wasti, S. A. (2009). Precarious manhood and displays of physical aggression. *Personality and Social Psychology Bulletin, 35*(5), 623-634.

Boyarin, D. (1992). The great fat massacre: Sex, death, and the grotesque body in the Talmud. In Eilberg-Schwartz, H. (Ed.), *People of the body: Jews and Judaism from an embodied perspective* (pp. 69-100). New York: State University of New York Press.

Breiding, M. J., Black, M. C., & Ryan, G. W. (2008). Chronic disease and health risk behaviors associated with intimate partner violence - 18 U.S. states/territories, 2005. *Annals of Epidemiology, 18*, 538-544.

British Broadcasting Corporation (2014). Pakistani woman stoned to death by family. May 27. www.bbc.com/news/av/world-asia-27594425/pakistani-woman-stoned-to-death-by-family.

British Broadcasting Corporation (2015). Afghan woman accused of adultery is stoned to death. November 3. www.bbc.com/news/world-asia-34714205.

Bronner, L. L. (1993). From veil to wig: Jewish women's hair covering. *Judaism, 42*(4), 465-477.

Bruce, D. B., Sestir, M. A., & Davis, E. B. (2005). Correlates and consequences of exposure to video game violence: Hostile personality, empathy, and aggressive behavior. *Personality and Social Psychology Bulletin, 31*(11), 1573-1586. https://doi.org/10.1177/0146167205277205.

Buga, G. A., Amoko, D. H., & Ncayiyana, D. J. (1996). Sexual behaviour, contraceptive practice and reproductive health among school adolescents in rural Transkei. *South African Medical Journal, 86*, 523-527.

Bulanda, R. E. (2004). Paternal involvement with children: The influence of gender ideologies. *Journal of Marriage and Family, 66*(1), 40-45. https://doi.org/10.1111/j.0022-2455.2004.00003.x.

Bureau of Justice Statistics (2016). www.bjs.gov/index.cfm?ty=dcdetail&iid=245.

Burnham, T. C., Chapman, J. F., Gray, P. B., McIntyre, M. H., Lipson, S. F., & Ellison, P. T. (2003). Men in committed, romantic relationships have lower testosterone. *Hormones and Behavior, 44*, 119-122.

Bushman, B. J., & Anderson, C. A. (2001). Media violence and the American public: Scientific facts versus media misinformation. *American Psychologist, 56*, 477-489.

Bushman, B. J., & Huesmann, L. R. (2006). Short-term and long-term effects of violent media on aggression in children and adults. *Archives of Pediatrics & Adolescent Medicine, 160*(4), 348-352. doi:10.1001/archpedi.160.4.348.

Buss, D. M., & Shackelford, T. K. (1997). Human aggression in evolutionary psychological perspective. *Clinical Psychology Review, 17*(6), 605-619.

Butler, D., & Geis, F. L. (1990). Nonverbal affect responses to male and female leaders: Implications for leadership evaluations. *Journal of Personality and Social Psychology, 58*(1), 48-59.

Cairns, R. B., Cairns, B. D., Neckerman, H. J., Ferguson, L. L., & Gariépy, J.-L. (1989). Growth and aggression: I. Childhood to early adolescence. *Developmental Psychology, 25*(2), 320-330. https://doi.org/10.1037/0012-1649.25.2.320.

Campbell, A. (2002). *A mind of her own: The evolutionary psychology of women*. New York: Oxford University Press.

Campbell, C., & Schwarz, D. F. (1996). Prevalence and impact of exposure to interpersonal violence among suburban and urban middle school students. *Pediatrics, 98*, 396-402.

Cannon, E. A., Bonomi, A. E., Anderson, M. L., & Rivara, F. P. (2009). The intergenerational transmission of witnessing intimate partner violence. *Archives of Pediatrics & Adolescent Medicine, 163*(8), 706-708.

Carlo, G., Raffaelli, M., Laible, D. J., & Meyer, K. A. (1999). Why are girls less physically aggressive than boys? Personality and parenting mediators of physical aggression. *Sex Roles, 40*(9-10), 711-729.

Carlo, P. (2016). *The night stalker: The life and crimes of Richard Ramirez*. New York: Kensington.

Carmo, R., Grams, A., & Magalhães, T. (2011). Men as victims of intimate partner violence. *Journal of Forensic and Legal Medicine, 18*(8), 355-359.

Carnagey, N. L, Anderson, C. A., & Bushman, B. J. (2007). The effect of video game violence on physiological desensitization to real-life violence. *Journal of Experimental Social Psychology, 43*, 489-496.

Carr, J. L., & VanDeusen, K. M. (2004). Risk factors for male sexual aggression on college campuses. *Journal of Family Violence, 19*(5), 279-289.

Catalano, S., Smith, E., Snyder, H., & Rand, M. (2009). Selected findings: Female victims of violence. Washington, DC: U.S. Department of Justice, Bureau of Justice Statistics. www.bjs.gov/content/pub/pdf/fvv.

Centers for Disease Control and Prevention (2003). Costs of intimate partner violence against women in the United States. Atlanta, GA: CDC, National Center for Injury Prevention and Control. www.cdc.gov/violenceprevention/intimatepartnerviolence/consequences.html.

Centers for Disease Control and Prevention (2012). Violence against women in Latin America and the Caribbean: A comparative analysis of population-based data from 12 countries. https://stacks.cdc.gov/view/cdc/22295.

Centers for Disease Control & Prevention (2015). Intimate partner violence surveillance uniform definitions and recommended data elements. www.cdc.gov/violenceprevention/pdf/ipv/intimatepartnerviolence.

Chaiken, S., Liberman, A., & Eagly, A. H. (1989). Heuristic and systematic information processing within and beyond the persuasion context. In Uleman, J. S., & Bargh, J. A. (Eds.), *Unintended thought.* New York: Guilford Press, pp. 212-252.

Chan, K. L. (2011). Gender differences in self-reports of intimate partner violence: A review. *Aggression and Violent Behavior, 16*(2), 167-175.

Chang, L.-Y., Wang, M.-Y., & Tsai, P.-S. (2016). Neighborhood disadvantage and physical aggression in children and adolescents: A systematic review and meta-analysis of multilevel studies. *Aggressive Behavior, 42*(5), 441-454.

Charles, P., & Perreira, K. M. (2007). Intimate partner violence during pregnancy and 1-year post-partum. *Journal of Family Violence, 22*, 609-619. doi:10.1007/s10896-007-9112-0.

Choi, Y. J. (2015). Religion as coping with IPV: Korean American clergy practices regarding intimate partner violence: Roadblock or support for battered women? *Journal of Family Violence, 30*(3), 293-302.

Cikara, M., Eberhardt, J. L., & Fiske, S. T. (2011). From agents to objects: Sexist attitudes and neural responses to sexualized targets. *Journal of Cognitive Neuroscience, 23*, 540-551. http://dx.doi.org/ 10.1162/jocn.2010.21497.

Civile, C., & Obhi, S. S. (2015). Power, objectification, and recognition of sexualized women and men. *Psychology of Women Quarterly.* Advance online publication. http://dx.doi.org/10.1177/ 0361684315604820.

Claes, J. A., & Rosentlial, D. M. (1990). Men who batter: A study in power. *Journal of Family Violence, 5*, 215-224.

Cline, V. B., Croft, R. G., & Courrier, S. (1973). Desensitization of children to television violence. *Journal of Personality and Social Psychology, 27*, 360-365.

Cohen, J. (1988). *Statistical power analysis for the behavioral sciences* (2nd ed.). Hillsdale, NJ: Erlbaum.

Coie, J. D., & Dodge, K. A. (1998). Aggression and antisocial behavior. In Damon, W. (Series Ed.), & Eisenberg, N. (Vol. Ed.), *Handbook of child psychology, Vol.3, Social, emotional and personality development* (5th ed.). New York: Wiley.

Comstock, G., & Scharrer, E. (2007). *Media and the American child.* San Diego: Academic Press.

Cooley-Quille, M. R., Turner, S. M., and Beidel, D. C. (1995). Emotional impact of children's exposure to community violence: A preliminary study. *Journal of the American Academy of Child & Adolescent Psychiatry, 34*, 1362-1368.

Coxell, A., King, M. B., Mezey, G. C., & Kell, P. (2000). Sexual molestation of men: Interviews with 224 men attending a genitourinary medicine service. *International Journal of STD and AIDS, 11*, 574-578.

Crick, N. R., & Grotpeter, J. K. (1995). Relational aggression, gender, and social-psychological adjustment. *Child Development, 66*, 710-722.

Cuddy, A. J.C., Wolf, E. B., Glick, P., Crotty, S., Chong, J., & Norton, M. I. (2015). Men as cultural ideals: Cultural values moderate gender stereotype content. *Journal of Personality and Social Psychology, 109*(4), 622-635.

Daly, M., & Wilson, M. I. (1988). *Homicide.* Hawthorne, NY: Aldine.

Daoud, N., Urquia, M. L., O'Campo, P., Heaman, M., Janssen, P. A., Smylie, J., & Thiessen, K. (2012). Prevalence of abuse and violence before, during, and after pregnancy in a national sample of Canadian women. *American Journal of Public Health, 102*(10). doi:10.2105/AJPH.2012.300843.

David, F., & Chin, F. (1998). *Economic and psychosocial influences of family planning on the lives of women in Western Visayas.* Iloilo City: Central Philippines University and Family Health International.

Davies, M. (2002). Male sexual assault victims: A selective review of the literature and implications for support services. *Aggression and Violent Behavior, 7*, 203-214.

Davis, K. C., Norris, J., George, W. H., Martell, J., & Heiman, J. R. (2006a). Men's likelihood of sexual aggression: The influence of alcohol, sexual arousal, and violent pornography. *Aggressive Behavior, 32*, 581-589.

Davis, K. C., Norris, J., George, W. H., Martell, J., & Heiman, J. R. (2006b). Rape-myth congruent beliefs in women resulting from exposure to violent pornography: Effects of alcohol and sexual arousal. *Journal of Interpersonal Violence, 21*(9), 1208-1223.

DeKeseredy, W. S., Saunders, D. G., Schwartz, M. D., & Alvi, S. (1997). The meanings and motives for women's use of violence in Canadian college dating relationships: Results from a national survey. *Sociological Spectrum, 17*, 199-222. https://doi.org/10.1080/02732173.1997.9982160.

DeKeseredy, W., & Schwartz, M. (1998). *Women abuse on campus: Results from the Canadian National Survey.* Thousand Oaks, CA: Sage.

Der, G., & Deary, I. (2006). Age and sex differences in reaction time in adulthood: Results from the United Kingdom Health and Lifestyle Survey. *Psychology and Aging, 21*(1), 62-73.

Dietz, T. L. (1998). An examination of violence and gender role portrayals in video games: Implications for gender socialization and aggressive behavior. *Sex Roles, 38*, 425-442.

Dill, K. E., & Thill, K. P. (2007). Video game characters and the socialization of gender roles: Young people's perceptions mirror sexist media depictions. *Sex Roles, 57*, 851-864. http://dx.doi.org/10 .1007/s11199-007-9278-1.

Dobash, R. E., & Dobash, R. P. (1980). *Violence against wives: A case against the patriarchy.* London: Open Books.

Dobash, R. P., Dobash, R. E., Wilson, M., & Daly, M. (1992). The myth of sexual symmetry in marital violence. *Social Problems, 39*, 71-91.

Dodge, K. A. (1985). Attributional bias in aggressive children. In Kendall, P. C. (Ed.), *Advances in cognitive-behavioral research and therapy*, Vol. 4. San Diego: Academic Press, pp. 73-110.

Dodge, K. A. Pettit, G. S., & Bates, J. E. (1995). Social information-processing patterns partially mediate the effect of early physical abuse on later conduct problems. *Journal of Abnormal Psychology, 104*, 632-643.

Donnerstein, E. (1984). Pornography: Its effect on violence against women. In Malamuth, N. M., & Donnerstein, E. (Eds.), *Pornography and sexual aggression*. San Diego: Academic Press, pp. 53-81.

Donnerstein, E., & Berkowitz, L. (1981). Victim reactions in aggressive erotic films as a factor in violence against women. *Journal of Personality and Social Psychology, 41*, 710-724.

Duncan, L., Peterson, B., & Winter, D. (1997). Authoritarianism and gender roles: Toward a psychological analysis of hegemonic relationships. *Personality and Social Psychology Bulletin, 23*, 41-49. doi:10.1177/0146167297231005.

Dutton, D. G., Nicholls, T. L., & Spidel, A. (2005). Female perpetrators of intimate abuse. *Journal of Offender Rehabilitation, 41*(4), 1e31.

Duvvury, N., Callan, A., Carney, P., & Raghavendra, S. (2013). Intimate partner violence: Economic costs and implications for growth and development. Women's Voice, Agency, & Participation Research Series No. 3. The World Bank. https://openknowledge.worldbank.org/bitstream/handle/10986/16697/825320WP0Intim00Box379862B00PUBLIC0.

Eagly, A. H. (1987). *Sex differences in social behavior: A social role interpretation.* Hillsdale, NJ: Erlbaum.

Eagly, A. H., & Steffen, V. J. (1986). Gender and aggressive behavior: A meta-analytic review of the social psychological literature. *Psychological Bulletin, 100*(3), 309-330. doi:10.1037/0033-2909.100.3.309.

Eagly, A. H., & Wood, W. (1999). The origins of sex differences in human behavior: Evolved dispositions versus social roles. *American Psychologist, 54*, 408-423.

Edwards, K. M., & Sylaska, K. M. (2013). The perpetration of intimate partner violence among LGBTQ college youth: The role of minority stress. *Journal of Youth and Adolescence, 42*, 1721-1731. doi:10.1007/s10964-012-9880-6.

Eisenberg, N., & Lennon, R. (1983). Sex differences in empathy and related capacities. *Psychological Bulletin, 94*, 100-131.

Eisler, R. M. (1995). The relationship between masculine gender role stress and men's health risk: The validation of a construct. In Levant R. F., & Pollack, W. S. (Eds.), *A new psychology of men* (pp. 207-228). New York: Basic Books.

Eisler, R. M., Franchina, J. J., Moore, T. M., Honeycutt, H., & Rhatigan, D. L. (2000). Masculine gender role stress and intimate abuse: Effects of gender relevance of the conflict situation on men's attributions and affective responses. *Psychology of Men and Masculinity, 1*, 30-36.

Elbagir, N., Leposo, L., & Mackintosh, E. (2018). Trump's ban on global abortion funding has led to more abortions. CNN. www.cnn.com/2018/05/24/health/trump-mexico-city-policy-abortion-ban-kenya-asequals-intl/index.html.

Elliott, D. M., Mok, D. S., & Briere, J. (2004). Adult sexual assault: Prevalence, symptomatology, and sex differences in the general population. *Journal of Traumatic Stress, 17*, 203-211.

Ellsberg, M. C. (1997). *Candies in hell: Domestic violence against women in Nicaragua*. Umeå, Sweden: Umeå University.

Ellsberg, M. C., Peña, R., Herrera, A., Liljestrand, J., & Winkvist, A. (1999). Wife abuse among women of childbearing age in Nicaragua. *American Journal of Public Health, 89*(2), 241-244. doi:10.2105/AJPH.89.2.241-10.2105/AJPH.89.2.241.

Ellsberg, M., Peña, R., Herrera, A., Liljestrand, J., & Winkvist, A. (2000). Candies in hell: women's experiences of violence in Nicaragua. *Social Science & Medicine, 51*(11), 1595-1610. https://doi.org/10.1016/S0277-9536(00)00056-3.

El-Zanaty, F., et al. (1995). *Egypt demographic and health survey 1995*. Calverton, MD: Macro International.

Entertainment Software Association (2018). US video game industry revenue reaches $36 billion in 2017. Press Release. www.theesa.com/article/us-video-game-industry-revenue-reaches-36-billion-2017/.

Ernst, A. A., Weiss, S. J., Del Castillo, C., Aagaard, J., Marvez-Valls, E., D'Angelo, J., ..., Coffman, B. (2007). Witnessing intimate partner violence as a child does not increase the likelihood of becoming an adult intimate partner violence victim. *Academic Emergency Medicine, 14*(5), 411-418.

Eron, L. D. (1986). Interventions to mitigate the psychological effects of media violence in aggressive behavior. *Journal of Social Issues, 42*, 155-169.

Eron, L. D., Huesmann, L. R., & Zelli, A. (1991). The role of parental variables in the learning of aggression. In Pepler, D. J., & Rubin, K. H. (Eds.), *The development and treatment of childhood aggression* (pp. 169-188). Hillsdale, NJ: Erlbaum.

Ewing, L. L., Gorski, R. A., Sbordone, R. J., Tyler, J. V., Desjardins, C., & Robaire, B. (1979). Testosterone-estradiol filled polydimethylsiloxane subdermal implants: Effect on fertility and masculine sexual and aggressive behavior of male rats. *Biology of Reproduction, 21*(4), 765-772. https://doi.org/10.1095/biolreprod21.4.765.

Ferguson, C. J. (2007a). Evidence for publication bias in video game violence effects literature: A meta-analytic review. *Aggression and Violent Behavior, 12*, 470-482.

Ferguson, C. J. (2007b). The good, the bad and the ugly: A meta-analytic review of positive and negative effects of violent video games. *Psychiatric Quarterly, 78*, 309-316.

Finneran, C., Chard, A., Sineath, C., Sullivan, P., & Stephenson, R. (2012). Intimate partner violence and social pressure among gay men in six countries. *Western Journal of Emergency Medicine, 13*(3), 260-271. doi:10.5811/westjem.2012.3.11779.

Fiske, S. T., & Taylor, S. E. (1991). *Social cognition* (2nd ed.). New York: McGraw-Hill.

Forbes, G., Zhang, X., Doroszewicz, K., & Haas, K. (2009). Relationships between individualism–collectivism, gender, and direct or indirect aggression: A study in China, Poland, and the US. *Aggressive Behavior, 35*(1), 24-30. https://doi.org/10.1002/ab.20292.

Fortune, M. M. (2001). Religious issues and violence against women. In Renzetti, C. M., Edleson, J. L., & Bergen, R. K. (Eds.), *Sourcebook on violence against women*. London: Sage, pp. 371-385.

Fox, J. A., & Zawitz, M. W. (1999). *Homicide trends in the United States*. Washington, DC: Bureau of Justice Statistics, United States Department of Justice.

Franchina, J. J., Eisler, R. M., & Moore, T. M. (2001). Masculine gender role stress and intimate abuse: Effects of masculine gender relevance of dating situations and female threat on men's attributions and affective responses. *Psychology of Men and Masculinity, 2*, 34-41.

Furnham, A. (2003). Belief in a just world: Research progress over the past decade. *Personality and Individual Differences, 34*, 795-817.

Futures without Violence (2018). IPV is a leading health issue. http://ipvhealth.org/health/ipv-health/?gclid=CjwKCAjwwJrbBRAoEiwAGA1B_elmO2QOKvxO5SikQ_deMgLLRwOLBizx1XeZKlarVSQV2WmtMes5PBo-CILgQAvD_BwE. Retrieved August 5, 2018.

Garcia-Moreno, C., Jansen, H. A. F. M., Ellsberg, M., Heise, L., & Watts, C. H. (2006). Prevalence of intimate partner violence: Findings from the WHO Multi-Country Study on Women's Health and Domestic Violence. *The Lancet, 368*, 1260-1269.

Garn, S., & Clark, L. (1953). The sex difference in the basal metabolic rate. *Child Development, 24*, 215-224.

Gassin, E. A. (2015). Eastern Orthodox Christianity and men's violence against women. In Johnson, A. J. (Ed.), *Religion and men's violence against women*. New York: Springer Science + Business Media, pp. 163-175.

Geen, R. G., & O'Neal, E. C. (1969). Activation of cue-elicited aggression by general arousal. *Journal of Personality and Social Psychology, 11*, 289-292.

Gentile, D. A. (Ed.) (2003). *Media violence and children*. Westport, CT: Praeger.

Gentile, D. A., Saleem, M., & Anderson, C. A. (2007). Public policy and the effects of media violence on children. *Social Issues and Policy Review, 1*, 15-61.

Gerbner, G., Gross, L., Morgan, M., & Signorielli, N. (1994). Growing up with television: The cultivation perspective. In Bryant, J., & Zillmann, D. (Eds.), *Media effects*. Hillsdale, NJ: Erlbaum, pp. 17-41.

Gervais, S. J., Vescio, T. K., & Allen, J. (2012). When are people interchangeable sexual objects? The effect of gender and body type on sexual fungibility. *The British Journal of Social Psychology, 51*, 499-513. http://dx.doi.org/10.1111/j .2044-8309.2010.02016.x.

Gilligan, C. (1982). *In a different voice: Psychological theory and women's development*. Cambridge, MA: Harvard University Press.

Goldberg-Looney, L. D., Perrin, P. B., Snipes, D. J., & Calton, J. M. (2016). Coping styles used by sexual minority men who experience intimate partner violence. *Journal of Clinical Nursing, 25*(23-24), 3687-3696.

Goldman, K. (2001). *Beyond the synagogue gallery: Finding a place for women in American Judaism*. Cambridge, MA: Harvard University Press.

Gonzalez, M. S. (1998). Domestic violence in Cuetzalan, Mexico: Some research questions and results. In *Third Annual Meeting of the International Research Network on Violence Against Women, Washington, DC, 9-11 January 1998*. Takoma Park, MD: Center for Health and Gender Equity, pp. 36-41.

Goodnight, B. L., Cook, S. L., Parrott, D. J., & Peterson, J. L. (2014). Effects of masculinity, authoritarianism, and prejudice on antigay aggression: A path analysis of gender-role enforcement. *Psychology of Men & Masculinity, 15*(4), 437-444.

Gorman-Smith, D., & Tolan, P. (1998). The role of exposure to community violence and developmental problems among inner-city youth. *Development and Psychopathology, 10*, 101-116.

Guerra, N. G., Huesmann, L. R., & Spindler, A. (2003). Community violence exposure, social cognition, and aggression among urban elementary school children. *Child Development, 74*(5), 1561-1576. https://doi.org/10.1111/1467-8624.00623.

Gursoy, R. (2010). Sex differences in relations of muscle power, lung function, and reaction time in athletes. *Perceptual and Motor Skills, 110*(3), 714-720.

Hakimi, M., Hayati, E. N., Marlinawati, V. U., Winkvist, A., & Ellsberg, M. C. (2001). *Silence for the sake of harmony: Domestic violence and women's health in Central Java, Indonesia*. Yogyakarta, Indonesia: Gadjah Mada University.

Heenan, M., & Murray, S. (2006). Study of reported rapes in Victoria 2000-2003: Summary research report. State of Victoria (Australia), Victoria Police. www.police.vic.gov.au/retrievemedia.asp?Media_ID=19462.

Heflick, N. A., Goldenberg, J. L., Cooper, D. P., & Puvia, E. (2011). From women to objects: Appearance focus, target gender, and perceptions of warmth, morality and competence. *Journal of Experimental Social Psychology, 47*, 572-581. http:// dx.doi.org/10.1016/j.jesp.2010.12.020.

Heise, L., Ellsberg, M., & Gottemoeller, M. (1999). *Ending violence against women*. Baltimore, MD: Johns Hopkins University School of Public Health.

Heise, L., & Garcia Moreno, C. (2002). Violence by intimate partners. In Krug, E. G., et al. (Eds.), *World report on violence and health*. Geneva: World Health Organization, pp. 87-121.

Hellmuth, J. C., Jaquier, V., Swan, S. C., & Sullivan, T. P. (2014). Elucidating posttraumatic stress symptom profiles and their correlates among women experiencing bidirectional intimate partner violence. *Journal of Clinical Psychology, 70*, 1008-1021. http://dx.doi.org/10.1002/jclp.22100.

Herek, G. (1986). On heterosexual masculinity: Some psychical consequences of the social construction of gender and sexuality. *American Behavioral Scientist, 29*, 563-577. doi:10.1177/000276486029005005.

Hines, D.A., Brown, J., & Dunning, E. (2007). Characteristics of callers to the domestic abuse helpline for men. *Journal of Family Violence, 22*, 63e72.

Hofstede, G. (1983). National cultures in four dimensions: A research-based theory of cultural differences among nations. *International Studies of Management & Organization, 13*(1-2), 46-74. doi:10.1080/00208825.1983.11656358.

Holmes, M. R. (2013). Aggressive behavior of children exposed to intimate partner violence: An examination of maternal mental health, maternal warmth and child maltreatment. *Child Abuse and Neglect, 37*, 520-530. doi:10.1016/j.chiabu.2012.12.006.

Homer, M. S. (1972). Toward an understanding of achievement-related conflicts in women. *Journal of Social Issues, 28*, 157-176.

Horon, I. L., & Cheng, D. (2001). Enhanced surveillance for pregnancy-associated mortality - Maryland, 1993-1998. *Journal of the American Medical Association, 285*(11), 1455-1459. doi:10.1001/jama.285.11.1455.

Huddy, L., & Terkildsen, N. (1993). Gender stereotypes and the perception of male and female candidates. *American Journal of Political Science, 37*(1), 119-147.

Huesmann, L. R. (1998). The role of social information processing and cognitive schema in the acquisition and maintenance of habitual aggressive behavior. In Geen, R. G., & Donnerstein E. (Eds.), *Human aggression: Theories, research, and implications for social policy*. San Diego, CA: Academic Press, pp. 73-109.

Hyde, J. S. (1984). How large are gender differences in aggression? A developmental meta-analysis. *Developmental Psychology, 20*, 722-736.

Hyde, J. S. (1986). Gender differences in aggression. In Hyde, J. S., & Linn, M. C. (Eds.), *The psychology of gender: Advances through meta-analysis* (pp. 51-66). Baltimore: Johns Hopkins University Press.

Intons-Peterson, M. J., Roskos-Ewoldsen, B., Thomas, L., Shirley, M., & Blut, D. (1989). Will educational materials reduce negative effects of exposure to sexual violence? *Journal of Social and Clinical Psychology, 8*(3), 256-275.

James, L., Brody, D., & Hamilton, Z. (2013). Risk factors for domestic violence during pregnancy: A meta-analytic review. *Violence and Victims, 28*(3), 359-380.

Jewkes, R., Penn-Kekana, L., Levin, J., Ratsaka, M., & Schrieber, M. (2001). The prevalence of physical, sexual and emotional violence against women in three South African provinces. *South African Medical Journal, 91*, 421-428.

Jewkes, R., Vundule, C., Maforah, F., & Jordaan, E. (2001). Relationship dynamics and teenage pregnancy in South Africa. *Social Science & Medicine, 52*(5), 733-744.

Johnson, H. (1996). *Dangerous domains: Violence against women in Canada*. Ontario: International Thomson Publishing.

Johnson, M. P. (1995). Patriarchal terrorism and common couple violence: Two forms of violence against women. *Journal of Marriage and the Family, 57*, 283-294.

Johnson, M. P., & Ferraro, K. J. (2000). Research on domestic violence in the 1990s: Making distinctions. *Journal of Marriage and the Family, 62*, 948-963.

Kalof, L. (1999). The effects of gender and music video imagery on sexual attitudes. *The Journal of Social Psychology, 139*, 378-385.

Keane, F. E., Young, S. M., Boyle, H. M., & Curry, K. M. (1995). Prior sexual assault reported by male attenders at a department of genitourinary medicine. *International Journal of STD and AIDS, 6*, 95-100.

Kheetan, D. (2017). Rape laws in the Middle East. *The Gazelle*, September 16. www.thegazelle.org/issue/118/opinion/middle-east-column.

Kilmartin, C. T. (2000). *Sexual assault in context: Teaching college men about gender*. Holmes Beach, FL: Learning Publications.

Kim, D., Pan, Y., & Park, H. S. (1998). High- versus low-context culture: A comparison of Chinese, Korean, and American cultures. *Psychology & Marketing, 15*(6), 507-521. https://doi.org/10.1002/(SICI)1520-6793(199809)15:6<507::AID-MAR2>3.0.CO;2-A.

Kirsh, S. J. (2006). *Children, adolescents, and media violence: A critical look at the research*. Thousand Oaks, CA: Sage.

Knight, G. P., Fabes, R. A., & Higgins, D. A. (1996). Concerns about drawing causal inferences from meta-analyses: An example in the study of gender differences in aggression. *Psychological Bulletin, 119*(3), 410-421. https://doi.org/10.1037/0033-2909.119.3.410.

Kornadt, H.-J. (1991). Aggression motive and its developmental conditions in Eastern and Western cultures. In Bleichrodt, N., & Drenth, P. J. D. (Eds.), *Contemporary issues in cross-cultural psychology*. Leiden, Netherlands: Swets & Zeitlinger, pp. 155-167.

Krahe, B., Schutze, S., Fritscher, I., & Waizenhofer, E. (2000). The prevalence of sexual aggression and victimization among homosexual men. *Journal of Sex Research, 37*(2), 142-150.

Kumagai, F., & Straus, M. A. (1983). Conflict resolution tactics in Japan, India, and the USA. *Journal of Comparative Family Studies, 14*, 377-392.

Lamborn, S. D., Mounts, N. S., Steinberg, L., & Dornbusch, S. M. (1991). Patterns of competence and adjustment among adolescents form authoritative, authoritarian, indulgent, and neglectful families. *Child Development, 62*, 1049-1065.

Lanis, K., & Covell, K. (1995). Images of women in advertisements: Effects on attitudes related to sexual aggression. *Sex Roles, 32*, 639-649. https://doi.org/10.1007/BF01544216.

Larimer, M. E., Lydum, A. R., Anderson, B. K., & Turner, A. P. (1999). Male and female recipients of unwanted sexual contact in a college student sample: Prevalence rates, alcohol use, and depression symptoms. *Sex Roles, 40*, 295-308.

Larrain, S. H. (1994). *Violencia puertas adentro: La mujer golpeada. (Violence behind closed doors: The battered women.)* Santiago: Editorial Universitaria.

382 *Aggression*

Lassek, W., & Gaulin, S. (2009). Costs and benefits of fat-free muscle mass in men: Relationship to mating success, dietary requirements and natural immunity. *Evolution and Human Behavior*, *30*, 322-328.

Linz, D. G., Donnerstein, E., & Penrod, S. (1988). Effects of long-term exposure to violent and sexually degrading depictions of women. *Journal of Personality and Social Psychology*, *55*(5), 758-768.

Löckenhoff, C. E., Chan, W., & McCrae R. R.(and 40+ others) (2014). Gender stereotypes of personality: Universal and accurate? *Journal of Cross-Cultural Psychology 45*(5), 675-694. doi:10.1177/0022022113520075.

Loomba-Albrecht, L., & Styne, D. M. (2009). Effect of puberty on body composition. *Current Opinion in Endocrinology Diabetes and Obesity*, *16*, 10-15.

Maccoby, E. E., & Jacklin, C. N. (1974). *The psychology of sex differences*. Stanford, CA: Stanford University Press.

Maccoby, E. E., & Martin, J. A. (1983). Socialization in the context of the family: Parent child interaction. In Mussen, P. H. (Series Ed.), & Hetherington, E. M. (Vol. Ed.), *Handbook of child psychology, Vol.4, Socialization, personality, and social development* (4th ed.). New York: Wiley.

MacKay, N. J., & Covell, K. (1997). The impact of women in advertisements on attitudes toward women. *Sex Roles*, *36*, 573-583. https://doi.org/10.1023/A:1025613923786.

Magdol, L., Moffitt, T. E., Caspi, A., Newman, D. L., Pagan, J., & Silva, P. A. (1997). Gender differences in partner violence in a birth cohort of 21-year-olds: Bridging the gap between clinical and epidemiological approaches. *Journal of Consulting and Clinical Psychology*, *65*, 68-78.

Malamuth, N. M. (1981). Rape fantasies as a function of exposure to violent sexual stimuli. *Archives of Sexual Behavior*, *10*(1), 33-47.

Malamuth, N. M. (1984). Aggression against women: Cultural and individual causes. In Malamuth, N. M., & Donnerstein, E. (Eds.), *Pornography and sexual aggression*. San Diego: Academic Press, 19-52. https://doi.org/10.1016/B978-0-12-466280-3.50008-7.

Malamuth, N. M., & Ceniti, J. (1986). Repeated exposure to violent and nonviolent pornography: Likelihood of raping ratings and laboratory aggression against women. *Aggressive Behavior*, *12*(2), 129-137.

Malamuth, N. M., & Check, J. V. P. (1981). The effects of mass media exposure on acceptance of violence against women: A field experiment. *Journal of Research in Personality*, *15*(4), 436-446. https://doi.org/10.1016/0092-6566(81)90040-4.

Malamuth, N., Hald, G., & Koss, M. (2012). Pornography, individual differences in risk and men's acceptance of violence against women in a representative sample. *Sex Roles*, *66*, 427-439.

Martos, J., & Hégy, P. (1998). Gender roles in family and culture: The basis of sexism in religion. In Martos, J., & Hégy, P. (Eds.), *Equal at the creation: Sexism, society, and Christian thought* (pp. 3-24). Toronto: University of Toronto Press.

Matasha, E., Ntembelea, T., Mayaud, P., Saidi, W., Todd, J., Mujaya, B., & Tendo-Wambua, L. (1988). Sexual and reproductive health among primary and secondary school pupils in Mwanza, Tanzania: Need for intervention. *AIDS Care*, *10*, 571-582. https://doi.org/10.1080/09540129848433.

McCloskey, L.A., & Lichter, E.L. (2003). The contribution of marital violence to adolescent aggression across different relationships. *Journal of Interpersonal Violence*, *18*, 390-412.

McLean, I. A., Balding, V., & White, C. (2005). Further aspects of male-on-male rape and sexual assault in greater Manchester. *Medicine, Science and the Law*, *45*, 225-232.

Meltzoff, A. N., & Moore, M. K. (2000). Imitation of facial and manual gestures by human neonates: Resolving the debate about early imitation. In Muir, D., & Slater, A. (Eds.), *Infant development: The essential readings*. Malden, MA: Blackwell, pp. 167-181.

Mercy, J. A., Abdel Megid, L. A., Salem, E. S., & Lotfi, S. (1993). Intentional injuries. In Mashaly, A. Y., Graitcer, P. L., & Youssef, Z. M. (Eds.), *Injury in Egypt: An analysis of injuries as a health problem*. Cairo: [Publisher not given], pp. 6-83.

Messinger, A. M. (2011). Invisible victims: Same-sex IPV in the National Violence Against Women Survey. *Journal of Interpersonal Violence*, *26*(11), 22-28.

Michau, L. (1998). Community-based research for social change in Mwanza, Tanzania. In *Third Annual Meeting of the International Research Network on Violence Against Women, Washington, DC, 9-11 January 1998*. Takoma Park, MD: Center for Health and Gender Equity, pp. 4-9.

Miczek, K. A., DeBold, J. F., Haney, M., Tidey, J., Vivtan, J., & Weerts, E. M. (1993). Alcohol, drugs of abuse, aggression and violence. In Reiss, A. J., & Roth, J. A. (Eds.). *Understanding and preventing violence. Vol. 3. Social influences*. Washington, DC: National Academy Press, pp. 377-570.

Mikula, J. (2003). Gender and videogames: The political valency of Lara Croft, continuum. *Journal of Media & Cultural Studies*, *17*, 79-87.

Milburn, M. A., Mather, R., & Conrad, S. D. (2000). The effects of viewing R-rated movie scenes that objectify women on perceptions of date rape. *Sex Roles*, *43*, 645-664. https://doi.org/10.1023/A:1007152507914.

Miller, T. R., Cohen, M. A., & Wiersema, B. (1996). Victim costs and consequences: A new look (NCJ 155282). U.S. Department of Justice, Office of Justice Programs, National Institute of Justice. www.ncjrs.gov/pdffiles/victcost.

Minton, H. L. (1986). Femininity in men and masculinity in women: American psychiatry and psychology portray homosexuality in the 1930's. *Journal of Homosexuality, 13*(1), 1-21.

Mooney, J. (1993). *The hidden figure: Domestic violence in north London*. London: Middlesex University.

Mooney, J. (1994). *The hidden figure: Domestic violence in north London*. London: Islington Council.

Moore, T. M., & Stuart, G. L. (2004). Effects of masculine gender role stress on men's cognitive, affective, physiological, and aggressive responses to intimate conflict situations. *Psychology of Men & Masculinity, 5*(2), 132-142. https://doi.org/10.1037/1524-9220.5.2.132.

Moreno, M. F. (1999). La violencia en la pareja. (Intimate partner violence.) *Revista Panamericana de Salud Pública, 5*, 245-258.

Moretti, M. M., Osbuth, I., Odgers, C. L., & Reebye, P. (2006). Exposure to maternal vs. paternal partner violence, PTSD, and aggression in adolescent girls and boys. *Aggressive Behavior, 32*, 385-395.

Morley, R. (1994). Wife beating and modernization: The case of Papua New Guinea. *Journal of Comparative Family Studies, 25*, 35-52.

Morse, B. J. (1995). Beyond the Conflict Tactics Scale: Assessing gender differences in partner violence. *Violence and Victims, 10*, 251-272.

Mosher, D. L., & Sirkin, M. (1984). Measuring a macho personality constellation. *Journal of Research in Personality, 18*, 150-163.

Muñoz-Rivas, M. J., Graña, J. L., O'Leary, K. D., & Pilar González, M. (2007). Aggression in adolescent dating relationships: Prevalence, justification, and health consequences. *Journal of Adolescent Health, 40*(4), 298-304. https://doi.org/10.1016/j.jadohealth.2006.11.137.

Murnen, S. K., Wright, C., & Kaluzny, G. (2002). If "boys will be boys," then girls will be victims? A meta-analytic review of the research that relates masculine ideology to sexual aggression. *Sex Roles, 46*(11-12), 359-375.

Nagoshi, J. L., Adams, K. A., Terrell, H. K., Hill, E. D., Brzuzy, S., & Nagoshi, C. T. (2008). Gender differences in correlates of homophobia and transphobia. *Sex Roles, 59*, 521-531.

National Television Violence Study (1996). (Vol. I). Thousand Oaks, CA: Sage.

National Television Violence Study (1997). (Vol. 2). Studio City, CA: Mediascope.

National Television Violence Study (1998). (Vol. 3). Santa Barbara, CA: Center for Communication and Social Policy, University of California.

Nelson, E., & Zimmerman, C. (1996). Household survey on domestic violence in Cambodia. Phnom Penh, Cambodia: Ministry of Women's Affairs and Project Against Domestic Violence.

Norton, J. (1997). "Brain says you're a girl, but I think you're a sissy boy": Cultural origins of transphobia. *Journal of Gay, Lesbian, and Bisexual Identity, 2*, 139-164.

Nowakowski Sims, E., Dodd, V. J. N., & Tejeda, M. J. (2008). The relationship between severity of violence in the home and dating violence. *Journal of Forensic Nursing, 4*, 166-173.

Orobio De Castro, B., Veerman, J. W., Koops, W., Bosch, J. D., & Monshouwer, H. J. (2002). Hostile attribution of intent and aggressive behavior: A meta-analysis. *Child Development, 73*(3), 916-934. https://doi.org/10.1111/1467-8624.00447.

Osakue, G., & Hilber, A.M. (1998). Women's sexuality and fertility in Nigeria. In Petchesky, R., & Judd, K. (Eds.), *Negotiating reproductive rights*. London: Zed Books, pp. 180-216.

Osofsky, J. D., Wewers, S., Hann, D. M., & Fick, A. C. (1993). Chronic community violence: What is happening to our children? *Psychiatry 56*, 36-45.

Paik, H., & Comstock, G. (1994). The effects of television violence on antisocial behavior: A meta-analysis. *Communication Research, 21*, 516-546.

Parrott, D. J., Adams, H. E., & Zeichner, A. (2002). Homophobia: Personality and attitudinal correlates. *Personality and Individual Differences, 32*, 1269-1278.

Parrott, D. J., & Gallagher, K. E. (2008). What accounts for heterosexual women's negative emotional responses to lesbians? Examination of traditional gender role beliefs and sexual prejudice. *Sex Roles, 59*, 229-239.

Parrott, D. J., & Zeichner, A. (2003). Effects of hypermasculinity on physical aggression against women. *Psychology of Men & Masculinity, 4*, 70-78.

Parrott, D. J., & Zeichner, A. (2008). Determinants of anger and physical aggression based on sexual orientation: An experimental examination of hypermasculinity and exposure to male gender role violations. *Archives of Sexual Behavior, 37*, 891-901.

Patel, S., Long, T. E., McCammon, S. L., & Wuensch, K. L. (1995). Personality and emotional correlates of self-reported antigay behaviors. *Journal of Interpersonal Violence, 10*, 354-366.

384 *Aggression*

Peek-Asa, C., Wallis, A., Harland, K., Beyer, K., Dickey, P., & Saftlas, A. (2011). Rural disparity in domestic violence prevalence and access to resources. *Journal of Women's Health, 20*(11), 1743–1749. doi:10.1089/jwh.2011.2891.

Pepper, B. I., & Sand, S. (2015). Internalized homophobia and intimate partner violence in young adult women's same-sex relationships. *Journal of Aggression, Maltreatment & Trauma, 24*(6), 656–673.

Peter, J., & Valkenburg, P. M. (2007). Adolescents' exposure to a sexualized media environment and their notions of women as sex objects. *Sex Roles, 56*(5-6), 381–395.

Peterson, Z. D., & Muehlenhard, C. L. (2004). Was it rape? The function of women's rape myth acceptance and definitions of sex in labeling their own experiences. *Sex Roles, 51*, 129–144. http://dx.doi .org/10.1023/B:SERS.0000037758.95376.00.

Piaget, J. (1976). Piaget's theory. In Inhelder, B., Chipman, H. H., & Zwingmann, C. (Eds.), *Piaget and his school.* Berlin and Heidelberg: Springer.

Pimlott-Kubiak, S., & Cortina, L. M. (2003). Gender, victimization and outcomes: Reconceptualizing risk. *Journal of Consulting and Clinical Psychology, 71*, 528–539.

Plant, M., Plant, M., & Miller, P. (2005). Childhood and adult sexual abuse: Relationships with "addictive" or "problem" behaviours and health. *Journal of Addictive Diseases, 21*, 25–38.

Pleasance, C. (2017). Woman, 19, is sentenced to death by stoning for adultery after she was 'raped at gunpoint by her cousin' in Pakistan. *Daily Mail*, May 30. www.dailymail.co.uk/news/article-4555734/Woman-19-sentenced-die-raped-Pakistan.html.

Polimeni, A.-M., Hardie, E., & Buzwell, S. (2000). Homophobia among Australian heterosexuals: The role of sex, gender role ideology, and gender role traits. *Current Research in Social Psychology, 5*, 1–10.

Poonwala, I. (2007). *The Pillars of Islam: Laws pertaining to human intercourse.* Oxford: Oxford University Press.

Porter, N., & Geis, F. (1981). Women and nonverbal leadership cues: When seeing is not believing. In Mayo, C., & Henley, N. M. (Eds.), *Gender and nonverbal behavior.* Springer Series in Social Psychology. New York: Springer.

Pratto, F., & Walker, A. (2004). The bases of gendered power. In Eagly, A. H., Beall, A. E., & Sternberg, R. J. (Eds.), *The psychology of gender.* New York: Guilford Press, pp. 242–268.

Prentice, D. A., & Carranza, E. E. (2002). What women and men should be, shouldn't be, are allowed to be, and don't have to be: The contents of prescriptive gender stereotypes. *Psychology of Women Quarterly, 26*, 269–281. doi:10.1111/ 1471-6402.t01-1-00066.

Reidy, D. E., Shirk, S. D., Sloan, C. A., & Zeichner, A. (2009). Men who aggress against women: Effects of feminine gender role violation on physical aggression in hypermasculine men. *Psychology of Men & Masculinity, 10*, 1–12. http://dx.doi.org/10.1037/a0014794.

Reidy, D. E., Sloan, C. A., & Zeichner, A. (2009). Gender role conformity and aggression: Influence of perpetrator and victim conformity on direct physical aggression in women. *Personality & Individual Differences, 46*, 231–235.

Renner, L. M., & Slack, K. S. (2006). Intimate partner violence and child maltreatment: Understanding intra- and intergenerational connections. *Child Abuse & Neglect, 30*(6), 599–617.

Rennison, C. M. (2002). Rape and sexual assault: Reporting to police and medical attention, 1992-2000 [NCJ 194530]. U.S. Department of Justice, Office of Justice Programs, Bureau of Justice Statistics. www.bjs.gov/content/pub/pdf/rsarp00.

Riggio, H. R., Groskopf, C., Dennem-Tigner, J., & Garcia, A. (2015). Religiosity and rape myth acceptance: Mediating role of traditional gender ideology. Paper presented at the annual meeting of the Western Psychological Association, Las Vegas, NV, April.

Rizzolatti, G., Fadiga, L., Gallese, V., & Fogassi, L. (1996). Premotor cortex and the recognition of motor actions. *Brain Research. Cognitive Brain Research, 3*, 131–141.

Rodgers, K. (1994). Wife assault: The findings of a national survey. *Juristat Service Bulletin, 14*, 1–22.

Rollero, C. (2013). Men and women facing objectification: The effects of media models on well-being, self-esteem and ambivalent sexism. *Revista de Psicología Social, 28*(3), 373–382.

Rosenthal, R. (1991). *Meta-analytic procedures for social research.* Newbury Park, CA: Sage.

Ross, L. E. (Ed.) (2014). *Continuing the war against domestic violence.* Boca Raton, FL: CRC Press.

Rozee, P. D., & Koss, M. P. (2001). Rape: A century of resistance. *Psychology of Women Quarterly, 25*, 295–311.

Ruble, D. N., & Martin, C. L. (1997). Gender development. In Damon, W. (Series Ed.), & Eisenberg, N. (Vol. Ed.), *Handbook of child psychology, Vol. 3, Social, emotional and personality development* (5th ed.). New York: Wiley.

Rudman, L. A., Moss-Racusin, C. A., Phelan, J. E., & Nauts, S. (2012). Status incongruity and backlash effects: Defending the gender hierarchy motivates prejudice toward female leaders. *Journal of Experimental Social Psychology, 48*, 165–179.

Rule, A. (2008). *The stranger beside me*. New York: Simon & Schuster.

Sadowa, K. (2015). Violence against women in Afghanistan following the liberation of the country from under the Taliban occupation – an outline of the problem. *Opolskie Studia Administracyjno-Prawne, 13*(3), 119-134.

Saltzman, L. E., Johnson, C. H., Gilbert, B. C., & Goodwin, M. M. (2003). Physical abuse around the time of pregnancy: An examination of prevalence and risk factors in 16 states. *Maternal and Child Health Journal, 7*(1), 31-43. doi:10.1023/A:1022589501039.

Sánchez, F. J., Westefeld, J. S., Liu, W. M., & Vilain, E. (2010). Masculine gender role conflict and negative feelings about being gay. *Professional Psychology: Research and Practice, 41*(2), 104-111.

Sanday, P. R. (1996). Rape-prone versus rape-free campus cultures. *Violence Against Women, 2*, 191-208.

Saunders, D. G. (1986). When battered women use violence: Husband-abuse or self-defense? *Violence and Victims, 1*, 47-60.

Scharrer, E. (2004). Virtual violence: Gender and aggression in video game advertisements. *Mass Communication and Society, 7*, 393-412.

Schuler, S. R., Hashemi, S. M., Riley, A. P., & Akhter, S. (1996). Credit programs, patriarchy and men's violence against women in rural Bangladesh. *Social Science & Medicine, 43*(12), 1729-1742. https://doi.org/10.1016/S0277-9536(96)00068-8.

Schoenau, E., Neu, C., Rauch, F., & Manz, F. (2001). The development of bone strength at the proximal radius during childhood and adolescence. *The Journal of Clinical Endocrinology and Metabolism, 86*(2), 613-618.

Schwab-Stone, M. E., Ayers, T. S., Kasprow, W., Voyce, C., Barone, C., Shriver, T., & Weissberg, R. P (1995). No safe haven: A study of violence exposure in an urban community. *Journal of the American Academy of Child & Adolescent Psychiatry, 34*(10), 1343-1352.

Schwalbe, M., & Wolkomir, M. (2001). The masculine self as problem and resource in interview studies of men. *Men & Masculinities, 4*(1), 90-103. https://doi.org/10.1177/1097184X01004001005.

Schwartz, M. D. (1987). Gender and injury in spousal assault. *Sociological Focus, 20*, 61-75.

Sell, A., Hone, L. S. E., & Pound, N. (2012). The importance of physical strength to human males. *Human Nature, 23*, 30-44. doi:10.1007/s12110-012-9131-2.

Sen, P. (1999). *Ending the presumption of consent: Nonconsensual sex in marriage*. London: Centre for Health and Gender Equity.

Sengupta, S. (2017). One by one, marry-your-rapist laws are falling in the Middle East. *The New York Times*, July 22. www.nytimes.com/2017/07/22/world/middleeast/marry-your-rapist-laws-middle-east.html.

Shamim, I. (1992). Dowry and women's status: A study of court cases in Dhaka and Delhi. In Viano, E. C. (Ed.), *Intimate violence: Interdisciplinary perspectives* (pp. 265-275). Washington, DC: Hemisphere.

Shuster, S., Black, M., & McVitie, E. (1975). The influence of age and sex on skin thickness, skin collagen and density. *British Journal of Dermatology, 93*, 639-643.

Silverman, J. G., Raj, A., Mucci, L., & Hathaway, J. (2001). Dating violence against adolescent girls and associated substance use, unhealthy weight control, sexual risk behavior, pregnancy, and suicidality. *Journal of the American Medical Association, 286*(5), 572-579.

Singer, D. G., & Singer, J. L. (Eds.) (2001). *Handbook of children and the media*. Thousand Oaks, CA: Sage.

Sinn, J. S. (1997). The predictive and discriminate validity of masculine ideology. *Journal of Research in Personality, 31*, 117-135.

Slater, M. D., Henry, K. L., Swaim, R. C., & Anderson, L. L. (2003). Violent media content and aggressiveness in adolescents: A downward spiral model. *Communication Research, 30*(6), 713-736.

Smith, S. G., Chen, J., Basile, K. C., Gilbert, L. K., Merrick, M. T., Patel, N., ..., Jain, A. (2012). The National Intimate Partner and Sexual Violence Survey: 2010-2012 State Report. Atlanta, GA: Division of Violence Prevention, National Center for Injury Prevention and Control, Centers for Disease Control and Prevention.

Smuts, B. (1995). The evolutionary origins of patriarchy. *Human Nature, 6*, 1-32. https://doi.org/10.1007/BF02734133.

Spitzberg, B. H., & Cupach, W. R. (2006). The state of the art of stalking: Taking stock of the emerging literature. *Aggression and Violent Behavior, 12*, 64-86.

St. Lawrence, J. S., & Joyner, D. J. (1991). The effects of sexually violent rock music on males' acceptance of violence against women. *Psychology of Women Quarterly, 15*, 49-63.

Stankiewicz, J. M., & Rosselli, F. (2008). Women as sex objects and victims in print advertisements. *Sex Roles, 58*, 579-589. http://dx.doi.org/10.1007/ s11199-007-9359-1.

Stark, E., & Flitcraft, A. (1996). *Women at risk: Domestic violence and women's health*. Thousand Oaks, CA: Sage.

Starkey, A. D. (2015). The Roman Catholic Church and violence against women. In Johnson, A. J. (Ed.), *Religion and men's violence against women*. New York: Springer Science + Business Media, pp. 177-193.

Stermer, S. P., & Burkley, M. (2015). SeX-Box: Exposure to sexist video games predicts benevolent sexism. *Psychology of Popular Media Culture, 4*(1), 47-55. https://doi.org/10.1037/a0028397.

Stevenson, M. R., & Medler, B. R. (1995). Is homophobia a weapon of sexism? *Journal of Men's Studies, 4*, 1-8.

Stotzer, R. L., & MacCartney, D. (2016). The role of institutional factors on on-campus reported rape prevalence. *Journal of Interpersonal Violence, 31*(16), 2687-2707.

Strack, F., & Deutsch, R. (2004). Reflective and impulsive determinants of social behavior. *Personality and Social Psychology Review, 8*, 220-247.

Straus, M. A. (1990). The Conflict Tactics Scale and its critics: An evaluation and new data on validity and reliability. In Straus, M. A., & Gelles, R. (Eds.), *Physical violence in American societies: Risk factors and adaptations to violence in 8145 families* (pp. 49-73). New Brunswick, NJ: Transaction Publications.

Straus, M. A. (2008). Dominance and symmetry in partner violence by male and female university students in 32 nations. *Children and Youth Services Review, 30*, 252-275.

Straus, M. A., & Gelles, R. J. (1988). How violent are American families? Estimates from the National Family Violence Resurvey and other studies. In Hotaling, G. T., Finkelhor, D., Kirkpatrick, J. T., & Straus, M. A. (Eds.), *Family abuse and its consequences: New directions in research* (pp. 14-36). Newbury Park, CA: Sage.

Sullivan, T. P., Cavanaugh, C. E., Buckner, J. D., & Edmondson, D. (2009). Testing posttraumatic stress as a mediator of physical, sexual, and psychological intimate partner violence and substance problems among women. *Journal of Traumatic Stress, 22*, 575-584.

Sullivan, T. P., Weiss, N. H., Price, C., Pugh, N., & Hansen, N. B. (2018). Strategies for coping with individual PTSD symptoms: Experiences of African American victims of intimate partner violence. *Psychological Trauma: Theory, Research, Practice, and Policy, 10*(3), 336-344.

Swami, V., Coles, R., & Wyrozumska, K. (2010). Oppressive beliefs at play: Associations among beauty ideals and practices and individual differences in sexism, objectification of others, and media exposure. *Psychology of Women Quarterly, 34*(3), 365-379. https://doi.org/10.1111/j.1471-6402.2010.01582.x.

Swan, S. C., Gambone, L. J., Caldwell, J. E., Sullivan, T. P., & Snow, D. L. (2008). A review of research on women's use of violence with male intimate partners. *Violence and Victims, 28*, 301-314.

Szymanski, D. M. (2005). Heterosexism and sexism as correlates of psychological distress in lesbians. *Journal of Counseling and Development, 83*, 355-360.

Tanner, J. M. (1989). *Foetus into man: Physical growth from conception to maturity* (2nd ed.). Ware, UK: Castlemead.

Tapper, K., & Boulton, M. J. (2004). Sex differences in levels of physical, verbal, and indirect aggression amongst primary school children and their associations with beliefs about aggression. *Aggressive Behavior, 30*(2), 123-145.

Theodore, P. S., & Basow, S. A. (2000). Heterosexual masculinity and homophobia: A reaction to the self? *Journal of Homosexuality, 40*, 31-48.

Thomas, J. R., & French, K. E. (1985). Gender differences across age in motor performance: A meta-analysis. *Psychological Bulletin, 98*, 260-282.

Thomas, M. H., Horton, R. W., Lippincott, E. C., & Drabman, R. S. (1977). Desensitization to portrayals of real life aggression as a function of television violence. *Journal of Personality and Social Psychology, 35*, 450-458.

Tiwari, P., & Mehrotra, S. (2016). Honour deaths: The story from then till now. *Social Sciences International Research Journal, 2*(1), 426-433.

Tjaden, P., & Thoennes, N. (1998). Prevalence, incidence, and consequences of violence against women: Findings from the National Violence against Women Survey. Research in Brief. Department of Justice, Washington, DC. National Institute of Justice, Centers for Disease Control and Prevention (DHHS/PHS), Atlanta, GA.

Tjaden, P., & Thoennes, N. (2000). *Full report of the prevalence, incidence, and consequences of violence against women: Findings from the National Violence Against Women Survey.* Washington, DC: National Institute of Justice, Office of Justice Programs, United States Department of Justice and Centers for Disease Control and Prevention.

Tjaden, P., Thoennes, N., & Allison, C. J. (1999). Comparing violence over the life span in samples of same-sex and opposite-sex cohabitants. *Violence and Victims, 14*(4), 413-425.

Torjesen, P. A., & Sandnes, L. (2004). Serum testosterone in women as measured by an automated immunoassay and a RIA. *Clinical Chemistry, 50*(3), 678; author reply 678-679. doi:10.1373/clinchem.2003.027565.

Triandis, H. C. (1995). *Individualism and collectivism.* Boulder, CO: Westview Press.

Turner, P. J., & Gervai, J. (1995). A multidimensional study of gender typing in preschool children and their parents: Personality, attitudes, preferences, behavior, and cultural differences. *Developmental Psychology, 31*, 759-772. doi:10.1037/0012-1649.31.5.759.

U.N. Women (2011). Progress of the world's women: In pursuit of justice. www.unwomen.org/en/digital-library/publications/2011/7/progress-of-the-world-s-women-in-pursuit-of-justice.

Uniform Crime Report (2011). Crime in the U.S., Table 66. https://ucr.fbi.gov/crime-in-the-u.s/2011/crime-in-the-u.s.-2011/tables/table_66_arrests_suburban_areas_by_sex_2011.xls.

United Nations Office on Drugs and Crime (2018). Crime and criminal justice. www.unodc.org/unodc/en/data-and-analysis/crime-and-criminal-justice.html.

United States Department of Justice (2012). An updated definition of rape. www.justice.gov/archives/opa/blog/updated-definition-rape.

United States Department of Justice (2018). Sexual assault. www.justice.gov/ovw/sexual-assault.

United States Department of Justice (1995). *Uniform crime reports for the United States*. Washington, DC: U.S. Printing Office.

Vaes, J., Paladino, M. P., & Puvia, E. (2011). Are sexualized females complete human beings? Why males and females dehumanize sexually objectified women. *European Journal of Social Psychology, 41*, 774-785.

Vandello, J. A., Bosson, J. K., Cohen, D., Burnaford, R. M., & Weaver, J. R. (2008). Precarious manhood. *Journal of Personality and Social Psychology, 95*(6), 1325-1339.

Vivian, D., & Langhinrichsen-Rohling, J. (1994). Are bidirectionally violent couples mutually victimized? A gender-sensitive comparison. *Violence and Victims, 9*(2), 107-124.

Ward, I. (1995). *Politics of the media*. New York: Macmillan.

Ward, L. M. (2002). Does television exposure affect emerging adults' attitudes and assumptions about sexual relationships? Correlational and experimental confirmation. *Journal of Youth and Adolescence, 31*(1), 1-15.

Ward, L. M. (2003). Understanding the role of entertainment media in the sexual socialization of American youth: A review of empirical research. *Developmental Review, 23*, 347-388.

Warriner, K., Nagoshi, C. T., & Nagoshi, J. L. (2013). Correlates of homophobia, transphobia, and internalized homophobia in gay or lesbian and heterosexual samples. *Journal of Homosexuality, 60*(9), 1297-1314.

Websdale, N., & Chesney-Lind, M. (1998). Doing violence to women: Research synthesis on the victimization of women. In Bowker, L. H. (Ed.), *Masculinities and violence* (pp. 55-81). Thousand Oaks, CA: Sage Publications.

Wegner, D. M., & Bargh, J. A. (1998). Control and automaticity in social life. In Gilbert, D., Fiske, S., & Lindzey, G. (Eds.), *The handbook of social psychology* (pp. 446-496). New York: McGraw-Hill.

Weiner, B. (1980). A cognitive (attribution)-emotion-action model of motivated behavior: An analysis of judgments of help-giving. *Journal of Personality and Social Psychology, 39*, 186-200. http://dx.doi.org/10.1037/0022-3514.39.2.186.

Weiner, B., Perry, R. P., & Magnusson, J. (1988). An attributional analysis of reactions to stigmas. *Journal of Personality and Social Psychology, 55*, 738-748. http://dx.doi.org/10.1037/0022-3514.55.5.738.

Weissler, C. (1992). *Mitzvot* built into the body: Tkhines for Niddah, pregnancy, and childbirth. In Eilberg-Schwartz, H. (Ed.), *People of the body: Jews and Judaism from an embodied perspective* (pp. 101-116). New York: State University of New York Press.

Wells, J. (2007). Sexual dimorphism of body composition. Best practice & research. *Clinical Endocrinology & Metabolism, 21*(3), 415-430.

Wemple, S. F. (1992). Women from the fifth to the tenth century. In Klapisch-Zuber, C. (Ed.), *Silences of the Middle Ages*, vol. II of *A history of women in the West*. Cambridge, MA: Harvard University Press, pp. 169-201.

Williamson, L. M., Dodds, J. P., Mercey, D. E., Hart, G. J., & Johnson, A. M. (2008). Sexual risk behaviour and knowledge of HIV status among community samples of gay men in the UK. *AIDS, 22*(9), 1063-1070. doi:10.1097/QAD.0b013e3282f8af9b.

Wilson, B. J., Smith, S. L., Potter, W. J., Kunkel, D., Linz, D., Colvin, C. M., & Donnerstein, E. (2002). Violence in children's television programming: Assessing the risks. *Journal of Communication, 52*(1), 5-35.

Wood, W., & Eagly, A. H. (2002). A cross-cultural analysis of the behavior of women and men: Implications for the origins of sex differences. *Psychological Bulletin, 128*, 699-727.

Wood, K., & Jewkes, R. (2001). "Dangerous" love: Reflections on violence among Xhosa township youth. In Morrell, R. (Ed.), *Changing men in Southern Africa*. Pietermaritzburg, South Africa: University of Natal Press.

World Health Organization (2002). World report on violence and health. http://apps.who.int/iris/bitstream/handle/10665/42495/9241545615_eng.pdf?sequence=1.

World Health Organization (2010). Maternal deaths worldwide drop by third. Report, September 15. Geneva/New York.

Yilo, K., & Straus, M. A. (1984). The impact of structural inequality and sexist family norms on rates of wife-beating. *Journal of International and Comparative Social Welfare*, *1*(1), 16-29. doi.org/10.1080/17486838408412648.

Yoshihama, M., Horrocks, J., & Bybee, D. (2010). Intimate partner violence and initiation of smoking and drinking: A population-based study of women in Yokohama, Japan. *Social Science & Medicine*, *71*(6), 1199-1207. doi.org/10.1016/j.socscimed.2010.06.018.

Yukawa, S., & Yoshida, F. (1999). The effect of media violence on aggression: Is aggressive behavior mediated by aggressive cognitions and emotions? *Japanese Journal of Psychology*, *70*(2), 94-103.

Zimmerman, K. (1995). *Plates in a basket will rattle: Domestic violence in Cambodia. A summary*. Phnom Penh, Cambodia: Project Against Domestic Violence.

12 Occupational Roles and Power

Global, Historical Sexism	394
Working Families	396
Household Responsibilities and Childcare	396
Parental Leave	400
Work-Family Conflict	401
Occupational Stereotypes	402
Sexism on the Job	403
Stereotypes, Emotions, and Power	403
Ambivalent Sexism	406
The Glass Ceiling	407
Leadership	408
Women in Politics	409

INEQUALITIES AND INJUSTICES

American Sexism and Hillary Rodham Clinton

There is little doubt that most Americans were at least somewhat shocked when Donald Trump defeated Hillary Rodham Clinton in 2016 to become President of the United States (see Figure 12.1). The vast majority of polls predicted that Clinton would be the winner (Smith, 2017), especially given her substantive professional experience in U.S. politics (e.g., serving as a state Senator, serving as Secretary of State under President Obama), especially compared to Mr. Trump. But the scholar in me was always very concerned that Secretary Clinton would be defeated, based simply on the ubiquitous nature of sexism in the United States. Many aspects of traditional American culture emphasize masculinity and male dominance, in the family, in the corporation, in the church, in the legal system, in the government (Sidanius, Levin, & Pratto, 1996). Being raised in such a culture, it is nearly impossible for any person to not develop automatic, implicit beliefs about women and men that operate at an unconscious, uncontrolled level, including beliefs that men should be in charge and granted authority. Such thinking is highly schematic; it is based on automatic,

Figure 12.1 Former U.S. Secretary of State, Hillary Clinton
Source: Etienne Laurent/EPA-EFE/Shutterstock

immediate retrieval of cognitive structures representing categories into consciousness so they may be used to process current information. Schemas that are **accessible** are easily brought into mind based on environmental cues or motivation. People who are **sexist** have beliefs about women (usually negative) and men (usually positive) that are easily, rather instantly retrieved, and thus likely to be used in processing information about any particular person or event (Fiske & Taylor, 1991).

Implicit ideas about leadership are linked with maleness and strength; as such, male qualities can trigger perceptions of strength and "rightness" when it comes to decisions about who should lead (Mazur & Stevens, 1975; Nosek, Banaji, & Greenwald, 2002; Spezio et al., 2008). In primate groups, physically stronger males are often the dominant animal in the group, the so-called **alpha male** (Smuts, Cheney, Seyfarth, Wrangham, & Struhsaker, 1987). In the past, with human societies governed more by brute strength than laws, power was often determined by physical strength (Henrich & Gil-White, 2001). Women are simply and rather automatically viewed as being less competent than men, based on physical size differences and **implicit** responding to those differences (Fiske, 2017). Further, masculine facial features (e.g., square jaw, large brow and nose, facial hair) signal dominance in humans (Perrett et al., 1998), and testosterone is linked with both dominant facial features and dominant behavior (Mazur & Booth, 1998; Penton-Voak & Chen, 2004). Research indicates that when people do not have current or strong opinions about any particular candidates in an election, they are more likely to vote for candidates with more dominant faces than those with less dominant faces (Little, Burris, Jones, & Roberts, 2007; Riggio & Riggio, 2010).

Implicit sexism operates at a rather unconscious level, although awareness of implicit cognitive processes certainly helps one in attempting to control such automatic or habitual thoughts. **Explicit sexism** against Hillary Clinton is also obviously part of her failure to win the Presidential election. Explicit sexism is more effortful than implicit sexism; it is conscious, intentionally formulated, and knowingly enacted. It is obvious. The sexist vitriol against Secretary Clinton was rampant during the election, with candidate Trump calling her "nasty," and referring to her as "disgusting" for using the bathroom, not to mention the social media attacks on her and her service as Secretary of State. I'm sure that some of you heard people refer to her as being "too emotional" to run the country, a typical **legitimizing myth**, a lie used to subordinate women and deny them power (Pratto & Walker, 2004). Candidate for Vice President Mike Pence mentioned on several occasions "the broadshouldered leadership of Donald Trump" (The Washington Post, 2016), suggesting that this masculine physical feature is somehow linked with greater ability to lead the country. In a truly equal society, where women and men are regarded and treated as equal to each other in terms of rights and opportunities, there should be as many female Presidents as there are male Presidents, especially since there are no differences in intelligence between women and men (Born, Bleichrodt, & Van der Flier, 1987) and since the job does not require physical strength. But alas, the sexism in the United States was too powerful. I don't know if I will live to see a female American President, but I certainly hope I do.

CRITICAL THINKING

Different But Equal: Job Requirements and Women's Equality

As indicated throughout this book (Chapters 1, 7, 11), size and strength differences between women and men are real, they are substantial, and they permit physical and **social dominance** of women by men.

The average man has 50-80% greater upper body strength and 30-60% greater lower body strength than the average woman (Lassek & Gaulin, 2009). The effect sizes for throwing distance and for throwing velocity between women and men are around 2.00, a huge difference (Thomas & French, 1985). Because of these and other physical advantages (Sell et al., 2012), including larger lung capacity (Gursoy, 2010), men perform better than women at tasks that involve physical strength, including fighting, lifting and carrying, and running, including in formal occupations. Many occupations require physical strength, including construction, law enforcement, the military, firefighting, mining, forestry, and so on, a primary reason why men tend to dominate in these professions compared to women. How about President of the United States? Does that require physical strength, besides basic physical health? Not really, but people still respond to powerful positions in terms of physical strength and stature (see "Inequalities and Injustices").

In the interests of fairness, the huge physical differences between women and men are considered when hiring within strength-necessary professions, right? Wrong. Fire departments require the same physical abilities in female and male applicants. All firefighter applicants must pass a physical abilities test called the **Candidate Physical Abilities Test (CPAT)**, which involves eight tasks, all of which involve muscular strength and aerobic capacity (e.g., climbing stairs carrying 25 pounds, dragging a 25-pound hose, carrying heavy equipment). All of the CPAT tasks are completed while the applicant is wearing a 50-pound vest to simulate the weight of a breathing apparatus (National Testing Network, 2012). Now there certainly are women who are strong and fit and capable of passing the CPAT and becoming successful firefighters; however, there are obviously fewer women than men who can pass such physical standards. Similarly, police departments set the same physical standards for female and male (and women who have) applicants, including a measure called the Physical Abilities Test (PAT) involving push-ups, sit-ups, sprinting, and distance running (National Testing Network, 2012). It is understandable that these jobs require physical strength and how important that strength is when lives are in danger. However, physical strength requirements for occupations necessarily lead to most women being effectively locked out of certain professions. Do you think it is important for physical standards for certain jobs to be revisited or revised to be more inclusive of women? Why or why not? Try to take both sides of the argument.

BONUS BOX

Puzzles in Northern India: Training Boys and Girls in Spatial Skills

There is a significant amount of research indicating that men and boys outperform women and girls in spatial reasoning tasks (cognitive tasks that require visual mental representations) (Hegarty & Sims, 1994; Levine, Huttenlocher, Taylor, & Langrock, 1999; Voyer, Voyer, & Bryden, 1995). Typically the largest sex differences are found in tasks that require mental rotation (rotating objects mentally in the mind as three-dimensional objects) (Levine et al., 1999; Linn & Peterson, 1985). Differences between women and men, girls and boys in terms of spatial abilities also tend to be rather large compared to other gender differences (Collaer & Hines, 1995). Such differences have been found in 4-month-old infants, with infant boys better at recognizing a previously seen object in a different position than infant girls (Moore & Johnson, 2008). In addition, neurological studies indicate that the right cerebral hemisphere is more specialized for spatial abilities (Bogen & Gazzaniga, 1965; Searleman, 1977; Witelson, 1976), and that men have greater right hemisphere specialization than women (de Lacoste, Hovarth, & Woodward, 1991; Levine et al., 1999; Wada, 1974). Research indicates that hormones are important in development of spatial reasoning, especially androgens (Hampson, Rovelt, & Altman, 1998). Sex differences in spatial abilities are also found in other species, most notably rats (Barrett & Ray, 1970; Cowley & Griesel, 1963; Dawson, 1972). These research findings support a substantial biological basis for spatial reasoning (McGee, 1979).

There is also evidence, however, that socialization plays an important part in development of spatial reasoning skills. Spatial skills can be taught (Sorby, 2009; Voyer et al., 1995), and boys and men generally have greater opportunities for spatial development than girls and women (Baenninger & Newcombe, 1989; Huttenlocher, Newcombe, & Vasilyeva, 1999). In addition, because girls and women are stereotyped as having poorer spatial skills compared to boys and men, **stereotype threat** hinders the performance of girls and women (Steele, 1997).

One interesting study examined gender differences in spatial abilities (specifically solving a block puzzle) among people in two isolated and primitive tribes in India, the Karbi and the Khasi (Hoffman, Gneezy, & List, 2011). The people in the two tribes are similar genetically, geographically, and culturally, however the Karbi are **patrilineal** (property is inherited by men) while the Khasi are **matrilineal** (property is inherited by women). In the Karbi tribe, women are not allowed to own property; in the Khasi tribe, men are not allowed to own property and working men must give their earnings to their mothers or wives. In the patrilineal group, men on average had 3.7 years more education than women, while there was no difference in education in the matrilineal group. Participants in each tribe (over 1,200 people in total) were paid to solve a four-piece block puzzle (when combined showing a picture of a horse) as quickly as possible. Even when controlling for the gender differences in education in the Karbi tribe, results indicated significant differences between women and men in solving the puzzle in the Karbi tribe, favoring men, while there were no differences between women and men in the matrilineal tribe, the Khasi, an **interaction effect**. Results such as these support that while there are biological foundations for spatial reasoning that differ somewhat by sex, socialization and culture also affect development of spatial skills and differences in them.

LEARN MORE

Girls and Women in STEM Fields

Women are increasingly outnumbering men in pursuing and earning bachelor's and post-baccalaureate degrees (Goldin, Katz, & Kuziemko, 2006). While the number of women pursuing degrees in **STEM** fields (science, technology, engineering, math) is increasing, men still outnumber women in STEM, especially in the physical sciences (physics, chemistry, geosciences), engineering, and mathematics. Over 80% of female scientists are experts in life and social sciences (e.g., biology, psychology) (National Science Board, 2010). What explains these differences? Some argue that girls and women, because of their gender, are just not as interested in such disciplines, either because of so-called natural preferences or because of **gender socialization** (Blau, Brinton, & Grusky, 2006). Choices about family life are much more influential for the educational and career choices of women (Mason & Ekman, 2007; Reskin, 1993). As such, they may choose careers that they think are more amenable to bearing and raising children, which may not include fields that are male-dominated and less responsive to women's career issues and biological functions (Taylor, 2010). Further, girls and women are socialized to believe that they are not good at science and math, especially compared to boys and men (Beilock, Gunderson, Ramirez, & Levine, 2010). As such, girls and women tend to underestimate their abilities, even when theirs are equal to those of boys and men (Beilock et al., 2010; Correli, 2001, 2004; Fiorentine

& Cole, 1992). These self-doubts about necessary abilities may lead girls and women to not consider academic disciplines or careers involving those abilities (Cech, Rubineau, Silbey, & Seron, 2011; Correli, 2001; Steinpreis, Anders, & Ritzke, 1999). Research indicates that unlike women, men do not underestimate their own abilities (McCarty, 1986; Reuben, Sapienza, & Zingales, 2014).

Other explanations for the STEM gender gap focus on features of the disciplines themselves, including their domination by men and discrimination inherent within them (Settles, Cortina, Malley, & Stewart, 2006). In male-dominated institutions, there are few female role models, mentors, and colleagues, and social support is low (Bettinger & Long, 2005; Neumark & Gardecki, 1998). Female professionals in traditionally male-dominated institutions report feeling isolated from male colleagues (Zuckerman, Cole, & Bruer, 1991). In addition, gender will always be highlighted in situations where one gender dominates; as such, women's gender will always be a focus in social and organizational behaviors toward them in such environments (Randel, 2002). Job requirements within such disciplines are unlikely to accommodate women's potential additional family needs, like pregnancy or caring for infants and children (Hogan, Zippel, Frehill, & Kramer, 2010; Mason & Ekman, 2007). False beliefs about women (legitimizing myths) reinforce male domination and lead to active exclusion of women from the discipline, whether individual men are consciously aware of their sexism or not (Richeson & Ambady, 2001). Women who do gain entrance to the career may be excluded from collaborations and opportunities because of false beliefs about women's lack of abilities (Fox, 2001). Interviews with professionals indicate that mentoring, discrimination, and traditions within the discipline are important factors affecting gender segregation in STEM fields (Ecklund, Lincoln, & Tansey, 2012).

Global, Historical Sexism

Even a cursory knowledge of history reveals that women have been oppressed since the very beginnings of civilization. Girls all over the world were routinely denied formal education up until the 20th century, in the United States up until the 19th century. Even when offered to girls, education was a privilege afforded only to certain girls, those of particular wealth, stature, or social rank; poorer girls were likely to become low-paid domestic servants (Riordan, 1990). Until around 1940 in the United States, the largest category of women's paid work was low-paid domestic work (May, 2017). The earliest schools for girls and women in the United States focused on training for caretaking professions, particularly teaching young children and nursing (Madigan, 2009). Many universities in the United States were not open to female applicants up until the 1970s (Antonoff, 2017). Millions of girls in poorer countries around the world are still being deprived of even primary education (grades 1 through 5) (Dorius & Firebaugh, 2010). A study of 113 million school-aged children indicated that 60% of girls aged 6 to 11 years were not enrolled in any school, with most of these girls living in Africa and the Middle East (UNESCO, 2004). With such great disparities in access to formal education, it goes without saying that boys and men, being more educated, would historically be considered more competent and more capable in a variety of money-making endeavors. In addition, property rights throughout history have strongly favored sons over daughters, with men accumulating wealth over time and women deprived of personal and family wealth (Meinzen-Dick, Brown, Sims Feldstein, & Quisumbing, 1997). With their disproportionate access to education and wealth, achieved through brute force and institutionalized oppression, it is not surprising that men have accumulated and held power all over the world and across time. In formal governmental and national roles with real power, men have clearly dominated. How many female Popes have there been, for example? How many Empresses versus Emperors, Queens instead of Kings? How many female Presidents of the United States? A bare glance at today's world statistics on government positions reveals clear male domination, with scant government power around the world afforded to women, including in wealthy, technologically advanced countries. While such inequalities are indeed changing around the world, differences between women and men are still quite large, especially in terms of political power (Dorius & Firebaugh, 2010).

The United Nations (2004) asserted a Millennium Development Goal of promoting gender equality around the world and empowering girls and women, with four key indicators of progress: decreasing inequality in literacy based on gender; increasing equality in primary, secondary, and tertiary (higher) education; increasing numbers of women in parliamentary seats held; and increasing numbers of women among wage earners in non-agricultural work. The World Economic Forum (2018) focuses on similar dimensions to reach gender parity: educational attainment, economic opportunity and participation, political power, and health and longevity. Across these four dimensions, the World Economic Forum estimates gender parity to be around 68%, with an average gap of 32% around the world, favoring men. According to the 2017 Global Gender Gap report, based on current trends around the world, gender parity will be reached globally in 202 years for economic equality, and 107 years for political empowerment. The countries with the greatest gender equality currently are Iceland, Norway, Sweden, Finland, Nicaragua, Rwanda, Namibia, the Philippines, New Zealand, and Ireland.

In most countries around the world, while the gender gap still exists, it is decreasing, with women's economic and social positions improving and moving closer, but very slowly, to those of men (Hausmann, Tyson, & Zahidi, 2007). The international gender wage gap is currently 13.8, meaning that for every one monetary unit that men make for paid work, women make only .862, with 48.5% of women and 75% of men worldwide working full-time (International Labour Organization, 2018; Organisation for Economic Co-operation and Development, 2018; World Bank, 2018) (see Figure 12.2). The gender wage gap is higher in the United States, with women making around 82 cents for every dollar that men make nationally (OECD, 2018). Women's gains around the world are particularly strong in terms of success in higher education, with women outnumbering men as college and university students in the United States and other advanced nations (Dorius & Firebaugh, 2010; Freeman, 2005). As such, women are gaining higher professional positions and making more money, with women the primary breadwinners in around one-fourth of United States families (Goings, 2008). Women are still lacking in higher executive positions in organizations (Catalyst, 2009; Foust-Cummings & Pomeroy, 2008; Goings, 2008). Gender inequality is greatest in areas that are developing (countries with lower life expectancies, education rates, per capita income, and less advanced technologies; O'Sullivan & Sheffrin, 2003). Population growth is highest in these poorer regions of the world, with women having greater numbers of children and fewer economic opportunities (Dorius & Firebaugh, 2010). Access to contraception has a powerful and positive influence on women's abilities to become educated and to earn higher incomes (Goldin & Katz, 2002; Miller, 2010), with access to contraception much less likely in developing regions of the world (Jayachandran, 2015). These same regions tend to be dominated by traditional religions, which tend to place girls and women in inferior, subjugated,

Figure 12.2 Women perform as well as men in the workplace but are frequently paid less for the same job
Source: Monkeybusinessimages/iStock Photo

subservient positions to boys and men. These traditional religious ideas and practices prevent cultural change and advancement of gender equality (Ingelhart & Norris, 2003; Jayachandran, 2015; Lopez-Carlos & Zahida, 2005).

Working Families

Household Responsibilities and Childcare

Families are not just people who are genetically related to each other, but people who live together for any extended period of time. People who share living spaces share life; they interact daily and share property, objects, food, and time with each other. Families are not necessarily happy or even functional; conflict in families is common (Johnson, 1995; see Chapter 10). It is obviously impossible to change to whom one is genetically related; one cannot choose one's parents, one is literally stuck with the parents (and their relatives) one is born to (barring the possibility of adoption, but then you're stuck with them too). It is also not possible for many people to change their living situation; poverty, young age, disabilities, and other factors restrict freedom to escape high-conflict or dysfunctional living situations. For children, families are usually ascribed, they are not chosen. For adults, families and unhappy living situations may be chosen to some degree, but not easily escaped. People who marry at younger ages (especially younger than 20 years old) are less likely to report positive marriages, more likely to report marriage and life problems, and more likely to experience divorce (Santhya, 2011; Wolfinger, 2015). Unwanted children often suffer poorer quality families with young parents and lower income (Trias, 1982).

Occupational Roles and Power 397

Single girls and women who have children are especially likely to live in poverty (United States Census Bureau, 2014). Other families are loving, supportive, and happy; escape is not needed or even considered. Such families tend to involve older (but not too old; Wolfinger, 2015), educated adults who marry or live together by choice and who want and plan for children (Guo & Huang, 2005; Stanley, Amato, Johnson, & Markman, 2006).

In any family, to function well, there must be some kind of caretaking, including caring for the less competent and capable members (e.g., babies, children, disabled and elderly or sick relatives). This caretaking must also involve someone responsible for maintaining food supplies and preparing meals, and maintaining cleanliness of the living space to prevent disease. Across history, girls and women have generally been assigned the bulk of **family work** (work directed toward caring for the family and living spaces; Coltrane, 2000), while boys and men have typically been assigned work requiring physical strengths (lifting, running speed, etc.) and intelligence, especially work outside the home for pay (Becker, 1981). Across history, girls and women have been nearly exclusively responsible for caring for infants and children, particularly given the physical capacity to feed children that men lack. Evolutionarily, women have a greater investment in every individual offspring, because of their inability to easily produce many offspring. Men of course could literally produce a viable zygote (or three or four, maybe more) every single day, thus are less invested in any particular zygote, fetus, infant, or child (Geary, 2000). As such, it makes sense that women would be more involved in caring for offspring and more motivated to be involved and that men would be less involved and less motivated to care for offspring. As caretaking of infants and others generally occurs within the living space (the family home), such roles often also involve maintenance of the living space, provision of meals, and so on. The **social roles** that are created through this **division of labor** then come to define what **femininity** and **masculinity** involve, how they are defined, what women and what men are presumed to be like (Eagly, 1987), creating expectations that individuals and social structures then use to guide their behavior toward girls and women, boys and men (Fiske & Taylor, 1991). In this way, **stereotypes** of women's and men's family and work roles, and the qualities believed to be involved in such roles, serve to support and justify the division of labor by gender and a hierarchal social structure with men in control of women, a process termed **system justification** (Jost & Banaji, 1994). Further, through socialization, individuals incorporate prescriptions and proscriptions regarding social roles into their individual identities (Cinamon & Rich, 2002; Cross & Madson, 1997). Gendered social roles are more likely to be emphasized and followed in more traditional cultures, including in countries that are less technologically advanced, poorer, and characterized by traditional religions (Jayachandran, 2015).

Modernly, with advancements in technology, educational opportunities, and intellectual (rather than physical) occupations, family work is less typically but still primarily relegated to girls and women. While some women and some men do take on the role of **stay-at-home parent**, the typical family in Western and wealthier countries around the world consists of two adults who work outside the home and their child(ren) (Jacobs & Gerson, 1998). In the United States, numbers of women in the workforce and earning university degrees have increased greatly (Johns, 2013), with women now earning a majority of college degrees (Goldin et al., 2006; U.S. Congress Joint Economic Committee, 2010). Increasingly, individuals and couples are choosing not to have children at all (Centers for Disease Control and Prevention, 2018). These changes affect family work and who is deemed responsible for most of it.

Working mothers are more commonly required to cope with multiple roles than working fathers (Barnett & Hyde, 2001). As a group, employed women have greater combined work and family demands than employed men (Duxbury, Higgins, & Lee, 1994; Shelton, 1990), including greater responsibility for housework and childcare (Konrad, 2003). Current research indicates that women spend up to 60% more time engaged in unpaid work caring for the home than men (Fletcher, 2017; Office for National Statistics, 2016). Among heterosexual couples, women engage in substantially more household chores than men, regardless of career, income, age, or stage of life (Horne, Johnson, Galambos, & Krahn, 2017). Despite the fact that men likely dirty just as many dishes, use the shower and toilet just as much, and spend just as much time living in living spaces, women are still cleaning up after them. Although he used the shower as often as I did, and we both worked outside the home full-time, my ex-husband used to say, "I cleaned the shower *for you*," as if I had primary or even sole responsibility for that task. Hmmmmmmm, he *used to* say. Women also engage in more child and other care within the home than men, even when they work the same number of hours outside of the home (Milkie, Raley, & Bianchi, 2009; Offer & Schneider, 2011; Raley, Bianchi, & Wang, 2012; Yavorsky, Dush, & Schoppe-Sullivan, 2015). Women are more likely than men to provide care for elderly relatives (Family Caregiver Alliance, 2001; National Alliance for Caregiving and AARP, 2009) and for disabled relatives (Sharma, Chakrabarti, & Grover, 2016).

Why do these gender disparities in responsibility for family work persist, especially in wealthier, more advanced, less traditional countries? The "stay-at-home" mom role tends to be rather derogated in modern, technologically advanced cultures (Cuddy, Fiske, & Glick, 2004), being viewed as high in warmth (i.e., likable) but low in competence (Fiske, Cuddy, Glick, & Xu, 2002). Most Americans report viewing mothers as the parent most responsible for childcare (Deutsch & Saxon, 1998). Few Americans think that mothers with very young children should work full-time (Pew Research Center, 2015). Individually, women tend to value childcare and household work more than men do, while men tend to value family work that occurs outside the home (e.g., caring for automobiles) (Kroska, 2003). Endorsement of traditional gender roles by women and men is associated with greater housework and childcare disparities within families (Gunter & Gunter, 1991). Research indicates that dual-earner families in which both parents work are characterized by more egalitarian views on gender roles and more symmetrical distribution of home and work roles between parents compared to families with mothers who are not employed outside the home (Perry-Jenkins, 1993) (see Figures 12.3a and 12.3b).

In poorer countries, traditional gender roles in the family are often strongly emphasized within traditional religious ideologies, thus making them more powerfully imposed on girls and women in families (Para-Mallam, 2010). If a god or powerful person says you are subservient to men, that you will be punished if you are not, and that you are immoral if you act in ways proscribed by the religion, then one is fearful of violating such norms. Family work responsibilities prevent women's active participation in education and the labor force; as such, imposition of excessive family work on girls and women functions to maintain gender disparities by preventing education and occupational opportunities for them (Morrison & Lamana, 2006). Girls and women, especially in developing countries, cannot possibly attain social and financial equality with men if they are continually impressed into positions of un- or low-paid domestic and family service, more so than boys and men. Gendered, traditional social roles then are a primary cause of inequality and oppression of girls and women (Lerner, 1986).

Young people today are more likely to report egalitarian attitudes about family work. Studies indicate that daughters of employed mothers are more career oriented, more likely to pursue nontraditional occupations, and more egalitarian in sex-role attitudes than daughters of homemaker mothers (Tsuzuki & Matsui, 1997). Young adult women and men who grew up with mothers employed full-time outside the home report less traditional family attitudes, including planning

Figures 12.3a and 12.3b Couples are more likely to share childcare responsibilities in dual-earner households
Source: Pixdeluxe/iStock Photo and FatCamera/iStock Photo

fewer children and more egalitarian division of family work. Young people who grow up completing household chores themselves, which is more likely to occur in dual-earner families, report greater feelings of self-efficacy (views of the self as a competent person in general) (Riggio, Valenzuela, & Weiser, 2010). Riggio and Desrochers (2006) found that both young women and men with continuously working mothers reported greater parenting self-efficacy (views of the self as a competent parent in the future) than young people who grew up with mothers who were not employed outside the home. Young women with employed mothers reported expecting to spend less time per week with families than young women with nonemployed mothers, while men with employed mothers reported expecting to spend more time with their families than men with nonemployed mothers. Men with consistently nonemployed mothers were particularly likely to report lower feelings of self-efficacy. As rates of women completing higher education and working outside the home increase, their children are raised with strong, accomplished, hard-working female role models, models they see for themselves and their families in the future (Riggio, 2006).

Parental Leave

Women who work are much more likely to adjust their careers to accommodate family responsibilities and parenting compared to working men. First, pregnancy and childbirth are life-threatening events; surviving both requires adequate prenatal care, rest, medical care, and other accommodations (World Health Organization, 2008). Pregnancy and childbirth complications are *the* leading cause of death among women aged 15 to 19 years in developing countries (Mayor, 2004). These activities also take time; pregnancy lasts for 40 weeks to full term, childbirth may require extended hospital stays, and both may require bed rest (staying off one's feet for the majority of the day) because of risks of complications (Meher, Abalos, Carroli, & Meher, 2005; Sosa, Althabe, Belizán, & Bergel, 2015). Most women must miss at least some work, which affects career advancement, during pregnancy and after (Equality and Human Rights Commission, 2018). Infancy lasts for fully one year, and breastfeeding is recommended throughout infancy for maximal developmental benefits (Centers for Disease Control & Prevention, 2018). Within the United States, workers are entitled to 12 weeks of unpaid parental leave (an inclusive term for maternity and paternity leave) under the Family Medical Leave Act (McKay, 2018). Under a plan proposed by the Trump Administration, organizations would provide less than three weeks of paid parental leave at full pay, with the United States being one of the only advanced countries in the world not offering paid leave to parents, subsidized by the government, for several months, even years (England, 2017). Around 38% of U.S. work organizations offer paid parental leave, usually limited to five or six weeks (Trimarchi, 2017).

Research indicates that women who take maternity leave suffer negative setbacks in their employment and career progression. Organizations may view working mothers as a burden on the organization, or not as vital to organizational success as men who cannot become pregnant (Equality and Human Rights Commission, 2018). Many employers have an idea that workers should be available whenever they are needed and that they should be devoted to their work (Bailyn, 1993). Working women are likely to delay or forgo having children altogether as a way to advance their careers, and around 20% of women who are mothers report being discriminated against by their employer (Equality and Human Rights Commission, 2018). Men's decisions about having children and being a father are comparatively unrelated to their career decisions (Van der Horst, Van der Lippe, & Kluwer, 2014).

Although very few jobs in the United States offer paid paternity leave to male workers (Okerlund, 2018), research indicates that men are not likely to ask for or use such benefits even when they are offered. One report indicates that around 76% of fathers take only one week or even less of leave after the birth or adoption of a child (Harrington, Van Deusen, Sabatini Fraone, Eddy, & Haas, 2014). Men may feel that taking leave will damage their careers, much as it damages those of mothers (Butler & Skattebo, 2004; Wayne & Codeiro, 2003). In one experiment, male employees requesting parental leave were perceived as poor organizational citizens and as feminine (weak, uncertain) and low in masculinity compared to male employees not requesting such leave. Men requesting leave were also more at risk for imposition of job penalties (e.g., demotion) specifically because they were perceived as more feminine (Rudman & Mescher, 2013). Additional research indicates that men who request and take parental leave from their work organization are viewed as feminine and correspondingly viewed more negatively as workers (Vandello, Hettinger, Bosson, & Siddiqi, 2013). This is unfair and unfortunate for fathers and children, with taking paternity leave positively linked with fathers' engagement and involvement with and sense of responsibility for their children over time, especially in disadvantaged groups (Knoester, Petts, & Pragg, 2019). Women are much more likely than men to reduce their work hours, take time off work, turn down a promotion, or quit a job entirely to care for family members. They are also more likely to report that such work reductions negatively affected their career progression (Pew Research Center, 2015). With these kinds of gender disparities in family caretaking, it is not surprising that women make less money, have fewer opportunities for high-level career positions, and have less social and political power than men.

Work-Family Conflict

Work-family conflict or imbalance involves conflict between work and family roles, and when work intrudes into or disrupts family life and vice versa (Ford, Heinen, & Langkamer, 2007; Greenhaus & Beutell, 1985). Work-family conflict is highly stressful (Allen, Herst, Bruck, & Sutton, 2000); having a family emergency while on the job or having to leave family events for work responsibilities can obviously affect one's sense of happiness, well-being, and life satisfaction, especially when such conflict happens frequently. Work stress is strongly predictive of family satisfaction (Ford et al., 2007). Repeated experiences of work-family conflict result in worker stress and lower job satisfaction, affecting worker productivity and individual and organizational outcomes (Kahn & Byosiere, 1992; King, Botsford, & Huffman, 2009). Because women may view family roles as more central to their identity than work roles, while men tend to view work more than family roles as central to their identity, women and men experience work-family conflict differently (Van der Lippe, Jager, & Kops, 2006). Cinamon and Rich (2002) found that women reported more frequent and more disruptive interference with family from work than did men. Additional research indicates that women experience greater strife between family and work life than men (Crompton, 2002). An organizational culture that is supportive of working parents and families may have meaningful effects on reducing work-family conflict and its negative outcomes (Den Dulk, Peper, Kanjuo Mrčela, & Ignjatović, 2016). Although working from home creates greater flexibility for working women and men, especially if they are parents, research indicates that working from home creates greater work-family conflict, especially for women (Van der Lippe & Lippényi, 2018).

As we've discussed throughout this book, single women and their children are the greatest segment of the population living in poverty anywhere in the world (United Nations, 2010; United

States Census Bureau, 2014). The average cost of 40 hours of childcare in the United States is approximately $1,445.00 per month, a substantial portion of any average person's monthly salary (Business Broker Network, 2019). The cost of raising a child increased by approximately 40% from 2000 to 2010, with average cost of raising a child from birth to 17 years old (not including college costs) in the United States being $233,610 (Im, 2018). If a woman, particularly a young woman who is not educated and does not come from wealth, becomes pregnant when she doesn't want to be pregnant, the best option for a woman's independent future and any potential future success she might have is a safe, legal, medical abortion. It is impossible for poor girls and women to be pregnant, give birth, and stay home to care for an infant without assistance of some kind and without sinking deeper into poverty. Depriving women of **bodily integrity**, forcing girls and women to endanger their lives with pregnancy and childbirth, and essentially depriving them of their rights to liberty and pursuit of happiness, is not only oppressive, it is morally wrong. Girls and women will have sex, that is for certain, just as boys and men will have sex. Boys and men are not forced to undergo life-threatening physical conditions of pregnancy and childbirth; they are not forced to put their life on hold during pregnancy and afterward to care for young children. This is an oppression reserved nearly exclusively for women around the world, since the dawn of time (United Nations, 2010). Pregnancy and childbirth are not punishments for boys and men having unprotected sex; they shouldn't be punishments for women either. Lack of access to reliable contraception and legal abortion are leading causes of women's poverty around the world (Goldin & Katz, 2002; Jayachandran, 2015; Miller, 2010).

Occupational Stereotypes

Beliefs that certain occupations require particular feminine or masculine traits (**occupational stereotypes**) support a traditional division of labor by gender, with girls and women relegated to domestic roles and boys and men trained, educated, and provided with employed work outside the home (Eagly & Steffen, 1984). Some jobs require greater physical strength; the average man performs better than the average woman on such tasks, given the obvious large differences in physical strength between women and men (Sell, Hone, & Pound, 2012). Such jobs involve physical labor (digging, lifting, etc.), or efficiency associated with strength. But with technological advancements there are declining numbers of these jobs, and such jobs are not necessarily associated with higher incomes or prestige (Cejka & Eagly, 1999). Activities requiring male sexual qualities include **sex work** and sperm donation. There are even fewer jobs that actually require physical qualities of girls and women. The only ones I can think of are egg donation (which isn't really an occupation); **surrogate mother** (again, probably not a great career, with a lot of physical risks), **wet nurse** (a lactating woman who provides milk to other people's children), and sex worker (a very dangerous job, with female and male prostitutes suffering rape, assault, and homicide at elevated rates compared to others; Deering et al., 2014).

Although physical strength is not required in most jobs these days, occupations around the world are still segregated by gender. Studies of occupational stereotypes indicate that occupations considered the most masculine in the United States in 1975 (mean ratings between 1 and 2 on a 7-point scale, with 1 = *masculine* and 7 = *feminine*) were miner, highway maintenance worker, heavy-equipment operator, U.S. Supreme Court Justice, building contractor, construction worker, mining engineer, railroad conductor, boat captain, and auto mechanic. The four occupations rated as most feminine (mean ratings between 6 and 7) were manicurist, registered nurse, receptionist, and private secretary (Shinar, 1975). These same results were found by Beggs and Doolittle in

1993 in the U.S. In 2000 in Spain and France, Sastre and colleagues found 10 occupations rated between 1 and 2 (highly masculine): miner, highway maintenance worker, heavy-equipment operator, construction worker, boat captain, auto mechanic, electrician, race-car driver, carpenter, and fisher. Only one occupation was seen as highly feminine (greater than 6 on the scale), that of manicurist. Other jobs seen as more masculine included police sergeant, bell captain, and orchestra conductor, while those viewed as more feminine included private secretary, librarian, and nurse (Sastre, Fouquereau, Igier, Salvatore, & Mullet, 2000). Although some of the masculine-rated jobs do require some physical strength, there is little strength involved in being an orchestra conductor, an electrician, or a bell captain, and female race-car drivers outperform men quite frequently (Petrány, 2014). It is also unclear what feminine qualities are required to be a librarian or a secretary, except perhaps quietness and obedience. Across these three studies, fewer jobs are rated as either highly feminine or highly masculine over time, and variability in ratings of various occupations has decreased, indicating increasing gender neutrality in ratings.

Additional studies have examined how people evaluate occupations in terms of the characteristics they require and if those qualities are perceived as feminine or masculine. In an earlier study, Glick (1991) found that the best predictor of ratings of an occupation's prestige was the association of the job with masculine personality characteristics. Cejka and Eagly (1999) first asked participants to identify female- and male-typed physical, personality, and cognitive characteristics (see Table 12.1). Then they asked participants to indicate how much they believed that those qualities were linked with success in various occupations. Like the findings of Glick (1991), the degree to which masculine personality qualities (e.g., competitive, unexcitable, aggressive) were viewed as essential to job success was a significant predictor of ratings of an occupation's prestige. The degree to which masculine cognitive qualities (e.g., analytical, exact) were viewed as essential to a job's success was also a significant predictor of occupational prestige. Cejka and Eagly also found that the necessity of masculine qualities for a job was significantly predictive of participants' estimated and actual incomes associated with such jobs. A job's requirement of feminine personality and cognitive qualities was not associated with ratings of occupational prestige, and the requirement of female physical qualities was linked negatively with prestige ratings. Finally, beliefs that gender stereotypic qualities are necessary for successful job performance were strongly predictive of the actual distributions of women and men in such occupations in the United States obtained from Census data, indicating that occupational stereotypes correspond with and justify segregation of paid work and professions by gender. Girls and boys, women and men express occupational preferences that are similarly consistent with occupational stereotypes (Lippa, 1995; Lippa & Connelly, 1990; Miller & Hayward, 2006). Currently in the United States, occupations dominated by women include elementary and middle school teacher, secretary and administrative assistant, and registered nurse. Occupations dominated by men include truck driver, manager, production worker, and electrician (United States Department of Labor, 2015).

Sexism on the Job

Stereotypes, Emotions, and Power

Stereotypes affect every aspect of individuals' lives, including interactions with and perceptions of and by other people at work. Gender stereotypes describe what women and men should be like, how they should and should not behave, and they have the same power of setting up

404   *Occupational Roles and Power*

Table 12.1 Description of gender-stereotypic dimensions

Gender-stereotypic dimension

Characteristics of dimension	Masculine Physical	Feminine Physical	Masculine Personality	Feminine Personality	Masculine Cognitive	Feminine Cognitive
Attributes in dimension	Athletic	Pretty	Competitive	Affectionate	Analytical	Imaginative
	Burly	Sexy	Daring	Sympathetic	Mathematical	Intuitive
	Rugged	Gorgeous	Unexcitable	Gentle	Good with numbers	Artistic
	Muscular	Dainty	Dominant	Sensitive	Exact	Expressive
	Tall	Soft voice	Adventurous	Nurturing	Good at reasoning	Perceptive
	Vigorous	Cute	Stands up under pressure	Sentimental	Abstract	Verbally skilled
	Brawny	Petite	Aggressive	Warm in relations	Creative	Problem solving
				Good with others		
	Strong	Beautiful	Courageous	Helpful to others		Tasteful
				Sociable		
				Understanding		
				Cooperative		
				Supportive		
				Kind		
				Outgoing		

Source: Cejka, M. A., & Eagly, A. H. (1999). Gender-stereotypic images of occupations correspond to the sex segregation of employment. *Personality and Social Psychology Bulletin, 25*, 413-423.

expectations and particular reactions when women and men are working. Because stereotypes of women include negative beliefs that legitimize their oppression, women's work lives are negatively affected when traditional gender stereotypes are used to evaluate them. Individuals use stereotypes to process information about other individuals; women as workers may be perceived as women first, with gender being a primary category used to process information about women (Eagly & Kite, 1987). Women's work is considered that, work by a woman, not just work. As such, when women workers defy or violate gender stereotypes, their work behavior may be judged negatively because they are not acting "ladylike" or like a woman. Because men are stereotypically and rather automatically viewed as more competent and more typically engaged in work (Eagly, 1983; Fiske, 2017), men's paid work is seen as normative or expected rather than as an option, as it is seen for women (Bridges & Etaugh, 1995; Wood & Eagly, 2002). Women at work may self-fulfill gender stereotypes if they perceive that others hold traditional gender stereotypes (Cikara & Fiske, 2009; von Baeyer, Sherk, & Zanna, 1981). When stereotypes operate in the workplace, they affect processes in face-to-face interviews (Latu, Mast, & Stewart, 2015), recruitment and hiring practices (Heilman, Manzi, & Braun, 2015), evaluations of performance (Ridgeway & Correll, 2004), considerations for advancement (Johns, 2013; Kunkel, Dennis, & Waters, 2003), and termination decisions (Gupta, Mortal, Silveri, Sun, & Turban, 2018), nearly always in favor of men's power to the disadvantage of women (Foschi, 2000; Correll & Benard, 2006).

Occupational Roles and Power   405

Table 12.2 Gendered display rules

	Positive emotions	Negative emotions
Women	Nurturance, warmth, joy/elation, compassion, admiration, cheerfulness	Fear, embarrassment, anxiety, vulnerability, bewilderment, worry, insecurity, jealousy, shame, envy
Men	Confidence, pride	Anger, stubbornness, resolve

Source: Ragins, B. R., & Winkel, D. E. (2011). Gender, emotion and power in work relationships. *Human Resource Management Review, 21,* 377-393.

Working women are often perceived as competitive and competent, but not warm or likable (Bridges, Etaugh, & Barnes-Farrell, 2002; Eckes, 2002; Etaugh & Poertner, 2002). They are considered less dedicated to their children and families (Etaugh & Nekolny, 1990), especially when they work for their own personal goals and achievements and not because of financial necessity (Bridges & Etaugh, 1995). Some scholars assert that perceptions of working women involve **envious prejudice**, where they are respected as competent but disliked at the same time because of their success and perceptions of low warmth (Glick & Fiske, 2001). One experiment found that when working women became mothers, they were judged as higher in warmth but lower in competence compared to working women who were not also mothers. In contrast, judgments of the competence of working men were not affected by them becoming fathers, yet becoming a father resulted in increased ratings of working men's warmth (Cuddy, Fiske, & Glick, 2004). Similarly, working women who request flexibility on the job to accommodate childcare needs are perceived as having lower career dedication and potential for advancement than working women on traditional work schedules (Rogier & Padgett, 2004). Judgments of competence and **agency** (energy and ability to accomplish goals) are highly predictive of hiring and promotion decisions, with men and childless people favored as employees over women and those with children (Cartwright, Hussey, Roche, Dunne, & Muphy, 2017; Cuddy et al., 2004; Heilman & Wallen, 2010; Moss-Racusin, Phelan, & Rudman, 2010).

Women's and men's emotions are perceived differently at work. As we've discussed in previous chapters (see Chapter 9), women generally report experiencing more intense and frequent emotions than men (Brebner, 2003; Brody & Hall, 2000; Kelly & Hutson Comeaux, 1999). Women report experiencing fear, shame, guilt, and sadness more than men, emotions associated with lack of power and independence (Brody & Hall, 2000; Fischer, Rodriguez Mosquera, van Vianen, & Manstead, 2004). In contrast, men report more commonly experiencing anger and pride, emotions associated with power (Fischer & Jansz, 1995; Tiedens, 2001). In addition to experiencing emotions more than men, women are also more emotionally expressive than men (Brebner, 2003; Brody & Hall, 2000). Gender stereotypes dictate which emotions are appropriate or desirable from women and men, with women expected to be warm, compassionate, and nurturing, and men expected to be proud and confident (Brescoll & Uhlmann, 2008; Hess, Adams, & Kleck, 2005). Such expectations are called **display rules** and they are used by individuals in various contexts, including at work (Ragins & Winkel, 2011; see Table 12.2). Emotions expected from men are associated with power in relationships, whereas those expected from women are associated with interdependence, caretaking, and low power overall (Conroy, Elliot, & Pincus, 2009; Hess, Blairy, & Kleck, 2000; Overbeck, Neale, & Govan, 2010). Men who express anger at work are perceived as powerful, decisive, and assertive, while women who express anger at work are evaluated negatively as harsh and overemotional (Brescoll & Uhlmann, 2008; Sinaceur & Tiedens, 2006). As such, women who display emotions considered appropriate to their gender at work are perceived as having low power and authority, which will necessarily affect their actual levels of organizational power (Fischer, 2000; Johnson & Shulman, 1988; Shields, 2000), while women who display more masculine-typed emotions at work are also perceived negatively (Rudman & Fairchild, 2004; Rudman & Glick, 2001). Once again, stereotypes serve to justify a patriarchal system where women are never evaluated as positively as men and men hold the bulk of power.

So why do emotions work to create power for men but not for women? A central cause involves beliefs about emotions and their controllability. For men, who are perceived as strong and competent, emotions are viewed as controllable; men carefully decide when to be emotional and then use their emotions to accomplish goals (Côté & Hideg, 2011; Gibson & Schroeder, 2002). Men's emotions are important because they are selective; men are viewed as controlling their emotions, which affects perceptions of power and influence (Hareli & Rafaeli, 2008; Tiedens, Ellsworth, & Mesquita, 2000). To compound this effect, powerful people (most commonly men) express more positive emotions (Berdahl & Martorana, 2006), are granted greater latitude by others in emotional expression (Tiedens et al., 2000), and their emotions often have the effect of increasing their power (Côté & Hideg, 2011; George, 2000). In contrast, women are viewed as *characteristically* emotional and emotionally expressive; that is, their emotions are not strategic or so important that they must be expressed, but are part of who they are all the time (Wood & Eagly, 2010). As such, women's emotions are not chosen strategies or communication of something important, but may be viewed as irrational, as linked to personality and not to real circumstances, and as likely to spin out of control (Shields, 2005). Women's emotions can thus be disregarded and viewed as a character flaw, rather than as important information about the task at hand, and women's power is limited (Carli, 2006; Ragins & Winkel, 2011). I am Vice Chair on a committee that I have been a member of for over 10 years, and I recently sent an email to the committee Chair about a flawed practice that could result in several negative outcomes, an argument I carefully outlined in my email. Later that day in a meeting with the committee, the Chair (a woman) announced that I was "*cranky*" that morning, an instant and fierce weapon that portrayed me as an irrational, emotional female (probably menstruating) whose opinion is not important. One word, and my competence and power as a professional were diminished, through an accusation of emotionality.

Ambivalent Sexism

Recall from Chapter 7 our discussion of ambivalent sexism, the co-existence of both positive (benevolent) and negative (hostile) attitudes toward women specifically because they are women. Benevolent sexism involves views of women as warm and desirable, but low in competence. Hostile sexism involves perceptions of women as aggressive and attempting to overtake, control, and diminish men (Glick & Fiske, 1996). In the workplace, benevolent sexism leads to perceptions of women as weak and incompetent, as less effective workers who need greater assistance by management. Women perceived as assertive and competent at work are generally judged as not likable (Rudman & Fairchild, 2004; Rudman & Glick, 2001). Both forms of sexism in the workplace promote power differences, with men afforded greater power, both through perceptions of others and incorporation of such beliefs by women into their own self-concepts (Becker, 2010; Cikara & Fiske, 2009). Benevolent sexist beliefs are linked with men assigning fewer challenging work tasks to female than male employees, which limits women's opportunities for learning and advancement on the job (King et al., 2012). Women exposed to benevolent and hostile sexism in a work context experience anxiety (Pacilli, Spaccatini, Giovannelli, Centrone, & Roccato, 2018), and women who are professionally successful are often liked less and perceived as interpersonally hostile compared to men of equal success (Heilman, Wallen, Fuchs, & Tamkins, 2004). While benevolent sexism is linked to support of gender equity employment practices, it contributes to continued gender segregation and power differentials by extending only to promotion of women into feminine job positions (Hideg & Ferris, 2016). Both hostile and benevolent sexism are linked with more negative judgments toward women making sexual harassment claims at work, but particularly hostile sexism (O'Connor, Gutek, Stockdale, Geer, & Melancon, 2004; Russell & Trigg, 2004). One study found that regardless of their endorsement of hostile or benevolent sexist beliefs, men as a group were especially likely to have negative judgments toward female sexual harassment complainants when they acted assertively in their complaint (Wiener et al., 2010).

The Glass Ceiling

The **glass ceiling** is a term that describes an apparently invisible but solid structure that prevents women from attaining the highest levels of organizational power. It is invisible because it is hidden from plain sight and artificial, not based on women's actual work experiences, capabilities, and talents (Johns, 2013). In the corporate world, as of November 2018, the number of Fortune 500 companies headed by women was only 26; that's 26 out of 500, or 5.2%. The number had decreased from 2017, when it was 32 out of 500 (6.4%) (Bellstrom, 2018). Women comprise only 17% of board members in Fortune 500 companies, 16% of board members in the top 500 companies in Canada, and 17.8% of board members in the largest companies in the European Union (Catalyst, 2013a, 2013b; European Commission Justice, 2014). Around 40% of top Canadian companies had no female board members at all (Catalyst, 2013a). Numbers are even smaller for women of color, with African-American women comprising less than 0.5% of corporate officers in Fortune 500 companies (Mejia, 2018). Although the majority of employees within the health care industry are female, only 13% of U.S. health care organizations have female CEOs (Stone, Miller, Southerlan, & Raun, 2019). Although women comprise one-half of people working in professional and management occupations (United States Department of Commerce, Economic and Statistics Administration, 2001), research indicates that women in executive positions are lacking across organizations (Catalyst, 2009; Foust-Cummings & Pomeroy, 2008; Goings, 2008).

What causes this massive disparity in wealth, opportunity, and power by gender? There are a few explanations. First, if one is sexist, the argument may be that women are simply inferior; they are incapable of leading and succeeding the way men do because of their ascribed qualities (e.g., emotionality, low intelligence, lack of stamina, all of the myths used to legitimize oppression). In refutation of this simplistic argument, evidence from nearly 22,000 companies in 91 countries around the world indicates that for-profit organizations are significantly more successful when women hold leadership positions (Noland, Moran, & Kotschwar, 2016). Research on group effectiveness indicates that groups that include women are more successful than all-male groups (Knouse & Dansby, 1999). In addition, women are outperforming men in terms of earning of university degrees, especially advanced degrees (Goldin et al., 2006), powerful evidence that women are just as intellectually capable as men (along with abundant research indicating no gender differences in general intelligence; Halpern & LaMay, 2000). Research evidence refutes this **old-fashioned sexist** argument.

408 *Occupational Roles and Power*

Other explanations for the ridiculous difference in numbers of female and male leaders focus on **patriarchy** and oppression. As we've discussed throughout this book, **social dominance** theory explains that hierarchies often exist within societies, with the people at the top (men in this case) enjoying a disproportionate share of that society's resources (power, wealth) and the people at the bottom of the hierarchy (women and those who do not identify as men) suffering a disproportionate share of society's shortcomings and liabilities (poverty, lack of opportunity) (Pratto & Walker, 2004). To maintain their social dominance, men (and women who support patriarchy) directly discriminate against girls and women; they provide messages (legitimizing myths) through socialization that girls and women are inferior and incapable, and that they should serve men in domestic roles; they deny access to education and training; they deny access to jobs through discriminatory hiring, training, promotion, collaboration, and termination practices. The empirical evidence from scholars and international organizations reviewed throughout this chapter (and this book) concerning all of the above strongly supports a social dominance explanation for the so-called glass ceiling.

Many countries around the world have developed employment equity policies to increase the hiring and promotion of women in work organizations (Yang, D'Souza, Bapat, & Colarelli, 2006). Such policies may include **affirmative action**, meaning female employees are hired over male employees if they are equally qualified. Much research indicates that employees often have negative attitudes toward such equity policies, attitudes linked to hostile sexism (Harrison, Kravitz, Mayer, Leslie, & Lev-Arey, 2006; Konrad & Hartmann,2001; Son Hing et al., 2011). In addition, although explicit stereotypes of women have become more positive over time (Stoker, Van der Velde, & Lammers, 2012), implicit negative stereotypes about women as weak and low in competence persist in affecting judgments about women, especially in leadership roles (Latu et al., 2011; Nosek, Banaji, & Greenwald, 2002; Rudman & Kilianski, 2000). When women are CEOs in corporations, they are significantly more likely to be fired than their male counterparts (called the **glass cliff**). Further, male CEOs are likely to be fired when organizations are doing poorly; female CEOs are more likely to be fired, regardless of the organization's current success (Gupta et al., 2018).

Leadership

Scholars who study leadership have identified various leadership styles or types, with some more effective than others. Some leaders are **transactional**; they work with subordinates in a give and take style, with an exchange-based relationship. Subordinates are told what to do in their jobs, corrected when necessary, and are rewarded for meeting work goals. Other leaders are hands-off; they set goals and let employees try to meet them, with little interference or control over subordinates' behavior. This is termed **laissez-faire** leadership (Bass, 1981). These styles are not highly effective in modern work organizations that involve advanced technology, globalization, and increasing workforce diversity and education (Kanter, 1997). The most effective leaders are **transformational** in their style; they are future-oriented, they foster subordinates' commitment to the organization, they support developing skills and abilities and creativity of subordinates, they empower subordinates, and they are inspirational. They are role models for subordinates and make them feel proud to belong to the group (Avolio, 1999; Bass, 1998). Being in charge does not just mean telling people what to do anymore; good leaders are increasingly viewed as coaches and teachers of subordinates (Eagly, 2007). Meta-analyses indicate that transformational leadership is significantly more effective in enhancing subordinate performance than other leadership styles (Judge & Piccolo, 2004).

Women as leaders are often caught in a so-called "double bind" because of gender stereotypes (Eagly, 2007, p. 4). As indicated previously, women are expected to be communal (loving, understanding, warm, caretaking), while leaders are expected to be agentic, which comprises more masculine-typed behaviors (strong, decisive, unemotional). As such, women as leaders, in expressing strength, confidence, and toughness, may be disliked because they violate the communality stereotype. This is especially true when leadership roles are feminized and seen as requiring feminine qualities (Rudman & Glick, 2001). It is mainly male co-workers and employees who have a problem with female leaders, who struggle to be leaders while trying to keep male co-workers comfortable (Catalyst, 2001). However, transformational leadership does involve communal behaviors, including consideration of needs of individual subordinates. Meta-analyses indicate that female leaders tend to be higher in transformational leadership than men, particularly in terms of individualized consideration (supporting and encouraging subordinates), although differences are small (Eagly, Johannesen-Schmidt, & van Engen, 2003). Other studies of leader effectiveness indicate that context is important, with men more effective as leaders in male-dominated industries or in masculine-typed roles, and women more effective as leaders in fields that are less dominated by men and in less masculine roles (Eagly, Karau, & Makhijani, 1995). Across the 20th century, most Americans reported a preference for a male rather than a female boss (Carroll, 2006). Recent research indicates that most Americans currently report no preference (55%), with a very slight (2%) difference in the number of people who prefer a male to a female boss (Brenan, 2017).

Women in Politics

In spite of the potential "backlash" (Rudman, 1998) against female leaders because they behave assertively, confidently, or authoritatively (Rudman & Fairchild, 2004; Rudman & Glick, 2001), women's engagement in politics is increasing around the world (see Figures 12.4a and 12.4b). The 2016 Presidential election and comments by candidate and now President Trump about women ("grab 'em by the pussy"; that women are "pigs," "dogs," "low IQ," "horse-faced") have inspired American women to engage in politics in record numbers. In 2016, the United States House of Representatives had 85 female members out of 435 members (19.5%); in 2019, that number had increased to 102 female Representatives (23.4%). The number of female Senators increased from 20 in 2016 (20%) to 25 in 2019, a record high. Equality is a long way off, however. There are similar disparities in other branches of the U.S. government. Unfortunately, in the nearly 230-year history of the United States Supreme Court, only four women have served (see Figure 12.5), versus 110 men over that time period. And of course, there has never been a female Vice President or President of the United States (see "Inequalities and Injustices"). There are currently nine women serving as governors in the 50 U.S. states. As you can see for yourself, these numbers are not even approaching 50%. The inequities are obvious; these numbers aren't even close to representing one full half of the human race. These disparities result from centuries of patriarchy and oppression of women. There have also been very few members of the U.S. Congress who are people of color and who are openly gay or bisexual, evidence of historical and systemic racism and heteronormativity in the United States.

Women's political power (at least in terms of holding powerful positions) varies around the world. The World Economic Forum (2018) reports that 17 out of 149 countries currently have female heads of state (11.4%), and that women's participation in parliaments and as ministers (heads of government departments) around the world is low (24% and 18%, respectively).

410 *Occupational Roles and Power*

Figures 12.4a and 12.4b German Chancellor Angela Merkel and New Zealand Prime Minister Jacinda Ardern
Source: Isopix/Shutterstock and Mark Baker/AP/Shutterstock

Gender parity in terms of political power has been reached in five countries (Bahamas, Colombia, Jamaica, Laos, the Philippines). In terms of holding parliamentarian and other legislative seats, France, Sweden, Canada, and Slovenia have nearly reached gender parity, followed closely by Denmark, Norway, Finland, Iceland, the Netherlands, and Spain. Mexico and New Zealand also report comparatively greater numbers of female parliamentarians. The United States is much lower in terms of women's participation in politics as department heads (16%)

Occupational Roles and Power 411

Table 12.3 Not allowed to vote until when? History of women's suffrage around the world

- **1893** New Zealand
- **1902** Australia
- **1906** Finland
- **1913** Norway
- **1915** Denmark
- **1917** Canada
- **1918** Austria, Germany, Poland, Russia
- **1919** Netherlands
- **1920** United States
- **1921** Sweden
- **1928** Britain, Ireland
- **1930** South Africa
- **1931** Spain
- **1934** Turkey
- **1944** France
- **1945** Italy
- **1947** Argentina, Japan, Mexico, Pakistan
- **1949** China
- **1950** India
- **1954** Colombia
- **1957** Malaysia, Zimbabwe
- **1962** Algeria
- **1963** Iran, Morocco
- **1964** Libya
- **1967** Ecuador
- **1971** Switzerland
- **1972** Bangladesh
- **1974** Jordan
- **1976** Portugal
- **1989** Namibia
- **1990** Western Samoa
- **1993** Kazakhstan, Moldova
- **2005** Kuwait
- **2006** United Arab Emirates
- **2015** Saudi Arabia

Source: Data taken from www.infoplease.com/us/gender-sexuality/womens-suffrage.

and members of Congress (24%) (OECD, 2018). The World Bank (Kumar, 2015) reports that the highest rate of participation by women in parliaments occurs in Rwanda (63.8% of parliamentary seats), followed by Andorra (50%), Cuba (48.9%), Sweden (45%), and South Africa (44.8%). The fewest parliamentary seats held by women is in Yemen (.3%), Onan (1.2%), the Solomon Islands (2%), Papua New Guinea (2.7%), and Comoros (3%). And please remember, women around the world were not granted the right to vote in elections (suffrage) for the vast majority of recorded history (see Table 12.3). In the United States, women were granted the right to vote in 1920 through the 20th Amendment to the Constitution, so it is only 100 years that women have even been considered to participate in American politics. Black women and men could not vote in South Africa until the end of apartheid in the early 1990s (Myre, 1991).

Figure 12.5 The only four women to ever serve on the U.S. Supreme Court since 1789
Source: Wiki

Women were granted the right to vote in Kuwait in 2005, in the United Arab Emirates in 2006, and in Saudi Arabia in 2015.

Even as a record number of women (and people of color) are running for and being elected to office in the United States, blatant sexism is directed toward them. Alexandria Ocasio-Cortez, the youngest woman ever elected to Congress, was called a "little girl with a big mouth" by the Chairperson of a political action committee on national television (Papenfuss, 2019), a characterization of her as an emotional, irrational child, a diminishment of her as an educated woman with a mind and an opinion, who was fairly elected to a powerful office. Rush Limbaugh referred to her as "uppity" (Rozsa, 2019), and Whoopi Goldberg suggested that she "sit still" and "learn the job" (McCarthy, 2019), suggesting that the Congressperson shouldn't use her voice or express herself in her newly elected position. Representative Ocasio-Cortez was also socially attacked for appearing in a video where she was dancing, taken when she was in college (May, 2019). A woman dancing is a target of social ridicule? Can women do *anything* without being attacked or demeaned? Elizabeth Warren, Senator from Massachusetts, has recently announced that she will run for President in 2020. A major concern identified in the media is the degree to which Senator Warren is *likable* (at the same time when we have arguably the most unlikable male President in the history of the United States) (Lewis, 2019) (see Figure 12.6). One of the first female Muslim members of Congress (along with Ilhan Omar), Rashida Tlaib, said on camera that she was going to Washington D.C. to "impeach the motherfucker" (meaning Trump) (see Figures 12.7a, 12.7b and 12.7c). Responses from government officials and media personalities were immediately scathing, especially from Trump supporters, in spite of Trump's obvious, repeated (even daily) history of cursing, name-calling, and even worse behaviors (Blest, 2019). It is very clear that people who support patriarchy, including conserving the current political and social hierarchy in the United

Figure 12.6 United States Senator Elizabeth Warren
Source: Jack Kurtz/ZUMA Wire/Shutterstock

States, are quite fearful of, and therefore hostile toward, women, especially when they are in or trying to acquire positions of real power (Okimoto & Brescoll, 2010).

Chapter Summary

In the service of maintaining patriarchy, women's educational and occupational opportunities have been severely limited across the span of history and around the world. Modernly, girls and women are denied education and access to occupational training in many areas of the developing world. Across history, women's work has been primarily limited to family work with no pay or domestic work for low pay. In modern, technologically advanced societies, most women are employed full-time outside the home, including when they are mothers, yet the gender pay gap persists. Women's careers are strongly affected by pregnancy, childbirth, and raising children, while those of men are not. Women are still largely responsible for childcare and housework in dual-earner families, even when they work as many hours or make as much or more money than their male partners. Women and men who take parental leave are commonly perceived negatively by employers, but especially women. Women who return to work after having a child are viewed as less committed to their families, while the same is not true for men who become fathers. Occupational stereotypes have changed over time and are becoming more gender neutral, but stereotypes of feminine (e.g., manicurist) and masculine (e.g., construction worker) jobs have been documented around the world. Gender stereotypes affect perceptions of workers, with women disadvantaged in interviews,

Figures 12.7a, 12.7b, and 12.7c New U.S. Congresspeople Ilhan Omar, Alexandria Ocasio-Cortez, and Rashida Tlaib
Source: Preston Ehrler/SOPA Images/Shutterstock; Evan Agostini/Invision/AP/Shutterstock; Michael Reynolds/EPA-EFE/Shutterstock

Occupational Roles and Power   415

hiring, promotion, and demotion decisions. Most biases against working and leading women occur because feminine stereotypes do not match expectations about competence and assertive, agentic behaviors in positions of power. Because of the clash between feminine stereotypes and ideas about power and leadership, and despite evidence supporting the effectiveness of female leaders, there are still few female leaders in the corporate world and in governments around the world. The United States lags behind other countries (Iceland, Sweden, Finland, Nicaragua, Rwanda, Namibia, the Philippines, etc.) in gender equality in financial, political, and social power.

Thoughtful Questions

- How can physical standards for particular jobs be discriminatory against women? Against men?
- Describe the difference between implicit and explicit attitudes.
- Do you think sexism affected the outcome of the 2016 U.S. Presidential election? Why or why not? Provide evidence to support your point of view.
- Explain the challenges faced by women and men in working families.
- How is maternal employment linked with young adults' family expectations and self-efficacy?
- Explain parental leave and how it is differentially used by women and men. Explain how pregnancy and taking leave affects women's and men's career choices and progression.
- Explain the link between access to contraception and abortion, and women's poverty.
- Explain how emotional expression at work is linked with power for women and men.
- Explain the glass ceiling, including evidence that it exists and explanations for why it exists.
- Describe various leadership styles, including how they may overlap with gender stereotypes.
- Describe the research on leadership effectiveness and gender.
- Describe the current state of women's participation in politics around the world.

Glossary

Accessible: the degree to which a schema is easily retrieved and used for processing information. For sexists, gender stereotypes are highly accessible schemas.

Affirmative action: employment policies that favor the hiring of an equally-qualified person from a minority or oppressed group rather than a white male.

Agency: energy, motivation, and ability to accomplish goals.

Agentic: traits involved in action (assertiveness, decisiveness, strength, rationality), typical of stereotypes of masculinity around the world.

Alpha male: the dominant male in a primate group, usually based on greater physical size and strength.

Ambivalent sexism: the psychological co-existence of positive and negative attitudes toward women, of benevolent and hostile sexism.

Apartheid: a formal system of institutionalized racism and white supremacy in South Africa in the latter half of the 20th century, used by minority whites to oppress black people and others so as to accumulate wealth and power.

416 Occupational Roles and Power

Ascribed: qualities or conditions that one is born with or into; ascribed qualities can be unchangeable (e.g., physical features and abilities). Usually contrasted with **achieved** qualities or conditions, which can be gained through work, effort, talent, and so on.

"Backlash": negative feelings toward professional women or female leaders when they behave in leader-like ways (e.g., assertively, authoritatively).

Benevolent sexism: sexism involving warmth, trust, and desire for intimacy, along with paternalistic ideas that subordinate women.

Bodily integrity: the right of individuals to not have their physical body violated; the right of individuals to have personal autonomy and self-determination over their own physical body.

Candidate Physical Abilities Test (CPAT): a standardized physical abilities test required of applicants to firefighter training programs.

Communal: traits involved in caretaking (emotionality, sensitivity, nurturance), typical of stereotypes of femininity around the world.

Developing: countries with lower life expectancies, education rates, per capita income, and less advanced technologies.

Discrimination: any attitude, act, or institutional structure that subordinates a person because of their group membership. For example, sexism involves treating people differently because of their gender.

Display rules: norms governing emotional expression in various contexts.

Division of labor: the assignment of tasks to women and men based on physical capabilities. Gendered division of labor was especially adaptive for prehistoric human groups.

Domestic work: work within a home or living space, including cleaning, food preparation, childcare.

Double bind: women leaders are expected to be like women (communal), but primary stereotypes of leaders are agentic.

Dual-earner families: families that include two partnered adults who work for money outside of the home.

Egalitarian: ideals that include valuing of equality, including gender equality. Egalitarian cultures value women and men equally.

Envious prejudice: negative feelings toward a group based on their success.

Explicit sexism: sexist attitudes that are based on consciously-held thoughts and beliefs about members of a particular sex; sexist attitudes that are obvious and explicitly stated.

Families: people who are genetically or legally related to each other; people who live together for any extended period of time.

Family work: work directed toward caring for the family and living spaces.

Femininity: the content of stereotypes of women; women are viewed as soft, caring, gentle, kind, emotional.

Feminist: a person who promotes and strives for equality between women and men. Feminist approaches emphasize global historical patriarchy in the oppression of women.

Feminization: causing something to be more feminine (more gentle, loving, kind), which is evaluated depending on one's view of feminine qualities as desirable.

Gender: the social construction of what it means to be female, male, or another gender; ideas about **femininity** and **masculinity** that are developed within a particular culture, including traditions, roles, and expectations of behavior for women and girls, men and boys.

Gender gap: the substantial difference in financial, political, and social power between women and men across history and around the world.

Occupational Roles and Power   417

Gender parity: where members of every gender enjoy equal rights, privileges, and opportunities.

Gender segregation: the process of separating people by gender, in education, workplaces, places of worship, etc.

Gender socialization: the process of teaching children and young people cultural expectations of gender; occurs through social institutions like the family, education, religion, government, art, media, etc.

Gender stereotypes: schemas about the characteristics of women and men.

Glass ceiling: a term that describes an apparently invisible but solid structure that prevents women from attaining the highest levels of organizational power. It is invisible because it is hidden from plain sight and artificial, not based on women's actual work capabilities and talents.

Glass cliff: the fact that female CEOs are more likely to be fired than male CEOs.

Head of state: the chief representative or leader of a government (e.g., a President, a Prime Minister).

Heteronormativity: discriminatory ideology, actions, and institutional structures that oppress people who are not heterosexual.

Hostile sexism: sexism involving negative feelings accompanied by negative stereotypes of women and heterosexual hostility.

Implicit sexism: sexist attitudes that are based on emotions and implicit associations between concepts; implicit attitudes are activated automatically, with little conscious awareness or control.

Inclusive: not excluding any member or group from a particular activity.

Infancy: from birth to approximately 1 year. Infants are completely helpless, have no self-awareness, and need constant care.

Interaction effect: when the effect of one independent variable on an aspect of behavior changes depending on the level of a second independent variable.

Irrational: a judgment or idea that is not based on facts and circumstances, but related to lack of careful thought and excessive emotionality.

Laissez-faire: a hands-off leadership style, with little interference or control over subordinates' behavior.

Legitimizing myths: false beliefs about a group that legitimize their oppression by another group (e.g., women are too emotional to be good leaders).

Masculinity: the content of stereotypes of men; men are viewed as hard, strong, tough, unemotional, independent.

Maternity leave: time off work (paid or unpaid) to care for a newly born or adopted child specifically for new mothers.

Matrilineal: a social system where property is only inherited by women, very rare throughout history.

Mental rotation: spatial skill that involves rotating objects mentally in the mind as three-dimensional objects.

Minister: the head or director of a government department.

Norms: formal and informal rules for behavior; **gender norms** specify rules of behavior based on gender.

Occupational stereotypes: beliefs about the traits, qualities, and characteristics of people in particular occupations.

418 Occupational Roles and Power

Old-fashioned sexism: open and obvious prejudice and discrimination against women.

Parental leave: time off work (paid or unpaid) to care for a newly born or adopted child (an inclusive term for **maternity** and **paternity** leave).

Parenting self-efficacy: a feeling of competence as a parent.

Parliament: a legislative body within a government.

Paternity leave: time off work (paid or unpaid) to care for a newly born or adopted child specifically for new fathers.

Patriarchy: a hierarchical structure where men control the majority of power and wealth; supported by false ideas (**legitimizing myths**) and practices that subordinate and oppress women.

Patrilineal: a social system where property is only inherited by men, with most cultures around the world historically being patrilineal.

Poverty: lacking in material possessions and money, such that meeting basic needs (e.g., for food, shelter, medical care) is affected.

Racism: any attitude, act, or institutional structure that discriminates against a person because of their race or ethnicity.

Role model: a person whom one observes and models one's behavior after. Parents are particularly important role models for their children growing up.

Schematic: human information-processing that relies on use of **schemas**, mental knowledge structures that contain everything a person knows about a particular topic or subject. **Stereotypes** are schemas containing information about the traits, qualities, and characteristics of large social groups.

Self-efficacy: a feeling of competence, a "can do" feeling. Self-efficacy can be a general feeling of competence, or a feeling of competence within a particular domain (e.g., **parenting self-efficacy** is a sense of one's competence as a parent).

Sex work: paid work involving sexual behavior.

Sexism: treating someone differently because of their sex; any attitude, act, or institutional structure or process that subordinates a person because of their sex.

Sexist: a person who endorses sexist ideology (negative ideas about women) and engages in behaviors that subordinate individuals because of their sex.

Social dominance: a theory that explains inequality within society. It asserts that in hierarchical structures, the people at the top enjoy a disproportionate share of society's resources (power, wealth), while the people at the bottom of the hierarchy suffer a disproportionate share of society's shortcomings and liabilities (poverty).

Social roles: roles for women and men that develop within society based on biological, physiological characteristics, including reproductive roles and physical size and strength.

Social support: the perception that one is cared for by others; emotional and other kinds of support provided by people (family, friends, co-workers, bosses, other relatives, clergy, counselors, etc.).

Spatial reasoning tasks: cognitive tasks that require visual mental representations, including mental rotation and navigation.

"Stay-at-home" mom: a stereotype subcategory of women, viewed as moral and warm, but low in competence.

Stay-at-home parent: a mother or father who chooses to forgo work outside of the home, instead working primarily at home, engaged in **family work.**

STEM: an abbreviation for science fields (science, technology, engineering, math).

Stereotype threat: when someone's performance is compromised by their awareness of a group stereotype (e.g., a woman's performance on a math test is poorer when she is made aware of the "girls are bad at math" stereotype).

Stereotypes: shared beliefs in a society about the traits, qualities, and characteristics of large social groups. **Gender stereotypes** are schemas about the characteristics of women and men.

Suffrage: the right to vote in elections.

Surrogate mother: a woman who bears a child for someone else. A surrogate mother may provide her own egg(s) for fertilization or a fertilized egg may be implanted in her uterus.

Transactional: a leadership style that involves exchange between leaders and subordinates, where subordinates are told what to do and rewarded for doing it.

Transformational: a leadership style involving **individualized consideration** (considering the needs of individual workers); **intellectual stimulation** (stimulating subordinates' creativity); **idealized influence** (engendering trust in subordinates and serving as a role model); and **inspirational motivation** (inspiring and motivating subordinates).

Unconscious: cognitive processing of information that occurs outside of conscious awareness.

Wet nurse: a lactating woman who provides milk to other people's children.

Work-family conflict: conflict between work and family roles; when work intrudes into or disrupts family life and vice versa.

References

Allen, T. D., Herst, D. E. L., Bruck, C. S., & Sutton, M. (2000). Consequences associated with work-to-family conflict: A review and agenda for future research. *Journal of Occupational Health Psychology, 5,* 278-308.

Antonoff, S. R. (2017). *The college finder*. New York: Ballantine.

Baenninger, M., & Newcombe, N. (1989). The role of experience in spatial test performance: A meta-analysis. *Sex Roles, 20*(5), 327-344.

Bailyn, L. (1993). *Breaking the mold: Women, men, and time in the new corporate world*. New York: Free Press.

Barrett, R. J., & Ray, O. S. (1970). Behavior in the open field, Lashley III maze, shuttle box, and Sidman avoidance as a function of strain, sex, and age. *Developmental Psychology, 3,* 73-77.

Becker, G. S. (1981). *A treatise on the family*. Cambridge, MA: Harvard University Press.

Bogen, J. E., & Gazzaniga, M. S. (1965). Cerebral commisurotomy in man: Minor hemisphere dominance for certain visio-spatial functions. *Journal of Neurosurgery, 23,* 394-399.

Born, M. P., Bleichrodt, N., & Van der Flier, H. (1987). Cross-cultural comparison of sex-related differences on intelligence tests: A meta-analysis. *Journal of Cross-Cultural Psychology, 18*(3), 283-314.

Brody, L. R., & Hall, J. A. (2000). Gender, emotion, and expression. In Lewis, M., & Haviland-Jones, J. M. (Eds.), *Handbook of emotions: Part IV: Social/personality issues* (2nd ed.). New York: Guilford Press, pp. 325-414.

Business Broker Network (2019). A map of the average child care costs by state. www.businessbroker.net/blog/good-info-for-new-buyers-and-sellers/average-child-care-costs-state-map.

Cejka, M. A., & Eagly, A. H. (1999). Gender-stereotypic images of occupations correspond to the sex segregation of employment. *Personality and Social Psychology Bulletin, 25*(4), 413-423. https://doi.org/10.1177/0146167299025004002.

Centers for Disease Control & Prevention (2018a). Birth data. www.cdc.gov/nchs/nvss/births.htm.

Centers for Disease Control & Prevention (2018b). Pregnancy Mortality Surveillance System. www.cdc.gov/reproductivehealth/maternalinfanthealth/pregnancy-mortality-surveillance-system.htm.

Collaer, M. L., & Hines, M. (1995). Human behavioral sex differences: A role for gonadal hormones during development? *Psychological Bulletin, 118,* 55-107.

Coltrane, S. (2000). Research on household labor: Modeling and measuring the social embeddedness of routine family work. *Journal of Marriage and the Family, 62*(4), 1208-1233. https://doi.org/10.1111/j.1741-3737.2000.01208.x.

Cowley, J. J., & Griesel, R. D. (1963). The development of second-generation low protein rats. *Journal of Genetic Psychology, 103,* 233-242.

Cuddy, A. J.C., Fiske, S. T., & Glick, P. (2004). When professionals become mothers, warmth doesn't cut the ice. *Journal of Social Issues, 60*(4), 701-718. ttps://doi.org/10.1111/j.0022-4537.2004.00381.x.

Dawson, J. L.M. (1972). Effects of sex hormones on cognitive style in rats and men. *Behavior Genetics, 2,* 21-42.

de Lacoste, M. C., Horvath, D. S., & Woodward, D. J. (1991). Possible sex differences in the developing human fetal brain. *Journal of Clinical and Experimental Neuropsychology, 13,* 831-846.

Den Dulk, L., Peper, B., Kanjuo Mrčela, A., & Ignjatović, M. (2016). Supervisory support in Slovenian and Dutch organizations: A contextualizing approach. *Community, Work & Family, 19*(2), 193-212.

Dorius, S. F., & Firebaugh, G. (2010). Trends in global gender inequality. *Social Forces, 88*(5), 1941-1968.

Duxbury, L., Higgins, C., & Lee, C. (1994). Work-family conflict: A comparison by gender, family type, and perceived control. *Journal of Family Issues, 15,* 449-466.

Eagly, A. H. (1987). *Sex differences in social behavior: A social role interpretation* . Hillsdale, NJ: Erlbaum.

Eagly, A. H., Karau, S. J., & Makhijani, M. G. (1995). Gender and the effectiveness of leaders: A meta-analysis. *Psychological Bulletin, 117,* 125-145.

England, C. (2017). Paid maternity leave: US is still one of the worst countries in the world despite Donald Trump's family leave plan. *The Independent,* March 1. www.independent.co.uk/news/world/americas/paid-maternity-leave-us-worst-countres-world-donald-trump-family-leave-plan-women-republican-social-a7606036.html.

Equality and Human Rights Commission (2018). Pregnancy and maternity discrimination research findings. www.equalityhumanrights.com/en/managing-pregnancy-and-maternity-workplace/pregnancy-and-maternity-discrimination-research-findings.

Family Caregiver Alliance (2001). On pay gap, millennial women near parity – for now. Selected Caregiver Statistics (Fact Sheet). San Francisco: FCA.

Fiske, S. T. (2017). Prejudices in cultural contexts: Shared stereotypes (gender, age) versus variable stereotypes (race, ethnicity, religion). *Perspectives on Psychological Science, 12*(5), 791-799.

Fiske, S. T., Cuddy, A. J., Glick, P., & Xu, J. (2002). A model of (often mixed) stereotype content: Competence and warmth respectively follow from perceived status and competition. *Journal of Personality and Social Psychology, 82*(6), 878-902. doi:10.1037//0022-3514.82.6.878.

Fiske, S. T., & Taylor, S. E. (1991). *Social cognition* (2nd ed.). New York: McGraw-Hill.

Fletcher, R. (2017). Women spend 50% more time doing unpaid work than men: Statistics Canada. CBC News, June 1. www.cbc.ca/news/canada/calgary/men-women-housework-unpaid-statistics-canada-1.4141367.

Ford, M. T., Heinen, B. A., & Langkamer, K. L. (2007). Work and family satisfaction and conflict: A meta-analysis of cross-domain relations. *Journal of Applied Psychology, 92*(1), 57-80. doi:10.1037/0021-9010.92.1.57.

Geary, D. C. (2000). Evolution and proximate expression of human paternal investment. *Psychological Bulletin, 126,* 55-77. http://dx.doi.org/10.1037/0033-2909.126.1.55.

Glick, P., & Fiske, S. T. (1996). The ambivalent sexism inventory: Differentiating hostile and benevolent sexism. *Journal of Personality and Social Psychology, 70,* 491-512. doi:10.1037/0022-3514. 70.3.491.

Goldin, C. D., & Katz, L. F. (2002). The power of the pill: Oral contraceptives and women's career and marriage decisions. *J. Polit. Econ. 110,* 730-770.

Greenhaus, J. H., & Beutell, N. J. (1985). Sources of conflict between work and family roles. *Academy of Management Review, 10,* 76-88.

Gunter, B. G., & Gunter, N. C. (1991). Inequities in household labor: Sex role orientation and the need for cleanliness and responsibility as predictors. *Journal of Social Behavior & Personality, 6*(3), 559-572.

Halpern, D. F., & LaMay, M. L. (2000). The smarter sex: A critical review of sex differences in intelligence. *Educational Psychology Review, 12*(2), 229-246.

Hampson, E., Rovet, J. F., & Airman, D. (1998). Spatial reasoning in children with congenital adrenal hyperplasia due to 21-hydroxylase deficiency. *Developmental Neuropsychology, 14,* 299-320.

Harrington, B., Van Deusen, F., Fraone, J. S., Eddy, S., & Haas, L. (2014). *The new dad: Take your leave: Perspectives on paternity leave from fathers, leading organizations, and global policies.* Boston: Boston College Center for Work & Family.

Hausmann, R., Tyson, L. D., & Zahidi, S. (2007). *The global gender gap report.* Geneva: World Economic Forum.

Hegarty, M., & Sims, V. K. (1994). Individual differences in mental animation during mechanical reasoning. *Memory & Cognition, 22,* 411-430.

Heilman, M. E., Wallen, A. S., Fuchs, D., & Tamkins, M. M. (2004). *Penalties for success: Reactions to women who succeed at male gender-typed tasks. Journal of Applied Psychology, 89*(3), 416-427.

Henrich, J., & Gil-White, F. J. (2001). The evolution of prestige: Freely conferred deference as a mechanism for enhancing the benefits of cultural transmission. *Evolution and Human Behavior, 22*(3), 165-196.

Hoffman, M., Gneezy, U., & List, J. A. (2011). Nurture affects gender differences in spatial abilities. *Proceedings of the National Academy of Sciences of the United States of America, 108*(36), 14786-14788.

Horne, R. M., Johnson, M. D., Galambos, N. L., & Krahn, H. J. (2017). Time, money, or gender? Predictors of the division of household labour across life stages. *Sex Roles, 78.* doi:10.1007/s11199-017-0832-1.

Huttenlocher, J., Newcombe, N., & Vasilyeva, M. (1999). Spatial scaling in young children. *Psychological Sciences, 10*(5), 393-398.

Im, J. (2018). Americans are having fewer kids because it's too expensive – here's how much child care costs in every state. CNBC, July 9. www.cnbc.com/2018/07/06/how-much-child-care-costs-in-every-state-in-america.html.

Ingelhart, R., & Norris, P. (2003). *Rising tide: Gender equality and cultural change around the world.* Cambridge: Cambridge University Press.

International Labour Organization (2018). *World employment social outlook: Trends for women 2018: Global snapshot* . Geneva: ILO.

Jayachandran, S. (2015). The roots of gender inequality in developing countries. *Annual Review of Economics, 7,* 63-88. doi:10.1146/annurev-economics-080614-115404.

Johnson, M. P. (1995). Patriarchal terrorism and common couple violence: Two forms of violence against women. *Journal of Marriage and the Family, 57,* 283-294.

Kahn, R. L., & Byosiere, P. (1992). Stress in organizations. In Dunnette, M. D., & Hough, L. M. (Eds.), *Handbook of industrial and organizational psychology,* Vol. 3 (2nd ed., pp 571-650). Palo Alto, CA: Consulting Psychologists Press.

Konrad, A. M. (2003). Family demands and job attribute preferences: A 4-year longitudinal study of women and men. *Sex Roles, 49,* 35-46.

Kroska, A. (2003). Investigating gender differences in the meaning of household chores and child care. *Journal of Marriage and Family, 65*(2), 456-473.

Levine, S. C., Huttenlocher, J., Taylor, A., & Langrock, A. (1999). Early sex differences in spatial skill. *Developmental Psychology, 35,* 940-949.

Linn, M. C., & Petersen, A. C. (1985). Emergence and characterization of sex differences in spatial ability: A meta-analysis. *Child Development, 56,* 1479-1498. doi:10.1111/j.1467-8624.1985.tb00213.x.

Little, A. C., Burriss, R. P., Jones, B. C., & Craig, S. (2007). Facial appearance affects voting decisions. *Evolution and Human Behavior, 28,* 18-27.

Lopez-Carlos, A., & Zahida, S. (2005). *Women's empowerment: Measuring the global gender gap.* Geneva: World Economic Forum.

Madigan, J. C. (2009). The education of girls and women in the United States: A historical perspective. *Advances in Gender and Education, 1,* 11-13.

Mayor, S. (2004). Pregnancy and childbirth are leading causes of death in teenage girls in developing countries. *British Medical Journal, 328*(7449), 1152. doi:10.1136/bmj.328.7449.1152-a.

Mazur, A., & Booth, A. (1998). Testosterone and dominance in men. *Behavioral and Brain Sciences, 21,* 353-371.

McGee, M. G. (1979). Human spatial abilities: Psychometric studies and environmental, genetic, hormonal, and neurological influences. *Psychological Bulletin, 86*(5), 889-918. http://dx.doi.org/10.1037/0033-2909.86.5.889.

McKay, D. R. (2018). Your rights under FMLA: What you need to know about the Family and Medical Leave Act. The Balance Careers. www.thebalancecareers.com/fmla-rights-as-employee-525699.

Meher, S., Abalos, E., Carroli, G., & Meher, S. (2005). Bed rest with or without hospitalisation for hypertension during pregnancy. *Cochrane Database of Systematic Reviews.* doi:10.1002/14651858.CD003514.pub2.

Meinzen-Dick, R. S., Brown, L. R., Sims Feldstein, H., & Quisumbing, A. R. (1997). Gender, property rights, and natural resources. *World Development, 25*(8), 1303-1315. doi:10.1016/S0305-750X(97)00027-2.

Mejia, Z. (2018). Just 24 female CEOs lead the companies on the 2018 Fortune 500 – fewer than last year. CNBC.com. www.cnbc.com/2018/05/21/2018s-fortune-500-companies-have-just-24-female-ceos.html.

Milkie, M. A., Raley, S. B., & Bianchi, S. M. (2009). Taking on the second shift: Time allocations and time pressures of U.S. parents with preschoolers. *Social Forces, 88,* 487-517. doi:10.1353/sof.0.0268.

Miller, G. (2010). Contraception as development? New evidence from family planning in Colombia. *Economic Journal, 120,* 709-736.

Moore, D. S., & Johnson, S. P. (2008). Mental rotation in human infants: A sex difference. *Psychological Science, 19*(11), 1063-1066. https://doi.org/10.1111/j.1467-9280.2008.02200.x.

Morrison, A., & Lamana, F. (2006). *Gender issues in the Kyrgyz labor market.* World Bank Background Paper for Kyrgyz Poverty Assessment. Washington, DC: World Bank.

National Alliance for Caregiving and AARP (2009). Caregiving in the US. www.caregiving.org/data/FINALRegular ExSum50plus.

National Testing Network (2012). *Physical abilities tests for law enforcement and corrections: Candidate Physical Abilities Test (CPAT).* NTN Tests. www.nationaltestingnetwork.com/publicsafetyjobs/ntn-test-pat.cfm.

OECD (2018). The global gender gap report. Paris: Organisation for Economic Co-operation and Development. https://data.oecd.org/earnwage/gender-wage-gap.htm.

Offer, S., & Schneider, B. (2011). Revisiting the gender gap in time-use patterns: Multitasking and well-being among mothers and fathers in dual-earner families. *American Sociological Review, 76*, 809-833. doi:10.1177/00031224114 25170.

Office for National Statistics (2016). Women shoulder the responsibility of 'unpaid work'. www.ons.gov.uk/employmentandlabourmarket/peopleinwork/earningsandworkinghours/articles/womenshouldertheresponsibilityofunpaidwork/2016-11-10.

Okerlund, R. (2018). Why don't men take paid paternity leave? And what can we do to change that? ParentMap, August 21. www.parentmap.com/article/why-paid-paternity-leave-men-statistics.

O'Sullivan, A., & Sheffrin, S. M. (2003). *Economics: Principles in action* . Upper Saddle River, NJ: Prentice Hall.

Para-Mallam, F. J. (2010). Promoting gender equality in the context of Nigerian cultural and religious expression: Beyond increasing female access to education. *Compare, 40*(4), 459-477.

Penton-Voak, I. S., & Chen, J. Y. (2004). High salivary testosterone is linked to masculine male facial appearance in humans. *Evolution and Human Behavior, 25*, 229-241.

Perrett, D., Lee, K., Penton-Voak, I., Rowland, D., Yoshikawa, S., Burt, D., ... Akamatsu, S. (1998). Effects of sexual dimorphism on facial attractiveness. *Nature, 394*, 884-887.

Perry-Jenkins, M. (1993). Family roles and responsibilities: What has changed and what has remained the same? In Frankel, J. (Ed.), *The employed mother and the family context* (pp. 245-259). New York: Springer-Verlag.

Pew Research Center (2015). The American family today. *Social & Demographic Trends*, December 17. www.pewsocialtrends.org/2015/12/17/1-the-american-family-today/. Retrieved January 4, 2018.

Pratto, F., & Walker, A. (2004). The bases of gendered power. In Eagly, A. H., Beall, A. E., & Sternberg, R. J. (Eds.), *The psychology of gender* . New York: Guilford Press, pp. 242-268.

Raley, S., Bianchi, S. M., & Wang, W. (2012). When do fathers care? Mothers' economic contribution and fathers' involvement in child care. *American Journal of Sociology, 117*, 1422-1459. doi:10.1086/663354.

Reskin, B. (1993). Sex segregation in the workplace. *Annual Review of Sociology, 19*, 241-270.

Reuben, E., Sapienza, P., & Zingales, L. (2014). How stereotypes impair women's careers in science. *Proceedings of the National Academy of Sciences of the United States of America*, March 10. https://doi.org/10.1073/pnas.1314788111.

Riggio, H. R. (2006). Structural features of sibling dyads and attitudes toward sibling relationships in young adulthood. *Journal of Family Issues, 27*, 1233-1254.

Riggio, H. R., & Desrochers, S. J. (2006). Maternal employment: Relations with young adults' work and family expectations and self-efficacy. *American Behavioral Scientist, 49*(10), 1328-1353.

Riggio, H. R., Valenzuela, A. M., & Weiser, D. A. (2010). Household responsibilities in the family of origin: Relations with self-efficacy in young adulthood. *Personality and Individual Differences, 48*, 568-573.

Riordan, C. (1990). *Girls and boys in school: Together or separate?* New York: Teachers College Press.

Searleman, A. (1977). A review of right hemisphere linguistic capabilities. *Psychological Bulletin, 84*, 503-528.

Sell, A., Hone, L. S. E., & Pound, N. (2012). The importance of physical strength to human males. *Human Nature, 23*, 30-44. doi:10.1007/s12110-012-9131-2.

Settles, I. H., Cortina, L. M., Malley, J., & Stewart, A. J. (2006). The climate for women in academic science: The good, the bad, and the changeable. *Psychology of Women Quarterly, 30*, 47-58.

Sharma, N., Chakrabarti, S., & Grover, S. (2016). Gender differences in caregiving among family - caregivers of people with mental illnesses. *World Journal of Psychiatry, 6*(1), 7-17. doi:10.5498/wjp.v6.i1.7.

Sidanius, J., Levin, S., & Pratto, F. (1996). Consensual social dominance orientation and its correlates within the hierarchical structure of American society. *International Journal of Intercultural Relations, 20*(3-4), 385-408.

Smith, A. (2017). A group of major pollsters just released an autopsy report to explain why the polls were such a disaster in 2016. *Business Insider*, May 7. www.businessinsider.com/trump-hillary-clinton-why-polls-wrong-2017-5.

Smuts, B. B., Cheney, D. L., Seyfarth, R. M., Wrangham, R. W., & Struhsaker, T. T. (Eds.) (1987). *Primate societies*. Chicago: University of Chicago Press.

Sorby, S. A. (2009). Educational research in developing 3-D spatial skills for engineering students. *International Journal of Science Education, 31*(3), 459-480.

Sosa, C. G., Althabe, F., Belizán, J. M., & Bergel, E. (2015). Bed rest in singleton pregnancies for preventing preterm birth. *Cochrane Database of Systematic Reviews, 3*, CD003581. doi:10.1002/14651858.CD003581.pub3.

Stanley, S. M., Amato, P. R., Johnson, C. A., & Markman, H. J. (2006). Premarital education, marital quality, and marital stability: Findings from a large, random household survey. *Journal of Family Psychology, 20*(1), 117-126.

Steele, C. M. (1997). A threat in the air: How stereotypes shape intellectual identity and performance. *American Psychologist, 52*, 613-629.

Steinpreis, R. A., Anders, K. A.,& Ritzke, D. (1999). The impact of gender on the review of the curricula vitae of job applicants and tenure candidates: A national empirical study. *Sex Roles, 41,* 509-528.

Taylor, C. J. (2010). Occupational sex composition and the gendered availability of workplace support. *Gender & Society, 24,* 189-212.

Thomas, J. R., & French, K. E. (1985). Gender differences across age in motor performance: A meta-analysis. *Psychological Bulletin, 98,* 260-282.

Trimarchi, M. (2017). Survey: 38% of employers offer paid parental leave. *The Independent,* May 17. www.independent.co.uk/news/world/americas/paid-maternity-leave-us-worst-countres-world-donald-trump-family-leave-plan-women-republican-social-a7606036.html https://www.bna.com/survey-38-employers-n73014451081/.

Tsuzuki, Y., & Matsui, T. (1997). Factors influencing intention to continue work throughout the life span among Japanese college women: A path analysis. *College Student Journal, 31,* 216-223.

United Nations (2004). Human Development report 2004: Cultural liberty in today's diverse world. New York: United Nations Publications.

United Nations Educational, Scientific and Cultural Organization (UNESCO) (2004). EFA Global Monitoring Report 2003/04: Gender and education for all – The leap to equality. Paris: UNESCO.

Van der Horst, M., Van der Lippe, T., & Kluwer, E. (2014). Aspirations and occupational achievements of Dutch fathers and mothers. *Career Development International, 19*(4), 447-468.

Van der Lippe, T., Jager, A., & Kops, Y. (2006). Combination pressure: The paid work-family balance of men and women in European countries. *Acta Sociologica, 49*(3), 303-319.

Van der Lippe, T., & Lippényi, Z. (2018). Beyond formal access: Organizational context, working from home, and work-family conflict of men and women in European workplaces. Social Indicators Research. https://doi.org/10.1007/s11205-018-1993-1.

Voyer, D., Voyer, S., & Bryden, M. P. (1995). Magnitude of sex differences in spatial abilities: A meta-analysis and consideration of critical variables. *Psychological Bulletin, 117,* 250-270.

Wada, J. A. (1974). Morphologic asymmetry of human cerebral hemispheres: Temporal and frontal speech zones in 100 adult and 100 infant brains. *Neurology, 24,* 349.

The Washington Post (2016). Mike Pence talks a lot about Donald Trump's shoulders and strength. October 5. www.washingtonpost.com/video/politics/mike-pence-talks-a-lot-about-donald-trumps-shoulders-and-strength/2016/10/05/de5a8604-8b41-11e6-8cdc-4fbb1973b506_video.html?noredirect=on&utm_term=.3088568b680a.

Witelson, S. F. (1976). Sex and the single hemisphere: Specialization of the right hemisphere for spatial processing. *Science, 193,* 425-427.

Wood, W., & Eagly, A. H. (2010). Gender. In Fiske, S. T., Gilbert, D. T., & Lindzey, G. (Eds.), *The handbook of social psychology* (5th ed., pp. 629-667). New York: Wiley.

World Bank (2018). Labor force participation rate, male (% of male population ages 15+) (modeled ILO estimate), world. Washington, DC: The World Bank Databank.

World Health Organization (2008). *Education material for teachers of midwifery: Midwifery education modules* (2nd ed.). Geneva.

Yavorsky, J. E., Dush, C. M. K., & Schoppe-Sullivan, S. J. (2015). The production of inequality: The gender division of labor across the transition to parenthood. *Journal of Marriage and Family, 77*(3), 662-679.

Zuckerman, H., Cole, J., & Bruer, J. (1991). *The outer circle: Women in the scientific community.* New York: W.W. Norton.

13 Current Issues and Social Problems

Sex and Gender in Continuing Social Problems	424
Maintaining Patriarchy: Right-Wing Authoritarianism and Fascism in the United States	426
The Backlash against Feminism	430
Online Sexism and Anti-Feminism Movements	431
The "Pro-Life" Movement in the United States	432
The Fight for LGBTQ Equality	435
Traditionalism and LGBTQ Oppression	437
Control through Poverty: Indifference to and Oppression of Poor People	438
Violence against Women and Children: A Global Epidemic	440
Changing Attitudes, Fighting Oppression	441

Sex and Gender in Continuing Social Problems

Well, dear student, we made it all the way to the end of this book! I'm sure you're relieved and I am too. This chapter is intentionally last, so please read it after you've read most or all of the book. This is a different chapter to write, different from the others, because I can rely on information you've already learned from this book (I hope) in explaining current social problems. In this chapter I will focus on current issues affecting women, the poor, racial minorities, and LGBTQ individuals, particularly within the United States. I am doing so because, as I write this, Americans are facing bigger threats to our democracy than ever before, threats that are increasing around the world. Through the capitalist economic system, a small group of powerful men (around eight of them) control 50% of all of the world's wealth (Oxfam International, 2017). Poverty and homelessness in the U.S. are increasing (Nadasen, 2017; The Guardian, 2017), along with wealth inequality overall, with the wealthiest 1% of Americans possessing 37% of the wealth in the United States (Wolff, 2010) (see Figure 13.1). Thousands of immigrants are fleeing dangerous, impoverished living conditions in Central and South America, Syria, and other areas around the world, many trying to immigrate into the U.S. The U.S. Supreme Court, through the Citizens United decision, has enabled the wealthiest individuals to have the greatest influence in American government (Cillizza, 2014). Powerful men are lying to the American people about climate change, immigrants, health care, and international politics (Cillizza, 2018; Klein, 2018; Roberts, 2018). Powerful men around the world are maintaining patriarchy and establishing plutocracy (rule by the wealthy). I am frightened and concerned for the future of my country, the world's people, and our planet, feelings that are growing every day.

Current Issues and Social Problems 425

Figure 13.1 Homelessness is rising across the United States as wealth inequality continues to increase
Source: Timothy A. Clary/AFP via Getty Images

I will not assume that you agree with me about everything, dear student, that is not required or desirable. However, a concern for the well-being of humankind within every person is highly desirable and so beneficial to society. **Liberalism** is linked with education, with highly educated people tending to be more liberal than the less educated (Weil, 1985). Educated people think **divergently**; they recognize that there is more than one solution to problems, more than one way of being (McCrae, 1987). As such, they are **skeptical** (thoughtful), **open-minded** and willing to change their minds based on evidence (Beyer, 1995). In addition, educated people value freedom, justice, and equality. They tend to be higher in **social interest**, a desire to relate positively with others that includes empathy, caring, and compassion toward other people, society, and the world (Ansbacher, 1992; Todman & Mansager, 2009). These feelings of affinity and common welfare are the bases of the democratic process (Nicoll, 1996). Educated people do not hate others based on their economic condition, their skin color, their ethnicity, their genitals, or their sexuality. And educated people have a greater responsibility to act, to speak out, to protest, and to create knowledge that supports the well-being of others, particularly those in our world with less power, who need more from those with much (children, the poor, disabled and sick people, the elderly). This is the power of education to improve conditions for humanity, to know how important it truly is to love one another, to treat neighbors with concern and equality. And so, with that being said, in this chapter I will address current issues surrounding the maintenance of patriarchy in the United States, including **sexism** and anti-feminism, anti-LGBTQ sentiment and **hate crimes**, negative attitudes and actions toward poor people, and violence against women.

426 *Current Issues and Social Problems*

All of these continuing social problems involving equality and social justice involve sex, gender, sexuality, socioeconomic status, and race.

Maintaining Patriarchy: Right-Wing Authoritarianism and Fascism in the United States

As you probably already know after reading some or all of this book, there are particular individual trait-like qualities that underlie support of a hegemony or hierarchy within a society. Hegemony is a social structure where one group dominates all other groups. Patriarchy is clearly hegemonic; men (particularly those with white skin) dominate all other groups politically, financially, and socially, all over the world. Some people prefer such a hierarchy, usually the people who are favored by such a hierarchy (men, white people). Such people are said to be high in social dominance orientation (SDO), a preference for inequality between groups (Sidanius, Levin, & Pratto, 1996). Research indicates that men and white people are higher in SDO than women and people of color (Miller, Smith, & Mackie, 2004; Pratto, Sidanius, & Levin, 2006). SDO is linked with endorsement of racist and sexist ideology, because viewing some groups as inferior is the entire basis of racism and sexism (Duriez & Van Hiel, 2002; Nicol & Rounding, 2013). Multiple studies conducted around the world have documented that men are less egalitarian, more racist, more punitive, and more politically conservative than women, attitudes that support patriarchy (see Sidanius, Pratto, & Bobo, 1994). Scholars assert that SDO involves a stable perception of the world as competitive and a valuing of winning, a worldview that stems from a tough-minded personality and experiences of inequality and competition (Duckitt, 2005). SDO is linked with support of President Trump (Crowson & Brandes, 2017). Education about inequalities and injustices may help to change people's minds about patriarchy and equality, with greater formal education predictive of more negative attitudes toward injustice (Dambrun, Kamiejski, Haddadi, & Duarte, 2009; Ekehammar, Nilsson, & Sidanius, 1987). Such attitudes are difficult to change, especially among people who are highly identified with a dominant group that they perceive as winning (Riggio, 2007).

Another personality dimension linked to support of patriarchy is right-wing authoritarianism (RWA) (see Table 13.1), a quality that originally was said to develop from learning and emotional experiences in early childhood (Adorno, Frenkel-Brunswik, Levinson, & Sanford, 1950). RWA involves one's perception of, interaction with, and motivation toward authority, initially learned in relations with parents, the original authorities. Authoritarian parents (who raise authoritarian

Table 13.1 Characteristics of right-wing authoritarianism

Blind submission to authority
Rigid conservatism
Strong respect for status and tradition
Strict adherence to middle-class conventions
Aggression and hatred against unconventional people
Convergent thinking
View outgroups (especially racial groups) as inferior
View women as inferior to men

Source: Adorno, T. W., Frenkel-Brunswik, E., Levinson, D., & Sanford, N. (1950). *The authoritarian personality*. New York: Harper & Brothers.

children; Friedson, 2016) are suspicious and mistrustful of their children; they view children as naturally bad and in need of domination and punishment. Authoritarian parents use physical punishment in disciplining their children (Ellison, Bartkowski, & Segal, 1996; Flynn, 1994; Grogan-Kaylor & Oti, 2007). They emphasize obedience and conformity by their children (Lareau, 2011). For the young child, especially one who is just learning about obedience and self-control (around age 2–4 years; Erikson, 1950), this physical punishment makes no sense and leads to scary and threatening feelings of anger and fear toward parents. The child's developing ego (sense of self, conscious awareness of the world) is too fragile and immature to cope in a healthy way with such threatening feelings, and instead uses psychological defense mechanisms to protect the self. Eventually, defense mechanisms result in changed feelings of anger and fear toward parents into idealizations of parents (reaction formation); views of people not like oneself as scary and threatening (displacement); and views of people not like oneself as hostile, angry, fearsome, dangerous (projection). Yes, this is a very Freudian explanation (see Chapter 6) (Silverberg, 1952). Because attitudes from such early learning are implicit, operating automatically and typically without awareness, they are very powerful in affecting feelings, thoughts, and behavior (Jonathan, 2008; Rowatt & Franklin, 2004; Rowatt et al., 2006). Research indicates that formal education does decrease authoritarianism and it increases democratic, liberal values (Sanborn & Thyne, 2014; Schuman, Bobo, & Krysan, 1992).

People high in RWA experience powerful feelings of obedience to authority and strong respect for tradition and hierarchy (Altemeyer, 1998). They feel safer having strong, powerful authority figures, whom they see as superior and belonging in authority. In this way, they are conformists (Duckitt, Wagner, du Plessis, & Birum, 2002). They enjoy being obedient to such authority figures, as long as it is *their* traditional authority, whatever that might be (e.g., a god, a religion, a powerful man). They feel safe within the status quo; they want to maintain hierarchy because it benefits their group and allows them to feel certain about their beliefs and superior to other groups. They are highly averse to change and to differences of any kind among people (Stenner, 2009). As such, they are rigidly conservative; they see different, progressive, and unconventional people and groups as threatening to their way of life, and they feel aggression and hatred toward such groups (Duckitt, Wagner, du Plessis, & Birum, 2002).

RWA is associated with viewing the world as dangerous, with one's group and way of life under threat from outsiders (Duckitt et al., 2002; Sibley et al., 2007). People who are high in RWA endorse racist and sexist ideology. They believe that people who are not white are inferior to white people; and they are open about their racism, openly referring to other groups as inferior (Altemeyer, 1998; Duriez & Van Hiel, 2002). They believe that women are characteristically inferior; as such they are higher in blatant, hostile sexism (Nicol & Rounding, 2013). They endorse statements like "Women seek to gain power by getting control over men" (see Chapter 7; Glick & Fiske, 1996). They are openly heterosexist, with strong negative emotional reactions to LGBTQ individuals (Altemeyer & Hunsberger, 1992; Altemeyer, 2003; Rowatt et al., 2006), especially to gay men who threaten their idealized hypermasculinity and the legitimacy of male dominance (Connell, 1995). They think convergently, a very simplistic, low-effort way of thinking that results in a view of the world as right-wrong, black-white, good-bad (Rubinstein, 2002). Whatever they are is seen as good, and everything else is seen as bad. People high in RWA tend to be lower in intelligence (Heaven, Ciarrochi, & Leeson, 2011) and higher in religious fundamentalism (Hunsberger, 1996). As I'm sure you have realized in reading about RWA, Americans who strongly favor President Trump tend to be high in RWA (Crowson & Brandes, 2017) (see Figure 13.2).

428 Current Issues and Social Problems

Figure 13.2 Supporters of Donald Trump express anger toward outgroups, especially those that are not traditional
Source: Sean Rayford/Getty Images

Table 13.2 Warning signs of fascism

1. Powerful and continuing nationalism
2. Disdain for human rights
3. Identification of enemies as a unifying cause
4. Rampant sexism
5. Controlled mass media
6. Obsession with national security
7. Obsession with crime and punishment
8. Religion and government intertwined
9. Corporate power protected
10. Labor power suppressed
11. Disdain for intellectuals and the arts
12. Rampant cronyism and corruption

Source: Data taken from United States Holocaust Memorial Museum.

People who are high in RWA favor rigid, hierarchical government systems, including in its most extreme forms. **Fascism** is a far-right, authoritarian governmental system that is based on extremely hierarchical and **traditional** attitudes. The Nazi Party was fascist (Kershaw, 2000) (see Figure 13.3). Looking at Table 13.2, it is rather easy to find examples of the ideologies and actions by President Trump, his Administration, and his supporters that fit with the primary features of fascism (I will address them in order). His primary slogan ("Make America Great Again!") and his

Current Issues and Social Problems 429

Figure 13.3 The fascist Nazi party leader, Adolf Hitler
Source: Hulton Deutsch/Getty Images

attitudes in general are highly **nationalistic** (Antle, 2019), as are his economic policies (Evans, 2019). He and his followers show little concern for human rights, which involve concerns for civil rights and rights of every person to life, liberty, and pursuit of happiness. **Hate crimes** in the United States have increased for the third straight year in a row, with most based on skin color or apparent race. Hate crimes increased 17% from 2016 to 2017. The majority of perpetrators of these crimes are white men (Federal Bureau of Investigation, 2017). Trump's primary platform is **jingoistic**; he identifies immigrants from Latin America and Muslims as enemies who are a threat to Americans (Fabian, 2018; Johnson & Hauslohner, 2017). Trump constantly portrays immigrants as criminals to cause fear (Rizzo, 2019). He has referred to violent **white supremacists** as "very fine people" (Scott, 2018). Do I need explain how sexist it is to refer to women as animals, as ugly, as stupid? His followers don't seem to mind, with individual endorsement of sexist and racist ideology the most powerful predictors of support for Trump for President (Schaffner, Macwilliams, & Nteta, 2018). Sexist, racist, and heterosexist ideology are lies used as tools to **legitimize** and sustain patriarchy (Pratto & Walker, 2004; Rich, 1986).

Trump and his followers despise the mainstream media. Trump has suggested a state-owned media organization and using his power as President to shut down NBC and other media outlets that criticize him (Mindock, 2017). The border wall that Trump and his followers are obsessed with led to the U.S. government being shut down (the longest shutdown in American history; Politi, 2019). The Trump Administration has created a Conscience and Religious Freedom division at the

430 *Current Issues and Social Problems*

Department of Health and Human Services, specifically to advance policy that limits women's right to choose abortion and that allows religious discrimination in service provision, especially of contraception (McGraw, 2018); it regularly hosts leaders of **evangelical Christianity** in the White House (Brody & Browder, 2018); it has eased enforcement of the **Johnson Amendment**, which prohibits churches from engaging in political campaigns (Fabian & Jagoda, 2017); and it is anti-abortion based on religious ideology (North, 2018). According to whitehouse.gov, President Trump is "standing up for the **sanctity** of life" (women's lives apparently have no sanctity). The Trump tax cut, passed by a Republican Congress in 2017, favors corporations and the super-wealthy, resulting in a tremendous increase in the national debt (Tankersley, 2018). Trump and his Administration favor **deregulation**, allowing corporations to exploit consumers and poison the environment (Popovich, Albeck-Ripka, & Pierre-Louis, 2018). Trump and the **GOP** are viru-lently anti-union; they promote so-called "right to work" laws that disallow **labor union** con-tracts (Jamieson, 2017). The Trump Administration supports cutting funding to the National Endowment for the Arts and Humanities (Boucher, 2018) and to the National Science Foundation (Diep, 2018). Trump himself regularly and publicly denies climate change, showing his disdain for science (Wright, 2018). And despite his proposed intention to "drain the swamp" (Samuels, 2018), the Trump Administration and Cabinet offices are staffed by personal friends, family members, and people who made large donations to the Trump campaign (Prins, 2016), **cronyism** at its very worst. Looks like Mr. Trump is batting 1.000 when it comes to fascism. The current government of the United States is supporting sexism, racism, heterosexism, and financial oppression in its pursuit of wealth and power. Fascism and right-wing authoritarianism are increasing around the world (National Public Radio, 2017). We have our work cut out for us, dear student.

The Backlash against Feminism

A **feminist** is a person who espouses and works toward women's social, political, and financial equality to men. A 2016 national poll indicated that around 6 in 10 women and around one-third of men describe themselves as a feminist or a strong feminist (Cai & Clement, 2016), an increase from previous years (McCabe, 2005). Educated women are particularly likely to be feminist (Solomon, 1985; Walsh & Heppner, 2006), perhaps one reason why girls and women have been denied access to formal education around the world for centuries, including today (Brine, 1999). Identifying as a feminist is associated with positive psychological outcomes. When compared to more traditional women, feminists report greater overall well-being (Yakushko, 2007) and greater self-esteem and self-efficacy (Eisele & Stake, 2008). Feminism increases feelings of empowerment (Downing & Roush, 1985), and feminists actually earn more money than women who are not feminist (Walsh & Heppner, 2006). Sexism is less stressful for women who are femi-nists (Zucker & Bay-Cheng, 2010).

Given these positive outcomes, why don't all people identify as a feminist? What is so terrible about women being considered equal to the other half of the human race, especially in terms of rights, opportunities, respect, and social value? Feminists are sometimes called *feminazis*, equat-ing women seeking equality to mass murderers and fascists (ironically, the people who use words like feminazi are more like Nazis in their values than feminists; Smith & Winter, 2002). Labels like these are perceived negatively, even by people who actually value women's equality (Ramsey et al., 2007). Other people view feminism as rather obsolete, as no longer needed because women are already equal (Swirsky & Angelone, 2014), a form of **modern sexism** (Martínez & Paterna-Bleda, 2013). The women's movement began in 1848 in the United States, with a pinnacle in the

Current Issues and Social Problems   431

development of the Equal Rights Amendment (ERA) in 1921. The ERA has been ratified in 37 states, with most states not ratifying it being in the South (Alice Paul Institute, 2018). A testament to the state of women's lack of equality in the U.S., the ERA has never passed both houses of the U.S. Congress. If sexism is no longer a problem, then pass the ERA!

Feminists are not necessarily well-liked, research indicates, including by other women. Research has documented a "backlash" effect, whereby women who behave in non-feminine ways are evaluated negatively (Rudman, 1998). A primary trigger of backlash is any violation of the expectation (and prescription) that women should be nice. This is an essential weapon used to maintain hegemony in general, the prescriptive stereotyping of the subordinate group as communal (accommodating, cooperative, deferent) (Jackman, 1994; Ridgeway & Erickson, 2000). In women, agentic qualities (being assertive, active, decisive) are seen as incompatible with warmth and kindness; women judged as highly competent are commonly perceived as "socially deficient" (Rudman & Glick, 2001, p.743). This same incompatibility between competence and warmth is not found for evaluations of men (Cuddy, Fiske, & Glick, 2004). Being a feminist obviously requires not being accommodating, deferential, and cooperative. Protesting the hierarchy is the opposite of deference. Protesting social injustice, calling out sexism and misogyny, that requires assertion and a decided lack of meekness. People who are sexist obviously do not enjoy being called sexist or called out for their mistreatment of women; like most oppressors, they prefer silence from the oppressed.

People who are highly traditional, which necessarily supports the patriarchal status quo, are especially averse to strong, agentic women and evaluate them very negatively (Glick & Fiske, 1996). Around 40% of Americans, women and men, describe feminists as angry and as unfairly blaming men for women's lack of equality (Cai & Clement, 2016). Attacking women's emotions is a typical tactic of sexists, who use emotionality to diminish women and their voices (Ragins & Winkel, 2011). Female feminists are called unattractive, manly, and man-hating (Bashir, Lockwood, Chasteen, Nadolny, & Noyes, 2013; Kamen, 1991; Six & Eckes, 1991), attacks and lies used to dismiss women's presence, voice, and power. Recent research indicates that people view feminist women as being physically masculine and feminist men as being physically feminine, especially men and people reporting greater hostile sexism (Gundersen & Kunst, 2018). Pat Robertson, the American evangelical Christian leader (founder of the Christian Broadcasting Network), claimed that feminists are anti-family and that feminism "encourages women to leave their husbands, kill their children, practice witchcraft, destroy capitalism, and become lesbians" (Associated Press, 1992). Punishing women for feminism is a method of maintaining control, another barrier that feminist women and men must overcome in the continuing fight for equality.

Online Sexism and Anti-Feminism Movements

One would hope that the online world would be free of sexism, but when people are involved, sexism happens. Research indicates that sexism is an issue on social networking sites, in blogs and online forums, and obviously, in video games (Fox & Tang, 2015; Marwick, 2013; Pedersen & Macafee, 2007; Penny, 2014; Shaw, 2014). Portrayals of women as sex objects are everywhere online (Morahan-Martin, 2000), and some scholars argue that the online world is characterized by a culture of misogyny (Barak, 2005; Bartow, 2009; Franks, 2012; Ritter, 2009). Just as in the real world, online sexism is not only openly hostile (Pew Research Center, 2014), but benevolent (Blumell, Huemmer, & Sternadori, 2018), passive and indirect (Barak, 2005), and often occurs cloaked as "humor" (Marwick, 2013). Sexist jokes, online or off, are not funny and they cause harm. They make women feel bad about themselves and have similar emotional effects on women as direct sexual harassment (Boxer & Ford, 2010; LaFrance & Woodzicka, 1998; Swim, Hyers, Cohen, & Ferguson, 2001). Men exposed to sexist humor tend to view sexism as more acceptable and engage in more discrimination against women, a perpetuation of sexism (Ford, Boxer, Armstrong, & Edel, 2008; Ford, Wentzel, & Lorion, 2001). Men who are exposed to sexist hashtags online are more likely to discriminate against female job applicants in later "unrelated" tasks (Fox, Cruz, & Lee, 2015). Just as in the real world, sexism and harassment online serve to maintain patriarchy by excluding, marginalizing, and silencing women (Megarry, 2014).

Anti-feminist movements are social movements by people, mainly men, which discourage feminism through a variety of forms of sexism. They portray feminism as stemming from a hatred of men and involve a rejection of the idea that sexism exists (Ford, 2009). They see men's domination of women as natural or determined by God, and they oppose women's sexual freedom, women's bodily autonomy, and women's rights in general (Clatterbaugh, 2004, 2007). Some anti-feminists see women's increasing social, political, and financial power as causing a **feminization** of society which is dangerous to the well-being of men (Blais & Dupuis-Déri, 2012). Anti-feminism online is characteristic of an "online male supremacist ecosystem," according to the Southern Poverty Law Center (Janik, 2018). A social media trend in 2014 included the hashtag #WomenAgainstFeminism, which argued that sexism does not exist, that men do not oppress women, and that feminism is hatred of men (**misandry**) (Brosnan, 2014; Kim, 2014). The so-called **alt-right** movement, which is essentially fascism, neo-Nazism, and white supremacy but relabeled so as to make it more palatable on the surface, is virulently anti-feminist and blatantly hostile toward women (McAfee, 2016; Romo, 2017; Stack, 2017). Not surprisingly, members of these groups are also highly prejudiced against LGBTQ people (National Public Radio, 2016; Signorile, 2016). Related to the alt-right are online communities of men who call themselves **incels** (involuntary celibates). These men assert that attractive women only seek out men who are attractive or who have money; that men have a right to sex with women; and they express deep misogyny (Cain, 2018; Ling, Mahoney, McGuire, & Freeze, 2018). Men who identify as incels have been involved in several homicidal attacks targeting women (Garcia-Navarro, 2018; Hudson, 2018). Some writers argue that online sexism is attractive to angry young men, who are then more likely to become involved in white supremacist groups (Romano, 2018). These highly misogynistic groups are prevalent on social media sites like Reddit (Kini, 2017) and 4chan (Beran, 2018).

The "Pro-Life" Movement in the United States

Reading any chapter of this book will give you an idea about my stance on safe, legal abortion and its accessibility to women. Most countries around the world have statutes that make abortion safe and legal under certain conditions, with fewer countries allowing abortions by request (see Table 13.3). Abortion by request is legal in the United States, France, China, North Korea, Cuba, Tunisia, South Africa, and Mozambique, just to name a few. Since the passage of *Roe v. Wade* in 1973, religious groups in the U.S. (mainly those associated with evangelical Christianity) have been trying to overturn it and find other ways of limiting girls' and women's access to abortion services. These groups are also against sex education for youth and access to safe, reliable contraception (Barkan 2006; Finke & Adamczyk, 2008). Their basic message is consistently "just don't do it," an **abstinence-only approach** for education and basically for every adult who is unmarried (in a heterosexual marriage, of course). These people view any sexuality that occurs outside of straight marriage as **fornication** (see Chapter 7), and they want to control the sexual

Table 13.3 Countries with legal abortion by request

Albania	Lithuania
Armenia	Luxembourg
Australia (varies by state)	Macedonia
Austria	Mexico (varies by state)
Azerbaijan	Moldova
Bahrain	Mongolia
Belarus	Montenegro
Belgium	Mozambique
Bosnia and Herzegovina	Nepal
Bulgaria	Netherlands
Cambodia	North Korea
Canada	Norway
Cape Verde	Portugal
China	Romania
Croatia	Russian Federation
Cuba	Serbia
Cyprus	Singapore
Czech Republic	Slovakia
Denmark	Slovenia
Estonia	South Africa
France	Spain
Georgia	Sweden
Germany	Switzerland
Greece	Tajikistan
Guyana	Tunisia
Hungary	Turkey
Ireland	Turkmenistan
Italy	Ukraine
Kazakhstan	United States
Kosovo	Uruguay
Kyrgyzstan	Uzbekistan
Latvia	Vietnam

Source: Data taken from https://web.archive.org/web/20160415084202/ http://www.un.org/en/development/desa/population/publications/pdf/policy/ WorldAbortionPolicies2013/WorldAbortionPolicies2013_WallChart.pdf. (accessed January 14, 2018).

behavior of the masses, because of their personal religious beliefs. Please try to understand the tyranny of this. These people want to control what I, what you, and what everyone does with their genitals with other people (they don't like **self-pleasuring** either). They, with their holy book, will dictate what everyone does sexually and they will prohibit and stop what they do not approve of (homosexual or bisexual behaviors, women having sexual freedom, etc.). They've been doing this for centuries. It is infuriating to me.

The **"pro-life" movement** is pro-fetus and pro-forced pregnancy (see Figure 13.4). The same people who claim to be pro-life are against free prenatal care for poor women, free childbirth services for poor women, free childcare and preschool for the poor, even free school lunches for poor kids. Their real concern is not for children, otherwise they would support these programs for poor children and their moms (and they wouldn't keep immigrant children in detention camps, see below). Their real concern is about women having sex; they want to stop women's free

Figure 13.4 The "pro-life" movement in the United States is against women's bodily autonomy and sexual freedom
Source: Zach Gibson/Bloomberg via Getty Images

sexuality, allowing traditional patriarchy and domination of women who should have no control over their own bodies, sexuality, and reproduction. Efforts by these groups to limit access to abortion include state requirements for abortions to occur in hospitals, for parents to consent, for state-mandated pre-abortion counseling, even requiring clinics to have hallways and doorways of a certain width (Berg, 2016; Guttmacher Institute, 2019). These kinds of efforts, mainly by traditional, more religious states (e.g., Alabama, Missouri, Texas, Virginia), have made getting an abortion in those places nearly impossible, especially for poor girls and women (Berg, 2016). Arkansas has passed a new law outlawing all abortions after 14 weeks and requiring women to obtain their husband's consent to have an abortion (Mallon, 2017). Abortion by request is illegal in many countries, with abortion only being allowed when there is risk to the mother's life or a fetal abnormality (United Nations, 2013).

As you already know, access to safe and reliable contraception, and abortion, is crucial for girls' and women's social, political, and financial success (Jayachandran, 2015; Miller, 2010). Restricting women's sexual health and freedom because of someone else's supernatural beliefs is the height of hubris and oppression. Almost immediately after being inaugurated, President Trump signed an executive order limiting federal funding for international groups that provide information about and access to abortion services (BBC News, 2017). The Trump Administration is attempting to prohibit distribution of federal family planning funds to abortion providers in the United States (Levey, 2018). The Administration has succeeded in appointing two Supreme Court Justices, Neil Gorsuch and Brett Kavanaugh, both very conservative politically (Higgens, 2018; Hurley, 2017). Kavanaugh was appointed and approved by the Republican Senate despite allegations of sexually assaulting a woman when they were teenagers (Abramson, 2018). Supreme Court Justice Ruth

Bader Ginsberg recently underwent surgery for lung cancer (Totenberg, 2018), at age 85 years, and may be close to retiring, opening up yet another spot on the Court, with dwindling numbers of more liberal judges. The war on women in the United States is real, and the fight for equality begins and ends with **sexual agency** and accessible reproductive health care.

Feminist scholars have consistently asserted that men's domination of women is rooted in their control of women's sexuality (Rudman, Fetterolf, & Sanchez, 2013). Men across time have consistently controlled women's sexuality through religion, laws, and other normative social structures, and they're still doing it. Spousal consent for an abortion is required in many countries, including Japan, South Korea, and Turkey (Center for Reproductive Rights, 2017). Research indicates that men who are sexist, especially those having negative feelings about women in general, are more likely to view their control of women's sexuality as a good thing. Greater hostile sexism is predictive of support for policies allowing men to control their pregnant partner's decisions, including having or not having an abortion. Hostile sexism is also predictive of support for men not providing financially for a child if a pregnant partner chooses not to have an abortion (Petterson & Sutton, 2018). Additional research indicates that greater social dominance orientation among women and men is linked with beliefs that men should dominate in sexual encounters and that men should control contraception (Rosenthal & Levy, 2010; Rosenthal, Levy, & Earnshaw, 2012). Christian men are also particularly likely to believe that they should dominate and control women's sexuality, with women's sexual behaviors judged as either "good" or "bad," and men's sexuality viewed as less controllable (Conrad, 2006). Traditional religious ideologies support male control of women's sexuality, along with other traditional social structures. American Christianity is intent on controlling American girls and women, an ongoing oppression that affects all American women today.

The Fight for LGBTQ Equality

All over the world, cultures are broadly **heteronormative**; heterosexuality is viewed as typical, normal, and more natural than other sexualities. The world is also dominated by a **cis-normative** system, whereby people who are **cisgender** (their chosen gender identity matches the gender category assigned to them at birth) are considered typical and more normal than other identities, including **transgender** (their gender identity is different from the gender category assigned at birth) (Worthen, 2018) (see Table 13.4 for a list of gender terms). Both of these systems are hierarchical and involve social dominance of groups with less power. Although some cultures have embraced homosexuality, including ancient Greece (Halperin, 2005), and honored people identifying as both female and male (e.g., Native American **two-spirit people**; Jacobs, 1997), LGBTQ people have been greatly oppressed all over the white patriarchal world and for centuries (Bornstein, 1994; Bronski, 2011). Unfortunately, as a numerical minority (3.5% of people describe themselves as homosexual or bisexual, Gates, 2011; .6% as transgender; Flores, Herman, Gates, & Brown, 2016), they are rather easily oppressed.

Although LGBTQ people are winning their civil right to marry whom they choose around the world, including in the United States (*Obergefell v. Hodges*, 2015), and in more than 20 other countries (most recently, Australia, Colombia, and Germany, all in 2017; Pew Research Center, 2017), they have no civil rights in many areas of the world, and are routinely targets of physical aggression, including murder (Thompson, 2019; United Nations Refugee Agency, 2019). LGBTQ individuals, mainly gay men, are being arrested, detained, and apparently imprisoned and tortured in the Russian area of Chechnya (Eleftheriou-Smith, 2017; Peter, 2017; Walker,

436 *Current Issues and Social Problems*

Table 13.4 Various terms referring to gender identity, sexuality, and sexual orientation

1. **LGBTQ:** an expansive term referring to people who do not identify as heterosexual and/or as cisgender. An abbreviation for lesbian, gay, bisexual, transgender, queer/questioning.
2. **Gay:** homosexual, often referring to homosexual men.
3. **Lesbian:** a homosexual woman.
4. **Straight:** a heterosexual person.
5. **Cis:** an abbreviation of **cisgender** (one's gender identity matches the gender category assigned at birth).
6. **Cishet:** an abbreviation of cisgender heterosexual.
7. **Trans:** an abbreviation of **transgender** (one's gender identity does not match the gender category assigned at birth).
8. **Genderqueer:** a person who identifies as neither gender or a combination of female and male.
9. **Genderfluid:** someone who feels that their gender is changeable and variable over time.
10. **Non-binary:** a term for someone whose gender is not female or male or limited to any combination of the gender binary. May include transgender, genderfluid, and genderqueer individuals.
11. **Intersex:** someone who is born with ambiguous genitals.
12. **Pansexual:** an orientation of someone who is attracted to people regardless of their gender.
13. **Bisexual:** someone attracted to people of their own gender and another gender.
14. **Sapiosexual:** someone whose sexual attraction is based on others' intelligence rather than gender.

Source: Adapted from list of terms featured in www.cosmopolitan.com/sex-love/a20888315/genders-identity-list-definitions/

2017a, 2017b). In 2016, 53 people were murdered, 43 others wounded, in a mass shooting by a man expressing virulent hatred toward gay men (Hanks, 2016) (see Figure 13.5). Several witnesses and people who knew the killer assert that he himself was a gay man (another example of **reaction formation**) (Hennessy-Fiske, Jarvie, & Wilber, 2016; Pilkington & Elgot, 2016). An openly gay Latin rapper named Kevin Fret was murdered in Puerto Rico recently, which the Puerto Rico Trans Youth Coalition called a hate crime (Guy, 2019). A transgender immigrant from Honduras (Roxsana Hernandez Rodriguez) seeking asylum in the U.S. died while in the custody of Immigration and Customs Enforcement (ICE). She was apparently beaten and not provided medical attention (Grinberg, 2018). Research indicates that violence against transgender people is likely to begin early and continue throughout their lives, with a particularly high risk for sexual violence (Stotzer, 2009). Hate crimes against LGBTQ individuals in the United States have increased under the Trump Administration and its hypermasculine, fascist orientation, with most perpetrators being men and most victims being gay men (Federal Bureau of Investigation, 2017). The Southern Poverty Law Center (2018) links the rise in all hate crimes in the U.S., especially crimes against racial minorities, to the election of President Trump.

President Trump shows his blatant, outright **heterosexism** by oppressing the LGBTQ community by threatening to ban them from military service (Block, Strangio, & Esseks, 2018), despite the fact that there are tens of thousands of LGBTQ people currently serving the United States in the armed forces, with 6.1% of armed force members identifying as LGBTQ (Meadows et al., 2018). Previously, the policy of "Don't ask, don't tell" required that LGBTQ people must hide their gender identity or sexuality while serving in the military. This ridiculous policy was dropped in 2011 (Waters, 2018). Why is it necessary to hide or ban LGBTQ people from serving their country? The legitimizing myth is that these people (especially gay and transgender men) will threaten the heterosexuality of straight men through seduction (Miller, 1994). The reality is that transgender women are at much greater risk for sexual violence, precisely from straight men (Stotzer, 2009),

Figure 13.5 Victims of the Pulse Nightclub shooting in Orlando, FL. From Diebelius, 2017
Source: Hugh Peterswald/Pacific Press Via Zuma Wire/Shutterstock

because gay men and transgender women threaten the masculinity of men with a precarious sense of manhood (Vandello & Bosson, 2013; Leverenz, 1986). Republicans' and conservative groups' continuing outrage about transgender people using public restrooms of their choice also legitimizes stigmatization and exclusion of LGBTQ people by portraying them as pedophiles or sexual predators (Brown, 2017; Johnson, 2019). The reality is that men who identify as straight comprise the vast majority of rapists and sexual offenders in the United States, including apparently in public restrooms (Uniform Crime Report, 2011).

Traditionalism and LGBTQ Oppression

Along with other historically and currently oppressed groups, **LGBTQ** Americans are in a battle for the most basic freedoms. Hate groups in the United States who target LGBTQ people portray them as dangerous to children (usually with claims of pedophilia), to public health (with lies about HIV, AIDS), and to traditional social institutions (Southern Poverty Law Center, 2017). Research indicates that conservatism and its endorsement of the traditional hierarchy are associated with more negative attitudes toward LGBTQ people and their having civil rights equal to those of others. Research has documented links between being Republican (Ender, Rohall &, Matthews, 2015; Flores, 2015), authoritarian and conservative (Norton & Herek, 2013), and endorsement of traditional gender ideology with negative attitudes toward LGBTQ people (Nagoshi et al., 2008). Other research indicates that people report feeling uncomfortable and disgusted when thinking about LGBTQ people (Gadarian & Van der Vort, 2017; Gillig & Murphy, 2016; Miller et al., 2017). Men are significantly more likely than women to report negative attitudes, because of the strong emphasis on masculinity in defining male heterosexuality (Norton & Herek, 2013). Indeed, threatening men's sense of masculinity in a laboratory experiment increased their reported opposition to transgender rights, revealing that men's own sense of identity is linked with feelings they have about other gender identities (Harrison & Michelson, 2019). Hypermasculinity is linked with strongly negative attitudes toward gay men and transgender people, because they violate expectations of masculinity and power (Connell, 1995).

Traditional institutions, including Christianity in modern America, are openly opposed to any sexuality outside of married heterosexuality and view transgender identities as sinful and wrong. Greater religiosity is linked with more negative attitudes toward homosexual (Whitehead, 2018) and transgender individuals (Ender et al., 2015). Focus on the Family, a mainstream Christian organization, asserts that sexuality is not a right, that sex is for reproduction, that heterosexual married sex is the only option, and that Biblical rules should be followed (Stanton, 2014). I'm not arguing that all Christians or all branches of Christianity are anti-LGBTQ, because that's not true, and support for same-sex marriage and LGBTQ equality is growing among Christian groups in the U.S. (Vandermaas-Peeler, Cox, Fisch-Friedman, Griffin, & Jones, 2018). But there is a clear link between traditional Christian ideology and negative sentiment toward LGBTQ people. Religious organizations have also been involved in movements aiming to limit or deny the civil rights of LGBTQ people, including to marry a same-sex partner (Pew Research Center, 2012) and to adopt children (Focus on the Family, 2009). Twenty-one states have so-called religious exemption laws that allow individuals, businesses, and non-profit organizations to not comply with state laws because of religious beliefs (Miller, 2018), including adoption agencies (Hubbard, 2018). Fifty-one LGBTQ hate groups are currently listed by the Southern Poverty Law Center, nearly all of them religious in nature.

Control through Poverty: Indifference to and Oppression of Poor People

It's no accident that poverty exists. Poverty is created by **capitalism**, the control of the means of production and life necessities by a few people with lots of money who use the means of production to produce monetary profit and wealth more than anything else. The "bottom line" (profits) has taken over the American business culture, with worker, environmental, and societal well-being falling by the wayside. Time and again in American businesses, large corporations close manufacturing or distribution sites, laying off hundreds or even thousands of workers, while CEOs and top executives walk away with huge golden parachute packages of millions of dollars (Jones, 2010; Siemaszko, 2018). Corporations raid or blatantly steal worker pension or retirement benefits, in favor of giving a few people millions of dollars (Adams, 2012). American worker wages have stagnated, while CEO compensation has risen dramatically, to an average of $13,940,000 per year for a CEO of an S&P 500 Index company, 361 times that of the average worker (Hembree, 2018). The American business culture is a **greed** culture based on getting as much as you possibly can, workers, customers, and the environment be damned. This necessarily results in a large section of society living in poverty; it is much harder for people to become super-rich when wealth is fairly distributed. And the people who are most likely to be in poverty, that's not an accident either. Women and their children, racial minority groups, the elderly and disabled, impoverishing them enables greater wealth for the super-rich and simultaneously serves to oppress them and keep them from positions of power. The **individualistic** capitalist system also provides a set of legitimizing myths, not just about women, and racial and sexual minorities, but about poor people, with responsibility for poverty shifted onto its victims (they are lazy, they are stupid, they aren't capable of wealth) and for wealth onto its holders (I worked hard, I deserve more, I am

Current Issues and Social Problems 439

special) (Gilbert & Mallone, 1995). The American Protestant work ethic of hard work and the myth that rich people work harder than others also justify wealth inequality in the U.S., individual, internal attributions that do not consider external, situational, uncontrollable causes of poverty (Rosenthal, Levy, & Moyer, 2011). Poverty is lowest in advanced democratic countries that follow socialist policies for public goods, like education, health care, and corrections (Matthews, 2015).

We've already discussed at length how women as a group are kept in poverty around the world, including through denying access to education (Dorius & Firebaugh, 2010; UNESCO, 2004) and sexual health care (Jayachandran, 2015; Miller, 2010). Women and children are more likely to live in poverty in the advanced world than any other group (Cook, 2014). Women of color (and their children) are particularly likely to live in poverty in technologically-advanced, wealthy countries, including the United States, where 21.4% of African American women, 18.7% of Latina American women, and 22.8% of Native American women live in poverty (Patrick, 2017). Historically, black and Latina women have been exploited in domestic servitude, black women as an extension of slavery (Bloom, 2015; May, 2017) and Latina women as undocumented immigrants or citizens who lack access to education (Carrillo, 2017). There are currently approximately two million domestic workers in the United States, nearly all of them black American or Latina immigrant women, many of whom suffer extremely low wages and abusive working conditions (Bick, 2017). Media images of black and Latina women have also commonly placed them into domestic roles (Rodriguez, 2018). Latino men, like Latina women, are more likely to be in service roles, including gardening and landscape work (Ramirez & Hondagneu-Sotelo, 2013), and portrayed as such in the media (Rodriguez, 2018).

Black men as a group are marginalized in the United States through institutionalized racism in the criminal justice system (Brewer & Heitzeg, 2008), with black men comprising 37% of men in prison (Bureau of Justice Statistics, 2013). Black men are more likely to be detained and arrested by police, and convicted of a crime, and receive harsher sentences, compared to white men accused of similar crimes (Brunson & Miller, 2006; Pettit & Western, 2004; Welch, 2007). Rios (2007) argues that black and Latino men are hypercriminalized in the United States. The for-profit prison industry in the U.S. is making record profits (Picchi, 2018), a public social service that is profiting from incarcerating people. Separating black men from their families helps to maintain poverty of African American families (see Pattillo, Western, & Weiman, 2004), who are already financially disadvantaged because of huge differences in inherited wealth across history between white and black Americans due to slavery and discrimination (Shapiro, Meschede, & Osoro, 2013). Black children, girls and boys, are criminalized in American schools, and are much more likely to be disciplined, including suspended and expelled from school (Monroe, 2005; Morris, 2016). Institutionalized racism in educational institutions and historic lack of access to higher education have obviously contributed to disadvantage and poverty among African and Latinx Americans (Allen, 1988; Huber, Johnson, & Kohli, 2006; Katz, 1999).

The current situation of immigrants at the American southern border is another example of cruelty toward the poor and profiting from them. Immigrants to the United States, generally only those with brown or black skin, are portrayed as criminals, a process called crimmigration (Stumpf, 2006). Donald Trump's Department of Homeland Security began a program of separating immigrant families seeking asylum at the southern border, taking children away from parents, including children in infancy (Burke & Mendoza, 2018; Domonoske & Gonzales, 2018). In December 2018, it was estimated that between 13,000 and 15,000 children were housed in detainment camps in the United States (Chalabi, 2018; Driver, 2018), with other children sent to adoption agencies or foster homes (Associated Press, 2019; Joyce, 2018). Private corporations are

440   *Current Issues and Social Problems*

providing the equipment, staff, and provisions for the detainment camps, the tent cities, which is estimated to cost the government up to $775 per day, per person (Urbi, 2018). These immigrant groups are legally seeking **asylum**, currently allowed under U.S. law; imprisoning people for seeking asylum is a violation of international and U.S. law (Tan, 2018). Trump shut down the U.S. government because Congress did not agree to funding $5 billion for a giant wall that is not even logistically feasible or physically possible in many border areas (Garfield, 2017). Trump repeatedly calls asylum-seekers criminals, drug dealers, dangerous, and terrorists, lies that justify their imprisonment and create fear in the American people (Jansen & Gomez, 2018). He refers to them as animals (Korte & Gomez, 2018), a **dehumanization** tactic that makes their oppression and violence against them more psychologically permissible (Haslam, 2006). Separating children from their parents is extremely psychologically and emotionally damaging to children, especially very young children (Rutter, 1971). The long-term consequences of such separations will not be good, not for the individuals and families involved and not for the communities where these people will one day be adults. In addition, at this writing two children have died in the custody of U.S. Border Patrol (Schnell & McCoy, 2018), with more immigrants dying in 2017 in ICE detention than in any other year since 2009 (Chen, 2018). These people are not wealthy; if they were, they wouldn't be so easily oppressed by their own and our government. Imprisoning and abusing people who need help is the essence of the deepest oppression, it is cruel, and it is decidedly un-American.

Violence against Women and Children: A Global Epidemic

I won't beleaguer you with another recitation of the statistics on violence (including sexual violence) from all over the world, which disproportionately affects children and women (see Chapter 11). But I will remind you of some facts. Rape and violence are truly global epidemics. The organization Know Violence in Childhood (2017) estimates that around 1.7 billion children experience some form of physical or sexual abuse over the course of one year. The World Health Organization (2013) reports that worldwide, around 35% of women have experienced physical or sexual abuse by an intimate partner or non-partner at some point in their lives (not including verbal abuse or sexual harassment). **Human trafficking** involves abducting people and selling them to others as slave labor or for sexual exploitation. It is also a global epidemic, being the second largest criminal enterprise internationally, yielding an estimated $150 billion each year to traffickers and involving 24.9 million victims (International Labor Organization, 2014). Women and girls account for 71 per cent of victims trafficked for labor or sexual exploitation (United Nations Office on Drugs and Crime, 2016). Girls and women make up 99% of victims trafficked for the commercial sex industry (International Labor Organization, 2014). The majority of perpetrators in all of these worldwide problems are men, who use violence to physically control and oppress women, as has been the case since the dawn of time.

So how do we reduce violence, if we cannot stop it entirely? The World Health Organization (2002) describes multiple factors that may be addressed to combat interpersonal violence around the world. Understanding the risk factors for violence, including poverty, a history of family violence, family instability, and alcohol and substance abuse, is obviously important. Addressing these social problems is also obviously important, which requires substantial financial investment by private and public organizations. Poverty will always be a huge social problem in a capitalist system; public goods must be distributed and subsidized by the government. Public health prevention programs may also help, preventing violence before it occurs. Such prevention programs can focus on risk factors for violence as well as education and training about the importance of not hurting other people, stress management, improving communication in families, and so on. Actively fighting against complacency and the social acceptance of violence may involve challenging cultural and social traditions, norms, and ideas that permit and even promote violence, including ideas about men as always dominant, always in charge, or allowed to physically force wives and children, and women in general. Changing negative stereotypes about girls and women is also critical. WHO (2002) asserts that the health care sector should be largely responsible around the world for combatting the epidemic of interpersonal violence.

I would add to WHO's recommendations greater societal, family, educational, and personal efforts toward training boys and men to respect girls and women and to not hurt them or exploit them with physical strength. Enough victim-blaming; the only people responsible for interpersonal violence are the perpetrators. Interpersonal violence is simply *never* okay and no one *ever* deserves to be victimized. With men the primary perpetrators of violence all over the world, the greater responsibility to reduce, even stop, interpersonal violence is very clearly theirs. The question remains, are the world's men willing to give up their disproportionate share of power, in the interests of equality, peace, harmony, nonviolence? Certainly not all of them, possibly many of them, hopefully more of them in the future. Women's responsibility is to use our minds and voices to fight back, refuse, stand up, resist, to call out and confront sexism whenever we can, wherever we are. Yes we can!

Changing Attitudes, Fighting Oppression

On the individual and group levels, changing attitudes (persuasion) can work. The best way to change attitudes (and keep them changed) is from within a group using evidence-based information. First, one must be an ingroup member; people routinely and rather automatically reject information they perceive as coming from someone who is in an outgroup (a group to which one does not belong). Ingroup members are listened to most of the time, however, even if they are a minority within the ingroup, simply because they are a part of the group and entitled to leniency (not outright rejection of their point of view; Crano & Chen, 1998). The majority in an ingroup has the power to compel, to force others to go along with their point of view. Ingroup members comply with the majority because they fear rejection by the apparent majority (a process called normative social influence; Deutsch & Gerard, 1955). The minority of a group cannot compel the majority because they don't have the social power, and so instead they must use information to influence the majority, to try to change their minds. This is the second necessity for persuasion, that the argument is solid, based on clear, verifiable evidence that comes from a credible (expert and trustworthy) source (McGinnies, 1973). This is called informational social influence, when minds are changed by facts (Deutsch & Gerard, 1955). The third requirement of minority social influence is that the minority persist (Crano & Chen, 1998). Although the majority is likely to reject a minority message up front, because being part of the minority is less attractive and less powerful, because of the leniency contract the majority must listen and therefore process the message. And in that, change begins; the message is processed, and so has entered the mind. Rejected up front, the minority must persist and come back with their message, again requiring the majority to think about it. Over time, this repeated processing may actually change existing attitudes, cause the majority to recognize that there are multiple ways of doing things (a liberalizing effect on thought), and the minority position may be adopted by the group. This entire process is called minority social influence and it is a very effective way to change attitudes and beliefs (Crano, 1994).

442 *Current Issues and Social Problems*

We can see minority social influence happening in educational settings, particularly higher education. Students may not necessarily agree with all of the messages and information they are receiving at college or university. In fact, some information may be highly troubling to students, particularly when it conflicts with cherished or very strongly held beliefs. Students who come from religious traditions may have learned to doubt science and explanations provided by science, including **evolutionary** theory, because it conflicts with beliefs provided by the religion (e.g., about **creation** of Earth and life on it). Students may believe that patriarchy is normal and preferable. A student once asked me in class, "What's wrong with men having all the power?" a question reflecting his implicit belief in the rightness of patriarchy. Education works to challenge these beliefs first, when universities and individual faculty, staff, and administrators are **inclusive** and impart a sense of belonging to students, creating an ingroup. As a member of the ingroup, students trust their teachers and give them the leniency of listening, even if they don't agree with them. Second, students must listen and process the information provided by their teachers, or they can't get the grade and earn the degree, often a primary motive for students. Student processing of information that teachers, credible and trustworthy sources, impart is essential to student success. Even if they don't believe information or don't want to believe information up front, they must process the information again and again to be successful in any course. Repeated processing may eventually lead to specific and overall attitude change, and perhaps later change on a massive scale, a change in entire belief systems, as the mind is opened to multiple possible solutions and a departure from dichotomous thinking. That is the power of formal education, to change minds and change thinking about the world and humankind.

The same processes of minority social influence may operate on the individual level, as each of us works to become more knowledgeable and impart our knowledge to others. Remember, a primary goal of psychology is to work toward improving the well-being of humankind. Challenging the status quo, challenging traditions and hierarchies that promulgate and support hatred and oppression, that is the duty of every educated person. Remember, you must try to stay in the ingroup with as many people as possible, so your messages are not rejected. View humanity as an ingroup, think of yourself as a member of the family of humankind, and portray yourself as such to others. In that way, your messages are more likely to be listened to and heard. Yes, you must call out tyranny, including identifying some people as tyrants. But to stay in the ingroup, you must try your hardest to be assertive and outspoken without attacking people. Try to attack ideas and oppression, rather than individual people. Provide evidence-based information in your assertions and arguments, the best of which is provided by science. Through informational social influence, you yourself can change people's minds. Use your power wisely, students; some people are intolerant, which we must never tolerate. But be open-minded, kind-hearted, compassionate, and flexible in your thinking, and be brave, never stop using your mind and voice to stop injustice and make positive change. I know you can do it, and I am so very proud of you. Thank you for reading my book!

Chapter Summary

Major social problems around the world reflect the oppression of women and minority groups by men (patriarchy). While the number of women and men describing themselves as feminist is increasing, female feminists are disliked by many people because their behaviors are not feminine. Men who identify as feminist are often seen as feminine and weak, anathema to most men, especially those high in hypermasculinity. Women and feminists are ridiculed, harassed, and attacked online, including by men with extreme hostile sexism. The pro-life movement in the United States arose in response to *Roe v. Wade*, which made abortion legal in the United States. The pro-life movement uses religious ideology to control women's sexuality, legitimizing myths that enable the social, political, and financial oppression of women. LGBTQ individuals are gaining rights around the world, rights they should never have been deprived of in the first place. However, violence against LGBTQ people is rampant worldwide and escalating. Religious ideology is involved in oppression of LGBTQ people. Poverty worldwide disproportionately affects women and children, especially women of color and their children. Women of color are limited in opportunity and have historically been disproportionately represented as domestic workers. Men of color are criminalized and incarcerated at disproportionate rates in the United States, keeping minority families in poverty for generations. Violence against women is a global epidemic that disproportionately affects women and children, with men overwhelmingly the perpetrators of violence. Violence prevention depends on public health prevention programs and changing norms about patriarchy and violence. Individual change involves emphasis on respecting all people, committing to not using violence, changing attitudes about violence and women through education, and activism. Minority social influence is a powerful weapon to use against hate and oppression.

Thoughtful Questions

- Explain how the Trump Administration is fascist.
- Explain links between social dominance orientation, right-wing authoritarianism, and racism, sexism, and heterosexism.
- Discuss the current state of equality of LGBTQ people around the world.
- Discuss legitimizing myths used to oppress LGBTQ people.
- How are women and racial minorities pushed into and kept in poverty by patriarchy?
- Explain the criminalization of black and Latinx people in the U.S.
- Explain how feminists are perceived in the United States.
- Discuss anti-feminist movements, including online groups like incels.
- Describe the pro-life movement in the U.S., including the role of evangelical Christianity.
- Describe Trump's treatment of immigrant families at the southern U.S. border.
- Explain how communities, organizations, and individuals can work to stop interpersonal violence.
- Explain how minority ingroup members can change attitudes held by the majority in a group.
- Explain how education works through minority social influence processes.

Glossary

Abstinence-only education: sex education in schools that focuses on abstinence as the only way to completely prevent disease and pregnancy. Such programs do not provide sufficient information about sexual health.

Alt-right: essentially fascism, neo-Nazism, and white supremacy but relabeled so as to make it more palatable on the surface. Such groups are virulently anti-feminist, blatantly hostile toward women, racist, and show hatred of LGBTQ people.

444 *Current Issues and Social Problems*

Anti-feminist movements: social movements by people, mainly men, which discourage feminism through a variety of forms of sexism.

Assertion: behaviors that involve exercising and displaying one's will and action toward one's goals.

Asylum: protection granted by a country to a person who is a political refugee from their native country.

Attribution: an explanation of cause.

Authoritarian parents: parents who are suspicious and mistrustful of their children and who emphasize obedience and use harsh disciplinary practices.

Capitalism: an economic system based on private/corporate ownership of the means of production (including of food, water, and other necessities) and their operation for profit.

Cisgender: people whose gender identity matches the gender assigned to them at birth.

Cis-normative: a hierarchical structure whereby **cisgender** individuals are regarded as normative (typical, normal), while **transgender** people are considered as not normative (not typical, not normal).

Citizens United: a decision by the United States Supreme Court that free speech is unfairly restricted when financial contributions to political campaigns are limited (558 U.S. 310 [2010]).

Conformist: a person who conforms to social custom and the expectations of others.

Convergent thinking: simplistic thinking that involves thinking in black or white, right or wrong categories. The opposite of dimensional, creative, complex thought (**divergent thinking**).

Creationism: the religious idea that a deity created the universe, the Earth, and all life on Earth through magical processes.

Credibility: when a source of information is viewed as both an expert on a topic and as trustworthy (having nothing to gain from persuasion). Credible sources are more persuasive and influence through provision of information.

Criminalized: to be perceived as or made to appear as a criminal.

Crimmigration: the portrayal of immigrants seeking asylum as criminals.

Cronyism: the corrupt practice of placing friends, relatives, and financial contributors in positions of power without regard to their actual qualifications.

Defense mechanisms: strategies the ego uses to protect itself from frightening experiences and threats.

Dehumanization: denying that a person or group possesses positive human qualities; portrayal of a person or group as less than human, having less inherent value than other people.

Displacement: an ego defense mechanism whereby negative feelings are displaced onto a substitute target rather than the actual target. For example, abused children take their feelings of anger toward their parents and direct them toward other children at school.

Divergent thinking: thinking that involves multiple right answers or multiple optional outcomes. Complex, dimensional, effortful thinking that underlies creativity.

Egalitarian: ideals that include valuing of equality, including gender equality. Egalitarian cultures value women and men equally.

Ego: the self; the conscious mind that reaches a compromise between reality, pleasure, and morality; the self. According to Erikson (1950), the ego emerges during early childhood, during toddlerhood.

Equal Rights Amendment (ERA): a proposed amendment to the U.S. Constitution that states that civil rights may not be denied on the basis of sex (whether one is female, male, or other).

Equality: when different groups enjoy equal status, opportunities, and rights.

Ethnicity: a group with a common cultural tradition or nationality.

Evangelical Christianity: a collective of various denominations of Protestantism in the United States that emphasize that one must be born again (be saved), that the Bible is the holy word of God, and the importance of evangelism (sharing their religion with others).

Evolutionary theory: the scientific explanation that life on our planet evolved over millions and millions of years from earlier, simpler forms. Evolutionary theory is supported by evidence in every branch of science and is accepted as fact by the vast majority of scientists.

Femininity: the content of stereotypes of women; women are viewed as soft, caring, gentle, kind, emotional.

Feminism: advocating social, political, legal, and economic rights for women equal to those of men.

Feminist: a person who promotes and strives for equality between women and men. Feminist approaches emphasize global historical patriarchy in the oppression of women.

Feminization: causing something to be more feminine (more gentle, loving, kind), which is evaluated depending on one's view of feminine qualities as desirable.

Fornication: a negative term describing sexual relations between two people who are not married; or sexual behavior engaged in for pleasure, not for reproduction.

Gender: the social construction of what it means to be female, male, or another gender; ideas about **femininity** and **masculinity** that are developed within a particular culture, including traditions, roles, and expectations of behavior for women and girls, men and boys.

Gender identity: one's identification as female, male, both, or neither.

GOP: the "Grand Old Party," another name for the Republican Party.

Greed: powerful and selfish desire for something, usually money.

Hate crime: as defined by the FBI, a "criminal offense against a person or property motivated in whole or in part by an offender's bias against a race, religion, disability, sexual orientation, ethnicity, gender, or gender identity" (www.fbi.gov/investigate/civil-rights/hate-crimes).

Hegemonic patriarchy: a social system that promotes and justifies men's control and dominance of the majority of a society's financial, social, and political power.

Hegemony: a social structure where one group dominates every other group.

Heteronormative: when heterosexuality is considered normal and preferred in a society; the rules of sexuality are inherently heterosexual, to the neglect of other sexualities.

Heterosexism: an ideology embodied in institutional practices that work to the disadvantage of sexual minority groups.

Homelessness: the state of not having a reliable, safe place to live; lacking an actual structure to live in. Reliable and safe includes adequate shelter from the elements and access to water.

Hostile sexism: sexism involving negative feelings accompanied by negative stereotypes of women and heterosexual hostility.

Human trafficking: the criminal enterprise that involves abducting people and selling them to others as slave labor or for sexual exploitation.

Hypercriminalized: when ordinary, everyday behaviors are viewed as inherently risky, deviant, threatening, or criminal, across social contexts (Rios, 2007).

Hypermasculinity: extreme masculinity including endorsement of violence, callous sexual attitudes toward women, and risk-taking.

Implicit: cognitive ideas and processes that are so well-practiced or so commonly used that they have become automatic (occurring unintentionally and sometimes without conscious awareness).

446   *Current Issues and Social Problems*

Incels: involuntary celibates. Such groups of men online express misogyny, a right to sex from women, rage at women for sexual rejection, and promotion of violent acts toward women.

Inclusive: attitudes and practices that include all people, with no individuals or groups excluded from participation.

Individualism: a cultural valuing of individual goals, achievements, responsibilities, and freedoms. Usually compared to **collectivism**, a cultural valuing of group goals over individual outcomes.

Informational social influence: when a person's thoughts, feelings, or behaviors change as the result of the actions of another person or group because of information they provide. Informational social influence occurs because the influence source is viewed as an expert who can be trusted to provide accurate information.

Ingroup: a group to which one belongs.

Jingoism: extreme patriotism that is aggressive toward other nations and groups, which are viewed as threats to national interests.

Johnson Amendment: a provision in the United States tax code that prohibits non-profit organizations, including religious organizations, from opposing or endorsing any political candidates.

Labor union: an organized group of workers engaged in a particular type of work; collectives of workers have power to negotiate contracts with employers. Unions are formed to protect worker rights and ensure fair working conditions and pay.

Legitimizing myths: false beliefs about a group that justify their continued oppression.

LGBTQ: lesbian, gay, bisexual, transgender, queer/questioning.

Liberalism: a personal philosophy or worldview that emphasizes equality and freedom, and the importance of protecting weaker people from harm by the powerful.

Liberalizing: an opening up of thought processes into dimensional thinking and multiple possible solutions. Thinking changes from simple, **convergent**, dichotomous thinking to **divergent**, creative thinking.

Majority: the numerical majority of a group that influences the group through social rewards and punishments.

Masculinity: the content of stereotypes of men; men are viewed as hard, strong, tough, unemotional, independent.

Minority: the numerical minority of a group that influences the group through provided information.

Minority social influence: the process by which a minority of an ingroup influences the majority. Because the majority listens to the minority, if the minority persists over time, the majority may adopt the minority point of view despite initial rejection through repeated processing of the message.

Misandry: hatred of men. A **misandrist** is a person who hates men. Anti-feminist groups often claim that feminism stems from misandry.

Misogyny: hatred of women. A **misogynist** is a person who hates women.

Modern sexism (aka neosexism): beliefs that women have already achieved equality, and that women who say otherwise are whining or trying to gain unfair advantage.

Nice: pleasing, agreeable, kind. A **prescription** for women, not for men.

Normative social influence: when a person's thoughts, feelings, or behaviors change as the result of the actions of another person or group because of social rewards. Normative social influence occurs out of fear of social rejection or loss of social reward from the influence source.

Current Issues and Social Problems   447

Open-minded: a person who is not closed-minded; an openness to new ideas, new experiences, and new information.

Outgroup: a group to which one does not belong. Messages from outgroup members are routinely ignored.

Patriarchy: a hierarchical structure where men control the majority of power and wealth; supported by false ideas (**legitimizing myths**) and practices that subordinate and oppress women.

Persuasion: attitude change that results from social influence.

Plutocracy: political rule by the wealthiest in society.

Poverty: lacking in material possessions and money, such that meeting basic needs (e.g., for food, shelter, medical care) is affected.

Prescriptions: commands to be a certain way; ideas about what women and men should be like.

Projection: an ego defense mechanism whereby a person projects threatening feelings and impulses onto others. For example, a person full of hate and anger views outgroups as full of hate and anger.

"Pro-life" movement: social movements, largely religious groups, who are trying to make abortion services illegal in the United States.

Public goods: social institutions that serve individual and public good, including education, health care, and corrections. Such institutions when fully funded and run fairly advance society.

Race: categories for grouping people based on skin color and other phenotypic (apparent) characteristics.

Racism: any attitude, act, or institutional structure that subordinates a person because of their skin color or ethnicity.

Reaction formation: an ego defense mechanism whereby a person's outward behavior is the opposite of their true inclination.

Right-wing authoritarianism (RWA): beliefs, feelings, and motives favoring obedience to traditional authorities.

Sanctity: a religious belief that something is sacred or holy.

Self-pleasuring (masturbation): stimulation of one's own genitals, usually to orgasm.

Sex: biological sex; one's sexual **genotype** (genetic profile) and **phenotype** (the physical appearance of a trait).

Sexism: any act, attitude, or institutional structure that subordinates a person because of their sex or gender identity.

Sexual agency: ability to control and direct one's own sexual behaviors.

Skeptical: to be habitually thoughtful.

Social interest: a desire to relate productively and positively with other people.

Social justice: fairness in availability of opportunities and privileges within a society.

Social problems: societal issues that cause harm to people, such as discrimination and poverty.

Socialism: an economic and political system where the means of production, distribution, and exchange are controlled by the community as a whole, not by individuals. **Democratic socialism** allows individual ownership of the means of production but not of public goods (health care, education, corrections); these should be controlled by a democratic government.

Socioeconomic status: one's overall economic and financial status in a society.

448 *Current Issues and Social Problems*

Status quo: the way things are, the current state of affairs.

Traditional: having to do with older ways of doing things. Traditionally, men have power over women and women are subordinate to men.

Transgender: people whose gender identity does not match the gender assigned to them at birth.

Wealth inequality: the unequal distribution of wealth in a society produced by capitalism.

References

Abramson, A. (2018). Brett Kavanaugh confirmed to Supreme Court after fight that divided America. *Time Magazine*, October 7. http://time.com/5417538/bett-kavanaugh-confirmed-senate-supreme-court/.

Adams, T. F. (2012). Stealing the nest egg. *Labor Notes*, February 7. www.labornotes.org/blogs/2012/02/stealing-nest-egg.

Adorno, T. W., Frenkel-Brunswik, E., Levinson, D., & Sanford, N. (1950). *The authoritarian personality*. New York: Harper & Brothers.

Alice Paul Institute (2018). Ratification info, state by state. www.equalrightsamendment.org/era-ratification-map.

Allen, W. R. (1988). Improving black student access and achievement in higher education. *The Review of Higher Education*, *11*(4), 403-416.

Altemeyer, B. (1998). The other 'authoritarian personality'. In Zanna, M. P. (Ed.), *Advances in experimental social psychology* (Vol. 30, pp. 47-92). New York: Academic Press.

Altemeyer, B. (2003). Why do religious fundamentalists tend to be prejudiced? *International Journal for the Psychology of Religion*, *13*(1), 17-28.

Altemeyer, B., & Hunsberger, B. (1992). Authoritarianism, religious fundamentalism, quest, and prejudice. *The International Journal for the Psychology of Religion*, *2*, 113-133.

Ansbacher, H. L. (1992). Alfred Adler's concepts of community feeling and of social interest and the relevance of community feeling for old age. *Individual Psychology: The Journal of Adlerian Theory, Research & Practice*, *48*(4), 402-412.

Antle, W. J. (2019). Donald Trump's nationalist moment: Voters are primed for country, border, and sovereignty – and this president is listening. *The American Conservative*, January 3. www.theamericanconservative.com/articles/donald-trumps-nationalist-moment/.

Associated Press (1992). Robertson letter attacks feminists. *New York Times*, August 26. www.nytimes.com/1992/08/26/us/robertson-letter-attacks-feminists.html.

Associated Press (2018). Deported parents may lose kids to adoption, investigation finds. NBC News, October 9. www.nbcnews.com/news/latino/deported-parents-may-lose-kids-adoption-investigation-finds-n918261. Retrieved January 15, 2019.

Barak, A. (2005). Sexual harassment on the internet. *Social Science Computer Review*, *23*(1), 77-92.

Barkan, S. E. (2006). Religiosity and premarital sex in adulthood. *Journal for the Scientific Study of Religion*, *45*(3), 407-417.

Bartow, A. (2009). Internet defamation as profit centre: the monetization of online harassment. *Harvard Journal of Law and Gender*, *32*(2), 383-429.

Bashir, N. Y., Lockwood, P., Chasteen, A. L., Nadolny, D., & Noyes, I. (2013). The ironic impact of activists: Negative stereotypes reduce social change influence. *European Journal of Social Psychology*, *43*, 614-626. https://doi.org/10.1002/ejsp.1983.

Batchelor, T. (2017). Russian police round up LGBT activists demonstrating against persecution of gay men in Chechnya. *The Independent*, May 1. Retrieved January 15, 2019.

Beran, D. (2018). Who are the incels of 4chan and why are they so angry? *Pacific Standard Magazine*, May 3. https://psmag.com/news/who-are-the-incels-of-4chan-and-why-are-they-so-angry. Retrieved January 13, 2019.

Berg, M. (2016). These 4 types of TRAP laws are dangerously chipping away at abortion access under the guise of 'women's health'. *Planned Parenthood*, June 15. www.plannedparenthoodaction.org/blog/these-4-types-of-trap-laws-are-dangerously-chipping-away-abortion-access-under-the-guise-of-womens-health.

Beyer, B. K. (1995). *Critical Thinking*. Bloomington, IN: Phi Delta Kappa Educational Foundation. http://dx.doi.org/10.1037/1524-9220.5.2.121.

Bick, C. (2017). Invisible women: Domestic workers underpaid and abused. Al Jazeera, October 21. www.aljazeera.com/news/2017/10/invisible-women-domestic-workers-underpaid-abused-171019104144316.html. Retrieved January 14, 2019.

Blais, M., & Dupuis-Déri, F. (2012). Masculinism and the antifeminist countermovement. *Journal of Social, Cultural and Political Protest*, *11*(1): 21-39. doi:10.1080/14742837.2012.640532.

Block, J., Strangio, C., & Esseks, J. (2018). Breaking down Trump's trans military ban. American Civil Liberties Union, March 30. www.aclu.org/blog/lgbt-rights/transgender-rights/breaking-down-trumps-trans-military-ban.

Bloom, E. (2015). The decline of domestic help. *The Atlantic*, September 23. www.theatlantic.com/business/archive/2015/09/decline-domestic-help-maid/406798/. Retrieved January 14, 2019.

Blumell, L. E., Huemmer, J., & Sternadori, M. (2018). Protecting the ladies: Benevolent sexism, heteronormativity, and partisanship in online discussions of gender-neutral bathrooms. *Mass Communication & Society*, 22(3), 365–388. doi.org/10.1080/15205436.2018.1547833.

Bornstein, K. (1994). *Gender outlaws: On men, women, and the rest of us* . London: Routledge.

Boucher, B. (2018). Trump's 2019 budget aims to zero out funding for the NEA and NEH – again: The agencies avoided the reaper's scythe last year. Will they survive again? Artnet News, February 12. https://news.artnet.com/art-world/trump-2019-budget-nea-neh-1222685.

Boxer, C. F., & Ford, T. E. (2010). Sexist humor in the workplace: A case of subtle harassment. In Greenberg, J. (Ed.), *Insidious workplace behavior* (pp. 175–206). Boca Raton, FL: Routledge.

Brewer, R. M., & Heitzeg, N. A. (2008). The racialization of crime and punishment: Criminal justice, color-blind racism, and the political economy of the prison industrial complex. *American Behavioral Scientist*, 51(5), 625–644. https://doi.org/10.1177/0002764207307745.

Brine, J. (1999). *Undereducating women: Globalizing inequality.* Maidenhead, UK: Open University Press.

British Broadcasting Corporation (2017). Trump's order on abortion policy: What does it mean? BBC News, January 24. www.bbc.com/news/world-us-canada-38729364. Retrieved January 10, 2019.

Brody, D., & Browder, J. (2018). Why the Trump White House hosted a huge dinner for evangelicals Monday. Christian Broadcasting Network, August 27. www1.cbn.com/cbnnews/politics/2018/august/why-the-trump-white-house-is-hosting-a-huge-dinner-for-evangelicals-tonight.

Bronski, M. (2011). *A queer history of the United States,* Boston: Beacon Press.

Brosnan, G. (2014). #BBCtrending: Meet the 'Women Against Feminism'. BBC News, July 24. Retrieved October 24, 2018.

Brown, A. (2017). Republicans, Democrats have starkly different views on transgender issues. Pew Research Center. www.pewresearch.org/fact-tank/2017/11/08/transgender-issues-divide-republicans-and-democrats/.

Brunson, R. K., & Miller, J. (2006). Gender, race, and urban policing: The experience of African American youths. *Gender & Societym* 20(4), 531–552. https://doi.org/10.1177/0891243206287727.

Bureau of Justice Statistics (2013). Prisoners in 2013. www.bjs.gov/index.cfm?ty=pbdetail&iid=5109. Retrieved January 14, 2019.

Burke, G., & Mendoza, M. (2018). Babies, young children separated from parents at border sent to 'tender age' shelters in Texas. *The Globe and Mail*, June 19. www.theglobeandmail.com/world/us-politics/article-babies-young-children-separated-from-parents-at-border-sent-to/. Retrieved January 15, 2019.

Cai, W., & Clement, S. (2016). What Americans think about feminism today. *The Washington Post*, January 27. www.washingtonpost.com/graphics/national/feminism-project/poll/.

Cain, Patrick (2018). What we learned from Alek Minassian's incel-linked Facebook page – and what we'd like to know. Global News, April 24. https://globalnews.ca/news/4164340/alek-minassian-facebook-page/. Retrieved January 13, 2019.

Carrillo, T. (2017). Latinas in domestic service. Oxford Bibliographies. www.oxfordbibliographies.com/view/document/obo-9780199913701/obo-9780199913701-0127.xml. Retrieved January 14, 2019.

Center for Reproductive Rights (2017). Interactive map of the world's abortion laws. World Abortion Laws 2017. Retrieved from http://worldabortionlaws.com/map/.

Chalabi, M. (2018). How many migrant children are detained in US custody? *The Guardian*, December 22. www.theguardian.com/news/datablog/2018/dec/22/migrant-children-us-custody. Retrieved January 15, 2019.

Chen, M. (2018). More immigrants died in detention in fiscal year 2017 than in any year since 2009: According to a new report, subpar medical care is contributing to deaths in ICE detention. *The Nation*, June 20. www.thenation.com/article/immigrants-died-detention-fiscal-year-2017-year-since-2009/. Retrieved January 15, 2019.

Cillizza, C. (2014). How Citizens United changed politics, in 7 charts. *Washington Post*, January 22. www.washingtonpost.com/news/the-fix/wp/2014/01/21/how-citizens-united-changed-politics-in-6-charts/?utm_term=.42592594d6be.

Cillizza, C. (2018). Donald Trump didn't tell the truth 83 times in 1 day. CNN Politics, November 2. www.cnn.com/2018/11/02/politics/donald-trump-lies/index.html.

Clatterbaugh, K. (2004). Antifeminism. In Kimmel, M., & Aronson, A. (Eds.), *Men and masculinities: A social, cultural, and historical encyclopedia* (pp. 35-37). Santa Barbara, CA: ABC-CLIO.

Clatterbaugh, K. (2007). Anti-feminism. In Flood, M., Kegan Gardiner, J., Pease, B., & Pringle, K. (Eds.), *International encyclopedia of men and masculinities* (pp. 21-22). London and New York: Routledge.

Conrad, B. K. (2006). Neo-institutionalism, social movements, and the cultural reproduction of a mentalité: Promise keepers reconstruct the madonna/whore complex. *The Sociological Quarterly, 47*(2), 305-331. https://doi.org/10.1111/j.1533-8525.2006.00047.x.

Cook, L. (2014). Who are America's poor? U.S. News & World Report, September 18. www.usnews.com/news/blogs/data-mine/2014/09/18/census-bureau-data-sheds-light-on-americas-poor.

Crano, W. D. (1994). Context, comparison, and change: Methodological and theoretical contributions to a theory of minority (and majority) influence. In Moscovici, S., Mucchi-Faina, A., & Maass, A. (Eds.), *Minority influence* (pp. 17-46). Chicago: Nelson-Hall.

Crano, W. D., & Chen, X. (1998). The leniency contract and persistence of majority and minority influence. *Journal of Personality and Social Psychology, 74*(6), 1437-1450.

Crowson, H. M., & Brandes, J. A. (2017). Differentiating between Donald Trump and Hillary Clinton, voters using facets of right-wing authoritarianism and social-dominance orientation: A brief report. *Psychological Reports, 120*(3), 364-373.

Cuddy, A. J.C., Fiske, S. T., & Glick, P. (2004). When professionals become mothers, warmth doesn't cut the ice. *Journal of Social Issues, 60*(4), 701-718. ttps://doi.org/10.1111/j.0022-4537.2004.00381.x.

Dambrun, M., Kamiejski, R., Haddadi, N., & Duarte, S. (2009). Why does social dominance orientation decrease with university exposure to the social sciences? The impact of institutional socialization and the mediating role of 'geneticism'. *European Journal of Social Psychology, 39*(1), 88-100. https://doi.org/10.1002/ejsp.498.

Deutsch, M., & Gerard, H. B. (1955). A study of normative and informational social influences upon individual judgment. *The Journal of Abnormal and Social Psychology, 51*(3), 629-636.

Diebelius, G. (2017). Pictures from inside Pulse nightclub reveal devastation of worst mass shooting in US history. Metro UK. https://metro.co.uk/2017/01/18/pictures-from-inside-pulse-nightclub-reveal-devastation-of-worst-mass-shooting-in-us-history-6387858/.

Diep, F. (2018). Why did the National Science Foundation propose slashing its own social science budget? Social science advocates and Democratic lawmakers suggest the White House was behind the NSF's proposed budget cuts. *Pacific Standard Magazine*, March 19. https://psmag.com/news/national-science-foundation-social-science-budget.

Domonoske, C., & Gonzales, R. (2018). What we know: Family separation and 'zero tolerance' at the border. National Public Radio, June 19.

Dorius, S. F., & Firebaugh, G. (2010). Trends in global gender inequality. *Social Forces, 88*(5), 1941-1968.

Downing, N. E., & Roush, K. L. (1985). From passive acceptance to active commitment. *The Counseling Psychologist, 13*, 695-709.

Driver, A. (2018). 13,000 migrant children in detention: America's horrifying reality. CNN, October 1. www.cnn.com/2018/10/01/opinions/13000-migrant-children-horrifying-reality-driver/index.html. Retrieved January 15, 2019.

Duckitt, J. (2005). Personality and prejudice. In Dovidio, J. F., Glick, P., & Rudman, L. A. (Eds.), *On the nature of prejudice: Fifty years after Allport* (pp. 395-412). Malden, MA: Blackwell.

Duckitt, J., Wagner, C., Du Plessis, I., & Birum, I. (2002). The psychological bases of ideology and prejudice: Testing a dual process model. *Journal of Personality and Social Psychology, 83*, 75-93.

Duriez, B., & Van Hiel, A. (2002). The march of modern fascism. A comparison of social dominance orientation and authoritarianism. *Personality and Individual Differences, 32*(7), 1199-1213. http://dx.doi.org.mimas.cal-statela.edu/10.1016/S0191-8869(01)00086-1.

Eisele, H., & Stake, J. (2008). The differential relationship of feminist attitudes and feminist identity to self-efficacy. *Psychology of Women Quarterly, 32*, 233-244.

Ekehammar, B., Nilsson, I., & Sidanius, J. (1987). Education and ideology: Basic aspects of education related to adolescents' sociopolitical attitudes. *Political Psychology, 8*(3), 395-410. http://dx.doi.org.mimas.cal-statela.edu/10.2307/3791042.

Eleftheriou-Smith, L. (2017). More than 100 gay men 'sent to prison camps' in Chechnya. *The Independent*, April 11. www.independent.co.uk/news/world/europe/chechnya-gay-men-concentration-camps-torture-detain-nazi-ramzan-kadyrov-chechen-russia-region-a7677901.html.

Ellison, C. G., Bartkowski, J. P., & Segal, M. L. (1996). Conservative Protestantism and the parental use of corporal punishment. *Social Forces, 74*, 1003-1028.

Ender, M. G., Rohall, D. E., & Matthews, M. D. (2015). Cadet and civilian undergraduate attitudes toward transgender people: A research note. *Armed Forces and Society, 42*(2), 427-435. https://doi.org/10.1177/0095327X15575278.

Erikson, E. (1950). *Childhood and society* . New York: Norton & Company.

Evans, P. (2019). Behind Trump's rhetoric of economic nationalism. *Global Dialogue: Magazine of the International Sociological Association*, 7(4). http://globaldialogue.isa-sociology.org/behind-trumps-rhetoric-of-economic-nationalism/.

Fabian, J. (2018). Trump: Migrant caravan 'is an invasion'. The Hill, October 29. https://thehill.com/homenews/administration/413624-trump-calls-migrant-caravan-an-invasion.

Fabian, J., & Jagoda, N. (2017). Trump eases ban on political activity by churches. The Hill, May 4. https://thehill.com/homenews/administration/331902-trump-eases-ban-on-political-activity-by-churches.

Federal Bureau of Investigation, Criminal Justice Information Services Division (2017). 2017 hate crime statistics. https://ucr.fbi.gov/hate-crime/2017.

Finke, R., & Adamczyk, A. (2008). Cross-national moral beliefs: The influence of national religious context. *The Sociological Quarterly, 49*(4), 617–652.

Flores, A. (2015). Attitudes toward transgender rights: Perceived knowledge and secondary interpersonal contact. *Politics, Groups, and Identities, 3*, 398–416. https://doi.org/10.1080/21565503.2015. 1050414.

Flores, A., Herman, J. L., Gates, G. J., & Brown, T. N. T. (2016). How many adults identify as transgender in the United States? https://williamsinstitute.law.ucla.edu/wp-content/uploads/How-Many-Adults-Identify-as-Transgender-in-the-United-States.

Flynn, C. P. (1994). Regional differences in attitudes toward corporal punishment. *Journal of Marriage and the Family, 56*, 314–324.

Focus on the Family Issue Analysts (2009). Adoption: Cause for concern. www.focusonthefamily.com/socialissues/family/adoption/adoption-cause-for-concern.

Ford, L. E. (2009). *Encyclopedia of women and American politics* . New York: Infobase Publishing.

Ford, T. E., Boxer, C. F., Armstrong, J., & Edel, J. R. (2008). More than 'just a joke': The prejudice-releasing function of sexist humor. *Personality and Social Psychology Bulletin, 34*, 159–170. http://dx.doi.org/10.1177/0146167207310022.

Ford, T. E., Wentzel, E. R., & Lorion, J. (2001). Effects of exposure to sexist humor on perceptions of normative tolerance of sexism. *European Journal of Social Psychology, 31*, 677–691. http://dx.doi.org/10.1002/ejsp.56.

Fox, J., Cruz, C., & Lee, J. Y. (2015). Perpetuating online sexism offline: Anonymity, interactivity, and the effects of sexist hashtags on social media. *Computers in Human Behavior, 52*, 436–442.

Fox, J., & Tang, W. Y. (2015). Women's experiences with harassment in online video games: Rumination, organizational responsiveness, withdrawal, and coping strategies. Paper presented at the 65th annual conference of the International Communication Association, June, San Juan, Puerto Rico.

Franks, Mary Anne (2012). Sexual harassment 2.0. *Maryland Law Review, 71*(3), 655–704.

Friedson, M. (2016). Authoritarian parenting attitudes and social origin: The multigenerational relationship of socioeconomic position to childrearing values. *Child Abuse & Neglect, 51*, 263–275.

Gadarian, S. K., & Van der Vort, E. (2017). The gag reflex: Disgust rhetoric and gay rights in American politics. *Political Behavior, 23*, 1–23. https://doi.org/10.1007/s11109-017-9412-x.

Garcia-Navarro, L. (2018). What's an 'incel'? The online community behind the Toronto van attack. National Public Radio, Weekend Edition, April 29. www.npr.org/2018/04/29/606773813/whats-an-incel-the-online-community-behind-the-toronto-van-attack. Retrieved May 5, 2019.

Garfield, L. (2017). Trump's $25 billion wall would be nearly impossible to build, according to architects. *Business Insider*, January 14. www.businessinsider.com/trump-wall-impossible-build-architects-2017-1. Retrieved January 15, 2019.

Gates, G. J. (2011). How many people are lesbian, gay, bisexual and transgender? The Williams Institute. https://williamsinstitute.law.ucla.edu/research/census-lgbt-demographics-studies/how-many-people-are-lesbian-gay-bisexual-and-transgender/. Retrieved January 13, 2019.

Gilbert, D. T., & Mallone, P. S. (1995). The correspondence bias. *Psychological Bulletin, 117*, 21–38.

Gillig, T. K., & Murphy, S. T. (2016). Fostering support for LGBTQ youth? The effects of a gay adolescent media portrayal on young viewers. *International Journal of Communication, 10*, 3828–3850. http://ijoc.org/index.php/ijoc/article/view/5496.

Glick, P., & Fiske, S. T. (1996). The ambivalent sexism inventory: Differentiating hostile and benevolent sexism. *Journal of Personality and Social Psychology, 70*, 491–512. doi:10.1037/0022-3514. 70.3.491.

Grinberg, E. (2018). Transgender immigrant who died in ICE custody was beaten and deprived of medical attention, family says. CNN, November 27. www.cnn.com/2018/11/27/us/transgender-asylum-seeker-wrongful-death-claim/index.html. Retrieved January 15, 2019.

Grogan-Kaylor, A., & Oti, M. D. (2007). The predictors of parental use of corporal punishment. *Family Relations, 56*(1), 80–91.

Guardian (2017). America's homeless population rises for the first time since the Great Recession. *The Guardian*, December 6. www.theguardian.com/us-news/2017/dec/05/america-homeless-population-2017-official-count-crisis.

Gundersen, A. B., & Kunst, J. R. (2019). Feminist ≠ feminine? Feminist women are visually masculinized whereas feminist men are feminized. *Sex Roles, 80*(5/6), 291–309. http://dx.doi.org.mimas.calstatela.edu/10.1007/s11199-018-0931-7.

452 *Current Issues and Social Problems*

Guttmacher Institute (2019). An overview of abortion laws. www.guttmacher.org/state-policy/explore/overview-abortion-laws?gclid=CjOKCQiAg_HhBRDNARIsAGHLV51OAJyh_G9bQms96RrXw3H6mnMzPKWQaH9diato UlPUKtFFGbe18ZMaAtfvEALw_wcB.

Guy, J. (2019). Kevin Fret: Rapper shot to death in Puerto Rico at 24. CNN, January 11. www.cnn.com/2019/01/11/americas/kevin-fret-gay-rapper-dead-scli-intl/index.html. Retrieved January 15, 2019.

Halperin, D. M. (2005). Homosexuality. In Hornblower, S., & Spawforth, A. (Eds.), *The Oxford classical dictionary* (3rd rev. ed.). Oxford: Oxford University Press.

Hanks, D. (2016). Orlando shooter's father points to men kissing in Miami to explain son's anger. *Miami Herald*, June 12.

Harrison, B. F., & Michelson, M. R. (2019). Gender, masculinity threat, and support for transgender rights: An experimental study. *Sex Roles, 80*, 63–75. https://doi.org/10.1007/s11199-018-0916-6.

Haslam, N. (2006). Dehumanization: An integrative review. *Personality and Social Psychology Review, 10*(3), 252–264. https://doi.org/10.1207/s15327957pspr1003_4.

Heaven, P. C. L., Ciarrochi, J., & Leeson, P. (2011). Cognitive ability, right-wing authoritarianism, and social dominance orientation: A five-year longitudinal study amongst adolescents. *Intelligence, 39*(1), 15–21. https://doi.org/10.1016/j.intell.2010.12.001.

Hembree, D. (2018). CEO pay skyrockets to 361 times that of the average worker. *Forbes Magazine*, May 22. www.forbes.com/sites/dianahembree/2018/05/22/ceo-pay-skyrockets-to-361-times-that-of-the-average-worker/#79906f17776d.

Hennessy-Fiske, M., Jarvie, J., & Wilber, D. Q. (2016). Orlando gunman had used gay dating app and visited LGBT nightclub on other occasions, witnesses say. *Los Angeles Times*, June 13.

Higgins, T. (2018). Trump nominates Brett Kavanaugh to the Supreme Court. CNBC, July 9. www.cnbc.com/2018/07/05/trump-picks-brett-kavanaugh-for-supreme-court.html.

Hubbard, R. (2018). More states say religious agencies can turn down same-sex couples for adoptions. National Public Radio, June 11. www.npr.org/2018/06/11/614425204/more-states-say-religious-agencies-can-turn-down-same-sex-couples-for-adoptions.

Huber, L. P., Johnson, R. N., & Kohli, R. (2006). Naming racism: A conceptual look at internalized racism in U.S. schools permalink. *Journal Chicana/o Latina/o Law Review, 26*(1), 183–206. https://escholarship.org/uc/item/2828k8g3.

Hudson, L. (2018). The internet is enabling a community of men who want to kill women. They need to be stopped. *The Verge*, April 25. www.theverge.com/2018/4/25/17279294/toronto-massacre-minassian-incels-internet-misogyny. Retrieved January 13, 2019.

Hunsberger, B. (1995). Religious fundamentalism, right-wing authoritarianism, and hostility toward homosexuals in non-Christian religious groups. *The International Journal for the Psychology of Religion, 6*(1), 39–49. doi.org/10.1207/s15327582ijpr0601_5.

Hurley, L. (2017). Brett Kavanaugh confirmed to Supreme Court after fight that divided America: Trump's Supreme Court appointee Gorsuch plots rightward course. Reuters, December 19. www.reuters.com/article/us-usa-court-gorsuch/trumps-supreme-court-appointee-gorsuch-plots-rightward-course-idUSKBN1EE0IJ.

International Labor Organization (2014). Forced labor, modern slavery and human trafficking. ILO. www.ilo.org/global/topics/forced-labour/lang--en/index.htm. Retrieved January 15, 2019.

Jackman, M. R. (1994). *The velvet glove: Paternalism and conflict in gender, class, and race relations*. Berkeley and Los Angeles: University of California Press.

Jacobs, S. (1997). *Two-spirit people: Native American gender identity, sexuality and spirituality*. Champaign: University of Illinois.

Jamieson, D. (2017). Republicans want to pass a national right-to-work law. Huffington Post, February 1. www.huffingtonpost.com/entry/republicans-pursue-national-right-to-work-law-while-they-hold-the-reins-in-washington_us_5891fb30e4b0522c7d3e354d.

Janik, R. (2018). 'I laugh at the death of normies': How incels are celebrating the Toronto mass killing. Hatewatch, Southern Poverty Law Center. www.splcenter.org/hatewatch/2018/04/24/i-laugh-death-normies-how-incels-are-celebrating-toronto-mass-killing. Retrieved April 25, 2018.

Jansen, B., & Gomez, A. (2018). President Trump calls caravan immigrants 'stone cold criminals.' Here's what we know. *USA Today*, November 26. www.usatoday.com/story/news/2018/11/26/president-trump-migrant-caravan-criminals/2112846002/. Retrieved January 15, 2019.

Jayachandran, S. (2015). The roots of gender inequality in developing countries. *Annual Review of Economics, 7*, 63–88.

Johnson, D. (2019). Transgender bathroom debate. Minnesota Psychological Association. www.mnpsych.org/index.php?option=com_dailyplanetblog&view=entry&category=industry%20news&id=207:transgender-bathroom-debate. Retrieved January 15, 2019.

Johnson, J., & Hauslohner, A. (2017). 'I think Islam hates us': A timeline of Trump's comments about Islam and Muslims. *The Washington Post*, May 20. www.washingtonpost.com/news/post-politics/wp/2017/05/20/i-think-islam-hates-us-a-timeline-of-trumps-comments-about-islam-and-muslims/?utm_term=.b3c257ffc236.

Jonathan, E. (2008). The influence of religious fundamentalism, right-wing authoritarianism, and Christian orthodoxy on explicit and implicit measures of attitudes toward homosexuals. *The International Journal for the Psychology of Religion, 18*(4), 316-329. https://doi.org/10.1080/10508610802229262.

Jones, R. (2010). CEOs lay off thousands, rake in millions. CNBC. www.nbcnews.com/id/38935053/ns/business-us_business/t/ceos-lay-thousands-rake-millions/.

Joyce, K. (2018). The threat of international adoption for migrant children separated from their families. *The Intercept*, July 1. https://theintercept.com/2018/07/01/separated-children-adoption-immigration/. Retrieved January 15, 2019.

Kamen, P. (1991). *Feminist fatale* . New York: Donald I. Fine.

Katz, H. R. (1999). Teaching in tensions: Latino immigrant youth, their teachers, and the structures of schooling. *Teachers College Record, 100*(4), 809-840.

Kershaw, I. (2000). *Hitler, 1889-1936: Hubris*. New York and London: W.W. Norton & Company.

Kim, E. K. (2014). Is feminism still relevant? Some women saying they don't need it. Today, July 30. NBC. Retrieved October 24, 2018.

Kini, A. N. (2017). How Reddit is teaching young men to hate women. Vice, November 15. www.vice.com/en_us/article/gyj3yw/how-reddit-is-teaching-young-men-to-hate-women. Retrieved January 13, 2019.

Klein, E. (2018). Republicans used to have a health care plan. Now all they have are lies. Why Republicans can't tell the truth about their health care plans. Vox, October 31. www.vox.com/policy-and-politics/2018/10/31/18044692/republicans-health-care-preexisting-conditions-lies-trump.

Know Violence in Childhood (2017). Ending violence in childhood: Global report. http://globalreport.knowviolenceinchildhood.org/. Retrieved January 15, 2019.

Korte, G., & Gomez, A. (2018). Trump ramps up rhetoric on undocumented immigrants: 'These aren't people. These are animals.' *USA Today*, May 6. www.usatoday.com/story/news/politics/2018/05/16/trump-immigrants-animals-mexico-democrats-sanctuary-cities/617252002/. Retrieved January 15, 2019.

Kramer, A. E. (2017). Russians protesting abuse of gay men in Chechnya are detained. *The New York Times*, May 1. Retrieved January 15, 2019.

LaFrance, M., & Woodzicka, J. A. (1998). No laughing matter: Women's verbal and nonverbal reactions to sexist humor. In Swim, J., & Stagnor, C. (Eds.), *Prejudice: The target's perspective* (pp. 61-80). San Diego: Academic Press.

Lareau, A. (2011). *Unequal childhoods: Class, race and family life* . Berkeley: University of California Press.

Leverenz, D. (1986). Manhood, humiliation, and public life: Some stories. *Southwest Review, 71*(4), 442-462.

Levey, N. N. (2018). Trump administration moves to put new restrictions on abortion services. *The Los Angeles Times*, May 18. www.latimes.com/politics/la-na-pol-trump-abortion-rule-20180518-story.html. Retrieved January 10, 2019.

Ling, J., Mahoney, J., McGuire, P., & Freeze, C. (2018). The 'incel' community and the dark side of the internet. *The Globe and Mail*, April 24. www.theglobeandmail.com/canada/article-the-incel-community-and-the-dark-side-of-the-internet/. Retrieved January 13, 2019.

Longman, M. (2017). The 12 early warning signs of fascism. *Washington Monthly*, January 31. https://washingtonmonthly.com/2017/01/31/the-12-early-warning-signs-of-fascism/.

Mallon, M. (2017). A husband can block his wife's abortion under a new Arkansas law. *Glamour Magazine*, February 3. www.glamour.com/story/a-husband-can-block-his-wifes-abortion-under-a-new-arkansas-law.

Martínez, C., & Paterna-Bleda, C. (2013). Masculinity ideology and gender equality: Considering neosexism. *Anales De Psicología/Annals of Psychology, 29*(2), 558-564. https://doi.org/10.6018/analesps.29.2.141311.

Marwick, A. (2013). Gender, sexuality, and social media. In Senft, T., & Hunsinger, J. (Eds.), *The social media handbook* (pp. 59-75). New York: Routledge. www.tiara.org/blog/wp-content/uploads/2014/03/Marwick_gender_sexuality_chapter_2013.

Matthews, D. (2015). Denmark, Finland, and Sweden are proof that poverty in the US doesn't have to be this high. Vox, November 11. www.vox.com/policy-and-politics/2015/11/11/9707528/finland-poverty-united-states. Retrieved January 14, 2019.

May, V. (2017). Domestic workers in U.S. history. *Oxford research encyclopedia of American history*. doi:10.1093/acrefore/9780199329175.013.431.

McAfee, T. (2016). What is the Alt-Right anyway? A user's guide. *People Magazine*, August 25.

McCabe, J. (2005). What's in a label? The relationship between feminist self-identification and 'feminist' attitudes among U.S. women and men. *Gender and Society, 19*, 480-505. doi:10.1177/0891243204273498.

McCrae, R. R. (1987). Creativity, divergent thinking, and openness to experience. *Journal of Personality and Social Psychology, 52*(6), 1258-1265. http://dx.doi.org.mimas.calstatela.edu/10.1037/0022-3514.52.6.1258.

McGinnies, E. (1973). Initial attitude, source credibility, and involvement as factors in persuasion. *Journal of Experimental Social Psychology, 9*(4), 285-296. https://doi.org/10.1016/0022-1031(73)90066-8.

McGraw, M. (2018). Trump administration announces new 'conscience and religious freedom' division at HHS. ABC News, January 18. https://abcnews.go.com/Politics/trump-administration-announce-conscience-religious-freedom-division-hhs/story?id=52434480.

Meadows, S. O., Engel, C. C., Collins, R. L., Beckman, R. L., Cefalu, M., Hawes-Dawson, J., …, Williams, K. M. (2018). *2015 Department of Defense Health Related Behaviors Survey* . Santa Monica, CA: Rand Corporation. www.rand.org/pubs/research_reports/RR1695.html. Retrieved January 15, 2019.

Megarry, J. (2014). Online incivility or sexual harassment? Conceptualising women's experiences in the digital age. *Women's Studies International Forum, 47*, 46-55.

Miller, D. A., Smith, E. R., & Mackie, D. M. (2004). Effects of intergroup contact and political predispositions on prejudice: Role of intergroup emotions. *Group Processes & Intergroup Relations, 7*, 221-237.

Miller, G. (2010). Contraception as development? New evidence from family planning in Colombia. *Economic Journal, 120*, 709-736.

Miller, L. L. (1994). Fighting for a just cause: Soldiers' views on gays in the military. In Scott, W. J., & Stanley, S. C. (Eds.), *Gays and lesbians in the military: Issues, concerns, and contrasts* (pp. 69-85). New York: Aldine de Gruyter.

Miller, P. R., Flores, A. R., Haider-Markel, D. P., Lewis, D. C., Tadlock, B. L., & Taylor, J. K. (2017). Transgender politics as body politics: Effects of disgust sensitivity and authoritarianism on transgender rights attitudes. *Politics, Groups, and Identities, 5*, 4-24. https:// doi.org/10.1080/21565503.2016.1260482.

Miller, S. (2018). 3 years after same-sex marriage ruling, protections for LGBT families undermined. *USA Today*, June 4. www.usatoday.com/story/news/nation/2018/06/04/same-sex-marriage-ruling-undermined-gay-parents/650112002/.

Mindock, C. (2017). Donald Trump threatens to shut down NBC and other TV news networks that criticise him. *The Independent*, October 11. www.independent.co.uk/news/world/americas/us-politics/trump-nbc-license-ban-tweet-cnn-shut-down-fake-news-threat-latest-a7994861.html.

Monroe, C. R. (2005). Why are 'bad boys' always Black? Causes of disproportionality in school discipline and recommendations for change. *The Clearing House: A Journal of Educational Strategies, Issues and Ideas, 79*(1), 45-50. doi:10.3200/TCHS.79.1.45-50.

Morahan-Martin, J. (2000). Women and the internet: Promise and perils. *CyberPsychology and Behavior, 3*, 683-691. http://dx.doi.org/10.1089/ 10949310050191683.

Morris, M. (2016). *Pushout: The criminalization of black girls in schools.* New York: The New Press.

Nadasen, P. (2017). Extreme poverty returns to America. *The Washington Post*, December 21. www.washingtonpost.com/news/made-by-history/wp/2017/12/21/extreme-poverty-returns-to-america/?utm_term=.25d47d670357.

Nagoshi, J. L., Adams, K. A., Terrell, H. K., Hill, E. D., Brzuzy, S., & Nagoshi, C. T. (2008). Gender differences in correlates of homophobia and transphobia. *Sex Roles, 59*, 521-531.

National Public Radio (2016). What you need to know about the Alt-Right movement. NPR, August 26. www.npr.org/2016/08/26/491452721/the-history-of-the-alt-right. Retrieved January 13, 2019.

National Public Radio (2017). Decline in democracy spreads across the globe as authoritarian leaders rise. NPR, August 3. www.npr.org/2017/08/03/541432445/decline-in-democracy-spreads-across-the-globe-as-authoritarian-leaders-rise?t=1543339813832.

Nicol, A. A. M., & Rounding, K. (2013). Alienation and empathy as mediators of the relation between social dominance orientation, right-wing authoritarianism and expressions of racism and sexism. *Personality and Individual Differences, 55*(3), 294-299.

Nicoll, W. G. (1996). School life-style, social interest, and educational reform. *Individual Psychology: Journal of Adlerian Theory, Research & Practice, 52*(2), 130-149.

Norton, A. T., & Herek, G. M. (2013). Heterosexuals' attitudes toward transgender people: Findings from a national probability sample of U.S. adults. *Sex Roles, 68*, 738-753. https://doi.org/10.1007/s11199-011-0110-6.

Oxfam International (2017). Just 8 men own same wealth as half the world. www.oxfam.org/en/pressroom/pressreleases/2017-01-16/just-8-men-own-same-wealth-half-world.

Patrick, K. (2017). National snapshot: Poverty among women & families. National Women's Law Center. https://nwlc.org/wp-content/uploads/2017/09/Poverty-Snapshot-Factsheet-2017.pdf. Retrieved January 14, 2019.

Pattillo, M., Western, B., & Weiman, D. (Eds.) (2004). *Imprisoning America: The social effects of mass incarceration.* New York: Russell Sage Foundation.

Pedersen, S., & Macafee, C. (2007). Gender differences in British blogging. *Journal of Computer-Mediated Communication, 12*, 1472-1492. http://dx.doi.org/10.1111/ j.1083-6101.2007.00382.x.

Penny, L. (2014). *Unspeakable things: Sex, lies, and revolution*. New York: Bloomsbury.

Peter, L. (2017). Chechen police 'kidnap and torture gay men' – LGBT activists. BBC News, April 11.

Petterson, A., & Sutton, R. M. (2018). Sexist ideology and endorsement of men's control over women's decisions in reproductive health. *Psychology of Women Quarterly, 42*(2), 235–247.

Pettit, B., & Western, B. (2004). Mass imprisonment and the life course: Race and class inequality in U.S. incarceration, *American Sociological Review, 69*(2), 151–169. https://doi.org/10.1177/000312240406900201.

Pew Research Center (2012). Religious groups' official positions on same-sex marriage. www.pewforum.org/2012/12/07/religious-groups-official-positions-on-same-sex-marriage/.

Pew Research Center (2014). Online harassment. www.pewinternet.org/2014/10/22/online-harassment/.

Pew Research Center (2017). Gay marriage around the world. www.pewforum.org/2017/08/08/gay-marriage-around-the-world-2013/.

Picchi, A. (2018). One winner under Trump: The private prison industry. CBS News, February 21. www.cbsnews.com/news/one-winner-under-trump-the-private-prison-industry/. Retrieved January 15, 2019.

Pilkington, E., & Elgot, J. (2016). Orlando gunman Omar Mateen 'was a regular at Pulse nightclub'. *The Guardian*, June 14.

Politi, D. (2019). Congratulations, Trump! This is now the longest government shutdown in U.S. history. Slate, January 12. https://slate.com/news-and-politics/2019/01/this-is-the-longest-government-shutdown-in-u-s-history.html.

Popovich, N., Albeck-Ripka, L., & Pierre-Louis, K. (2018). 78 environmental rules on the way out under Trump. *The New York Times*, December 28. www.nytimes.com/interactive/2017/10/05/climate/trump-environment-rules-reversed.html.

Pratto, F., Sidanius, J., & Levin, S. (2006). Social dominance theory and the dynamics of intergroup relations: Taking stock and looking forward. *European Review of Social Psychology, 17*, 271–320.

Pratto, F., & Walker, A. (2004). The bases of gendered power. In Eagly, A. H., Beall, A. E., & Sternberg, R. J. (Eds.), *The psychology of gender* . New York: Guilford Press, pp. 242–268.

Prins, N. (2016). The magnitude of Trump's cronyism is off the charts – even for Washington: The President-elect's incomplete cabinet is already the richest one ever. *The Nation Magazine*, December 9. www.thenation.com/article/the-magnitude-of-trumps-cronyism-is-off-the-charts-even-for-washington/.

Ragins, B. R., & Winkel, D. E. (2011). Gender, emotion and power in work relationships. *Human Resource Management Review, 21*(4), 377–393. https://doi.org/10.1016/j.hrmr.2011.05.001.

Ramirez, H., & Hondagneu-Sotelo, P. (2013). Mexican gardeners in the USA. In Kilkey, M., Perrons, D., & Plomien, A. (Eds.), *Gender, migration and domestic work* (pp. 122–148). London: Palgrave Macmillan.

Ramsey, L. R., Haines, M. E., Hurt, M. M., Nelson, J. A., Turner, D. L., Liss, M., & Erchull, M. J. (2007). Thinking of others: Feminist identification and the perception of others' beliefs. *Sex Roles, 56*, 611–616. doi:10.1007/s11199-007-9205-5.

Rich, A. (1986). Compulsory heterosexuality and lesbian existence. In Rich, A. (Ed.), *Blood, bread, and poetry: Selected prose 1979–1985* (pp. 23–75). New York: Norton.

Ridgeway, C. L., & Erickson, K. G. (2000). Creating and spreading status beliefs. *American Journal of Sociology, 106*, 579–615.

Riggio, H. R. (2007). Political party, strength of identification, and knowledge and evaluation of Bush v. Gore. *Journal of Applied Social Psychology, 38*(1), 234–279.

Rios, V. M. (2007). The hypercriminalization of Black and Latino male youth in the era of mass incarceration. In Marable, M., Steinberg, I., & Middlemass, K. (Eds.), *Racializing justice, disenfranchising lives* (pp. 409–421). New York: Palgrave Macmillan.

Ritter, B. A. (2009). The new face of sexual harassment. In Torres-Coronas, T., & Arias-Oliva, M. (Eds.), *Encyclopedia of human resources information systems: Challenges in e-HRM* (pp. 655–660). Hershey, PA: IGI Global.

Rizzo, S. (2019). The Trump administration's misleading spin on immigration, crime and terrorism. *The Washington Post*, January 7. www.washingtonpost.com/politics/2019/01/07/trump-administrations-misleading-spin-immigration-crime-terrorism/?utm_term=.2b0a361d4450.

Roberts, D. (2018). Why conservatives keep gaslighting the nation about climate change: Republican climate rhetoric shifts (again), but the goal remains the same. Vox, October 31. www.vox.com/energy-and-environment/2018/10/22/18007922/climate-change-republicans-denial-marco-rubio-trump.

Rodriguez, C. E. (2018). *Latin looks: Images of Latinas and Latinos in the U.S.* Abingdon, UK: Media Routledge.

Romano, A. (2018). How the Alt-Right's sexism lures men into white supremacy. Vox, April 26. www.vox.com/culture/2016/12/14/13576192/alt-right-sexism-recruitment. Retrieved January 13, 2019.

Romo, V. (2017). 'Ghost skins' and masculinity: Alt-Right terms, defined. National Public Radio, September 6.

Rosenthal, L., & Levy, S. R. (2010). Understanding women's risk for HIV infection using social dominance theory and the four bases of gendered power. *Psychology of Women Quarterly*, *34*, 21–35. doi:10.1111/j.1471-6402.2009.01538.x.

Rosenthal, L., Levy, S. R., & Earnshaw, V. A. (2012). Social dominance orientation relates to believing men should dominate sexually, sexual self-efficacy, and taking free female condoms among undergraduate women and men. *Sex Roles*, *67*(11/12), 659–669. doi 10.1007/s11199-012-0207-6.

Rosenthal, L., Levy, S. R., & Moyer, A. (2011). Protestant work ethic's relation to intergroup and policy attitudes: A meta-analytic review. *European Journal of Social Psychology*, *41*, 874–885.

Rowatt, W. C., & Franklin, L. M. (2004). Christian orthodoxy, religious fundamentalism, and right-wing authoritarianism as predictors of implicit racial prejudice. *The International Journal for the Psychology of Religion*, *14*(2), 125–138.

Rowatt, W. C., Shen, M. J., LaBouff, J. P., & Gonzalez, A. (2013). Religious fundamentalism, right-wing authoritarianism, and prejudice: Insights from meta analyses, implicit social cognition, and social neuroscience. In Paloutzian, R. F., & Park, C. L. (Eds.), *Handbook of the psychology of religion and spirituality* (2nd ed., pp. 457–475). New York: Guilford Press.

Rowatt, W. C., Tsang, J., Kelly, J., LaMartina, B., McCullers, M., & McKinley, A. (2006). Associations between religious personality dimensions and implicit homosexual prejudice. *Journal for the Scientific Study of Religion*, *45*, 397–406.

Rubinstein, G. (2003). Authoritarianism and its relation to creativity: A comparative study among students of design, behavioural sciences and law. *Personality and Individual Differences*, *34*(4), 695–705. http://dx.doi.org.mimas.calstatela.edu/10.1016/S0191-8869(02)00055-7.

Rudman, L. A. (1998). Self-promotion as a risk factor for women: The costs and benefits of counterstereotypical impression management. *Journal of Personality and Social Psychology*, *74*(3), 629–645. https://doi.org/10.1037/0022-3514.74.3.629.

Rudman, L. A., Fetterolf, J. C., & Sanchez, D. T. (2013). What motivates the sexual double standard? More support for male versus female control theory. *Personality and Social Psychology Bulletin*, *39*, 250–263. doi:10.1177/0146167212472375.

Rutter, M. (1971). Parent-child separation: Psychological effects on the children. *The Journal of Child Psychology and Psychiatry*, *12*(4), 233–260. https://doi.org/10.1111/j.1469-7610.1971.tb01086.x.

Samuels, B. (2018). Trump:'It may not look like it, but we are draining the swamp'. The Hill, April 12. https://thehill.com/homenews/administration/382883-trump-it-may-not-look-like-it-but-we-are-draining-the-swamp.

Sanborn, H., & Thyne, C. L. (2014). Learning democracy: Education and the fall of authoritarian regimes. *British Journal of Political Science*, *44*(4), 773–797. https://doi.org/10.1017/S0007123413000082.

Schaffner, B. F., Macwilliams, M., & Nteta, T. (2018). Understanding White polarization in the 2016 vote for president: The sobering role of racism and sexism. *Political Science Quarterly*, *133*(1), 9–34. https://doi.org/10.1002/polq.12737.

Schnell, L., & McCoy, K. (2018). DHS chief slams immigration system in wake of 2nd migrant child death, orders more medical exams of kids in custody. *USA Today*, December 26. www.usatoday.com/story/news/nation/2018/12/26/guatemalan-boy-death-medical-checks-immigrant-children-custody/2413058002/. Retrieved January 15, 2019.

Schuman, H., Bobo, L., & Krysan, M. (1992). Authoritarianism in the general population: The education interaction hypothesis. *Social Psychology Quarterly*, *55*(4), 379–387. doi:10.2307/2786954.

Scott, E. (2018). President Trump, 'angry mobs' and 'very fine people'. *The Washington Post*, October 8. www.washingtonpost.com/politics/2018/10/08/president-trump-angry-mobs-very-fine-people/?utm_term=.2245aee55f20.

Shapiro, T., Meschede, T., & Osoro, S. (2013). The roots of the widening racial wealth gap: Explaining the Black-White economic divide. Institute on Assets and Social Policy. http://health-equity.lib.umd.edu/4120/1/racialwealthgapbrief.

Shaw, A. (2014). The internet is full of jerks, because the world is full of jerks: What feminist theory teaches us about the internet. *Communication and Critical/Cultural Studies*, *11*, 273–277. http://dx.doi.org/10.1080/14791420.2014.926245.

Sibley, C. G., Wilson, M. S., & Duckitt, J. (2007). Effects of dangerous and competitive worldviews on right-wing authoritarianism and social dominance orientation over a five-month period. *Political Psychology*, *28*(3), 357–371. http://dx.doi.org.mimas.calstatela.edu/10.1111/j.1467-9221.2007.00572.x.

Sidanius, J., Levin, S., & Pratto, F. (1996). Consensual social dominance orientation and its correlates within the hierarchical structure of American society. *International Journal of Intercultural Relations*, *20*(3-4), 385–408.

Sidanius, J., Pratto, F., & Bobo, L. (1994). Social dominance orientation and the political psychology of gender: A case of invariance? *Journal of Personality and Social Psychology*, *67*(6), 998–1011. http://dx.doi.org.mimas.calstatela.edu/10.1037/0022-3514.67.6.998.

Siemaszko, C. (2018). While Sears executives get $25 million in bonuses, laid-off workers struggle during Christmastime. NBC News, December 18. www.nbcnews.com/news/us-news/while-sears-executives-get-25-million-bonuses-laid-workers-struggle-n949446.

Signorile, M. (2016). Donald Trump's hate-fueled, Alt-Right army hates 'faggots' too. Huffington Post, September 21. www.huffingtonpost.com/entry/donald-trumps-hate-fueled-alt-right-army-hates-faggots-too_us_57e11904e4b04a1497b67558. Retrieved January 13, 2019.

Silverberg, W. V. (1952). *Childhood experience and personal destiny: A psychoanalytic theory of neurosis.* New York: Springer.

Six, B., & Eckes, T. (1991). A closer look at the complex structure of gender stereotypes. *Sex Roles, 24*(1/2), 57-71. https://doi.org/10. 1007/bf00288703.

Smith, A. G., & Winter, D. G. (2002). Right-wing authoritarianism, party identification and attitudes toward feminism in student evaluations of the Clinton-Lewinsky story. *Political Psychology, 23*(2), 355-383. http://dx.doi.org.mimas.calstatela.edu/10.1111/0162-895X.00285.

Solomon, B. M. (1985). *In the company of educated women: A history of women and higher education in America.* New Haven, CT: Yale University Press.

Southern Poverty Law Center (no date). Hate map by ideology. SPLC. www.splcenter.org/hate-map/by-ideology. Retrieved January 13, 2019.

Southern Poverty Law Center (2017). Anti-LGBTQ. www.splcenter.org/fighting-hate/extremist-files/ideology/anti-lgbt. Retrieved January 13, 2019.

Southern Poverty Law Center (2018). Report: Rise in hate violence tied to 2016 Presidential election. www.splcenter.org/hatewatch/2018/03/01/report-rise-hate-violence-tied-2016-presidential-election. Retrieved January 15, 2019.

Stack, L. (2017). Alt-right, alt-left, antifa: a glossary of extremist language. *The New York Times*, August 15.

Stanton, G. (2014). 10 things everyone should know about a Christian view of homosexuality. Focus on the Family. www.focusonthefamily.com/about/focus-findings/sexuality/10-things-everyone-should-know-about-a-christian-view-of-homosexuality.

Stenner, K. (2009). Three kinds of 'Conservatism'. *Psychological Inquiry, 20*, 142-159.

Stotzer, R. L. (2009). Violence against transgender people: A review of United States data. *Aggression and Violent Behavior, 14*(3), 170-179. https://doi.org/10.1016/j.avb.2009.01.006.

Stumpf, J. (2006). The crimmigration crisis: Immigrants, crime, and sovereign power. *American University Law Review, 56*, 367-419.

Swim, J. K., Hyers, L. L., Cohen, L. L., & Ferguson, M. J. (2001). Everyday sexism: Evidence for its incidence, nature, and psychological impact from three daily diary studies. *Journal of Social Issues, 57*, 31-53. http://dx.doi.org/10.1111/0022-4537.00200.

Swirsky, J. M., & Angelone, D. J. (2014). Femi-Nazis and bra-burning crazies: A qualitative evaluation of contemporary beliefs about feminism. *Current Psychology, 33*(3), 229-245.

Tan, M. (2018). ICE is illegally imprisoning asylum seekers. American Civil Liberties Union. www.aclu.org/blog/immigrants-rights/ice-and-border-patrol-abuses/ice-illegally-imprisoning-asylum-seekers.

Tankersley, J. (2018). How the Trump tax cut is helping to push the federal deficit to $1 trillion. *The New York Times*, July 25. www.nytimes.com/2018/07/25/business/trump-corporate-tax-cut-deficit.html.

Thomas, S. S. (2018). 13 gender-related terms you need to know. *Cosmopolitan Magazine*, May 23. www.cosmopolitan.com/sex-love/a20888315/genders-identity-list-definitions/.

Thompson, J. (2018). Persecution and identity – Stories of LGBT asylum seekers. Torture Abolition and Survivors Support Coalition (TASSC) International. www.tassc.org/news-blog/2018/9/13/persecution-and-identitystories-of-lgbt-asylum-seekers. Retrieved January 13, 2019.

Todman, L. C., & Mansager, R. (2009). Social justice: Addressing social exclusion by means of social interest and social responsibility. *The Journal of Individual Psychology, 65*(4), 311-318.

Totenberg, N. (2018). Justice Ruth Bader Ginsburg undergoes surgery for lung cancer. National Public Radio, December 21. www.npr.org/2018/12/21/679065534/justice-ruth-bader-ginsburg-undergoes-surgery-for-lung-cancer.

United Nations (2013). World abortion policies. https://web.archive.org/web/20160415084202/http://www.un.org/en/development/desa/population/publications/pdf/policy/WorldAbortionPolicies2013/WorldAbortionPolicies2013_WallChart.pdf. Retrieved January 13, 2019.

United Nations Office on Drugs and Crime (2016). Global report on trafficking in persons 2016.

United Nations Refugee Agency (2019). LGBTI claims. www.unhcr.org/en-us/lgbti-claims.html. Retrieved January 13, 2019.

U.N. Women (2018). Facts and figures: Ending violence against women. www.unwomen.org/en/what-we-do/ending-violence-against-women/facts-and-figures. Retrieved January 15, 2019.

UNESCO (2004). Gender and education for all: The leap to equality. https://en.unesco.org/gem-report/report/2003/gender-and-education-all-leap-equality.

Uniform Crime Report (2011). Crime in the U.S 2011; Table 66. https://ucr.fbi.gov/crime-in-the-u.s/2011/crime-in-the-u.s.-2011/tables/table_66_arrests_suburban_areas_by_sex_2011.xls.

Urbi, J. (2018). This is how much it costs to detain an immigrant in the US. CNBC, June 20. www.cnbc.com/2018/06/20/cost-us-immigrant-detention-trump-zero-tolerance-tents-cages.html. Retrieved January 15, 2019.

Vandello, J. A., & Bosson, J. K. (2013). Hard won and easily lost: A review and synthesis of theory and research on precarious manhood. *Psychology of Men & Masculinity*, *14*(2), 101-113.

Vandermaas-Peeler, A., Cox, D., Fisch-Friedman, M., Griffin, R., & Jones, R. P. (2018). Emerging consensus on LGBT issues: Findings from the 2017 American Values Atlas. Public Religion Research Institute, May 1. www.prri.org/research/emerging-consensus-on-lgbt-issues-findings-from-the-2017-american-values-atlas/.

Walker, S. (2017a). Chechen police 'have rounded up more than 100 suspected gay men'. *The Guardian*, April 2.

Walker, S. (2017b). People are being beaten and forced to 'sit on bottles' in anti-gay 'camps' in Chechnya. *The Independent*, May 26.

Walsh, W. B., & Heppner, M. J. (Eds.) (2006). *Handbook of career counseling for women*. Mahwah, NJ: Erlbaum.

Waters, M. (2018). We finally have data about the number of LGBT people in the military. The Outline, August 2. https://theoutline.com/post/5680/us-military-lgbt-population-size?zd=1&zi=ji7rypzy. Retrieved January 15, 2019.

Weil, F. (1985). The variable effects of education on liberal attitudes: A comparative-historical analysis of anti-Semitism using public opinion survey data. *American Sociological Review*, *50*(4), 458-474. http://dx.doi.org.mimas.calstatela.edu/10.2307/2095433.

Welch, K. (2007). Black criminal stereotypes and racial profiling. *Journal of Contemporary Criminal Justice*, *23*(3), 276-288. https://doi.org/10.1177/1043986207306870.

Whitehead, A. L. (2018). Homosexuality, religion, and the family: The effects of religion on Americans' appraisals of the parenting abilities of same-sex couples. *Journal of Homosexuality*, *65*(1), 42-65.

WhiteHouse.Gov (2018). President Donald J. Trump is standing up for the sanctity of life. Law & Justice, January 19. www.whitehouse.gov/briefings-statements/president-donald-j-trump-standing-sanctity-life/.

Wolff, E. N. (2010). *Recent trends in household wealth in the United States: Rising debt and the middle-class squeeze – an update to 2007*. Annandale-on-Hudson, NY: Levy Economics Institute of Bard College.

World Health Organization (2002). World report on violence and health. www.who.int/violence_injury_prevention/violence/world_report/en/summary_en.

World Health Organization (with Department of Reproductive Health and Research, London School of Hygiene and Tropical Medicine, South African Medical Research Council) (2013). Global and regional estimates of violence against women: Prevalence and health effects of intimate partner violence and non-partner sexual violence. [For individual country information, see The World's Women 2015, Trends and Statistics, Chapter 6, Violence against Women. United Nations Department of Economic and Social Affairs, and UN Women Global Database on Violence against Women.]

Worthen, M. G. F. (2018). Transgender under fire: Hetero-cis-normativity and military students' attitudes toward trans issues and trans service members post DADT. *Sexuality Research and Social Policy*, *3*, 1-20. https://doi.org/10.1007/s13178-018-0340-2.

Wright, P. (2018). Trump dismisses his administration's climate report, says the Earth will cool. The Weather Channel, November 6. https://weather.com/science/environment/news/2018-11-06-trump-denies-administrations-climate-change-report.

Yakushko, O. (2007). Do feminist women feel better about their lives? Examining patterns of feminist identity development and women's subjective well-being. *Sex Roles*, *57*, 223-234.

Zucker, A., & Bay-Cheng, L. Y. (2010). Minding the gap between feminist identity and attitudes: The behavioral and ideological divide between feminists and non-labelers. *Journal of Personality*, *78*, 1895-1924. doi:10.1111/j.1467-6494.2010.00673.x.

INDEX

ability 88
abortion 59-60, 75, 167-8, 402, 430, 432-5
absent fathers 300
abstinence-only 224-5, 432
abuse *see* child abuse
accessibility 128, 142
accommodation 93, 95, 352
achievement ideology *see* Protestant work ethic
achondroplasia dwarfism 50, 54
acne 69, 75
adaptation 6, 18
adenosine triphosphate (ATP) 5, 18
adolescent sexuality *see* sexuality development
adoption 167
adoption studies 267-8
adult attachment 306-8
adult sexuality *see* sexuality in adulthood
agency 95-6, 104
aggression 22, 125, 141, 165, 267, 362, 370; biological
    basis 348-50; children 362; gender roles
    359-62; masculinity 350, 359, 361-2, 365-7;
    media violence 351-4; parenting 355-7; religion
    357-9; rewarding 344-5; socialization of 350-5;
    towards LGBTQ 361-2; violent pornography
    368-9; *see also* intimate partner violence; rape
agreeableness 212, 260, 272
AIDS/HIV 224, 225
Ainsworth, M. 304-5
albinism 52-4
allele 43-7, 49-50, 54
Allen's Rule 15-16, 18
allosomes *see* sex chromosomes
alt-right movement 432
ambivalent sexism 171-4, 182, 406-7
amniotic fluid 71, 75

amniotic sac 71, 75
anaphase 25-6, 34
Androgen Insensitivity Syndrome (AIS) 68-9, 75
androgyny 274
Angleman Syndrome 43, 54
animal behavior 134, 205
anorgasmia 220, 223
anti-feminist movements 432
Antisocial Personality Disorder 263, 279
anxiety 274
anxious-ambivalent attachment 305-8
Archer, D. 176-7
arousal *see* sexual arousal
ascending reticular activating system (ARAS) 262,
    267, 279
asexual reproduction 204-5
assertiveness 274, 345
assignment *see* gender assignment
assimilation 93-4, 104, 352
associative networks 88-9, 104
atheism 84
athletics 256
attachment theory 270; in adulthood 306-8; in
    infancy 303-6
attention 86-8
attitudes 157-8; changing 441-2
attraction 316-18
attributions 94, 104, 346
Australopithecus Afarensis 10-11
Australopithecus Africanus 10-11
authoritarianism 137, 142, 173-4, 426-30
autosomal genetic disorders 48-9; dominant 49-50,
    54; recessive 50-2, 54
autosomes 28, 30, 34, 44
avoidant attachment 305-8

460 Index

babyfacedness 101, 104
backlash effect 431
Bandura, A. 125, 352
Barty, B. 50, 52
BDSM 204, 229
Beckwith-Wiedemann Syndrome 43, 54
behavioral genetics 267-8
belief bias 85-6, 104
belief in a just world 346
benevolent sexism 101, 171-4, 277, 406-7
Bergmann's Rule 15-16, 18
Best, D. L. 95
Bianchi, K. 369
Big Five see Five Factor Model
biogeography 6, 18
biological differences 162-8
biological sex 63-4, 75, 87; gender theories 124-5;
    genes 64-5
biosocial theories 130-4, 261-3
bipedalism 9
blaming see victim blaming
blastocyst 71
bodily integrity 59, 75, 402
body humors 261
body image 175-6, 213, 218-19, 354
body shape and size 15-16
bonding 218, 229, 265-7, 303-4
Bosson, J. K. 277
brain development 66-7
Brebner, J. 275
bulbourethral glands 71, 75
Bundy, T. 369

Caldera, Y. M. 126
capitalism 438-9
casual sex see hooking-up
Cattell, R. B. 258
Cejka, M. A. 403
cell life cycle 25, 34
cells 23, 33-4; kinds of human body cells 22; meiosis
    25-7; meiosis and variability 27-9; mitosis
    25-6; nondisjunction 29-33; structure and
    function 23-5
cellular membrane 23, 34
centrioles 25, 37
centromere 25, 35
cervix 70, 75
child abuse 301-2, 306, 440
child marriage 165

child sexuality 206-7
childbirth 72-3, 99-100, 130, 254-5
childcare 402
children's athletics 256
China 170
Chodorow, N. 140
Christianity see religion
chromatin 23, 35
chromosomal abnormalities 48, 54
chromosomes 23, 28, 35, 43, 54
Cinamon, R. G. 401
circumcision 61, 75, 200-2
cis-normativity 435
cleavage furrow 26, 35
Clinton, H. 389-91
codominance 46, 55
cognition 87-8, 104
cognitive abilities, gender differences 275-6
cognitive development theory 127-8
Cohen, J. 114
collectivism see individualism-collectivism
color blindness 47, 55
coming out 297-8
commitment 318-19
common ancestry 5-6, 18
common couple violence 362-3
communality 95, 104, 172
communication 315
competence 101, 104
comprehensivity 121, 142
confirmation bias 85, 93-4, 104
conflict and resolution 127
Congenital Adrenal Hyperplasia (CAH) 60-1,
    68, 75
conscientiousness 260, 272
consciousness 88
contraception 133, 215, 223-6, 430, 434-5;
    reversible inhibition of sperm under guidance
    (RISUG) 61-2, 77
creationism 16-17, 18
Cri du Chat Syndrome 31, 35
critical thinking: genes and social power 39-40;
    implicit attitudes and unconscious bias 157-8;
    job requirements 391-2; maternal mortality
    254-5; single mothers and absent fathers
    299-301; stereotypes about atheists 84; top ten
    myths about evolution 2-4
cronyism 430
crossing over 27-8, 35

Index   461

culture 268, 270, 273-4; intimate partner violence 364-5; sexuality 212-13; *see also* individualism-collectivism
cystic fibrosis (CF) 50-1, 55
cytokinesis 26, 35
cytoplasm 25, 35

Darwin, C. 5-6
Davis, M. J. 213
Dawood, K. 220
de la Chapelle Syndrome 68, 75
deletion 48, 55
depression 276-8, 323
deregulation 430
desensitization 353
development 395
Dinnerstein, D. 140
discounting 94, 104
discrimination 89, 104, 123; LGBTQ 202-4; *see also* sexism
disorganized attachment 305-6
dispositional attributions 39-40, 55
dispositional (trait) approach 257-8
dissociation 306
distraction 86-7
division of labor 100, 102, 104, 138-9, 397
divorce 312-13, 323
DNA (deoxyribonucleic acid) 7, 18, 24, 40-2; *see also* genetics
dominant allele 44-6, 55
double standard 210, 226-7
Down Syndrome 32, 35
dual-earner families 398, 400

Eagly, A. 130, 132, 362, 403
education 221-2, 272, 298, 394-5, 425-6, 439-42; STEM fields 393-4
egalitarianism 132, 271, 311
Egypt 170
ejaculation 71
elaboration 88, 104
Electra Complex 120
embryo 71, 74
emotional display rules 405-6
emotional labor 315, 325; *see also* family work
emotional stability 260, 264, 272
emotionality 95, 104, 164-5, 263, 274-5, 405-6; *see also* personality
empathy 84, 104, 274

employment equity policies 408
endometrium 70, 75
endoplasmic reticulum (ER) 25, 35
environment *see* socialization
epididymides 71, 75
epigenetics 52-3, 55
epistasis 52, 55
equal protection 178
Equal Rights Amendment (ERA) 430-1
estrogens 65, 75, 124-5, 266-7
eukaryotic cells 23-4, 35
evolution 5, 17-18, 121; basic principles and supporting evidence 5-8; beginning of life on earth 4; controversy 16-17; hominids and *Homo* species 2, 10-15; human variation 15-16; humans 8-10; skulls 10; timeline 8; top ten myths 2-4
evolutionary psychology 123, 142
evolutionary theory 5, 18, 122
explicit sexism 390-1
extraversion 209, 260-3, 272, 317
eye color 16
Eysenck, H. J. 261-3

face structure 100-1
faceism 176-7
factor analysis 258-9, 280
falsifiability 121-2, 142
familiarity 317
family conflict theory 362-3
family influences *see* parenting
family relationships 311-13, 396-7
family roles 116-18, 397; work-family conflict 401-2
family work 397-400
fascism 428-30
female gender role stress (FGRS) 277, 281
female genital mutilation (FGM) 202, 227-8, 230
femininity 87, 95-7, 104, 164-5, 274-5, 344; *see also* gender roles; gender stereotypes; gender stereotypes
feminism 102, 105, 170-1, 174; anti-feminist movements 432; backlash against 430-1; feminist theory 139-40, 362-3
fertile (follicular) phase 71
fertilization 71, 75
Fetal Alcohol Syndrome (FAS) 73-4, 75
fetal brain development 66-7, 124
fetus 71-2
Finneran, C. 348
Five Factor Model (FFM) 259-61, 272-4

foreskin 200-2
fornication 133, 142, 206
fossil 7, 18
fragile state 254, 281
Franklin, R. 40-1
Freud, S. 119-20, 122, 252-4
Friedman, H. 100-1
friendships 315-16
functionality 89, 105

Galapagos finches 5-6
gametes 26, 35
gaslighting 83, 101, 105, 156
gender 63-4, 76, 87, 122, 124
gender assignment 60-1
gender behaviors 66, 76, 313-15
gender constancy 127-8, 143
gender differences: cognitive abilities 275-6; friendships 316; intimate partner violence 362-3; love schemas 319-21; mental health 276-8; parenting 308-11; personality and emotions 272-5; physical health 276; social interaction and communication 313-15
gender dysphoria 112-14, 143
gender gap 395-6
gender identity 66-7, 76, 87, 122, 124, 127-8
gender neutrality 311
gender parity 395, 410, 417
gender role strain 140-1, 143, 277, 365
gender roles 122, 270-1, 308-11; aggression 359-62; family work 397-400; gay men 346-7; intimate partner violence 365; sexuality 207
gender schema theory 128-9, 270-1
gender schematic 91, 105, 129
gender stereotypes 87, 89, 94-7, 103, 105, 135, 271, 274; family roles 116-18; prescriptive and proscriptive 97-9; purposes of 102-3; relationship behaviors 319; sources of 99-101; in the workplace 403-4
gender theories 120-3, 141; biological 124-5; biosocial 130-4; cognitive development theory 127-8; feminist approaches 139-40; gender role strain 140-1; gender schema theory 128-9; parental investment 131-4; precarious manhood 140-1; psychoanalysis 119-20, 122; social dominance theory 134-9; social learning/social cognitive theory 125-7; social role theory 129-31
gender-congruent behavior 123, 126, 143, 310-11
gender-incongruent behavior 122-3, 126, 143, 310-11

genes 23-4, 35, 43, 55; biological sex 64-5
genetic disorders 67-9; autosomal genetic disorders 48-52; sex-linked genetic disorders 47-8
genetics 7-8, 43-4, 53-4; and aggression 22; behavioral 267-8; epigenetics 52-3; Human Genome Project (HGP) 41-2; imprinting 42-3; one-trait crosses 44-6; sex-linked traits 46-7; simple and polygenic inheritance 46; social power 39-40; variability 27-9
Genghis Khan 131
genital tubercle 65, 76
genotype 44, 55, 87
glans penis 200-2
glass ceiling 407-8
Glick, P. 403
global equality 179-80
Golgi apparatus 25, 35
gonads 26, 35, 63, 66; and hormones 65
Greece 170
gynocentric approach 140, 143

Hall, J. A. 316
haploid 26, 35
Hazan, C. 307-8
health 276-8, 323; intimate partner violence 363-4
health care 251-2, 441
healthy sexuality 178, 203-4, 217-18
Hebl, M. R. 174
hegemonic patriarchy see patriarchy
hemizygotic 44, 55
hemophilia 48, 55
heritability 267-8
heteronormativity 161, 177-9, 183, 214, 348, 435
heterosexism 177-9, 436
heterozygous 44-5, 55
heuristic value 121, 143
HEXACO model 261, 263
hierarchy 134-5, 427
Holmes, M. R. 356
homeostasis 66, 76
hominids and Homo species 2, 10-15
Homo Erectus 12
Homo Floresiensis 14
Homo Habilus 12
Homo Heidelbergensis 12-13
Homo Neanderthalensis 12-14
Homo Sapiens 14-15
Homo Sapiens Denisovans 14
homologous chromosomes 24, 26, 35, 43, 55

homologous forms 7, 19
homozygous 44-5, 55
honesty-humility 261, 263
hooking-up 219
hormonal disorders 67-9
hormones 62-3, 76, 124-5; aggression 349; fetal
    brain development 66-7; and gonads 65;
    personality 263-7
Horney, K. 139-40
hostile attribution bias 356, 372
hostile sexism 171, 173-4, 183, 226, 277, 406-7,
    431, 435
housewife/mother 95, 105, 116-18, 172
human evolution see evolution
Human Genome Project (HGP) 41-2
human sexual reproduction see sexual reproduction
human sexuality see sexuality
human trafficking 440
Huntington's disease 49, 55
Huston, A. C. 126
hyperfemininity 359, 361
hypermasculinity 165, 176, 178-9, 213, 277, 345, 359,
    361-2, 367
hypogonadism 63, 67, 76
hypothalamus 66, 76
Hyse, J. S. 114

ideal self 96
immigrants 439-40
implicit attitudes 157-8, 389-90
Implicit Attitudes Test (IAT) 158, 184
implicit bias 94, 105
implicit knowledge structure 118, 143
imprinting 42-3
incels 432, 446
incomplete dominance 46, 55
individual differences 114, 257
individualism 39, 55, 252, 438-9
individualism-collectivism 96, 270, 273, 350
inequalities and injustices: coming out and identity
    formation 297-8; global 179-80; health care
    251-2; Hillary Clinton and sexism 389-91;
    ignoring and blaming women 154-6; intimate
    partner violence in the cave 1; physical strength
    115-16; reproductive health 59-60; rewarding
    male aggression 344-5; Rosalind Franklin 40-1;
    sex differences 114-15; son preference 21-2;
    vagina shame 198-200; words used only for
    women 82-3

infant attachment 303-6
infantilizing 101, 105
information-processing 88-9; schematic
    processing 90-4
informational social influence 441-2
instrumentality 95-6, 105
intelligence 275-6
internalization 102, 105
internalized homonegativity 347-8
interpersonal relationships: family relationships
    311-13; friendships 315-16; social interaction and
    communication 313-15; see also parenting
intersectionality 278, 282, 298
intersex 32, 36, 60-1, 63, 76
intimacy 318-19
intimate partner violence 1, 127, 362-5; child
    exposure to 356-7; cultural factors 364-5;
    gender differences 362-3; gender roles 365;
    health consequences 363-4; LGBTQ 347-8;
    men as victims of 347-8
intimate relationships: attachment 307-8; attraction
    316-18; love 318-21
introversion 209, 261-3
Islam see religion

Jacob's Syndrome 22, 33, 36
Japan 170
jealousy 132, 318
job requirements 391-2
Johansen, D. 10

Khasi tribe 393
Klinefelter Syndrome 33, 36
knowledge 88-9

labia 69
labioscrotal swelling 65, 76
lactose persistence 16, 19
language 226-7
Laumann, E. O. 221
laws 163-5, 206
leadership 390-1, 408-9
legitimizing myths 102, 135, 157-8, 164,
    275-6, 391
LGBTQ: aggression towards 361-2, 435-7;
    coming out and identity formation 297-8;
    discrimination 202-4, 298, 361-2, 435-8; gay
    men and masculine norms 346-7; heterosexism
    177-9; intimate partner violence 347-8; intimate

464 *Index*

relationships 320-1; minority stress 278; rape victims 366; religious condemnation 216, 298, 347; sexual health 224-5
life on earth 4
Liu, W. M. 347
long-term memory 88, 105
love 318-21; *see also* intimate relationships
love schemas 319
love styles 319-20

Maccoby, E. E. 315
Main, M. 305
male circumcision 200-2
mansplaining 101, 105
Marfan Syndrome 49-50, 55
marital rape 133, 358, 367
marital timing 321
marriage 206, 231, 321-3
masculine discrepancy stress (MDS) 277
masculinity 87, 95-6, 106, 140-1, 164-5, 274-5, 344-7; aggression 350, 359, 361-2, 365-7; *see also* gender roles; gender stereotypes; hypermasculinity; gender stereotypes; hypermasculinity
masturbation (self-pleasuring) 69, 76, 201-2, 206, 220-1
maternal mortality rate 254-5
maternal stress 73
mathematics 275-6
matriarchy 161, 184
media 271; Donald Trump 429; sexism in 175-7, 354-5; sexuality 213-16, 221-2, 354-5; violence 351-4
meiosis 25-7, 36, 204-5; nondisjunction 29-33; and variability 27-9
melanin 15, 19
menstruation 69, 76, 198-200
mental health 162, 276-8, 297-8, 302, 306-7; intimate partner violence 356-7
mental rotation 275, 282, 392
metaphase 25-6, 36
#MeToo movement 159-60, 182
minority social influence 441-2
minority stress 277-8
misogyny 170, 184, 432; *see also* right-wing authoritarianism; sexism
mitochondria 25, 36
mitosis 25-6, 36
modeling 126-7, 143

modern sexism 174-5, 184, 430
monogamy 317-18
monosomy 30, 33, 36
moral authority 84, 106
morality 4, 19, 206
morbidity 276
motivated tactician 88, 106
motivation 88
Müllerian ducts 65, 76
Müllerian inhibiting substance (MIS) 65, 76
Murnen, S. K. 227
muscular dystrophy (MD) 47-8, 56
mutation 48, 56

nationalism 428-9
natural selection 6, 19
neglect 301-2
neosexism *see* modern sexism
Nettle, D. 220
neural tube 73, 76
neurofibromatosis 49, 56
neuroticism 212, 260, 263-4, 272
Niebes-Davis, A. J. 213
nondisjunction 29-33
normal distribution 64
norms *see* gender roles; heteronormativity; social norms
#NotAllMen 159-60, 182
nuclear envelope 23, 36
nucleus 23, 36
nutrition 73

objectification *see* sexual objectification
O'Brien, M. 126
observational learning *see* social learning/social cognitive theory
Ocasio-Cortez, A. 412, 414
occupational roles 138-9, 274; emotional display rules 405-6; family work 397-400; gender gap 395-6; gender stereotypes 403-4; glass ceiling 407-8; job requirements 391-2; leadership 408-9; parental leave 400-1; sexism 403-9; work-family conflict 401-2
occupational stereotypes 402-3
Oedipus Complex 119-20
old-fashioned sexism 171, 184
Omar, I. 412, 414
one-trait cross 44-6, 56
online sexism 431-2

oocytes 69, 76
oogenesis 29, 36
open relationships 204
open system 4, 19
openness 260-1
oppression see LGBTQ; racism; sexism
optic neuropathy 48, 56
organelles 23, 25, 36
orgasm 219-20
Out-of-Africa hypothesis 14, 19
ovaries 69, 77
ovulation 69, 71, 77
oxytocin 125, 144, 220, 264-7, 303-4

pair bonding 4, 19
Pancultural Adjective Checklist 95-6
parental investment 131-4, 144, 309-10
parental leave 400-1
parenting 125-8, 166-7, 270-1; aggression 355-7;
    attachment 303-6; authoritarian 426-7; family
    relationships 311-13; gender differences 308-11;
    sexuality 210-12; single mothers 299-301
parsimony 122, 144
part-whole fallacy 4, 19
passion 318-19
paternity uncertainty 132, 206, 299, 318
patriarchy 102, 163-4, 169-71, 184, 345, 442;
    anti-feminism 431-2; glass ceiling 408;
    global culture 135, 161, 181, 364-5; right-wing
    authoritarianism 426-30
peer influences 209-10
Pence, M. 16
penis 70-1, 77, 200-2
persistent Müllerian duct syndrome 65, 77
personal constructs 91, 106
personality 209, 278; behavioral genetics 267-8;
    biological bases of 261-3; defining 256-9;
    Five Factor Model (FFM) 259-61, 272-4;
    gender differences 272-5; hormones 263-7;
    psychodynamic theory 252-4; religiosity 272;
    socialization 268-72
personality psychology 119
persuasion 441
phenotype 44, 56, 87, 106, 124
phenylketonuria (PKU) 51-2, 56
physical attraction 317-18
physical strength 115-16, 131, 162-5, 349
pituitary gland 66, 77
placenta 71, 77

play 128, 310-12, 315
Pleck, J. H. 140
point mutations 48, 56
polar body 29, 36
political power 137-9, 180, 389-91, 395, 409-13
Pollet, T. V. 220
Poly-X Syndrome 33, 36
polygenic inheritance 46, 56
pornography 215-16, 222; violent
    pornography 367-9
poverty 179, 184, 268-9, 438-40; abortion
    and unwanted pregnancy 167-8, 224, 402;
    aggression 357; child abuse 302; intimate
    partner violence 364-5; maternal mortality
    254-5; personality 268-9, 273, 278; rape 366;
    single mothers 299-300
Prader-Willi Syndrome 42-3, 56
Pratto, F. 137
precarious manhood 140-1, 144, 165, 277, 345, 361
pregnancy 71-4, 99-100, 130, 166-8, 174, 254-5,
    401-2; parental leave 400-1
prejudice 91, 94, 106, 114; see also sexism
prenatal health 73-4
prescriptions 97-9, 106
primates 4, 8-9, 19
prison industry 439
pro-life movement 432-5
property rights 394-5
prophase 25-6, 36
proscriptions 97-9, 106, 308-9
prosocial behavior 84, 106
prostate gland 71, 77
Protestant work ethic 102, 106, 439
prototypes 89, 106, 116-17
pseudoautosomal genes 44, 56
psychoanalysis: gender theories 119-20, 122, 139-40;
    personality 252-4
psychoticism 263, 268
puberty 69, 77, 206-9
punctuated equilibrium 3, 19
Punnet Square 44-6, 56
Puts, D. A. 220

racial minority groups 277-8
racism 93-4, 129, 171-2, 426-7, 429, 439
rape 156, 208-9, 365-8, 440; male victims 366;
    marital rape 133, 358, 367; #MeToo movement
    159-60, 182; poverty 366; rape culture 367-8;
    rape myths 215, 272, 346, 355, 367-8; religion

358-9; serial sexual predators 369; token resistance 214-15; underreporting of 366, 368; victim blaming 345-6

recessive allele 44-6, 56

reciprocity 4, 19, 315-17

Reidy, D. E. 359

Reimer, D. 60-1

relationships see interpersonal relationships; intimate relationships; parenting

religion 84-6, 99, 164-5, 169-70, 177-9, 255, 271-2, 347; aggression against women 357-9; fascism 429-30; pro-life movement 432-5; sexuality 201, 206, 216, 220-3, 226, 227, 297-8, 433-5, 438

religiosity 272

representation 175-7

reproduction see sexual reproduction

reproductive health 59-60, 223-6, 302

reproductive rights 59-60, 167-8, 172, 255, 402, 430, 432-5

reproductive systems 69-71

respect 101

reversible inhibition of sperm under guidance (RISUG) 61-2, 77

Rich, Y. 401

Richters, J. 219-20

right-wing authoritarianism (RWA) 173-4, 184, 426-30

Rios, V. M. 439

risky sexual behaviors 208-9, 211-12, 219, 232, 300-1

RNA (ribonucleic acid) 4, 19, 25, 37

Robertson, P. 431

roles 89, 106

romance novels 213-15

romantic relationships see intimate relationships

Rome 170

Sahelenthropus Tchadensis 10

Sánchez, F. J. 347

Sanghani, R. 83

schema accessibility 91, 106

schemas 89, 91, 106, 117-18, 128-9, 352-3, 389-90

schematic processing 90-4, 129

Schmitt, D. P. 273

science 17, 441-2; sexism in 160-1; see also theory

scripts 89, 106

secondary sex characteristics 33

secure attachment 304-5, 307-8

self-concept 102, 106, 126, 303

self-disclosure 316

self-efficacy 400

self-esteem 303, 306

self-pleasuring see masturbation

seminal vesicles 71, 77

sensation-seeking 262-3, 283

serial sexual predators 369

sex (biological) 63-4, 75, 87; gender theories 124-5; genes 64-5

sex chromosomes 28, 32-3, 36, 44, 64-5, 67-9

sex differences 114-15, 132; aggression 348-50, 362; attachment 306-7; biological 162-8, 392-3; sexuality 218

sex differentiation 63-7, 77; genetic and hormonal disorders 67-9; puberty 69

sex education 224-5, 301

sex toys 204

sex-determining region of Y (SRY) 44, 56, 64-5, 67-8

sex-influenced traits 47, 56

sex-linked genetic disorders 47-8

sex-linked traits 46-7, 56

sexism 103, 116, 120, 123, 161-2, 180-2, 394-6; ambivalent sexism 171-4, 182, 406-7; benevolent sexism 101, 171-4, 277, 406-7; control of sexuality 226-8; glass ceiling 407-8; global equality 179-80; heterosexism 177-9; history of 168-71, 394-5; hostile sexism 171, 173-4, 183, 226, 277, 406-7, 431, 435; ignoring and blaming 154-6; implicit attitudes and unconscious bias 157-8; laws 163-5; the media 175-7; modern sexism 174-5, 184, 430; occupational roles 403-9; old-fashioned sexism 171, 184; online sexism 431-2; physical strength 162-5; politics 389-91, 412-13; reproductive roles 166-8; right-wing authoritarianism 427; in science 160-1; types of 171-5; US election 2016 389-91; see also gender stereotypes

sexting 210

sexual agency 226

sexual arousal 205, 216-17

sexual assault 366; see also rape; sexual violence

sexual attraction 217, 316-18

sexual desire 216-17

sexual experiences 217-19

sexual minority groups see LGBTQ

sexual objectification 162, 175-7, 184, 354-5

sexual orientation 66-7, 177-9

sexual reproduction 204-5; childbirth 72-3; fertilization 71; gender assignment 60-1;

parental investment 131-4, 318; pregnancy 71-4, 99-100, 130; prenatal health 73-4; reproductive rights 59-60; reproductive systems 69-71; sex differentiation in utero 63-7; sexism 166-8; *see also* pregnancy

sexual scripts 212-16

sexual self-esteem 217

sexual violence 156, 208-9, 440; #MeToo movement 159-60, 182; rape 365-8; rape myths 215, 272, 346, 355, 367-8; religion 358-9; serial sexual predators 369; token resistance 214-15; victim blaming 345-6; violent pornography 368-9

sexuality 204-6, 228-9; contraception and reproductive health 223-6; control of 226-8, 433-5; double standard 210; gender roles 207; kinks 204; language 226-7; media 213-16; religion 201, 206, 216, 220-3, 226, 227, 438; uncontrolled 205-6

sexuality in adulthood: arousal 216-17; attraction 217; experiences 217-19; hooking-up 219; masturbation (self-pleasuring) 220-1; orgasm 219-20; social and cultural influences 221-3

sexuality development 206-7; child sexuality 206-7; family influences 210-12; first sexual experiences 208; individual qualities 208-9; peer influences 209-10; personality 209; social and cultural influences 212-16

sexually dimorphic nucleus (SDN) 66-7, 77

sexually transmitted diseases (STDs) 202, 206, 208, 223-6, 232

sexually transmitted infections (STIs) 224

shame 198-200, 206, 223

Shaver, P. R. 307-8

short-term memory 86, 88, 106

sibling relationships 313

sickle-cell anemia 46, 56

sickle-cell trait 46

simple inheritance 46, 56

single mothers 299-302, 312-13, 401-2

sister chromatids 25, 37

skin color 15

slut-shaming 227, 232

Smedslund, J. 85

social cognition 87, 101

social dominance orientation (SDO) 103, 106, 135, 137, 169, 426

social dominance theory 102, 106, 134-9, 164, 350, 408

social influence 441-2

social learning/social cognitive theory 101, 107, 122, 125-7, 270, 309, 352

social norms 163-4; sexual scripts 212-16; *see also* gender roles; gender stereotypes; heteronormativity

social power 39-40

social role theory 99, 107, 129-31, 309, 350

socialization 89, 91, 101, 107, 125-7; aggression 350-5; communication and social interaction 313-15; personality 268-72; sexuality in adulthood 221-3; sexuality development 212-16; spatial reasoning 392-3; *see also* parenting; religion; religion

sodomy 206

Solomon, J. 305

son preference 21-2

spatial reasoning skills 392-3

Spearman, C. 258

spermatids 71, 77

spermatogenesis 29, 37, 69

spindle apparatus 25, 37

stalking 364

stay-at-home mother 398

Steffan, V. J. 362

STEM fields 393-4

stereotype threat 276, 393-4

stereotypes 84, 89, 93-4, 107, 135, 157; occupational 402-3; *see also* gender stereotypes

Sternberg, R. J. 318-19

stigmatization 205, 232

stoicism 275

Strange Situation measure 304-5

straw person 3, 19

stress 73, 277-8, 401

struggle for existence 6, 19

subtyping 94, 96-7, 107

Superego 120, 145

suprachiasmatic nucleus (SCN) 66-7, 77

survival of the fittest 6, 19

Sutherland, J. D. 4

Swaab, D. F. 67

swinging 204

Swyer Syndrome 67-8, 77

synapsis 27, 37

Taung Child 11

Tay-Sachs Disease 51, 56

telophase 25-6, 37

468 *Index*

teratogens 73-4, 77
testability 121-2, 145
testes 65, 70-1, 78
testis determining factor (TDF) 65, 78
testosterone 33, 37, 65-6, 78, 124-5, 263-5, 267, 349
tetrad 26, 37
theories of gender *see* gender theories
theory 3-4, 19, 120-2
#TimesUp 160, 182
Tlaib, R. 412, 414
token resistance 214-15
toys 128, 310-11
trait approach *see* dispositional approach
traits 89, 107
transformational leadership 408-9
transgender 112-14, 145, 177-8, 435-7
trinucleotide repeat disorders 48, 56
trisomy 30, 32-3, 37
Trump, D. 154-6, 177-8, 389-91, 412, 426-30, 434, 436, 440
tubal ligation 70, 78
Turner Syndrome 33, 37
twin studies 267-8

unconscious bias 157-8
United States 170-2, 180
universal health care 252
urethra 69, 71, 78
urogenital groove 65, 78
uterine (Fallopian) tube 69-70, 78
uterus 70, 78

vagina 69, 78, 198-200
Vandello, J. A. 277

variability 27-9, 37, 64
variation 6, 15-16, 19
vas deferens 70-1, 78
Vasalgel 61-2, 78
vasectomy 71, 78
vesicle 25, 35
victim blaming 345-6, 366
video games 176, 353-4
Vilain, E. 347
violence *see* aggression; intimate partner violence; sexual violence
virginity 206
vulva 69, 78

Walker, P. L. 1
warmth 101
wealth inequality 424; *see also* poverty
Welling, L. L. M. 220
Westefeld, J. S. 347
white supremacists 91-2, 107, 432
Williams, J. E. 95
Wolffian ducts 65, 78
women's rights 172
Wood, W. 130, 132
work *see* occupational roles
working memory *see* short-term memory
working models 303, 308
work-family conflict 401-2
World Health Organization (WHO) 251-2, 441
Wundt, W. 261

Zebrowitz, L. A. 100-1
Zerjal, T. 131
zygote 71, 78